Dictionary of
Brazilian
Literature

Dictionary of
Brazilian
Literature

IRWIN STERN

Editor-in-Chief

Greenwood Press

NEW YORK • WESTPORT, CONNECTICUT • LONDON

Library of Congress Cataloging-in-Publication Data

Dictionary of Brazilian literature.

Bibliography: p.
Includes index.
1. Brazilian literature—Dictionaries.
I. Stern, Irwin.
PQ9506.D53 1988   869'.09'981   87–17744
ISBN 0–313–24932–6 (lib. bdg. : alk. paper)

British Library Cataloguing in Publication Data is available.

Library of Congress Catalog Card Number: 87–17744
ISBN: 0–313–24932–6

First published in 1988

Greenwood Press, Inc.
88 Post Road West, Westport, Connecticut 06881

Printed in the United States of America

The paper used in this book complies with the
Permanent Paper Standard issued by the National
Information Standards Organization (Z39.48–1984).

10 9 8 7 6 5 4 3 2 1

To F.E.R.
Amar se aprende amando

Contents

Contributors   ix

Preface   xv

Map of Brazil   xviii

Chronology   xix

Glossary of Frequently Used Brazilian Words   xxxi

Key to Bibliographical References   xxxiii

Introduction: Brazilian Literature in Cultural Perspective   xxxvii

Dictionary of Brazilian Literature   1

Index   369

Contributors

Severino João Albuquerque is an assistant professor of Portuguese at the University of Wisconsin–Madison. In Brazil he has had poetry and short fiction published, and in the United States he has contributed articles and book reviews on Brazilian and Portuguese literature to *Hispania*, *Latin American Theatre Review*, *Romance Notes*, *Modern Drama*, *Luso-Brazilian Review*, and other publications. He is completing a book on the contemporary Latin American theater.

Onésimo Teotónio Almeida holds a Ph.D. in philosophy from Brown University, where he teaches at the Center for Portuguese and Brazilian Studies. He has completed a book on the theoretical issues concerning national thought with regard to Portugal: *A obsessão da portugalidade*. He is also interested in the issues of values, ideologies, and worldviews. His book *The Labyrinth of Ideology* is forthcoming.

Ana Luiza Andrade is an assistant professor of Brazilian literature at Harvard University. She holds a Ph.D. from the University of Texas at Austin and previously taught at Yale University. Her book on the narratives of Osman Lins was published in Brazil in 1987 by Editora Ática of São Paulo. Her current research interest is the works of Clarice Lispector.

Norwood Andrews, Jr., is professor of Romance languages at Texas Tech University, where he has taught since 1970. He has had numerous works published on Luso-Brazilian literature and is an officer of the Order of the Southern Cross of Brazil.

Lee Boyd has a degree in physics. She is currently writing a biography of Villa-Lobos.

Keith H. Brower is an assistant professor of Spanish and Portuguese at Dickinson College. His primary research has dealt with the twentieth-century Latin American novel. He has had work published on the theater of Machado de Assis.

E. Bradford Burns, a professor of history at the University of California, Los Angeles, is the author and editor of five books on Brazil, including *A History of Brazil* (2nd ed., 1980).

Bobby J. Chamberlain is associate professor in the Department of Hispanic Languages and Literature at the University of Pittsburgh. He also has taught at the University of Michigan and the University of Southern California. Twice a Fulbright-Hays scholar in

Brazil, he is the author (with Ronald M. Harmon) of *A Dictionary of Informal Brazilian Portuguese* (1984). He is currently finishing a book on the characterization of women in the fiction of Jorge Amado.

Leslie Damasceno is instructor in Portuguese at Princeton University. She is a specialist in the contemporary Brazilian theater and has had material published on Viana Filho's dramatic works.

Mary L. Daniel has been head of the Luso-Brazilian Studies program of the University of Wisconsin–Madison since 1977 and has served as editor of the *Luso-Brazilian Review* since 1978. Her published works include a book and monographs on João Guimarães Rosa and studies on Osman Lins, Érico Veríssimo, Eça de Queiroz, Machado de Assis, and other nineteenth- and twentieth-century authors. She spends her summers as guest consultant and translator with the Summer Institute of Linguistics (Wycliffe Bible Translators) in Brazil.

Joan Dassin, Ph.D., studies the politics and culture of contemporary Brazil. She has written about cultural policies of the modernist movement, as well as censorship, the press, and the arts during the military regime. She edited the English version of *Brasil: nunca mais* (*Torture in Brazil*, 1986), a documentary history of repression from 1964 to 1972. Dassin has intermittently lived and worked in Brazil since 1971. Currently, she is the staff associate to the Joint Committee on Latin American Studies of the Social Science Research Council.

Paul Dixon is associate professor of Spanish and Portuguese at Purdue University. He has written about Machado de Assis, Luís de Camões, and contemporary Brazilian authors, including Clarice Lispector, Nelson Rodrigues, João Cabral de Melo Neto, and João Guimarães Rosa.

Earl E. Fitz is an associate professor of Portuguese, Spanish, and Comparative Literature at Pennsylvania State University. He has written about several Brazilian writers, including Clarice Lispector, Jorge Amado, Graciliano Ramos, and Mário de Andrade and is the author of *Clarice Lispector* (1985). Fitz is currently at work on a book about Machado de Assis.

René P. Garay is an assistant professor of Romance languages at the City College of New York. He has worked on medieval Portuguese literature and contemporary Brazilian literature.

John Gledson is senior lecturer in the Department of Hispanic Studies and the Institute of Latin American Studies at the University of Liverpool. He has had books published on Carlos Drummond de Andrade and Machado de Assis: *Poesia e poética de Carlos Drummond de Andrade* (1981), *The Deceptive Realism of Machado de Assis* (1984), and *Machado de Assis: Ficção e história* (1986), as well as articles on other aspects of Brazilian literature.

Heloísa Buarque de Hollanda is professor of communications at the Federal University of Rio de Janeiro and director of the university's Interdisciplinary Center for Contemporary Studies. She has had many works published on the relationship of dictatorship to literature and on the cultural scene in Brazil during the past twenty years. She has also worked in film and video.

K. David Jackson is an associate professor of Portuguese at the University of Texas, Austin. He has written about the modernist generation, has translated Oswald de Andrade, and has organized important English-language anthologies of contemporary Brazilian literature.

Randal Johnson is associate professor of Portuguese at the University of Florida. He has had several books published on Brazilian cinema, including *Cinema novo × 5* (1984), and, most recently, *The Film Industry in Brazil: Culture and the State* (1987). He has also written about contemporary figures such as Mário de Andrade and Nelson Rodrigues.

James H. Kennedy is lecturer in Portuguese and Spanish at Howard University. His essays on teaching methodology and Luso-Brazilian literature have appeared in *Hispania*, *Phylon*, *Ponto & Vírgula*, and *Présence Africaine*. He is the author of the textbook *Relatos latinoamericanos* (1986).

Harriet E. Manelis Klein is professor of anthropology at Montclair State College. Her research interests include South American Indian languages, discourse analysis, and lexicography. Her major published works include *South American Indian Languages: Retrospect and Prospect*, coedited with L. Stark (1985); and *Una gramática de la lengua toba: Morfología verbal y nominal* (1978).

Edgar C. Knowlton, Jr., is professor of European languages at the University of Hawaii in Manoa. He also has taught linguistics in Kuala Lumpur and Caracas under a U.S. State Department grant. In addition to doing a prize-winning translation from Portuguese of Sá de Meneses's *Malaca conquistada*, he is the author of many articles on Brazilian literature and a book on the Argentine writer Esteban Echeverría.

Dale A. Koike is assistant professor of Spanish and Portuguese linguistics at the University of Texas at Austin. She has done extensive research on sociolinguistic and pragmatic aspects of contemporary Brazilian Portuguese and is presently coediting a collection of studies in Portuguese linguistics.

Marisa Lajolo is professor of Brazilian literature at the University of Campinas, São Paulo. She has had many studies published on literary theory, contemporary Brazilian writers, and the development of children's literature.

Naomi Lindstrom is associate professor of Spanish and Portuguese and of Latin American Studies at the University of Texas, Austin, where she heads the Politics of Culture study group at the Institute of Latin American Studies. She is the author of *Literary Expressionism in Argentina* (1977), *Macedonio Fernández* (1981), and other studies and is a translator of Latin American literature.

Luiza Lobo is professor of literary theory at the State University of Rio de Janeiro. She has had several volumes of short stories and two books on Sousândrade published. Her reviews, articles, and essays have appeared in Brazil, Italy, Portugal, and the United States. She has translated into Portuguese the works of Virginia Woolf, Edgar Allen Poe, William Golding, Jane Austen, and others.

Maria Angélica Guimarães Lopes is assistant professor of Portuguese and Spanish at the University of South Carolina in Columbia. She is the Brazilian short story editor for the Library of Congress *Handbook of Latin American Studies* (a yearly publication) and has written about Machado de Assis and twentieth-century Brazilian fiction, in particular works by João Alphonsus, Aníbal Machado, and recent writers.

José López-Heredia is professor of Romance languages at Baruch College of the City University of New York. In addition to developing his study of Raul Pompéia's fiction, he has worked on French and Spanish literature and has had several collections of short stories published in Spanish, for example, *Milagro en el Bronx y otros relatos* (1984).

Elizabeth Lowe is assistant professor at Miami-Dade Community College. With a Ph.D. in comparative literature from the City University of New York, Lowe is the author of *The City in Brazilian Literature* (1982), scholarly articles on Latin American literature, and translations of fiction from Spanish and Portuguese.

Naomi Hoki Moniz is assistant professor of Portuguese at Georgetown University. She has written extensively on contemporary Brazilian fiction, particularly on women's literature and Brazilian immigrant literature.

Maria Luísa Nunes is associate professor of Portuguese at the State University of New York, Stony Brook. She has published extensively on Portuguese and Brazilian literature: *The Craft of an Absolute Winner* (1983), *Lima Barreto: Bibliography and Translations* (1979), *Portuguese Colonial in America* (1982), and *Becoming True to Ourselves: Cultural Decolonization and National Identity in the Literature of the Portuguese-Speaking World* (Greenwood Press, 1987).

Marta Peixoto is associate professor of Portuguese at Yale University. She has had a book about João Cabral de Melo Neto published, as well as articles on other contemporary Brazilian authors.

Charles A. Perrone is an assistant professor of Portuguese and Luso-Brazilian culture and literature in the Department of Romance Languages and Literature at the University of Florida, Gainesville, and is an affiliated faculty member of the Center for Latin American Studies. He is a specialist in the interrelationship of music and literature in Brazil.

Júlio Machado Pinto is professor of English literature at the University of Minas Gerais. He has written about the contemporary Brazilian semiotics movement and has applied this theory to the study of works by Jorge de Lima, Ledo Ivo, and other writers.

Richard A. Preto-Rodas is director of the Division of Language at the University of South Florida, Tampa. He has taught at the Universities of Michigan, Florida, and Illinois and has had many monographs and articles published on aspects of Spanish, Portuguese, Brazilian, and Lusophone African literature.

Frances Elizabeth Rand is a research associate and cochair of the Brazil Seminar at Columbia University. She has had articles published on the nineteenth-century Brazilian businessman Baron Mauá and is writing a doctoral thesis on the subject. She is also completing a book about Anglo-Argentine affairs in the midnineteenth century and another one on Cuba's relations with the Palestine Liberation Organization. Rand was a visiting lecturer at the Brazilian Historical and Geographical Institute and a deputy director of the House of Brazil in London. She has done much freelance research.

Raymond S. Sayers is professor emeritus of Romance languages and comparative literature at Queens College and the Graduate School of the City University of New York.

Among his major published works is *The Negro in Brazilian Literature* (1956). In addition, he has edited studies of both Portuguese and Brazilian literature and was appointed to the Order of Rio Branco in 1986, thus receiving the highest award accorded by the Brazilian government to a foreigner for contributions in the area of Brazilian culture.

Jaime H. da Silva was born on Fayal in the Azores Islands and was educated at the University of Pennsylvania and Harvard University. Since 1983 he has been an assistant professor of Portuguese at the University of Puerto Rico, Río Piedras. He has had material published about and has lectured on the works of the Portuguese poet Fernando Pessoa, as well as contemporary Brazilian poets.

Malcolm Silverman is associate professor of Spanish and Portuguese at San Diego State University. He has published many articles on contemporary Brazilian fiction, *Moderna ficção Brasileira*, both volumes. He is also the editor of a collection of contemporary Brazilian short stories, *O novo conto brasileiro*.

Irwin Stern is editor-in-chief of the *Dictionary of Brazilian Literature* (1988). He is lecturer in Portuguese and Brazilian literature at Columbia University, where he is also a member of the Institute of Latin American and Iberian Studies of the School of International Affairs. Among his major published works on Portuguese and Brazilian literature are *Júlio Dinis e o romance português (1860–1870)* (1972) and *Modern Spanish and Portuguese Literatures* (1988), coedited with Marshall J. Schneider. He also has had articles published in *World Literature Today*, *Colóquio/Letras*, *Review*, *The New York Times*, and other publications.

Ricardo Lobo Sternberg is assistant professor of Portuguese at the University of Toronto. He has written about contemporary Brazilian poetry and is the author of *The Unquiet Self: Self and Society in the Poetry of Carlos Drummond de Andrade* (1986), as well as many other studies on contemporary Brazilian and Portuguese poets.

Jon M. Tolman is professor of Portuguese and associate director of the Latin American Institute at the University of New Mexico, Albuquerque. He has written about modernism and contemporary Brazilian fiction.

David H. Treece was a temporary full-time lecturer in Portuguese and Brazilian Studies at the University of Glasgow, Scotland. He is presently working for Survival International, a human rights organization that campaigns for the rights of tribal peoples.

Luiz Fernando Valente was born in Rio de Janeiro and was educated in Brazil and the United States. He holds a Ph.D. in comparative literature from Brown University, where he has taught since 1982. A specialist in twentieth-century narrative, his articles have appeared in *Luso-Brazilian Review*, *Hispania*, and *Hispanic Review*. He is currently working on a book about the uses of parody in twentieth-century Brazilian literature.

Nelson H. Vieira is professor and director of the Center for Portuguese and Brazilian Studies at Brown University. He has had numerous articles published on Dalton Trevisan, Jorge Amado, Roberto Drummond, Sérgio Sant'Anna, Moacir Scliar, and others. A translator of short stories, novels, and plays, he is presently completing the English translation of Sérgio Sant'Anna's novel *Amazona*. Besides having an ongoing interest in modern Jewish-Brazilian prose, he is also preparing a manuscript on the Brazilian autobiographical novel. Among his published works are *The Promise* (1981), *Roads to Today's Portugal* (1983), and *Brasil e Portugal: a imagem recíproca* (1987).

Jon S. Vincent is professor of Spanish and Portuguese at the University of Kansas, Lawrence. He is the author of the Twayne series volume on *João Guimarães Rosa* (1978) and has authored numerous other papers and articles, principally in the field of Brazilian prose fiction.

María Tai Wolff is assistant professor of Romance languages at the University of Michigan. She has worked on contemporary Latin American literature from a comparative perspective with special emphasis on nineteenth- and twentieth-century Brazilian literature.

Preface

The *Dictionary of Brazilian Literature* contains approximately 300 entries in English covering the most significant writers, literary schools, and related cultural movements in Brazilian literary history, with an emphasis on twentieth-century and very contemporary figures. It has been prepared with the cooperation of leading American and British Brazilianists, as well as distinguished Brazilian literary scholars.

The volume is specifically oriented toward the English-reading public. It presents the literature within the sociocultural context of Brazilian life throughout the centuries. The length of the entries is determined primarily by the writer's or the movement's significance in the literature and secondarily by my desire to present information about as many writers and themes as possible within the space allowed. Thus writers whose careers are forgotten today or those that are very recent are discussed or mentioned in general thematic or movement entries.

Each entry provides concise, factual information. More extensive entries, in addition, offer a critical perspective for placing the writer within the literature. I have attempted to provide as many English translations and critical resources as possible, offering a wide range of opinions. Conflicting critical opinions do appear, and I hope that they will stimulate the user to read the work(s) in question and reach his or her own conclusion.

The volume is divided into the following sections: List of Contributors, Preface, Map, Chronology, Glossary of Frequently Used Brazilian Terms, Key to Bibliographical References, Introduction, Dictionary of Brazilian Literature, and Index.

The Introduction presents a global perspective on the development of Brazilian literature within the culture. It ends with an annotated bibliography of bibliographies, dictionaries, histories, and general studies about Brazilian literature, history, and culture, as well as a listing of readily available collections of selections from Brazilian literature in translation and in the original Portuguese.

Two types of entries appear: theme or movement entries and author entries. Theme or movement entries include not only the standard literary movements (e.g., Modernism, Romanticism, Symbolism) but also the sociocultural movements that have a special significance for the literature (e.g., Dictatorship and Literature; Popular Culture; Portugal and Brazil: Literary Relations; Positivism and Literature; Slavery and Literature). The theme or movement entries begin with an overview of the subject's roots in the international literary context, followed by a discussion of its specific characteristics and development in Brazil, with brief references to the major writers and less remembered figures associated with the theme or movement. The entry's bibliography lists other sources of information on the topic, in English whenever possible.

Author entries are alphabetized by the writer's actual last name, the best-known last name, or the last or only name of his or her pseudonym, basically following the Library of Congress cataloguing system for Portuguese names. The only exceptions are the following: (1) authors whose last name is Filho or Neto are listed by their last two names (e.g., Adonias Filho, Coelho Neto, Melo Neto, Lopes Neto); and (2) the traditionally accepted compound last name Qorpo-Santo is listed as such. Cross-referencing of names is provided in the body of the text and in the index. Each name is followed by the birth and death date when known, and, when appropriate, by the designation *BAL: date*, indicating that the writer was a member of the Brazilian Academy of Letters, with the date of his or her initiation. The first reference to the writer will give the person's traditionally accepted last or best-known name, and subsequent references will be to the last name once again. The initial paragraph of the entry presents a brief biographical note, followed by a discussion of the writer's major works. Depending on the significance of his or her achievement, a concluding paragraph offers an evaluation of the writer's achievement within the literature.

Citation of the author's works in the entry is done according to the following pattern: (a) works with English translations give the title in English followed by the date of the translation—*Os sertões* (1902; *Rebellion in the Backlands*, 1944); (b) works without English translations also give the title in English but have no translation date—*Assunção de Salviano* (1954; The Assumption of Salviano). Further references to translated works in that entry are to the English title. All other citations are made to the Portuguese title.

The bibliography of most entries is divided into two or three parts: (a) Additional selected works by the author: Only selected works with the date of their first edition are offered because of space limitations; (b) Translations: References listed are to other translated works by the writer that are not included in the body of the text but appear in a selected group of bibliographies, anthologies, collections, or reviews. Citations refer to the editor(s)' last name(s) or the accepted abbreviations for reviews. Check the "Key to Bibliographical References" for exact information. (c) Criticism: This section includes primarily English sources when available, including major book-length studies of the literature or culture in English, although important Portuguese (and Spanish or French) sources are also listed. Once again, frequently cited critical works are referred to by the last name of the author(s) or editor(s) or the accepted abbreviations for reviews. Check the "Key to Bibliographical References" for exact information. All entries are signed by their authors; unsigned entries were prepared by the editor-in-chief.

Cross-referencing among the entries is accomplished by the use of the asterisk* (e.g., *Romanticism or Antônio *Torres), with the asterisk preceding the first word of the actual entry title or by the word *See* (e.g., *See* Arcadias) at the end of paragraphs or in the text following a tangential reference. Portuguese words and foreign words appear in italics with a translation, except for those that are often cited and appear in the glossary. The index includes all writers mentioned in the dictionary, including authors who do not have a separate entry.

Several additional procedures have been adopted to facilitate use of this volume and allow space for a greater number of entries: (a) References to *Rio* or *São Paulo* are to the cities, unless otherwise indicated. References to *Minas* are to the state of Minas Gerais. *Coimbra* refers to the University of Coimbra, Portugal. (b) All spellings have been modernized, except for the names of contemporary writers who have a preferred or now-standard spelling (e.g., Antônio Callado, Affonso Ávila, Sérgio Sant'Anna). (c) Every effort has been made to verify the birth and death dates and dates of publication. This matter is complicated not only by the discrepancies among generally reliable sources but also by the difficulty in locating materials. I have relied primarily on the *Library of Congress Catalogue*. All translations, with the exception of a poem by C. Meireles, were done by the author or the editor.

This task would have been impossible without the help of the following people. I am greatly indebted to each of the contributors who fulfilled his or her task with clarity, reliability, and cordiality. Haydée Piedracueva, Latin American Collection bibliographer, and Gladys Markoff-Sotomayor, Latin American Collection cataloguer, at Butler and Lehman Libraries of Columbia University, offered continuous support and cooperation in obtaining titles; the Reference Room librarians at Butler Library were also very helpful. My colleagues in Brazil, Heloísa Buarque de Hollanda, professor of communications, Federal University of Rio de Janeiro, and Luiza Lobo, professor of literary theory, State University of Rio de Janeiro, kept me up to date on new writers and a myriad of other issues. Professor Raymond S. Sayers, professor emeritus of Romance languages and comparative literature, Queens College and the City University of New York, was also a source of information, support, and encouragement throughout the project. Frances Rand, my wife, good-naturedly tolerated my moodiness and lack of free time. She supplied tender care, close friendship, wise counsel, occasional editorial work, an article, and well-informed collegial debate about relevant historical issues. Finally, I accept all blame for misinterpretations and errors of fact and judgment that may appear.

Irwin Stern

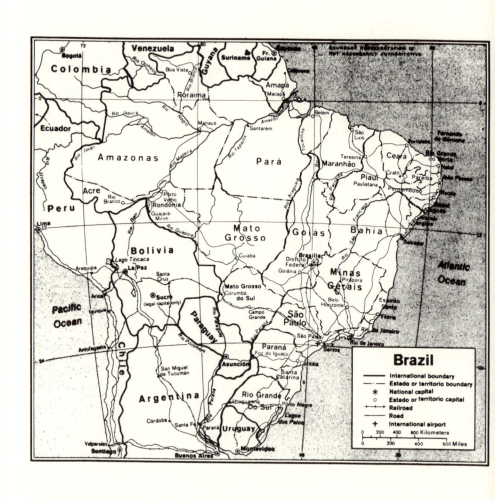

Brazil

——— International boundary
—·—·— Estado or territorio boundary
⊛ National capital
○ Estado or territorio capital
+++ Railroad
——— Road
+ International airport

0   200   400   600 Kilometers
0   200   400   600 Miles

Chronology

References to writers under the column Brazilian Literature are to the name listed in the index and used for the main entry in the text. Where similar names exist, the first initials, first name, or composite last names are used for clarification.

DATE	BRAZILIAN HISTORY	BRAZILIAN LITERATURE	FOREIGN LITERATURE
1500	Discovery of Brazil	P. V. de Caminha's *Letter*	
1502			Gil Vicente's first dramatic dialogue
1534	First captaincies	Birth of Father Anchieta	
1539	First African slaves arrive in Brazil		
1554	Fathers Nóbrega and Anchieta establish a school in São Paulo		
1557		Father Anchieta's *Diálogo sobre a conversão do gentio*	
1565	City of Rio founded		
1570		Death of Father Nóbrega	
1572	Two capitals for Brazil: Bahia in the North and Rio in the South		Camões's *Os Lusíadas*
1577	Bahia becomes capital of Brazil		

1580	Portugal and Brazil fall to Spanish control		Montaigne's "Des Cannibales"
1583	English invasions begin	Father Anchieta's *Auto de São Lourenço*	
1600			Shakespeare's *Hamlet*
1601	*Bandeirantes* explore the interior	B. Teixeira's *Prosopopéia*	
1608	Sugar boom	Birth of Father A. Vieira	
1616			Second part of Cervantes's *Don Quijote*
1624	Dutch invasions begin		
1636		Birth of G. de Matos and Botelho de Oliveira	Calderón de la Barca's *El alcalde de Zalamea*
1640	Portugal regains independence from Spain		
1650		Father A. Vieira's "Sermão de Santo Antônio"	
1654	The Dutch leave Brazil		
1670			Molière's *Le Bourgeois gentilhomme*
1690	Gold discovered in Minas		Locke's "Essay on Human Understanding"
1699			Fénelon's *Les Aventures de Télémaque*
1705		B. de Oliveira's *Música do Parnasso*	
1710	Mascates War		
1712			Birth of Rousseau
1720	Vila Rica revolt		
1724		Academy of the Forgotten	
1741		Birth of B. da Gama	

1744		Birth of T.A. Gonzaga	
1749			Fielding's *Tom Jones*
1752		Orta's *As aventuras de Diófanes*; Aires's *Reflexões sobre a vaidade dos homens*	
1759	Jesuits expelled from the Portuguese empire by the Marquis of Pombal		Sterne's *Tristram Shandy*; Voltaire's *Candide*
1763	Capital transferred to Rio		
1768		C. M. da Costa's *Obras*	
1769		B. da Gama's *O uraguai*	
1774		Birth of H. da Costa	Goethe's *Werther*
1778			Voltaire and Rousseau die
1781		Durão's *Caramuru*	
1789	Mineiran Conspiracy		
1792	Exile of participants in conspiracy	Gonzaga's *Marília*	
1799		Silva Alvarenga's *Glaura*; second part of Gonzaga's *Marília*	Schiller's *Wallenstein*
1808	Portuguese court settles in Rio	H. da Costa's *Correio Brasiliense*	Goethe's *Faust* (first part)
1811		Birth of Gonçalves de Magalhães	Austen's *Sense and Sensibility*
1812			Grimms' fairy tales
1815	Brazil raised to kingdom status		
1817			Byron's *Manfred*
1818			Scott's *Ivanhoe*
1822	Independence of Brazil; D. Pedro I declared emperor		
1824	First Constitution		
1827			Hugo's *Cromwell*

1830			Stendhal's *Le Rouge et le noir*
1831	D. Pedro I abdicates		Hugo's *Notre Dame de Paris*
1836		*Niterói: Revista Brasiliense* appears in Paris; Gonçalves de Magalhães's *Suspiros poéticos e saudades*	
1839		Birth of Machado de Assis	
1840	D. Pedro II assumes throne		José de Espronceda's *El diablo mundo*
1842	Revolts in São Paulo and Minas Gerais	Martins Pena's *O juiz da paz na roça*	Gogol's *The Overcoat*
1844		J.M. de Macedo's *A moreninha*	Sarmiento's *Facundo*
1845	Farrapos War ends	Publication of Gonzaga's *Cartas chilenas*	Poe's "The Raven"; Merimée's *Carmen*
1846		Gonçalves Dias's *Primeiros cantos*	Balzac's *Cousin Bette*
1850	Queiroz Law prohibiting slave traffic		Dickens' *David Copperfield*; Melville's *Moby Dick*
1852	Telegraph system in Brazil; Baron Mauá begins Amazonian steamship service; war against Argentine dictator Rosas	M.A. de Almeida's *Memórias de um sargento de milícias*	Stowe's *Uncle Tom's Cabin*; Dumas Fils's *La Dame aux camélias*
1853		Álvares de Azevedo's *Lira dos vinte anos*	
1855	Coffee boom begins		Whitman's *Leaves of Grass*
1857		Alencar's *O guarani*	Flaubert's *Madame Bovary*
1859		Casimiro de Abreu's *Primaveras*	Baudelaire's *Les Fleurs du mal*
1861		Fagundes Varela's *Noturnas*	
1864	Paraguayan War begins	Death of Gonçalves Dias	Goncourt Brothers' *Renée Mauperin*

1870	Republican movement begins	Castro Alves's *Espumas fluctuantes*	
1871	Law of the Free Womb	Death of Castro Alves	
1876		Assis's *Helena*	Twain's *Adventures of Tom Sawyer*
1877	Major drought in Northeast		Tolstoy's *Anna Karenina*; Zola's *L'Assommoir*
1878		"Battle" of Parnassus	Eça de Queiroz's *O primo Basílio*
1880	Abolitionist campaign begins		Zola's *Le Roman expérimental*; Dostoevsky's *The Brothers Karamazov*
1881		Assis's *Memórias póstumas de Brás Cubas*; Aluísio Azevedo's *O mulato*	James' *The Portrait of a Lady*
1882	Rubber boom		Maupassant's *Contes*
1883		Castro Alves's *Os escravos*	
1885	Law of the Sixty Year Olds		
1888	Golden Law freeing slaves; large-scale immigration begins	Bilac's *Poesias*; A. Caminha's *O missionário*; J. Ribeiro's *A carne*; Pompéia's *O ateneu*	
1889	Proclamation of the Republic		
1890	Separation of church and state	Aluísio Azevedo's *O cortiço*	
1891	New Constitution	Assis's *Quincas Borba*	Wilde's *The Picture of Dorian Gray*
1893	Naval revolt	Cruz e Sousa's *Missal* and *Broquéis*	Heredia's *Les Trofées*
1896	Brazilian Academy of Letters founded		
1897	Battle of Canudos		
1899		Assis's *Dom Casmurro*	

1902		E. da Cunha's *Os sertões*; Graça Aranha's *Canaã*	Conrad's *Heart of Darkness*
1904	Baron Rio Branco negotiates boundaries	Assis's *Esaú e Jacó*	
1908		Death of Assis; publication of his *Memorial de Aires*	Wells's *Tono Bungay*
1909		Lima Barreto's *Recordações do escrivão Isaías Caminha*	G. Stein's *Three Lives*
1915		Lima Barreto's *Triste fim de Policarpo Quaresma*	Maugham's *Of Human Bondage*
1917	Brazil enters First World War	Monteiro Lobato's "Paranóia ou mistificação"	Pound begins *The Cantos*
1918		Monteiro Lobato's *Urupês*; death of Bilac	Apollinaire's *Calligrames*
1920	First Brazilian university		
1922	Lieutenants' Revolt—Rio	Week of Modern Art; *Klaxon* founded; death of Lima Barreto	Joyce's *Ulysses*; Eliot's *The Waste Land*
1924	Prestes Column	"Manifesto de poesia pau-brasil," by O. de Andrade	"Manifeste du surréalisme," by Bréton
1926		Regionalist Manifesto	Hemingway's *The Sun Also Rises*
1927		M. de Andrade's *Amar, verbo intransitivo*	Woolf's *To the Lighthouse*
1928		O. de Andrade's "Manifesto antropófago"; M. de Andrade's *Macunaíma*; J.A. de Almeida's *A bagaceira*; C. Ricardo's *Martim Cererê*	Huxley's *Point Counterpoint*; Brecht's *Three-penny Opera*

1929			Faulkner's *The Sound and the Fury*; Hesse's *Steppenwolf*
1930	Getúlio Vargas takes power	R. de Queiroz's *O quinze*; Bandeira's *Libertinagem*; Drummond de Andrade's *Alguma poesia*	
1931		Bopp's *Cobra Norato*; death of Graça Aranha	Woolf's *The Waves*; H. Miller's *Tropic of Cancer*
1932		Rego's *Menino do engenho*; Camargo's *Deus lhe pague*	
1933	Integralist Party formed	G. Ramos's *Caetés*; Freyre's *Casa grande e senzala*; A. Fontes's *Os Corumbas*	Malraux's *La Condition humaine*; O'Neill's *Ah, Wilderness!*
1934	University of São Paulo founded	G. Ramos's *São Bernardo*; death of Coelho Neto	
1935		É. Veríssimo's *Caminhos cruzados*	
1936		S. Buarque de Hollanda's *Raízes do Brasil*; G. Ramos and Jorge Amado imprisoned; Bandeira's *Estrela da manhã*	Bernanos's *Jornal d'un curé de campagne*
1937	Creation of Vargas's "New State"	Jorge Amado's *Capitães de areia*; O. de Andrade's *O rei da vela*	Steinbeck's *Of Mice and Men*
1938	Unsuccessful Integralist revolt	G. Ramos's *Vidas secas*; É. Veríssimo's *Olhai os lírios do campo*; Mendes's *A poesia em pânico*	Sartre's *La Nausée*
1939		D. Silveira de Queiroz's *Floradas na serra*	Sarraute's *Tropismes*

1940	Vargas supports the Axis	Drummond de Andrade's *Sentimento do mundo*	Hemingway's *For Whom the Bell Tolls*; Greene's *The Power and the Glory*; R. Wright's *Native Son*
1941	Vargas supports the Allies	M. de Andrade's *Poesias*	
1942	Brazil enters the war	C. Meireles's *Vaga música*; Jorge Amado's *Terras do sem-fim*	Camus's *L'Étranger*; Cela's *La familia de Pascual Duarte*
1943		N. Rodrigues's *Vestido de noiva*	
1944		C. Lispector's *Perto do coração selvagem*; Élis's *Ermos e gerais*	Borges's *Ficciones*
1945	Vargas deposed	Melo Neto's *A rosa do povo*; death of M. de Andrade; Generation of 1945	Orwell's *Animal Farm*
1946		Rosa's *Sagarana*	
1947		J. de Lima's *Poemas negros*	Camus's *La Peste*; C. Cullen's *On This I Stand*
1948		Brazilian Comedy Theater founded; death of Monteiro Lobato	A. Miller's *Death of a Salesman*; Sábato's *El túnel*
1949		É. Veríssimo's *O continente*	Orwell's *1984*
1950	Vargas elected president		Paz's *El laberinto de la soledad*
1952		Concretists organize *Noigandres*	Hemingway's *The Old Man and the Sea*
1953	Petrobrás created	C. Meireles's *Romanceiro da Inconfidência*; deaths of G. Ramos and J. de Lima	Neruda's *Poesía política*; A. Miller's *The Crucible*; Beckett's *Waiting for Godot*
1954	Vargas's suicide; Kubitschek government	Gullar's *A luta corporal*	W. Steven's *Poems*
1956	Brasília planned	Rosa's *Grande sertão: veredas*	

1958	Brazil wins World Soccer cup	Concrete Poetry Manifesto; Guarnieri's *Eles não usam black-tie*; Jorge Amado's *Gabriela, cravo e canela*	Pasternak's *Dr. Zhivago*; Lampedusa's *Il gattopardo*
1959		Cândido's *Formação da literatura brasileira*	Richler's *The Apprenticeship of Duddy Kravitz*; Grass's *The Tin Drum*
1960	Inauguration of Brasília as capital	C. Lispector's *Laços de família*	Robbe-Grillet's *Dans le labyrinthe*
1961	Jânio Quadros renounces presidency	Jorge Amado's *Os velhos marinheiros*; Lins's *O fiel e a pedra*; Popular Culture Centers founded	Heller's *Catch-22*; Salinger's *Franny and Zooey*
1962		Rosa's *Primeiras estórias*	Burgess's *A Clockwork Orange*
1963	Peasant revolts	Antônio's *Malagueta, Perus e Bacanaço*	Cortázar's *Rayuela*
1964	Military regime begins	C. Lispector's *A paixão segundo GH*; J.C. de Carvalho's *O coronel e o lobisomem*	Bellows's *Herzog*
1965	Institutional Act 2 creates two political parties	D. Trevisan's *O vampiro de Curitiba*; É. Veríssimo's *O senhor embaixador*	Bishop's *Questions of Travel*
1966		Melo Neto's *Morte e vida Severina*	Malamud's *The Fixer*
1967	Press censorship	Callado's *Quarup*; death of Rosa	Asturias's *El señor presidente*; García-Márquez's *Cien años de soledad*
1968	Student revolts; Institutional Act 5	C. Buarque's *Roda viva*; death of Bandeira	
1969	Political repression, torture, and imprisonment under military regime	Gullar's *Vanguarda e subdesenvolvimento*	Roth's *Portnoy's Complaint*; Vargas Llosa's *Conversación en la catedral*

1970	Propaganda of a Brazilian "economic miracle"; second World Cup championship	Dourado's *O risco do bordado*	
1971	Large foreign bank loans to Brazil begin	Callado's *Bar Don Juan*; Ubaldo Ribeiro's *Sargento Getúlio*	
1972		Jorge Amado's *Teresa Batista cansada da guerra*; Nava's *Baú de ossos*	Sarduy's *Cobra*
1973	Oil problem hits Brazil	Lins's *Avalovara*; L.F. Telles's *As meninas*	Solzhenitsyn's *The Gulag Archipelago*
1974	General Geisel assumes power	Rubião's *O pirotécnico Zacarias*	K. Rexroth's *New Poems*
1975		Loyola Brandão's *Zero*; Melo Neto's *Museu de tudo*; Louzeiro's *Lúcio Flávio, passageiro da agonia*	
1976		Gullar's *Poema sujo*; M. Souza's *Galvez, imperador do Acre*	Puig's *El beso de la mujer araña*
1977		Death of C. Lispector; publication of her *A hora da estrela*	
1979	Political amnesty begins under General Figueiredo	Ângelo's *A casa de vidro*; Gabeira's *O que é isso, companheiro?*	
1980	Metalworkers strike; gold discovered in Amazon	Death of V. de Moraes; Gullar's *Toda poesia*; R. Fonseca's *O cobrador*; A. do Nascimento's *O quilombismo*	Moravia's *Impegno controvoglia*; Jong's *Fanny*; death of Barthes
1981	Political *abertura* begins; rampant inflation	Callado's *Sempreviva*; D. Ribeiro's *O mulo*	Vargas Llosa's *La guerra del fin del mundo*; Thomas's *The White Hotel*

1982	Elections for Congress, state and local offices	Dias Gomes's *Sucupira, ame-a ou deixe-a*; Santiago's *Em liberdade*	Theroux's *The Mosquito Coast*; Sylvia Plath's *Journals*
1983	IMF constraints on Brazil result in rioting and unemployment	Ana Cristina César's *A teus pés*; Francis's *Filhas do segundo sexo*; Steen's *Corações mordidos*	Cela's *Mazurka para dos muertos*
1984	Campaign for direct presidential elections begins	Deaths of J. Andrade and Nava; R. Fonseca's *A grande arte*	Barnes's *Flaubert's Parrot*; Updike's *The Witches of Eastwick*
1985	Death of Tancredo Neves; Sarney becomes president	Callado's *Concerto carioca*; Noll's *Bandoleiros*; S. Sant'Anna's *Junk Box*; H. de Campos's *Galáxias*: death of H. Lisboa	Fuentes's *Gringo viejo*; LeGuin's *Always Coming Home*; Sir S. Spender's *Collected Poems*
1986	*Cruzado* currency	R. Fonseca's *Bufo & Spallanzani*	Nobel Prize to Soyinka; death of J. Génet; García Márquez's *El amor en los tiempos del cólera*
1987	Constituent assembly meets	Deaths of Gilberto Freyre, Drummond de Andrade and Leon Hirzsman	

Glossary of Frequently Used Brazilian Words

antropofagia	Anthropophagy, the cannibalist movement in *modernism
caboclo	A poor inhabitant of the interior, usually of mixed Indian and white ancestry
caipira	A poor inhabitant of the interior
carioca	An inhabitant of the city of Rio de Janeiro and/or any characteristic attributed to the city or resident
crônica	A short prose sketch of daily life (see entry)
gaúcho	An inhabitant of any of the southern states of Brazil (Santa Catarina, Paraná, Rio Grande do Sul) or any characteristic attributed to the area or resident
mineiro	An inhabitant of the state of Minas Gerais and/or any characteristic attributed to the state or resident
paulista	An inhabitant of the state of São Paulo and/or any characteristic attributed to the state or resident
saudade	Nostalgia or longing for the past, a person, or a place (see entry)
sertaneja, sertanejo	An inhabitant of the *sertão* and/or any characterstic attributed to the place or person
sertão	The barren hinterland of Brazil
tropicalismo	A cultural movement of the late 1960s and early 1970s that sought to reevaluate Brazilian life (see entry)
ufanismo	The ultrachauvinistic nativism of Brazilian civilization (see entry)

Key to Bibliographical References

AH	*American Hispanist*
BA	*Books Abroad*
BHS	*Bulletin of Hispanic Studies*
Bishop/Brasil	*An Anthology of Twentieth-Century Brazilian Poetry*. Edited by Elizabeth Bishop and Emanuel Brasil. Middletown, Conn.: Wesleyan University Press, 1972.
Brasil/Smith	*Brazilian Poetry: 1950–1980*. Edited by Emanuel Brasil and William Jay Smith. Middletown, Conn.: Wesleyan University Press, 1983.
BRMMLA	*Bulletin of the Rocky Mountain Modern Language Association*
Brookshaw	Brookshaw, David. *Race and Color in Brazilian Literature*. Metuchen, N.J.: Scarecrow Press, 1986.
BSG	*Brazil Studies Guides*. Edited by Sam Adamo and Jon M. Tolman. Albuquerque, New Mex.: Institute of Latin American Studies, University of New Mexico, 1984–1986.
BSUF	*Ball State University Forum*
CL	*Comparative Literature*
CLS	*Comparative Literature Studies*
Coutinho	*A literatura no Brasil*. Organized by Afrânio Coutinho. 2d ed. 6 vols. Rio: Editorial Sul-Americana, 1968–1970. (Third edition in progress).
Coutinho/Rabassa	Coutinho, Afrânio. *An Introduction to Literature in Brazil*. Translated by Gregory Rabassa. New York: Columbia University Press, 1969.
Donoso/Henkin	*The Triquarterly Anthology of Contemporary Latin American Literature*. Edited by José Donoso and William Henkin. New York: Dutton, 1969.
Driver	Driver, David Miller. *The Indian in Brazilian Literature*. New York: Hispanic Institute in the United States, 1943.

ESPSL   *Estado de São Paulo Suplemento Literário*

Ellison   Ellison, Fred. *Brazil's New Novel: Four Modern Masters.*
                           Berkeley: University of California Press, 1954.

Fremantle   *Latin American Literature Today.* Edited by Anne Fremantle.
                           New York: Times Mirror, 1977.

Foster/Foster   *Modern Latin American Literature.* 2 vols. Edited by David
                           W. Foster and Virginia Ramos Foster. New York: Ungar, 1975.

Goldberg   Goldberg, Isaac. *Brazilian Literature.* New York: Knopf,
                           1922.

Grossman   *Modern Brazilian Stories.* Translated and edited by William
                           Grossman. Berkeley: University of California Press, 1967.

Haberly   Haberly, David. *Three Sad Races.* Cambridge: Cambridge University Press, 1983.

HAHR   *Hispanic American Historical Review*

HLAS   *Handbook of Latin American Studies*

Hower/Preto-Rodas   *Empire in Transition: The Portuguese World in the Time of
                           Camões.* Edited by Alfred Hower and Richard A. Preto-Rodas.
                           Gainesville, Fla.: University Presses of Florida, 1985.

HR   *Hispanic Review*

Hulet   *Latin American Poetry in English Translation.* Organized and
                           edited by Claude Hulet. Washington, D.C.: Pan American
                           Union, 1965.

I & L   *Ideologies & Literature*

JIAS   *Journal of Inter-American Studies and World Affairs*

JL (Rio)   *Jornal de Letras*

KRQ   *Kentucky Romance Quarterly*

LALR   *Latin American Literary Review*

LATR   *Latin American Theatre Review*

LBR   *Luso-Brazilian Review*

Loos   Loos, Dorothy Scott. *The Naturalist Novel of Brazil.* New
                           York: Hispanic Institute in the United States, 1963.

Lowe   Lowe, Elizabeth. *The City in Brazilian Literature.* Madison,
                           N.J.: Fairleigh Dickinson University Press, 1982.

Martins   Martins, Wilson, *The Modernist Idea.* Translated by Jack Tomlins. New York: New York University Press, 1971.

MGSL   *Minas Gerais Suplemento Literário*

MLJ   *Modern Language Journal*

MLR   *Modern Language Review*

Monegal/Colchie   *Borzoi Anthology of Latin American Literature.* 2 vols. Edited
                           by Emir Rodríguez Monegal with the assistance of Thomas
                           Colchie. New York: Knopf, 1977.

Neistein/Cardozo	*Poesia brasileira moderna: A Bilingual Anthology.* Edited by José Neistein. Translations by Manuel Cardozo. Washington, D.C.: Brazilian American Cultural Institute, 1972.
Nist	*Modern Brazilian Poetry: An Anthology.* Edited by John Nist with the assistance of Yolanda Leite. Bloomington: Indiana University Press, 1962.
NYT	*New York Times*
NYTBR	*New York Times Book Review*
Patai	Patai, Daphne. *Myth and Reality in Brazilian Literature.* Madison, N.J.: Fairleigh Dickinson University, 1982.
PLL	*Papers on Language and Literature*
PMLA	*Publication of the Modern Language Association*
PPNCFL	*Proceedings* of the Pacific Northwest Council on Foreign Languages
PT	*Poetics Today*
RCB	*Revista de cultura brasileña* (Madrid)
REH	*Revista de estudios hispánicos*
RF	*Romanische Forschugen*
RHM	*Revista hispánica moderna*
RI	*Revista iberoamericana*
RIB	*Revista interamericana de bibliografía*
RLA	*Revista de letras da Faculdade de Assis (São Paulo, Brasil)*
RLC	*Revue de Littérature comparée*
RLV	*Revue des Langues vivantes*
RMLA/LAMR	*Revista de música latinoamericana/Latin American Music Review*
Roett	*Brazil in the Sixties.* Edited by Riordan Roett. Nashville: Vanderbilt University Press, 1963.
RomN	*Romance Notes*
Sayers	Sayers, Raymond S. *The Negro in Brazilian Literature.* New York: Hispanic Institute in the United States, 1956.
SLAPC	*Studies in Latin American Popular Culture*
Solt	*Concrete Poetry: A World View.* Edited by Mary Ellen Solt. Bloomington: Indiana University Press, 1968.
SSF	*Studies in Short Fiction*
Tolman (1978)	*Literary Review.* Special Brazil Issue. (Winter 1978). Edited by Jon M. Tolman.
Tolman (1984)	*Literary Review.* Special Issue on Brazilian Stories: 1956–1977. (Summer 1984). Edited by Jon M. Tolman.

TQ	*Texas Quarterly*
VV	*Village Voice*
WLT	*World Literature Today*
Woodbridge	"A Bibliography of Brazilian Poetry in English Translation." Edited by Hensley C. Woodbridge. *LBR*. Supplementary Issue (1978), pp. 161–188.

Introduction: Brazilian Literature in Cultural Perspective

Setting eyes in the year 1500 upon the newly discovered Portuguese territory, later to be called Brazil, Pero Vaz de *Caminha provided a fascinating first view of the new land and the Brazilian Indians (*brasilíndios*) through ingenuously vivid comparisons with the fruits, animals, and people of Portugal. Nonetheless, he often faltered: "I do not know how to describe what I see here."[1] (*See* Portugal and Brazil: Indianism; Literary Relations.)

Almost five hundred years later, this inability to comprehend the Brazilian reality persists. For example, Fernando *Gabeira returned from exile following an amnesty declared by the military dictatorship in 1979 and titled the initial volume of his *memoirs of political activities, torture, and exile *O que é isso, companheiro* (What's This, Pal?). In 1980 Affonso Romano de *Sant'Anna published the poem "Que país é este? ("What Kind of Country Is This?") on the front page of an important newspaper, in which he questioned the military's leadership of the nation. Ironically, the statement had been taken from a speech of a minister of the regime and it became a popular slogan until 1985. (*See* Dictatorship and Literature.)

This constant self-evaluation and definition and self-redefinition and reevaluation of Brazil by Brazilian writers has been one of the significant preoccupations as the country has grown from a colony to an independent nation to a world power: What is Brazil? Who are we? Where are we going? (*See* Philosophy of National Identity.)

Caminha's first words of bedazzlement and nativist sentiment, today called *ufanismo*, were echoed by subsequent chroniclers and visitors throughout the centuries. While Pero de Magalhães Gandavo (*see* Historiography) was convinced that the newly discovered inhabitants of this earthly Garden of Eden, the Tupi-Guarani Indians, had "neither faith nor laws nor a king," other visitors, such as the sixteenth-century French traveler Jean de Léry (*see* Travel Literature) commented on their practice of cannibalism. In fact, the first Portuguese bishop in Brazil, D. Pedro Fernandes Sardinha, was eaten by the Caeté Indians in 1556.

Léry, however, saw cannibalism as no worse than the greed for wealth that prevailed among his own countrymen.

Father Manuel da *Nóbrega sought a biblical origin for the Indians' existence. Nóbrega and Father José de *Anchieta proselitized the Indians to Roman Catholicism; in the process they learned and wrote in the *Indian languages. In a letter from São Paulo dated 1554, Father Anchieta described the Jesuits' dedication to their flock in the face of hardships: "We are in such difficult straits that it is often quite necessary for the Brothers to give grammar lessons outdoors; although the cold outdoors bothers us, inside there is heavy smoke [from the fires], but we prefer to suffer the inconvenience of the cold outside than the smoke indoors."[2] It is not surprising, therefore, that upon commenting on this dedication in our own time, Gilberto *Freyre described Jesuit Roman Catholicism as the "cement of Brazilian unity." (*See* Religion and Literature.)

The material wealth of the new land was pinpointed by many chroniclers. Sugar cane and brazilwood, the origin of the colony's name, were immediately exploited for international trade, thus beginning Brazil's first economic cycle. Descriptions of mineral riches were accompanied by tales of ferocious tropical insects. In 1534 hereditary captaincies were awarded by the king to noblemen, bestowing upon them almost royal power over their new territories while obliging the "captains" to develop these at their own expense. While this system failed, the personal ownership of huge tracts of land, *latifundia*, began to set the stage for the development of Brazilian social classes and slavery. (*See* Slavery and Literature.)

Illusions of a potential new political grandeur led the young Portuguese King Sebastian into battle and to death in 1578. His throne legitimately fell to King Philip II of Spain. The Spanish political dominion over Portugal and its empire lasted sixty years, 1580–1640. Colonization of Brazil continued, at times rapaciously. Although the Amazon River was discovered and explored by Francisco de Orellana between 1539 and 1541, it was only a full century later, in 1637, that Pedro Teixeira led an expedition up the river to Quito; he founded the city of Tabatinga in 1639 at the point where modern-day Peru, Colombia, and Brazil meet. Father Acuña, a Spanish priest, wrote the first detailed description of the "river-sea" of the mythological giant women, commenting that: "the great river excludes no one from its vast treasures, but rewards all who wish to take advantage of them."[3]

The settlement of the North was begun as a purely defensive measure. The city of Belém was founded at the mouth of the Amazon in 1616; the province of Maranhão was created, comprising modern Maranhão, Ceará, and Pará states. Nevertheless, this area of the colony was conquered by the Dutch with the aid of some settlers and Indians. They supported the administration of Maurice of Nassau (1637–1644), which ruled over the coastline as far south as Bahia. It was not until 1654 that the Dutch were finally expelled from Brazil, leaving behind their cultural mark—in art and architecture—which is still visible today.

A Portuguese colonial government was established at that time and lasted until the era of Brazil's independence. (*See* Art and Literature.)

Beset by coastal invasions by the English and French in the early seventeenth century, the colonial government, the settlers, and Jesuits united to repulse them. A century after discovery a sense of a national character distinct from that of the Portuguese was being defined. Writings on the natural resources and the flora and fauna in a "new" Portuguese language—the *língua geral* (*see* Portuguese Language of Brazil)—as well as the literary style of the chroniclers revealed this nativism. In 1627 Friar Vicente do Salvador (*see* Historiography) wrote a *História do Brasil* (History of Brazil) in which he criticized the "European" rulers for favoring their African possessions and complained about recently arrived settlers (*colonos*), who came in search of quick wealth. However, he also lamented: "But this is not only true about those who come from there [Portugal], but also about those who were born here—both use the land not as masters but as profit seekers, only abusing it and abandoning it once it is destroyed."[4]

By this time, the colony was becoming divided socially between the Portuguese settlers (*renóis*), people born in Brazil of Portuguese parents (*mazombos*), and the growing number of mestizos and mulattoes, respectively of Portuguese/Indian or Portuguese/African blood. Although black slaves had begun to appear in Brazil in the middle of the sixteenth century, Indians were the major source of forced labor during the early colonial period. Their rapid decimation due to illnesses or brutal treatment was recognized and lamented by Nóbrega and Anchieta; however, it was Father Antônio *Vieira who, at mid-century, brought this issue to the direct attention of the Portuguese King Afonso VI in both his sermons and letters: "In the period of forty years on the coast and in the interior more than two million Indians have been killed, and more than five-hundred settlements as large as cities have been destroyed—and no one has been punished."[5] Vieira insisted further that the mistreatment of these Indians, the king's subjects, was solely for the benefit of the ruling nobles appointed by the king himself. Vieira echoed Anchieta's and Nóbrega's calls for more humane treatment.

Seventeenth-century Brazilian letters were directly influenced by the variations of the *baroque. Whereas Vieira's rhetoric addressed major issues of Portuguese, Brazilian, and international politics, Gregório de *Matos's pen touched on the increasingly unjust social conditions within the colony: "Dear Bahia / noble and opulent city / Stepmother to its native born / and mother to foreigners."[6] Matos denounced the pretensions of the "white" Brazilian society of Bahia. By his time miscegenation had become a pronounced feature of Brazilian life: Africans were gradually becoming the preponderant element in an ever more complex, multitiered society. Slavery was not limited to plantation life but was also prevalent in the city. Colonies of rebellious slaves (*quilombos*) dotted the country. The best organized was Palmares in Alagoas (1672–1694), an attempt to re-create an African tribal state in the New World. Vieira aptly remarked at the time that "Brazil has the body of America and the soul of Africa."[7]

Although the Jesuits had created institutions of higher learning in the colony, until the midnineteenth century the sons of the well-to-do sought a university education in Portugal at Coimbra. Most, however, rejected Portugal as a foreign place and returned to Brazil. The colony's rapid economic growth during the eighteenth century stimulated the construction of homes, churches, bridges, dams, and other infrastructures. This boom was due partly to the successful explorations of Brazilian pioneers of all races (*bandeirantes*), who traveled Brazil's rivers in search of Indian slaves, gold, diamonds, and other wealth. In 1711, André João Antonil (*see* Historiography) described the mad rush of gold prospectors (*garimpeiros*) to the interior:

Each year the fleets bring many Portuguese and foreigners who take over the mines. From towns, villages, the seacoast and the interior of Brazil, whites, browns, blacks and many Indians, who serve the *paulistas*, come to the mines. They are a mixture of all conditions of mankind: male and female, young and old, rich and poor, nobles and peasants, laymen, clergy and religious people of diverse orders, many of whom have neither convent nor house in Brazil. Over all these people there is no effective secular control or well-ordered government.[8]

Political, social, and economic conflicts increasingly divided the society. Although several black slave uprisings in the seventeenth century—the most famous led by Zumbi in Palmares—had been quelled, violent backlashes against new influxes of Portuguese settlers or against the economic policies of the Portuguese monarchy itself occurred. Manuel Beckmann, a rich landowner and merchant, attempted to declare the independence of Maranhão; he was hanged in 1684. The War of Emboabas in Minas in 1709 involved a clash of interests between "Brazilians" and newcomers over mining claims. The Mascates War, 1710–1711, pitted the "traditional" sugar aristocracy of Recife against the merchant classes, made up principally of recent Portuguese immigrants.

In 1750 King D. José I appointed Sebastião José de Carvalho, the future marquis of Pombal, as prime minister of Portugal. Pombal pursued aggressive economic policies throughout the empire; he created two new Brazilian regional trading companies to compete with the Dutch and the English entrepreneurs. Furthermore, he banished the Jesuits from Portugal and Brazil in 1759, accusing them of empire building. Pombal's expulsion of the Jesuits assuaged some critics of Portugal's political and social policies, but it also led to the massacre of Indians who had been proselitized. (The expulsion of the Jesuits from South America and the destruction of their Indian missions are treated in the film *The Mission.*) Pombal increased the economic burdens of the colonists. After his fall from power in 1777, Queen D. Maria I further tightened the economic noose on the Brazilians, prohibiting any industrialization and requiring higher production and duties on gold, by then the mainstay of the Portuguese economy.

The loosely knit eighteenth-century *academies and *arcadias, groups of intellectuals in Rio, Bahia, and Minas, absorbed the ideals of the French *philosophes*: the concepts of nationhood, free thought, and social justice secured by equitable political, economic, and legal institutions. Brazil's newest intellectuals discussed, debated, and wrote about Brazilian concerns. In addition, American independence from England and the prerevolutionary activities in France led them to conclude that their "nation" was unfairly subjugated by the mother country and that the Brazilian was every inch the equal of the Portuguese, or better. Alvarenga *Peixoto wrote in one of his more famous poems: "The most outstanding heroes/Are now among our compatriots;/And your [the Portuguese] blood, which thrives in this land,/Already produces the best fruits of Europe."[9] Domingos Caldas Barbosa, while in Portugal, recognized that in love matters the Brazilian surpassed the Portuguese: "I thought that the pleasure of love/Was always the same pleasure,/But a Brazilian love,/I know not why, is sweeter. . . . The pleasures of this land [Portugal]/Taste always like bread and cheese,/They are not like in Brazil/where even desire is sweet."[10] The *Mineiran Conspiracy of 1789 sought to gain Brazilian freedom; other failed revolts of a similar nature followed in Rio and Salvador.

Contemporaneously, a modest native urban cultural base was being formed, consisting of schools, small theater groups, public spaces with sculpture. Following the arrival of the Portuguese royal family in Rio in 1808, as a result of the invasion of the Iberian Peninsula by Napoleon's forces, Brazil was raised to the status of kingdom, equal to Portugal. Dom João, then prince regent, opened Brazilian ports and trade to businessmen and ships of all friendly nations. Social and cultural life in the Court was enriched by several French cultural missions, which included artists, architects, and scholars. A royal press was established in 1808. Journals and magazines appeared lauding the colony's new status. The opposition—those intellectuals favoring independence or a special role for Brazil within the Portuguese empire—were forced into exile. Most notable among them was Hipólito da *Costa, who, in England, carried out his campaign for an improved political future for Brazil.

Anti-Portuguese emotions ran high when King João VI was finally obliged to return to Portugal in 1821, leaving his son Dom Pedro as regent. Although, initially, there was an attempt to return Brazil to its colonial status, the nationalist sentiment of the local elite forced Dom Pedro to declare independence on September 7, 1822. The United States recognized the newly independent Empire of Brazil in 1824, the same year that the first Brazilian Constitution was drafted, ensuring the continuation of a strong monarchical government in the New World. In 1825, Portugal accepted the existence of the new nation; spiritually and economically, however, Portugal has never recovered from the loss. The following year, 1826, England also recognized Brazil in exchange for Dom Pedro I's agreement to several commercial treaties which were of questionable value to his young nation. Newspapers soon began to circulate throughout the country: the *Diário de Pernambuco* (1825), the Rio newspapers *Jornal do Comércio* (1827) and *Aurora Fluminense* (1827), as well as the *Observador Constitucional* (1830) in São Paulo and others in Bahia. Translations of foreign literature appeared in the 1830s.

The early years of Dom Pedro I's reign were guided by some of the wisest and most conciliatory spirits of Brazilian history, notably the stalwart José Bonifácio de Andrada e *Silva. Nonetheless, two distinct political factions developed: the federalists, who supported autonomy for the individual provinces, and the centrists, generally aristocrats who defended the concept of a strong central government represented by the emperor. In the international arena, Dom Pedro I was unsuccessful. His resignation of the throne in 1831, in favor of his son the future Dom Pedro II, derived from his decision to defend his right to the Portuguese throne.

The interval until the ascension of Dom Pedro II, called the Regency (1831–1840), was characterized by the intensification of regionalist/centrist conflicts around important economic issues. Several of these conflicts erupted into civil wars: the Cabanagem (1835–1840) in Pará; the Sabinada (1837–1838) in Bahia; the Balaiada (1838–1841) in Maranhão, Ceará, and Piauí; and, the most serious, the Farroupilha Revolt (1835–1845) in Rio Grande do Sul.

The ideals of ending negro slavery and civilizing the Indians always existed in some measure during the Empire. José Bonifácio, the "godfather" of his country, had espoused these generally unpopular goals in the early days of independence: "Reason and law dictate that [the slaves] be gradually converted from their vile status to free and active men. Then the inhabitants of this land will be transformed from their cruelness, which they frequently manifest on this point, into Christians. . . . [The Indians] are . . . capable of civilization as soon as the proper methods are adopted and there is true faith and zeal in carrying them out."[11]

During the Regency Brazilian *romanticism began—not in Brazil but in France. Gonçalves de *Magalhães and other founders of the literary review *Niterói: Revista Brasiliense* (1836; *see* Reviews) used the motto "Tudo pelo Brasil e para o Brasil" (Everything on behalf of Brazil and for Brazil). In the review's second (and final) issue, J. M. Pereira da Silva attempted to improve the public's attitude toward the significant role that "poets" would play in the new nation's future: "It is necessary for Brazil to rid itself of prejudices about poets which Portugal bequeathed us upon discovery, suggesting that they are useless men for the society and ignoring their mission and influence. . . . It is up to Brazil to begin to appreciate its men, remembering that the poet, to earn his name, must be an historian, philosopher, politician and artist."[12]

Dom Pedro II's ascension to the throne in 1840 helped to bring political order, as well as cultural advancement to the nation. The Brazilian Historical and Geographical Institute, founded in 1838, received the emperor's lifelong patronage. New schools and theater groups appeared. Artists and musicians received imperial support and grants; some based their works on literary themes, thus initiating an intimate relationship between *art and literature and *music and literature. Many contemporary intellectuals were considered to have "sold out" to the emperor's conservative, European-oriented perspective. Throughout his reign, Dom Pedro II, whose legacy to Brazil is still vigorously debated, practiced a policy of conciliation. He supported the two established elite political parties, which alternated in power, and avoided action on many controversial political, economic, and social issues. Despite Dom Pedro II's ability at manipulation, the narrowness of the political system was a factor in the downfall of the empire. (*See* Theater History.)

It was only in the final phase of Brazilian romanticism, from the 1850s onward, that a growing abhorrence of the massive contradictions of the Brazilian social reality inspired wider protests. The status of the slave in Brazil attracted worldwide and national attention. Thomas Ewbank, a North American traveler to Brazil in the 1850s, described a slave auction with great compassion for the "commodity":

I have repeatedly passed an auction store at the corner of Ourives and Ouvidor [Streets]. Today printed bills were hanging by the door. I stepped in. . . . They [the Africans] were of every shade, from deep Angola jet to white or nearly white, as one young woman facing me appeared. She was certainly superior in mental organization to some of the buyers. The anguish with which she watched the proceedings and waited her turn to be brought out, exposed, examined and disposed of was distressing."[13] (*See* Travel Literature.)

The great romantic poet Antônio Gonçalves *Dias extolled his land's uniqueness in his "Canção de exílio" [Song of Exile], but he also exposed the facade of the avowed "liberal" regime of Dom Pedro II. In the poetic dialogue "Meditação" (Meditation), an elderly Brazilian lauds the nation's glories, while a young Brazilian boldly tempers his views: "A large part of its [Brazil's] population is made up of slaves and its wealth consists of slaves—and its smile, the success of its businessmen, of its farmers, and the food of all its inhabitants is bought at the expense of the slaves' blood!"[14] In 1850, under extreme international pressure, the Queiroz Law put an end to the import of slaves. (*See* Slavery and Literature.)

Although historians view the 1850s and 1860s as a politically stable period of development for the empire—steamship railroad service and a telegraph system began in the 1850s—serious internal and international problems arose: a bitter one-year revolution in Pernambuco, beginning in 1848, set the inhabitants of the city against those of the backlands (*sertão*); a war in the River Plate (1850–1852) succeeded in deposing the aggressive Argentine dictator Rosas; between 1864 and 1870 the Paraguayan War, considered Latin America's costliest, allied Brazil, Argentina, and Uruguay against Paraguay, which lost most of its male population; in the Northeast a periodic drought became severe in 1877, devastating the area and its inhabitants.

Sílvio *Romero considered the post–Paraguayan War period to be a watershed for the nation:

The Paraguayan War revealed to all the immense defects of our military organization and the backwardness of our social progress, repugnantly uncovering the wound of slavery . . . everything is put into discussion: the sophisticated election machine, the billyclub system of police and courts, and the innumerable economic problems. . . . A collection of new ideas swarmed over us from all points on the horizon.[15]

The birth of the coffee economy signaled the end of the dominant political and economic role of northeastern Brazil. A new wealthy class was forming, consisting partly of merchants and of entrepreneurs enriched by speculation. The ''new nobility'' achieved both riches and power—but often subsequent ruin. The republican movement made strides in Brazil during the 1870s, due to the growing dissatisfaction with the inequities of Brazilian life. The authors of the Republican Manifesto of 1870 summed up the situation:

Privilege invades all aspects of society—in synthesis, it is the fabric of our society and politics—privilege of religion, privilege of race, privilege of intellect, privilege of position. . . . Despite a half century of existence as an independent national community, Brazilian society today faces the problems of its political organization as if it had just now emerged from colonial chaos.[16]

In fiction, poetry, essays, and *crônicas*, the literary and intellectual community debated every aspect of the Brazilian identity. *Realism and *naturalism, as well as *Parnassianism and *symbolism, were, once again, ''imported'' literary movements, but they assumed a significant Brazilian quality through the often graphic presentation of a society composed of contrasting elements: rural and urban, slave and free citizen, coastal and interior, farmer and bureaucrat, immigrant, Indian, mulatto, and black and white. Aluísio *Azevedo described the aim of his naturalistic fiction: ''to combat all the inimical evils, vices, defects and prejudices of my land, while stressing its beauty and virtue.''[17]

The ''first'' republic, born under the philosophical sign of positivism, replaced the empire in 1889. It was led by a series of oligarchic, despotic reserve officers (*coronéis*) who were, at times, as ineffective in controlling their state militias as they were in resolving the nation's difficulties. A military revolt in 1893 favored the return of the monarchy. A workforce to replace the newly freed slaves was sought through an open immigration policy, which brought more than 100,000 immigrants a year to Brazil until the turn of the century. Spanish, Portuguese, Italians, Japanese, and Chinese were contracted at home and arrived to work as indentured laborers on rubber plantations in the Amazon and coffee plantations in the South. (The film *Gaijin* describes the arrival of the first Japanese immigrants to Brazil at the beginning of the twentieth century.) Some overcame their condition as immigrants and became leaders in the industrialization of Brazil; still others became labor leaders. The Canudos rebellion in Bahia, begun in 1896, was reminiscent of the Palmares *quilombo* of two centuries before. The government crushed the rural poor participants and their leader, Antônio Conselheiro, in a most dramatic episode of class warfare, narrated by Euclides da *Cunha. (*See* Film and Literature; Immigrants and Literature; Positivism and Literature.)

The questions about the Brazilian identity remained little changed four centuries after discovery: What is Brazil? Who are we? What is our past and our future? By the early twentieth century the past seemed to have become indelibly engraved on the nation's future: economic instability; social instability; political instability. The Amazonian rubber boom (1870–1910) went bust. The elite society life of the *belle-époque* ended together with the First World War. Urban industrial workers were forming unions, but faced great obstacles.

A national sense of Brazilian culture slowly developed. Increasingly, the middle class would "sanitize" and imitate the cultural expressions of the lower classes, for example, the *samba*. While the identification of a "Brazilian language" was attributed—justly so—to the romantics, for example, José de Alencar, the concept gained wider acceptance thanks to the prose of Cunha's *Os sertões* and to Monteiro Lobato's attack on *gramatiquice*, traditional continental Portuguese grammar rules which seemed irrelevant for Brazil.

Influences from abroad once again set the pace for a new generation's debate about Brazil. Graça *Aranha's comments attracted widespread interest:

The history of civilization in Brazil could be written in four lines, so simple and so insignificant has been its contribution to the luminous history of the human spirit. All cultural efforts in the immense territory in which we have encamped, can be reduced to three essential facts: . . . discovery, national independence and the abolition of slavery. Like the rest of America, Brazil had a simple economic destiny.[18]

Ronald de *Carvalho wrote:

Our duty is to destroy the bias in favor of Europe, the worst and most noxious of all our ills. We must give to the history of the American peoples that preeminence in our thoughts which we now give to other countries. We must stop thinking 'European.' We must think American. . . . Our duty is to fight all these deviations, crowning the work of our political independence by achieving independence of thought.[19]

Paying homage to some romantic precursors and to some contemporaries, the modernists (*see* Modernism) also invoked those age-old questions: Who are we? What do we represent as a nation? Many orientations—most echoes of the past— were proposed during the 1920s. Was Brazil symbolized by its Indians' cannibalistic heritage? Was *regionalism the greatest asset or the most serious liability? Were Brazilian fauna and flora the most representative features of the country? What about *popular culture and folklore? Who was the typical Brazilian—the Portuguese, the Indian, the African, the mulatto, the *caboclo*, or the *caipira* of São Paulo? What should be the role of Roman Catholicism in Brazilian life? And the role of the Afro-Brazilian rites? In the midst of the heated intellectual debate, with sides definitively drawn, one insightful, superior voice emerged— that of Mário de *Andrade.

Uprisings against the authoritarian republican government of Artur Bernardes (1922–1929) were followed by the Prestes Column march through Brazil (1924– 1926), a protest against electoral manipulations; it marked the middle class's exasperation with the failures of the republic. The stock market crash of 1929 rocked the Brazilian economy and led to the revolution of 1930. The critic

Nelson Werneck Sodré (*see* Critics and Criticism) related the political and literary situation and commented:

The modernist movement had been the initial action, the vanguard action, in a break with the artistic manifestations of a colonial society . . . living off external influences and subordinating its creations to foreign models . . . In Brazil, there began to exist a "people" in the modern sense, and only the people could grant vitality to any form of expression which was intended to reflect the collective national physiognomy. We were entering the phase in which only what is popular is national.[20]

In 1937 Getúlio Vargas assumed dictatorial powers, and he proceeded to manipulate and co-opt culture for the duration of his "New State" (*Estado Novo*). Dissidents inevitably were jailed or forced into exile. The cultural focus turned away from the people (*povo*) and returned to the elites. Cultural events became a series of Hollywoodesque musicals and spectacles; for example, Heitor *Villa-Lobos leading 30,000 schoolchildren in a singing demonstration. Opposition to the regimes's policies could be found in the fiction of the *social novelists of the 1930s, and the sociological reevaluations of the Brazilian reality published by Gilberto *Freyre and Caio Prado Júnior.

Vargas changed sides during World War II. In 1940, he supported the Axis; then, anticipating its defeat, he turned to the Allies. The war years brought many foreign intellectuals to Brazilian shores in search of safety. Vargas was deposed by the military in 1945, the year of Mário de Andrade's death, and the date given for the birth of a new era of Brazilian literature known as Postmodernism. (*See* Postmodernism in Poetry.) An unsteady political course brought Vargas back to power in 1950 as a populist president. He promoted workers' rights and unions, among other social reforms. Further problems with the military led to his suicide in 1954. (*See* Foreign Writers and Brazil.)

The post-Vargas period of the 1950s and early 1960s was characterized by political and economic development, cultural expansion, and a look to the future represented by the new capital, Brasília. The *samba* attained real international popularity through the *bossa-nova*. The *cinema-novo* generation was inspired by the Brazilian reality: poverty, messianism, and unemployment. Brazil won the World Cup Soccer championship in 1958 and was in the international spotlight. Concretism (*see* Postmodernism in Poetry), a worldwide cultural movement, had its major impetus in Brazil. (*See* Film and Literature; Soccer and Literature.)

Serious imbalances persisted and intensified as the nation's population grew from 60 million to 100 million, in the mid-1970s, to 140 million by 1987. The government of João Goulart (1961–1964) sought basic social reforms, including land redistribution and peasant rights. Termed pro-communist by some, it was overthrown by the military, which then took charge of the country for twenty-one years, empowering itself through five successive Institutional Acts which curtailed the rights of citizens, instituted a bizarre mechanism of censorship, and tacitly allowed for the use of torture.

While many novelists, poets, and dramatists sought ingenuous and subtle ways to protest the regime's tactics, others sought (or were forced to seek) exile as a means of protest, among them Chico *Buarque, Augusto *Boal, and Ferreira *Gullar. The Monteiro *Martins began a collection of stories about the 1970s with a citation from *Macbeth*: "Alas, poor country! / Almost afraid to know itself. It cannot / be called our Mother, but our grave; / where nothing / But who knows nothing, is once seen to smile.[21] (*See* City and Literature; Dictatorship and Literature.)

Modernization and urbanization took place under the military government. Several years of very high growth rates, known as the "economic miracle," ended in the early 1970s. Through extensive borrowings abroad, a series of major national development projects were initiated. The early 1980s found Brazil in a severe economic recession; though the picture improved slightly in the middle of the decade, the inflation rate soon shot up again.

A political liberalization (*abertura*) began under the presidency of General João Baptista Figueiredo (1979–1985). A general amnesty allowed exiles to return but also prevented the prosecution of the military officers or police for crimes committed during the dictatorship. A widespread intellectual undertaking became that of recording and analyzing the experiences of the previous decades, often through *memoirs and *autobiographies.

A democratically inspired civilian government was established in 1985, under President José Sarney, a poet and fiction writer. Though politically pressured as a result of continuing economic hardship, this government is promoting a fair, free, and effective multiparty electoral system under a new liberal constitution. Nationalistic Brazilian economists have presented new plans for economic rebirth and for some governmental relief from the heavy burdens of servicing the immense foreign debt. They have stressed the social and political need to ensure an adequate subsistence throughout the population.

Those centuries-old questions about national identity continue to be debated today, while new ones have been added, for example, what will be the role of women in a new Brazilian society? The unrelenting euphoria about Brazil's future is basically unshaken in face of a multiplicity of serious problems. Today's literature actively participates in the analysis of the contradictions that make up the nation: an amazingly original civilization, in many ways still living in its past while striving hard for paradise in the twenty-first century. (*See* New Writers)

NOTES

1. Caminha, Pero Vaz de. *Vocabulário da "Carta" de Pero Vaz de Caminha*. Seguido da reprodução fac-similar da leitura diplomática do manuscrito. Edited by Sílvio Batista Pereira. Rio: INL/MEC, 1964.

2. Anchieta, Padre José de. *Cartas, informações, fragmentos, histórias e sermões do Padre Joseph de Anchieta, S. J. (1554–1594)*. Rio: Civilização Brasileira, 1933. p. 43.

3. Acuña, Padre Cristóbal de. "A New Discovery of the Great River of the Ama-

zons." In *Expeditions into the Valley of the Amazons*. Edited by Clements R. Markham. London: Haklyut Society, 1859. p. 133.

4. Salvador, Friar Vicente do. *História do Brasil*. São Paulo and Rio: Weisflog, 1918. p. 27.

5. Vieira, Padre Antônio. *Obras escolhidas*. Lisbon: Sá da Costa, 1951–1954. V:48.

6. *Antologia dos poetas brasileiros da fase colonial*. Edited and organized by Sérgio Buarque de Hollanda. Rio: INL, 1953. I: 108.

7. Cited in E. Bradford Burns. *A History of Brazil*. New York: Columbia University Press, 1970. p. 43.

8. Antonil, André João [João Antônio Andreoni]. *Cultura e opulência do Brasil*. São Paulo: Companhia Editora Nacional, 1967. p. 264.

9. *Antologia dos poetas brasileiros da fase colonial*. II:49.

10. *Ibid*. II:301.

11. Silva, José Bonifácio de Andrada e. *O pensamento vivo de José Bonifácio*. Introduction by Octávio Tarquínio de Sousa. São Paulo: Martins, 1961. pp. 63–64, 88.

12. *Niterói: Revista Brasiliense* (1836).

13. Ewbank, Thomas. *Life in Brazil; or A Journal of a Visit to the Land of the Cocoa and the Palm*. New York: Harper, 1856. pp. 282, 283.

14. Dias, Antônio Gonçalves. "Meditação." *Poesia completa e prosa escolhida*. Rio: Aguilar, 1959. p. 743.

15. Romero, Sílvio. "Provocações e debates." In Mendonça, Carlos Sussekind de. *Sílvio Romero: sua formação intelectual (1851–1880)*. São Paulo: Companhia Editora Nacional, 1938. p. 48.

16. "Manifesto Republicano." In Salles, Alberto. *Política republicana*. Rio: 1882. pp. 502, 503.

17. Cited in Massaud Moisés. *História da literatura brasileira: romantismo, realismo*. São Paulo: Cultrix/EDUSP, 1984. p. 350.

18. Aranha, José Pereira da Graça. *A esthetica da vida*. Rio/Paris: Garnier, 1925. p. 166.

19. Carvalho, Ronald de. *Estudos brasileiros*. 1ª série. Rio: Anuário do Brasil, 1929. p. 63.

20. Sodré, Nelson Werneck. *História da literatura brasileira: seus fundamentos econômicos*. 4ª ed. Rio: Civilização Brasileira, 1964. p. 531.

21. Martins, Júlio César Monteiro. *Muamba*. Rio: Ânima, 1985.

BIBLIOGRAPHY

Bibliographies

Bryant, Solena V., compiler. *Brazil*, World Bibliographical Series. Oxford, England: Clio Press, 1985.

Carpeaux, Oto Maria. *Pequena bibliografia crítica da literatura brasileira*. (Many editions; best overall general bibliography of works and criticism in Portuguese.)

Levine, Robert M., ed. *Brazil, 1822–1930: An Annotated Bibliography for Social Historians*. New York: Garland, 1983.

———. *Brazil since 1930*. New York: Garland, 1980.

Brazilian History and Documentation

Burns, E. Bradford, ed. *A Documentary History of Brazil*. New York: Alfred A. Knopf, 1966.
———. *A History of Brazil*. 2nd ed. New York: Columbia University Press, 1980.

Dictionaries of Literature

Foster, David W., and Ricardo Reis. *A Dictionary of Contemporary Brazilian Authors*. Tempe, Ariz.: Center for Latin American Studies, Arizona State University, 1981. (Articles on twentieth-century and very contemporary figures.)
Moisés, Massaud, and José Paulo Paes. *Pequeno dicionário da literatura brasileira*. 2d ed. São Paulo: Cultrix, 1979. (A comprehensive dictionary of Brazilian literature in Portuguese.)

Histories of Literature

Bandeira, Manuel. *A Brief History of Brazilian Literature*. Translated by Ralph E. Dimmick. New York: Charles Frank Publications, 1964.
Coutinho, Afrânio. *A literatura no Brasil*. 2d ed. 6 vols. Rio: Sul-Americana, 1968–1970.
———. *An Introduction to Literature in Brazil*. Translated by Gregory Rabassa. New York: Columbia University Press, 1969.
Moisés, Massaud. *História da literatura brasileira*. São Paulo: Cultrix/EDUSP, 1981– .
Veríssimo, Érico. *Brazilian Literature: An Outline*. New York: Macmillan, 1945.

Guides to Brazilian Language and Literature

Tolman, Jon M., and Ricardo Paiva. *Brazilian Literature and Language Outlines. Brazil Studies Guides*. Edited by Sam Adamo and Jon M.Tolman. Albuquerque, New Mex.: Institute of Latin American Studies, University of New Mexico, 1984–1986.

General Critical and Cultural Studies of Brazilian Literature

Adamo, Sam, and Jon M. Tolman, eds. *Brazil Studies Guides*. 15 vols. Albuquerque, New Mex.: Center for Latin American Studies, University of New Mexico, 1984–1986.
Azevedo, Fernando de (BAL: 1967). *Brazilian Culture*. New York: Macmillan, 1950.
"Brazil, Twentieth-Century Giant." *The Courier*, UNESCO: December, 1986. (Special issue on Brazilian Culture.)
Franco, Jean. *The Modern Culture of Latin America: Society and the Artist*. Middlesex, Eng.: Penguin, 1967.
Martins, Wilson. *História da inteligência brasileira*. 7 vols. São Paulo: Cultrix/Editora da Univerdade de São Paulo, 1978–1981.
Putnam, Samuel. *Marvelous Journey: A Survey of Four Centuries of Brazilian Writing*. New York: Alfred A. Knopf, 1948.

Selections from Brazilian Literature

Hulet, Claude. *Brazilian Literature*. 3 vols. Washington, D.C.: Georgetown University Press, 1974–1975. (Portuguese selections are preceded by English introductions.)

Cândido, Antônio, and J. Aderaldo Castello. *Presença da literatura brasileira*. (Many editions of this classic all-Portuguese compilation have been published since the 1960s.)

History of Book Publication in Brazil

Hallewell, Laurence. *Books in Brazil: A History of the Publishing Trade*. Metuchen, N.J.: Scarecrow Press, 1982.

Dictionary of
Brazilian
Literature

A

ABOLITIONISM. *See* Slavery and Literature.

ABREU, CAIO FERNANDO (b. 1948). From Rio Grande do Sul State, Abreu is an extremely popular contemporary novelist and short story writer. His appeal has been very strong among members of his own generation owing to his treatment of issues confronting them: his handling of sexual questions, his references to *popular culture, his use of slang and scatology, and his staccatolike prose. Nonetheless, he cites a literary debt to Clarice *Lispector and Osman *Lins, as well as to contemporary Brazilian musicians such as Chico *Buarque. (*See* Music and Literature; New Writers.)

Limite branco (1970; Open Limit), his first novel, is a seemingly autobiographical account of a struggling adolescent in the industrializing urban environment of modern Brazil. The stories in *Inventário do irremediável* (1970; Inventory of the Irremediable), awarded the Chinaglia Literary Prize (*see* Prizes) in 1969, also focus on the existential problems of life in big cities. (*See* Autobiography; City and Literature.)

The story "A margarida" (The Sunflower), from the volume *O ovo apunhalado* (1975; The Stabbed Egg), is a lively satire of the influences of modern advertising. The ad man oversees and promotes the rise and fall of canned sunflowers. *Pedras de Calcutá* (1977; Stones of Calcutta) and *Morangos mofados* (1982; Musty Strawberries), his most successful collections to date, evoke the sociopolitical repression of the society during the military dictatorship. The story "Sargento Garcia" (Sargent Garcia), from the latter collection, offers a startling view of Brazilian life through a case of (in)voluntary homosexual rape. In *Triângulo das águas* (1983; Triangle of the Waters), the setting is São Paulo, the scene of nighttime encounters, high culture, and magic.

BIBLIOGRAPHY: Translations: *Now the Volcano*, 1979.

ABREU, CASIMIRO JOSÉ MARQUES DE (1839–1860). Casimiro de Abreu was the illegitimate son of a wealthy Portuguese businessman living in Rio. After a brief sojourn in Lisbon, Abreu spent the rest of his life in Rio as a reluctant student of commerce. He died there from tuberculosis at the age of twenty-one, a year after publishing his first book of poetry, *Primaveras* (1859; Spring Songs).

Abreu belongs to the second romantic generation, who adopted a bohemian life-style, exploring in both reality and literature the darker, more destructive aspects of human existence. Within this context, Abreu's work represents a move toward greater musicality and sentimentalism. Stimulating his readers' sensibility without offending their morality, he succeeded in translating the passionate intensity and despair of his contemporaries into a wistful and elegiac melancholy. Sexual arousal and frustration are conveyed euphemistically at the level of delicately ambiguous titillation. Separation, exile, and regret, meanwhile, are dealt with by appealing to a tradition of writing on *saudade*. (*See* Romanticism.)

A wave of articles and reeditions of the poetry followed Abreu's death, and poems such as "Minha terra" (My Land) and "Meus oito anos" (Eight Years Old) remain well known even today. Apart from the Parnassians who attacked his sentimentalism and stylistic "incorrectness," critics have been unanimous in their admiration of his ability to identify universal areas of individual human experience. (*See* Parnassianism.)

BIBLIOGRAPHY: Additional selected works by Abreu: *Camões e o jau*, 1856 (*Camões and the Man of Java*. In *Boletim do Instituto Luís de Camões* [Macau], 1972); *Carolina*, 1856; *A virgem loura*, 1857; *Obra completa*, 1940. Translations: Hulet. Criticism: Magalhães Júnior, Raimundo. *Poesia e vida de Casimiro de Abreu*. Rio de Janeiro: Instituto Nacional do Livro, 1972; Sayers.

DAVID H. TREECE

ACADEMIES. The academy, in the sense of a society for reading, discussion, and critique of cultural works, was part of the *baroque movement of the early eighteenth century. In both the major and minor works of the movement there is a notable nativist intent that is revealed through a discussion of the issues of Brazilian existence as an entity distinct from Portugal. In fact studies appeared on cotton farming, tobacco, natural resources of Minas, and the nature of the Amazonian region.

The first Brazilian academy was the Academy of the Forgotten (1724–25); its name suggests that Brazilians were "outcasts" from the Portuguese academies. Among its notable members was the historian Rocha Pita. (*See* Historiography.) One member of the Academy of the Select, organized in Rio (1751–1752), was Ângela do Amaral Rangel (1725?–?), perhaps the first Brazilian woman poet to have her verses published. The works of some of its other members are known through the very rare volume *Júbilos da América* (1754; Joyous Poems of America), published by the Academy. Another ephermeral academy was the Brazilian Academy of the Reborn (1759–1760), which included among its members: the historian Friar Jaboatão (1695–1763?), who prepared an important description of the early activities of Franciscan missionaries in colonial Brazil; Friar Gaspar de Madre de Deus (1715–1800), who wrote a history of the captaincy of São Vicente; and, as a corresponding member, Cláudio Manuel da *Costa. Other academies included the Academy of the Happy (1736–1740), the Scientific Academy of Rio (1772–1790), and the Literary Society of Rio (1786–1794), whose members, such as Silva *Alvarenga, eventually dedicated themselves to political and philosophical concerns and were involved in an independence plot similar to the *Mineiran Conspiracy. The number of the groups offers an idea of the growing role of intellectual thought during Brazil's third century. (*See* Religion and Literature.)

Although other academies appeared in Bahia, Rio, and São Paulo into the early nineteenth century, only in 1896 was the *Brazilian Academy of Letters established in Rio. Other modern humanistic academies included the Brazilian Academy of Philology and the Brazilian Academy of Philosophy. (*See* Philosophy of National Identity; Portuguese Language of Brazil.)

BIBLIOGRAPHY: Criticism: Castelo, J. Aderaldo. In Coutinho, I.

ADONIAS FILHO [ADONIAS AGUIAR FILHO] (b. 1915; BAL: 1965). Adonias Filho spent his youth on a farm in the cacau region of southern Bahia, the site of many of his novels and short stories (e.g., *Memórias de Lázaro*, [1952; *Memories of Lazarus*, 1969]). He has served in numerous positions in the Brazilian cultural establishment, including director of the National Book Institute, the National Library, and the Federal Culture Council.

Adonias Filho's work draws from but transcends the regionalist narrative that was prevalent among the *social novelists of the 1930s and 1940s, and in many ways, his roots are closer to those of the psychological novel that began to gain force in the late 1930s, with writers such as Otávio de *Faria and Lúcio *Cardoso. His psychological approach is intensified by an almost theological focus, concentrating on the metaphysical drama of his brutish, primitive characters who are often guided by their instincts in a blind struggle against fate in a godless, nightmarish world of violence and are motivated by revenge or envy. The fatalism of his world is existential, far from the biological determinism of nineteenth-century *naturalism. (*See* Regionalism.)

O forte (1965; The Fortress) and *Luanda beira Bahia* (1971; Luanda at the Shore of Bahia) trace Bahian historical, ethnic, and mythical roots. The former incarnates the history of Bahia in an old fortress, and the latter traces Bahia's African origins by linking Brazil with Angola and Mozambique. *Noite sem madrugada* (1983; Night without Dawn) transfers the urban jungle to the city of Rio in a Kafkaesque tale of terror and entrapment. (*See* Slavery and Literature.)

The author's narratives are relayed in a dense, poetic, elliptic style tending to deny linear structures and juxtapose multiple levels of time and space in the creation of an oneiric atmosphere conducive to the development of nightmarish violence.

BIBLIOGRAPHY: Additional selected works by Adonias Filho: *Os servos da morte*, 1945; *Corpo vivo*, 1962; *As velhas*, 1975; *O largo da palma*, 1981. Criticism: Connor, Susan Hill. "From Anti-Hero to Hero: The Rebirth Archetype in *Corpo Vivo*." *LBR* (Winter, 1979), pp. 224–232; Deveny, Thomas. "Narrative Techniques in Adonias Filho's *Memórias de Lázaro*." *Hispania* (May, 1980), pp. 321–327; Ellison, Fred. "The Schizophrenic Narrator and the Myth of Renewal in *Memórias de Lázaro*." *From Linguistics to Literature: Romance Studies Offered to Francis M. Rogers*. Edited by Bernard H. Bichakjian. Amsterdam: John Benjamins B.V., 1981; Foster/Foster, I; Patai.

RANDAL JOHNSON

AIRES, MATIAS [MATIAS AIRES DA SILVA DE EÇA] (1705–1763). Born in São Paulo, where he completed his early education, his family, including his sister Maria Teresa Margarida da Silva e *Orta, moved to Lisbon in 1717. He later studied law, mathematics, science, and Hebrew in France.

Reflexões sobre a vaidade dos homens (1752; Reflections on Man's Vanity) is a major work of the Luso-Brazilian Enlightenment. (*See* Arcadias.) In the book, which is autobiographical, Aires analyzed his own and man's irrational behavior and ridiculous illusions in a pessimistic and misanthropic manner. As a moralist in the style of LaRochefoucauld, he had a style that reflected *baroque literary techniques; nonetheless, his *Problemas de arquitetura civil* (1770; Problems of Civil Architecture) reveals his "enlightened" interest in the sciences. (*See* Arcadias; Autobiography.)

BIBLIOGRAPHY: Additional selected works by Aires: *Lettres bohèmiennes*, 1759. Criticism: Lima, Alceu Amoroso. "Introdução." *Reflexões sobre a vaidade dos homens*. São Paulo: Livraria Martins, 1942.

ALBUQUERQUE, JOSÉ MEDEIROS E (1867–1934; BAL: 1897). Educated in his native Pernambuco, in Rio, and in Lisbon, Albuquerque was a journalist and a diplomat. In the latter position, he spent many years in Europe, where he gained fame as an orator.

Although he cultivated all genres, only a few of his short stories with Brazilian rural and city themes are considered notable, for example, "As calças do raposo" (The Wolf's Pants). Many of these stories have surprise endings in the style of Maupassant. His *memoirs, *Quando eu era vivo* (1942; When I Was Alive), are irreverent views of his own bohemian existence in turn-of-the-century Europe. Albuquerque also wrote detective fiction: *Se eu fosse Sherlock Holmes* (1932; If I Were Sherlock Holmes).

BIBLIOGRAPHY: Additional selected works by Albuquerque: *Poesias*, 1905; *Laura*, 1923; *Surpresas*, 1934. Translations: Goldberg. Criticism: Sales, Antônio. *Retratos e lembranças*. Fortaleza: s.d.

ALCÂNTARA MACHADO. *See* Machado, Antônio de Alcântara.

ALEGRE, APOLINÁRIO PORTO (1844–1890). Alegre, son of Araújo Porto *Alegre, was active in the republican and abolitionist causes in his native Rio Grande do Sul. He was the primary activist of the Parthenon Literary Society, the center of *gaúcho* cultural life between 1868 and 1885. (*See* Slavery and Literature.)

Considered a precursor of southern *regionalism, Alegre published poetry about the *gaúchos*, for example, *Paisagens* (1875; Landscapes). His novel *O vaqueano* (1872; The Cowboy) is a good regional historical novel presenting events of the Farroupilha Revolt (1835–1845).

BIBLIOGRAPHY: Additional selected works by Alegre: *Bromélias*, 1874; *A tapera*, 1876; *Epidemia política*, 1882. Criticism: César, Guilherme. *História da literatura do Rio Grande do Sul*. Porto Alegre: Globo, 1956.

ALEGRE, MANUEL ARAÚJO PORTO (1806–1879). Born in Rio Grande do Sul, Araújo Porto Alegre moved to Rio in 1826 to study art with the Jean-Baptiste Debret, director of the recently founded Brazilian Academy of Fine Arts. He accompanied Debret to Europe in 1831. (*See* Art and Literature.)

While in Paris he came under the influence of the french romantics. In 1836 he started the literary review *Niterói: Revista Brasiliense* with Gonçalves de *Magalhães and Alberto Torres Homem. (*See* Reviews Romanticism.) Like Maglhães, whose literary works he imitated, the patriotic intent of his poetry is readily evident. In *Brasilianas* (1836; Brazilian Poems), there are pompous tableaux of little poetic force. The epic poem *Colombo* (1866; Columbus), considered his major work, purports to bring a new aesthetic to Brazilian literature, but in reality it is a poor copy of the poems by Friar *Durão and Basílio da *Gama.

Although his reputation as a precursor of romanticism, an artist, and an architect remains firm, his literary work, so acclaimed during his lifetime, has become largely ignored, although a few excerpts are still anthologized.

BIBLIOGRAPHY: Criticism: Driver; Magalhães, Basílio de. *Manuel de Araújo Porto Alegre*. Rio: AGIR, 1945.

MARIA ANGÉLICA GUIMARÁES LOPES

ALENCAR, JOSÉ DE (1829–1877). Alencar was born in Mecejana, Ceará. His father, a leading liberal politician, moved the family to Rio in 1838. After completing work toward a law degree in São Paulo, in 1850, Alencar entered a law office in Rio. In 1853 he began writing for the newspapers there. His first serialized fiction (*folhetim*) appeared a year later, and in 1856 it was published in book form: *Cinco minutos* (1856; Five Minutes). This was Alencar's first little novel (*romancete*, to use his own term). That same year, under the pseudonym "Ig," Alencar also published a series of critiques of Gonçalves de *Magalhães's epic poem *A confederação dos tamoios*, which set off a heated literary polemic about *Indianism.

These events marked the beginning of a very active literary career. However, Alencar was also a politician of some note. In 1860 he was elected as a conservative deputy for Ceará. He later served in the Imperial Cabinet as minister of justice, from 1868–1870, resigning his position and effectively abandoning politics after a conflict with the emperor. Throughout this period, though, Alencar continued to write at an astonishing pace. In 1857 the first edition of *O guarani*

(The Guarani Indian) appeared. Within the next two years, three plays were produced and published. Between 1860 and 1875 Alencar had thirteen novels published, as well as numerous other literary and political works. He died of tuberculosis, leaving behind, in the final lines of the last work published in his lifetime—*O sertanejo* (1875; The Backlandsman)—the promise to recount yet more tales.

Alencar's program for a national literature might be viewed in three major critical statements: the *Cartas sobre "A confederação dos tamoios"* (1856; Letters on the Confederation of the Tamoios); his "literary *autobiography" *Como e por quê sou romancista* (written in 1873; published in 1893; How and Why I Am a Novelist); and the "Bênção paterna" (Paternal Blessing) to his novel *Sonhos d'Ouro* (1872; Dreams of Gold). In the first work, Alencar called for the creation of a true Brazilian literature, "in which everything would be new, both ideas and form, both imagery and verse construction." In the "Bênção paterna," the writer suggested that this national expression would be the product of the indigenous past and the spirit of the Portuguese colonizers and that foreign elements and the influx of "civilization" would enrich it further. He affirmed the great importance of contact with Brazil's splendid natural beauty for his project, as well as the roles of the Brazilian novelist Joaquim Manuel de *Macedo, and foreign novelists such as Sir Walter Scott, Vicomte Chateaubriand, James Fenimore Cooper, and Honoré de Balzac in his own literary formation.

Alencar's novels, beyond representing individual themes, are a series of efforts and experiments in the production of this national fiction. The melodramatic elements, the use of elaborate descriptions, the portrayal of extravagant sentiments and heroism, place most of his works clearly within *romanticism. However, despite a shared goal and stylistic similarities, Alencar's novels cover a wide range of themes and settings.

His own remarks in the "Bênção paterna," together with the classifications made by the editor of the Aguilar edition of his complete works, divide his fiction into four main groups. The "Indianist" novels *Iracema* (1865; *Iracema, The Honeylips: A Legend of Brazil*, 1886; reprint, 1978) and *Ubirajara* (1874; Ubirajara) present the "myths and legends of this land before and during its conquest." These works are notable for their highly poetic language. In *Iracema*, an anagramic name for America, Alencar reworks words from the Tupi *Indian language and modifies standard sentence construction to create a suitably indigenous Portuguese. Chateaubriand's *Atala* is a possible precursor for this area of Alencar's fiction. (*See* Portuguese Language of Brazil.)

The Indianist works are sometimes included as a subset of his "historical" novels, which depict "the interaction of an invading people with the American land" and the "slow growth of the American people" up to Brazil's independence. *O guarani*, sometimes classified among the Indianist novels; *As minas de prata* (1861–1866; The Silver Mines); *Guerra dos Mascates* (1873; The Mascates's Revolt); and other fragments make up this group, for which the novels of Scott and Cooper are important models. Aside from the ever-popular

O guarani—made into an opera by the Brazilian composer Carlos Gomes (*See* Music and Literature)—these works are the least known of Alencar's novels. The attempt to use the forms of the romantic historical novel to create a heroic "medieval" past for Brazil from real events of its colonial history seems to result in somewhat strained, artificial works, which are not as compelling as the author's other creations.

In the final two groups, Alencar sees the "childhood" of Brazil's own literature. The "regionalist" novels *O gaúcho* (1870; The Gaucho), *O tronco de Ipê* (1871; The Ipê Trunk), *Til* (1872; Til), and *O sertanejo* depict the traditions, customs, and language of Brazil's backlands and frontiers, which remain untouched by the outside influences of the city and foreign ideas. These works' observation and analyses of the Brazilian landscape and social patterns approximate them to the fiction of *realism; yet their dramatic plots are clearly romantic.

This romantic-realist combination is also characteristic of the final group, the "urban" novels. For Alencar, these "human-comedy" scenes of upper-class life in Rio present Brazilian society in its "adolescence." *Cinco minutos, A viuvinha* (1857; The Little Widow), *Lucíola* (1862; Lucíola), *Diva* (1864; Diva), *Sonhos d'Ouro, Senhora* (1875; Madam), and *Encarnação* (1877; Encarnação) reflect the struggle between the national spirit and foreign invasion. They depict a society still in transition toward its own individual identity to which ideas and peoples from abroad, as yet not fully assimiliated, will contribute. Furthermore, *Lucíola, Diva, Senhora*, and *Encarnação* make up Alencar's series of bold profiles of women (*perfis de mulher*), which influenced even Machado de *Assis. (*See* Feminism and Literature.)

The urban novels are often praised as excellent psychological studies; yet they also feature startling, even perverse, plot twists, vivid and bizarre scenes, and, in several cases, a consequential sociopolitical backdrop. Critics have suggested George Sand as an influence for these works, but Balzac is also a strong presence here.

Two other areas of Alencar's works reflect his interest in a national literature. The idea of a Brazilian Portuguese language preoccupied him throughout his career: reflections on the language of the Indians or of different regions of Brazil, on philology, and even on orthography frequently appear in the notes and prefaces to his novels, in the novels themselves, and in explanatory letters and statements. Alencar was also concerned with a renewal of national theater. In works such as *Verso e reverso* (1857; Back and Reverse), *O demônio familiar* (1857; The Family Devil), and *As asas de um anjo* (1858; The Wings of an Angel), he attempted to create a Brazilian high comedy. *O jesuíta* (written in 1863; performed in 1873; The Jesuit), a historical drama, encountered political and critical opposition—and the indifference of the public. (*See* Religion and Literature; Theater History.)

Critics universally acknowledge Alencar as one of the most important writers of the nineteenth century, calling him "the patriarch of Brazilian literature." (See Critics and Criticism.) Yet debate continues over his overall literary sig-

nificance and over the merit of individual works. Unfortunately, this more judg-
mental treatment of Alencar often seems to overshadow discussion of fictional
technique, intertextual elements, and the specific issues he addressed. Such close
study remains to be accomplished for most of his fiction. Alencar indeed explores
problems of narrative strategies, plot construction, and narrative production and
exchange. Furthermore, his relationship to the literature of European romanticism
and realism is not one of naive imitation. Although his adaptation of Scott's
historical novel, for example, may not be fully successful, in Alencar's works
a more sophisticated transformation—and even subversion or parody—of nineteenth-century novelistic style and devices is also present.

Perhaps Alencar's importance for Brazilian literature lies in this critical perspective on the writing of fiction. He was aware of the situation of a professional
writer in a country with a limited reading public and of the problems of creating
a national literature for a culturally diverse and rapidly changing country. A
careful reader of the work of both his compatriots and European novelists, he
recognized the possibilities that different literary models offered for his own
project. Whatever his final success as a novelist and in creating a national
literature, Alencar enriched Brazilian literature (and our understanding of it)
through his "research" as an observer of his country's landscape and society
and as a reader and a writer.

Assis described Alencar's contribution as follows: "No writer has possessed
a higher degree of Brazilian soul. And it is not only because he dealt with our
themes. There is a way of being and feeling which gives [his works] an intimate
note of nationality, independent of their external appearance" (*Páginas recolhidas*, [Rio, 1942], p. 279). His presence still haunts contemporary Brazilian
culture. For example, a recent film on the status of Brazil's Indians today has
the symbolic title *Iracema*. Mário de Alencar, his son (1872–1925; BAL: 1905),
was a poet who also wrote a partial biography of his father. (*See* Biography and
Biographers; Film and Literature.)

BIBLIOGRAPHY: Additional selected works by Alencar: *Obra completa*, 4 vols.
1959. Translations: Monegal/Colchie, I; Criticism: Alencar, Heron de. In Coutinho, II;
Driver; Haberly; Pierson, Colin. "José de Alencar: Realistic Dialogue and Characterization in the Anti-Slavery Thesis Play." *LBR* (Summer, 1981), pp. 161–172; Sayers;
Schwarz, Roberto. *Ao vencedor as batatas: Forma literária e processo social nos inícios
do romance brasileiro*. São Paulo: Duas Cidades, 1977; Wasserman, Renata Mautner.
"The Red and the White: The 'Indian' Novels of José de Alencar." *PMLA* 98 (1983),
pp. 815–827; idem. "Re-inventing the New World: Cooper and Alencar." *CL* (Spring,
1984), pp. 130–152.

MARÍA TAI WOLFF

ALMEIDA, GUILHERME DE (1890–1969; BAL: 1930). One of the most
widely read modernist poets, Almeida, from São Paulo, was a lawyer, journalist,
and film critic. In 1958 he was voted the "Prince of Brazilian Poets" by a panel
of critics. (*See* Critics and Criticism; Film and Literature; Modernism.)

Almeida participated in the 1922 Week of Modern Art (*see* Modernism), joining forces with the group of Graça *Aranha. He helped found the *review *Klaxon*. In Almeida's first five collections, the influence of *impressionism and penumbrism, later *symbolism, is clearly evident. *Meu* (1925; Mine) and *Raça* (1925; Race) are his major free-verse contributions to modernism. In the former the poet organizes a world of visual images in an effort to come to terms with national identity; the latter is a lyrical celebration of racial mixtures, as in the poem "Nós" (We): "We. White—Green—Black: / simpleness—laziness—superstition."

Elsewhere, the poet exhibits varied interests, excelling in the composition of diverse styles or forms. Known for his versatile and virtuoso imitations, he wrote impressions of Greek antiquity, medieval songs, popular ballads, and Japanese haiku and wrote in the classical styles of the Portuguese poet Luís de Camões in *Camoniana* (1956; Poems in the Style of Camões). His *Do sentimento nacionalista na poesia brasileira* (1926; On the Nationalistic Sentiment in Brazilian Poetry) is a major study of the origin and development of a national consciousness in literature. (*See* Portugal and Brazil: Literary Relations.)

BIBLIOGRAPHY: Additional selected works by Almeida: *Nós*, 1917; *Você*, 1931; *A rua*, 1962; *Rosamor*, 1965. Translations: Hulet, Woodbridge. Criticism: Ataíde, Tristão de. *Primeiros estudos*. Rio: AGIR, 1948, pp. 155–161; *ESPSL* (Special Issue dedicated to Almeida), November 9, 1968.

CHARLES A. PERRONE

ALMEIDA, JOSÉ AMÉRICO DE   (1887–1980; BAL: 1966). José Américo held important positions in the Brazilian government and was once a candidate for the presidency, events that he described in his *memoirs, *Ocasos de sangue* (1954; Chances for Blood). Although his literary career is limited to three novels, his *A bagaceira* (1928; *Trash*, 1978) is a milestone of Brazilian fiction and has garnered for him an important place among the regionalist writers and the *social novelists of the 1930s. (*See* Regionalism.)

Almeida's cultural background was conditioned by *positivism and his readings of Euclides da *Cunha. His intense social preoccupations caused him to document realities of life in his native Paraíba, *A Paraíba e seus problemas* (1922; Paraíba and Its Problems), and to present these realities in fiction. *Trash* was the first modern novel of the periodic droughts plaguing northeastern Brazil. Although its characters and situations would often—and more effectively—reappear in later works of the drought *cycle, Almeida's novel has a sociological and poetic level that makes it unique. Critics have often stated, however, that Almeida's novel belongs to literary history rather than to literature itself. (*See* Critics and Criticism.)

BIBLIOGRAPHY: Additional selected works by Almeida: *O boqueirão*, 1935; *Coiteiros*, 1936. Criticism: Scott-Buccleuch, R. L. "Foreword." *Trash* by José Américo de Almeida. London: Peter Owen, 1978, pp. 5–9.

ALMEIDA, JÚLIA LOPES DE (1862–1934). Almeida's opus includes novels, short stories, dramas, and didactic works. Her career spanned forty years when there were few women writers. She was married to the poet and dramatist Filinto de Almeida (1857–1945; BAL: 1897), with whom she coauthored the novel *A casa verde* (1896; The Green House). (*See* Theater History.)

Simplicity and superficiality, mixed with a good dose of *romanticism, are dominant notes of her writings. Her detractors label her literature monotonous and her style lacking in any personal trait or characteristic. Several works do stand out from her vast production. Her collection of short stories *Ânsia eterna* (1903; Eternal Anxiety) reveals a great preoccupation with death and the macabre. *A falência* (1901; Bankruptcy) is an engaging story set against the spiral of inflationary speculation that pervaded life in nineteenth-century Brazil. It offers a woman writer's perspective on the condition of Brazilian women of her time. (*See* Feminism and Literature.)

Almeida's best work is *A família Medeiros* (1901: The Medeiros Family), a family saga whose backdrop is the era of abolitionism in the state of São Paulo; it also features a strong female character. She also penned an interesting epistolary novel, *Correio da roça* (Mail from the Hills). (*See* Naturalism; Realism; Slavery and Literature.)

BIBLIOGRAPHY: Additional selected works by Almeida: *Contos infantis*, 1886; *A viúva Simões*, 1897; *Livro das donas e donzelas*, 1906; *A herança*, 1909; *A Silveirinha*, 1916. Criticism: Brookshaw; Loos.

MARIA LUÍSA NUNES

ALMEIDA, MANUEL ANTÔNIO DE (1831–1861). For most of his short life, Almeida was influenced by economic necessity. Trained in medicine, he nevertheless became a journalist and for a while was administrator of the National Typography. It was there that he befriended Machado de *Assis, a young man of similar background, aspirations, and (liberal) political beliefs.

In spite of the aura of struggle and tragedy (he drowned) that surrounds Almeida, he was the greatest purely comic novelist of nineteenth-century Brazil. He belonged to the second romantic generation, which came of age in the 1850s, a significant period of physical and cultural expansion in his native city of Rio. (*See* City and Literature; Romanticism.)

He is the author of one novel, *Memórias de um sargento de milícias* (1854–1855; *Memoirs of a Militia Sergeant*, 1959), originally serialized in 1852–1853 in the *Correio Mercantil* newspaper. Its military-sounding title is deceptive. It is set in Rio during the reign of Dom João VI (c. 1820) and concerns the escapades of Leonardo, a young rogue, the "product of a nudge and a pinch," who in spite of the machinations of the older generation and his own passing fancy for the flirtatious Vidinha, eventually gets Luizinha, the girl he really loves. As in many comic masterpieces, the novel's plot is predictable, but the relaxed and unpretentious style of narration and the equally relaxed moral standards portrayed in the novel give it a charm and a value of its own.

One of the objects of the *Memoirs of a Militia Sergeant* is documentary. We are treated to descriptions of gypsies, religious processions, and even to a scene in which Leonardo's father, Leonardo-Pataca, goes through what nowadays would be called a *macumba*, an Afro-Brazilian religious rite, in an attempt to win the love of a gypsy girl. Yet as the literary critic Antônio Cândido has pointed out in his seminal article on the book, "Dialética da malandragem" (The Dialectics of Roguery), the novel's real aims are more fundamental. (See Critics and Criticism.) The shifting and unstable relations between the characters represent a world remarkably free of guilt or even of genuine figures of authority. According to Cândido, this indolent, carefree world is representative of the free men and women of Rio at that time, and the novel thus takes its form from the thing it (almost) ignores, slavery. (*See* Religion and Literature; Slavery and Literature.)

The contrast with Almeida's more successful contemporaries, Joaquim Manuel de *Macedo and José de *Alencar, who are much more clearly romantic, is obvious: there can be no doubt that Almeida is, for the twentieth century, the most readable of the three. In fact *modernism's Mário de *Andrade and Marques *Rebelo were responsible for revaluing *Memoirs of a Militia Sergeant*, which had been generally ignored since the latter part of the nineteenth century. Numerous modern editions are witness to its continuing interest and value.

BIBLIOGRAPHY: Translations: Monegal/Colchie, I. Criticism: Aiex, Nola Kortner. "*Memórias de um sargento de milícas* as Menippean Satire." *KRQ* 28 (1981), pp. 199–208; Cândido, Antônio. "Dialética da malandragem." *Revista do Instituto de Estudos Brasileiros* (São Paulo) 8 (1970), pp. 67–89; Parker, J. M. "The Nature of Realism in *Memórias de um sargento de milícias*." *BHS* 48 (1971), pp. 128–150; Sayers.

JOHN GLEDSON

ALPHONSUS, JOÃO [JOÃO ALPHONSUS DE GUIMARÃES] (1901–1944). Son of the poet Alphonsus de *Guimaraens and great-nephew of Bernardo *Guimarães, Alphonsus was educated in Minas and received a law degree.

Alphonsus adhered to *modernism and collaborated on several *mineiro* literary *reviews with Carlos Drummond de *Andrade, Pedro *Nava, and others. Among his best-known short stories are: "Galinha cega" (Blind Chicken), which appeared in the *review *Terra Roxa e Outras Terras* in 1926 and is notable for its colloquial language and its profundity of human feeling transposed to the animal; and "Foguetes ao longe" (Fireworks in the Distance), from his collection *Eis a noite!* (1943; It's Nightime), a marvelous psychological tale of a marital relationship.

Alphonsus's other fiction, for example, *Totônio Pacheco* (1934; Totônio Pacheco), presents simple people—usually civil servants, the lower middle classes—from an endearing yet ironic, sometimes skeptical, perspective, which has led critics to compare him to Machado de *Assis.

BIBLIOGRAPHY: Additional selected works by Alphonsus: *Rola-moça*, 1938. Criticism: Sadlier, Darlene. "The Pattern of Contradiction as Narrative Technique in João Alphonsus's 'Foguetes ao longe.' " *SSF* (Spring, 1981), pp. 171–177.

ALVARENGA, MANUEL INÁCIO DA SILVA (1749–1814). Born in Minas and educated at Coimbra, Silva Alvarenga, who used the Arcadian pseudonym Alcindo Palmireno, wrote *O desertor* (1774; The Desertor), a heroic-comic poem in neoclassic style, as a defense of the university reforms initiated by the marquis of Pombal. He later returned to Brazil, where he lectured on rhetoric and poetics in Rio. (*See* Arcadias.)

Involved in a plot for the independence of Brazil, he was arrested as a proponent of the ideals of the French Revolution. Jailed in 1794, he was granted a pardon by Queen Maria I in 1797 and returned to teaching and practicing law.

The collection of poems to his beloved, *Glaura* (1799; Glaura), was rated as superior to Tomás Antônio *Gonzaga's contemporary *Marília de Dirceu*, owing to the native Brazilian elements—birds, animals, and trees—that appear in them, in spite of their repetitious form. Other poems attest to his interest in the physical sciences, for example, "As artes" (The Arts).

BIBLIOGRAPHY: Additional selected works by Alvarenga: *Obra poética de Manuel Inácio da Silva Alvarenga*. 2 vols. Rio, 1864. Criticism: Arinos, Afonso. "Prefácio." *Glaura* de Silva Alvarenga. Rio: Instituto Nacional do Livro, 1944; Sayers.

ALVARENGA PEIXOTO. *See* Peixoto, Inácio José de Alvarenga.

ALVERNE, FRIAR FRANCISCO DE MONTE [RELIGIOUS NAME OF FRANCISCO JOSÉ DE CARVALHO] (1784–1858). Rio-born Monte Alverne professed as a Franciscan monk when his city became the seat of the Portuguese empire in 1808. He became a favorite in the royal Court owing to his inspirational, glittering oratory.

The four volumes of his *Obras oratórias* (1853–1854; Oratorical Works) and his *Compêndio de filosofia* (1859; Compendium of Philosophy) introduced eighteenth- and nineteenth-century philosophers to Brazil (Etienne Condillac, John Locke, Immanuel Kant, and Friedrich Hegel), but he did so without any originality, development, or method.

Alverne's importance, however, extends beyond oratory. As a professor of philosophy and theology at São José Seminary, he played a role in shaping the nation's political destiny during the Regency (1831–1840); he was indirectly instrumental in the founding of Brazilian *romanticism through his disciples Gonçalves de *Magalhães and Araújo Porto *Alegre, whose feelings for nature, patriotism, and religiosity derived partially from his teachings.

BIBLIOGRAPHY: Criticism: Lopes, Roberto B. *Monte Alverne: Pregador imperial*. Rio: Vozes, 1958.

MARIA ANGÉLICA GUIMARÃES LOPES

ALVES, ANTÔNIO DE CASTRO (1847–1871). A poet, playwright, and orator, Castro Alves is remembered as the last and greatest of the romantic poets and as one of the most valiant opponents of the institution of slavery in Brazil. Born on a large plantation into a family of slaveowners and landlords, he was taken at an early age to the city of Salvador, where he was educated at a private school. He studied law in Recife and São Paulo successively, but he left university life before taking a degree. (*See* Romanticism; Slavery and Literature.)

His personal life contributed both scandalously and pathetically to his reputation through his love affair with an older actress (and minor poet), Eugênia Câmara (1837–1879), begun when he was sixteen; his tuberculosis, which dated from the same year and which was to cause his death; and a hunting accident, which led to the amputation of his foot. His handsome appearance made him a popular public image; the early death of his mother and the insanity and suicide of a favorite brother also affected him as a poet. (*See* Theater History.)

During his lifetime, Alves had only one volume of poetry published, but before that he had already become known through poems published in periodicals and recited at antislavery and patriotic rallies. The published volume was *Espumas flutuantes* (1870; Floating Spume), a collection of bucolic, erotic, and patriotic lyrics that excluded his antislavery poems. The antislavery poems appeared posthumously in *A cachoeira de Paulo Afonso* (1876; The Waterfalls of Paulo Afonso); in *Vozes da África, O navio negreiro*, and *Tragédia no lar* (1880; Voices of Africa, The Slave Ship, and Tragedy in the Home); and in *Os escravos* (1883; The Slaves). Abolition and republicanism are the two themes of his patriotic, historical drama in prose, *Gonzaga* (1875; Gonzaga), about the figure of the *Mineiran Conspiracy, written for Câmara.

The writer's life as a poet coincides with a period in which Brazil was in a state of ferment because of the Paraguayan War and the increasingly powerful antislavery and republican campaigns, which reached a crest in the year of his death and into which he threw himself unsparingly. It is obvious that he should have been called the poet of the slaves. He is also known as the leader of the condor poets (*condoreiros*), who used the condor, strong and high flying, as the symbol of their highly charged and rhetorical social verse. He translated some of the contemporary French and Spanish romantic poets, including Victor Hugo, whom along with Lord Byron he especially admired. He believed that he, like Victor Hugo, could play the part of a prophet of social change, and he also saw himself in the role of a Byronic hero, a melancholic, indomitable figure who, in spite of many love affairs, was doomed to a solitary and melancholy existence. Although he did not have Byron's wealth of experience in public life, like Byron he was handsome and was a fighter for the liberty of the oppressed. (*See* Condorism.)

Alves's fine poetry of nature is reflective and gentle, marked by a tranquil, subtle beauty. His erotic verse is sensual and abounds in feminine images such as the scent of rich perfumes, the soft texture of youthful skin, and the sheen of luxuriant hair, images that are startling by comparison with those of his predecessors; his pantheistic, sensual appreciation of external nature brings it great immediacy. In general, the vocabulary, verse forms, and meters also recall the earlier generations of romantics. Like Alvares de *Azevedo, Junqueira *Freire, Casimiro de *Abreu, and Fagundes *Varela, he enjoyed experimenting with a great variety of meters and patterns. He used the familiar romantic poetic vocabulary as, for example, adjectives like *tétrico*, macabre, *funéreo*, funereal, *sombrio*, somber, *alvinitente*, and snowy white. Inversions are everywhere as are attributives used ornamentally before their nouns. There are scores of spectacular antitheses and, especially in the social verse, daring hyperboles.

The poetry of the symbolists is foreshadowed in his intermittent use of synesthesia, for example, "larga harmonia embalsava os ares" ("a broad harmony perfumed the breezes"). Occasionally, through his use of colloquialisms, he struck a conversational note in which he half mocked his amatory nature, as in "A canção do boêmio" (The Song of the Bohemian). However, his references to himself are more frequently melancholic and often confessions of his fear of an early death. Thus the beautiful "Mocidade e morte" (Youth and Death) is a kind of duet in which his expression of absorbing sensual desires in decasyllabic octaves is contrasted with the tolling gloom of couplets prophesying death. (*See* Symbolism.)

Although romantic poetry is read in Brazil less than it was, Alves maintains a lofty position in the national literature.

BIBLIOGRAPHY: Additional selected works by Alves: *Obra completa*, 1960. Translations: Hulet. Criticism: Braga, Thomas. "Castro Alves and the New England Abolitionists Poets." *Hispania* (December, 1984), pp. 585–593; Brookshaw; Haberly; Sayers.

RAYMOND S. SAYERS

AMADO, JORGE (b. 1912; BAL: 1961). Amado came of age in the southern cacau region of Bahia. The events that he depicted in his novels—land wars, local political bossism, and banditry—were part of his childhood environment. Taught by a private teacher in Ilhéus, he later frequented a Jesuit high school in Bahia, the Colégio Antônio Vieira. He went on to study law in Rio, embarking on a career in journalism and fiction.

As a member of the Aliança Nacional Libertadora (National Liberating Alliance) political party, Amado emerged as a writer of the Left. He also served as a federal congressman until the outlawing of the Communist party in Brazil (1947). Amado went into exile in Buenos Aires and Uruguay and later in France, the USSR, and the people's republics of Eastern Europe until his permanent return to Brazil in the 1950s. In 1950 he was awarded the Stalin Prize for Literature.

Amado's literary career now spans six decades from the thirties to the eighties, an epoch covering various phases in Brazilian literature. He was initially associated with other *social novelists of the 1930s; however, he made a change from the strictly protest aspect of his novels upon his return to Brazil in the 1950s. During the military dictatorship (1964–1985), he wrote a more allegorical social novel, but in the eighties he has reminisced about the cacau lands, as in his novel *Tocaia Grande* (1984; *Showdown*, 1988). The achievement of Amado is a style that has evolved as his alone. (*See* Dictatorship and Literature; Regionalism.)

Terras do sem fim (1942; *The Violent Land*, 1945) is possibly the most significant novel of Amado's early period. Set in southern Bahia, it recounts the story of the struggle to possess the rich cacau lands with various subplots often in the form of lyrical love stories. This work treats the social and political problems of the region with poetic force. Other novels of this early period treat social problems using the language of the masses, with a richness of popular and folkloric elements, as in *Mar morto* (1936; *Sea of Death*, 1984). (*See* Folklore and Literature.)

In his so-called proletarian phase, which continued until 1958, Amado championed the workers and the poor of the cacau zone and of Salvador da Bahia, his beloved city and the site of African culture in Brazil. The African religions brought to Brazil by the former slaves are partially elaborated in each of his novels to make up a complete picture of the Afro-Brazilian ritual *candomblé*. The food of the *orixás* or gods, the dancers, the musical instruments, and the ceremonies of the gods are given detailed descriptions. Other aspects of folklore, such as *capoeira*, a martial art brought from Angola, and the presence of popular types such as the trickster (*malandro*) are also notable in Amado's fiction, as in *Jubiabá* (1935: *Jubiaba*, 1984). (*See* City and Literature; Religion and Literature.)

With *Gabriela, cravo e canela* (1958; *Gabriela, Clove, and Cinnamon*, 1962), Amado passed to a more picaresque phase of his art. In this novel the principal local pastime is a fundamental and all-pervasive interest in sexual activity. This sensuality along with the local foods that Gabriela prepares are the basic requisites to a contented life in Ilhéus, the site of the novel. Although the course of attaining and keeping these pleasures does not always run smoothly, it is what gives atmosphere and character to the story. Basic to the novel is the possession of freedom to pursue these values. Anything that inhibits freedom is viewed as negative to the well being of the characters and is set up for defeat at the hands of the forces of a free and unconventional life-style filled with poetry and lyricism.

The love story of the cinnamon-colored Gabriela and the Syrian barkeeper, Nacib, is full of humor and makes an early gesture in Brazilian letters to illustrate the parallels between progress and liberation of women. Although one contemporary Brazilian feminist critic, Walnice Galvão (*see* Critics and Criticism), has specifically pinpointed novels such as *Tereza Batista cansada de guerra* (1972; *Tereza Batista Home from the Wars*, 1975) and *Tiêta do Agreste* (1977; *Tiêta*, 1979) as presenting a sadistic and prurient vision of women that reads like a sex manual and is obviously the product of a former slavocratic society like Brazil, Amado's reflections on the treatment of women do no more than mirror an undeniable reality of Brazilian life. (*See* Feminism and Literature; Slavery and Literature.)

The theme of a free and untrammeled life-style is taken up in other novels of Amado's picaresque period, such as *A morte e a morte de Quincas Berro d'Agua* (1962; *The Two Deaths of Quincas Wateryell*, 1965) and *Os pastores da noite* (1964; *Shepherds of the Night*, 1967). The bohemian night life of Salvador, the cronyism of its free spirits, and a caricature of all that is self-satisfied bourgeois living make up the protest of these works. Amado's primary function in such novels is to exhalt the freedom to pursue a life unrestricted by bourgeois values and to entertain his readership with stories of a part of Brazil that abounds in colorful local characters.

Another controversial aspect of Amado's writing has emerged in the very portrayal of his free spirits. Detractors have seen his perusal of Bahia's local characters as an exploitation of misery and an idealization of poverty. This criticism of his work is possibly more evident to insiders of the local scene than to other readers, who respond to the humor and unmaterialistic values of his *bons vivants*.

A final controversial aspect of Amado's art is his unqualified approbation of Bahia's tradition of miscegenation. In *A tenda dos milagres* (1969; *The Tent of Miracles*, 1978), he confronted the resistance encountered and the hypocrisy inherent in this issue of Brazilian society. Although most of Bahia's elite have black ancestry, they are often very racist and project schemes such as sending all blacks and mulattoes back to Africa. Based on historical models, Amado's characters explore the perennial dilemma of Brazilian society—to be or not to be a mulatto. Amado's views on the subject are perhaps not what the majority of Brazilians accept. Ever since colonial times, whitening has been not only a personal goal but a political prescription for dealing with the color problem. Amado's mulatto hero in this novel, Pedro Archanjo, who is based on a self-styled ethnographer, Manuel Querino, represents all that is good about Bahian society and speaks out against the fascism of his era (World War II). His role in African religions and folklore is paramount, and as a historical figure, foreigners seek to discover more about him long after his death. For Amado, the mixing of races is not only an absolute boon, but the results are an esthetic improvement over the originals.

Amado has emerged as the best-known Brazilian novelist of the twentieth century, and his novels have been widely translated. His concern for the poor and the underdog has made him a champion of the oppressed. He has captured the spirit and the flavor of his native region of Bahia, and the city of Salvador in particular, and has provided entertainment and a strong dose of local color to his readership while creating a unique style of novel writing. He has succeeded in popularizing the regional novel within and beyond Brazil's frontiers. Although his contribution is surrounded by controversy, his achievement cannot be underrated. Amado is without a doubt the great popular writer of twentieth-century Brazil.

BIBLIOGRAPHY: Additional selected works by Amado: *O país do carnaval*, 1931; *Cacau*, 1933; *Suor*, 1934; *Capitães de areia* (1937; *Captains of the Sand*, 1988); *São Jorge dos Ilhéus*, 1942; *Seara Vermelha*, 1946; *Os subterrâneos da liberdade*, 1952; *Os velhos marinheiros* (1961; *Home is the Sailor*, 1964); *Dona Flor e seus dois maridos* (1966; *Dona Flor and Her Two Husbands*, 1969); *Farda, fardão, camisola de dormir* (1979; *Pen, Sword, Camisole*, 1985); *Gato malhado e a andorinha Sinhá* (1982; *The*

Swallow and the Tom Cat: A Love Story, 1982); *The Miracle of the Birds*, 1983; *O sumiço da santa* (in progress). Criticism: Brookshaw; Chamberlain, Bobby J. "Salvador, Bahia, and the Passion According to Jorge Amado." *The City in the Latin American Novel*. Edited by Bobby J. Chamberlain. East Lansing, Mich.: Michigan State University Press, 1980, pp. 69–82; Ellison; Fitz, Earl E. "The Problem of the Unreliable Narrator in Jorge Amado's *Tenda dos milagres.*" *KRQ* 30 (1983), pp. 311–321; Foster/Foster, I; Nunes, Maria Luísa. "The Preservation of African Culture in Brazilian Literature: The Novels of Jorge Amado." *LBR* (Summer, 1973), pp. 86–101; Patai; Rougle, William. "Soviet Critical Response to Jorge Amado." *LBR* (Winter, 1984), pp. 35–56; Stern, Irwin. "Magical Socialism" (Review of translations of *Sea of Death* and *Jubiaba*). *NYTBR* (October 21, 1985), p. 7.

MARIA LUÍSA NUNES

AMÁLIA, NARCISA [NARCISA AMÁLIA DE OLIVEIRA CAMPOS] (1852–1924). The daughter of a literary man, Joaquim Jácome de Oliveira Campos Filho, and a private elementary teacher, Narcisa Amália separated from both of her husbands. She moved permanently to Rio in 1888, where she worked as a municipal teacher.

Author of the poems *Nebulosas* (1872; Clouds) and editor of the literary magazine *A Gazetinha de Resende* (The Resende Gazette), Narcisa Amália was a nineteenth-century intellectual woman. As a poet, she can be classified as part of the romantic movement influenced by Victor Hugo and *Alves. Her poetry is descriptive of Brazil's tropical nature in all its grandeur and evokes the Indian god Tupã. It further evokes virgin forests and the sea, and like Alves's poetry, it shows empathy for the African slaves. (*See* Indianism; Romanticism; Slavery and Literature; *Ufanismo*.)

Amália had very strong social tendencies and waged a tenacious struggle to combat the prejudices obstructing the social and political ascent of women. She participated freely in nineteenth-century culture, possessing a knowledge of antiquity, the Renaissance, and the idealism of the romantics. Although somewhat forgotten in the twentieth century, she was considered a great talent in her time. She was a precursor to the feminist movements of the twentieth century and may be ranked among the best of the nineteenth-century romantic idealists. (*See* Feminism and Literature.)

BIBLIOGRAPHY: Criticism: *Narcisa Amália*. Edited by Antônio Simões Reis. Rio: Simões, 1949; Sayers.

MARIA LUÍSA NUNES

ANCHIETA, FATHER JOSÉ DE (1534–1597). A Spanish-born Jesuit educated at Coimbra, Anchieta went to Brazil in 1553 and spent the rest of his life there as a missionary. His piety gained him the nickname of "the Brazilian Apostle." He studied all aspects of Indian life and published the first grammar of the Tupi language, *Arte de gramática da língua mais usada na costa do Brasil* (1595; modern edition, 1933; Grammar of the Language Most Used on the Coast of Brazil), as well as letters, memoranda, historical notes, sermons, poetry, and plays—in Portuguese, Tupi, Castilian, and Latin. (*See* Indian Languages; Indianism.)

As a literary artist Anchieta was tied to the Middle Ages. His vernacular poetry preserves the traditional verse forms of popular balladry rather than following the learned forms that entered the Iberian Peninsula from Renaissance Italy. A poem in Latin dedicated to the Virgin Mary, "De Beata Virgine Dei Matre Maria," is considered his finest achievement. His plays draw heavily from the medieval religious theater, both in form and in the extraliterary, catechizing intent that they share with his other works. His *Auto na festa de São Lourenço* (staged 1583; A Play for St. Lawrence's Day), moreover, is the best surviving work from sixteenth-century Brazil's remarkable Jesuit theater. (*See* Religion and Literature; Theater History.)

Thematically present in Anchieta works is the so-called *ufanismo* initiated by Pero Vaz de *Caminha. Because he wrote in Brazil for others who lived there, rather than for Europeans who did not, Anchieta is often considered the father of Brazilian literature. His biography was written by another Jesuit, Father Simão de Vasconcelos (1596(?)–1671). (*See* Biography and Biographers.) Fagundes *Varela based his romantic epic poem *Anchieta ou o evangelho na selva* (1875) on Anchieta's life and works.

BIBLIOGRAPHY: Additional selected works by Anchieta: *A província do Brasil*, 1585 (modern edition, 1946); *Informações e fragmentos históricos do Padre Joseph de Anchieta*, 1886, 1933; *Capitania de São Vicente*, 1946. Criticism: Carvalho, Armando de. In Coutinho, I; Dominian, Helen G. *Apostle of Brazil: The Biography of Padre José de Anchieta*. New York: Exposition Press, 1958; Driver; Fernández, Oscar. "José de Anchieta and Early Theatre Activity in Brazil." *LBR* (Summer, 1978), pp. 26–43; Gilet, Joseph. "José de Anchieta: The Brazilian Dramatist." *HR* (April, 1953), pp. 155–160; Preto-Rodas, Richard. "Anchieta and Vieira: Drama as Sermon, Sermon as Drama." *LBR* (December, 1970), pp. 96–103.

NORWOOD ANDREWS, JR.

ANDRADA E SILVA. *See* Silva, José Bonifácio de Andrada e.

ANDRADA E SILVA (THE YOUNGER). *See* Silva (The Younger), José Bonifácio de Andrada e.

ANDRADE, CARLOS DRUMMOND DE (1902–1987). Born in the now immortalized town of Itabira do Mato Dentro, in Minas, into an old family of landholders who later lost much of their wealth, Drummond de Andrade studied first in his hometown and, subsequently, in Belo Horizonte and Rio. He returned to Belo Horizonte, where he began to collaborate as a journalist and poet in regional and national newspapers and reviews. In 1922 a short story of his won a literary *prize.

From 1923 to 1925 Andrade pursued a course of study in pharmacology in Belo Horizonte, completing work toward the degree but never practicing the profession. The following year he returned to his birthplace and taught at a local secondary school, but the sojourn was brief. Andrade also worked as an editor and, afterwards, as editor-in-chief of the *Diário de Notícias* newspaper, switching in 1929 to another daily, the *Minas Gerais*. In 1928 he began a parallel career as a civil servant in the State Department of Education, maintaining his activities as a newspaper editor.

Even when he went to Rio in 1934 to serve as an assistant to the head of his department, who had been named national minister of education, he never interrupted his active participation in publications such as *Revista Académica, Euclydes,* and *A Manhã.* After leaving his government post, Andrade became codirector of the leftist *Tribunal Popular*, but this active political involvement was short lived. In the same year he initiated a new career as a civil servant in the directorship of the National Historic and Artistic Patrimony, where he attained permanent status in 1952, retiring ten years later after serving as head of the Division of History. From 1969 onwards Andrade wrote *crônicas* for the Rio daily *Jornal do Brasil*. He was a translator of French authors such as François Mauriac, Pierre Laclos, Honoré de Balzac, Marcel Proust, Maurice Maeterlinck, and Jean-Baptiste Molière in addition to García Lorca. His translations of Molière and Lorca were awarded literary prizes.

Although not a direct participant in the vanguard Week of Modern Art (*see* Modernism), Andrade came into contact with many of the principal figures involved when they visited the historical sites of Minas. In 1925, along with Emílio Moura (1901–1971), Martins de Almeida, Ciro dos *Anjos, and Gregoriano Canedo, he founded the literary review *A Revista*, which served as the organpiece of *mineiro* modernism.

The inclusion of his poem "No meio do caminho" ("In the Middle of the Road," in *In the Middle of the Road: Selected Poems of Carlos Drummond de Andrade,* 1965) in the July 1928 issue of the Oswald de *Andrade's *Revista de Antropofagia* marked Andrade's national literary debut. His first volume of poems, *Alguma poesia* (1930; Some Poetry) is imbued with many of the characteristics of modernism: a perceived dichotomy of Western culture into European and American branches; a very strong, anti-European posturing and an equally ebullient Brazilian nationalism; a satirical view of bourgeois mores, in common with European modernists; and an emphasis on the need for a new poetic diction in Portuguese that reflects Brazilian colloquial and syntatical norms. Andrade's individual voice also shows a futurist rejection of mummified Western culture and a strong sense of poetic calling. (*See* Portuguese Language of Brazil.)

This nationalist posturing wanes with the subsequent *Brejo das almas* (1930; Fen of Souls), in which the poet communicates a skeptical reconsideration of the possibility of a Brazilian national identity, underscoring a common notion articulated early on by writers such as Euclides da *Cunha. There is always a renascent illusion in the midst of disillusionment, and often there is a theme of love but equally often tinged by irony. Much of the imagery is conveyed in apocalyptic language, and love tends to be a devouring, rather than constructive, passion. (*See* Philosophy of National Identity.)

In *Sentimento do mundo* (1940; Sentiment of the World), the apocalyptic visions are continued but are limited more to the urban uniformity of modern life. There is a questioning of life and a flirtation with suicide as a possible solution. This desperation with the *world*—a word constantly present—is connected to a growing consciousness of social injustices and to a sense of alienation resulting from the poet's insightful apartness. (*See* City and Literature.)

Poesias (1942; Poems) reiterates the earlier anticity sentiments and assumes a stoical stance before the disintegration of many illusions. The struggle with ideals and realities has another side, a struggle with words and a discomfiture with his own poetic diction. At the same time, there is a calming reconciliation with ancestors, a theme that will, henceforth, surface over and over. Indeed, the first volume of prose *Confissões de Minas* (1944; Confessions from Minas) initiates the poet's retrenchment into a privatistic and regional inwardness, which, though interrupted, would reassert itself later. (*See* Regionalism.)

That interruption, the collection *A rosa do povo* (1945; The People's Rose), is strongly influenced by the European struggle against the fascist ideology. It is the one book in which Andrade was tempted by a leftist order and in which he celebrated, in particular, Soviet victories. Although the poet attacked capitalist, bourgeois society and its degenerate and decomposing lyricism, and although he searched for a new, broader, and more populist perception of beauty and the inclusion in poetry of new subjects, he failed to acquiesce to an all-encompassing ideology. Rather, he endeavored to purge himself of an interest in ancestors and the past; yet he sensed both the permeating presence of "family" in his veins and the voluptuousness of life and the overpowering, indecipherable world. In the end, words and not matter triumph, as does the myth, even a celluloid and popular one like Chaplin's Tramp, the mythic hero of this volume.

The intellectual tensions and social-realist interest of *A rosa do povo* yield in *Claro enigma* (1951; Clear Enigma) to a depoliticization of Andrade's verse, and there is a clear affirmation and use of a complex poetic idiom with persistent metaphysical themes. The title oxymoron underscores the metaphysical exploration of the book and the unabashed and unapologetic intellectual and private nature of the poetic exercise. Even unpleasantness must be delved into; poetry should even cause pain and suffering. The plenitude of loving is existence, but the acts of loving are not to be made public. Andrade, here, is no longer concerned with the modernist obsession with Brazilian nationalism and identity. In fact, there is a provincialization of the focus of the poetic architect who turns toward the places of Minas so as to prop up the collapse of the baroque edifices of a decaying and threatened style, the foundation of Brazil.

At the same time, there is a desire to preserve only the externals of baroque Minas and not the social and ecclesiastical edifications of slavery and repression. The cohabitation of present and past is also geneological and leads Andrade to a consideration of the domestic continuity, which is the collapsing but always salvagable and self-sustaining family. Here, the poetic idiom becomes colloquial, gastronomic, and hearth bound. The generational conflict whereby offspring are "a negative mode" of reaffirming parents is a liturgical offering whose daily ritual of interaction at the table becomes a sacramental illusion of transcending, oxymoronic empty fullness. When presented with a climactic opportunity to grasp the mechanics of the world, the poet looks askance at the materialist temptation to comprehend, to reduce the universe; he opts for the hermetic science of poetry. (*See* Slavery and Literature.)

Firm in his stance, in *Fazendeiro do ar* (1954; Planter of Air), Andrade elaborated upon the metaphysics of poetry as a craft and mission, undermined by the tragic feeling that poetry is a slow, "secret death." The focus often is upon recently deceased friends and there is an imagistic concentration upon Death's earthly monuments—cemeteries—and artifacts—urns.

A vida passada a limpo (1959; Life in a New Copy), as the title suggests, prepares a new, cleaner copy of themes previously considered, beginning with a catalog of subjects that will not be the object of the song. Thus Andrade returns to the list of topics and images in the first volume of modernist derision. "Nothing" and a nudity that transcends bodies are to bear his attention; in other words, there must be a reencounter with the unavoidable Self and a re-vision. The collection has a predominant sense of exile in Rio from Minas. Andrade dwells upon the constant cycle of procreation, but ironically. For the first time in his verse the olfactory senses are examined and given their Proustian connotations. Social poetry resumes prominence both in a critical view of consumer society and in a broader, mythopoetic context. The long elegy on the life and death of the Rio landmark, the Hotel Avenida, is Andrade's social poem *par excellence*. In it, the physical and, after its destruction, mnemonic structure represents the flow of time as measured by societal constraints and as measured against the poet "Self" or "Work," an edifice in which the poet "I" comes and goes as a guest in the undemolishable and universal poetic structure.

Lição das coisas (1962; Lesson about Things) contains Andrade's most experimental verse some of which show influences from concretism (*see* Postmodernism) and from *surrealism. The division of the book is into "elements" of which consists the lesson on "Things," both primary and socially contextual. The symbiosis sought is that of the first poem, "The Word and the Land."

Later works are multivaried. *As impurezas do branco* (1973; The Impurities of White) satirizes the modern idolatry of technological communication; ironically the author apologizes for being the "survivor" of his generation, and proposes a series of cultural heroes. His last works, including *memoirs in prose, O observador do escritório* (1985; The Office Observer), confirmed the continued vigor, both imagistic and verbal, of Andrade's gift for poetry. There is an unpublished collection of erotic verse, *O amor natural* (Natural Love), which was referred to by the bard in interviews. This production of outstanding quality highlighted Andrade's undisputed place as "The Master," the term of endearment and respect accorded him by young Brazilian poets. It also demonstrated

Andrade's undeniable prominence as one of the major voices in the Portuguese language. Moreover, because of his friendship and collaboration with Elizabeth Bishop (*see* Foreign Writers and Brazil), who included seven translations of Andrade's verse in her *Complete Poems*, as well as several volumes of poems in translation, Andrade is the best known and most disseminated Brazilian poet in the United States.

BIBLIOGRAPHY: Additional selected works by Andrade: *O gerente*, 1945; *Contos de aprendiz*, 1951; *Passeios na ilha*, 1952; *A bolsa e a vida*, 1962; *Cadeira de balanço*, 1966; *José e outros*, 1967; *Caminhos de João Brandão*, 1970; *O poder ultrajovem*, 1972; *Menino antigo—Boitempo II*, 1973; *O marginal Clorindo gato e a visita*, 1978; *Esquecer para lembrar—Boitempo III*, 1979; *Contos plausíveis*, 1981; *Amar se aprende amando*, 1985; *O observador no escritório*, 1985. Translations: Bishop/Brasil; Hulet; *The Minus Sign: Selections from the Poetic Anthology*, 1981; Tolman (1978); Woodbridge; *Souvenir of the Ancient World*, 1976; *Traveling in the Family*, 1986. Criticism: Coelho, Joaquim-Francisco. *Terra e família na poesia de Carlos Drummond de Andrade*. Belém: Universidade Federal do Pará, 1973; Foster/Foster, I; Gledson, John. *Poesia e poética de Carlos Drummond de Andrade*. São Paulo: Duas Cidades, 1981; Martins; Stern, Irwin. "A Poet for All Brazilians." *Review* 32 (1984), pp. 16–17; Sternberg, Ricardo Lobo. *The Unquiet Self: Self and Society in the Poetry of Carlos Drummond de Andrade*. Valencia: Albatross/Hispanófila, 1987; Williams, Frederick G. "Carlos Drummond de Andrade, Jorge de Sena, and International Prizes: A Personal Correspondence." *Carlos Drummond de Andrade and His Generation*. Santa Barbara: University of California, Jorge de Sena Center for Portuguese Studies, 1986. Pp. 38–57.

JAIME H. DA SILVA

ANDRADE, JORGE (1922–1984). Born in the interior of São Paulo, the site of many of his dramas, Andrade studied law but abandoned it in favor of a career as a dramatist. In 1954 he won the Saci Prize for his most successful play: *A moratória* (1955; The Moratorium). (*See* Prizes.) He went on to compose a series of dramas—which he later organized into a dramatic cycle collected in *Marta, a árvore e o relógio* (1970; Marta, the Tree and the Watch)—narrating the social history of São Paulo from settlement in the eighteenth century through the present. (*See* Theater History.)

Andrade's dramas were both theatrically and structurally original for the Brazilian stage. *A moratória* presented the disintegration of the traditional rural families and the coffee plantation system as a result of national political and economic foul play, as well as the 1929 Depression. Its staging is notable: a two-level set in which the past and present actions run concurrently, allowing the audience to participate in the family's decline. *Pedreira das almas* (1958; Quarry of Souls), set in the nineteenth-century describes a mine worker's plight when caught in a divisive situation between the government—which wants to close the mines—and a guardian of traditional values who aims to preserve her idyllic past. Characters here, and in other dramas, often feel more comfortable in the decadent, yet noble, past than in the present. Andrade uses traditional folk and popular music as background to enforce the concept of the past. *Vereda da salvação* (written 1954; performed 1964; Path of Salvation), based on a true event in Minas, describes a group of poor Brazilians led by a messianic figure into confrontation with the government. *Senhora na boca de lixo* (written 1963; performed 1968; Woman Caught Up in Trash) is a condemnation of wealthy Brazilians who look abroad for culture, rejecting national values and traditions.

Andrade's plays may be considered dramas of social protest; nonetheless, each one has a deep psychological content: for example, Joana in *Milagre na cela* (1977; Miracle in the Cell) psyches herself up to avoid confession even under torture. Although historical events are the prime topic of his plays, they are developed within the framework of mythical and even biblical references, which provide an astoundingly emotional depth to the cycle. Andrade turned to writing scripts for television during the years of the military dictatorship's censorship. His *O Grito* (The Scream) was an immensely popular serial. (*See* Dictatorship and Literature.)

BIBLIOGRAPHY: Additional selected works by Andrade: *O telescópio*, 1954; *Os ossos do barão*, 1964; *Rastro atrás*, 1967; *As confrarias*, 1970; *O sumidouro*, 1970; *O incêndio*, 1979. Criticism: Clark, Fred M. "Tragedy and the Tragic: Andrade's *Pedreira das almas*." *LATR* (Fall, 1981), pp. 21–30; Mazarra, Richard. "The Theater of Jorge Andrade." *Dramatist in Revolt: The New Latin American Theater*. Austin: University of Texas Press, 1976, pp. 205–220; Moser, Gerald. "Jorge Andrade's São Paulo Cycle." *LATR* (Fall, 1971), pp. 17–24; Pinto, Paul. "Jorge Andrade's Three Enigmas." *Hispania* (September, 1984), pp. 364–376; Unruh, Vicky. "Andrade's *Milagre na cela*: Theatre Space and Body Movement." *LATR* (Fall, 1981), pp. 45–51.

ANDRADE, MÁRIO DE (1893–1945). Andrade was heralded as the "pope" of Brazilian *modernism, one of the most astute analysts of Brazilian culture and civilization, and a premier literary figure. The influence of his vast opus is continually being assessed. His works include prominent Brazilian fiction and poetry and prime analyses of Brazilian music, art, folklore, and ethnography, as well as short fiction and works for the theater. (*See* Art and Literature; Folklore and Literature; Music and Literature; Theater History.)

Born and brought up in São Paulo, Andrade received a degree in piano (music was his life's passion) from the Conservatory of São Paulo in 1917. That same year he began his career as an art critic and a poet: *Há uma gota de sangue em cada poema* (There's a Drop of Blood in Every Poem), published under the pseudonym Mário Sobral, reflects on the suffering caused by World War I with distinct echoes of *Parnassianism. Several short stories also followed. He began his "discovery" of Brazil about the same time, traveling to the colonial cities of Minas, where he visited the poet Alphonsus de *Guimaraens.

Soon he was drawn into the premodernist revolution being orchestrated by Oswald de *Andrade (no relation). Oswald had returned from Paris drunk with the "futurist" spirit proclaimed by Filippo Tommaso Marinetti. He "presented" a poem from Mário de Andrade's then unpublished *Paulicéia desvairada* (1922; *Hallucinated City*, 1968) in an article titled "Meu poeta futurista" ("My Futurist

Poet''). The poem revealed Mário's break with the themes and structures of the reigning symbolist-Parnassian schools. In the article Oswald rhetorically asked the reader: ''Did you discover the change in rhythm, the new form, the daring sentence? We can say that not only does France have its Paul Fort, its [Paul] Claudel. . . . we also have our own remodelers renewing pathways of expression and exctasy!'' (In Mário da Silva Brito, *Antecedentes da Semana de Arte Moderna*. Rio: Civilização Brasileira, 1964, pp. 230–231). Mário's embarrassment led him to a quick and honest denial of the direct association with the Futurists: ''The poet of *Hallucinated City* is not a Futurist. . . . He will allow you to call him extravagant, original, up-to-date, crazy . . . but will not allow you to link him to the smelly stable of any school.'' (In Mário da Silva Brito, *Antecendentes da Semana de Arte Moderna*, p. 238). (*See* Modernism; Parnassianism; Symbolism.)

Mário de Andrade's attitudes toward his contemporary literature and writers were devastatingly clear and expressed in his series of articles: ''Mestres do Passado'' (1921; ''Masters of the Past''). The Brazilian literary ''past'' for Andrade included some of the most distinguished names of the moment: Francisca *Júlia (''the least inspired of the Parnassians''); Raimundo *Correia (''He surely was a bit more inspired than Francisca Júlia''); Alberto de Oliveira (*See* Parnassianism) (''Alberto de Oliveira was persecuted during his life by one great unhappiness: he had nothing to say''); Olavo *Bilac (''I don't consider him one of the great poets of the language. I liked him. . . . But he doesn't hold my attention because he moves me only occasionally. I'm not sure why he doesn't move me more. Perhaps it is his excessive perfection''); and Vicente de Carvalho (*See* Parnassianism) (''Empty ideas, empty plays on words and an unfeeling hammer banging out empty meters''). His conclusion about the artistic moment repeatedly thunders ''May the Past Masters be Damned Forever'' but finishes with a touch of meekness: ''Might we be perhaps at a moment of transition?'' (In Mário da Silva Brito, *Antecedentes da Semana de Arte Moderna*, pp. 254–309). Andrade's own intense modernist activities begin at this point.

In 1924 he took another trip to Minas, this time in the company of ''that ultimate traveler'' Blaise Cendrars. (*See* Foreign Writers and Brazil.) In a 1925 newspaper interview (In *O turista aprendiz* [São Paulo: 1976], p. 18), he summed up the initial achievements of that ''heroic'' phase of modernism:

The Brazilian modernist killed the *saudade* for Europe, the *saudade* for its talents and the ideals, for the past. . . . The Brazilian modernist lives, he does not relive. For this reason the poem of small ideas and the poem of evocations died. And because ''we live'' we are necessarily living in Brazil that is our land, family, present and tradition. This is very important: to feel and to live Brazil not only in its physical reality but also in its historical emotivity.

That same year he assumed a professorship in music and aesthetics at the Conservatory. In 1926 the stories of *Primeiro andar* (First Floor) were published, followed in 1927 by the novel *Amor, verbo intransitivo* (*Fräulein*, 1933), a novel that coldly "dissects" the social and moral prejudices of a *paulista* family, which brings a German governess to complete their children's formal (and sexual) education.

By 1928 Andrade was recognized as the "pope" of modernism, and he began a *crônica* column called "Taxi" in the *Diario Nacional*. For about three months in 1928 and again in 1929, he traveled through northern Brazil and the Amazon collecting ethnological material on regional cultures: dances, legends, and religious customs. The diary of these travels was published under the title *O turista aprendiz* (1976; The Apprentice Tourist). That same year the novel *Macunaíma, herói sem nenhum caráter* (*Macunaíma*, 1984), his most famous work, was published. Initially, he subtitled it as *story* but later used the term *novel* and, finally, *rhapsody*. (*See* Indian Languages; Indianism.)

After 1935 the center of his dynamic activities was the Culture Department of the City of São Paulo, which he had helped found and of which he was the first director. In this capacity, he created the São Paulo Library and a Record Library, children's playground, the National Historical Site Commission, and the São Paulo Society for Ethnography and Folklore. Andrade described his activities and goals in this office in an interesting article published in *Bulletin of the Pan American Union* (December 1935). Among his many achievements was his invitation to the French anthropologist Claude Lévi-Strauss to teach at the recently founded University of São Paulo. Lévi-Strauss published several important works (e.g., *Tristes tropiques*) related to Brazilian Indian life and structural anthopology as a result of his residence in Brazil.

Dismissed from his position by the Vargas regime, Andrade moved to Rio in 1938 to assume a professorship of history and philosophy of art at the short-lived University of Brazil, as well as to head the National Book Institute's preparation of a Brazilian Encyclopedia. After 1940 he carried out further extensive historical, artistic, folkloric, and ethnological research during trips through several areas of Brazil. He was a founding member of the Brazilian Society of Writers in 1942.

Any analysis of Andrade's work, however brief, must reflect on not only his philosophy of Brazilian civilization but also the specific moment in Brazilian cultural history. He himself analyzed this conjuncture at several points in his career. In *A escrava que não é Isaura* (1926; The Slave Who Is Not Isaura, a play on the title of Bernardo *Guimarães's antislavery novel), he evaluated how the Brazilian modernist movement broke with old literary traditions and established a "new Brazilian literature." Citing the poetry of Manuel *Bandeira, Guilherme de *Almeida, Ronald de *Carvalho, Sérgio *Milliet, and others, he noted that they fulfilled the requirement of a real national literature: they viewed Brazil through Brazilian eyes; they wrote in Brazilian Portuguese, free of influence from Portugal; they created artistic forms that reflected both the language and spirit of Brazil. These ideas would be sounded throughout his critical writings, lectures, and personal correspondence, including, for example, his *Aspectos da literatura brasileira* (1943; Aspects of Brazilian Literature); his collection of literary criticism, *O empalhador de passarinho* (1944; The Bird Stuffer); and his *Cartas a Manuel Bandeira* (1958; Letters to Manuel Bandeira). In all of these works he revealed an immense knowledge of contemporary trends in European and North American culture. (*See* Portugal and Brazil: Literary Relations; Portuguese Language of Brazil.)

It was not until the 1927 publication of his *Clã do jaboti* (Clan of Jaboti), poetry based on national folklore and traditions and written in a truly popular language, that Andrade's modernist tendencies became clearly evident. *Macunaíma*, his rhapsody of Brazilian folklore, broke with all traditions of earlier prose fiction and created a prose full of indigenous terms, neologisms, and proverbs. Macunaíma is a black Indian hero of the Tapanhumas tribe who becomes a white man in order to pursue his stolen treasure in the city. "I made a point of showing and stressing that Macunaíma, being the Brazilian he is, has no character," he wrote to Manuel Bandeira in 1927. "Quite secretly, I really think that the satire, besides being directed at the Brazilian in general, some of whose characteristics he shows, systematically hiding the good ones, for sure always seemed to me to also be a more universal satire about contemporary man." Andrade's satire of the Brazilian and universal man has indeed been right on target. The work has made successful transitions to the contemporary Brazilian reality through film and stage. (*See* Film and Literature; Theater History.)

As fascinated as Andrade was by the reality of his Brazil, São Paulo—his city—would attract his prime literary attention in the last years of his life: "When I die I want to be / Buried in my city, / Don't tell my enemies, / *Saudade.* / Bury my feet on Aurora Street / Leave my sex in Paissandu / On Lopes Chaves, forget / my head" ("When I Die," from *Lira paulistana* [1946; São Paulo Lyre]).

BIBLIOGRAPHY: Additional selected works by Andrade: The *Obras completas* (*Complete Works of Mário de Andrade*) was published in twenty volumes by Livraria Martins of São Paulo. Translations: Grossman. Criticism: Albuquerque, Severino João. "Construction and Destruction: *Macunaíma.*" *Hispania* (March, 1987), pp. 67–72; Foster, David W. "Some Formal Types in the Poetry of Mário de Andrade." *LBR* (December, 1965), pp. 75–95; Hart, Thomas R. "The Literary Criticism of Mário de Andrade." *The Disciplines of Criticism: Essays in Literary Theory, Interpretation, and History.* Edited by Peter Demetz et al. New Haven: Yale University Press, 1968, pp. 265–288; Johnson, Randal. "Macunaíma as Brazilian Hero." *LALR* (1978), pp. 38–44; Martins; Proença, M. Cavalcanti. *Roteiro de Macunaíma.* Rio: Civilização Brasileira, 1969; Wasserman, Renata R. Mautner. "*Preguiça* and Power: Mário de Andrade's *Macunaíma.*" *LBR* (Summer, 1984), pp. 99–116.

ANDRADE, OSWALD DE (1890–1954). Known for his wit ("Tupy or not Tupy, that is the question") and for his joke-poems (*poemas-piadas*), Andrade wrote poetry, prose, manifestoes, and works for the theater that satirized Brazilian society while forging a modernist theory of Brazilian culture in a vanguardist style that has influenced subsequent writing. (*See* Indianism; Modernism.)

Andrade's biography can be shaped in phases united by his vigorous personality: family and education (1890–1911); travel and independence (1912–1916); premodernist (*See* Modernism) ferment (1917–1921); modernist action (1922–1930); social commitment (1931–1944); and humanistic and philosophical studies (1945–1954). Commenting on Andrade's personality, his editor, the novelist and literary critic Geraldo Ferraz (b. 1905), author of *Doramundo* (1956; Doramundo) and *Km 63* (1979; Kilometer 63), stated that his temperament searched for positions of dominance, yet succeeded only in forging instruments that revealed his revolt, through sarcasm and parody directed at the bourgeois latifundiary system of which he was a part. (*See* Critics and Criticism.)

His early interest in writing was perhaps strengthened by his maternal uncle, the novelist Inglês de *Sousa, although a formative European trip in 1912 brought Andrade into contact with cubism, futurism, and other vanguard tastes. As a young journalist, Andrade published the polemical political journal *O Pirralho* (1912–1917), which included a column by Juó Bananére (pseudonym of Alexandre Ribeiro Marcondes Machado) (1892–1933) in the Italo-Portuguese dialect of the Italian immigrants to São Paulo. Later he defended Anita Malfatti, discovered the sculptor Vítor Brécheret, and "launched" poet Mário de *Andrade. (*See* Art and Literature; Immigrants and Literature; Modernism.)

Andrade's artist's studio was the center of premodernist ferment, captured in the scrapbook-diary *O perfeito cozinheiro das almas deste mundo* (1918–1919; The Perfect Chef of this World's Souls). He played a leading role in the 1922 Week of Modern Art (*see* Modernism) reading from his novel *Os condenados* (1922; The Condemned), in which one character was modeled on sculptor Brécheret, before several return trips to Europe and Tarsila do Amaral's (one of his six wives) Parisian *atélier*. He finished his cubist novel *Memórias sentimentais de João Miramar* (1923; *Sentimental Memoirs of John Seaborne*, 1979) in Italy and published the *Pau Brasil* (Brazilwood) poems in Paris in 1925. Andrade's "Manifesto de poesia pau brasil" was published in 1924 ("Manifesto of Pau-Brasil Poetry," in *LALR* [January-June, 1986], pp. 184–197); he began his "great nonbook" *Serafim Ponte Grande* (1926; *Seraphim Grosse Pointe*, 1979), and he launched literary cannibalism with his *Manifesto antropófago* (Manifesto of Anthropophagy) in 1928. His creative talent worked through synthesis, satire, and originality applied to a fictionalization of his own intellectual and personal experience.

In the 1930s Andrade turned to Marxist social criticism in expressionist theater that carried modernist parody of language and mores to plastic and dramatic extremes. *O rei da vela* (1937; The Candle King) subjects São Paulo's *nouveau-riches* capitalists and decadent rural aristocracy to a psychosexual exposé in a panorama of perversions that also criticizes North American imperialism. The sensational production of this play in 1967 by the Teatro Oficina (*see* Theater History) set the spirit of Oswaldian satire at the heart of cultural *tropicalismo*. In *A morta* (1937; *The Dead Woman*, 1980), he exhorted the audience in the final scene to face its own corruption by setting fire to the theater. With Patrícia *Galvão (Pagu), another of his wives, Andrade edited a radical newspaper, *O*

Homem do Povo (The Man of the People), which closed when attacked by students at the law school. The social-mural novels of the series "Marco-Zero" (1943, 1945; Point Zero) were written during this period.

In turning to humanistic and philosophic studies in the 1940s, Andrade explored the concept of utopia as a natural consequence of these vanguardist writings: *A marcha das utopias* (1953; The Progress of Utopias). The primitivist idea in his *Manifesto antropófago* is again explored in the realms of social theory and psychology in *A crise da filosofia messiânica* (1950; The Crisis of Messianic Philosophy), which introduced the German philosopher Herbert Marcuse's notions of technology, leisure, and play into a discussion of matriarchical organization.

According to his editor, the cycle of Andrade's most authentic and great works begins with *Sentimental Memoirs of John Seaborne*, passes through the *Pau Brasil* poems, and closes with *Seraphim Grosse Pointe*, which the critic Antônio Cândido (*see* Critics and Criticism) considers "the most powerful application of social satire [in Brazilian literature]." Cândido characterized Andrade's style of "satire-criticism" as a search for moveable structures through rapid and surprising disarticulations, supported by a heterogeneous, fragmentary style. (In *Estouro e libertação*. São Paulo: Martins, 1944, pp. 11–30). *Sentimental Memoirs of John Seaborne* is set in twentieth-century Brazil and recreates the first half of the hero's life in memoirs that the "young poet" has written at a symbolic midpoint in his life. Starting with childhood, Seaborne wrote memoirs to reconstruct a critical consciousness of a recreated world through which he could rediscover essential or significant values. *Seraphim Grosse Pointe* is a satirical, systematic destruction of modernist society. Seraphim's adventures transmute Seaborne's alienation into rebellion against bourgeois values. Seraphim travels to the Middle East and Europe and returns to Brazil in a spirited revolt against conformity and repression. Andrade later called the work the "grande finale of the bourgeois world among us." In his searing preface of 1933, he offered the text as "A document . . . A drawing . . . Necrology of the bourgeoisie. Epitaph of what I was."

In a poem written on the day of Andrade's death ("Oswaldo morto" [Dead Oswaldo], In *Dentro da noite veloz*. Rio: 1975), the poet Ferreira *Gullar saw him as "an angel with banana leaf wings." Oswald's work, neglected at the time of his death, has seen a renaissance dating from the 1950s, in concrete poetry (*see* Postmodernism in Poetry), theater—José Celso's production of *O rei da vela*—, film—Joaquim Pedro de Andrade's *O homem do pau brasil*, and the resurgence in studies of modernism. (*See* Film and Literature.)

BIBLIOGRAPHY: Additional selected works by Andrade: *Primeiro caderno do aluno de poesia Oswald de Andrade*, 1927; *O homem e o cavalo*, 1934; *Os romances do exílio: a escada vermelha*, 1934; "Cântico dos cânticos para flauta e violão," 1944; *A Arcádia e a Inconfidência*, 1945; *Ponta de lança*, 1945; *Obras completas*, 10 vols. 1970–. Translations: Bishop/Brasil; Hulet; Monegal/Colchie, II; Woodbridge; Criticism: Burgess, Ronald D. "Birth. Life. *A Morta*. de Andrade." *LBR* (Winter, 1985), pp. 103–110; Campos,

Haroldo de. "The Rule of Anthropophagy: Europe under the Sign of Devoration." Translated by María Tai Wolff. *LALR* (January-June, 1986), pp. 42–60; idem. "Seraphim: A Great Non-Book." In *Seraphim Grosse Pointe*. Austin: New Latin Quarter, 1979, pp. 113–131; Clark, Fred M. "Oswald and Mayakovsky: *O homem e o cavalo* and *Mystery-Bouffe*." *REH* (May, 1982), pp. 241–256; Foster/Foster, I; Jackson, K. David. "Rediscovering the Rediscoverers: João Miramar and Serafim Pointe Grande." *TQ* (Autumn, 1976), pp. 162–173; Maharg, James. "From Romanticism to Modernism: The *poemaspiadas* of Oswald de Andrade as Parodies." *LBR* (Winter, 1976), pp. 220–230; Morse, Richard. "Triangulating Two Cubists: William Carlos Williams and Oswald de Andrade." *LALR* (January-June, 1986), pp. 175–183.

K. DAVID JACKSON

ÂNGELO, IVAN (b. 1936). Born into a large family of modest economic means in Minas, Ângelo spent most of his childhood in the Belo Horizonte, where he developed his literary interests.

In 1956–1957 he joined with a group of young writers interested in cinema and literature that founded the *review *Complemento*. Involved with leftist currents and the populist thrust of the early Brazilian 1960s, Ângelo and his band of intellectuals, including Fernando *Gabeira, attracted attention in literary circles. Pursuing a journalistic career since 1958, Ângelo wrote a daily literary column and also short stories that led to a collection coauthored with Silviano *Santiago: *Duas faces* (1961; Two Faces). With the 1964 military coup, the literary group disbanded, and he moved to São Paulo, where he now works as one of the chief editors of the *Jornal da Tarde* newspaper. (*See* Film and Literature.)

From 1961 to 1976, given the increasingly repressive climate of censorship, Ângelo did not publish any fiction. Having outlined a novel in 1963, which was the beginning of his best-seller *A festa* (1976; *The Celebration*, 1982), Ângelo ceased to write and only returned to this narrative ten years later. This novel is a *tour-de-force* of language and narrative structure as well as a mirror of the fear, injustice, and repression in Brazil of the early 1970s. Composed of a series of texts, stories, fragments, and parallel incidents, some of which are even related to the early part of the century (thereby showing recurrent sociohistorical patterns), the author suggested the sociopolitical causes for the cultural deterioration of the 1970s. Focusing on the behavior of a gallery of characters in a nonlinear narrative intended to keep the reader alert and responsible for deciphering the many interpretations the novel offers, *The Celebration* is to a degree evocative of the structure in *Hopscotch* by Argentine Julio Cortázar, but, above all, it stands as a veritable testimony to a very dark period in recent Brazilian history. (*See* Dictatorship and Literature.)

In 1979 Ângelo published *Casa de vidro* (*Tower of Glass*, 1986), a collection of five interlocking short novellas that address the issue of oppression from several perspectives in a masterful language suggestive of the nation's quintessential dilemmas. A modern-day "history" of Brazil, this volume underscores Ângelo's interest in dramatizing social, historical, political, and cultural issues.

BIBLIOGRAPHY: Additional selected works by Ângelo: *A face horrível*, 1986. Translations: *The Massachusetts Review* (December, 1986). Criticism: Monegal, Emir Rodríguez. "Writing under the Censor's Eye." *WLT* (Winter, 1979), pp. 19–22; Slater, Candace. "A Triple Vision of Brazil." *Review* (January-May, 1984), pp. 13–15.

NELSON H. VIEIRA

ANÍSIO, CHICO [FRANCISCO ANÍSIO DE OLIVEIRA PAULO FILHO] (b. 1931). A leading stage and television figure from Maranhão, Anísio has successfully transposed his humor and some of his theatrical personalities (e.g., Santelmo, Coronel Limoeiro, the Mayor of Chico City) into fictional creations.

Anísio's most popular collection has been *O enterro do anão* (1973; The Dwarf's Internment). In the title story, a dwarf's burial turns into black comedy when the hearse carrying his body breaks down on the streets of Rio. Hours go by, jokes and puns fly, and the cortege diminishes until the problem—a lack of gasoline—is discovered. The stories in *Feijoada no Copa* (1976; Black Bean Stew at the Copa) both censure and satirize upper-class Brazilians for their insensitivity to the reality around them. The collection *Teje preso* (1975; *Teje Jailed*) concerns northeastern life and admirably mixes the folkloric with the comic and poetic in a typical northeastern language. The title story centers on the madcap search for a prisoner to occupy a cell for the inauguration of the new jail by the governor. (*See* Folklore and Literature; Regionalism.)

BIBLIOGRAPHY: Additional selected works by Anísio: *O batizado da vaca*, 1972; *Carapau*, 1978; *O telefone amarelo*, 1979; *É mentira, Terta?* 1986.

ANJOS, AUGUSTO DOS (1884–1914). Born four years before the abolition of slavery, Anjos spent his childhood and early youth on the family's decaying sugar plantation in Pernambuco. He graduated with high honors from the law school of Recife but chose the precarious professions of poet, teacher, and an occasional journalist. In Recife he became well acquainted with contemporary scientific and philosophical theories. Anjos derives his fame from his one book, the often-reprinted *Eu* (1912; I). After some years as an impecunious teacher, he obtained a permanent position in a provincial town, where four months later he died.

Although in his earlier, less successful poems, Anjos paid tribute to the prevailing schools of *Parnassianism and *symbolism and demonstrated an admiration for Baudelaire, Cruz e *Souza, and the sonnet form, few of the poems that he selected for inclusion in *Eu* may be linked to either school of poetry. Nor is he to be considered a "scientific" poet, in spite of his scientific erudition and his mastery of the vocabulary of the sciences, especially that of organic science. He does not attempt to explain scientific theory or discoveries but rather concerns himself with deep philosophical problems of human existence. He belongs to the philosophical tradition of the Portuguese poet Antero de Quental. (*See* Portugal and Brazil: Literary Relations.)

In the sonnet "A um germén" (To a Germ), the germ's development to the point of attaining a soul serves as a symbol for man's wretched destiny: a state of nothingness is preferable to the "supreme misfortune of having a soul." Although he was not a satanist, he imitated Baudelaire's use of physical putrefaction and decay in his image of a world that is a decaying body being eaten by assassin worms. Contemporary critics are fascinated by the power of this existentialist cry of agony uttered in a style that is at once colloquial and clinical. (*See* Critics and Criticism.)

BIBLIOGRAPHY: Additional selected works by Anjos: *Eu e outras poesias*, 1919; *Toda a poesia* (with a study by Ferreira Gullar), 1976. Translations: Hulet. Criticism: Magalhães Júnior, Raimundo. *Poesia e vida de Augusto dos Anjos*. Rio: Civilização Brasileira, 1977; Vidal, Ademar. *O outro Eu de Augusto dos Anjos*. Rio: José Olympio, 1967.

RAYMOND S. SAYERS

ANJOS, CIRO DOS   (b. 1906; BAL: 1969). Anjos received his law degree in his native Minas. He has spent virtually his entire adult life in government service in both state and federal administrations and also was instrumental in founding the University of Brasília.

As a novelist, Anjos is viewed by many critics as the reincarnation of Machado de *Assis. This in large part is due to the nature of his first two novels, *O amanuense Belmiro* (1937; *Diary of a Civil Servant*, 1988) and *Abdias* (1945; Abdias), both of which are semiautobiographical novels of the author's intellectual development (*Künstlerroman*). Both Belmiro and Abdias, a literature professor at a girls' school, are similar to Assis's intelligent, introspective narrators-protagonists. They are prone to self-analysis, filled with self-doubt, incapable of action, and content to be timid nonparticipants in the world that surrounds them. Their skepticism, which projects an air of sadness, is laced with self-ridicule and a subtle humor again reminiscent of Assis. (*See* Autobiography.)

A third novel, *Montanha* (1956; Mountain), aims its criticism outward—at Brazilian political practices—and probably for this reason it has never enjoyed the popular success of his earlier works. Anjos's introspective and insightful novels stand out amid the more socially minded fiction produced during the 1930s and 1940s. (*See* Social Novelists of the 1930s.)

BIBLIOGRAPHY: Additional selected works by Anjos: *A criação literária*, 1954. Criticism: Fernandes, Ronaldo. "*O amanuense Belmiro*." *MGSL* (December 11, 1982), p. 6; Masin, Léa Sílvia dos Santos. "*Abdias*: o sentido existencial." *MGSL* (September 10, 1970), p. 10.

KEITH H. BROWER

ANTÔNIO, JOÃO   (b. 1937) Antônio spent his childhood and adolescence in São Paulo's lower middle-class neighborhoods. He developed a lifelong passion for popular music from his father, and the tones and rhythms of this musical heritage are a structuring element in Antônio's fiction. (*See* Music and Literature.)

The game of snooker is also a metaphorical and thematic device in Antônio's narratives. It is the unifying element in his first collection of short stories,

Malagueta, Perus e Bacanaço (1963; Names of Working-Class Neighborhoods in São Paulo). These tales of three young picaresque pool players and the stories in *Leão de chácara* (1975; The Bouncer) are set in the grey wastes of São Paulo's industrial zones and in Rio slums. These locations are the homes of the under-dogs, the marginalized of Brazilian society during the years of the military dictatorship and its "economic miracle." (*See* City and Literature.)

Antônio has also written reportage pieces that describe in even greater realistic detail the depths of an alienated existence. Of note is his *Calvário e porres do pingente Afonso Henriques de Lima Barreto* (1977; Calvary and Drunkedness of the Drinker Afonso Henriques de Lima Barreto), which emphasizes Lima *Barreto's favorite drinking spots in Rio. His most recent collection of stories is also dedicated to Lima Barreto: *Abraçado no meu rancor* (1986; Embraced in My Anger); the story "Sufoco" ("Suffocation") attacks racial prejudice in soccer life in Brazil, as well as the negative aspects of Brazilian "North Americanization." (*See*: Dictatorship and Literature; Soccer and Literature.)

Antônio is an iconoclast who espouses a radically independent theory of Brazilian culture. True Brazilian cultural identity, he claims, comes from the streets and not from government "cultural planners." What is needed, he insists, is a new "recipe" for literature that can be consumed by the Brazilian people. (*See* Philosophy of National Identity.)

BIBLIOGRAPHY: Additional selected works by Antônio: *Malhação do Judas carioca*, 1975; *Casa de loucos*, 1976; *Meninão do caixote*, 1983. Translations: Tolman (1984). Criticism: Lowe; Tolman (1984).

ELIZABETH LOWE

ARANHA, JOSÉ PEREIRA DA GRAÇA   (1868–1931; BAL: 1897). From northeastern Maranhão State, a lawyer by profession and a student of the *Recife School of philosophy by avocation, Graça Aranha embodied a peculiar turn-of-the-century fascination with the ideas of progressive evolution and cosmic harmony.

As a young magistrate in the state of Espírito Santo, Aranha collected data for his first and best-known work, the novel *Canaã* (1902; *Canaan*, 1920), which depicts life in the German settlements of the region. A *roman à thèse*, *Canaan* involves two German immigrants who represent opposing points of view concerning the future of Brazil: one maintaining that Aryan superiority will eventually dominate while the other foresees a merger of peoples and customs leading to a future national harmony embracing both settlers and natives. Although much of the novel falls into an ideological dialogue involving interlocutors who tend to be abstract mouthpieces, there are several chapters that reveal a sensitive technique characteristic of *symbolism and *impressionism in capturing a delicate moment, and others show the author as a careful observer of social customs and local reality. (*See* Immigrants and Literature.)

The success of *Canaan* served to launch the author on a career of diplomatic service to Brazil, from 1910 to 1920, which permitted Aranha to study the rich cultural vanguard of the period in several European capitals. After his return to Brazil in 1920, *A estética da vida* (1920; The Aesthetics of Life) was published representing a defense of intuition and artistic appreciation as an antidote to alienation. The tract's echoes of revolutionary movements such as primitivism, futurism, and other forms of antitraditionalism endeared the author to an ill-defined movement of young artists and intellectuals opposed to conventional cultural norms and determined to bring Brazil into the mainstream of modern life. Declaring himself a supporter of youth and modernity and unalterably opposed to the academic spirit, the author-statesman was lionized by the younger generation as the standard-bearer of what has been subsequently designated as *modernism. It is clear today that this outburst of innovation involving the arts and letters of Brazil took place independently of Aranha, whose contribution, while significant, was fortuitous and adventitious.

The heady early twenties served as a background for Aranha's high-spirited lecture "Aesthetic Emotion in Modern Art," during the Week of Modern Art (*see* Modernism), which led to his break with the *Brazilian Academy of Letters, at the time the most conservative voice in Brazilian culture. By the end of the decade the author had completed a second novel, *A viagem maravilhosa* (1929; The Wonderful Journey), an attempt to capture the modern temper with a syntax that tends to be antitraditional, nervous, and dynamic. The plot involves an emancipated married woman, her lover, and the woman's dull husband. The lovers are shown as superior beings thanks to their passion for ecstasy and aesthetic sensitivity. As in *Canaan*, the characters are little more than puppets exposing their creator's well-known views.

The place of Aranha in Brazilian letters remains a matter of some controversy. His works are decidedly uneven in quality with brilliant moments outweighed by unconvincing, abstract characters. As a thinker, he displays considerable inconsistency in his failure to appreciate modern art even while celebrating the modern spirit. His bright hopes for cosmic harmony and the evolution of human kind are dimmed by a persistent racism, which led him to deplore miscegenation in Brazil.

There is, then, some truth to the observation that Aranha lacked not only the lyric qualities necessary to be a creative writer but also the discipline to achieve originality as a thinker. Nonetheless, his contribution to the development of a national Brazilian consciousness in the modern era and his moral leadership at the inception of modernism can neither be discounted nor overlooked. (*See* Philosophy of National Identity.)

BIBLIOGRAPHY: Additional selected work by Aranha: *Malazarte*, 1911; *O espírito moderno*, 1925. Translations: In *Contemporary Latin American Philosophy*. Edited by Aníbal Sánchez-Reulet. Albuquerque: University of New Mexico Press, 1954, pp. 101–18. Criticism: Aiex, Anoar. "Graça Aranha and Brazilian Modernism." *Tradition and Renewal: Essays on Twentieth-Century Latin American Literature and Culture*. Edited by Merlin Forster. Urbana, Ill.: University of Illinois Press, 1975, pp. 51–67; Brookshaw; Cruz Costa, João. "Graça Aranha." *History of Ideas in Brazil*. Translated by Suzette

Macedo. Berkeley: University of California Press, 1964, pp. 252–257, passim; Eakin, Marshall C. "Race and Ideology in Graça Aranha's *Canaã*." *I & L* (September–November, 1980), pp. 3–15; Foster/Foster, I; Munn, B. W. "Graça Aranha, Nabuco, and Brazilian Rapproachement with the United States." *LBR* (December, 1969), pp. 66–72.

RICHARD A. PRETO-RODAS

ARAÚJO PORTO ALEGRE. See Alegre, Araújo Porto.

ARCADIAS. The term *arcadias* refers to the neoclassical cultural and philosophical groups that surfaced in colonial Brazil in the last half of the eighteenth century, an era generally referred to as the Enlightenment. (*See* Portugal and Brazil: Literary Relations.)

The *Arcádia Lusitana* (Lusitanian Arcadia) was founded in Lisbon in 1756, under the patronage of King José I (ruled 1750–1777). Its members considered themselves "shepherds" and took Greek or Latin pastoral pseudonyms. They held meetings in gardens or parks to symbolize their return to "nature" and "natural literature." They were intimately linked to and an outgrowth of the *academies of the earlier part of the century. The arcadias' break with the staid baroque cultural tradition allowed for more abstraction in thought and a personal, even emotional tone. Writers returned to classical poetic forms—the eclogue, odes, sonnets, and so on—in imitation of the great Renaissance poets, for example, Luís de Camões, and thus the movement was also known as neoclassicism.

No arcadian school actually took root in Brazil. Rather, arcadian attitudes toward culture among Brazilian intellectuals of the time resulted from their studies and travels in Europe, as well as through their contact with the Lusitanian Arcadia. Encouraged by the philosophers of the French Enlightenment to conceive of a unique Brazilian national sentiment and inspired by successful revolutions in the United States and in France, members of this loosely formed group of intellectuals—clergyman, lawyers, doctors, and scientists—were involved in unsuccessful movements to gain Brazilian independence from Portugal, for example, the *Mineiran Conspiracy.

These intellectuals surveyed the "Brazilian situation" as part of the arcadian all-inclusive concept of "literature." For example, Father Prudêncio do Amaral's (1675–1715) early eighteenth-century treatise on sugarcane agriculture in Brazil (*Sachari Opificio Carmen*) was published in 1781, and Francisco de Melo Franco (1757–1823) censured the "retrograde" government of Queen Dona Maria I in his *O reino de estupidez* (1785; The Kingdom of Stupidity). Father Sousa Caldas (1762–1814) wrote a zoological study of Brazilian birds, *As aves* (178?; The Birds) and was later imprisoned for his written defense of the Brazilian Indians. (*See* Indianism.)

Lyric and epic poetry, a major Brazilian inheritance from Portuguese cultural tradition, was particularly rich. Among the poets who adopted arcadian pseudonyms were Tomás Antônio *Gonzaga, Alvarenga *Peixoto, Basílio da *Gama, and Silva *Alvarenga. The arcadian view of the superiority of the bucolic existence to urban life found a voice in the sonnets of Cláudio Manuel da *Costa. Costa and Silva Alvarenga also theorized briefly on the arcadian aims of their poetry. The major works of epic poetry were Basílio da *Gama's *O uraguai* and Santa Rita *Durão's *Caramuru*. Philosophical treatises on morals and women's education appeared, and grammars of the "Brazilian language" were published in Portugal in the late 1780s. (*See* Feminism and Literature; Portuguese Language of Brazil.)

Minas was the most important New World center of music at the time, according to one critic, and Latin America's greatest eighteenth-century artist was the Brazilian Aleijadinho ("the Little Cripple") (1720–1814), the one-armed sculptor of Ouro Preto. (*See* Art and Literature; Music and Literature.)

The failed Mineiran Conspiracy resulted in the imprisonment and banishment of many of these Brazilian nationalist artists and thinkers. Their literary techniques and themes, nonetheless, continued to flourish as Brazil entered the nineteenth century and reached independence. The first generation of romantic writers were late arcadians. Thus the Arcadias may be considered a transitional period in Brazil from the baroque mentality of political and cultural conservatism toward the century characterized by liberalism, national and personal self-affirmation, and *romanticism. (*See* Philosophy of National Identity.)

BIBLIOGRAPHY: Criticism: Burns, E. Bradford. "Concerning the Transmission and Dissemination of the Enlightenment in Brazil." *The Ibero-American Enlightenment*. Edited by A. Owen Aldridge. Urbana: University of Illinois Press, 1971, pp. 256–281; idem. "The Intellectuals as Agents of Change and the Independence of Brazil, 1724–1822." *From Colony to Nation*. Edited by A.J.R. Russell-Wood. Baltimore: Johns Hopkins University Press, 1975, pp. 211–246; Martins, Wilson. *Historia da inteligência brasileira*. São Paulo: Editora Cultrix, 1977–1978; Moog, Clodomir Viana. *Bandeirantes and Pioneers*. New York: Braziller, 1964.

ARINOS, AFONSO [AFONSO ARINOS DE MELO FRANCO] (1868–1916; BAL: 1901). Arinos grew up in the *sertão* of Minas. He studied law in São Paulo. After practicing law, teaching, and traveling to Europe on several occasions, he moved permanently to Paris in 1904.

Although Arinos wrote poetry, several works of fiction and drama, and collections of essays, today he is primarily known for only one prose work: *Pelo sertão* (1898; Through the Backlands). Rather than writing stories with plots, Arinos presented "tales and landscapes" of backlands existence. Considered the founder of *mineiro* *regionalism, his tales possess a painterly quality of an artist fascinated by nature. These tales display a high level of *ufanismo*, as he attempts to capture the unique characteristics of backlands life. Lacking psychological depth, Arinos's regionalism does not attain a universal level. Also of note is his novel *Os jagunços* (1898; The Backlands Bandits). (*See* Cycles.)

Arinos's son, Afonso Arinos de Melo Franco (b. 1905; BAL: 1958), is a historian and postmodernist poet; he wrote an important *biography of his father: *Um estadista da república* (1955; A Statesman of the Republic). (*See* Postmodernism in Poetry.)

BIBLIOGRAPHY: Additional selected works by Arinos: *Lendas e tradições brasileiras*, 1917; *Obra completa*, 1969. Translations: Hulet. Criticism: Ataíde, Tristão de. *Afonso Arinos*. Rio: 1922; Severino, Alexandrino. "Major Trends in the Development of the Brazilian Short Story." *SSF* (Winter, 1971) pp. 199–208.

ART AND LITERATURE. The relationship between Brazilian art and literature has been most intense since *modernism. Nonetheless, the plastic arts have experienced cultural movements parallel to literature throughout Brazilian literary history. Furthermore, many writers have been artists and art critics, while artists have dedicated themselves to illustrations for works of literature.

Folkloric art, painting and sculpture—inspired by biblical and, on occasion, nativist themes—have flourished in Brazil since the colonial days. The first artists were Portuguese and foreign priests or missionaries and travelers who sketched and painted scenes of frontier life. With the Dutch presence in northern Brazil during the early seventeenth century, Frans Post (1612–1680) painted his orderly "Landscape of Pernambuco with the Master's House" (1665). The prime figure of eighteenth-century art was Antônio Francisco Lisboa, known as Aleijadinho, the "Little Cripple" (1738–1814), a one-armed sculptor who worked on famous soapstone statues of the saints and other religious works in colonial Minas. (*See* Academies; Arcadias; Baroque; Folklore and Literature; Minas School; Regionalism; Religion and Literature; Travel Literature.)

Upon the arrival of the Portuguese royal family in Rio, the relationship between art and literature became more formalized. Dom João VI "imported" a French cultural mission (1816) led by Jean-Baptiste Debret (1768–1848). Aside from sketching Brazilian life of the time in his *Voyage pittoresque et historique au Brésil* (1833–1839; Picturesque and Historical Voyage to Brazil), he established the Academy of Fine Arts, which was later led by his disciple, the romantic poet Manuel Araújo Porto *Alegre. Literally hundreds of other foreign artists appeared in Brazil and recorded many facts of urban, rural, and tribal life. Among the most important were Maria Graham (1785–1842) and Johann Moritz Rugendas (1802–1858).

Brazilian painters and writers were inspired by academic subjects as well as by popular legends of the nation's past during the nineteenth and early twentieth centuries. *Indianism was a popular theme with painters as well as writers: Vítor Meireles (1832–1903) painted *Moema* (1861); Rodolfo Amoedo (1857–1941) painted the *Ultimo tamoio* (1883; The Last Tamoio Indian) and *Marabà* (1882); and Antônio Parreiras (1860–1937) painted *Iracema* (1909). Luís Gonzaga *Duque was a novelist and also the major art critic of the turn of the century. His critical works include *A arte brasileira* (1888; Brazilian Art) and *Contemporâneos* (1929; Contemporaries). Duque's criticism also appeared in important art reviews of the time, among them *O Pierrot* (1890), *Neo-Revista* (1895), *Galáxia*

(1896), and *O Mercúrio* (1898). The artist Maurício Jubim (1875–1923) illustrated works by the symbolist poets, including Cruz e *Sousa. Historical portraiture of events of the Brazilian past as well as portraits of contemporary political figures and writers were also common, for example, Belmiro de Almeida's (1858–1935) portrait of Parnassian Alberto de Oliveira. (*See* Parnassianism.) Raul *Pompéia and Aluísio *Azevedo were also accomplished caricaturists. (*See* Symbolism.)

A few examples can attest to the fact that *modernism and postmodernism (*see* Postmodernism in Poetry) have been the eras of most intense contacts between art and literature. Anita Malfatti's (1896–1972) 1917 vanguard art exhibit led to Monteiro *Lobato's attack on foreign imports into Brazilian culture, which was mistakenly viewed as an attack on the newly forming modernist group. Oswald de *Andrade inspired works by Tarsila de Amaral (1886–1973) with his use of brazilwood (*pau-brasil*) and anthropophagical themes, while she did a portrait of him, her future husband, in 1922; Amaral, Cândido Portinari (1903–1962), Di Cavalcanti (1897–1976), and Lasar Segall (1891–1957) all did important portraits or sketches of Mário de *Andrade, who was also a major art critic and student of Brazilian art both past and contemporary, known especially for *Aspectos das artes plásticas no Brasil* (1965; Aspects of Plastic Arts in Brazil). Mário de Andrade, more than any predecessor, recognized art as an important cultural phenomenon. He, along with Alcântara *Machado and Sérgio *Milliet, helped to establish *A Vida de Spam*, the journal of the Pro-Modern Art Society, which was founded by modernist painters in 1932. Ismael Nery (1900–1934), although best known as an artist, was also a poet; he married Adalgisa *Nery. Writers Paulo *Prado and Ronald de *Carvalho were middlemen in the planning of the plastic arts exhibitions at the Week of Modern Art (*see* Modernism), and Graça *Aranha led off the week with a lecture on the trends in modern art. Gastão *Cruls, a nonmodernist, did extensive research into indigenous art.

Since the 1930s, many writers have been artists in their own right, for example, Millôr *Fernandes, Pedro *Nava, and Luís *Jardim. Cornélio *Pena is known to have designed the cover for his novel *Fronteira*. Other writers have been important art critics including Manuel *Bandeira, Jorge de *Lima, Murilo *Mendes, Luís Martins, Walmir *Ayala, and Jacob Klintowitz (b. 1941). Augusto de *Campos's and Haroldo de *Campos's concrete poetry movement (*see* Postmodernism in Poetry) has a base in the international plastic arts movement. In fact, the Brazilian concrete artists, who considered themselves the continuators of the artistic and cultural trends of the modernist generation of 1922, exhibited their paintings at the Museum of Modern Art in São Paulo in 1956. *Tropicalismo* was a general cultural movement of the late 1960s that also had some effect in the plastic arts. Rodrigo de Haro (b. 1941) has been successful both as a painter and as a poet. (For his translations, *see* "Key to Bibliographical References": Hulet.)

Many artists have been illustrators for literary works, for example, Cícero

Dias (b. 1908); Carybé (b. 1911), whose illustrations of Mário de Andrade's *Macunaíma* and Jorge *Amado's novels are widely known; Oswaldo Goeldi (1895–1961), who did drawings for Raul *Bopp's *Cobra Norato*; Percy Lau (b. 1908); Percy Deane (b. 1921), who illustrated Graciliano *Ramos's *Memórias do cárcere* (1966 edition); and Poty (b. 1924), who was the illustrator of Guimarães *Rosa's *Sagarana*. Since the 1960s, many collections of *crônicas* (e.g., works by Sérgio *Porto, Chico *Anísio, Carlos Eduardo *Novaes) have been enhanced with the humorous drawings of Ziraldo (b. 1932), who recently published his first novel, *Vito Grandam* (1987; Vito Grandam); Vilmar (b. 1931), Jaguar (b. 1932), and others.

Also of note are the works of popular artists of the Northeast, which appear in *cordel* literature, among them Damásio Paulo. (*See* Folklore and Literature.)

BIBLIOGRAPHY: Criticism: Amaral, Aracy. "The Modernist Period." *Art and Artists* (April, 1976), pp. 32–35; Ayala, Walmir. *Brazil through Its Arts*. Rio: Nórdica, 1982; DeFiore, Ottaviano C. *Architecture and Sculpture in Brazil. BSG*; Lemos, Carlos, et al. eds. *The Art of Brazil*. New York: Harper & Row, 1983; Pontual, Roberto. *Dicionário das artes plásticas no Brasil*. Rio: Civilização Brasileira, 1969; Rego, Stella de Sá, and Maguerite Itamar Harrison. *Modern Brazilian Painting. BSG*.

ASSIS, JOAQUIM MARIA MACHADO DE (1839–1908). Machado de Assis was the son of relatively poor parents. He was mulatto—his mother was white (from the Azores Islands) and his father predominantly black—although it is probable that his family had been free for one or two generations. They were dependents (*agregados*) of a powerful family who lived on the outskirts of Rio. The young Assis, obviously ambitious and tenacious, entered the field of letters, specifically, journalism, one of the few careers that could give him a modicum of independence in the Brazil of the 1850s. He was helped by one of the most admirable figures of the time, the first important Brazilian publisher, Francisco de Paula Brito (1809–1861), also mulatto and founder of the *Petalógica*, a literary club.

Assis adopted liberal political views and, in the 1860s, worked for the *Diário do Rio de Janeiro*, with famous republican supporters such as the journalists and politicians Quintino Bocaiúva (1836–1912) and Saldanha Marinho (1816–1895). At this time, Assis was an active poet, short story writer, and dramatist, although very much an apprentice in all these modes, as he himself was well aware (as evidenced by the apologetic tone not only of prefaces but of letters to friends).

The end of the 1860s and early 1870s were a crucial period for Assis. In 1869 he married Carolina Xavier de Novais, an Azorean and sister of a Portuguese poet; the marriage, although childless, seems to have been harmonious. Her death in 1904 left her husband, according to him, utterly disconsolate. In 1868 he also had obtained a bureaucratic post, which he kept throughout his life in spite of sudden changes of government during both the empire and the republic. In 1869 his first collection of stories, *Contos fluminenses* (Stories about the

Inhabitants of the State of Rio) was published, followed in 1872 by his first novel, *Ressurreição* (Resurrection). Although it might have been difficult to sense it from these works, they were the first steps toward the goal he was ultimately to reach. He is, as no one would dispute, the greatest master of both forms to have written in Brazil.

Three other novels were published in the 1870s—*A mão e a luva* (1874; *The Hand and the Glove*, 1970); *Helena* (1876; *Helena*, 1984) and *Iaiá Garcia* (1878; *Iaiá Garcia*, 1977); a further collection of stories; and his third book of poetry, *Americanas* (1875; American Poems). According to critic Roberto Schwarz (*See* Critics and Criticism), this phase (generally, and misleadingly, called romantic) is in fact an exploration of the oppressive nature of the Brazilian patriarchal family and of the relation between masters and dependents. The fact that love is used as a plot device is less important than the exploration itself, and, indeed, progressively and above all in the second part of *Iaiá Garcia*, we begin to see that love itself is not an absolute: what is often true with this deliberate but determined writer, intellectual convictions gradually make themselves felt at plot level and enforce change. (*See* Romanticism.)

Romantic love was never much more than a device for Assis; at that time he did not know—nor is it in the least surprising that he did not know—how to write novels without it. Some of his stories, most notably "A parasita azul" (The Blue Parasite), the opening story from *Histórias da meia-noite* (1874; Midnight Stories), are much more clearly satirical than are these conventional novels. But they show, what is equally significant, that Assis had not yet found an adequate generic mold for such attitudes.

He found that mold in 1880 with the publication of his first great novel, *Memórias póstumas de Brás Cubas* (*Epitaph of a Small Winner*, 1952). It purports to be an autobiography, written from beyond the grave, by a member of the Brazilian oligarchy. Formally, it is a complete break with the Brazilian literary past and with his own time. If anything, in its willfully intrusive narrator, who decides to begin the story with his death, it harks to the eighteenth century, to writers like Laurence Sterne or Denis Diderot, or to the classical tradition of Menippean satire, to which Assis owed a conscious debt. But in a sense this is the least of it; such things are catalysts. His break with the usual way of writing novels in his time allowed an exploration of unsuspected areas of reality that are at best hinted at earlier. In part, this is a matter of psychological acuity. He observes human beings in their pettiest, most cynical, and most self-serving state, without seeing them as simple animals incapable of making choices. But he is not simply a moralist, however subtle. We are also given a remarkably full and complex picture of *carioca* society in the first half of the nineteenth century, as seen by the rich. Even the changing mores of the upper classes are focused in the adulterous affair between Brás Cubas and Virgília, spurred on by a melodramatic, self-indulgent romanticism, as well as by sexual passion, that is half-permitted, half-ignored, in an increasingly urban, if theoretically traditional, society.

Critics and biographers (*see* Biography and Biographers; Critics and Criticism) have attributed Assis's sudden access to greatness in 1880 to the crisis in his health that preceded it—he had to leave Rio for a while in 1878–1879. Underlying such explanations there usually lurk romantic notions of suffering genius, which Assis himself would most likely have abhorred. It seems much more sensible to explain the change as both a consequence of a lifelong desire—expressed in a critical article titled "Instinto de nacionalidade" (1872; Instinct of Nationality)—to produce an art that would be Brazilian in a more than superficial sense and that would make the writer "A man of his time and of his country," as well as a result of the very real difficulties that stood in the way, given the narrative models at his disposal and the nature of the society around him.

One aspect of this struggle is worth emphasizing: his rejection of the most obvious alternative model to romanticism presented by European culture, *naturalism. In 1878 he had two perceptive and highly critical articles published on the Portuguese Eça de Queiroz's (1845–1890) novel *O primo Basílio* (1878; *Cousin Bazilio*, 1953), which he took to be representative of the movement. (His opinions of Zola seem to have been almost unprintable.) It is significant that it is no minor product of the movement that he attacks, for it is the doctrine itself, which deprives characters of freedom and also of morality, that disgusts Assis. It is easy to portray him as either conservative and intolerant or as a farseeing precursor of existentialism on the basis of these articles. In fact, he was neither. He saw people as both free and predetermined and some (slaves, for instance) as more determined than others and thus, logically, less responsible for their actions. His rejection of naturalism (which extends to all deterministic and progressivist theories that dominated the nineteenth century) may well have come from the implicit or explicit racism in some of them, for his own status as a mulatto epileptic was hardly a comfortable identity at that stage in human intellectual history. His rejection of naturalism makes him an exception among the great novelists of the Hispanic world at the time and goes a long way to explaining his uniqueness. (*See* Portugal and Brazil: Literary Relations.)

Epitaph of a Small Winner produced a sudden unleashing of energy or was itself the first product of that unleashing: some of his greatest short stories, including "O Alienista" (1881–1882; "The Psychiatrist," in *The Psychiatrist and Other Stories*, 1963) and "O espelho" (1882; "The Looking Glass," in *The Psychiatrist . . .*), soon followed. In them, "philosophical" concerns with the boundaries of madness or the existence of the soul are given comically trivial settings—a colonial Brazilian backwater or an abandoned plantation house. During the 1880s Assis wrote numerous short stories, by no means all in this vein. His perception of human capacity for self-delusion and thus for perversion is extraordinary for his time, as shown by the scene of Fortunato torturing mice in "A causa secreta" (1885; "The Secret Heart," in *The Psychiatrist . . .*) or, on a less macabre level, by Dona Paula's vicarious enjoyment of her niece's suffering in the story that bears her name, or, again, by the almost subterranean (or deliberately controlled?) frustrations of Conceição in "Missa do galo" (1894;

"Midnight Mass," in *The Psychiatrist* . . .). Sex is a more frequent subject in these stories (and in the novels) than is frequently recognized (again, his "prudish" dismissal of Eça de Queiroz should deceive no one); yet it is sex seen as an integral part of the personality; frequently, it is an expression of a desire to dominate or even to prey on others.

But if *Epitaph of a Small Winner* was part of a sudden release of creative powers, the final encounter of form with content, it also produced problems, the most obvious being where to go from there, since there can be no doubt that Machado saw himself as a novelist above all. The first movement toward a solution is perhaps surprising: a short novel called *Casa velha* (1885–1886; Old House). This story of injustice and family exclusiveness in the period of Assis's birth (1839) might seem romantic. In fact, it is an attempt to write a serious, realistic, historical novel. Assis obviously did not think it was successful, for he never had it published in book form, but the attempt itself shows that a fundamentally realist desire to portray his own environment and his own century persisted.

Months after finishing *Casa velha*, in 1886, Assis began the serialization of his second great novel, *Quincas Borba* (1891; *Quincas Borba: Philosopher or Dog?* 1954). This work is often regarded as less interesting or problematic than *Epitaph of a Small Winner* and *Dom Casmurro* (1890; *Dom Casmurro*, 1971), of which it is fully the equal. (The reasons for this view tend to be trivial: this novel does not have the cachet of a first-person narrator, for instance.) *Quincas Borba* recounts the career of the foolish Rubião, who inherits a huge amount of the money and a crazed (deterministic) philosophy from Quincas Borba, a character who had already appeared in *Epitaph of a Small Winner*, and takes both to Rio. There he is slowly but surely fleeced by the fascinating "limited company of crooks," the ambitious businessman Cristiano Palha and his seductive wife, Sofia. Around these three central characters we are shown a variety of people in various stages of social climbing and falling. The plot is complex, and this in itself shows a break with *Epitaph of a Small Winner*, which is genuinely episodic. To a great extent this is because the paternalistic society of the novel is gradually being replaced by one that is marginally more mobile.

Quincas Borba is set in 1867–1871, a period of important political, intellectual, and social change in Brazil, a fact that is apparently only marginal to its greatness. Yet the central plot itself, by which unexpected and undeserved wealth gets in to the hands of a rapacious parasite, is a parable of the history of the Second Reign (that of Dom Pedro II). The wealth and apparent political stability brought by the coffee boom failed to produce real progress, and profits were diverted into the hands of speculators tied to international capital.

Little of such a political or historical meaning is present on the surface of *Quincas Borba*. Assis's greatest fiction is characterized by a coherence of many levels of meaning and action, private and public, roving with dizzying ease from philosophical generalization to trivial realistic detail within the same phrase. Such a complex unity is the product of conscious effort—*Quincas Borba* was considerably rewritten between 1886 and 1891—but we should not overlook the fact that Assis's confidence and success as a novelist is born of a sense of the coherence and consistency of many levels of meaning and truth. To give one example, his nationalism (however skeptical) is the perfect accompaniment for his equally persistent antideterminism, which in turn has its roots in his personal life, and so on.

Dom Casmurro is perhaps the most triumphant illustration of this many-layered harmony: it is the most consistently realistic of all of Assis's novels, in that a conscious attempt has been made to make the narrator, the style, and the story, all of one piece. In a sense, it transfers the plot of Quincas Borba (the fleecing of a man with inherited wealth by an upstart businessman) into a more narrowly familial context, removes the element of parable or folktale—the country cousin in the big city—present in the earlier novel and returns to that important nineteenth-century subgenre, the novel of adultery.

Bento, its narrator–hero, is the only son of a family grown wealthy on sugar that is now removed to a safer, more comfortable existence in Rio. He marries his childhood sweetheart, Capitu, thus forcing the breaking of a vow his mother had made to make him a priest. He finally becomes convinced that his wife has committed adultery with his best friend, Escobar, a businessman. His marriage to Capitu, the daughter of a civil servant, is below him on the social scale and leads him, unwary, into a world of social differences that he—generously?, selfishly? romantically?—would like to ignore and that in the end produce insecurity, pathological jealousy, and separation. With an ingenuity and perceptiveness springing from deep understanding, Assis gives the narration to Bento and so allows the romantic-youth-turned-cynical-determinist-in-old-age ("You, dear reader, will agree with me that the woman [Capitu] was in the girl, just as the fruit is in the rind") to reveal a truth of which he is largely unaware, although he is its prime exhibit. Bento is every privileged, spoiled child, cocooned by the preconceptions of his childhood to the extent of being unable to understand how the world outside really operates. Yet we, the readers, can see how it operates, although perhaps not entirely, for we can never be sure whether Capitu did or did not commit adultery (the question on which, understandably, much criticism of the novel focuses). However, to a very considerable extent, and, in fact, we know the world that emerges in this novel is as varied, detailed, and colorful as in any of Assis's works. The timorous, overprotective mother, Dona Glória; the carping, resentful, hanger-on cousin Justina; the trivial, vain, and gluttonous Father Cabral, and, above all, the hypocritical, scheming, pompous, dependent José Dias, Assis's definitive portrayal of the type, are all sensitive, revealing, and even sympathetic portraits in the best realist tradition.

The best of Assis's fiction combines, with apparent ease, the social, philosophical, psychological, and historical dimensions and makes them parts of a whole. Perhaps this explains why his last two novels, Esaú e Jacó (1904; Esaú and Jacó, 1966) and Memorial de Aires (1908; Counselor Ayres Memoirs, 1972), have found less favor with critics and readers, although they are works of great artistry and intelligence. Narrative complexity and surface difficulty is perhaps nowhere greater than in *Esaú and Jacó*. For instance, it is uncertain who is narrating, Assis or his official narrator, Counselor Ayres. The plot contains more obvious elements of political allegory than does any of his other works; also, it recounts the rival loves of two identical twins, Pedro and Paulo, one monarchist, the other republican, for a single girl, Flora. It is hard to imagine a less exciting plot, although the novel is full of interest both in its ideas and its characters. But the dull plot may be why Assis half disclaims paternity.

In *Counselor Ayres' Memoirs* he returns to a clear first-person narrator (Counselor Ayres again) and tells what apparently is a love story set against the background of abolition but actually is a damning account of the irresponsibility of the Brazilian upper class, members of which are always prepared to sacrifice the public good for their most trivial personal wants, a theme that had preoccupied Assis and that lies at the center of all of his novels after, and including, *Epitaph of a Small Winner*. These final works are a logical, if not perhaps a triumphant, conclusion to his work. Those who question and experiment as radically as Assis did, with aims as ambitious as he had, must expect to be the victims as well as the spokesmen of the world to which they open themselves. (*See* Slavery and Literature.)

This account of Assis's career and his fiction is not everyone's, but it is impossible, in the nature of the subject, to present one that is both conventional and objective. He was a successful writer in his time—*revered (consagrado)* is the word most usually used—and an establishment figure, the founder-president of the *Brazilian Academy of Letters, for example. Such an expert at disguise becomes, in effect, a literary chameleon, who adapts to many different kinds of environments and suits many different kinds of readers.

Critical orthodoxy has thus gone through recognizable stages in its view of Assis. For many years, the cynical, disabused writer in the mold of Anatole France dominated the scene; this even produced its own response, in an essay by Mário de *Andrade, who asked the wrong question—"Do you love Machado de Assis?"—and answered in a predictable negative. The modernist generation (*see* Modernism) produced a different, more interior view of an anguished writer, in the mold of (a certain) Dostoyevsky, in the essay of Augusto *Meyer. More recently, in the important critical works of Raymundo Faoro and above all Roberto Schwarz (*see* Critics and Criticism), Assis's connections with the social structure and the thought of his time have become the focus of study. This approach appears to be the most fruitful, in part because it is not one made obvious by the texts themselves. With Assis, what is on the surface tends to be superficial.

Strangely, for a writer so respected and admired (and read), his influence on later writers is not very visible. This may be true because of his extraordinary linguistic agility and humor, which defy plodding imitation. He is in touch with all levels of the language, from the most literary and archaic to the most everyday and popular. One need only look at his journalism, especially of the 1880s and

1890s, to see how intelligently he responded to public events and how flexible were the linguistic instruments at his command. He is, even on the surface, the complete man of letters—poet, short story writer, novelist, dramatist, journalist—but he is also that more elusive thing, a great writer: great and profoundly typical of the time and place that he aspired, tenaciously and from an early age, to represent. (*See also* Theater History.)

BIBLIOGRAPHY: Additional selected works by Assis: Poetry, drama, many newspaper articles and *crônicas beyond the works mentioned above were published. There is not a satisfactory complete works; the *Obra completa* published by Jackson and by Aguilar are both incomplete, although the latter is more reliable. Other short story collections: *Papéis avulsos*, 1882; *Histórias sem data*, 1884; *Várias histórias*, 1896; *Páginas recolhidas*, 1899; *Relíquias da casa velha*, 1906. Many of these stories have appeared in English translations, in collections and individually: Hulet. Criticism: Brookshaw; Caldwell, Helen. *The Brazilian Othello of Machado de Assis: A Study of "Dom Casmurro."* Berkeley: University of California Press, 1960; idem. *Machado de Assis*. Berkeley: University of California Press, 1970; Driver; Faoro, Raymundo. *Machado de Assis: a pirâmide e o trapézio*. São Paulo: Brasiliense, 1976; Foster/Foster, I; Gledson, John. *The Deceptive Realism of Machado de Assis: A Dissenting Interpretation of "Dom Casmurro."* Liverpool: Liverpool University Press, 1984; Haberly; Ishimatsu, L. C. *The Poetry of Machado de Assis*. Valencia, Spain/Chapel Hill, N.C.: Albatros Ediciones/Hispanófila, 1984; Nunes, Maria Luísa. *The Craft of an Absolute Winner: Characterization and Narratology in the Novels of Machado de Assis*. Westport, Conn.: Greenwood Press, 1983; Peixoto, Marta. "Aires as Narrator and Aires as Character in *Esaú e Jacó.*" *LBR* (Summer, 1980), pp. 79–92; Sayers; Schwarz, Roberto, *Ao vencedor as batatas*, São Paulo: Duas Cidades, 1977.

JOHN GLEDSON

ASSIS BRASIL. *See* Brasil, Assis.

ASSUNÇÃO, LEILAH [MARIA DE LOURDES TORRES DE ASSUNÇÃO] (b. 1943). A *paulista* with a degree in education, Assunção studied theater with the *Teatro Oficina* and began her career with the *Teatro Novo* (New Theatre Group) in the mid–1960s. (*See* Theater History.)

Rather than focusing on the social and political themes that characterized Brazilian drama of the 1960s, Assunção has been more preoccupied with the emotional and psychological questions about society that have general appeal. Several of her first plays, for example, *Feira* (1967; Fair), were prohibited by censorship. *Fala baixo, senão eu grito* (1959; Speak Softly, or I Shall Yell), awarded the Molière Theater Prize (*see* Prizes), is a tense drama between a middle-aged, unmarried woman and an intruder. Assunção revealed them both to be caught in individual webs of reality mixed with grotesque fantasies from which neither one can break out. *Amélia ou Roda cor-de-roda* (1973–1975; Amelia or Color Wheel), also the victim of censorship, deals with infidelity in a traditional Latin husband-wife relationship but with a new twist. Assunção attacked marriage as a bourgeois symbol from a feminine perspective. (*See* Dictatorship and Literature; Feminism and Literature.)

Assunção's *A Kuka de Kamaiorá* (1978; The Kuka of Kamaiorá) is a new turn of direction. In it she parodied a futuristic reality in a mythical Latin American country, a highly class-conscious dictatorship. This drama mixes classical elements, for example, a prophetic choir, with avant-garde theatrical techniques. Assunção is Brazil's leading woman playwright. Through allegory, irony, and humor she criticizes reality in a striking way. One critic has written that her dramas do not need directors but rather tamers.

BIBLIOGRAPHY: Additional selected works by Assunção: *Jorginho, o machão*, 1970; *Da fala ao grito*, 1977. Criticism: Milleret, Margo. "Entrapment and Flights of Fantasy in Three Plays by Leilah Assunção." *LBR* (Summer, 1984), pp. 49–56.

AUTOBIOGRAPHY. Among the true autobiographies written by Brazilian literary and cultural figures are works by Matias *Aires, Junqueira *Freire, José de *Alencar, Joaquim *Nabuco, Oswald de *Andrade, José Lins do *Rego, and Manuel *Bandeira.

Although autobiographical elements have entered into the works of the so-called psychological novelists of the nineteenth and twentieth centuries, Machado de *Assis, Raul *Pompéia, and Lima *Barreto, Brazilian writers have tended toward the *Künstlerroman* of *Bildungsroman*, in which there is a fictional presentation of the writer's youth and intellectual development, for example, novels by Ciro dos *Anjos and Fernando *Sabino; *Marcoré* (1957; *Marcoré*, 1970) by Antônio Olavo Pereira; Josué de Castro's (1908–1973) semiautobiographical novel of his youth in impoverished Recife: *Homens e caranguejos* (*Men and Crabs*, 1970); novels by Paulo *Francis, and Carlos Heitor *Cony; and *A idade da paixão* (1985; The Age of Passion) by Rubem Mauro Machado, a novel that describes growing up in Brazil in the predictatorship 1960s.

Partial autobiographies have been written by authors who returned from political exile during the last years of the dictatorship, for example, Fernando *Gabeira, or by those who describe their lives in Brazil during the years of the regime, for example, José Vicente's (b. 1945) autobiography of his life in the theater, *Reis da terra* (1984; Kings of the Land) and Herbert Daniel's narration of his homosexual life-style in Brazil and Paris: *Passagem para o próximo sonho* (Passage to the Next Dream). Surely one of the most curious autobiographies written in Brazil was Nelson *Rodrigues's fictional autobiography of his female literary alias Suzana Flag, *Minha vida* (1946; My Life). (*See* Biography; Dictatorship and Literature; Homosexuality and Literature; Memoirs; Theater History.)

BIBLIOGRAPHY: Criticism: Vieira, Nelson H. "Fictional Autobiography in the Novel *Marcoré*: Confessions of a Brazilian Soul." *LBR* (Summer, 1983), pp. 139–149.

ÁVILA, AFFONSO (b. 1928). Ávila is a leading art and cultural critic of the Brazilian *baroque and a student of its continued presence in Brazilian culture (e.g., *Resíduos seiscentistas em Minas* (1967; Seventeenth Century Residues in Minas). (*See* Arcadias; Art and Literature; Minas School.)

Mineiro Avila began his literary career as a member of the Generation of 1945. (*See* Postmodernism in Poetry.) In 1957 he was associated with the group that founded the *review *Tendência*: Silviano *Santiago, Rui *Mourão, the critic Fábio Lucas (*see* Critics and Criticism), Fritz Teixeira de Salles, and others. The movement was indirectly aligned with concretism and exerted, briefly, an influence on the concretists through which they turned to social questions. Ávila later collaborated on the review *Invenção* (1962–1967), the leading organ of the second phase of concretism. (*See* Postmodernism in Poetry.)

In his "Carta do solo: poema referencial" (Letter from the Earth: Referential Poem), included in his *O poeta e a consciência crítica* (1969; The Poet and His Critical Consciousness), Ávila revealed the influence of João Cabral de *Melo Neto's aesthetic on his work, stating that poetry is both an art object and a personal view of the poet's world. The visualist and semiotic influences of the concretists combine with his social interests in his poetry, as in *Código de Minas e poesia anterior* (1969; Minas Code and Earlier Poetry) and *Cantaria barroca* (1975; Baroque Stones) in which montage is used. One of Ávila's prime poetic techniques is parody, used for elucidation rather than for comic effect.

BIBLIOGRAPHY: Additional selected works by Ávila: *O açude e Sonetos da descoberta*, 1953; *Código nacional de trânsito*, 1972.

AYALA, WALMIR (b. 1933). Ayala, from Rio Grande do Sul, has lived in Rio since 1956. He has been very active in all literary genres, as well as being an anthologist of poetry and an art and music critic. (*See* Art and Literature; Music and Literature.)

Ayala had some seventeen volumes of highly metaphorical verse published between 1955 and 1971, but he rejected many of these poems and rewrote others in his *Poesia revisada* (1972; Revised Poetry). *Um animal de Deus* (1964?; An Animal of God) involves an unrevealed homosexual affection that leads the protagonist to an ambiguous desire for the priesthood. A collection of short fiction, *Ponte sobre o rio escuro* (1974; Bridge Over the Dark River), presents common people who suddenly discover a fateful truth about their existence. In the use of stream of consciousness and other stylistic techniques, his fiction reveals the influence of Osman *Lins and Clarice *Lispector. (*See* Homosexuality and Literature.)

Other works that Ayala has had published are *children's literature, *memoirs, plays, and an interesting collection of Indian legends about his native region, *Moça lua* (1974; Young Moon). (*See* Folklore and Literature; Indian Languages; Indianism; Regionalism; Theater History.)

BIBLIOGRAPHY: Additional selected works by Ayala: *Cantata*, 1966; *A nova terra*, 1980; *Brazil through Its Art*, 1982; *Águas como espadas*, 1983; *Os reinos e os vestes*, 1986. Translations: *Signals* (London). 1964.

AZEVEDO, ALUÍSIO (1857–1913; BAL: 1897). Born and brought up in northeastern Maranhão, Azevedo, brother of Artur *Azevedo, attained national prominence in Rio with his social and political caricatures in popular turn-of-the-century literary *reviews and magazines such as *Fígaro* and *Fon-Fon!* He returned to Maranhão upon his father's death and began a career as a journalist and author of *crônicas. After having many novels, short stories, and plays published, he began a diplomatic career in 1896, hoping that it would alleviate financial difficulties and allow him more time to write. Ironically, he published little after that date. He died in Buenos Aires.

Along with Inglês de *Sousa, Azevedo introduced *realism and *naturalism into Brazilian literature. Nonetheless, he also had several novels published in serials (folhetins), with characteristics of the romantic school: superificial characterizations and melodramatic adventures often verging on the fantastic and often employing theatrical devices. Filomena Borges (1884; Philomena Borges), which some critics believe was inspired by José de *Alencar's novel Senhora, parodies the conventions of middle-class marriage, and O coruja (1887; The Owl) views the decadence of the empire's politicians. In these and other novels, his concern was not with the "scientific examination" promoted by the naturalists but rather with a superficial interest in documentation. (See Romanticism.)

Three novels stand out among all of his works as important personal achievements with major literary repercussions. O mulato (1881; The Mulatto) was the first important Brazilian realist novel. Set in his native Maranhão, the writer narrates the events leading to the murder of Raimundo, a mulatto with a refined European education. Upon returning to Maranhão, Raimundo falls in love with his cousin Ana Rosa; however, a marriage is prohibited by her father because Raimundo is the son of a slave. As the plots unfolds, the racial prejudices of Brazil's middle class and its hypocritical church representatives are documented. Although Azevedo's characterization of Raimundo has been called "romantic" (some think it is based on the true story of poet Gonçalves *Dias's similar unfortunate love affair), the novel makes an effective sociological statement about Brazilian racial attitudes. Although naturalistic elements appear in O mulato, for example, Ana Rosa's graphic abortion and the theme of anticlericalism, melodrama tends to dominate.

In Casa de pensão (1884; The Pension), the thematic concerns of naturalism take firmer hold: environmental determinism, the power of sex, and money play important roles. Amâncio, a student from Maranhão, arrives in fascinating Rio only to be drawn to his death by "middle-class" forces at a student residence, which harbors all classes of people. While Azevedo creates several vivid characterizations in the naturalistic mold, for example, João Coqueiro and Amélia, Amâncio's behavior, like Raimundo's in O mulato, is symbolic of a collective societal dilemma rather than an individual problem.

O cortiço (1890; The Brazilian Tenement, 1926) is considered one of the essential novels of Brazilian literature as well as Azevedo's premier work. In it the influence of Émile Zola and the Portuguese Eça de Queiroz blends with his own creative originality to produce a forceful portrait of a society of outcasts preoccupied with sex, money, and, finally, social standing. João Romão, a Portuguese immigrant, leaves no stone unturned in his pursuit of wealth and position. No deceit, thievery, or trick is beneath him. His wealth is represented by his grocery store and home and the tenement housing he constructs next door. Its inhabitants are poor mulatto Brazilians, immigrants from Italy and Portugal, and the ex-slave Bertoleza, João Romão's longtime lover and financial conspirator. The brutal details of the tenement's life—from rampant promiscuity to the "national" racial hostilities between the Portuguese and Brazilians—intensify along with João Romão's wealth. Social position, the ultimate desire of the immigrant during the empire, is finally achieved through João's marriage to his arch rival's daughter Zulmira. Rejected by João and defenseless in face of her old master's appearance to recapture her, Bertoleza commits suicide. (*See* Immigrants and Literature; Portugal and Brazil: Literary Relations.)

Azevedo possessed an innate ability for fiction. His affiliation with the naturalistic school resulted from a desire "to combat all the inimical evils, vices, defects and prejudices of my land while stressing her beauty and virtue." (*apud* Massaud Moisés. *História da literatura brasileira: romantismo, realismo.* São Paulo: Cultrix/EDUSP, 1984, p. 350).

BIBLIOGRAPHY: Additional selected works by Azevedo: *O homem,* 1877; *Demônios,* 1893; *A mortalha de Alzira,* 1894; *O livro de uma sogra,* 1895. Criticism: Brookshaw; Loos; MacNicoll, Murray Graeme. "*O mulato* and Maranhão: The Socio-Historical Context." *LBR* (Winter, 1975), pp. 234–240; Meneses, Raimundo de. *Aluísio de Azevedo: Uma vida de romance.* São Paulo: Martins, 1958; Sayers.

AZEVEDO, ARTUR (1855–1908; BAL: 1897). Born in Maranhão and the brother of Aluísio Azevedo (with whom he often collaborated), Azevedo moved to Rio, where he had a career in government and became one the leading playwrights of his day. (*See* Theater History.)

Initially influenced by popular European imports, he later followed in the tradition of Brazilian national dramatists Martins *Pena and José Joaquim da *França Júnior. In general, Azevedo's plays are light-hearted comedies in a colloquial language. However, he also wrote several more serious dramas, particularly on the antislavery theme: *O escravocrata* (1884; The Slavocrat) and *O Liberato* (1888; Liberato). *O dote* (1907; The Dowry), his final drama, is based on a *crônica* of Júlia Lopes de *Almeida; in it, the resolution of a marital dilemma is presented from an interesting psychological perspective. His most popular and successful plays, though, presented the corrupting influence of city life on rural folk; most notable was *A capital federal* (1893; The Federal Capital). (*See* City and Literature; Slavery and Literature.)

Azevedo was also a popular short-fiction writer. His stories have a theatrical, anecdoctal style and possess the same humoristic, fast-paced, and light-hearted attitudes of his plays. Many have unexpected endings in the style of Guy de Maupassant; some critics have called them *crônicas.*

BIBLIOGRAPHY: Additional selected works by Azevedo: *Amor por anexins,* 1876; *A jóia,* 1879; *A almanjarra,* 1888; *Contos possíveis,* 1889; *Contos efêmeros,* 1893; *Teatro a vapor.* Criticism: Magalhães Jr., Raimundo. *Artur Azevedo e sua época.* São Paulo: Martins, 1956; Moser, Gerald. "Artur Azevedo's Last Dramatic Writings: The *Teatro a vapor* Vignettes (1906–1908)." *LATR* (Fall, 1976), pp. 23–35; Sayers.

AZEVEDO, MANUEL ANTÔNIO ÁLVARES DE (1831–1852). Álvares de Azevedo died of tuberculosis, the "romantic" disease, when he was less than twenty-one years old. Nonetheless, he is one of the major poets of the second generation of Brazilian *romanticism. While in high school, Azevedo was already actively writing poetry. In law school in São Paulo, he was a member of the "Epicurean Society," along with Bernardo *Guimarães, Aureliano Lessa (*see* Romanticism), and others, which had as its goal "the achievement of Byron's dreams."

Azevedo is often called the Brazilian Byron, owing to the realistic, skeptical, yet humorous tone of some of his poetry. Nonetheless, he is most celebrated for his ultraromantic (*see* Romanticism) verse, replete in visions and dreams of death and in extreme sentimentality, such as "Se eu morresse amanhã" (If I Were to Die Tomorrow), perhaps the best-known poem of his collection *Lira dos vinte anos* (1853; The Lyre of the Twenty Year Old).

Poesias diversas (Several Poems), the second part of this collection, and his works in prose, for example, *Noite na taverna* (1855; Night at the Tavern) and drama, *Macário* (1885; Macário) reflect the romantics' interest in the fantastic. Azevedo, all of whose work was published posthumously, remains one of the most widely read romantic poets today. (*See* Theater History.)

BIBLIOGRAPHY: Additional selected works by Azevedo: *Poema do frade*, 1862; *O conde Lopo*, 1886. Translations: Hulet. Criticism: Batchelor, Malcolm. "Álvares de Azevedo: A Transcendental Figure in Brazilian Literature." *Hispania* (May, 1956), pp. 149–156; Warren, Donald O. "On the Functions of the Poetic Sign in Álvares de Azevedo." *LBR* (Summer, 1980), pp. 93–106.

B

BANDEIRA, MANUEL (1886–1968; BAL: 1940). Although his native north-eastern Brazil and, in particular, the city of Recife frequently appear in his poetry, Bandeira's family moved to Rio when he was ten, and the poet spent most of his life there. Initially, he studied with José *Veríssimo; however, influenced by his father, an engineer, he intended to become an architect and enrolled in the Polytechnic Institute of São Paulo. His studies were cut short in 1904, when he fell ill with tuberculosis. Bandeira began to travel widely in search of a cure. He became a patient at a clinic in Switzerland, where he met the French poet Paul Éluard (1895–1952). He was appointed to the prestigious Colégio Pedro II in 1938, and in 1943 he became a professor of Hispanic-American literature at the University of Brazil.

A translator, an anthologist, an essayist, and a memoralist, Bandeira, however, is essentially a poet. Considered one of the greatest poets of this century, his premodernist (see Modernism) virtuosity in terms of form and rhythm was never abandoned but rather was transformed by the modernist sensibility. A friend of many of the modernists, Bandeira was a diligent correspondent as well. His correspondence with Mário de *Andrade is particularly interesting in revealing the sharpening modernist sensibility of both poets. Andrade called Bandeira the ''Saint John the Baptist of Modernism'' for his role as a precursor. He is honored as a friend and fellow poet in poems by many other contemporaries, such as Vinícius de *Moraes and Carlos Drummond de *Andrade. (See Memoirs.)

Bandeira, who was extremely prolific, self-published his first collection in 1917. His work exemplifies better than that of any other poet the transition from premodernism to modernism itself. His poetry is commonly divided into two not entirely distinct phases. The first phase encompasses his first three collections and is characterized by ''penumbrism,'' late symbolist themes, and *Parnassian forms. Written under the shadow of his illness, A cinza das horas (1917; The Ashes of the Hours) is marked by a finely tuned musicality coupled to the expression of sadness, of quiet melancholy expressed in rhymed and metered verses. The poems ''Paisagem noturna'' (Nocturnal Landscape) or ''Imagem''

(Image) represent well the temper of the book. *Carnaval* (1919; Carnival) imposes on the melancholic themes of the first book the carnival mask that does not entirely hide the suffering of the poet. Bandeira began to master a gentle irony that would characterize his work from then on. The harlequins, pierrots, and columbines in these poems give note that the poet is still tied to the *fin-de-siècle* images. On the other hand, the book includes the poem "Os sapos" (The Frogs), read during the Week of Modern Art (*see* Modernism), which, with its humorous criticism of Parnassian preoccupations with poetic rules, became a sort of modernist manifesto. *O ritmo dissoluto* (1924; Dissolute Rhythm) gathers poems written during the period of *Carnaval* and others written subsequently either under the impact of the modernism or as a consequence of Bandeira's natural development. It is his transitional book, with some poems reflecting the aesthetics that guided the preceding ones while others point to the development of the modernist Bandeira, that would be made definite with *Libertinagem* (1930; Libertinage). (*See* Symbolism.)

Libertinagem begins Bandeira's second phase of poetry and gathers poems written between 1924 and 1930, during the so-called heroic phase of the modernist movement. The book's modernist aesthetics are declared in "Poética" (Poetics): "I'm fed up with correct lyricism / Well behaved lyricism / Civil service lyricism with registers records files and demonstrations of appreciation to the director." Indeed, on occasion the poet completely abandoned meter, choosing instead to compose prose poems, such as "Nocturno da Rua da Lapa" (Lapa Street Nocturne) or the one-sentence poem "Madrigal tão engraçadinho" (Such a Cute Madrigal). Included in *Libertinagem* as well is one of Bandeira's best-known poems, "Vou-me embora pra Passárgada" ("I'm Leaving for Pasárgada"; *see* "Key to Bibliographical References": Fremantle). Written in the traditional Portuguese popular-verse form, the *redondilha*, the poem synthesizes many of the themes that would obsess the poet throughout his career: the plans of a normal life waylaid by disease; the polarity between a daily, banal reality and a city of dreams; and the strong eroticism that would permeate so many of Bandeira's love lyrics. (*See* Portugal and Brazil: Literary Relations.)

The poetry of *Libertinagem* clearly evidences the transition to the modernist aesthetic in several concrete ways. First, Bandeira shifted Brazilian literary diction to a colloquial, oral one, making his literary language true to the Portuguese spoken in Brazil as opposed to that spoken in Portugal. While he was on the forefront of this shift, he was influenced by the Portuguese poets, such as Luís de Camões (1524–1580), Cesário Verde (1855–1886), and António Nobre (1867–1900). He also brought the prosaic topic to poetry. Responding to the narrow poetical themes allowed by the Parnassians, Bandeira brought to poetry "trivial," everyday events such as in the poem "Poema tirado de uma notícia de jornal" (Poem Taken from a Newspaper Article). He revived interest in the "primitive" or popular aspects of Brazilian culture, which, again, the Parnassians and the symbolists had ignored. This would take the form not only of the use of children's rhyme but also of non-European myths and beliefs, such as in the poem "Macumba de Pai Zusé" (Priest Zusé's Macumba), inspired by the Afro-Brazilian rituals. Finally, humor ranging from fine irony to the outright joke appears as a response to the rhetorical, lofty tone of the predecessors. Bandeira and the other modernists, such as Oswald de *Andrade, delighted in the humorous stance, the joke-poem (*poema-piada*). (*See* Religion and Literature; Portuguese Language of Brazil.)

The books that followed, including *Estrela da manhã* (1936; Morning Star), *Estrela da tarde* (1963; Evening Star), and *Estrela da vida inteira* (1965; Whole Life Star), established Bandeira as one of the most important poets of the century. Although there is no dramatic change of direction from *Libertinagem* onwards, the poet continued to be open to new developments in Brazilian poetry. Thus, for instance, *Estrela da tarde* contains eight poems following the concretists dictums. (*See* Postmodernism in Poetry). As Bandeira himself pointed out (*Jornal do Brasil*. February 23, 1958), the shift, visually dramatic, does not represent a rupture with the poetry that preceded it: "I wrote a poem applying some touches of concretism to my surpassed poetic manner." His would always remain essentially a lyrical voice.

In addition to being recognized for his poetry, Bandeira is well known as a literary critic (*see* Critics and Criticism) and an anthologist with important collections of Brazilian romantic, Parnassian, and symbolist poetry. He did translations throughout his life (William Shakespeare, Stefan Zweig [*see* Foreign Writers and Brazil], Friedrich Schiller) both as a way to complement a teacher's meager salary and out of affinity with the work in question. Of his books of prose, perhaps the best known are his *Guia a Ouro Preto* (1938; Guide to Ouro Preto) and his *Itinerário de Passárgada* (1954; The Route to Pasárgada), an autobiography almost entirely devoted to his poetical development with frequent discussion of particular poems and the problems of composition. Bandeira's reputation has diminished somewhat after his death owing principally to the limited thematic range of his works. Nonetheless, post-modernist poets of the 1970s sought inspiration and orientation in his lyrics based on popular themes. (*See* Romanticism.)

BIBLIOGRAPHY: Additional selected works by Bandeira: *Lira dos cinquent'anos*, 1954; *De poetas e de poesia*, 1954; *Noções da história das literaturas* (1938; *A Brief History of Brazilian Literature*, 1958; revised 1964); *Poesia e vida de Gonçalves Dias*, 1962; *Andorinha, Andorinha*, 1966; *Poesia completa e prosa*, 1974. Translations: Bishop/Brasil; Fremantle; Hulet; *Recife: Manuel Bandeira*. Translated by Eddie Flintoff. London: Rivelin Grapheme Press, 1984; *This Earth, That Sky: Poems by Manuel Bandeira*. Translated by Candace Slater, 1988; Tolman (1978); Woodbridge. Criticism: Brower, Gary. "Graphics, Phonics, and the Concrete Universal in Manuel Bandeira's Poetry." *LBR* (May, 1966), pp. 19–32; Cândido, Gilda e Antônio. "Introdução." *Estrela da vida inteira*. Rio: José Olympio, 1966; Foster/Foster, I; Pontiero, Giovanni. "The Expression of Irony in Manuel Bandeira's *Libertinagem*." *Hispania* (December, 1965), pp. 843–849; idem. "Manuel Bandeira's European Diary: July-December, 1957." *LBR* (Winter, 1976), pp. 209–219.

RICARDO LOBO STERNBERG

BARBOSA, FATHER DOMINGOS CALDAS (1738–1800). The son of a Portuguese merchant and an African slave woman, Caldas Barbosa's father accepted him and later sent him to the Jesuit College in Rio. After a period of military service, Barbosa went to Lisbon. There he enjoyed the patronage of the brothers of the Viceroy of Brazil and gained popularity as an improvisor of poems and songs (*repentista*) sung to the accompaniment of his guitar. He subsequently took holy orders and became chaplain of the Court of Appeals.

As his fame as a *repentista* grew, he became the center of attraction at social functions and was elected the first president of the New Arcade, using the *nom de plume* Lereno. (*See* Arcadias; Portugal and Brazil: Literary Relations.)

Barbosa left formal poetry in the classical taste as well as several theatrical works. He is remembered principally for verse written in two popular Brazilian forms: sentimental songs (*modinhas*) and comic songs of Afro-Brazilian origin (*lundus*). His *Viola de Lereno* (1798; Lereno's Viola) is considered the first Brazilian verses to have an entirely local flavor, characterized by his innovative use of colloquial Brazilian Portuguese and Afro-Brazilian speech patterns and rhythms. He was probably the first to express the Afro-Brazilian folk experience and the rhythms of its music in literary form. (*See* Folklore and Literature; Music and Literature; Portuguese Language of Brazil; Theater History.)

BIBLIOGRAPHY: Additional selected works by Barbosa: *O remédio é casar*, 1793; *A vingança da cigana*, 1794. Criticism: Brookshaw; Malinoff, Jane M. ''Domingos Caldas Barbosa: Afro-Brazilian Poet at the Court of Dona Maria I.'' *From Linguistics to Literature: Romance Studies Offered to Francis M. Rogers*. Edited by Bernard H. Bichakjian. Amsterdam: John Benjamins B.S., 1981, pp. 195–203; Porter, Dorothy B. ''Padre Domingos Caldas Barbosa: Afro-Brazilian Poet.'' *Phylon*. 3d quarter (1951), pp. 264–271; Sayers.

JAMES H. KENNEDY

BARBOSA, RUI (1849–1923; BAL: 1897). After completing secondary school in Bahia, Barbosa studied law in Recife and São Paulo (1870). His law practice eventually gave way to a career in politics and international diplomacy. During the 1870s and 1880s he became increasingly involved in campaigns for educational reform, abolition of slavery, the separation of church and state, and federalism. Upon the declaration of the republic in Brazil in 1889, he was named provisional vice-president; subsequently, he held other official positions in the national and international arenas.

A founding member of the *Brazilian Academy of Letters, he was elected its president upon the death of Machado de *Assis. In his vast numbers of speeches and published articles he dealt preferentially with issues of the period such as civic responsibility and patriotism, moral education, justice, political liberalism in the British model, church-state relations, and Brazil's role vis-à-vis its South American neighbors, the United States, and Europe.

The causes he espoused and the institutions and individuals he criticized embody the wide spectrum of Brazilian life of his time. Barbosa's works are so voluminous and diverse in subject matter that he is most commonly read in anthology form by the contemporary public. His essayist style is considered a classic model, and his use of the Portuguese language is an example of impeccable purity, as in his "Oração aos moços" (1921; Speech to the Graduates). He has been lauded and criticized as both *baroque and *Parnassian, and his rhetoric has been compared to that of Father Antônio *Vieira.

BIBLIOGRAPHY: Additional selected works by Barbosa: *O Papa e o concílio*, 1877; *Queda do império*, 1889; *Cartas de Inglaterra*, 1896; *Páginas literárias*, 1918; *Cartas políticas e literárias*, 1919; *Obras completas*. 50 volumes. Rio: Casa Rui Barbosa, 1942–; *Obras selectas*. Rio: Casa Rui Barbosa, 1952. Criticism: Johnson, Phil Brian. "Up-Tight about Ruy: An Essay on Brazilian Cultural Nationalism and Mythology." *JIAS* (May, 1973), pp. 191–205; Turner, Charles W. *Rui Barbosa: Brazilian Crusader for Essential Freedoms*. New York: Abingdon-Cokesbury Press, 1946.

MARY L. DANIEL

BAROQUE. The term *baroque* refers to a subtle, complex form of rhetoric whose inspiration was the intricate style of the plastic arts during the late sixteenth century.

To an extent it was the odd result of the conflict between medieval and renaissance mentality and principally the Roman Catholic church's need for a preaching style to defend itself during the Counter-Reformation. In Portugal and in Brazil the baroque period lasted from the early seventeenth century—the publication of Bento *Teixeira *Prosopopéia* (1601; Personification)—through the mideighteenth century. Usually divided into three epochs of fifty years each, the variety of the movement is curiously reflected in historical events: the Spanish dominion over Portugal (1580–1640), followed by the gradual shift of the economic center of Brazil from the Northeast (Pernambuco, Bahia) to the center (Minas), and finally, the end of the Jesuits' domination over Luso-Brazilian cultural and educational channels.

Direct literary influences were the Spanish poets Luis de Góngora (1561–1627), Francisco de Quevedo (1580–1645), and Baltasar Gracián (1601–1658). Góngora's "cultism" was a literary language characterized by pure metaphors, plays on words, double meanings, and hyperbatons. Poetic forms associated with this movement were the acrostic, the diacrostic, the labyrinth, and so on. "Conceptism," the other leading form of baroque literature, was promoted by Quevedo and dwelled on antitheses and paradoxes, attempting subtle affirmations of contradictory or, sometimes, illogical truths.

Both of these orientations appeared in Brazilian poetry as early as the *Música do Parnaso* by Botelho de *Oliveira and, most importantly, in the poetry of Gregório de *Matos and in the prose of Father Antônio *Vieira and Matias *Aires. With the publication of Cláudio Manuel da *Costa's works in 1768, the baroque movement came to an end, and neoclassicism (*see* Arcadias) began. Notable also is the baroque achievement in music and the plastic arts, particularly the sculptors of the one-armed Aleijadinho. In spite of these formal rhetorical devices, Brazilian baroque writers did indeed reveal some nativist sentiments. (*See* Art and Literature; Music and Literature; *Ufanismo*.)

Finally, the term *baroque* is also used more generically with reference to a complex, difficult literary language; in this way it has been applied to the prose of Raul *Pompéia and Euclides da *Cunha, as well as to some more recent writers, for example, novelists João Guimarães *Rosa and Osman *Lins.

BIBLIOGRAPHY: Criticism: Coutinho/Rabassa; Morejón, Julio García. *Coordenadas do barroco*. São Paulo, 1965.

BARRETO, AFONSO HENRIQUES DE LIMA (1881–1922). Lima Barreto spent his childhood on the Ilha do Governador, an island near his native Rio, where his father worked at a mental institution. He completed his secondary education at the prestigious Colégio Pedro II and attended the Polytechnic Institute for a short period. He began to work as a journalist but principally earned his living for the greater part of his life as a civil servant in the War Ministry.

Burdened with the care of his father, who had gone insane, Barreto struggled in poverty. His nonconformance to the Brazilian racial hierarchy—in which a poor, dark-skinned mulatto ranked low—always caused him difficulties. In addition, the tedium of his civil service job combined with the mediocrity of Brazilian literary life and the lack of recognition accorded him in literary circles drove him to a bohemian life-style and the excesses of alcohol, which carried him to an early death at the age of forty-one.

Barreto was a premodernist (*see* Modernism) who wielded the banner of autonomy in language, a battle later taken up by Mário de *Andrade and Oswald de *Andrade. Thematically and stylistically, Barreto showed an originality far superior to his predecessors. He rejected *Parnassianism; indeed, his literary *review *Floreal* (1907) had objectives similar to the modernist review *Klaxon*. He had a great admiration for Monteiro *Lobato and his regionalist literature in which the men of the *sertão* were not simply picturesque but sought the truth of their significance in a language free from the "perfection of superior art." (*See* Portuguese Language of Brazil; Regionalism.)

Barreto did not like to be compared to Machado de *Assis, whom he considered stylistically overly indebted to the Portuguese tradition. Although he acknowledged Assis's merits, Barreto disliked the aridity of his soul and his lack of sympathy and of generous enthusiasms. Nor did he appreciate fiction in the style of his contemporary *Coelho Neto, whom he caricatured in *Recordações do Escrivão Isaías Caminha* (1909; Memoirs of the Clerk Isaías Caminha). (*See* Portugal and Brazil: Literary Relations.)

Barreto wanted not to create works of art but rather to document in fiction his drama as a mulatto in a society based on prejudice. Using ridicule and caricature, he hoped to point out to his society its foibles. His primary targets were the Brazilian bureaucracy, the world of journalism, Brazilian race relations, U.S. imperialism in Latin America and its oppression of blacks at home, the Brazilian republican oligarchy, São Paulo coffee policy, and so on.

Perhaps his most notable work is *Triste fim de Policarpo Quaresma* (1915; *The Patriot*, 1978), set during the early years of the Brazilian republic. This is a satirical novel that attacks republican society, agricultural policies, and the actions of the dictator Floriano Peixoto (1839–1895) during the naval rebellion of 1893. Its protagonist, Policarpo Quaresma, may be viewed as a superior being who desires only to know his country and to see its potential fulfilled or as a chauvinist whose schemes lead him to the madhouse and death. In reality, he is a kind of Don Quixote whose society does not understand him, and thus he is doomed to failure in his desires to recover a true Brazilian identity. In the end, the utopian Policarpo fails, but his dream lives on in the text that preserves it.

The role of women in Brazilian society is important in *The Patriot* and other novels. Barreto's antifeminism is a curious paradox. He was against the entrance of women into the bureaucracy and often satirized the Brazilian feminist movements as mere imitations of the British and American movements. Nonetheless, in a country where men could murder adulterous wives and be absolved by a jury, he was against uxoricide. Furthermore, in *Clara dos Anjos* (1923–1924; *Clara dos Anjos*, 1979), Barreto offered advice to Brazilian women about how to overcome society's enforced limitations and fulfill themselves, and in *The Patriot* and the satirical *Numa e a ninfa* (1915; Numa and the Nymph), women characters are markedly superior beings to their mates. (*See* Feminism and Literature.)

Vida e morte de M. J. Gonzaga de Sá (1919; *The Life and Death of M. J. Gonzaga de Sá*, 1979) is particularly striking and experimental. In the Foreword, Barreto addressed the reader directly and explained that he is the publisher of a biography of Sá written by his friend Augusto Machado. For Barreto, the classification of the work as biography was not exact if it implied a rigorous exactitude for facts and minute explanation for certain parts of the main character's life. Machado often speaks more of himself than he does of Sá, and this frequent appearance of the author disturbs Barreto. Augusto Machado is a young mulatto writer of plebeian origin. He rejects the gaudiness of the new Brazilian upper classes, who thrive on the imported intellectual and cultural legacy of Germany and Greece, and identifies himself with the grandeur of Brazil's tropical nature and its history of four centuries of slavery. The biographee, Sá, is the elderly, white scion of an old noble family, a skeptic, a privileged Voltairean whose characterization is a contrast to the venality of the republican bourgeoisie and to the dull bureaucracy at which he works. Machado and Sá are one moral and spiritual entity. They enjoy perfect communication and are equivalent to what is good in Brazilian society: artistic ability, racial tolerance, intelligence, nobility of the spirit, critical wit, self-analysis, and originality in their vision of Brazil. *The Life and Death of M. J. Gonzaga de Sá* is an innovation in Brazilian letters that captures the true image of Brazil by means of original narrative techniques in the literary context of the times. It shows a transition period between the traditional and modern eras and brilliantly and subtly delineates the origins, essences, and contradictions of the Brazilian myth of racial democracy.

Barreto wanted to write a novel about the work of blacks on a plantation along the lines of Émile Zola's *Germinal* (1885). In this work he would develop Negroidism (*negroísmo*) as a parallel to the *Indianism of *romanticism. But he delayed writing, and finally never authored what he thought would be his masterpiece. On the one hand, he feared that the work would bring him bitter trials, which he might not be able to overcome; on the other hand, he hoped that the realization of this work would bring him glory and even fame in Europe. Although he felt great love and sympathy for Brazil's blacks, he was aware that they did not understand his artistic identity or aspirations. Ultimately, Barreto was an artist, and his raised black consciousness was simply a part of this artistic identity.

BIBLIOGRAPHY: Additional selected works by Barreto: *Histórias e sonhos*, 1920; *Bagatelas*, 1923; *Coisas do reino de Jambon*, 1953. Criticism: Brookshaw; Herron, Robert. "*Isaías Caminha* as a Psychological Novel." *LBR* (December, 1971), pp. 26–38; Kinnear, J. C. "The 'Sad End' of Lima Barreto's Policarpo Quaresma." *BHS* (January, 1974), pp. 60–75; *Lima Barreto: Bibliography and Translations*. Edited by Maria Luísa Nunes. Boston: G. K. Hall, 1979; Nunes, Maria Luísa. "Lima Barreto's Theory of Literature." In *From Linguistics to Literature: Romance Studies Offered to Francis M. Rogers*. Amsterdam: Benjamins, 1981, pp. 223–234; Oakley, R. J. "*Triste Fim de Policarpo Quaresma* and 'The New California.'" *MLR* (October, 1983), pp. 838–849; Teixeira, Vera Regina. "Lima Barreto: Dead or Alive?" *WLT* (Winter, 1979), pp. 36–40.

MARIA LUÍSA NUNES

BARROSO, MARIA ALICE (b. 1926). All of Barroso's works are set in her native state and city of Rio. She has created, like Faulkner, whose influence on her style is noticeable, her own small town—Parada de Deus—which serves as a backdrop for the three-novel cycle that bears its name.

In terms of plot, theme, or structure, her novels reveal a distinguishable progression. *Os posseiros* (1955; The Squatters) deals with the lopsided system of land distribution, which perpetuates the farm laborers' plight in rural Brazil. It is classic socialist realism whose *engagé* approach, like that of the *social novelists of the 1930s, sacrifices character development for a sociopolitical message.

Three novels published in the 1960s might be considered a trilogy owing to their similar thematic and artistic preoccupations. In *História de um casamento* (1960; Story of a Marriage) content is subordinated to form. The conventional narrator-storyteller disappears, substituted instead by rotating viewpoints whose three narrator-characters are bound to and by an enigmatic catalyst, simply called M. A. *Um simples afeto recíproco* (1962; A Simple Mutual Affection) reinforces the psychological bent in the tender story of friendship between two people or poles at odds with conventional mores, told by multiple narrators in the "new novel" style. (*See* Feminism and Literature.)

Um nome para matar (1967; A Name to Murder), considered the author's best novel to date, traces the intertwined history of Parada de Deus and its decadent founding family, similar to Érico *Veríssimo's cycle, "Time and the Wind." *Quem matou Pacífico* (1969; Who Killed Pacifico) continued the violent story but with an almost picaresque flair, and *O globo da morte* (1981; The Globe of Death) envelops the cycle in a kind of circus motif.

BIBLIOGRAPHY: Additional selected works by Barroso: *Um dia vamos rir disso tudo*, 1976. Criticism: Boring, Phyllis Zatlin. "Maria Alice Barroso: A Study in Point of View." *LBR* (Summer 1977), pp. 30–39; Patai; Silverman, Malcolm. "Stylistic Evolution of Maria Alice Barroso's Works." *Hispania* (September, 1977), pp. 478–485.

MALCOLM SILVERMAN

BELL, LINDOLF (b. 1938). Bell, from southern Santa Catarina State, studied dramatic arts in São Paulo. This theatrical training emerged in his "Poetic Catechism," a program of literary activism initiated in 1964 and designed to take performance-poetry to the people in the streets, stadiums, schools, and other public places.

In 1969 he participated in the International Writing Program at the University of Iowa. Since then he has been involved in diverse projects, devising "object poems" for a São Paulo festival (1970), creating body poems (*corpoemas*), that is, poems printed on T-shirts; printing poster poems; and dedicating the Plaza of Poetry in Santa Catarina with texts engraved in stone (1981). After the impact of visually oriented concrete poetry (*see* Postmodernism in Poetry), Bell aimed at sharing the poetic experience with an aurally oriented audience. The catechetical in Bell's poetic project refers to its didactic and aural designs, not necessarily to any association with Catholic teaching, as is evident in his *Antologia da catequese poética* (1968; Anthology of Poetical Catechism). Still, Christian values such as hope, charity, and humility inform much of Bell's lyric poetry.

Longing for liberty, social justice, authenticity, and self-discovery is often present in Bell's poems. These attitudes are consistent with the *engagé* concerns of much of Brazilian art to counter elitism during the sociopolitical mobilizations of the early 1960s and the period of resistance following the military coup of 1964. (*See:* Dictatorship and Literature.)

BIBLIOGRAPHY: Additional selected works by Bell: *Os póstumos e as profécias*, 1962; *Curta primavera: narrativa lírica*, 1967; *Incorporação: doze anos de poesia, 1962–1973*, 1974; *O código das águas*, 1984. Translations: Brasil/Smith; Woodbridge. Criticism: Tomczak, Maria Joana. *Lindolf Bell e a catequese poética*. Florianópolis: ESC, 1978.

CHARLES A. PERRONE

BETHENCOURT, JOÃO (b. 1924). An agronomist by profession, Bethencourt studied theater in Rio and at Yale. He has distinguished himself as a professor at the National Conservatory of Theatre in Rio; as the director of several dramatic productions in Rio, London, and Lisbon; as a writer of plays, fiction, essays, and film scripts; and as a translator.

Although he is the author of a book of humorous essays (*A mãe que entrou em órbita* (1964; The Mother Who Went into Orbit) and a satiric novel, Bethencourt's first play, *As provas de amor* (1957; Tests of Love), verged on pure *surrealism. He is now known primarily as a writer of comedies. Often set in contemporary Rio, his plays satirize the moral inconsistencies of several character types of *carioca* society: doormen, politicians, military men, playboys, fortune seekers, and so on. In *Como matar um playboy* (1969; How to Kill a Playboy), for example, the "happy ending," so typical of his comedies, is tempered by a note of pessimism, perhaps related to his depiction of so many characters as opportunists. *O dia em que sequestraram o Papa* (1972; The Day They Kidnapped the Pope) has been a widely presented drama with a serious message: a plea for international peace.

BIBLIOGRAPHY: Additional selected works by Bethencourt: *As vidas de El Justicero, o cafajeste sem medo e sem mácula*, 1965; *A ilha de Circe (Mister Sexo)*, 1966; *Frank Sinatra 4815*, 1969; *Crime roubado*, 1974. Criticism: Cacciaglia, Mario. *Quattro secoli di teatro in Brasile*. Roma: Bulzoni, 1980, pp. 147–149.

PAUL DIXON

BILAC, OLAVO (1865–1918; BAL: 1897). Bilac had illustrious careers in government and literature. Among his notable activities was his support for obligatory military service as a means of decreasing the nation's high illiteracy rate. Although he was also an important orator and an author of patriotic *children's literature and *crônicas*, his poetry is considered the most representative— and most critics state that it is the finest—of Brazilian *Parnassianism. (*See* Critics and Criticism.)

Immediately upon the first publication of his *Poesias* (1888; Poems), Bilac was lauded by Raimundo *Correia and Alberto de Oliveira (*see* Parnassianism) as their equal in the pantheon of Parnassian poets. In his first poem of the collection, "Profissão de fé" (Profession of Faith), Bilac viewed his poetic task as similar to that of a goldsmith working with precious, delicate jewelry. He insisted upon the need for perfection in language and form to achieve simplicity of expression. "Via láctea" (Milky Way), a section of the 1888 collection, is generally considered the epitome of his lyrical production because it reveals the variety of his styles—from the exacerbated sentimentalism inherited from *romanticism to the sensualism characteristic of some of the symbolist poets. (*See* Symbolism.)

In his cult of art for art's sake, Bilac's thematics avoided daily reality, although he had been an ardent abolitionist. Instead, he subjectively cultivated philosophical and personal themes—which became more frequent in his later years— and historical themes, be they about the classical world of Rome or episodes or figures of Brazilian history. A prime example of this preoccupation with theme and form is his epic poem *O caçador de esmeraldas* (1902: The Emerald Hunter), which narrates the adventures of the *bandeirante*, an eighteenth-century Brazilian pioneer, Fernão Dias Pais Leme, in his search for emeralds and silver in the interior of Brazil. The epic consists of forty-six sextains with a strict AABCCB rhyme throughout. Critics have often commented on the lack of objectivity and epic passion in these verses, both of which were substituted with a general tone of coldness and impassivity. (*See* Slavery and Literature.)

Declared "the prince of Brazilian poets" in 1907, Bilac's star has dimmed somewhat since the advent of *modernism.

BIBLIOGRAPHY: Additional selected works by Bilac: *Poesias*, 2d ed., 1902; *Conferências literárias*, 1906; *Ironia e piedade*, 1916. Translations: Hulet; Woodbridge. Criticism: Driver; Foster/Foster, II; Gentil, Georges Le. "L'Influence Parnassienne au Brésil." *RLC* XI(1931), pp. 23–43.

BIOGRAPHY AND BIOGRAPHERS. Various biographies have been written about almost every major writer and many secondary figures of Brazilian literature from the colonial days to the present. Biography has played an essential role in literary criticism (*see* Critics and Criticism), not only helping critics to explain the background to an author's works but also, in the best cases, to clarify literary attitudes and themes as resulting from personal or contemporary national events. In some cases, "novelized biographies" or "psychobiographies" have appeared in which the author's or his major characters' thoughts, deeds, and "actual" words are melded by the biographer into the narration of his subject's life.

Although new biographical information appears continually as a result of research in personal or general libraries or archives, some full-fledged biographies are now considered classics. Included among them are Lúcia Miguel-Pereira's (*see* Critics and Criticism) life of Gonçalves *Dias; Jean-Michel Massa's biography of Machado de *Assis's youth; Josué *Montello's study of Assis's role in the founding and early years of the *Brazilian Academy of Letters; Joaquim *Nabuco's biography of his father and his daughter's, Carolina's, biography of him; and Marques *Rebelo's study of the life and works of Manuel Antônio de *Almeida. Raimundo de Magalhães, Jr. (*see* Criticism and Critics) specialized in biographies of important nineteenth-century writers, including Machado de Assis, Artur *Azevedo, João do *Rio, and Augusto dos *Anjos.

Standard biographies of early twentieth-century writers include Edgard Cavalheiro's two-volume biography of Monteiro *Lobato and Cassiano Nunes's shorter studies of Lobato and Francisco de Assis Barbosa's (BAL: 1970) biography of Lima *Barreto. Biographies of the leaders of *modernism have been infrequent. Augusto de Campos, however, recently published a biography of modernism's Patrícia *Galvão (Pagu). (*See* Autobiography; Memoirs.)

BIBLIOGRAPHY: Criticism: Vieira, Nelson H. "A Brazilian Biographical Bibliography." *Biography* (Fall, 1982), pp. 357–364.

BLACK LITERATURE. *See* Contemporary Black Literature.

BLOCH, PEDRO (b. 1914). Bloch arrived in Brazil from the Ukraine when he was three years old. Now a surgeon, he also has had a very active, but somewhat controversial, career as a dramatist. His initial plays were written for radio theater, for example, *Marilena versus Destino* (1940; Marilena versus Destino). Some twenty-five plays followed: light-hearted drawing-room comedies; superficial family psychological dramas, for example, *Roleta paulista* (1966; São Paulo Roulette) and *Dona Xepa* (1973; Madame Leftovers); and, most recently, generational conflicts, set principally in middle-class contemporary Rio, for example, *Bi, o sorriso perdido* (1986; Bi, the Lost Smile). (*See* Theater History.)

Bloch remains primarily known for *As mãos de Eurídice* (1951; *The Hands of Euridice*, 1957), which has been produced worldwide thousands of times. In a *tour de force* monologue on man's desperation in the modern world, the protagonist Gumersindo has been portrayed by leading actors. Bloch's goal is to unite actor and audience as participants in a drama that borders on the absurd fringes of reality.

Bloch has received several literary *prizes, including the *Brazilian Academy of Letters Artur *Azevedo Prize.

BIBLIOGRAPHY: Additional selected works by Bloch: *Morre um gato na China*, 1952; *Os enemigos não mandam flores* (1957; *Enemies Don't Send Flowers*, 1957); *O Problema*, 1961; *O menino falou e disse*, 1973; *Família em preto e branco*, 1985.

BOAL, AUGUSTO (b. 1931). Educated at Columbia University, Boal joined the Arena Theater of São Paulo in 1956 and began to work with Oduvaldo *Viana Filho, and Gianfrancesco *Guarnieri. An actor and dramatist, Boal, in addition, has been a dedicated "revolutionary theorist" of drama, whose influence has spread throughout Latin America and Europe. (*See* Theater History.)

While a member of Arena, he helped to develop the joker (*coringa*) system, used as a political consciousness-raising method of educating the oppressed masses. *A revolução na América Latina* (1960; Revolution in Latin America) is a satire on the plight of the poor, as well as a call to arms. *Arena conta Zumbi* (Arena Theater Tells about Zumbi) and *Arena conta Tiradentes* (Arena Theater Tells about Tiradentes), written with Guarnieri, were among his most successful collaborations. His *Arena conta Bahia* (Arena Theater Tells about Bahia) assumes a similar form and aim. All are based on a new look at Brazilian history, traditions, and legends. Zumbi had an immensely popular tour in the United States, Argentina, Mexico, and Peru.

In 1970 Boal began his newspaper theater (*teatro jornal*), in which he aimed "to show that any person even if he is not an artist, can make the theater a means of communication." (In *Categorias do teatro político.* [Rio: 1972], p. 12). The *teatro jornal* was the initial step in the development of his Theater of the Oppressed (*teatro do oprimido*). This theater owes a debt to the theories of

Paulo Freire. (*See* Philosophy of National Identity.) Boal's politically committed theatrical activities led him to a confrontation with the military dictatorship. Imprisoned in 1971, he was tortured and then released. He went into exile in Argentina and then Chile and Portugal and finally France, where he carried on his theatrical activities. There he experimented with forms of psychodrama—"invisible theater" and "theater forum"—with distinct political themes. The techniques of all these theatrical projects were described in his *Stop, c'est magique!* (1980; Stop, It's Magic). (*See* Dictatorship and Literature.)

During his years of exile, Boal's name was taboo in Brazil. With the political liberalization of the late 1970s and the easing of censorship, his play *Murro em ponto de faca* (1978; Hitting Your Head against a Brick Wall) was presented in São Paulo. In it he dramatized an autobiographical situation: the problems faced by Brazilian exiles from the military regime. Boal finally returned to Brazil in 1986, where he has been directing plays and organizing theater workshops. His recent play *O corsário do rei* (1985; The King's Pirate), with music by Edu Lobo and lyrics by Chico *Buarque, returned to his 1960s style of political theater, for which there is apparently no public in Brazil today. (*See* Autobiography; Music and Literature.)

Although critics may carp about Boal's theater, he is without doubt accepted as Latin America's leading theorist of political drama. His *Teatro do oprimido* (1974; Theater of the Oppressed, 1983), essays written between 1962 and 1973, and *200 exercícios e jogos para o ator e não ator com vontade de dizer algo através do teatro* (1980; 200 Exercises and Games for Actors and Nonactors Who Wish to Say Something Through the Theater) are now classic collections on the techniques and aims of political theater.

BIBLIOGRAPHY: Additional selected works by Boal: *Tio Patinhas*, 1968; "O que pensa você da arte da esquerda?" *LATR* (Spring, 1970), pp. 45–53; *Torquemada*, 1971. Criticism: Butler, Ross E. "Social Themes in Selected Contemporary Brazilian Dramas." *RomN* (Autumn, 1973), pp. 52–60; Driskell, Charles. "An Interview with Augusto Boal." LATR (Fall, 1975), pp. 71–78.

BOPP, RAUL (1898–1984). Bopp, from Rio Grande do Sul, studied law in Recife, Belém do Pará, and Rio, where he discovered the "real" Brazil; he was particularly impressed with the Amazon.

With Oswald de *Andrade in São Paulo, Bopp named Tarsila do Amaral's (*see* Art and Literature) painting of a primitivist savage the *Abaporu* (from the Tupi *Indian language meaning "man who eats"), thereby consolidating the cannibalist movement to which Bopp contributed his major work, the poem *Cobra Norato* (written in 1928; published in 1931; The Snake Norato).

As a modernist "cannibal" of the literary *review *Revista de Antropofagia* (Anthropophagical Review), Bopp turned his eyes toward the primitivist and mythical sphere of Brazil's interior, inspired by his own visit to Manaus. He, like Mário de *Andrade in his novel-rhapsody *Macunaíma*, selected a folk myth of the Amazon to lend linguistic and thematic dimensions to a poem that would evoke and define a mysterious, telluric Brazil. His rhythmic, Amazonian cobra revives the melodious vocabulary and folk verse of Brazil's vast interior, in which the modernists sought a diagnosis and therapeutic for urban, colonial culture. (*See* Folklore and Literature.)

The folk stories of "The Snake Norato" and "The Daughter of Queen Luzia" form the basis for the "poem-novel." His montage of Amazonian sounds and images is conveyed with vanguardist metaphor and concision, a stylistic trait common to the early modernist poetic spirit: "Here the school of trees / Is studying geometry" or "Toads with sore throats study aloud." (*Cobra Norato*, passim)

Bopp's interest in Brazilian folk culture and legend extends to his *Urucungo* (1932; Black Poems) and other poetry based on folklore (e.g., *Putirum* [1969; Putirum]. He is also the author of several books of *memoirs and criticism of the modernist movement, most notably *Vida e morte da antropofagia* (1977; Life and Death of Anthropophagy), a history of the "cannibal" school he helped found.

BIBLIOGRAPHY: Additional selected works by Bopp: *América*, 1942; *Poesias*, 1947; *Movimentos modernistas no Brasil*, 1966; *Coisas do Oriente*, 1971. Translations: Hulet. Criticism: Crespo, Ángel. "Raúl Bopp/*Cobra Norato*." *RCB* (March, 1966), pp. 5–53; Martins.

K. DAVID JACKSON

BORBA FILHO, HERMILO (b. 1917). Brought up in a traditional Pernambucan family, Borba Filho has been active in all literary areas, from popular poetry to theater to folklore. He has prepared many valuable, often scholarly, studies with music and photographic documentation of the popular theatrical traditions of northeastern Brazil. Most notable are his *Espetáculos populares do nordeste* (1966; Popular Shows of the Northeast) and *Apresentação do bumba-meu-boi* (1966; Presentation of Bumba-Meu-Boi (a traditional northeastern rural Christmastime pageant). (*See* Folklore and Literature; Regionalism; Theater History.)

Borba Filho's original plays and his fiction are also set in the northeast, whose character types, language, and humor are thoroughly representative. Additionally, he has published art criticism, including the English-language *Brazil through Its Art*. (*See* Art and Literature.)

BIBLIOGRAPHY: Additional selected works by Borba Filho: *João sem terra*, 1952; *O general está pintando*, 1973; *As meninas do sobrado*, 1976. Criticism: Mazarra, Richard A. "Hermilo Borba Filho's *A donzela Joana* and the Brazilianization of Joan of Arc" *BSUF* (Autumn, 1970), pp. 23–26.

BRAGA, RUBEM (b. 1913). Braga finished law school in Belo Horizonte in 1932. He has been a journalist since 1929 and reported on the São Paulo Revolution of 1932, as well as on the Brazilian expeditionary force in Italy during World War II. Active in politics, he suffered imprisonment but achieved appointments as ambassador to Morocco and chief of the Brazilian Trade Bureau in Chile.

Braga adapted his literary talents to the *crônica*. He has published many collections since the 1940s. The site is almost always his adopted city of Rio. Through a combination of irony and lyricism, he finds significance in the superficial. For example, in "Aula de inglês" (English Lesson), from the collection *Um pé de milho* (1948; A Corn Tree), the character, a Brazilian—perhaps the author himself—tries to learn English through linking sounds with images and popular psychology. In "Lembranças do braço direito" ("Recollections of a Right Arm," in *Atlantic Monthly* (February, 1956), pp. 140–141), he tells of a plane ride from Rio to São Paulo. When fog prevents the landing for some time, he narrates his emotions and those of fellow travelers.

BIBLIOGRAPHY: Additional selected works by Braga: *O conde e o passarinho*, 1936; *O homem rouco*, 1949; *Ai de Ti, Copacabana*, 1960; *Livro de versos*, 1980; *Crônicas de Espírito Santo*, 1984. Translations: *Mele: International Poetry Letter* (University of Hawaii). Edited by Stefan Baciu (August, 1983); Tolman (1978). Criticism: Bandeira, Manuel. "The Sardonic Brazilians." *Américas* (September, 1964).

EDGAR C. KNOWLTON, JR.

BRANDÃO, IGNÁCIO DE LOYOLA (b. 1936). Brandão was born in Araraquara, São Paulo. His career as a movie critic began at sixteen in his hometown. Four years later he moved to the state capital, where his first job was at the now-extinct *Última Hora*, a Center-Left newspaper that played a critical role in covering the sociopolitical events of the early 1960s, such as the students' and workers' movements, as well as living conditions in São Paulo's poorer suburbs. (*See* Film and Literature.)

Brandão, like many other contemporary Brazilian writers, has written most of his work under the authoritarian government; in fact, he declared himself to be a "child of dictatorship." His novels and stories read like *Bildungsroman*, that is, the story of a provincial young man who grows to discover the big city, the metropolis, its seedy night life, its misery, its despair and hope, for example, the collection of short stories *Depois do sol* (1965; After the Sun). (*See* Dictatorship and Literature.)

Zero (1975; *Zero*, 1984), his best-known work, was first published in Italy; after great success, it was published in Brazil but was subsequently censored. This book is a portrait of the "metropolis"—with echoes of Fritz Lang's movie of that title—a chaotic city supposedly a microcosm of Brazil, or what is called the fictitious region of América Latíndia. *Zero* is a powerful, overwhelming description of how the government and its repressive apparatus collaborate to torture and kill its detractors. While the masses live in squalor and suffer endemic hunger, the wealthy class frolics at bucolic country spas. The protagonist's name is José Gonçalves—the common John Smith—the anonymous individual who represents the oppressed collective and becomes a revolutionary searching for freedom. The narrative form shows Brandão's experience as a movie critic and journalist. Both media have provided the rhythms and visual effects for the novel: parallel columns, collage of newspaper clippings, drawings, comics' balloons, commercial jingles, all of which result in a fragmented, chaotic reading. (*See* City and Literature.)

Brandão's other popular novel, *Não verás país nenhum* (1981; *And Still the Earth*, 1985), has a title that is a pun on a famous verse of the nineteenth-century poet Olavo *Bilac. In the poem, the poet sings of the splendor of Brazilian natural riches to the future generations, while Brandão offers a darker view of a country "that they will not inherit." This novel is a prophetic vision of Brazil after it has devastated its natural environment. The story is set again in the big city now suffering shortages of its most basic needs—water and food—and is controlled by a brutal Orwellian Big Brother. (*See Ufanismo.*)

Throughout his career, Brandão's style and major concerns have aimed to portray the lives of people not only in Brazil but also in underdeveloped nations in general. He has written about their struggle to survive and to keep their dignity as human beings.

BIBLIOGRAPHY: Additional selected works by Brandão: *Bebel que a cidade comeu*, 1968; *Cadeiras proibidas*, 1969; *E o verde arrenbentou o muro*, 1984; *O beijo não vem na boca*, 1985; *O ganhador*, 1987. Criticism: Monegal, Emir Rodríguez. "Fiction under the Censor's Eye." *WLT* (Winter, 1979), pp. 19–22; Rohter, Larry. "Life under the Mili-Techs" (Review of *And Still the Earth*). *NYTBR* (September 29, 1985), p. 38; Silverman, Malcolm. "A ficção de Ignácio de Loyola Brandão." *Moderna ficção brasileira*. Rio: Civilização Brasileira, 1978, pp. 209–226.

NAOMI HOKI MONIZ

BRASIL, ASSIS [FRANCISCO DE ASSIS ALMEIDA BRASIL] (b. 1932). From Piauí State, Brasil is a journalist, novelist, and literary critic. (*See* Critics and Criticism.)

Brasil's most successful work of fiction has been *Beira rio, beira vida* (1965; Rivershore, Lifeshore), the first volume of his "Tetralogy of Piauí." In it the river folk attain a symbolic quality, as he denounces the general misery and suffering of the nation's poor through an effective use of language and imagery. *Os que bebem como os cães* (1975; Those Who Drink Like Dogs) began his "Terror Cycle." Set in a jail cell, the novel describes the character's gradual dehumanization. The novel clearly reflects conditions of Brazilian life during the military dictatorship. *Sodoma está velha* (1985; Sodom Is Old) is the second novel of his "Copacabana Quartet." Set in a rough shantytown (*favela*), the protagonist's life story is shockingly absorbing. (*See* Dictatorship and Literature.)

As a critic (*see* Critics and Criticism), Brasil has analyzed major Brazilian and foreign writers, from Clarice *Lispector and Carlos Drummond de *Andrade to James Joyce and William Faulkner, and he has published a critical history of recent Brazilian literature: *A nova literatura* (4 vols.; 1973–1975; The New Literature).

BIBLIOGRAPHY: Additional selected works by Brasil: *Verdes mares brancos*, 1953; *O salto do cavalo cobridor*, 1968; *O livro de Judas*, 1970; *A rebelião dos mortos*, 1975.

BRAZILIAN ACADEMY OF LETTERS. A modern outgrowth of *acade-mies of the *baroque era, the Brazilian Academy of Letters was established in Rio in 1896 in the offices of José *Veríssimo's *Revista Brasileira*. Dedicated to the "cultivation of the national language and literature," its motto is "Ad immortalitatem."

Modeled on the Académie Française, forty members are selected from among all professions—from politics through medicine—with the requirement that they must have published a literary work of merit. Furthermore, twenty-five must be from the city of Rio, and twenty corresponding members are also allowed. Each chair is named for its "patron," an important figure of early Brazilian culture, for example, Alvares de *Azevedo, Bernardo *Guimarães, Cláudio Manuel da *Costa, and Gregório de *Matos. The first officers included president: Machado de *Assis; general secretary: Joaquim *Nabuco; and treasurer: Inglês de *Sousa. The first female member, Rachel de *Queiroz, was admitted in 1977.

The academy holds regular meetings, issues a bulletin, awards literary *prizes, and offers opinions on aspects of language and culture. The current president is Austregésilo de Athayde (b. 1898); among its current members are the present president of Brazil and poet and prose writer José Sarney. (*See* Regionalism.)

Writers included in this dictionary who have been or are members of the academy are so indicated after their birth and death dates with the indication *(BAL: date of initiation if known)*.

BIBLIOGRAPHY: Criticism: Brookshaw; Montello, Josué. *O presidente Machado de Assis*. 2nd edition. São Paulo: Livraria Martins, 1985; Simons, Marlise. "Gossip with Icing: At Tea with Brazil's Literati." *NYT* (October 3, 1986), p. A2.

BUARQUE, CHICO [FRANCISCO BUARQUE DE HOLLANDA] (b. 1944). Chico is the son of the distinguished historian Sérgio Buarque de Hollanda. (*See* Historiography.) Since the mid–1960s he has been Brazil's leading poet-song-writer, recording artist, and an important writer of prose fiction and drama. His first theatrical project was the musical setting for *Morte e vida Severina* by João Cabral de *Melo Neto. In 1969 Buarque went into voluntary exile in Italy as a protest against the military regime. (*See* Dictatorship and Literature; Music and Literature; *Tropicalismo*.)

In the 1970s most of Buarque's songs were written for films (e.g., "O que será," "Bye-Bye Brasil") or for dramas he authored or coauthored, for example, *Gota d'agua* (1975; Drop of Water) with Paulo Pontes. Given the overriding sociopolitical concerns of these dramas and of many of his prominent songs, the author encountered problems with military censors. His 1974 novel *Fazendo modelo: novela pecuária* (Modelmaking: A Pecuary Novel), an allegorical vision of a dictatorial society akin to Orwell's *Animal Farm* (1945), was a best-seller. Buarque has also penned popular works of *children's literature. (*See* Film and Literature; Theater History.)

Buarque is primarily known as a composer and poet of song. Although he has never published a book of poetry, many consider him to be the best poet of

68

his generation. Buarque manipulates rhyme, rhythm, and sound effects master-fully. His sonorous song texts are also marked by structural ingenuity, irony, and ambiguity. The most prominent thematic concern is contemporary social reality, as in "Pedro Pedreiro" (1965; Peter the Stonemason), "Construção" (1970; ["Construction"] in *Tongues of Fallen Angels*. New York: New Directions, 1974), and "Vai passar" (1984; It Will Pass).

Depth of insight into feminine psychology is also notable in his lyrical repertory. Noting the broadly based respect that Buarque commands, Millor *Fernandes has called him "the only unanimous choice of the nation." (*See* Feminism and Literature.)

BIBLIOGRAPHY: Additional selected work by Buarque: *A banda: manuscritos*, 1966; *Roda viva*, 1967; *Ópera do malandro*, 1978; *A bordo do Rui Barbosa*, 1981. Criticism: Meneses, Adélia Bezerra de. *Desenho mágico: poesia e política em Chico Buarque*. São Paulo: HUCITEC, 1982; Patai, Daphne. "Race and Politics in Two Brazilian Utopias." *LBR* (Spring, 1982), pp. 66–81; Perrone, Charles A. "Lyric and Lyrics: The Poetry of Song in Brazil." Dissertation, University of Texas, 1985, pp. 77–118, 160–200; Woodyard, George. "The Dynamics of Tragedy in *Gota d'água*." *LBR*. Supplementary Issue (1978), pp. 151–160.

CHARLES A. PERRONE

BULHÕES, ANTÔNIO (b. 1925). Bulhões is a lawyer, translator, and screenwriter in Rio, which is the site of many of his works. His short fiction is notable for its fusion of psychology and philosophy in an erudite manner reminiscent of Machado de *Assis.

The stories in the collection *Outubro 65* (1966; October 65) delve into the complex relationships between husbands and wives. Bulhões footnoted the text and dialogues with commentaries, suggestions, and explanations of the events in a subtle attempt to influence the reader's perception. Another style is revealed in "Valsa" (Waltz) from his collection *Estudos para a mão direita* (1971; Etudes for the Right Hand). In it he eloquently evoked a nostalgia for the small-town life of preindustrial Rio of the 1940s. (*See* City and Literature.)

Bulhões's latest novel, *As quatro estações* (1986; The Four Seasons) is an emotional tale of psychological attitudes, dependencies, and relationships that develop in a tuberculosis clinic.

BIBLIOGRAPHY: Additional selected works by Bulhões: *Outra terra, outro mar*, 1968.

C

CABRAL DE MELO NETO, JOÃO. *See* Melo Neto, João Cabral de.

CALADO, FRIAR MANUEL (1584–1654). A Paulist brother who spent almost thirty years in Brazil, Calado wrote an epic poem, *O valeroso Lucideno e triunfo da liberadade* (1648; Brave Lucideno and Triumph of Liberty), which narrates João Fernandes Vieira's defense of the Brazilian territory of Pernambuco against Dutch invaders (1635–1646).

Calado was a witness to the events described; thus the poem has some historical value, regrettably diminished by the author's evidently subjective interpretations of them. Furthermore, Calado's narration reveals knowledge of Portuguese medieval chronicles and epics of the explorations, which are adapted to fit the *baroque style characteristic of his epoch. His inclusion of a Brazilian Indian character, Felipe Camarão, fighting alongside the Portuguese, and his use of colloquial Brazilian speech appear to be unconscious contributions to a nascent Brazilian self-identity. (*See*: Historiography; Indianism; Portugal and Brazil: Literary Relations; *Ufanismo.*)

BIBLIOGRAPHY: Criticism: Melo, José Antônio Gonsalves de. *Frei Manuel Calado do Salvador.* Recife, 1954.

CALLADO, ANTÔNIO (b. 1917). During World War II, Callado, from Niterói, Rio de Janeiro, worked in London as a journalist for the BBC. Upon returning to Brazil, he became one of the nation's leading and most respected journalists. Callado reported on the plight of Brazil's Indians and the northeastern peasants; he traveled to Cuba and to North Vietnam. He protested against the repression of the military regime and was jailed with other intellectuals such as Ferreira *Gullar. Callado also has been a distinguished visiting professor of Brazilian literature at Cambridge and Columbia universities. (*See* Dictatorship and Literature.)

All of Callado's works—both fiction and drama—are marked by a religiosity characteristic of a society permeated by Catholicism. This is most obvious in his first two novels in which there is concern about man's search for spirituality and grace, somewhat similar to Graham Greene's fiction, for example, *Assunção de Salviano* (1954; The Assumption of Salviano) and *Madona de cedro* (1957; Cedar Madonna). (*See* Religion and Literature; Theater History.)

Quarup (1967; *Quarup*, 1970), one of his most important novels, has had an enormous impact on Brazil's search for a populist and nationalistic expression of an authentic Brazilian identity. An allegory of Brazil and its people and institutions, *Quarup*'s title is taken from an Indian ritual of death and resurrection. Callado tries to encompass the diversity and complexities of problems that over-whelm the nation, while simultaneously seeking new paths to liberate its people. The novel presents a mosaic of diverse ideologies—from the past and the present—through its characters. Some view Brazil as a nation identified with Western Christian values; others see it as the land of the Indians, the poor peasants of the Northeast, or the modern developing country of the future; still others consider Brazil to be dominated and colonized by the interests of international economic groups. Nando, the protagonist, is a priest who wants to civilize and Christianize the Indians. The process of apprenticeship is long and arduous and takes him away from his dream of a mythical Paradise. As he discovers the reality of Brazil, Nando slowly starts to discover himself, his own sexuality. His metamorphosis from a priest to a man with a political mission to a revolutionary hero is complete. (*See* Indianism; Philosophy of National Identity.)

With *Quarup*, Callado brought a new perspective into Brazilian literature. Although many Brazilian authors have frequently presented characters in search of knowledge moving usually from the interior to the city, in *Quarup* Callado called for a move from the city to the heart of the country, a mythical center where the true identity of Brazil can be found.

Bar Don Juan (1971; *Bar Don Juan*, 1972) and *Reflexos do baile* (1978; Reflections on the Dance) are political novels attempting to make sense of contemporary Brazilian history and the chaos and frustration of intellectuals whose dream of a true social revolution has evaporated. *Sempreviva* (1981; *Sempreviva*, 1988), awarded the Goethe Institute Prize for Fiction in 1982 (*see* Prizes), is an outstanding portrait of Brazil as it attempts to regain direction after the immoralities of the military repression and torture.

Callado once declared that some of the most influential books in Brazilian literature were José de *Alencar's *Iracema*, Euclides da *Cunha's *Os sertões* (both written in the nineteenth century), and Mário de *Andrade's *Macunaíma*. These novels deal with precisely the issues that have been his prime concern and are at the heart of Brazil's search for an identity: the role of the Indian vis-à-vis its origins and future, the marginalized masses in the backlands, and the man of the New World and his attachment to European values. These issues reappear in Callado's most recent novels, but there is now a self-mocking darker and ironic view of the once held Utopia: *Expedição Montaigne* (1982; The Montaigne Expedition) and *Concerto carioca* (1985; Carioca Concert).

Callado's works, especially since *Quarup*, are the most comprehensive modern reflections on Brazil. He questions the ideologies that sustain the nation's political and economic institutions. His work is one of the most concertedly artistic productions of modern Brazilian literature. It also has inspired many other intellectuals, such as the film director Gláuber Rocha and his fellow novelist Darcy *Ribeiro.

BIBLIOGRAPHY: Additional selected works by Callado: *Pedro Mico*, 1957; *Uma rede para Iemanjá*, 1961; *Tempo de Arraes*, 1964; *Vietnã do Norte*, 1977; *A revolta da cachaça*, 1983. Criticism: Aiex, Nola Kortner. "From Rhetoric to Revolution: Antônio Callado's *Bar Don Juan.*" *Selecta* (1980), pp. 60–62; idem. "The Reality of a Myth: Antônio Callado's *Assunção de Salviano.*" *Perspectives on Contemporary Literature* (1979), pp. 131–137; Gallagher, David. "*Quarup.*" *NYTBR* (June 14, 1970), p. 4; Leite, Lígia Chiappini Moraes. "Quando a pátria viaja: uma leitura dos romances de Antônio Callado." *O nacional e o popular: literatura.* Edited by João Luiz Lafetá. São Paulo: Brasiliense, 1982, pp. 120–234.

NAOMI HOKI MONIZ

CAMARGO, JORACY (1898–1973; BAL: 1967). Camargo began acting when he was fourteen years old. After law school in his native Rio, he had a variety of official and other jobs, including the directorship of several of Rio's best theaters. (*See* Theater History.)

Camargo's career as an extremely prolific dramatist dates from the early 1930s. During the early decades of the century, Brazilian theater was dominated by vaudeville, musical reviews, and light comedies in praise of bourgeois values. Thus his allegorical drama *Deus lhe pague* (1932; May God Repay You) was an immediate success owing to its criticism of important social questions of the moment: urban poverty and capitalism. It aroused the censor's eye because of its attack on the status quo. Many of Camargo's following dramas would return to these social themes, for example, *O bobo do rei* (1930; The King's Jester); *O juízo final* (The Final Judgment); *Sindicato dos mendigos* (1939; Beggars' Union).

Camargo also penned less successful historical dramas related to the empire and the period of the Paraguayan War, for example, *A retirada da Laguna* (The Retreat from Laguna) and *Tamandaré* (Tamandaré), a biographical drama about an important admiral of the war. He also wrote family dramas such as *A pupila dos meus olhos* (The Apple of My Eye) and, *Figueira de inferno* (1954; Hell's Fig Tree), dealing with the question of sterility.

Although Camargo was the major dramatic voice before the appearance of Nelson *Rodrigues, his plays are rarely performed today.

BIBLIOGRAPHY: Additional selected works by Camargo: *Um corpo de luz*, 1945; *Bagaço*, 1946.

CAMINHA, ADOLFO (1867–1897). Caminha spent his life in Ceará and Rio, the cities in which his major novels take place. He had a brief career in the navy in Fortaleza, but the scandal surrounding his relationship with a married woman forced him to abandon his post. He subsequently became an employee of the

National Treasury in Fortaleza. In 1892 he was transferred to Rio, where he died of tuberculosis.

Caminha's earliest works (poems and short novels) reveal romantic tendencies. Nonetheless his three major novels clearly identify him as a naturalist in the style of Émile Zola, Eça de Queiroz, and Aluísio *Azevedo: they study human passions and instincts and the influence of the social and economic environment on the individual. To a certain extent his novels are *romans à clef*, with thinly disguised portraits of contemporary figures and some biographical background. (*See* Naturalism; Portugal and Brazil: Literary Relations; Romanticism.)

A normalista (1893; The Schoolgirl) is the account of a provincial girl seduced by her guardian. Although it has a somewhat peculiar happy ending, it seems to lack originality. *Bom crioulo* (1895; *Bom Crioulo*, 1982) explores the homosexual relationship between a black sailor and a younger, white cabin boy. Their story ends in betrayal and violence. It is by far the strongest of Caminha's novels and one of the most significant products of Brazilian naturalism. One critic suggested that it reaches beyond the limits of naturalism in the portrait of its protagonist, Amaro, and in the curiously muted presentation of its violent climax. Yet another critic thought the novel transcended the constraints of the literary movement in its theme and in its use of a black main character. However, *Bom Crioulo* also reveals significant limitations; for example, it relies upon contemporary "scientific racist doctrines" as a mode of explanation of events and characters. (*See* Critics and Criticism; Homosexuality and Literature.)

Tentação (1896; Temptation) depicts the friendship between two couples, a provincial pair who migrate to Rio, and the more sophisticated family that offers them a home. Into this domestic scene intrudes the "temptation" of adultery. (*See* City and Literature.)

Caminha is at his best in the forceful presentation of the less pleasant aspects of the urban environment and in his concern for the individual in an oppressive society. Nonetheless, his work displays little stylistic variation, a weakness that often undercuts even this element of social criticism.

BIBLIOGRAPHY: Additional selected works by Caminha: *Vôos incertos*, 1886; *No país dos ianques*, 1894; *Cartas literárias*, 1895. Criticism: Loos.

MARÍA TAI WOLFF

CAMINHA, PERO VAZ DE   (late fifteenth century-early sixteenth century). Caminha was a ship's chronicler (an *escrivão a bordo*) at the height of the Portuguese explorations. He sailed with the fleet of Pedro Álvares Cabral on a voyage to Africa and India. However, wind and water currents forced the fleet off course. Cabral happened upon Brazil on Easter day, May 1, 1500. The new land was first named Terra da Santa Cruz.

Caminha's letter of the discovery of Brazil—*Carta do achamento do Brasil* (1500)—was addressed to the Portuguese King Manuel. In it, he provided the very first glimpses of the breathtaking beauty and inherent wealth of the "earthly Eden," as well as the Portuguese amazement at the "pure, natural state" of the

Indians encountered. The narration proceeds in vivid episodes that narrate the initial social and economic contacts between the races, as well as the first Catholic mass.

Caminha's letter reveals the moral and educational background typical of late medieval-early Renaissance Portugal. For example, he commented upon the desire for political control of the land and the people. He suggested that this may be at odds with the declared "conquest-for-Christianity" aim of the Portuguese explorations. Nonetheless, this is but a fleeting suggestion. Artistically, Caminha's letter attests to his knowledge of the Greek and Roman classical writers, biblical tales, and contemporary Portuguese literature. (*See* Portugal and Brazil: Literary Relations.)

Notably, Caminha's letter is the original source for the "good-savage" theme in Western literature and *ufanismo*. Mario de *Andrade saluted Caminha's description of the new land by using selections from the letter in his own masterpiece *Macunaíma*.

BIBLIOGRAPHY: *Carta a El-Rei D. Manuel* (1500). Diplomatic edition, 1964. Translations: Monegal/Colchie, II. Criticism: Barradas de Carvalho, Margarida. "L'idéologie religieuse dans la 'Carta' de Pero Vaz de Caminha." *Bulletin des études portugaises* 22 (1959–1960), pp. 21–29; Stern, Irwin. In Hower/Preto-Rodas.

CAMPOS, AUGUSTO DE (b. 1931). Poet, critic, translator, Campos is also a cofounder, with his brother Haroldo de *Campos, of the concrete poetry movement (*see* Postmodernism in Poetry) and coauthor of its combative book-manifesto *Teoria da poesia concreta* (1965; Theory of Concrete Poetry). His more recent poetic works, dedicated to composers Anton von Webern (1883– 1945) and John Cage (b. 1912) attest to his attention to the interrelationships between music and poetry, as well as to his vanguard position in the area of art and language. (*See* Art and Literature; Music and Literature; Postmodernism in Poetry.)

Linguaviagem (1967; Languagetravel), *Poemóbiles* (1974; Poemobiles), and *Caixa preta* (1975; Black Box), exploring the new field of poem-objects, ally Brazilian poetry with experiments in the plastic arts. Guided by a dialectical spirit of antipoetry anthropophagy (*antipoesia antropofagia*), an allusion to Oswald de *Andrade's cannibal manifesto of 1928, Campos consumed the vanguard and produced an antidote for the "poetic" text.

Campos sought to integrate concrete poetry with the cultural movement *tropicalismo* in their mutual criticism of Brazilian society and culture. Popular musicians Caetano Veloso (b. 1942), Gal Costa (b. 1946), and others have sung poetic texts and translations by Campos. *Balanço da bossa* (1968; Balance of the Beat) is the most comprehensive analysis of music-culture-politics in Brazil of the 1950s and 1960s. The poem-sculpture "VIVA VAIA" (1972; Hurrah to Hissing) derives from a Caetano concert, and "CIDADE" (City) and other concrete poems constitute visual and graphic references to the skyline of São Paulo's urban jungle. (*See* City and Literature.)

Campos's color poems, *Poetamenos* (1953; Poetless), bring multiple dimensions and readings to the graphic text in a participatory, multilingual, and experimental environment. In "MEMOS" (Memos) the reader must decipher the poetic text disguised in the jumbled typography of a memo pad, whereas the "Pentahexagram to John Cage" transforms the musical staff into the Chinese "I-Ching." The "Eye" poem is an ordered collage of photos exploring the relationship between word-object-body. Campos's *EXPOEMAS* (1985; Expoems), which includes "Pós-Tudo" (Post-Everything), a poem that aroused another storm of controversy over the concept of the postvanguard artwork.

Campos has participated in the recovery of a Brazilian literary tradition of innovation in his studies of *Sousândrade, Pedro Kilkerry (*see* Symbolism), and, most recently, the feminist author, poet, and personality Patrícia *Galvão (Pagu). His translations range from Provençal poets to contemporaries. João Cabral de *Melo Neto dedicated his *Agrestes* (1985; Rural Poems) to Campos in homage to his linking two generations of innovative poets: the modernists and postmodernists. (*See* Modernism.)

BIBLIOGRAPHY: Additional selected works by Campos: *Noigandres*, 1952–1962; *Cantares de E. Pound*, 1960; *Re/Visão de Sousândrade*, 1964; *Luxo*, 1967; *Mallarmargem*, 1971; *Poesia 1949–1979*, 1979/1986; *e.e. cummings 40 POEM(A)S*, 1986. Translations: Brasil/Smith; Solt: Steiner, Wendy. *The Colors of Rhetoric*. Chicago: University of Chicago Press, 1982; Tolman (1978); Williams, Emmet, ed. *Anthology of Concrete Poetry*. New York: Something Else Press, 1967; Woodbridge. Criticism: Clüver, Claus. "KlangFarbenmelodie in Polychromatic Poems: A. von Webern and Augusto de Campos." *CLS* (September, 1981); idem. "Reflections on Verbivocovisual Ideograms." *PT* (1982), pp. 132–148; *Concrete Poetry: A World View*. Edited by Mary Ellen Solt. Bloomington: Indiana University Press, 1970, pp. 12–16, 95–98.

                                                                               K. DAVID JACKSON

CAMPOS, GEIR (b. 1924). Born in Espírito Santo State, Campos was a navy-ship pilot. He later studied law and philosophy in Rio and has been a journalist and translator of Franz Kafka, Walt Whitman, Rainer Rilke, and Bertolt Brecht.

Although initially associated with the so-called Generation of 1945 (*see* Postmodernism in Poetry), in the 1950s and 1960s he rejected the hermetic or avantgarde strictures of his contemporaries and began to publish a more direct poetry in traditional forms, such as the sonnet *Coroa dos sonetos* (1953; Crown of Sonnets). Campos's dedication to a sociopolitical role for the poet in "the brotherhood of working people" was revealed not only in his theoretical works, *Pequeno dicionário de arte poética* (1960; A Short Dictionary of the Poetic Art) but also in the poetry of his *Da profissão do poeta* (1956; About the Poet's Profession). This note has predominated in most of his latter poetry.

Campos has also written short fiction, for example, *Conto e vírgula* (1982; Story and Comma), and has had a drama published based on the life of Castro *Alves (1972). (*See* Theater History.)

BIBLIOGRAPHY: Additional selected works by Campos: *Rosa dos rumos*, 1950; *O sonho de Calabar*, 1959; *Cantigas de acordar mulher*, 1964; *Cantos do Rio*, 1982; *O que é tradução*, 1986. Translations: Hulet. Criticism: Ramos, Péricles de Silva. In Coutinho, III.

CAMPOS, HAROLDO DE (b. 1929). Campos is a connosieur of world literature whose critical works cover dozens of languages. One of the founders of concretism (*see* Postmodernism in Poetry), with his brother Augusto de *Campos, his work is both lyrical and specific, derived from a synchronic rereading of the modern tradition in poetry and the arts.

As a concretist, Campos explored ties with formalism of the avant-garde while finding themes in his native São Paulo and in a Brazilian tradition of satire and social criticism. His *Servidão de passagem* (1962; "Transient Servitude," in *Rites of Passage: Selected Translations*. London: Carcanet Press, 1976) criticizes Brazil's colonial class and social structure, although its poetic idea originated in a "right-of-passage" space near the poet's home. *Xadrez de estrelas* (1976; Checkerboard of Stars) borrows its title from the *baroque discourse of Father Antônio *Vieira to emphasize both the idea of meaningful structure and linguistic inventiveness in the poet's exploration of a textual universe or universe of text, in the tradition of James Joyce, Ezra Pound, and others. The quest for poetic Utopia through the act of writing is evidence in *Signantia: quase coelum* (1979; Signs: Resembling Sky), whereas *A educação dos cinco sentidos* (1985; The Education of the Five Senses), a title taken from Marx, returns to the concept of poetry as experience and vital criticism of life. (*See* Portugal and Brazil: Literary Relations.)

Ever more dedicated to translation, Campos has had published fragments of classics—including works by Goethe, Dante, James Joyce, Ezra Pound, Vladimir Maiakovski, and Stéphane Mallarmé—and the biblical *Genesis* since the 1970s. His activity as a literary critic (*see* Critics and Criticism) accompanies his poetry, embracing ten volumes of theory and practice applied to Latin American texts and to the modern tradition in world literature. He is known for his recovery of neglected figures in Brazilian literature, such as *Sousândrade, and for pioneering essays on the vanguardist poetry, prose, and theater of Oswald de *Andrade.

Campos major prose-poem or poem-prose work, the polyglotal *Galáxias* (1984; Galaxies), was composed over most of his career. It combines Joycean linguistic inventiveness with a poetic stream of consciousness style as a voyage through birth-death, day-night, space-nonspace, of his universe. Campos has been called a "cosmonaut of the signifier" in homage to the modernity and universality of his work and stature.

BIBLIOGRAPHY: Additional selected works by Campos: *Auto do possesso*, 1950; *Noigandres*, 1952–1962; *Morfologia do "Macunaíma,"* 1973; *Ideograma*, 1977; *A ruptura dos gêneros na literatura latino–americana*, 1977; *Deus e o diabo no Fausto de Goethe*, 1981. Translations: Brasil/Smith; *LALR* (January–June, 1986); Tolman (1978); Woodbridge. Criticism: Barbosa, João Alexandre. "Um cosmonauta do significante: navegar é preciso." In *Signantia: quase coelum*, by Haroldo de Campos. São Paulo:

Perspectiva, 1979, pp. 11–25; Jackson, Kenneth David. "Literature and Criticism of the Brazilian Concrete Poets." *PPNCFL* 29 (1979), pp. 104–105; Longland, Jean. "On Translating Haroldo de Campos." *Dispositio* (Spring-Summer, 1982), pp. 189–202; Sarduy, Severo. "Towards Concreteness." Translated by Amelia Simpson. *LALR* (Spring, 1986), pp. 61–69.

                                                                    K. DAVID JACKSON

CAMPOS, NARCISA AMÁLIA DE OLIVEIRA. *See* Amália, Narcisa.

CAMPOS, PAULO MENDES (b. 1922). A *mineiro*, Campos's first novel resulted from a childhood adventure, when he and a friend ran away to Mato Grosso. After an unsuccessful attempt at a military career, Campos returned to Minas, where he came into contact with João *Alphonsus, Carlos Drummond de *Andrade, Murilo *Rubião, and other important writers, including Mário de *Andrade. In Rio, since 1945, he has written newspaper columns and was a foreign correspondent.

Often linked with the Generation of 1945 (*see* Postmodernism in Poetry), his first collection of poetry, *A palavra escrita* (1955; The Written Word), included in a later volume, *O domingo azul do mar* (1958; The Blue Sunday of the Sea), verses both social themes and childhood remembrances.

Although he has had additional verse published, he has dedicated himself primarily to the *crônica* genre. In his narrations of Rio life, he aims for a definition of true Brazilian qualities. His "Brasileiro, homem do amanhã" (The Brazilian, Tomorrow's Man) and "Dar um jeitinho" (How to Fix a Situation), from his collection *O colunista do morro* (1965; The Columnist of the Shantytown Hill), are strikingly direct comments about Brazilian idiosyncrasies. They are considered classic *crônicas*, in both form and content, and basic reading about contemporary Brazilian life. (*See* City and Literature.)

BIBLIOGRAPHY: Additional selected works by Campos: *O cego de Ipanema*, 1960; *Quadrante*, 1962; *Homenzinho na ventania*, 1962. Translations: Hulet; Tolman (1978).

CÂNDIDO DE CARVALHO, JOSÉ. *See* Carvalho, José Cândido de.

CARDOSO, LÚCIO (1913–1968). A well-read youth from Minas, Cardoso had dabbled in several literary genres by his sixteenth birthday. He went on to become one of the most significant midtwentieth-century novelists. He also had poetry published that adhered to the spiritualist trends of *modernism during the 1930s. (*See* Religion and Literature.)

Cardoso began his career as a novelist in 1934, when the socially oriented northeastern regionalist novel dominated Brazilian prose fiction. His fiction showed little interest in these concerns, but instead he wrote introspective studies focusing on man's interaction with the world and with other men. (*See* Regionalism; Social Novelists of the 1930s.)

Maleita (1934; Malaria) and *Crônica da casa assassinada* (1959; Chronicle of the Assassinated House) are his best-known works. The latter novel concerns the destructive effect of Nina, a beautiful and disruptive intruder into the stable, traditional Meneses family. Constructed from numerous documents frequently arranged in a nonchronological fashion, the events of the story are told through the eyes and perspectives of several characters, including family members and neighbors. The gathered bits and pieces create a multidimensional picture of reality. It represents the author's most profound penetration into the human psyche, and its complex manner of presentation reveals the maturation of the writer as a craftsman.

Cardoso's novels continue the tradition of psychological fiction begun by Machado de *Assis. Introspection, characterized by a stronger concern for man as man and not simply as Brazilian, would play a significant role in the new Brazilian novel of Clarice *Lispector, for whom Cardoso served as mentor.

BIBLIOGRAPHY: Additional selected works by Cardoso: *Histórias da lagoa grande*, 1939; *Inácio*, 1944; *Angélica*, 1950; *O enfeitiçado*, 1954; *Poemas inéditos*, 1982. Criticism: Foster/Foster, I.

KEITH H. BROWER

CARDOZO, JOAQUIM (1897–1978). Born in Pernambuco, Cardozo studied engineering and was a planner-contributor to the construction of Brasília along with architect Oscar Niemeyer and writer Samuel *Rawet.

Cardozo's involvement in *modernism was due to his regionalist poetry, written in the 1920s, which evoked varied aspects of everyday life in Recife— churches, streets, and people. He was an editor of the modernist *review *Revista do Norte* (1924–1925), along with Ascenso *Ferreira, Luís *Jardim, and others. A collection of his poetry was not published until the mid–1940s. (*See* Modernism; Regionalism.)

A later collection of poems, *Signo estrelado* (1960; Starred Signal), contains more metaphysical and abstract verse on the regionalist theme. He soon returned to direct usage of northeastern traditions in poetry and popular dramas. *O coronel de Macambira* (1963; The Colonel from Macambira) is a highly personalized *bumba-meu-boi*, a traditional rural Christmastime pageant with music, singing, and dance; it was performed with great success throughout Brazil. (*See* Music and Literature.)

Cardozo's last poems had a declamatory purpose and touched on socioeconomic issues facing the Northeast, for example, the conflicts between the poor *sertanejos* and the large landholders.

BIBLIOGRAPHY: Additional selected works by Cardozo: *Poemas*, 1947; *Trivium*, 1970; Translations: Bishop/Brasil; Hulet; Woodbridge.

CARVALHO, JOSÉ CÂNDIDO DE (b. 1914; BAL: 1974). As a youth, Carvalho worked in Rio as a messenger at the International Exposition of 1922. Educated in public schools, he worked part time and about 1930 began a career in journalism. He continued his studies and earned a law degree in 1937. Soon he began to write prose fiction, and his early publications included *children's literature and interviews, as well as humorous—yet serious—vignettes similar to the popular Brazilian *crônicas*.

Carvalho's greatest achievement, however, is his multifaceted regionalistic work *O coronel e o lobisomem* (1964; The Colonel and the Werewolf), which earned three distinguished Brazilian literary *prizes. In this novel the author showed innovative linguistic usages (including word coinage) and an exceptional characterizational ability through his creation of the magnificent, exaggerating colonel. The novel fuses myth and magic realism and is particularly intriguing for its conflicting layers of truth and fiction. The linguistic and structural complexity of this achievement has caused comparison with writers like Guimarães *Rosa. (*See* Regionalism.)

Also of note is Carvalho's role as a translator; for example, he translated the work of Stefan Zweig into Portuguese. (*See* Foreign Writers and Brazil.)

BIBLIOGRAPHY: Selected additional works by Carvalho: *Olhe para o céu, Frederico!* 1939; *Pinóquio em procura de Branca Neve*, 1941; *Ninguém mata o arco-íris*, 1972; *Os mágicos municipais*, 1984; *O rei Baltazar* (in preparation). Criticism: Chamberlain, Bobby J. "Frontier Humor in *Huckleberry Finn* and Carvalho's *O coronel e o lobisomem*." *CLS* (Summer, 1984), pp. 201–216; Murphy, Terrence J. "Fact and Fantasy vs. *The Coronel*." *KRQ* 19 (1972), pp. 515–524.

EDGAR C. KNOWLTON, JR.

CARVALHO, RONALD DE (1893–1935). A sensitive and perspicacious thinker, Rio-born Carvalho studied law and began a diplomatic career in 1914. He participated in the Futurist (*see* Modernism) movement in Paris, and along with the Portuguese poets Fernando Pessoa and Mário de Sá-Carneiro, and Luís de Montalvor, he founded the ephemeral but extremely significant Luso–Brazilian avant-garde *review *Orpheu* (1915). (*See* Portugal and Brazil: Literary Relations.)

Earlier, Carvalho's symbolist verse—*Luz gloriosa* (1913; Glorious Light)—was published and he would return to symbolism again in 1919. Nonetheless, he became an avid participant in *modernism and was greatly admired by the young writers. Not only in his lecture at the Week of Modern Art (*see* Modernism), entitled "A revolta dos anjos" (The Revolt of the Angels), did he set the goals for movement, but he also played the role of wheeler-dealer between the artists and writers of São Paulo and Rio, including the musician Heitor *Villa-Lobos. (*See* Music and Literature; Symbolism.)

Carvalho published several collections of poetry in the modernist vein; most notable was *Toda a América* (1926; *All the Americas*), which in its presentation of Brazil, and all of the Americas, as well as in its use of popular language and themes reflects the influence of Walt Whitman: "Where are your poets, America? / . . . America, your poets don't belong to that race of servants who dance to the beat of Greeks and Latins!" As a literary critic (*see* Critics and Criticism), Carvalho produced *Pequena história da literatura brasileira* (1919;

A Short History of Brazilian Literature), which is notable for its premodernist (*see* Modernism) recognition of nativist sentiments in literature. He also authored what is probably the first English study of Brazilian fiction: "The Brazilian Novel" (in *Inter-America* [April, 1923], pp. 214–221).

Although he was initially influenced by the values established by an earlier generation of critics—Sílvio *Romero and José *Veríssimo— Carvalho's essential role in modernism was celebrated by its leading members, including Mário de *Andrade and Tasso da *Silveira.

BIBLIOGRAPHY: Additional selected works by Carvalho: *Estudos brasileiros*, 1924, 1931; *Jogos pueris*, 1926. Translations: Hulet; Woodbridge. Criticism: Foster/Foster, I; Lopes, Albert R., and Willis D. Jacobs. "Ronald de Carvalho: The Balanced Voice." *University of Kansas City Review* (Spring, 1953), pp. 163–168; Martins.

CARVALHO, WALTER CAMPOS DE   (b. 1915). A *mineiro*, Carvalho completed law school in São Paulo and has lived in Rio since the 1950s. His fiction presents odd characters in a reality in which absurd events are normal. In *A lua vem da Ásia* (1956; The Moon Comes from Asia), the character begins his tale by announcing that he had murdered his logic instructor, was absolved, and went to live under a bridge of the Seine, although he had never been to Paris!

In his later novels, Carvalho also touched on other "rational" absurdities of life. For example, *Vaca de nariz sutil* (1961; Cow with a Subtle Nose) presents a full-fledged discussion on the smells of death: excrement, vomit, and so on.

BIBLIOGRAPHY: Additional selected works by Campos: *Tribo*, 1954; *O púlcaro búlgaro*, 1964.

CASTRO, CONSUELO DE   (b. 1946). Castro holds degrees in sociology and politics that have served her well in her career as a dramatist of contemporary Brazilian sociopolitical events and dilemmas.

Castro's career began in the late 1960s under the influence of Plínio Marcos. *À prova de fogo ou a invasão dos bárbaros* (written 1968; produced 1974; Fireproof or the Invasion of the Barbarians) was awarded second place in the main theater *prize of 1968; however, the military government prohibited its production. In this drama, Castro analyzed the 1968 student protests against the military regime and the police repression, including the murder of several students, which followed. She is particularly interested in determining women's roles in these struggles—as leaders or as followers. The drama concludes that the students' youth and "innocence" about life prevented them from presenting an effective resistance. (*See* Dictatorship and Literature; Feminism and Literature.)

Castro's subsequent dramas have dealt with generational conflicts, as well as the role of women in modern marriage, for example, *O porco ensangüentando* (1971; The Bleeding Pig). Her greatest success has been *Caminho da volta* (1974; The Road Back) awarded the Molière Prize. (*See* Prizes.) Marisa, the protagonist, wants to improve her social status and is ready to prostitute herself to achieve that goal. Castro insists that in this consumerist society, few individuals can escape that same urge. This play was well received owing to its convincing themes and dialogue.

A cidade impossível de Pedro Santana (1975; The Impossible City of Pedro Santana) is the story of an idealistic architect who attempts to aid factory workers. He is unsuccessful—as are most of Castro's heroes and heroines; they are all conscious of society's ills but are unable to effect change due to the capitalist system's pursuit of money and social status. Castro is one of the most vibrant voices of the Brazilian stage today.

BIBLIOGRAPHY: Additional selected words by Castro: *A flor da pele*, 1969; *Aviso prévio*, 1986.

CASTRO ALVES, A.   *See* Alves, Antônio de Castro.

CEARENSE, CATULO DA PAIXÃO   (1863–1946). Poet and performing songwriter, Catulo lived until the age of fifteen in northern Brazil. This background weighs heavily in his poems and song texts. In Rio, he revitalized the sentimental ballad (*modinha*) and initiated a "backlands vogue" in song and poetry. His songs, performance style, and poetry were immensely popular throughout Brazil. Cearense's best-known works remain song texts such as "Luar do sertão" (Backlands Moonlight) and "Cabocla do Caxangá" (Hillbilly of Caxangá), with music by his contemporary João Pernambuco. (*See* Music and Literature.)

Cearense used an unusual, erudite vocabulary and put sophisticated, cultured, or "civilized" ideas in supposedly rustic lyric voices. The lexical peculiarities of the language of the *sertão* are more evident in his fifteen volumes of written verse. Accordingly, Manuel *Bandeira called him a "dialectal poet." (In "Ensaios literários." *Poesia completa e prosa de Manuel Bandeira*. Rio: 1967, p. 727). Cearense sought moving simplicity and the illusion of spontaneity. Although others objected to the falsity of the poet's rural poses, Mário de *Andrade called him "the greatest creator of images in Brazilian poetry."

BIBLIOGRAPHY: Additional selected works by Cearense: *Cantor fluminense*, 1887; *Meu sertão*, 1918; *Sertão em flor*, 1919; *Aos pescadores*, 1923; *Alma do sertão*, 1928; *Modinhas*, 1943. Criticism: Brookshaw; Maúl, Carlos. *Catulo: sua vida, sua obra, seu romance*. Rio: São José, 1971.

CHARLES A. PERRONE

CHAMIE, MÁRIO   (b. 1933). Chamie studied law and social sciences and currently teaches communications theory at the University of São Paulo. At home and abroad, he has lectured on various aesthetic issues, produced cultural programs for television, and contributed regularly to journals and newspapers. Until the early 1960s he collaborated with the concrete poets (*see* Postmodernism in Poetry) as an "independent avant-garde poet," but he broke with them to form what he considered to be a more humanistic and socially concerned poetic vanguard. He is known as the founder, theorist, and principal author of the praxis poetry project (*poesia praxis*), which published the *review Praxis. (See Post-modernism in Poetry.)

Praxis poetry is concerned with social-historical facts, links between words, and extralinguistic contexts, as well as reader response to the text. The poetry emerges from an elaborate theoretical framework that denies subjective lyricism and establishes a rational compositional process. Chamie conceives the poetic word as "energy" and the poem as a dynamic "product." The praxis poet does not write about themes; he should examine *áreas*, external facts or emotions, and seek all possible meanings and contradictions of these *áreas* in their lexical, syntactic, and semantic manifestations. Chamie typically manipulates mor-phemes, sound patterns, and the relationships of vocabulary items in the explo-ration of an *área* with social overtones.

Critic Assis *Brasil considers Chamie one of the most consequential poets of contemporary Brazil.

BIBLIOGRAPHY: Additional selected works by Chamie: *Espaço inaugural*, 1955; *Indústria: textos praxis, 1961–1964*, 1967; *Instauração praxis: manifestos, plataformas, textos e documentos críticos, 1959–1972*, 1974; *A linguagem virtual*, 1976; *A quinta parede*, 1986. Translations: Woodbridge. Criticism: Mário Chamie, "Poesia praxis: re-trospectiva e prospectiva." In *Poetas do modernismo*. Edited by Leodegário A. de Aze-vedo Filho. Brasília: INL/MEC, 1972, VI:205–290.

CHARLES A. PERRONE

CHILDREN'S LITERATURE. Until the end of the nineteenth century, the few children's books available in Brazil were imports from Portugal, often translations of Christoph von Schmid, the Grimm Brothers, Hans Christian An-dersen, and Edmondo De Amicis. Only in the last decade of the century did writers and publishers start producing a national children's literature. They had enthusiastic and concrete support from educational authorities. The increasing number of schools during the early republican years provided the necessary reading public for these books, which carried distinct nationalistic overtones, for example, Olavo *Bilac's *Contos pátrios* (1904; Patriotic Stories), Júlia Lopes de *Almeida's *Histórias de nossa terra* (1907; Stories of Our Nation), and Bilac's and Manuel Bonfim's (1868–1932) *Através do Brasil* (1910; Across Brazil). (*See* Portugal and Brazil: Literary Relations.)

Although the republican regime listed among its goals a break with the old rural structure of Brazilian society, a traditional, conservative image pervades these tales. Thales de Andrade's (1890–1977) *Saudade* (1919; Nostalgia) ex-emplifies the archaic ruralism, showing how much children's literature was outdated regarding economic and social activities then taking place in Brazil.

This anachronistic ideology of endorsing a past social pattern disappears only with Monteiro *Lobato. From his first children's story in 1921 to his last in 1944, Lobato's work is faithful to several features of the rural tradition of the genre but changes their meaning completely. His characters are modern minded, and the rural setting is merely the starting point for their breathtaking adventures. Agricultural production—the traditional characteristic of ruralism—is never presented as a worthy trend for the Brazilian economy in Lobato's plots. Wealth comes from petroleum, and so, as a metaphor for Brazil, Lobato brings to his books a discussion about modernization, which was then a national issue.

Lobato was also a successful publisher using modern marketing and merchandising devices. His characters question adult and school authority and criticize government wrongdoings in a contemporary language. They include popular movie stars like Shirley Temple (in *Memórias de Emília* [1936; Emilia's Memoirs], Tom Mix, and Felix the Cat (*Reinações de Narizinho* [1931; Narizinho's Pranks]) or literary characters like Louis Carroll's Alice (in *O picapau amarelo* (1939; The Yellow Woodpecker), Cervantes's Don Quixote (in *Dom Quixote das crianças* [1939; A Children's Don Quixote]), and James Matthew Barrie's Peter Pan (*Peter Pan*, 1939). (*See* Portuguese Language of Brazil.)

Regardless of Lobato's models, the 1930s were full of moralistic texts oriented toward adult values, except for Viriato Correia's (1884–1967; BAL: 1938) *Cazuza* (1938; Cazuza). Fables and folktales of Indian and black origin (perhaps due to *modernism) became very popular, representing the reverse side of the "modern spirit" of Lobato's works, for example, Osvaldo Orico's (1900–1981) *Histórias do pai João* (1933; Father John's Stories), José Lins do *Rego's *Histórias da velha Totonha* (1936; Old Totonha's Stories), and Lúcio *Cardoso's *Histórias da Lagoa Grande* (1939; Stories of Lagoa Grande). The narrative device of folktales told by old black women to white children revealed the anachronism of this literature and pointed out the cultural gap between the *old* and the *new* Brazil. The exception seems to be Graciliano *Ramos's *Alexandre e outros heróis* (1944; Alexander and Other Heroes), the only book of folk background in which teller and audience partake in the same cultural origin. (*See* Folklore and Literature.)

After 1945 the mass media and industrialization strongly affected Brazilian children's literature. The author who best represents this new situation is Isa Silveira Leal (b. 1910). The main character of her books is a teenage girl, Glorinha, who lives the modern life her readers dream of. But the ambitious project of "being modern" also had a hidden face. As the nation moved west—to a new capital and to development of the interior—Brazil was also drawing a new self-image, which stimulated a resurgence of rural stories and folktales, for example, Hernani Donato's (b. 1922) *Histórias dos meninos índios* (1951; Stories of Indian Children) and Francisco Marins's (b. 1922) *Expedição aos Martírios* (1952; Expeditions to Martirios).

With the imposition of strong censorship during the military regime, novels and songs related what was banished from the media and official documents. Within this context, the concern with contemporary problems reached children's literature, which began to present a world undergoing a crisis. Odette de Barros Mott's (b. 1913) *Justino o retirante* (1970; Justino the Refugee) swept the children's literature *prizes that year and started a new trend. Justino's story deals with the northeastern droughts, viewed through the eyes of a teenaged orphan who abandons his home in search of a better chance in life. Mott's next work, *A rosa dos ventos* (1971; The Weathervane), focuses on urban poverty, on youngsters entangled in drugs and sexual and family problems. (*See* Cycles; City and Literature; Dictatorship and Literature; Music and Literature.)

In the seventies this trend was further emphasized through books concerned with social issues like pollution, for example, Wander *Piroli's *Os rios morrem de sede* (1976; The Rivers are Dying of Thirst); parent's divorce, for example, Vivina Viana's (b. 1940) *O dia de ver meu pai* (1977; The Day to See My Father); or racial discrimination, for example, Mirna Pinsky's (b. 1943) *Nó na garganta* (1979; All Choked Up). Some social criticism comes out through irony and parody as in Ruth Rocha's (b. 1931) *O reizinho mandão* (1978; The Little Pushy King) and Ana Maria Machado's (b. 1942) *História meio ao contrário* (1979; A Somewhat to the Contrary Story).

Another contemporary trend confronts the psychological and emotional growth of its intended readers, either through first-person stories like Lygia Bojunga's (b. 1932) *A bolsa amarela* (1978; The Yellow Purse), through highly symbolic texts like Marina *Colasanti's (b. 1937) *Uma idéia toda azul* (1979; A Blue-Colored Idea), or even through regional cultures like the folk characters of Haroldo Bruno's (b. 1922) *O incrível rapto de Flor de Sereno* (1979; The Incredible Kidnapping of Flor de Sereno). Clarice *Lispector, in *A mulher que matou os peixes* (1968; The Woman Who Killed the Fish), and Osman *Lins introduced avant-garde narrative procedures into children's books of the sixties and seventies. (*See* Regionalism.)

More recently, children's literature has begun to bear a strong structural resemblance to comic strips and detective stories, notably through the high incidence of dialogues, a perfect sense of timing, and quick action. If Stella Carr's (b. 1932) *O caso da estranha fotografia* (1977; The Case of the Strange Photograph) and *O incrível roubo da loteca* (1978; The Incredible Robbery of the Lottery) take their structure from mystery books, João Carlos Marinho's (b. 1935) *O gênio do crime* (1969; The Crime Genius) and *Sangue fresco* (1983; Fresh Blood) promote a renewal of the genre through irony and, surprisingly, exaggerations.

In the Brazilian tradition, children's poetry has served as an excuse for displaying filial emotions, patriotic enthusiasm, and similar virtues. However, the past twenty years seem to have released texts from these constraints. Poets like Sidónio Muralha (1920–1982) in *A TV da bicharada* (1962; The Gang's TV), Cecília *Meireles's *Ou isto ou aquilo* (1964; This or That), Mário *Quintana's *Pé de pilão* (1968; A Nonsense Rhyme), Vinícius de *Moraes's *A arca de Noé* (1974; Noah's Ark), and José Paulo Paes's (*see* Postmodernism in Poetry) *É isso ali* (1985; That's It) represent a very innovative burst in contemporary Brazilian children's poetry. Also, Chico *Buarque's *Chapeuzinho amarelo* (1979; Little Yellow Riding Hood) adapts the traditional tale with linguistic inventiveness. In 1986 several extremely popular Brazilian lyricists and musicians have turned to children's literature: Martinho da Vila, João Bosco, Rita Lee, Toquinho, Tom Jobim, and Paulo Ricardo.

Important names in modern Brazilian children's theater are Lúcia Benedetti (b. 1914), author of a popular children's Christmas play, *Sigamos a estrela* (Let's Follow the Star); Stella *Leonardos; and Maria Clara Machado (b. 1921). The latter two writers stressed historical and folkloric regional traditions within an imaginative context. Also of note is Ana Elisa Gregori (b. 1931). (*See* Theater History.)

Of note also are the existence of a National Foundation for Children's and Juvenile Literature and also the great editorial investment in children's literature as evidenced by the quality illustrations prepared for recent children's stories and poems. Both publishers and readers view the genre in today's Brazil as having reached maturity.

BIBLIOGRAPHY: Criticism: Arroyo, Leonardo. *Literatura infantil brasileira. Ensaio de preliminares para sua história e suas fontes.* São Paulo: Melhoramentos, 1968; Coelho, Nelly Novães. *Dicionário crítico da literatura infanto-juvenil brasileira.* São Paulo: Edições Quíron, 1984; Lajolo, Marisa, and Regina Zilberman. *Literatura infantil brasileira: história e histórias.* São Paulo: Ática, 1984.

MARISA LAJOLO

CITY AND LITERATURE. There is a strong tradition of city literature in Brazil that dates from the colonial era, when Gregório de *Matos brilliantly satirized the dissolute society of Salvador, Bahia, in saucy verse.

The literary *academies of the eighteenth century were important institutions for the production and dissemination of a thematically and stylistically urban poetry. The satire of urban life was the intent of the *Cartas chilenas* by the arcadian (*see* Arcadias) poet Tomás Antônio *Gonzaga, implacable critic of Governor Luís da Cunha Meneses, whose inept administration of the then capital of Minas, Vila Rica, was the focus of this poetic treatise on civic disorder in the neoclassical tradition.

By that time, urban life in Brazil was sufficiently developed to allow the flight from the city to become a significant literary motif. Until the end of the nineteenth century, however, Brazilian literature of the coastal cities merely transposed European cultural and literary values to the Brazilian context. Machado de *Assis and the Brazilian naturalists and realists created an European-style *salon littéraire* in the tradition of Molière and George Meredith (1828–1909) that focused on urban characters in domestic conflict. (*See* Naturalism; Realism.)

According to Antônio Cândido (*see* Critics and Criticism), two of the most important periods of interaction between the city and literature in Brazil have been during *romanticism and *modernism. The young romantic writers, like Alvares de *Azevedo or Gonçalves *Dias, whose cult heroes were the Portuguese Almeida Garrett and Lord Byron sought to emulate the decadent, urbane lifestyle of the *bohème*. Like their European counterparts, these brilliant young men suffered a keen sense of alienation from society. They were tubercular, idealistic, and sensuous. They complained of tedium; they wrote in a range of voices from the sarcastic to the satanic. Sérgio Buarque de Hollanda (*see* Historiography) attributed the malaise of Brazilian romantic writers to the difficult transition from the rural to the urban way of life. Romantic literary conventions such as the themes of *Indianism or the inability to cope with everyday life found great resonance in the particularly Brazilian *saudade*, or nostalgia for a lost rural tradition. Another variant of romantic urban literature in Brazil is the picaresque novel, exemplified by Manuel Antônio de *Almeida's *Memórias de um sargento de milícias*, and the novel of courtship, illustrated by Joaquim Manuel de *Macedo's *A moreninha*. (*See* Portugal and Brazil: Literary Relations.)

The city is the fundamental element in the first phase of modernism; this urban theme was dedicated to the new Brazil taking the form of megalopolis, for example, Mário de *Andrade's *Paulicéia desvairada*. The city also became symbolic of what modernists thought was a dispersion of national character, personified by Mário de Andrade's *Macunaíma*, the "hero without character." The modernists saw the city as the "new backlands," the future and challenge of Brazilian society. With this regionalist aesthetic, the modernists did not intend to separate themselves from urban society but rather to challenge a decadent cultural oligarchy. (*See* Modernism; Regionalism.)

The transition to urban themes has been decisive since the late 1940s. Once the thematic and stylistic possibilities of the regionalist novel of the thirties were exhausted, literary interest and activity shifted to the city. Brazilian literature since the sixties has come to reject the simplistic solutions of the novel of the Northeast, in which man is the victim of social and political circumstance. The writer's mission is envisioned as much more complex and demanding than exhorting political and social change. He must transcend the narrow boundaries of a purely local sense of social injustice to take on the greater challenge of the problems of universal man in a chaotic and indifferent world. (*See* Social Novelists of the 1930s.)

The result has been a literature both national and universal. Foreign literary conventions once borrowed have been assimilated into the Brazilian experience. Marcel Proust, Franz Kafka, James Joyce, Ernest Hemingway, and William Faulkner have been cited as the major foreign influences on this new orientation in Brazilian literature.

Contemporary Brazilian city fiction has also been strongly shaped by the process of the 1964 military takeover, known as the Revolution, which ended with a return to civilian government in 1985. As the Revolution pressed to implement progress through technocratic modernization, it alienated the Brazilian intellectual and overtly suppressed him through censorship and other repressive acts. Norma Pereira Rego's recent novel *Ipanema Dom Divino* (1983; Ipanema the Divine Gift) is a fictional re-creation of the thriving intellectual life in Rio of the pre-1964 era. (*See* Dictatorship and Literature.)

The city is alternately portrayed as heaven and hell in contemporary Brazilian literature, a metaphorical bifurcation traditional in the canon of Western city literature. The persistent vision of the city-as-hell can be understood as reflective of an awareness of the reality of the encroaching megalopolis, fear of political repression, in the context of recent Brazilian history, as well as pessimism about the human condition and Brazilian society. José Carlos de Oliveira's very popular works, for example, *Terror e êxtase* (1979; Terror and Ecstasy), presented this situation throughout the years of the dictatorship.

Among the most influential of the urban writers to emerge since the 1960s are Rubem *Fonseca, Clarice *Lispector, Antônio *Callado, Osman *Lins, Ignácio de Loyola *Brandão, Víctor *Giudice, João *Antônio, Dalton *Trevisan, Sérgio *Sant'Anna, Lygia Fagundes *Telles, Nélida *Piñon, Antônio *Torres, Marcos *Rey, José *Louzeiro, and Monteiro *Martins, as well as the *new writers Anna Maria Martins and Márcia Denser. (*See also* Feminism and Literature.)

BIBLIOGRAPHY: Criticism: Lowe, Elizabeth. *The City in Brazilian Literature*. Madison, N.J.: Farleigh Dickinson University Press, 1982; Severino, Alexandrino. In Roett.

ELIZABETH LOWE

COELHO NETO, HENRIQUE (1864–1934; BAL: 1897). Coelho Neto was the son of an Indian mother and Portuguese father, a merchant, who had immigrated to northeastern Maranhão State. The future writer studied medicine and law before turning to journalism and teaching, where he found his talents lay. After his marriage in 1890, he began to devote himself seriously to a writing career, and he ultimately produced more than 110 published works, thus becoming the most prolific of Brazilian authors. He later acquired fame as a public lecturer, and between 1908 and the late 1920s he was elected as a federal deputy three times and also occupied several diplomatic and other governmental posts.

Throughout his many books, Coelho Neto displays a penchant for aesthetic eclecticism, eschewing total allegiance to any one of the literary currents then in vogue. Perhaps the most outstanding feature of his writing is his language, which critics (*see* Critics and Criticism) have called "*baroque," "symbolist," or "impressionist." His style is replete with detailed, often static descriptions of landscapes, in which a strong emphasis on opulence, elegance, and mystery is coupled with the author's choice of a rich and at times *recherché* vocabulary reminiscent of sixteenth-century Portuguese letters. (*See* Impressionism; Portugal and Brazil: Literary Relations; Symbolism.)

Many of the basic characteristics of his fiction are manifest in his early novel, *A capital federal* (1893; The Federal Capital), in which the young and bedazzled Anselmo abandons his rural roots and settles in cosmopolitan Rio. But the vice and corruption of the capital prove to be not as much to his liking as he had anticipated. Thus he returns to his bucolic provenance, convinced of the superiority of the Brazilian hinterland. Notwithstanding a certain ideological naiveté and shallowness of conception, the novel is notable for a number of reasons, not the least of which is the author's vivid portrait of the *carioca* life-style. (*See* City and Literature.)

Turbilhão (1906; Crowd) tells the tragic story of a humble *carioca* family: a widowed mother, Dona Júlia; an adolescent daughter, Violante; and a young man, Paulo, who works as a proofreader for a local newspaper to support them all. When to escape certain poverty Violante runs away with a rich man and later falls into prostitution, Dona Júlia, out of shame, decides to move to a new neighborhood where the truth will not be known and she can hide her disgrace. Paulo is a dreamer, who is easily seduced by vices and the pleasures of the flesh. He quits his job and takes up with Ritinha, the stereotypical sensuous Brazilian mulatta. Albeit founded on deterministic precepts, *Turbilhão* succeeds for the most part in avoiding the melodrama and partisanship typical of many novels of *romanticism and *naturalism and is considered by many critics as one of the finest of the Coelho Neto's works.

O rei negro (1914; The Black King) tells of Macambira, the son of an African king, and his life as a slave on a plantation in southeast Brazil. Despite his friendship with the slavemaster, Macambira's bride-to-be is raped by the slave-master's son, and Macambira himself is forced to flee after slaying the culprit. The story is full of tragedy and melodrama. At its best moments, it is gripping and powerful. Heroes are idealized in the manner of the romantics, while African folkways are exploited for picturesque and supernatural effects. Yet this is juxtaposed somewhat uneasily with the work's prevailing realist tone and with scenes at times reminiscent of naturalistic narration. Despite many noteworthy aspects, the novel ultimately fails to realize its full artistic potential. (*See* Realism; Slavery and Literature.)

Coelho Neto's fortunes as a Brazilian writer and intellectual took a drastic downward turn with the triumph of *modernism. From 1926 until his death, he was president of the *Brazilian Academy of Letters. In 1928 he was proclaimed the "Prince of Brazilian Prose Writers," as the result of a contest. In 1932 he was nominated unanimously by the academy for the Nobel Prize. But he was also one of the staunchest opponents of the new modernist aesthetics, a fact that earned him the scorn of many writers and, to this day, has hampered attempts, especially by Otávio de *Faria, to revive his flagging literary reputation.

BIBLIOGRAPHY: Additional selected works by Coelho Neto: *Rapsódias*, 1891; *Fruto proibido*, 1895; *Sertão*, 1896; *A conquista*, 1898; *A bico da pena*, 1904; *Esfinge*, 1908; *Vida mundana*, 1909; *A cidade maravilhosa*, 1928; *Fogo-fátuo*, 1929; *A árvore da vida*, 1929. Translations: Goldberg. Criticism: Brookshaw; Foster/Foster, I; Loos; Pierson, Colin M. "Coelho Neto: Introduction of African Culture into Brazilian Drama." *LATR* (Spring, 1976), pp. 57–62.

BOBBY J. CHAMBERLAIN

COLASANTI, MARINA (b. 1937). A television personality, journalist, essayist, and plastic artist, Colasanti has been a leading voice in feminist causes and issues since 1962. She founded the feminist review *Nova* in 1975.

E por falar em amor e outros contos (1984; And Speaking about Love and

Other Stories) and *Contos de amor rasgados* (1986; Torn-Up Love Stories) are
her first ventures into short fiction. She narrates the difficulties of love, emotions,
and man-woman relationships with only a trace of direct feminist concerns. The
latter collections has ministories (ninety-eight) that possess a sparse style and
occasional surrealist overtones. Colasanti has also written *children's literature.
(*See* Feminism and Literature; Surrealism.)

BIBLIOGRAPHY: Additional selected works by Colasanti: *Eu, sozinha,* 1968; *A mo-
rada do ser,* 1978; *A nova mulher,* 1980. Translations: Tolman (1984).

CONCRETISM. *See* Postmodernism in Poetry.

CONDÉ, JOSÉ (1918–1971). Condé left his native city of Caruaru, Pernambuco, to study in the state of Rio, where he earned a law degree in 1939. For
more than thirty years he contributed literary columns to Rio newspapers and
worked as an attorney for the Banking Institute. In 1949 he cofounded with his
brothers João and Elísio the *Jornal de Letras,* which for many years has been
one of the most important Brazilian monthly literary journals. (*See* Critics and
Criticism.)

Although Condé began to write fiction in the 1940s, he attained recognition
with his *Histórias da cidade morta* (1951; Stories of the Dead City) and *Os dias
antigos* (1955; Days Gone By), two collections of short fiction set in Santa Rita,
a fictional Northeast town caught in the economic stagnation of the postslavery
days. *Terras de Caruaru* (1960; Lands of Caruaru) is considered his finest novel.
This work of historical fiction provides an intimate sociological portrait of the
city of his birth and childhood. (*See* Regionalism.)

Other successful literary experiments include the magical realism of *Vento do
amanhecer em Macambira* (1962; Dawn Breeze in Macambira) and *Pensão Riso
da Noite* (1967; Night Laugh Pension), six picaresque tales about popular night
life in Caruaru. Less convincing are his explorations of bourgeois life in Rio,
Um ramo para Luísa (1959; A Bouquet for Luisa), and *Noite contra noite* (1965;
Night against Night). (*See* City and Literature.)

Condé avoided the social criticism or political activism of other contemporary
northeastern regionalists. He was an observer of life, principally interested in
the consequences of change upon his characters. (*See* Social Novelists of the
1930s.)

BIBLIOGRAPHY: Additional selected works by Condé: *Caminhos na sombra,* 1945;
Onda selvagem, 1950; *Como uma tarde em dezembro,* 1969; *Tempo vida solidão,* 1971.
Criticism: Cavalcanti, Valdemar, "Caruaru: A face humana." *JL* (Rio) (August, 1977),
p. 3; Pérez, Renard. "José Condé." *Escritores brasileiros contemporâneos.* Rio: Editora
Civilização Brasileira, 1970, I: 217–222.

SEVERINO JOÃO ALBUQUERQUE

CONDORISM. A term coined in Brazil by the historian Capistrano de Abreu
(*see* Historiography), *condorism* refers to a poetic movement that flourished
during *romanticism, principally between 1850 and 1870. Although its name is
truly American, a reference to the high-flying, undaunted, all-seeing condor of

the Andes, the movement's roots are to be found in the poetic forms and hyperbolic rhetoric of the sociopolitical poetry of Victor Hugo and other French romantic poets.

The contemporary Brazilian themes most-often versed in this style were patriotic—the emancipation of the slaves or the Paraguayan War (1864–1870)—as well as foreign ones dealing with liberal causes, for example, the liberation of Poland. Although it can be traced initially to the poetry of José Bonifácio de Andrada e *Silva, The Younger, and Paulo Eiro's (1836–1871) poetry, Castro *Alves is considered its prime exponent. Other romantic and ultraromantic (*see* Romanticism) poets who used this technique included Tobias Barreto de Meneses (*see* Recife School), Pedro de Calasãs (1837–1874), Vitoriano Palhares (1840–1900), and Quirino dos Santos (1841–1886).

BIBLIOGRAPHY: Criticism: Romero, Sílvio. "O condoreirismo de Tobias Barreto e Castro Aíves." *História da literatura brasileira*. 6th ed. Rio: José Olympio, 1960, pp. 1180–1349.

CONTEMPORARY BLACK LITERATURE. In contrast with the relative dearth of literature written by blacks during much of the twentieth century, from the late 1970s into the early 1980s Brazil experienced a considerable upsurge in the publication of works by writers of discernible African descent. In reflecting largely the collective experience of fellow Afro-Brazilians, these authors have continued and elaborated on themes established by earlier figures, such as Cruz e *Sousa and Lima *Barreto.

During the period 1920–1960 few Afro-Brazilians described the black experience. Lino Guedes (1897–1951) of Campinas, in São Paulo, wrote poetry that reflected black urban life and projected a sense of moral outrage rather than an attitude of protest. Solano Trindade (1908–1974) of Recife, a socially committed poet strongly influenced by the *négritude* movement in France, wrote verses asserting black racial identity and cultural pride, as well as explosive poems of social protest. Abdias do *Nascimento was instrumental in encouraging black participation in the theater during the post–World War II period. (*See* Theater History.)

Afro-Brazilian literary production came to a virtual halt during the 1960s as a result of the military regime's strict censorship policies and national security laws, which classified racial themes, among other subjects, as taboo. The return to democracy initiated in the late–1970s coincided with a marked rise in black consciousness among Afro-Brazilians and a growing disposition to challenge the country's racial status quo. As censorship eased, a small but vigorous vanguard of black writers began to produce militant newspapers and modest volumes of poetry with a view toward fostering in fellow Afro-Brazilians an increased awareness of questions such as the importance of African heritage, the inequalities of society, and racism. This initial body of poetry served as a catalyst. By the early 1980s black writers in major urban centers were producing significant works of prose and poetry reflecting primarily the reality, sentiments, and aspirations of Afro-Brazilians. (*See* Dictatorship and Literature.)

The largest number of works—principally collections and anthologies of poems and short stories—has been produced in São Paulo by a group known as *Quilombhoje*. Under the pen name Cuti, poet Luís Silva (b. 1951) has directed the publication of the group's annual anthology, *Cadernos Negros* (Black Notebooks), since its inception in 1978 and has two collections of poetry and a one-act play to his credit as well.

Well-established literary figures in São Paulo include the poets Eduardo de Oliveira (b. 1926) and Oswaldo de Camargo (b. 1936), the author of highly acclaimed works of poetry and prose fiction who also organized the recent anthology of Brazilian black literature from Caldas *Barbosa to Eli Semog (b. 1952): *A razão da chama* (1986; Reason for the Flame). Both Oliveira and Camargo have been instrumental in encouraging younger writers and have published in *Cadernos Negros* as well.

Cadernos Negros includes works of not only authors residing in São Paulo but also writers who promote Afro-Brazilian literature in other cities. Poets Semog and José Carlos Limeira (b. 1951) and prose writer Eustáquio Rodrigues (*Cauterizai meu umbigo* [1986; Cauterize My Navel] have been at the forefront of such activity in Rio. Poets Adão Ventura (b. 1946), author of *A cor da pele* (1981; The Color of the Skin) (for his translations, *see* "Key to Bibliographical References": Woodbridge), Oliveira Silveira (b. 1941); and Edu Omu Oguiam (b. 1953) have been outstanding in Belo Horizonte, Porto Alegre, and Salvador, respectively.

BIBLIOGRAPHY: Criticism: *Afro-Braziliana: A Working Bibliography*. Compiled by Dorothy B. Porter. Boston: G. K. Hall, 1978; Bastide, Roger. "Variations on Négritude." *Presénce africaine* (English edition) (Paris) 8 (1961), pp. 83–92; Brookshaw, David. *Race and Color in Brazilian Literature*. Metuchen, N.J.: Scarecrow Press, 1985; Dreller, Gerald. *The Afro-Brazilian: An Expression of Popular Culture in Selected Examples of Bahian Literature*. Urbana: University of Illinois, 1974; Kennedy, James H. "Recent Afro-Brazilian Literature: A Tentative Bibliography." *A Current Bibliography on African Affairs* (1984–1985), pp. 327–345; Litto, Frederic M. "Some Notes on Brazil's Black Theatre." *The Black Writer in Africa and the Americas*. Los Angeles: Hennessey & Ingalls, 1973, pp. 195–229; Malinoff, Jane. "Modern Afro-Brazilian Poetry." *Callaloo* (February-October, 1980), pp. 43–69; idem. "Poetry for the People: Lino Guedes and Black Folk Style in Early Twentieth-Century Afro-Brazilian Verse." *Research in African Literatures* (Fall, 1982), pp. 366–382; Preto-Rodas, Richard. "Negritude in Brazilian Poetry." *Negritude as a Theme in the Poetry of the Portuguese-Speaking World*. Gainesville: 1970, pp. 14–31.

JAMES H. KENNEDY

CONY, CARLOS HEITOR (b. 1926). Cony's education at a seminary, which led to his disillusionment with religion, is described in his mostly autobiographical novel *Informação ao crucificado* (1961; Information to the Crucified). Later he studied philosophy and began writing for newspapers and magazines. His outspoken denunciation of the post–1964 military regime led to his persecution and several arrests. (*See* Religion and Literature.)

Cony was an experience journalist by the time he turned to fiction. In fact, his first novels, *O ventre* (1958; The Womb) and *A verdade de cada dia* (1960; Everyday's Truth), won important literary *prizes. Cony's prose fiction is set primarily in his native Rio. He often portrays man's disenchantment with unsuccessful love affairs. His protagonists are often married men approaching middle age, claiming to be in search of life's meaning yet cynically involved in illicit romances. (*See* City and Literature.)

Only in *Pessach: a travessia* (1967; *Passover, the Crossing*, selection translated by Nelson H. Vieira in *Jewish Spectator* [Winter, 1984], pp. 30–32), his best work to date, does the protagonist's dissatisfaction at the personal level evolve into a political action. Paulo Simões, the partly autobiographical novelist living in the post–1964 dictatorship, unexpectedly joins an urban guerrilla group on his fortieth birthday. The political "crossing" of Simões (an anagram in Portuguese for Moses) is paralleled in his gradual acceptance of himself as a Jew. The next novel, *Pilatos* (1974; Pontius Pilate), marks a return to the despair, pessimism, and rejection of the earlier works. Its first-person narrator and protagonist is a castrated man who equates happiness with ignorance and, like Pontius Pilate, shuns responsibility for his action. (*See* Dictatorship and Literature.)

Cony has since had a "novel-news report" published, *O caso Lou* (1975; The Lou File), and a "movie-novel," *A noite do massacre* (1976; The Night of the Massacre), which are fictionalized accounts of two episodes of brutal violence in contemporary Rio. Cony's fiction has been the object of considerable praise but also of adverse criticism in Brazil because of his ruthless depiction of a desintegrating middle class.

BIBLIOGRAPHY: Additional selected works by Cony: *Tijolo de segurança*, 1960; *Matéria de memória*, 1962; *Da arte de falar mal: Crônicas*, 1963; *Antes o verão*, 1964; *Posto seis: Crônicas*, 1965. Criticism: Parker, John M. "The Novels of Carlos Heitor Cony." *LBR* (Winter, 1973), pp. 163–186; Patai; Vieira, Nelson H. "Judaic Fiction in Brazil: To Be or Not to Be." *LALR* (July-December, 1986), pp. 31–45.

SEVERINO JOÃO ALBUQUERQUE

CORREIA, RAIMUNDO (1859–1911; BAL: 1897). A member of the pantheon of Brazilian Parnassian poets, Correia, born in Maranhão, was a judge. He spent several years abroad in diplomatic posts, most notably in Lisbon. (*See* Parnassianism; Portugal and Brazil: Literary Relations.)

Correia's first collection of poetry, *Primeiros sonhos* (1879; First Dreams), includes the highly emotional sonnet "As pombas" (The Doves), which reveals *romanticism's great influence on him, from which he would never totally free himself. Correia ignored this collection in latter life. He evolved toward Parnassianism, but one commentator stated that it was "Parnassianism against Parnassianism." Correia himself attacked this literary "import," referring to it as "broken down"; nonetheless, he cultivated the sonnet form but never attained the *baroque style that was common to many of the movement writers.

The second part of his *Sinfonias* (1883; Symphonies) is notable because it dwells on metaphysical themes related to his disenchantment with worldly existence, but they are superficial. He returns to these themes again in the collection *Versos e versões* (1887: Verses and Versions), in poems such as "O misantropo" (The Misanthrope): "Why, since this atrocious hatred has come upon me, / Do I see betrayal in every look? / Perfidies in every human heart?"

In spite of his ranking among the Parnassians, Correia, like many other poets of the school, gradually crossed over to the opposing literary school—*symbolism. In fact, his poem "Plenilúnio" (Full Moon) is considered one of symbolism's most important works. The poet and novelist Ledo *Ivo spoke of the "lunarity" of this particular poem, defining this term as the quality of "enchantment of vocabulary which makes poetry another language within each language." (In "Apresentação." *Raimundo Correia: Poesia*. Rio: 1963, p. 13). The poem verses the theme of lunacy: "An ample moonshine overwhelms me, and I walk, / Swimming in a visionary light, / All over, a crazyman dragging the long blanket of my moonshine."

Critics have charged Correia with plagiarism with regard to themes and techniques "adapted" from earlier and contemporary national and foreign poets. In fact, Parnassians were known to assimilate others' verses, elevating them to a highly personal level. Correia's audience today is small but faithful.

BIBLIOGRAPHY: Additional selected works by Correia: *Aleluias*, 1891. Translations: Hulet.

COSTA, CLÁUDIO MANUEL DA (1729–1789). Born into a mining family in rural Minas, Costa studied at Coimbra. Returning to Vila Rica (modern Ouro Preto), he established a law practice and soon entered the colonial government. A leading figure of the *Minas School, in 1768 he published his collected poetry, *Obras poéticas* (Poetic Works; modern edition, 1903). His attempt at an epic poem narrating the founding of Vila Rica (*Vila Rica*, published in 1839) was unsuccessful. Arrested in 1789 as a leader of the independence minded *Mineiran Conspiracy, he took his own life while imprisoned.

During his years at Coimbra he was mainly influenced by *baroque poetic techniques. Costa spoke of establishing an "Overseas *Arcadia," and once in Brazil, he fashionably adopted an arcadian pseudonym, Glauceste Satúrnio. His sonnets are often amatory in the pastoral mode, but they also frequently strike a genuinely nativist note. His shepherd's lament becomes that of the eighteenth-century Brazilian, torn affectively between the homeland's immediate reality and the mother country's cultural heritage. (*See*: Portugal and Brazil: Literary Relations; *Ufanismo*.)

These gemlike sonnets, among the finest written in Portuguese, are his best work and were esteemed for their technical perfection during Brazil's period of *Parnassianism. Simultaneously, through the intimate relationship he established between nature and human emotions (e.g., "Fábula do Ribeirão do Carmo" ["Fable of Ribeirão do Carmo"]), Costa anticipated an important aspect of *romanticism. He is also believed to be the author of the poem that precedes the *Cartas chilenas* now attributed to Tomás Antônio *Gonzaga.

Brazil's first major neoclassical poet, and one of the finest in the Portuguese language, Costa also became the first Brazilian writer to gain international recognition when the Swiss historian Simonde de Sismondi (1773–1842) discussed him in 1812 and the American poet James Gates Percival (1795–1856) translated and published one of his sonnets in 1841.

BIBLIOGRAPHY: Additional selected works by Costa: *O Parnaso obsequioso*, 1768. Translations: Hulet. Criticism: Dutra, Waltensir. In Coutinho, I.

NORWOOD ANDREWS, JR.

COSTA, FLÁVIO MOREIRA DA (b. 1942). A *gaúcho*, Costa has published novels, many short stories, collections of poetry, and film criticism and has organized many anthologies, from southern regional literature to stories about soccer. (*See* Film and Literature: Regionalism; Soccer and Literature.)

Costa is a master of collage, to judge from his first novel *O desastronauta* (1971; The Disastronaut), in itself a play on the words "disaster" and "astronaut." The protagonist, Cláudio, narrates his life through memoirs (or "dismemoirs"), quotes, newspaper articles, and telephone conversations, proving that "I am chaos." The novel *As margens plácidas* (1978; The Placid Shores), coauthored with Roberto Grey, takes its title from the first words of the Brazilian national anthem and presents the post–1964 depression of the average Brazilian "asphixiated" by the military regime. (*See* Dictatorship and Literature.)

Costa's short fiction has dealt primarily with the lives of the poor. *Malvadeza Durão: contos malandros* (1981; Malvadeza Durão: Scoundrel Stories) is set in a shantytown (*favela*), where violence and poverty dominate, whereas *Os mortos estão vivos* (1984; *The Dead Are Alive*), with similar themes, is characterized by a quick paced, colloquial language.

BIBLIOGRAPHY: Additional selected works by Costa: *As armas e os barões*, 1974; *Os espectadores*, 1976. Translations: Tolman (1984); Woodbridge.

COSTA, HIPÓLITO DA [HIPÓLITO JOSÉ DA COSTA PEREIRA FURTADO DE MENDONÇA] (1774–1823). Brazilian-born Costa spent his life outside of Brazil. After graduating from Coimbra with degrees in philosophy (1796) and law (1798), he was sent by the Portuguese government to the United States to study agricultural systems and bridge construction. Subsequently, he spent two years in England. (*See* Portugal and Brazil: Literary Relations.)

Upon his return to Portugal, he began to expound upon the liberal philosophies and political systems he saw during his travels, and he was jailed as a Freemason, a liberal thinker opposed to the monarchy and the colonial status of Brazil. In 1805 he managed to escape and fled to England, where he began to publish, in 1808, *O Correio Brasiliense* (The Brazilian Post). With the independence of

Brazil in 1822, he entered the diplomatic corps; however, he died before assuming his first assignment as Brazilian consul general in England.

O Correio Brasiliense was a monthly publication totally written by Costa for some fourteen years; some issues ranged up to 236 pages. In a vivid style, Costa discussed not only political events but also religious, scientific, and artistic advancements with the aim of promoting Brazilian progress. Among his many foresightful positions were his early opposition to slavery in Brazil and his support for an interior capital for the nation. Costa is considered the link between the European Enlightenment's (*see* Arcadias) liberal concepts and the rise of liberalism in Brazil.

BIBLIOGRAPHY: Additional selected work by Costa: *Descrição da árvore açucareira e da sua utilidade e cultura*, 1811. Criticism: Rizzini, Carlos. *Hipólito da Costa e o "Correio Brasiliense."* 2 vols. São Paulo: Nacional, 1957.

COUTINHO, EDILBERTO (b. 1938). Paraíba-born Coutinho studied law but has been a journalist, short fiction writer, critic (*see* Critics and Criticism), and cultural historian. While a foreign correspondent in Spain, he interviewed Ernest Hemingway, who appears as a character in his story "Sangue na praça" (Blood in the Ring).

Although his first collections, published before he was twenty, have regionalist themes, his *Um negro vai à forra* (1977; A Black Man Stands Up) are innovative in theme and structure. The "games" people play—be they sexual or political games or games of domination—are an essential structural element of his short fiction. Interestingly, male characters are indecisive in all their activities—professional, sexual, and so on. The ups and downs of soccer life are the backdrop for the collection *Maracanã, Adeus* (Maracanã Stadium, Good-bye), which was awarded the Cuban Casa de las Americas short fiction *prize in 1980. (*See* Dictatorship and Literature; Homosexuality and Literature; Regionalism.)

Coutinho has also written literary theory and criticism. Most notable is his "rediscovery" of the late regionalist poet Carlos Pena Filho (1929–1960). He has also written popular biographies of the Brazilian Indian explorer Colonel Cândido Rondon (1865–1958).

BIBLIOGRAPHY: Additional selected works by Coutinho: Translations: Tolman (1984). Criticism: Foster, David W. *"Maracanã, adeus"* (book review). *WLT* (Summer, 1981), pp. 441–442; Tolman (1984).

COUTINHO, SÔNIA (b. 1939). A native of Bahia, Coutinho has published short fiction and literary criticism. She has been a translator of American and English literature, as well as the organizer of literary supplements.

Coutinho's short fiction has dealt primarily with women's situations, in particular the desire for freedom from the limiting rural life. *Uma certa felicidade* (1976; A Certain Happiness) presents tales of women who have come to Rio in search of independence and excitement but instead are confronted with loneliness, casual sex, and economic frustration. The story "Darling, ou do amor em Copacabana'' (Darling, or About Love in Copacabana) narrates the consumerist world of a beach doll whose attraction to a young boy is purely instinctual.

Coutinho's later stories turned to Afro-Brazilian culture as in *Os jogos de Ifā* (1980; The Games of Ifā), as well as to *surrealism as in *Os venenos de Lucrécia*, which was awarded the Jabuti Prize. (*See* Prizes.) The title story ("Lucrecia's Poisons," in *Michigan Quarterly Review* [Winter, 1986]) mixes imaginary and real time, space, and historical events and figures in the narration of an eternal woman's magical powers.

BIBLIOGRAPHY: Additional selected works by Coutinho: *Do herói inútil*, 1966; *Nascimento de uma mulher*, 1971. Translations: *Ploughshares* (Winter, 1986).

COUTO, RUI RIBEIRO (1898–1963; BAL: 1934). Couto, who studied law in São Paulo, was a journalist and government lawyer. He served in Europe during many years of his career in the Foreign Service.

Although he had novels and short stories published, Couto was primarily a poet. His first collection, *O jardim das confidências* (1921; The Garden of Secrets), appeared in the last stages of *symbolism. His later works reveal his adherence to *modernism and contain poems inspired by traditional Brazilian songs (*modinhas*) and popular themes of Brazilian life. Several of these works were set to music by Heitor *Villa-Lobos. For example, his "Modinha do exílio" (Song of Exile) laments the diplomat's "self-exile"; it is a tragicomic parody of "Canção de exílio" (Song of Exile), a well-known poem by Gonçalves *Dias: "Wherever I go / I can hear the sabiá bird / . . . It sings Brazilian songs. / It sings, and how it hurts me!" (In *Dia longo*. Lisboa: Portugália, 1944, p. 257.) (*See* Folklore and Literature.)

His novel *Cabocla* (1931; Backlandswoman) and his numerous collections of short fiction also invoke aspects of Brazilian life. The story "O bloco das mimosas borboletas" (The Dainty Butterflies Carnival Group) from *Baianinha e outras mulheres* (1927; Little Baiana Woman and Other Women) is a bittersweet tale of carnival's disruption of a sedate upper-middle-class family's life. (*See* Feminism and Literature.)

BIBLIOGRAPHY: Additional selected works by Couto: *Poesias unidas*, 1910; *O crime do estudante Batista*, 1922; *Prima Belinha*, 1940. Translations: Grossman; Hulet. Criticism: Bandeira, Manuel. "The Sardonic Brazilians." *Américas* (September, 1954).

CRESPO, ANTÔNIO GONÇALVES (1846–1883). Gonçalves Crespo, born in Rio, went to Lisbon in 1860 and remained there until his death. (*See* Portugal and Brazil: Literary Relations.)

He is most recognized for his 1870 collection *Miniaturas* (Miniatures), only a precursor to the Brazilian *Parnassianism but an important collection of verse for Portuguese Parnassianism. In these poems, he often evoked his Brazilian childhood, his mother, and his domestic life surrounded by slaves and parlor maids, (*mucamas*) in ultraromantic (*see* Romanticism) tones. Yet another theme is his personal difficulty in accepting his mulatto color. A later collection, *Noturnos* (1882; Nocturnes), develops similar themes within a broader artistic and thematic perspective.

BIBLIOGRAPHY: Additional selected works by Crespo: *Obras completas*, 1942. Criticism: Peixoto, Afrânio. "Prefácio." *Obras completas de Gonçalves Crespo*. Rio, 1942; Sayers.

CRITICS AND CRITICISM. The first commentators of Brazilian literature were foreign writers, critics, and travelers, who included Brazilian literature as part of their comments on Portuguese literature, for example, Friedrich Bouterwek's (1765–1828) *Geschichte der portugiesischen Poesia und Beredsamkeit*(1805); Simonde de Sismondi's (1773–1842) *De la littérature du midi de l'Europe* (1813); Ferdinand Denis's (1798–1890) *Résumé de l'histoire litteraire du Portugal et du Brésil* (1826), and the Portuguese Almeida Garrett's *Bosquejo da história da poesia e da língua portuguesa* (1826). (*See* Portugal and Brazil: Literary Relations; Travel Literature.)

Brazilians who dabbled in literary commentaries after independence were primarily concerned with identifying a nationalist orientation and sentiment for their newly independent country for example, Gonçalves de *Magalhães, Januário da Cunha Barbosa (1780–1846) who was extremely active in the independence movement, Torres Homem (*see* Romanticism), Fernandes Pinheiro (1825–1876), Dutra e Melo (1822–1846), and the novelists Joaquim Norberto de Sousa e Silva (1820–1891), José de *Alencar, and Machado de *Assis. (*See* Romanticism.)

With the exception of Alencar and Assis, these writers approached their tasks from an impressionistic viewpoint, which characterized most of Brazilian literary criticism until the mid–1950s. Impressionistic criticism exists without any formal aesthetic philosophy of art behind it; rather, it is based on extremely personal, often emotional, beliefs or prejudices that are tangential to the artistic process.

Modern literary criticism is said to begin with Sílvio *Romero. He, like other members of the *Recife School, for example, Tristão de Alencar Araripe Júnior (1848–1911), was influenced by the scientific theories then in vogue. Romero introduced a sociological approach into the study of Brazilian literature, stressing the role of miscegenation on Brazilian culture. Araripe Júnior believed that Brazilians were dramatically changed by their contact with the land, a phenomenon that he characterized as cloudiness (*obnubilação*). His application of this theory to literature itself was and still is debated. With the exception of several short essays and a collection of regionalist stores about Indians, *Contos brasileiros* (1868; Brazilian Stories), Araripe Júnior's work has fallen into oblivion. Other contemporary critics have had similar fates: Nestor Vítor dos Santos (1868–1932), who was "the" critic of Brazilian *symbolism; João Ribeiro (1860–1934; BAL: 1898); Afrânio *Peixoto; Humberto de Campos (1886–1934); Medeiros e *Albuquerque; and Capistrano de Abreu. (*See* Historiography.)

A more sophisticated form of impressionistic criticism was practiced by José

*Veríssimo. Although he lacked a formal critical philosophy, Veríssimo had a solid literary and cultural background and intuition. He applied this knowledge to an analysis of literature within a national, social and artistic context. Although ignored today, Veríssimo's *Estudos brasileiros* (1884–1889; Brazilian Studies) and his *História da literatura brasileira* (1916; History of Brazilian Literature) offer good insights into the contemporary artistic scene. Followers of Veríssimo's orientation have included Alceu Amoroso *Lima (Tristão de Athayde) and Ronald de *Carvalho, whose *Pequena história da literatura brasileira* was the first overview of the literature within a notable Brazilian linguistic style and nativist conception of the formation of literature. Other important names of the the the early part of this century included José Brito Broca (1903–1961), whose most important contribution is *1900: a vida literária no Brasil* (1956; 1900: Literary Life in Brazil); Lúcia Miguel-Pereira (1903–1959), also a novelist and biographer of Gonçalves *Dias, whose collection of essays, *Prosa de ficção: 1870–1920* (1950; Prose Fiction from 1870 to 1920), is considered a classic work of intelligent, sensitive scholarship; Álvaro Lins (1912–1970; BAL: 1955), whose *Jornal de crítica* (7 vols; 1941–1963; Critical Journal) tends to be polemical but reveals good critical intuition based on his constant consideration of the relationship between literature and culture; Mário de *Andrade and Sérgio *Milliet are the important critics of Brazilian literature and culture throughout the era of *modernism, whereas Alceu Amoroso Lima (Tristão de Atayde) was considered the "Dean" of Brazilian literary critics during the 1950s.

In 1956 literary criticism began to obtain a "professionalized" orientation in Brazil. Presently, there exist several schools of critical thought that either have been adapted from foreign schools—American, English, French—or that are intensely nationalistic.

Antônio Cândido [Antônio Cândido de Mello e Souza], (b. 1918), professor of sociology and literary theory at the University of São Paulo, uses a sociocultural orientation as the basis for his criticism, which he outlined in the introduction to his now classic *Formação da literatura brasileira (Momentos decisivos)* (3d ed.; 1969; The Development of Brazilian Literature [Decisive Moments]):

The attempt to simultaneously focus upon the work as a reality itself, and the context as a system of works, may seem too ambitious to some, owing to the strength with which the prejudice about the divorce between history and aesthetics, form and content, erudition and taste, objectivity and appreciation has taken root. A balanced criticism . . . must, to the contrary, seek to show that they are parts of a total explanation to the extent possible, which is the critic's ideal although it is never attained owing to the individual and methodological limits.

Based on this credo, Cândido's major works include his collection of essays, *Literatura e sociedade* (1965; Literature and Society), and his "Dialéctica da malandragem" (Dialectics of Roguery), the most important study on Manuel Antônio de *Almeida's *Memórias de um sargento de milícias*. His disciples include many eminent critics who have diligently pursued his critical goals, including João Alexandre Barbosa, who has authored many studies on *modernism and contemporary poetry; Walnice Galvão, a feminist critic, who recently completed a critical edition of Euclides da *Cunha's *Os sertões*; Davi Arrigucci, Jr., author of essays on literature of the dictatorship years, *Achados e perdidos* (1979; Lost and Found); João Luiz Lafetá, a student of *modernism and contemporary cultural criticism; Roberto Schwarz, one of the most important critical polemicists of the moment, who, aside from being a dramatist, has had a major study published on the development of Brazilian fiction in the nineteenth century, *Ao vencedor as batatas* (1977; To The Winner, The Potatoes); and Telê Porto Ancona Lopez, who has published extensively on the works of Mário de *Andrade. (*See* Dictatorship and Literature; Feminism and Literature; Theater History.)

Afrânio Coutinho (b. 1911; BAL: 1962), professor emeritus of Brazilian literature at the Federal University of Rio de Janeiro, has proposed Anglo-American "new criticism" adapted to the Brazilian situation as another important critical approach. In the preface to his edition of *A literatura no Brasil* (Literature in Brazil), arguably the most important critical overview of Brazilian literature published in Portuguese, he referred to the noted North American critics René Wellek and Austin Warren and concluded:

New criticism is not only a tool for analysis. It is a group of ideas and principles on the level of general aesthetics and literary doctrine; specific aesthetics of the genres; and analysis and methods of investigation. It includes postulates of a general order with regard to the concept of literature, its nature, function and aims, including a series of concepts, such as irony, the objective correlative, paradox, relevancy, sign structure, symbol, texture, tension, ambiguity, some of them old concepts with a different meaning, others new concepts.

Coutinho has also made significant contributions to the defense of a nationalistic criticism, defending the "national impulse" of Brazilian literature in many studies, such as those collected in *O conceito de literatura brasileira* (1981; The Concept of Brazilian Literature). He has also fought long and hard for the preeminence of the Portuguese of Brazil and Brazilian culture over European Portuguese language and literature. (*See* Portugal and Brazil: Literary Relations; Portuguese Language of Brazil.)

Wilson Martins (b. 1921) is another leading, productive voice in contemporary Brazilian criticism and intellectual history. A lawyer by profession, Martins later turned to literature and assumed a professorship at the University of Paraná. He is currently professor of Portuguese at New York University. Although he has lived primarily outside of Brazil for some twenty five years (a fact that his detractors often refer to), Martins is directly involved in the day-to-day literary fray. Martins judges a literary work on its supreme literary merit: quality. He does not deny the role of sociohistorical background in literature but rejects these external forces in the evaluation of specific works. Best known for his study *O modernismo* (3d ed., 1969; *The Modernist Idea*, 1971), Martins has also produced the encyclopedic *História da inteligência brasileira* (1977–1978; History of Brazilian Intellectual Culture) and a panoramic overview of literary criticism in Brazil: *A crítica literária no Brasil* (2d ed., 1983; Literary Criticism in Brazil).

Many twentieth-century critics with varying critical persuasions have shaped and are shaping Brazilian criticism today. Among them are Manuel Cavalcanti Proença (1905–1966), author of a major study of Mário de *Andrade's *Macunaíma*; the philosopher Euryalo Cannabrava (b. 1908), who, like Afrânio Coutinho, has been a proponent of a "professional" criticism that would bring together all aspects of Brazilian culture, as he describes in his *Estética e crítica* (Aesthetics and Criticism); Astrojildo Pereira (1890–1965), a founder of the Brazilian Communist party in 1922, whose criticism analyzed social issues: *Interpretações* (1944; Interpretations); Nelson Werneck Sodré (b. 1911), an ex-military officer, who, in addition to writing many studies of Brazilian history, has produced an analysis of Brazilian literature from a Marxist point of view: *História da literatura brasileira: seus fundamentos econômicos* (3d ed., 1969; History of Brazilian Literature: Its Economic Basis), as well as a major bibliographical resource for knowledge about Brazil: *O que se deve ler para conhecer o Brasil* (many updated editions; What One Should Read to Become Acquainted with Brazil); Oswaldino Marques (b. 1916), who produced an important study of Cassiano *Ricardo's poetry; Massaud Moisés (b. 1928), who has published important bibliographies and dictionaries of Brazilian and Portuguese literature, as well as works of literary theory; Benedito Nunes (b. 1929), who has produced many invaluable analysis of contemporary writers from a perspective of philosophical concepts, for example, studies of Clarice *Lispector, João Cabral de *Melo Neto; Gilberto Mendonça Telles (b. 1931), a poet (collected works in *Hora aberta* [1987; Open Hour]) as well as a critic, who has published comparative literary studies, for example, *Camões e a poesia brasileira* (1973; Camões and Brazilian Poetry), and organized an important collection of literary manifestoes related both to European and Brazilian culture; Fábio Lucas (b. 1931), a *mineiro*, who has penned important overviews of the social content of Brazilian literature, for example, *O caráter social da ficção do Brasil* (1985; The Social Character of Fiction in Brazil); Alfredo Bosi (b. 1936), professor of Brazilian literature at the University of São Paulo, who has produced important studies on poetic theory, for example, *O ser e o tempo da poesia* (1977; Being and Time in Poetry), and who has organized popular anthologies of Brazilian literature, for example, his *O conto brasileiro contemporâneo* (1975; The Contemporary Brazilian Short Story); Affonso Romano de *Sant'Anna; Luís Costa Lima (b. 1937) is principally a structuralist critic who led the battle to establish a strong school of literary theoreticians in Brazil during the 1970s: *Estruturalismo e teoria de literatura* (1973; Structuralism and Literary Theory), *Mimesis e modernidade* (1980; Mimesis and Modernity), and *Sociedade e disurso ficcional* (1986; Society and Fictional Discourse), and among whose critical monographs is a major analysis of the fiction of Cornélio *Pena (1976); Silviano *Santiago, who has done extensive comparative literary studies and analyzed questions of Latin American cultural dependency; José Guilherme Merquior (b. 1941; BAL: 1982), who has been one of the principal critical polemicists of the 1970s and 1980s, includes among his seventeen books of criticism and theory: *Razão do poema* (1965; *Reason for the Poem*), which analyzes poetry as a rational activity, *Arte e sociedade em Marcuse, Adorno, and Benjamin* (1969; Art and Society in Marcuse, Adorno and Benjamin), and *Formalismo e tradição* (1974; Formalism and Tradition); Carlos Nelson Coutinho (b. 1943), who is considered a disciple of Georgy Lukács's humanist cultural method, although he, like other Brazilians who employ this critical approach, are not orthodox Marxists. Coutinho argues against vanguardism and extreme artistic innovation; he favors literature as a lesson for man: *Literatura e humanismo* (1967; Literature and Humanism); Fausto Cunha (b. 1938), author of *Aproximações estéticas do onírico* (1967; Aesthetic Approaches to the Oneiric) and the recent science fiction novel *As noites marcianas* (1986; Martian Nights).

Other notable figures of criticism during the twentieth century are Agrippino Grieco (1888–1973); Otto Maria Carpeaux (*see*: Foreign Writers and Brazil); Eduardo Portella (b. 1932; BAL: 1981), editor of the *review *Tempo Brasileiro*; Antônio Soares Amora; Raymundo Faoro; José Aderaldo Castello; Franklin de Oliveira (b. 1916); Assis *Brasil; Flora Sussekind; Pedro Lyra (b. 1945); Nelson Ascher; Gilda de Mello e Souza; Lígia Chiappini Moraes Leite; Marisa Lajolo; Nadia B. Gottlieb; Norma S. Goldstein; Regina Zilberman; Maria Luísa Ramos; Paula Beiguelman; Heloísa Buarque de Hollanda; Nicolau Sevcenko; Luiza Lobo; Jorge Schwartz; Ester Schwartz, and others.

Aside from literary *reviews, which have included some critical studies of literature, there has been a tradition of journals dedicated to literary analysis. Among them are *Anhembi, Kriterion, Letras, Tempo Brasileiro, Revista de Letras* (Assis), *Jornal de Letras* (Rio), *Leia, Argumento, Almanaque, Opinião, Revista do Brasil, Travessia, Letras de Hoje*.

BIBLIOGRAPHY: Criticism: Heyck, Denis Lynn. "Afrânio Coutinho's *Nova Crítica*." *LBR* (June, 1978), pp. 90–104; Sayers, Raymond S. "Brazilian Literary Criticism Today." *LBR* (June, 1964), pp. 67–79.

CRÔNICA. Although the literal English translation of *crônica* is "chronicle," since the middle of the nineteenth century the word has been used to describe a "sketch" of life, be it historical, personal, or imaginary. As an open-ended genre, it has few fixed rules. Generally, its theme and content can range from the lightly poetic to the bitingly satiric or even to black humor; its language is highly colloquial; its length is most often less than 1,000 words; it offers no direct morale.

Initially, the *crônica* involved imperial life or national life as seen from Rio. It dwelled on customs, figures, and scandals of the Court. José de *Alencar began the first daily *crônica* column in a newspaper under the title "Ao correr da pena" (1851–1854; As the Ink Flows). He was followed by Manuel de

*Macedo and Machado de *Assis; the latter raised the popular form to an artistic one, seeing in it an "admirable fusion of the useful and futile." José Joaquim de *França Júnior, João do *Rio, Olavo *Bilac, and Henrique *Coelho Neto delightfully described Rio life of the 1890s, the "decadent" years. Júlia Lopes de *Almeida gave the form its first feminine perspective. (*See* Feminism and Literature.)

During early *modernism, 1922–1923, Menotti del *Picchia used his *crônica* in the *Correio Paulistano* newspaper to defend the aims of the movement. Most major and many minor writers have put pen to paper in popularizing this uniquely Brazilian genre, for example, Rachel de *Queiroz, Manuel *Bandeira, Carlos Drummond de *Andrade, Paulo Mendes *Campos, Ledo *Ivo, Luís Martins (1907–1985), Mariazinha Congílio, Carlos Heitor *Cony, Helena Silveira (b. 1911), Luís Fernando *Veríssmo, Carlos Eduardo *Novaes, and Marcelo Cerqueira. The short story writer Fausto Wolff's *crônicas* views Brazil's condition and his own situation with both humor and astonishment: *O dia em que comeram o ministro* (1982; The Day They Ate the Minister) and *Venderam a mãe gentil* (1984; They Sold the Gentle Mother).

BIBLIOGRAPHY: Criticism: Moser, Gerald. The *crônica*: A New Genre in Brazilian Literature." *SSF* (Winter, 1971) pp. 245–252; Rónai, Paulo. "Um gênero brasileiro: a crônica." *Crônicas brasileiras*. Gainesville, Fl.: Center for Latin American Studies, 1971, pp. 154–156.

CRULS, GASTÃO (1888–1959). The son of a Belgian scientist, Cruls's early inclination to science led him to study medicine. Influenced by contemporary European scientific theories then in vogue, which coincided with the progressive ideology of Brazil's new republican regime, Cruls accompanied Colonel Cândido Rondon's 1928 exploration into the interior of the Amazon. (*See* Positivism and Literature.)

Cruls's fiction combined the scientific power of observation with the imaginative sense of new discovery and created an early form of science fiction. In fact, he became best known to his contemporaries as the author of *Amazônia misteriosa* (1925; *The Mysterious Amazonia*, 1944) and as a "historian of fiction," or a writer of fiction whose purpose was to compose history.

In a fashion similar to that of other Latin American writers such as Jorge Luis Borges and Julio Cortázar, Cruls's fiction forced the reader to question the reversible nature of fiction and reality. The novel *A criação e o criador* (1928; The Creation and the Creator) shows the reversibility of fiction and reality, and Cruls himself appears as one of the characters. In his short story "Meu sósia" (My Double), from the collection *História puxa história* (1938; One Story Leads to Another), a narrator becomes obsessed with a "double" who precedes him in the library and asks for the same books (on the Amazon region) that he intends to read in order to write his own book. This obsession translates itself into the author's concern with the magic moment of involvement brought by fiction, the moment of union between reader and writer in the one and only common creative act.

Only tangentially related to the literary movements of his time, Cruls's place in modern Brazilian literature has still to be defined and thoroughly evaluated.

BIBLIOGRAPHY: Additional selected works by Cruls: *Coivara*, 1920; *Ao embalo da rede*, 1925; *Helena e Elza*, 1927; *Vertigem*, 1934; *De pai a filho*, 1954. Criticism: Andrade, Ana Luiza. "Uma leitura cúmplice: a função do duplo em 'Meu sósia' de Gastão Cruls." *KRQ* 28 (1981), pp. 417–425.

ANA LUIZA ANDRADE

CRUZ E SOUSA. *See* Sousa, João da Cruz e.

CUNHA, EUCLIDES DA (1866–1909; BAL: 1903). Cunha was orphaned at the age of three upon the death of his mother, Dona Eudóxia. He was of Portuguese and Bahian *sertanejo* ancestry. His father, Manuel Rodrigues Pimenta da Cunha, was an amateur poet and bibliophile, who imbued his son with a love of literature and knowledge. Cunha's early years were spent in the care of relatives in Rio and Bahia, where he received his primary and secondary education. It was at the Colégio Aquino in Rio that he came into contact with republican, abolitionist, and positivist ideas through the teachings of the Brazilian philosopher Benjamin Constant Botelho de Magalhães (1836–1881). In 1884 he enrolled at the Polytechnic School of Rio, where he received training as an engineer. But two years later he transferred to the War College to prepare for a military career. (*See* Positivism and Literature; Slavery and Literature.)

As a result of his strong republican sentiments, however, he openly insulted the minister of war on one occasion and was promptly dismissed from the army. Moving to São Paulo, he turned to journalism, writing a number of newspaper articles against the monarchy and in favor of a socialist society. But he soon returned to Rio to resume his engineering studies. With the proclamation of the republic, Cunha was allowed to rejoin the armed forces and was reinstated in the War College, where he graduated with a degree in mathematics and sciences in 1891. He served for a while as a military field engineer and rose to the rank of first lieutenant. In 1896 he resigned his commission to pursue a career in journalism and engineering. The next year he was sent as a war correspondent by the newspaper *O Estado de São Paulo* to cover the final phase of the army's suppression of the uprising of a religious cult in the backlands of Bahia State. His eyewitness accounts of the violent campaign would later serve as the basis for his masterpiece and a major work of Brazilian culture, *Os sertões* (1902; *Rebellion in the Backlands*, 1944). In 1909 he was shot to death in a duel with the lover of his estranged wife, a story recently narrated in a *memoir written by one of the lover's descendants: Judith Ribeiro de Assis, *Anna: história de um trágico amor* (1987; Anna de Assis: Story of a Tragic Love Affair).

Cunha's literary reputation rests almost exclusively on *Rebellion in the Backlands*. In it he chronicled the Canudos rebellion from its inception to its tragic outcome. The conflict had erupted when the impoverished disciples of a messianic figure, Antônio Maciel, known as "Conselheiro" ("the Counselor"), set up several small religious communities in the Bahia backwoods while awaiting the end of the world. Conselheiro preached a hodge-podge of mysticism and salvation and was said to perform miraculous cures. There were disputes with local ranchers, however, and the religious fanatics declined to pay taxes or respect civil or church authorities. It was alleged, too, that they harbored criminals, practiced free love, and advocated the overthrow of the newly proclaimed republic. A police force was dispatched by the state governor in 1896 to put down the "rebellion," but it sustained a crushing defeat. The federal government in Rio responded by sending two successive expeditionary forces, both of which met with a similar fate. Finally, a fourth expedition was assembled, well equipped with weapons and munitions, and succeeded in laying seige to Canudos, the rebels' last stronghold. The final battle was protracted and bloody; the government troops showed no mercy in taking their long-awaited revenge.

   Rebellion in the Backlands is, however, far more than a mere history of the event. On the one hand, it is also a geographical, geological, botanical, zoological, ethnographical, folkloric, psychological, and sociopolitical treatise of the region and its inhabitants, an attempt to explain the catastrophe from a scientific and quase-mechanistic perspective, in accordance with the ideas of the times. On the other hand, it is definitely a work of literature but displays some of the essential characteristics of several different literary genres without totally conforming to any of them. Like a novel, it presents an imaginative and sometimes fast-paced narration that is both vivid and suspenseful. Like an epic, it is broad in its scope and often heroic in its tone and in the stature it accords the two opposing camps, clearly intended to be a statement about the essence of Brazilian nationality. At times, it waxes poetic. On other occasions, it is essayistic and expository. But whether it assumes the cold, rational approach of a scientist, as it sometimes does, or takes the shape of an impassioned, critical indictment of Brazil's neglect and mistreatment of its less-privileged citizens, of the lack of professionalism of its army, and the incompetence of its press corps and government bureaucracy, the work is at all times marked by sincerity and a spirit of vigorous inquiry. Cunha, whose literary style has been variously characterized as prolix, pompous, convoluted, and *baroque, is always clearly in control of the narration. (*See* Folklore and Literature.)

   The volume is divided into three parts: "The Land," "Man," and "The Battle." It opens with a discussion of the backlands and their ecology and then moves to an examination of the human types that inhabit the area, an analysis of the psychology of the revolt's leader, and, finally, to an account of the roots of and events of the bloody conflict. The author's hypothesis is heavily deterministic. Cunha sees the rebellion as having been a natural, if not also an inevitable, outgrowth of a society flawed environmentally by the rigors of climate and genetically by the "deleterious" effects of racial admixture. (Racism was firmly ensconced even in the scientific thought of the epoch). In short, the region's fluctuation between periods of endemic drought and intervals of heavy flooding and the supposed "racial degeneration" brought about by miscegenation were said to account for the backlandsman's alleged behavioral oscillation between the extremes of impulse and apathy. The backlandsman was a barbarian, and Antônio Conselheiro was merely the personification of his barbarism.

Yet *Rebellion in the Backlands* is not simply a replay of the familiar "civilization versus barbarism" theme of the Argentine writer Domingo Faustino Sarmiento (1811–1888) in his poem of the *gaucho* cowboy Facundo (1845). For all of his elaborate theorizing, Cunha is unable to make all of the facts of the historic event fit neatly into his rigid framework. It is to his credit, then, that rather than attempting to gloss over the jagged edges so that the reality will conform to his ideological convictions, he prefers to remain faithful to the truth and in so doing provides one of the first great critical examinations of Brazilian society. He is quick to realize, for example, that the backlandsman is anything but a biological degenerate. Steeled by the harsh climate and intimately acquainted with the land, he proves himself a formidable opponent for the Brazilian army, although the latter is better equipped and supposedly better educated. Nor is Antônio Conselheiro viewed merely as a fanatic and sociopath. Cunha, while pointing to his shortcomings and decrying the error of his ways, nevertheless treats the charismatic religious leader much in the manner of a tragic hero.

Moreover, it soon becomes glaringly apparent that the backlandsman has no monopoly on barbarous behavior. In the end, it is the forces of "civilization" and "law and order" that Cunha sees as having committed the greater atrocities. Canudos, he believes, is a step backward in Brazilian history, a deplorable stumbling block to the national unity of the young republic, an attack on the very "bedrock of our race."

There are indeed two Brazils, he asserts: one coastal and modern, the other interior and primitive. The latter has been ignored by the former for almost four centuries, as if by denying its existence, by refusing to acknowledge its "blood relationship," a dreadful embarrassment could be avoided. Seeking to "civilize the barbarians" at the point of a sword is, in his opinion, only tantamount to admitting that society has failed in its duty to understand and incorporate the backward element. Canudos represents a nation turned against itself, a form of national suicide, and, at the same time, a cry of protest against what the author perceives as the insanity of this national disgrace. Only by undertaking an intensive educational campaign among the poor and ignorant of the backlands can the Brazilian nation hope to atone for the crime of Canudos, salvaging some good from the monstrous evil that had been wrought.

This influence of *Rebellion in the Backlands* has been both deep and wide. It has been called by some "the Bible of Brazilian nationality," by others one of the finest historical novels ever written in Latin America. The Brazilian *social novelists of the 1930s and later looked to the work as a kind of starting point, an inspiration on which they patterned many of their own harsh portraits of traditional Brazilian society. It is said also to have left its imprint on works of art and literature such as the *cinema novo* films of Gláuber Rocha and others and in the monumental *Grande sertão: veredas* by João Guimarães *Rosa. More recently , its mark may be seen as well outside of Brazil, for example, in the novel *Volverás a Región* (1967; *Return to Region*, 1985) by the Spaniard Juan Benet (b. 1927) and more directly in the Peruvian Mario Vargas Llosa's (b. 1936) so-called Brazilian novel *La guerra del fin del mundo* (1981; *The War of the End of the World*, 1984). (*See* Foreign Writers and Brazil.)

Cunha's importance not only to Brazilian literature but also to the history and evolution of Brazilian national thought, identity, and language cannot be overstated. In her critical comparison of the variations in the first editions of the work, critic Walnice Galvão (*see* Critics and Criticism) detailed Cunha's gradual acknowledgment of a uniquely Brazilian literary language, different from the "chaste" Portuguese of Portugal. Cunha was a scientist but one who was prepared to foresake all restrictive preconceptions and permit his human emotions, conscience, and sense of decency to prevail. He was also a military man but one who argued forcefully against the horrors and absurdity of war. *Rebellion in the Backlands* was seen by many Brazilians as a reflection of their own agonizing quest for national identity, and even today, almost a century later, it is regarded as a classic unequaled in Brazilian and Latin American letters. (*See* Portuguese Language of Brazil.)

BIBLIOGRAPHY: Additional selected works by Cunha: *Os sertões*, 1902 (Critical edition by Walnice Galvão, 1986); *Castro Alves e seu tempo*, 1907; *Contrastes e confrontos*, 1907; *À margem da história*, 1909; *Canudos (Diário duma expedição)*, 1939. Criticism: Amory, Frederic. "Euclides da Cunha as Poet." *LBR* (Winter, 1975), pp. 175–185; idem. "The Making of *Os sertões*." *RF* 68 (1966), pp. 126–141; Brookshaw; Foster/Foster, II; Putnam, Samuel. "Brazil's Greatest Book." *Rebellion in the Backlands*. Chicago: University of Chicago Press, 1944, pp. iii–xviii.

BOBBY J. CHAMBERLAIN

CYCLES. Dealing with a significant sociocultural or economic theme of Brazilian civilization, the origin of literary cycles can be traced to the regionalist movement of the late nineteenth century: Franklin *Távora's *O cabeleira* might be classified as the initial novel of the drought cycle and the backlands bandit (*jagunço*) cycle. The *social novelists of the 1930s and writers of the 1950s picked up these threads. Among the major modern literary cycles are the sugar cycle (Pernambuco), the drought cycle (Ceará), the *sertão* cycle (Bahia, Minas), the cocoa cycle (Bahia), and the gold-mining cycle (Minas). (*See* Regionalism.)

D

DA CUNHA, EUCLIDES. *See* Cunha, Euclides da.

DIAS, ANTÔNIO GONÇALVES (1823–1864). Dias was the illegitimate son of a Portuguese shopkeeper and a *cafusa*, a woman of Indian and African blood. Born while they were fleeing the xenophobic political reprisals that followed the declaration of independence in the northern state of Maranhão, he spent his early childhood alone with his mother on a small farm, surrounded by black slaves from the cotton plantations and detribalized Indians who came to trade in the towns and villages.

Dependent upon the support of his new stepmother and the generosity of his student friends, he was able to study law and modern languages at Coimbra. There he came into contact with the French romantics, in particular, Vicomte Chateaubriand, Alphonse Lamartine, Victor Hugo, and the Portuguese writers Almeida Garrett, António Feliciano de Castilho, and Alexandre Herculano, as well as those writers of the medievalist school of poetry associated with the magazine *O trovador* (The Troubadour). (*See* Portugal and Brazil: Literary Relations; Romanticism.)

Returning penniless to his home in 1845, he passed through a series of legal, teaching, and journalism posts arranged for him by friends in Rio. Stimulated by that cultural milieu with its academic resources, he had his first volume of poetry, *Primeros cantos* (1847: First Songs), published as well as a play, a historical work, and the ethnographical study *Brasil e Oceânia* (1852; Brazil and Oceania), assigned to him by the emperor Dom Pedro II in his capacity as patron of the Brazilian Historical and Geographical Institute.

After an unsuccessful proposal of marriage, which he attributed to a racial snub, Dias embarked on a series of unsatisfactory sexual encounters. Syphilis was added to an increasing list of his ailments, and his personal unhappiness remained unresolved when he did eventually marry. Various diplomatic and academic appointments took him on journeys to Europe and into the Brazilian interior. By the time of his death in a shipwreck, he was, contrary to his own sense of failure, a celebrated literary success both at home and abroad and had made some important contributions to Brazilian ethnography. Today he is regarded as the finest poet of his generation and, according to Manuel *Bandeira, "the Brazilian poet who most profoundly and extensively practiced our language." (In "A póetica de Gonçalves Dias." *Poesia completa e prosa escolhida de Gonçalves Dias*. Rio: 1959, p. 77.)

Dias's birth coincided with one of the manifestations of provincial unrest that had characterized the first twenty-five years of the empire, particularly the Regency period (1831–1840). Prolonged and bloody revolts throughout the nation expressed a violent disappointment at the failure of national independence to resolve the racial and class oppression and the regional inequalities that had been the mark of Portuguese colonial rule. These pressures for liberal reform and political decentralization were contained and to some extent neutralized with the ascension of the "liberal" Dom Pedro II in 1840. Indeed, the Indianist movement, which he enthusiastically patronized, can be seen as part of the process of consolidation of the imperial regime's political unity and cultural identity, which had been so fragile until then. (*See* Indianism.)

This process, the shift toward conservatism, which for many politicians actually involved a change of party loyalty, is nowhere more evident than in the first generation of Brazilian romantics, led by Gonçalves de *Magalhães. On the whole, these were writers whose financial security, ancestral respectability, and prestigious public careers made the transformation from liberal abolitionists to apologists for the imperial status quo an easy one.

Although also clearly present in Dias, that ideological compromise exists in a state of tension that gives his work an intensity not to be found elsewhere in those of his generation, except perhaps Teixeira e *Sousa. These two mestizos shared a similar background of social and racial disadvantage, their consciousness of which must explain the critical, pessimistic overtones that are clearly detectable in their writing. The romantics' massive reappraisal of preindependence history, including colonial relations between whites and Indians, is brought to bear on some of the oppressive contemporary realities upon which the prosperity of the empire depended. Mass black slavery, for example, is addressed along with the marginalization of the Indian in Dias's apocalyptic *Meditação* (1846; Meditation). The social alienation of a rootless, redundant colored and white middle class living under the feudal economy of nineteenth-century Brazil meanwhile lies at the heart of his poetry.

To this thematic core, Dias brought the literary training he had received in Portugal, in particular a neoclassical economy of style and expression that, nevertheless, did not prevent him from experimenting to great dramatic effect with rhythm-based meters in the Indianist poetry. In addition, his association with the European medievalists bore fruit in the form of the *Sextilhas de Frei Antão* (1848; Friar Antão's Sextains) and the theatrical works (e.g., the historical drama *Leonor de Mendonça* [1847; Leonor de Mendonça]), as well as determining the character of his Indian heroes. Although certainly overestimated, the role of the tribal warrior as a substitute for the medieval chivalresque knight in the search for traditional, nationalist values is nevertheless very real.

A number of his "Poesias americanas" (American Poems) and sections of his *Primeiros cantos* (First Songs) and *Ultimos cantos* (1851; Last Songs), such as "O canto do Piaga" (Song of the Piaga) and "Deprecação" (Prayer), convey the psychological impact and trauma of conquest on the country's Indian population. But if compared with the overtly historical poems (e.g., "À desordem de Caxias" [To the Disorder at Caxias], dealing with an event of the Balaiada), it becomes clear that they emerge from the same apocalyptic vision of socio-political conflict and disintegration. Both history and the Indians' eternal round of ritual war and reprisal are cyclical rather than progressive, subject to the cataclysmic punishment of a wrathful god.

Similarly, parallels can be drawn between the more obviously autobiographical love poetry and Indianist poems such as "Leito de folhas verdes" (Bed of Green Leaves) and "Marabà" (name for an Indian and white cross-breed), whose subject is the irremediable sexual frustration caused by separation and racial prejudice, respectively. Indeed, if the militarist ethic of Dias's Indianist poetry can be seen as a sublimation of the sexual impulse, it is also expressive of a tragic view of existence, the Tamoyo Indian's warning to his new-born son that "life is a struggle which brings down the weak and exalts the strong." (Canção do tamoio" [Song of the Tamoyo Indian] in *Poesia completa e prosa escolhida de Gonçalves Dias*, p. 372).

On the other hand, the Indianist poetry also represents an imaginative attempt to recover the absent or lost harmony of the two worlds that concern Dias: imperial and pre-Colombian Brazil. Rousseau considered the Venezuelan Caribs as an ideal intermediate stage in man's development, a perfect condition of physical and spiritual harmony. Many of Dias's poems evoke a similar world, in which, for all its wars and even because of them and their ritual of cannibalistic assimilation, the total integration of the individual within the community enjoys a perfect harmony.

Dias was responsible for "popularizing" literary Indianism within the restricted readership of the nineteenth century. The unprecedented sales and reeditions of his poetry during his own lifetime, as well as his success abroad, are proof of that. His "Canção de exílio" (Song of Exile), meanwhile, remains one of the best-known and most often parodied poems of Brazilian literature, the national anthem of exile and *saudade*.

But as his dedication to ethnography (including a Tupi-Portuguese dictionary, 1858) and historical research confirm, the originality and significance of his work extends beyond the exotically picturesque and patriotic. They lie in an appreciation of the fundamental gulf between Western civilization and that "other" society that it has nearly destroyed. Regardless of the documentary authenticity of the ideal world he created, it is that understanding which enabled him to convey life in his own society as an experience of alienation and marginalization.

BIBLIOGRAPHY: Additional selected works by Dias: *Os timbiras*, 1857; *Obras pós-*

tumas, 1868–1869. Translations: Hulet; Woodbridge. Criticism: Ackerman, Fritz. *A obra poética de Antônio Gonçalves Dias*. Translated by Egon Schaden. São Paulo: Conselho Estadual de Cultura, 1964; Haberly; Ricardo, Cassiano. In Coutinho, II; Sayers.

DAVID H. TREECE

DIAS GOMES. *See* Gomes, Alfredo Dias.

DICTATORSHIP AND LITERATURE (1964–1985). The 1964–1985 military dictatorship sharply conditioned cultural life in Brazil. The initial period, 1964–1968, presented relatively few problems of censorship or restrictions; in fact, it was a period of mild repression even known as the golden age of Brazilian popular protest culture. Movements such as *cinema novo*, protest and political music, and protest theater dominated the cultural production in opposition to the military regime. The outstanding authors of political literature of this moment were the novelists Antônio *Callado (*Quarup*), Érico *Veríssimo (*O prisioneiro*), and Carlos Heitor *Cony (*Pessach: a travessia*); the poets such as Ferreira *Gullar and Thiago de *Melo; and the dramatists such as Plínio *Marcos and Oduvaldo *Viana Filho. Of note also are the works of José Agrippino de Paula (e.g. *Lugar público* [1965; *Public Place*], a film/novel of the Brazilian reality; and *Pan-América* [1967; PanAmerica]). (*See* Film and Literature; Music and Literature; Theater History; *Tropicalismo*.)

In 1968 the Institutional Act Number 5, known as the "coup within the coup," implemented a total restriction on all civil rights and on the use of public spaces and imposed severe censorship on the press and other published material. Many writers, artists, intellectuals, and academics were exiled or arrested (e.g., Ferreira Gullar, Antônio Callado, Augusto *Boal), resulting in a cultural vacuum. Literature assumed an important role as an artistic response to repression. Given the limited public for literature in Brazil and the "private" nature of literary communication, the government had little to fear regarding literature's power to act as a political mobilizing force. Therefore, literature—with the exception of the theater—was allowed a larger degree of autonomy than the other communicative arts. Nonetheless, because of its metaphorical and allegorical possibilities, literature could manage to express protest and suggest analyses of political conditions in indirect ways. For these reasons, during the 1968–1978 period of censorship, literature was the medium that best encapsulated and registered resistance to the policies of dictatorship. A few books were censored—among them, *Zero* by Ignácio de Loyola *Brandão and *Em câmara lenta* (1977; In Slow Motion), a fictional description of torture by Renato Tapajós—for being politically subversive; *Feliz ano novo* by Rubem *Fonseca—considered pornography; and *A rebelião dos mortos* by Luiz Fernando *Emediato.

Prose fiction of 1968–1978 presented four marked trends:

1. *Testimonial literature.* Testimonies of the sociopolitical violence of the historical present used a strategy of structural fragmentation of narrative, for example, Antônio Callado's *Bar Don Juan* and *Reflexos do baile*, and /or fictional

allusions to specific realities for example, Érico Veríssimo's *Incidente em An-tares*, Oswaldo *França Jr.'s *Um dia no Rio*, and Rodolfo Konder's (b. 1939) *Cadeia para os mortos* (1977; Jail for the Dead) and *Tempo de ameaça* (1978; Threatening Times).

2. *Autobiographical narratives*. The repression of channels of expression resulted in a surge in *memoirs and autobiographies, both real and fictional. Whether or not this reflects the author's intention, their popularity attests to the reading public's need to reconstitute a more collective memory through the telling of personal experiences. For example the first volumes of Pedro *Nava's memoirs, *Balão cativo* and *Baú de ossos*, appeared during these years. Important fictional autobiographies of that moment included: Antônio Carlos Villaça's (b. 1928) *O nariz do morto* (1970; The Dead Man's Nose) and Abel Silva's (b. 1943) *O afogado* (1971; The Drowned One), as well as his collection of short stories, *Açogue das almas* (1973; Slaughterhouse of Souls). (*See* Autobiography).

3. *True-life portraits of the marginalized elements of society*. Outlaws, crim-inals, and society's outcasts became central characters of fiction. They appeared in an analogic manner to signify the marginality or "outlawed" character of Brazilian society, which had no rights within the law, for example, João *An-tônio's *Leão de chácara*, *Casa de loucos*, and *Calvário e porres do pingente Afonso Henriques de Lima Barreto*.

4. *Romances-reportagens, journalistic novels*. Due to press censorship and the ensuing hunger for facts and information, former reporters worked out a nonfiction fictional form to discuss recent events or facts that could not be fully told in the newspapers. These books (among them best- sellers) dealt with crimes or abuses emphasizing the violence of the penal system or the arbitrariousness of the police and were "read" as important denunciations of the brutality of political repression and torture, for example, José *Louzeiro's *Lúcio Flávio*, Parcifal de Souza's (b. 1943) *A prisão*, Almeida Filho's (b. 1946) *A sangue quente*, Carlos Heitor Cony's *O caso Lou*, or works by Aguinaldo *Silva.

These four narrative trends constituted recognizable subcategories of the Bra-zilian novel of resistance. Many other important works were characterized by a formal attention to narrative style: allegorical procedures and strategies were produced, among them Sérgio *Sant'Anna's *Memórias de Ralfo* and *Romance de geração*, Ivan *Ângelo's *A festa*, Roberto *Drummond's *A morte de D. J. em Paris*, Antônio *Torres's *Um cão univando para a lua*, Moacir *Scliar's *Mês de cães danados*, Raduan *Nassar's *Lavoura arcáica*, Carlos Sussekind's *Armadilha para Lamartine* (1976; Booby Trap for Lamartine), Gramiro de Ma-tos's *Os môrcegos estão comendo os mamões maduros* (1973; The Bats are Eating the Ripe Papayas), and some short stories by Lygia Fagundes *Telles and Ary Quintella (b. 1933). Along these lines, books by authors such as Rubem Fonseca and Renato Pompeu that thematically involved apparently gratuitous acts of violence, and by José J. *Veiga, who presented fantastic and absurd situations, were interpreted as directly referring to the political reality.

Others' uses of allegory are found in the new short stories, in which the descriptions of life and problems of women and sexual minorities presented the sense of exclusion from the legal process and civil rights to which the population as a whole was subjected under the dictatorship. Authors from this group of writers—Caio Fernando *Abreu, Domingos *Pellegrini Jr., Júlio César Monteiro *Martins, and Jeferson Ribeiro de Andrade (b. 1947), author of *Um homem bebe cerveja no bar do Odilon* (1978; A Man's Drinking Beer in Odilon's Bar), among others—were published in a landmark collection called *Histórias de um novo tempo* (1977; Stories about New Time). Works by women writers such as Lygia Fagundes *Telles and Nélida *Piñon also appeared.

By 1975 critics talked about a very welcome boom in novels, poems, and short stories consolidating the market and strengthening the editorial infrastructure of the publishing houses. Parallel to this mainstream editorial boom in prose fiction, there was an outburst of poetry by young writers, which came to be known as "marginal" poetry. This was one of the most important trends of the literature of resistance, since it also dealt largely with the feelings of exclusion, alienation, and helplessness fostered under the regime. The novelty of this poetry is its amazing creativity in the independent and home production of books, the creation of cooperatives, and the formation of writers' groups to promote their activities. The principal result of this new poetry, besides its power to mobilize and create a new public for poetry, was the way it represented the limitations of the generation that grew up under the fear and strictures imposed by the military regime. Known as the "poetry of suffocation," it succeeded in presenting the political dimensions of day-to-day events but doing so in a language characterized by humor and parody. Groups were formed in the second half of the 1970s throughout the country, and many of the poets are still productive today. The anthology *26 poetas hoje* (1976; *26 Poets Today*) brought these poets to the attention of a broader public, and some of them, such as Francisco Alvim, Antônio Carlos de Brito, Ana Cristina César, and Chacal, who recorded the repressive activities of the regime in their poems, were later published by important editorial houses. (*See* New Writers.)

This period comes to an end in December 1978 with the *abertura*, the political opening and the end of censorship, the declaration of a political amnesty, and the reorganization of national political parties. With the end of direct repression, there emerged a wave of biographical political memoirs written principally by exiles and former political prisoners. Most typical are Fernando *Gabeira's *O que é isso, companheiro?* (1980; What's This, Pal?), which has gone through more than twenty printings, and Alfredo Sirkis's (b. 1951) *Os carbonários* (1980; *The Carbonari). (*See* Biography; New Writers.)

BIBLIOGRAPHY: Criticism: Fernández, Oscar. "Censorship and the Brazilian Theater." *Educational Theater Journal* (October, 1973), pp. 285–298; *Index on Censorship* (London) (Issued dedicated to Brazil). (July/August, 1979); Miccolis, Leila. *Do poder ao poder*. Rio, 1987; Michalski, Jan. "Brazilian *Bizarreiros." Censorship* 2 (1966), pp.

25–29; Monegal, Emir Rodríguez. "Writing Fiction under the Censor's Eye." *WLT* (Winter, 1979), pp. 19–22; Severino, Alexandrino. In Roett; Sussekind, Flora. *Literatura e vida literária*. Rio: Zahar, 1985; Thomas, Earl W. In Roett.

HELOÍSA BUARQUE DE HOLLANDA

DINAH. *See* Queiroz, Dinah Silveira de.

DOURADO, AUTRAN (b. 1926). Dourado spent his early years in his native Minas, where he studied law. He was a member of the postmodernist group that published the *review *Edifício* (1947). Upon moving to Rio, he served as press secretary during Juscelino Kubitschek's presidency (1956–1961). His literary output includes novels, novelettes, and short stories, but he had a marked preference for the longer narrative; he also has written on the theory of fiction. (*See* Postmodernism in Poetry.)

Dourado's works are psychological and intimist, with a gothic bent enhanced by *mineiro* *regionalism. His admiration for the *baroque style is more than passing. *A barca dos homens* (1961; The Ship of Men), considered his finest novel to date, displays a combination of structural flexibility, rotating viewpoints, deep-set symbolism, and ambiguity—all hallmarks of Dourado's hermetic world, often situated geographically in his fictional town of Duas Pontes.

Interest in technical aspects of narration was evidenced in his first stories, *Nove histórias em tres grupos* (1957; Nine Stories in Three Groups), and in his novel *O risco do bordado* (1970; *Pattern for a Tapestry*, 1984). In this novel, similar to the Argentine Julio Cortázar's *Hopscotch*, Dourado broke the tale(s) into six related yet independent sections and suggested to the reader that they can be read straight through or that another order may be used to discover the "pattern for the tapestry" of João de Nogueira's initiation into manhood. Dourado has explained his approach to the organization of this novel in the volume *Uma poética do romance* (1976; A Poetics of the Novel).

Most at home with flow of consciousness, the author is apt to plunge his brooding, marginalized personnae—their names so often flagrantly symbolic—into decisive situations. Noteworthy in this respect are Dourado's "political novels," *Os sinos da agonia* (1974; The Bells of Agony) and the recent *A serviço del-Rei* (1984; In his Majesty's Service), as well as his *Ópera dos mortos* (1967; The Voices of the Dead, 1981).

BIBLIOGRAPHY: Additional selected works by Dourado: *Teia*, 1947; *Sombra e exílio*, 1950; *Uma vida em segredo*, (1964; *A Hidden Life*, 1969); *As imaginações pecaminosas*, 1981. Criticism: Patai; Pollock-Chagas, Jeremy E. "Rosalina and Amélia: A Structural Approach to Narrative." *LBR* (Winter, 1975), pp. 263–272; Pollitt, Katha. "*The Voices of the Dead.*" *NYTBR* (January 24, 1982), p. 13; Silverman, Malcolm. "Autran Dourado and the Introspective-Regionalist Novel." *RLV* 6 (1976), pp. 609–619.

MALCOLM SILVERMAN

DRUMMOND, ROBERTO (b. 1937). A noted sports journalist from Minas, Drummond's literary world was initially dominated by kitsch and pop culture—from Coca-Cola to Lifebuoy soap—one in which psychedelic dreams crisscross with reality in the make-believe land known as Brazil during the years of dictatorship. (*See* Dictatorship and Literature.)

Drummond's fiction falls within *tropicalismo's* search for a contemporary Brazilian identity and, consequently, evidences a debt to Oswald de *Andrade. Eternal carnival as a reality of Brazilian existence under the military dictatorship is the theme of his "psychedelic" novel *Sangue de Coca-cola* (1981; Blood of Coca-Cola), whereas the stories of *Quando eu fui morto em Cuba* (1982; When I Was Killed in Cuba) view the tortures, exiles, and persecutions of the 1970s. An even more tragically realistic side of his fiction is revealed in his *prize-winning short stories of people in no-escape situations, *A morte de D. J. em Paris* (1975; D. J.'s Death in Paris), as well as in his recent *Hitler manda lembranças* (1984; Hitler Sends Regards), in which the events of the Holocaust take on new significance in contemporary Minas.

BIBLIOGRAPHY: Additional selected works by Drummond: *O dia em que Ernest Hemingway morreu crucificado*, 1978.

DRUMMOND DE ANDRADE. *See* Andrade, Carlos Drummond de.

DUQUE, LUÍS GONZAGA (1863–1911). A passionate symbolist, Gonzaga Duque was Brazil's pioneer art critic. (See Art and Literature; Symbolism.)

Stylistically, his one novel *Mocidade morta* (1899; Dead Youth) is similar to his essays on art: replete with neologisms and archaisms, images and metaphors. Considered one of the prose masterpieces of Brazilian symbolism, Duque narrated—between tangential analyses of art works—the lives of artists during Rio's *belle-époque*. Teléforo de Andrade, one of Duque's bohemian artists, is a decadentist, a victim of the *mal du siècle*, and deals cynically with his own life and in his contacts with his clients—usually aristocracy and rich bourgeoisie.

A collection of stories in a similar vein, *Horto da mágoa* (1914; Site of Sorrow) was published posthumously.

BIBLIOGRAPHY: Additional selected works by Duque: *Arte brasileira*, 1887; *Contemporâneos*, 1929.

DURÃO, FRIAR JOSÉ DE SANTA RITA (1722–1784). Born in Brazil, Durão left it as a child and never returned. Growing up in Portugal, he entered the Augustinian order, received a doctorate in theology, and taught at Coimbra. Religious politics forced him into exile, primarily in Italy, from 1761 until, it is believed, 1777. In 1778 he returned to Coimbra. There, in 1781 he completed his single surviving literary work, *Caramuru*, a ten-canto epic poem in *ottava rima*. He wrote other works but destroyed them before he died.

Retrogressively modeled on *Os Lusíadas* of Luís de Camões (1524–1580) in intent as well as form, *Caramuru* purported to exalt Portuguese achievements in Brazil as Camões had exalted them in India and Asia. Thus whereas Camões had constructed his narrative around Vasco da Gama's adventurous voyage, Durão built his around Diogo Álvares Correia's discovery of Bahia (1510) and his adventures under his Indian name, Caramuru. (*See* Portugal and Brazil: Literary Relations.)

Unlike Basílio da *Gama, earlier in the century he rejected the ideological rationalism of the Enlightenment. (*See* Arcadias.) Instead, like Camões, he espoused the ideal of a Christian empire in which the Portuguese glorified God through the civilizing effect of their conquests. Nevertheless, his acceptance of eighteenth-century natural law and the savage's innate nobility is evident.

One line of Brazilian criticism has found him merely a prolix versifier of historical prose. His unusually accurate and often fluent descriptions of Brazilian nature, however, earn him a significant place among contributors to the theme of *ufanismo*. His remarkably authentic descriptions of native life, customs, and temperament simultaneously make him a major precursor of *Indianism, most notably as a precursor to Gonçalves *Dias's important Indianist work "I-Juca-Pirama" (1851). (*See* Historiography.)

BIBLIOGRAPHY: Additional selected works by Durão: *Caramuru: poema épico do descubrimento do Brasil* (1781; modern edition, 1957). Criticism: Cândido, Antônio. *Formação da literatura brasileira: momentos decisivos.* 2d ed. São Paulo: Livraria Martins Editora, 1964, I: 183–193; Driver; Hulet, Claude L. "The Noble Savage in *Caramuru.*" *Homage to Irving A. Leonard.* Michigan: Michigan State University, 1977, pp. 123–130.

                                                        NORWOOD ANDREWS, JR.

E

EÇA, MATIAS AIRES DE. *See* Aires, Matias.

ELIODORA, BÁRBARA (1759–1819). Little definitive information exists about Eliodora, who was married to Alvarenga *Peixoto and became known as the "Heroine of the *Mineiran Conspiracy." According to some critics, Peixoto's exile and death led her to madness. Still other critics believe that she aided him in writing or even wrote his poetry.

Only one of Eliodora's poems survives: "Conselho aos meus filhos" (Advice to my Children), probably written after her husband's exile. In it she advises the children "not to fool around with God nor the King: serve and obey."

Her beauty was renowned. Not only was she the subject of verse by her husband, but she was also admired in a poem by the Portuguese judge of the conspirators, the arcadian poet Cruz e Silva (1731–1799). (*See* Arcadias; Portugal and Brazil: Literary Relations.)

BIBLIOGRAPHY: Criticism: Leite, Aureliano. "A vida heróica de Bárbara Eliodora." *RCB* (September, 1960), pp. 301–308.

ÉLIS, BERNARDO [BERNARDO ELIS FLEURY DE CAMPOS CURADO] (b. 1915; BAL: 1975). A lawyer, Elis was cofounder of the Center for Brazilian Studies at the Federal University of Goiás and has been professor of Brazilian literature at both the Federal and Catholic universities of Goiás.

Élis has been credited with resuming the regionalist *cycle of the so-called center-west *sertão* during the 1940s, following in the tradition of Bernardo *Guimarães and Afonso *Arinos, as well as preparing the way for contemporaries such as Guimarães *Rosa, Mário *Palmério, and José J. *Veiga. The region that Élis writes about is the *gerais* and *cerrados*, the semiarid upland plains of Goiás and Minas states, which is characterized by a semifeudal economy based on cattle, by the violent struggle for power, and by the exploitation of the landless poor by powerful landowners. (*See* Regionalism.)

His collection of stories *Ermos e gerais* (1944; types of land in Goiás) was lauded by both Monteiro *Lobato and Mário de *Andrade. In the story "A mulher que comeu o amante" (The Woman Who Ate Her Lover), Élis narrated a brutal murder in a shockingly matter-of-fact style. The action seems both acceptable and normal within the perspective of the barren backdrop. Élis's other stories and his major novel *O trono* (1956; *The Trunk)* present a somber mood and an attraction to the grotesque. His style, notable for its expressiveness and originality, incorporates oral phraseology and regional dialect.

BIBLIOGRAPHY: Additional selected works by Élis: *Caminhos e descaminhos*, 1965; *Apenas um violão*, 1984.

LUIZ FERNANDO VALENTE

EMEDIATO, LUIZ FERNANDO (b. 1951). From Minas, Emediato was awarded the Esso Prize and the King of Spain International Prize for his coverage of warfare in Central America. (*See* Prizes.) He began his literary career by winning the Paraná State Short Story Prize.

The title story of his collection *Não passarás o Jordão* (1977; You Will Not Pass the Jordan) recounts the gravest moments of oppression and torture during the years of the military dictatorship, specifically the death of the journalist Wladimir Herzog while in police custody. Like Monteiro *Martins, Domingos *Pellegrini Jr., and Jeferson Ribeiro de Andrade, who were also included in the important collection *Histórias de um novo tempo* (1977; Stories for a New Time), Emediato focused on the situation of his own generation, which grew to adulthood during the years of dictatorship. After innocently supporting the regime for patriotic motives, this generation later called the reality and the "truth" of Brazilian life into question. (*See* Dictatorship and Literature.)

These themes are developed in the stories of *Rebelião dos mortos* (1978; Rebellion of the Dead) and *Geração abandonada* (1979; Abandoned Generation). The story "Verdes anos" (Youthful Years), a bittersweet tale of Brazilian adolescents confronting sex, drugs, and political confusion during the time of the regime, was made into a popular film. (*See* Film and Literature.)

BIBLIOGRAPHY: Additional selected works by Emediato: *Os lábios úmidos de Marilyn Monroe*, 1977.

ENEIDA [ENEIDA DE MORAIS] (1903–1971). Educated in Rio and her native city of Belém, Pará State, Eneida was associated with the Pará modernist group, known as Flaminaçu. She published a volume of modernist verse, *Terra verde* (1929; Green Land), whose twenty six poems are in praise of the Amazonian traditions of Pará. In Rio in 1930 she became acquainted with modernists of São Paulo and Rio. (*See* Modernism.)

Employment difficulties forced her to travel to São Paulo, where she became involved in the activities of the Brazilian Communist party, writing speeches and newspaper columns in support of workers' rights. Jailed briefly for these activities by the Vargas regime, between 1936 and 1937, she again returned to jail, where she met Graciliano *Ramos, who published her first story. She was repeatedly jailed during the next decade. In later years, Eneida became a defender of women's and writers' rights; traveled to the Soviet Union, Eastern Europe, and China; and had her impressions published in *Os caminhos da terra* (1959; The Earth's Road). (*See* Feminism and Literature.)

Eneida had several collections of *crônicas published, for example, *Cão da madrugada* (1954; Dawn's Dog), in which she describes her childhood in Belém and her residence in Paris, and *Aruanda* (1957; *Aruanda*), which has a similar theme. Her story "Clocló entre oceanos, mares e rios" (Clocló between the Oceans, Seas, and Rivers) in *Alguns personagens* (1954; Some Characters) is a poignant narration of her close relationship with her maid. Eneida also wrote *children's literature and a study of Rio's carnival.

BIBLIOGRAPHY: Additional selected works by Eneida: *História do carnaval carioca*, 1958.

ENLIGHTENMENT. *See* Arcadias.

F

FAGUNDES TELLES, LYGIA. *See* Telles, Lygia Fagundes.

FAGUNDES VARELA. *See* Varela, Luís Nicolau Fagundes.

FAILLACE, TÂNIA JAMARDO (b. 1939). A novelist and short fiction writer from Rio Grande do Sul, Faillace's literary world focuses on members of the lower middle class of Porto Alegre, who attempt to discover some meaning in their existence. (*See* City and Literature.)

Fuga (1964; *Flight*) views, in a poetic fashion, an adolescent girl's inability to cope with changes taking place in and around her. Faillace's collections of short fiction, which include *O 35° ano de Inês* (1971; Ines's 35th Year) and *Tradição, família, e outras estórias* (1978; Tradition, Family, and Other Stories), reveal an intense interest in the psychology of her characters, who exist in a society in great social and moral transition. In "O menor" (The Minor), from the latter collection, a youngster's personal and societal plight repeatedly lands him in jail. His interrogation, in dialogue form, employing the very colloquial language often used by Faillace, reveals how much traditional life has been shaken by Brazil's contemporary reality. (*See* Dictatorship and Literature; Feminism and Literature.)

Faillace's 1983 novel *Mário/Vera* (Mario/Vera) has autobiographical overtones: her relationship with a married man set against the sociopolitical dilemma of Brazil between 1962 and 1964. (*See* Autobiography.)

BIBLIOGRAPHY: Additional selected works by Faillace: *Adão e Eva*, 1965; *Vende a mim os pequenos*, 1977.

FARIA, OTÁVIO DE (1908–1984; BAL: 1972). Faria belongs to an important traditional Brazilian family. In 1931 he attained a law degree in his native Rio, and he began writing sociopolitical essays that adhered to the Catholic, conservative, authoritarian orientation of Plínio *Salgado's integralist politics and antisocialist fervor, for example, *Maquiavel e o Brasil* (1934; Maquiavelli and

Brazil). Among the important conservative influences on his writings were his relative Alceu Amoroso *Lima and European Catholic philosophers-novelists, including León Bloy, Georges Bernanos, and Graham Greene. (*See* Foreign Writers and Brazil; Religion and Literature.)

Although he published film criticism, his cycle of novels called the *Tragédia burguesa* (Bourgeois Tragedy) is his prime claim to literary fame. Begun in 1937 with *Mundos mortos* (Dead Worlds), the cycle, set against the events of Rio life of the 1930s, follows several characters from adolescence to adulthood. Each is representative of an ethical-moral attitude: Branco is a reverent man striving against evil, synonymous with the character Pedro Borges and the bourgeois values he represents. Branco and other "good" characters of the cycle are morally supported by Father Luís, who instills in them belief in and reliance on God. (*See* City and Literature; Film and Literature.)

Faria focuses on the psychological ramifications of his characters' behaviors, similar to his contemporaries Lúcio *Cardoso and Cornélio *Pena. Ultimately, he aims to show that society's decadence, frustration, and amorality are inevitable results of bourgeois pursuits. Regrettably, Faria's style is plodding, and his rhetoric is often tangential.

BIBLIOGRAPHY: Additional selected works by Faria: *Caminhos da vida*, 1939; *Os loucos*, 1952; *O retrato da morte*, 1961; *O cavaleiro da viagem*, 1971. Criticism: Montenegro, Olívio. *O romance brasileiro*. Rio: 1953.

FAUSTINO, MÁRIO [MÁRIO FAUSTINO DOS SANTOS E SILVA] (1930–1962). A native of Piauí State, Faustino was educated in Belém and began to write *crônicas* when he was sixteen. He was a professor of business, a diplomat, and a literary columnist for the *Jornal do Brasil*. He died in an airplane crash while on assignment for the newspaper.

Faustino had only one collection of poetry published, *O homem e sua hora* (1955; Man and His Time), in which he developed new poetic views based on traditional forms and themes. In doing so, he revealed a deep appreciation for the classics of Portuguese literature, including Luís de Camões and Fernando Pessoa, through the use of their poetry as a symbolic basis for his own. His unfinished post–1955 poetry reflects a personal interpretation of concretism. (*See* Portugal and Brazil: Literary Relations; Postmodernism in Poetry.)

This attitude toward poetry was developed in his "Poesia-Experiência" (Poetry-Experiment) column, which was published in the *Jornal do Brasil* between 1956 and 1958. These articles, along with several important studies of contemporary Brazilian and foreign poets, made Faustino an important critical voice. (*See* Critics and Criticism.)

BIBLIOGRAPHY: Additional selected works by Faustino: *Poesia de Mário Faustino*, 1966. Translations: Brasil/Smith, Woodbridge. Criticism: Nunes, Benedito, "Introdução." *Poesia de Mário Faustino*. Rio: Civilização Brasileira, 1966, pp. 3–35.

FEMINISM AND LITERATURE. Literature by women about women's lives and other themes has been produced since the colonial era, for example, Teresa Margarida da Silva e *Orta and Bárbara *Eliodora. In the midnineteenth century Maria Firmino dos Reis wrote one of the earliest Brazilian novels, *Ursula* (1855; Ursula), which despite its overly romantic plot introduced the problem of slavery. The poet Auta de Souza (1876–1901), included among the symbolists, wrote poems with a strong religious fervor. Other women writers such as Narcisa *Amália, Francisca *Júlia, and Carmen Dolores (*see* Naturalism) were enormously popular at the end of the nineteenth century but are almost totally forgotten today. However, within the past ten years, women's literature has become a strong force on the Brazilian cultural scene. Therefore, the effort to recover texts, the analysis of works produced by women who were feminists *avant-la-lettre*, is receiving serious critical consideration, for example, Gilka *Machado and Elisa Lispector. (*See* Slavery and Literature; Symbolism.)

The number and diversity of contemporary Brazilian women writers testifies to the vitality of this body of work, which appears to be more of an active process of exploration rather than a coherent literary progression within a historical tradition and development. For example, Clarice *Lispector, a giant in modern Brazilian literature, declared that she is a writer who happens to be a woman and that the accident of her gender does not influence the subject matter she treats or the forms she uses. A similar attitude was expressed by Nélida *Piñon.

Although one has a sense of common theme in the works of Rachel de *Queiroz, Clarice Lispector, Lygia Fagundes *Telles, Nélida Piñon, and Ana Maria Machado, they use various techniques in addressing the problems that women and writers face in Brazil. Although their works are included within a wide time span—the 1930s to the 1980s—two major approaches with different emphasis in the process of exploration of the feminine condition can be observed. One approach deals with oppression, focusing on the external restrictions, and the other approach is concerned with repression, that is, what has been repressed and the need to create a language capable of expressing their imaginary world. The search for a new language is most significant not as a style or in its syntax or grammar but in the investigation of a symbolic female system—a female mytho-poetics.

Oppression.   Rachel de Queiroz's *As tres Marias* provides a panorama of the Northeast of Brazil with three main characters and a number of secondary ones who live in a traditional patriarchical society. Of utmost importance in this novel is the problem of space, the social division between the public and the private in which women are relegated to the domestic sphere. The woman who chooses to abandon the "cloister" of Catholic social norms risks the loss of social acceptance as well as her own women friends.

Maria Alice *Barroso's *A história de um casamento* uses various narrators to relate their points of view about the central female character who does not have a name, only initials: M. A. Esther, an artist, loves her beauty; her father wants to mold her in the image of a mother and nurturer; Roberto, the bridegroom, sees her as a temptress and an angel, to be conquered and possessed by himself. M. A., however, has no voice. She is entirely invisible throughout the novel except when perceived and defined by others. Therefore, she is not only speechless but also nameless, a vessel to diverse ideologies that disregard her own self.

Lygia Fagundes Telles's *As meninas* is almost like a modern version of *As tres Marias* adapted to a recent setting: Brazil during the military dictatorship begun in 1964. The author carefully presented the issue of class as it corresponds to the situation of women. Ana Clara, a girl from the proletariat, represents the unsatisfied, immature youth who floats from one drug experience to the next and uses sexual freedom in a destructive manner. Lia, from the solid middle class, is politically active, a revolutionary trying to keep her dreams of a revolution alive. Lorena is the virginal rich girl, descendant of an aristocratic family troubled by personal problems. Although these women are living together, they are unable to learn from one another, much less act together in any concerted effort except for an afternoon tea. Like the female characters in *As tres Marias*, the women in *As meninas* are closed in the "convent"—a metaphor of their own closed lives. (*See* Dictatorship and Literature.)

Repression. The three novels above present the oppression felt by the women, and *As meninas* also shows women facing new challenges that require changes and new solutions outside prevalent normative thinking of Western philosophy, as well as its masculine order.

The novel *A casa da paixão* by Nélida Piñon is an ethical and aesthetic meditation about the major postulates of logocentrism. The author alludes to the tradition of a Christian framework that reduces sexuality to its reproductive function, to its heterosexual form, and to its legitimacy only in marriage. With her poetic prose, she recovers the body and the sensitive side of desire, which has been excluded from logical thought. Marta, the protagonist, is like a chameleon, a central metaphor to the changes—both physical and emotional—associated with her rite of passage from adolescence to womanhood. This process involves coming to terms with her body, appropriating her "house of passion," but also leaving the patriarchal home.

Clarice Lispector's first novel is *Perto do coração selvagem*, a title taken from Joyce and somewhat prophetic of her unrelenting search to be "close to the wild heart" of things. The prevalence of certain themes in her works could place her affiliation within existentialist-phenomenological philosophical currents. Her themes are the solitude and anguish of life, as well as the impossibility of communicating our despair to other humans. Lispector's style does not attempt to depict a material, tangible reality but a more fascinating ontological and emotional reality, closer to the essence of life that has been lost to modern man. She also uses irony to expose oppressive systems or traditions of thought in Western society, the futility of mental constructs that predetermine or obstruct the reality of what is seen. Therefore, Lispector touches on many issues and ideas that have concerned feminist authors. Furthermore, she creates a female voice that articulates her perception of the world within a literary tradition that has been dominated by males.

Ana Maria Machado's *Alice e Ulisses* (1983; Alice and Ulysses) reverses the roles that history and literature have traditionally ascribed these characters. Ulisses is a film director and Alice a film critic. He is in the traditional role of "story telling"; however, she is the one capable of critical thought. She is "curious" Alice in action, demanding answers, moving in the outside world. Ulisses becomes sentimental and incapable of moving beyond their domestic space. The reversal in these traditional roles is developed on many levels in the text: action, language, and characterization. The story is presented with humor, and it tries to reinterpret the myths of prototypical male or female and to create new models of behavior and response for them in literature.

Many other women writers use a true feminist voice to debate both personal and societal issues: for example, Edla van *Steen; Adélia *Prado; Tânia *Faillace; Lya *Luft; Leilah *Assunção; Marina *Colasanti; Sônia *Coutinho; Patrícia Bins, author of "Trilogy of Solitude," which includes the novels *Jogo de fiar* (1983; Trusting Game) and *Janela do sonho* (1986; Window of Dreams); Marilene Felinto (b. 1957), author of *As mulheres de Tijucopapo* (1982; The Women from Tijucopapo), about the lives of poor women and their children; Heloneida Studart (b. 1932), a pioneer in feminist writing in Brazil, for example, the essay *A mulher, brinquedo do homem* (1969; Woman, Man's Plaything) and the novel, *O pardal e um pássaro azul* (1975; The Sparrow and Blue Bird); Helena Parente Cunha's *A mulher no espelho* (1984; The Woman in the Mirror); as well as *new writers, for example, Márcia Denser (*See* New Writers.); Ledusha; Bruna Lombardi, author of a collection of erotic poetry, *O perigo do dragão* (1984; The Danger of the Dragon); Myriam Campello; Joyce Cavalcante, who has had published the feminist novel, *Costela de Eva* (1980; Eve's Rib) and the collection of stories *O discurso da mulher absurda* (1985; Discourse of the Absurd Woman). (*See* Memoirs.)

The dominant images present in the works of these women writers are the conquest and definition of freedom of movement, from the confinement of domestic spaces and objects (pianos, boxes, furniture) and rooms of madness, all metaphors of women's silent voice, to new places. Although these authors present a diverse range of fictional techniques and approaches, they are unified by the fact that they are all exploring the experiences of women in society and as writers.

BIBLIOGRAPHY: Criticism: Collins, Gina Michelle. "Translating Feminine Discourse: Clarice Lispector's *Agua Viva*." *Translation Perspectives: Selected Papers, 1982–1983*. Binghamton, N.Y.: SUNY Translation Program, 1984; Courteau, Joanna. "The Problematic Heroines in the Novels of Rachel de Queiroz." *LBR* (Winter, 1985), pp. 123–144; Hahner, June S. "The Nineteenth-Century Feminist Press and Women's Rights in Brazil." *Latin American Women: Historical Perspectives*. Westport, Conn.: Greenwood Press, 1978, pp. 254–285; idem. *Women in Brazil: Problems and Perspectives*. *BSG*; Moniz, Naomi Hoki. "Ética, estética e a condição feminina: *A casa de paixão*."

RIB (January–March, 1984), pp. 137–146; Pescatello, Ann. "The *brasileira*: Images and Realities in Writings of Machado de Assis and Jorge Amado." *Female and Male in Latin America: Essays.* Edited by Ann Pescatello. Pittsburgh: University of Pittsburgh Press, 1973, pp. 29–58.

NAOMI HOKI MONIZ

FERNANDES, MILLÔR (b. 1924). Artist, dramatist, novelist, poet, author of *crônicas*, in all these media, Rio-born Fernandes views Brazilian life from the angle of black humor.

It was as a cartoonist that Fernandes first gained wide popularity. His cartoons with satirical "analyses" of politicians and the political moment of the military dictatorship filled the pages of the major weekly newsmagazine during the depths of repression and censorship. Among his many collections of *crônicas* is *Fábulas fabulosas* (1976; Wonderful Fables), in which reality contains a comic depth and truth. (*See* Dictatorship and Literature.)

Fernandes coauthored, with director Flávio Rangel, *Liberdade, liberdade* (1965; Liberty, Liberty) a protest play directed against the military dictatorship. The work consists of important declarations—both from Brazilian and foreign history, statesmen, and dramatists—on the aims and purposes of liberty. With music by Chico *Buarque, the play was successful on national and international stages. *Duas tábuas e uma paixão* (1982; Two Boards and One Passion) is a fictional dramatization of a bombing that took place in 1982; it leads the protagonist, an actress named Cordélia, to recognize the need for political activism. That same year, Fernandes wrote *Vidigal*, a theatrical representation of Manuel Antônio de *Almeida's *Memórias de um sargento de milícias. (See* Theater History.)

In 1984 Fernandes turned his hand to poetry. Touching on all elements of Brazilian life—from bureaucracy to soap operas—he mixed fear with laughter: for example, "Anti-poética" (Anti-Poetics): "I sing about the empty dish / Laughter without teeth / Rio-Rio of the past / I sing about cancer without a cure." Fernandes is one of the most popular, original, and respected figures on the Brazilian cultural scene today.

BIBLIOGRAPHY: Additional selected works by Fernandes: *Tempo e contratempo*, 1954; *Um elefante no caos*, 1955; *O homem do princípio ao fim*, 1966; *Computa, computador, computa*, 1972; *Os órfãos de Jânio*, 1980. Criticism: Butler, Ross E. "Social Themes in Selected Contemporary Brazilian Dramas." *RomN* (Autumn, 1973), pp. 52–60.

FERREIRA, ASCENSO (1895–1965). Born in Pernambuco, Ferreira initially wrote poetry in the Parnassian mold but soon adhered to the tenets of *modernism. However, under the influence of the distinguished folklorist Luís de Câmara Cascudo, Ferreira turned to *regionalism inspired by traditional Pernambucan dances and one-act plays (*autos*), such as *bumba-meu-boi. (See* Folklore and Literature; Parnassianism.)

A recurrent theme of his works, such as the collection *Catimbó e outros poemas* (1927; name of a syncretic Afro-Indian-Brazilian religious rite and other poems), is *saudade* for the old-fashioned plantation life. His poetry, often in dialogue form, appeared in the literary *review *Revista de Norte*, which he organized with Joaquim *Cardozo. Ferreira was also known for his singing recitations of poetry; thus his latter collections were often sold with an accompanying record.

BIBLIOGRAPHY: Additional selected works by Ferreira: *Poemas*, 1951. Criticism: Brookshaw.

FERREIRA GULLAR. *See* Gullar, Ferreira.

FIGUEIREDO, GUILHERME DE (b. 1915). Figueiredo grew up in the state of São Paulo and studied law in Rio. He has been a diplomat, as well as a poet, a novelist, an essayist, a critic, and, most importantly, a dramatist. His very popular plays are often inspired by classical Greek themes and comment upon general human situations rather than specific Brazilian realities; in spite of his international success, some Brazilian critics (*see* Critics and Criticism) have classified his work as too "intellectualized."

Figueiredo's greatest success has been *A raposa e as uvas* (1953; *The Fox and the Grapes*, 1957) with Aesop as its main character in an allegory about the search for personal freedom and truth. *O asilado* (1961; The Asylum Seeker) deals with a true incident of a political activist; it was awarded the Martins *Pena Prize for Drama. (*See* Prizes.)

Figueiredo's prose works include a comic dissertation on the proverbial *chato*, the boring person or event: *Tratado geral dos chatos* (1962; General Treatise on Bores), as well as the novel *14 Tilsitt, Paris* (1975; 14 Tilsitt Street, Paris) in which a dog narrates his experiences in Paris with his master, a wealthy *paulista* coffee baron. Figueiredo satirizes the Brazilian-French relationship on both a personal, cultural, and political level.

Figueiredo also has published translations of plays by William Shakespeare, Jean-Baptiste Molière, and George Bernard Shaw, and he has written *children's literature. He has been president of the Brazilian Writers Association and a professor of drama. (*See* Theater History.)

BIBLIOGRAPHY: Additional selected works by Figueiredo: *Um violino na sombra*, 1936; *Lady Godiva*, 1948; *Um deus dormiu lá em casa*, 1949 (*A God Slept Here*, 1957); *Viagem*, 1955; *Os fantasmas*, 1956; *O homem e a sombra*, 1986. Criticism: Prado, Décio de Almeida. *Apresentação do teatro brasileiro moderno*. São Paulo, 1956.

FIGUEIREDO, JACKSON DE (1891–1928). Born in Sergipe, Figueiredo studied law in Bahia. Along with Tasso da *Silveira and Alceu Amoroso *Lima, he founded the "Catholic Renaissance," a movement that promoted Catholicism in Brazilian life and modernist literature. (*See* Modernism; Religion and Literature.)

An ardent polemicist and founder of the Catholic review *A Ordem* (1921; Order), Figueiredo established the Dom Vital Center. The novelist Otávio de *Faria cited a large literary and cultural debt to him.

BIBLIOGRAPHY: Additional selected works by Figueiredo: *A reação do bom senso*, 1923; *Aevum*, 1930. Translations: In *Contemporary Latin American Philosophy*. Edited by Aníbal Sánchez-Reulet. Albuquerque, New Mex.: University of New Mexico, 1954, pp. 237–251. Criticism: Abrantes, Jorge. *O pensamento político de Jackson de Figueiredo*. Recife, 1954.

FILM AND LITERATURE.   Relations between film and literature in Brazil are varied and multiple. Many twentieth-century writers are said to have written "cinematically." Some such as Menotti del *Picchia and Márcio *Souza have directed films. Others, including Jorge *Amado, Lúcio *Cardoso, and Nelson *Rodrigues, have written screenplays. Still others—Guilherme de *Almeida, Otávio de *Faria, Vinícius de *Moraes, and Ignácio de Loyola *Brandão—have been active film critics. A number of directors have also engaged in literary activity. Gláuber Rocha (1939–1981), for example, wrote numerous short stories and at least one novel, *Riverão sussuarana* (1978; Riverrun Sussuarana). Screenplays such as that of Arnaldo Jabor's *Tudo bem* (1978; Everything's Okay) are of literary quality and on the level of the best drama in Brazil today.

From almost the beginning of narrative film production in Brazil, the country's literary heritage has been a major source of thematic material. The incipient Brazilian film industry attempted to capitalize on the popularity or prestige of literary masterpieces to guarantee commercial success and give the new art form a degree of cultural legitimacy. Most of these early film adaptations of literary works tended to be mere cinematic transpositions or illustrations, which did little more than portray on film the story related verbally by the novel. In fact, this continues to be true for many adaptations made even today, especially those of a more commercial nature. Works were and are often chosen for adaptation because of their dramatic potential, their historical or patriotic interest, or their scandalous or erotic nature.

Virtually every major Brazilian novelist of the nineteenth and twentieth centuries has found his or her way onto the screen, although adaptations have not always reached the level of their literary sources. Starting in the second decade of the century, for example, Italo-Brazilian Vittorio Capellaro (1874–1943) made a series of films based on nineteenth-century classics such as the Visconde de *Taunay's *Inocência* (1915), Aluísio *Azevedo's *O mulato* (1917), Bernardo *Guimarães's *O garimpeiro* (1920), and José de *Alencar's *Iracema* (1919) and *O guarani* (1916; 1926). Among the writers whose works have most often been chosen for adaptation are Alencar (twelve films); Amado (seven films), including coproductions such as Bruno Barreto's *Gabriela*; and Nelson Rodrigues (fourteen films based on plays, novels, and screenplays). Even works by such apparently "uncinematic" writers as Lúcio *Cardoso have been adapted for film.

It was only with the *cinema novo* (new cinema) movement in the 1960s that a deeper and more creative mutual relationship between literature and film began to take shape in Brazil. *Cinema novo*'s roots are to be found not only in the political climate of the early 1960s, characterized by the euphoric developmental policies of President Juscelino Kubitschek (1902–1976) and the populism of Presidents Jânio Quadros (b. 1917) and João Goulart (1918–1976), but also in the long tradition of cultural and artistic nationalism, which dates from at least nineteenth-century *romanticism. In their attempt to create a strong national cinema that would be recognized both as art and as a meaningful form of intellectual discourse, filmmakers continually stressed their ties to the country's literary traditions, specifically to *modernism and the *social novelists of the 1930s. By anchoring themselves firmly to Brazil's literary heritage, they achieved the first true integration of cinema within the mainstream of Brazilian culture and created a level of artistic discourse frequently as important as that of the nation's literature.

Besides attempting to establish cultural credentials for the cinema and to attract a sometimes reticent audience, the high number of adaptations also derives from the infrastructure of the cinematic production process itself. Only recently has there emerged a reasonable number of screenwriters who provide raw material for film scripts. The lack of a qualified group of writers has resulted inevitably in the director being responsible for his or her own scripts, so that he or she is the *auteur* not only of the film but also of the script. Internationally acclaimed directors such as Joaquim Pedro de Andrade (b. 1932) and Nelson Pereira dos Santos (b. 1928) have relied heavily on literary sources, whereas others such as Gláuber Rocha and Carlos Diegues (b. 1940) have preferred to develop their own scripts, which are frequently of high literary quality.

The first masterpiece of *cinema novo* was Pereira dos Santos's *Vidas secas* (1963) based on the well-known homonymous novel by Graciliano *Ramos. Pereira dos Santos's adaptation was intended as an intervention in a contemporary political situation, namely, the debate then raging over agrarian reform. Working with what has since become known as the "aesthetic of hunger," Pereira dos Santos was able to find strikingly original equivalents for the stylistic elements of Ramos's prose.

Many other early *cinema novo* adaptations employ this strategy of making the literary source, regardless of its own time frame, relate directly to Brazil's contemporary social reality. Two other works by Ramos adapted to film, which further exemplify this strategy, have indelibly marked the development of Brazilian cinema. Leon Hirszman's (1938–1987) 1972 version of Ramos's *São Bernardo*, made during the most repressive period of military rule, is an exquisitely composed study of modes of artistic representation and of the reification of human beings in capitalist society. It also transcends a mere adaptation and creates an allegory of Brazilian society in the wake of the economic "miracle" of the late 1960s. Pereira dos Santos's cinematic realization of Ramos's *Memórias do cárcere* (1984) was seen as an eloquent critique of the abuses of the twenty-year period of military rule and authoritarianism. All of these films based on

Ramos's works are remarkable for their fidelity and respect for the original literary work. They reveal a convergence of ideological orientation with the distinguished social novelist of the 1930s. (*See* Dictatorship and Literature.)

Whereas many *cinema novo* participants tended to look toward the social or northeastern models, Joaquim Pedro de Andrade turned more toward the initial phase of modernism. In a 1966 interview he suggested that filmmakers would do well to reexamine the modernist movement of the 1920s in terms of the Brazilian sociopolitical situation of the late 1960s. His masterpiece, which results from just such a reevaluation, is his 1969 film version of Mário de *Andrade's Macunaíma*, a film as monumental to the *cinema novo* movement as the novel is to the modernist movement. The film not only continues the strategy of making the film relate more directly to contemporary society but also enters into a creative dialogue with the novel itself, emphasizing elements that are latent in it and thus revealing its vast interpretive possibilities. Joaquim Pedro de Andrade's step in the direction of greater contemporary realism is one indication of his political radicalization of Mário de Andrade's "rhapsody." The transformation of the character Ci from an Amazon warrior to an urban guerrilla is but one example of the director's faithful yet creative textual subversions.

Joaquim Pedro de Andrade's interest in modernism continued in 1982 with *O homem do pau-brasil* (*The Brazilwood Man*), based on the life and work of the modernist Oswald de *Andrade. In a cinematic *tour de force*, the director emphasized both the masculine and feminine components of Andrade's personality and literary ideology by casting two actors, one male and one female, in the role of Andrade, with both of them in scene at the same time. He also dramatized Andrade's theoretical matriarchal revolution, by having the phallus transferred from male to female at the end of the film.

Oswald de Andrade is also the subject of Júlio Bressane's (b. 1946) *Tabu* (1980), which creates an imaginary encounter between the modernist poet and the contemporary popular samba composer and sometime dramatist Lamartine Babo (1904–1963), introduced by the turn-of-the-century journalist João do *Rio. Their conversation is intercut with sequences from W. F. Murnau's (1889–1931) film of South Pacific isle, *Taboo* (1931), and with additional scenes from early pornographic films. *Tabu*, which takes literary-cinema relations to an extreme, is a veritable deconstruction of modernist *antropofagia* and the 1960s *tropicalismo*, itself a reelaboration of the major ideological concerns of *modernism. (*See* Music and Literature; Theater History.)

Filmmakers have approached literature still in other ways, going beyond traditional forms of adaptation based on individual works. Joaquim Pedro de Andrade's *Guerra conjugal* (1975; Conjugal Wars), for example, is based on sixteen short stories from seven volumes by Dalton *Trevisan. Walter Lima Jr.'s *Menino do engenho* (1965) borrows not only from José Lins do Rego's homonymous novel but also from the same author's *Fogo morto*. A Franco-Brazilian production, *Como era gostoso o meu francês* (How Tasty Was My Little Frenchman), was based somewhat on Hans Staden's (*see* Historiography; Travel Literature) chronicle of his life as a prisoner of Indians during the midsixteenth century. Jorge Bodansky's and Orlando Senna's (b. 1945) *Iracema* (1975) is not precisely based on Alencar's Indianist novel; nonetheless, the film draws inevitable parallels with an implicit radical critique of the romantic aesthetic of the original work, especially with respect to the Indian girl Iracema's relationship with a white man. The film, however, shows Iracema's prostitution and decadence, creating an analogy with official Brazilian policy toward the Amazon region and, by extension, the military government's economic policy in general. (*See* Indianism.)

Among the many other recent works of literature produced as films are José *Louzeiro's *Infância dos mortos*, under the title *Pixote*; Aguinaldo *Silva's *República dos assassinos*; Clarice *Lispector's *A hora da estrela;* and Chico *Buarque's *Ópera do malandro*.

Relations between film and literature also work the other way. Ignácio de Loyola Brandão's close relationship with film is revealed not only in his activity as a film critic in the 1960s but also in the fact that two of his works have had cinematic versions. His controversial novel *Zero* is in many ways a literary adaptation of Rogério Sganzerla's (b. 1946) 1968 underground classic *O bandido da luz vermelha* (The Red Light Bandit). Along the same lines, but perhaps in less creative fashion, João Felício dos Santos's (b. 1911) *Xica da Silva* (1976) is based on the film script the author wrote in collaboration with director Carlos Diegues.

In recent years, films for television have also begun to draw on the national literary tradition. Soap operas (*telenovelas*) have been based on Joaquim Manuel de *Macedo's *A moreninha*, Bernardo *Guimarães's *A escrava Isaura*, and Monteiro *Lobato's *Sítio do pica-pau amarelo*. The best-known of such adaptations is no doubt TV Globo's version of Jorge Amado's *Gabriela, cravo e canela*, which led to Bruno Barreto's 1976 cinematic version of *Dona Flor e seus dois maridos*, the actress Sônia Braga's rise to stardom, and to an ever increasing number of adaptations of the Bahian writer's works. TV Globo, the world fourth largest television network, has also produced a number of high-quality miniseries based on literary works, most notably João Cabral de *Melo Neto's *Morte e vida Severina*, Jorge Amado's *Tenda dos milagres*, and João Guimarães *Rosa's *Grande sertão: veredas*. (*See* Popular Culture.)

BIBLIOGRAPHY: Criticism: Burns, E. Bradford, et al. "History in the Brazilian Cinema." *LBR* (Summer, 1977), pp. 49–59; Johnson, Randal. *Cinema novo × 5: Masters of Contemporary Brazilian Film*. Austin: University of Texas Press, 1984; Kavanaugh, Thomas. "Imperialism and the Revolutionary Brazilian Cinema: Gláuber Rocha's *Antônio das Mortes*." *Journal of Modern Literature* 3 (1973), pp. 201–213; West, Dennis. *Contemporary Brazilian Cinema. BSG.*

RANDAL JOHNSON

FOLKLORE AND LITERATURE.   Brazil's uneven development raises major problems for planners of social policy, but in literature it brings some extraordinary opportunities. Within a single national literature coexist the most cosmopolitan of literary scenes and folkloric tales, balladry, and theatrical performance of undiminished vitality. This folklore deserves attention both for its own remarkable features and for the uses made of this source material by more erudite poets, novelists, and playwrights. (*See* Theater History.)

By far the most researched example of Brazil's folklore is the *literatura de cordel*, or ballad booklet. This variety of rhymed tale, told in verses of six or seven lines, is called *cordel* after the line of string on which it is displayed in bunches in the marketplace. The grassroots, on-a-string production of these inexpensive little chapbooks, with their folded pages in multiples of four and with rustic woodcuts, has fascinated investigators, as have the lives and ways of the folk poets who write these action-crammed stanzas.

Of more strictly literary interest, though, is the *cordel's* achievement in keeping alive the ballad tradition that has so largely died out in Europe and in synthesizing such diverse components. Traditional narratives harking to the Middle Ages come together with fabled or factual episodes from more recent European, Iberian, and Brazilian history, up to the most current events and public personalities. For example, an extensive *cordel* has flourished regarding the life of the Brazilian unofficial saint Father Cícero (1867–1934), as well as the story of Tancredo Neves, who died just as he was to assume the presidency of Brazil in 1985. (*See* Popular Culture.)

Although the Brazilian Northeast is traditional *cordel* territory, migration of northeasterners toward the coast and cities has spread the form widely. Their verse narratives may fascinate with lurid elements— treachery, revenge, dalliances, and ventures into the spirit realm—but the subject matter almost inevitably turns out to be leading toward some morale. However raucous or silly or scabrous the intervening stanzas may be, the beginning and end prove the essential seriousness of the form. The protagonist faces a difficult ethical choice, and the reader is well aware whether the resulting decision is morally correct. This narrative form continues to enjoy great popularity, with sales of 20,000 copies fairly common and 100,000 occasionally reached.

Traditional regional and national legends are another significant form of folklore. These orally transmitted tales present significant events and famous figures—both real and legendary—of Brazilian life. For example, Raul *Bopp's *Cobra Norato* is based on a popular Amazonian folk legend; both theater and film have recaptured the popularized tale of Zumbi, the leader of the seventeenth-century *quilombo* in Palmares, Alagoas; and one of the most popular southern legends, "O negrinho do pastoreio" (The Little Black Shepherd Boy), was developed into one of Simoes *Lopes Neto's best short stories. (*See* Film and Literature.)

The most outstanding all-around example of a writer attuned to Brazilian folklore, in all its regional and formal variety, is Jorge *Amado. His works are full of references to the fabled Afro-Brazilian religious syncretism, festival-day traditions, tales, rhymes, jokes, cuisine, and street life. The international success of entertaining novels such as *Dona Flor e seus dois maridos* demonstrates that a diverse audience can appreciate both the exoticism of Amado's treatment of folklore and his implied assertion that modern city dwellers inevitably develop their own mutated varieties of folklore. The dramatist Ariano *Suassuna exemplifies a more focused and specific use of folkloric material than Amado's wide embrace of Brazilian *popular culture.

Although many nineteenth-century writers, ethnographers, and scientists, for example, Gonçalves *Dias or João Barbosa Rodrigues (1842–1909), compiled folkloric tales, the first systematic investigations of them is owed to Sílvio *Romero, Melo Morais Júnior (1844–1919), and Celso de Magalhães (1849–1879), who published *Poesia popular brasileira* (1873; Popular Brazilian Poetry). Luís de Câmara Cascudo (1898–1986) produced a voluminous opus, which includes versions and analysis of folk legends of all areas of Brazil. Other prominent folklorists include Renato Almeida (b. 1895), Oneida Alvarenga (b. 1911), Edison Carneiro (1912–1972), Osvaldo Orico (1900–1972; BAL: 1937), Cecília *Meireles, Hermilo *Borba Filho, and the *paulista* folklorist Cornélio Pires (1884–1958).

BIBLIOGRAPHY: Criticism: Carvalho Neto, Paulo de. ''Historial del folklore de las luchas sociales en América Latina: Especial referencia al Brasil.'' *Cuadernos americanos* (July–August), 1973, pp. 133–156; Curran, Mark J. ''The Brazilian Democratic Dream: The View from Cordel.'' *LBR* (Winter, 1986), pp. 29–45; *Folk Literature of the Gê Indians.* 2 vols. Edited by Johannes Wilbert. Berkeley: University of California Press, 1979–1983; Seljan, Zora. ''Negro Popular Poetry in Brazil.'' *African Forum* (Spring, 1967), pp. 54–77; Slater, Candace. *Stories on a String: The Brazilian ''Literatura de cordel.''* Berkeley: University of California Press, 1982; idem. *Trail of Miracles.* (on Father Cícero). Berkeley: University of California Press, 1986; Thomas, Earl W. ''Folklore in Brazilian Literature.'' *Brazil.* Nashville: Vanderbilt University Press, 1953, pp. 91–135.

NAOMI LINDSTROM

FONSECA, RUBEM (b. 1925). Born in Minas to Portuguese parents, Fonseca and his family moved to Rio when he was a child, and he later earned degrees in law and public administration.

Fonseca, who started to work at age twelve, has been a criminal lawyer, professor, and researcher at the Getúlio Vargas Foundation, as well as an executive with a multinational company. He has been a firm advocate of cultural development and writers' rights in Brazil and has served as secretary of culture for the state of Rio de Janeiro from 1980 to 1981.

Fonseca is one of the most important writers who began to publish in the early 1960s, when Brazil was undergoing profound sociopolitical change. Two processes that greatly affected the contemporary Brazilian writer were urbanization and the military takeover of 1964. Fonseca, who has been accused of being a ''pornographer'' and whose volume of short stories, *Feliz ano novo* (1973; Happy New Year), was banned by General Ernesto Geisel's administration (1974–1979), has loomed as a major moralist and muralist of contemporary Brazilian society. (*See* Dictatorship and Literature.)

Writing in the tradition of the great city novelists, such as Balzac, Dickens, and Dostoyevsky, and with strong literary links to contemporary North American city and detective fiction writers, Fonseca's works focus on the big city, particularly Rio and São Paulo. He used the Brazilian urban setting to symbolize the general distress of modern man. Fonseca has created two particularly noteworthy characters who reappear throughout his work: Vilela and Mandrake. Vilela is the young vice squad cop (*delegado*), in *A coleira do cão* (1965; The Dog's Leash), who reappears in *O caso Morel* (1973; The Morel Case) as a freelance writer and private detective. Mandrake, a lawyer, appears in *A grande arte* (1983; *High Art*, 1986) and has a tough amoral attitude toward life. He is a model for street survival and yet full of tender brutality that makes him accessible to all social types. In Vilela and Mandrake the poet and criminal become one. (*See* City and Literature.)

Described by the American critic Jon Tolman as a "neonaturalistic" writer, Fonseca metaphorically portrays the modern Brazilian city as living hell, emphasizing violence, degradation, and social exploitation. This portrait of Brazil has shocked many who do not perceive in his works the context of Western city literature and who cling to a traditional regionalist view of Brazilian culture. Fonseca's reputation as a "pornographer" also comes from those who do not see the strongly romantic element in his fiction, which explores the psychological distance between the real and the ideal. In 1985 Fonseca was the recipient of the Brazilian Goethe Prize for Fiction. (*See* Naturalism; Prizes; Regionalism.)

BIBLIOGRAPHY: Additional selected works by Fonseca: *Os prisioneiros*, 1963; *Lúcia McCartney*, 1969; *O cobrador*, 1979; *Bufo & Spallanzani*, 1985. Translations: *Fiction* (Spring, 1975); *LALR* (January–June, 1986); *Review* (Fall, 1976); Tolman (1984). Criticism: Lowe; Tolman, Jon. "The Moral Dimension in Rubem Fonseca's Prose." *New World* 1 (1986), pp. 61–81; Vargas Llosa, Mario. "Thugs Who Know Their Greek" (Review of *High Art*). *NYTBR* (September 7, 1986), p. 7.

ELIZABETH LOWE

FOREIGN WRITERS AND BRAZIL. Chroniclers and travelers have written about Brazil since the colonial era. It was only in the nineteenth century, as a result of the opening of Brazil's ports to international traffic, that foreign writers began to arrive, for example, the British poet Robert Southey (1774–1843), who wrote a *History of Brazil (1810–1819)*; Sir Richard Burton (1821–1890), who translated Basílio da *Gama's epic; and the French literary critic Ferdinand Denis (1798–1890), who wrote a history of Brazilian literature (1826) and who documented folkloric traditions of the Indians. Toward the late 1830s works of foreign literatures began to appear in Portuguese translations. (*See* Critics and Criticism; Folklore and Literature; Historiography; Travel Literature.)

Only in the late nineteenth century did foreign writers and artists begin to include Brazil as part of their travel itineraries, for example, Louis Gottschalk and Sarah Bernhardt. Some of them took up permanent residence in Brazil, and others wrote about their voyages and experiences in *memoirs; still others used Brazil as the background or theme of their work(s).

In 1909 Anatole France (1844–1924) was received in Rio by literary circles but primarily by the liberal democrats, for example Rui *Barbosa, who lauded his antiauthoritarian, pro–free thought doctrines. The Portuguese novelist Ferreira de Castro arrived in Brazil in his teens, not as a writer but as an immigrant worker on rubber plantations in the Amazon. Several of his novels are related to Brazilian life: *Emigrantes* (1928; *Emigrants*, 1962); *A selva* (1930; *The Jungle*, 1934), and *O instincto supremo* (1968; The Supreme Instinct), which is about Colonel Rondon, the founder of the Indian Protection Service. Castro is greatly admired by Brazilian writers; his *The Jungle* was made into a film by Márcio *Souza. (*See* Film and Literature; Portugal and Brazil; Literary Relations.)

Among the literary visitors during the 1920s were Felippo Tommaso Marinetti, who had indirectly inspired Brazilian *modernism; Luigi Pirandello; and Rudyard Kipling, who later wrote *Brazilian Sketches* (1943). The Swiss writer Blaise Cendrars (1887–1961) became friendly with Oswald de *Andrade while the latter was in Paris in 1912. Cendrars came to "modernist" Brazil on several occasions, and he participated in the *Pau-Brasil* movement. He also traveled through northern Brazil with Mário de *Andrade; his memoirs of Brazil were published in *Etc . . . etc . . . (Um livro 100% brasileiro)* (1976; Etc . . . etc . . . [A 100% Brazilian Book]).

During World War II Brazil, under the Vargas regime, initially supported the Axis. Later, however, in an attempt at a careful balancing act, Vargas also allowed some refugees—principally wealthy or famous ones—to seek asylum in Brazil. The French Catholic philosopher and writer Georges Bernanos (1888–1948) lived in Brazil from 1938, from the fall of France until liberation in 1945. He was an immensely popular *confrère* of Brazilian Catholic writers, such as Jorge de *Lima, Augusto Frederico *Schmidt, Alceu Amoroso *Lima, and Geraldo França de *Lima, who served as his secretary. Bernanos lived in Barbacena, Minas, and wrote a weekly newspaper column on political-cultural-Brazilian-international themes.

Among the immigrants from Eastern Europe were the distinguished bibliographer of Brazilian literature Otto Maria Carpeaux (1900–1978), who authored the basic literary biobibliography *Pequena bibliografia crítica da literatura brasileira* (1949; now in 5th ed; Short Critical Bibliography of Brazilian Literature), and histories of world literature; and the translator and literary critic Paulo Rónai (b. 1907) (*see* Critics and Criticism), who was one of the founders of the Brazilian Association of Translators. A more tragic refugee from war-torn Europe of the time was Stefan Zweig (1881–1942). Zweig arrived in Brazil seeking asylum in 1940 and began to do research for his book *Brasil: país do futuro* (1941; *Brazil: Land of the Future*, 1941), which turned out to be a panegyric of Brazilian life under Vargas's dictatorial regime and which caused Brazilian intellectuals to snub him. Zweig had a few Brazilian contacts, for example, Gilberto *Freyre; Manuel *Bandeira, who translated some of Zweig's poems into Portuguese; the folklorist Osvaldo Orico; and the grammarian Antenor Nascentes, who helped Zweig with his Portuguese. Distraught by the war Zweig and his wife committed suicide in Brazil in 1942. (*See* Folklore and Literature; Portuguese Language of Brazil; Religion and Literature.)

Many Portuguese intellectuals sought asylum in Brazil during the regime of Antônio de Oliveira Salazar (1889–1971). Most notable for their writings on Brazilian life and literature are Adolfo Casais Monteiro and Jorge de Sena. The American poet Elizabeth Bishop (1911–1979) made her home in Petrópolis, outside of Rio, and in Ouro Preto, Minas, from the mid–1950s until her death. Not only did she translate *The Diary of "Helena Morley"* into English, but she was an avid translator of Brazilian poetry, notably that of Drummond de *Andrade, which she had published in *The New Yorker* and other North American journals. She also edited, along with Emanuel Brasil, an important bilingual anthology of Brazilian modernist poets. (*See* Memoirs.)

The Chilean poet and Nobel Prize winner Gabriela Mistral (1889–1957) was honorary cultural ambassador in Rio during the early forties and was a friend of many of the modernists, principally Cecília *Meireles. The Peruvian novelist Mario Vargas Llosa (b. 1936) has also been inspired by a Brazilian theme. The events of Canudos, as described by Euclides da *Cunha, are the subject of his novel *La guerra del fin del mundo* (1981; *The War of the End of the World*, 1984). The Argentine novelist Manuel Puig, who is now a resident of Rio, has had works published such as *Sangre del amor correspondido* (1982; *Blood of Unrequited Love*, 1985), which are set in Brazil.

With the extensive growth of the Brazilian publishing industry and reading public, translations of foreign writers have increased dramatically, thus making them regular travelers to São Paulo and Rio to launch their works on the Brazilian market.

BIBLIOGRAPHY: Criticism: Brown, Ashley. "Elizabeth Bishop in Brazil." *The Southern Review* (Autumn, 1977); Dines, Alberto. *Morte no paraíso* (about Stefan Zweig in Brazil). Rio: Nova Fronteira, 1985; Sarrazin, Hebert, ed. *Bernanos no Brasil*. Rio: Vozes, 1968.

FRANÇA JÚNIOR, JOSÉ JOAQUIM DA (1838–1890). Rio-born França studied law in São Paulo. He is known not only for his *crônicas* of Rio life, written in a light-hearted, easy-flowing language, but also for his comedies, equally spirited and popular. (*See* Theater History.)

Following the mode of his predecessor Martins *Pena and his contemporary Artur *Azevedo, França Jr. delighted in presenting the caricatures of character types of the empire: university students; wealthy ranchmen from São Paulo (*fazendeiros*); verbose, dullard politicians; and the proverbial "sharp" immigrant. *As doutoras* (1889; The Women Doctors), which satirized feminist issues of the time, is considered his most significant play, but it clearly falls within the limited conventions of his time and style of comedy. (*See* Feminism and Literature.)

Although his comedies are now considered simplistic, França Jr. was extremely popular in his day and rated among the most important Brazilian dramatists. Today his works are viewed principally as social documents, although the revival, in 1973, of his *Caiu o ministério* (1882; The Government Has Fallen), a political satire, temporarily rescued his name from obscurity.

BIBLIOGRAPHY: Additional selected works by França Júnior: *Meia hora de cinismo*, 1861; *Os candidatos*, 1881; *Amor com amor se paga*, 1882; *A estação da lotação*, 1898; *Teatro de França Júnior*, 1980; Criticism: Barman, Roderick J. "Politics on the Stage: The Late Brazilian Empire as Dramatized by França Júnior." *LBR* (Winter, 1976), pp. 244–260; Sayers.

FRANÇA JÚNIOR, OSWALDO (b. 1936). A prolific novelist and short-fiction writer, França Júnior's first publications coincided with the beginning of the military dictatorship in Brazil and, to a great extent, daringly commented upon it. (*See* Dictatorship and Literature.)

França's Júnior's novels have been concerned with the lives of lower middle classes, for example, a mechanic in *O homem do macacão* (1972; *The Man in the Monkey Suit)*, and they all emphasize a psychological approach to characterization. *Jorge, um brasileiro* (1967; *The Long Haul*, 1980) has been his most successful work. It narrates a trucker's determined journey along half-completed roads of the Brazilian interior, tested not only by the elements of nature but also by his fellow Brazilians' attempts to waylay him. The land of the military regime's "economic miracle" is also one of repression and violence, according to a later novel, *Um dia no Rio* (1969; A Day in Rio). A small-time businessman's schemes for wealth are paralleled with the university students' mass protests in Rio for more political freedom in the late 1960s immediately preceding the worst years of political and social repression. As the students are felled by the policemen's teargas and bullets, Márcio's schemes also fall apart.

Among França Júnior's recent novels in which psychology plays an important role are *Aqui e em outros lugares* (1980; Here and in Other Places) and *A procura dos motivos* (1982; In Search of the Motives). *O passo-bandeira* (1984; The Airplane) has autobiographical overtones; it deals with the career of a pilot in the Brazilian Air Force that is compromised and ended by his political views (as was França Júnior's). His latest collection, *As laranjas iguais* (1985; The Equal Oranges), consists of fantastic micro-ministories in which there are birds with golden beaks, blue women, and staircases without steps. (*See* Autobiography.)

BIBLIOGRAPHY: Additional selected works by França Júnior: *As lembranças de Eliana*, 1978: *Recordações de amar em Cuba*, 1986. Criticism: Monegal, Emir Rodríguez. "Writing under the Censor's Eye." *WLT* (Winter, 1979), pp. 19–22.

FRANCIS, PAULO [FRANZ PAULO HEILBORN] (b. 1930). Francis began his career as an actor in Rio in the early 1950s. He was a drama critic and theater director and has written cultural and political commentary and articles on the media for many publications. He was active in the Ministry of Culture under the government of President João Goulart (1963–1964). Persecuted during the military dictatorship (1964–1985), he moved to New York, from where he continues to contribute to Brazilian newspapers and magazines and, since 1982, has been the foreign policy commentator for the Globo television network. He is married to the writer Sônia Nolasco Ferreira. (*See* Dictatorship and Literature; New Writers; Theater History.)

In *O afeto que se encerra* (1981; The Enclosed Affection), a book of *memoirs, Francis discussed the influence that Catholicism and Marxism have had on him. That influence is readily evident in his fiction, which is written in the objective style of a political commentator. *Cabeça de papel* (1977; Paper Head) and *Cabeça de negro* (1979; Black Head Bomb), the first two novels of a planned trilogy, are somewhat autobiographical narrations in the first person. Hugo Mann, the protagonist, is one of the leftist intellectual *engagés* of Rio that resisted the system and despised those of his group who mingled with the rich and powerful during the post–1964 military regime.

In addition to writing *Filhas do segundo sexo* (1982; Daughters of the Second Sex), two novels about sex, politics, and the awakening of Brazilian women's consciousness in the 1980s, Francis has produced a series of polemical essays on modern Brazil, notably *O Brasil no mundo* (1985; Brazil in the World), in which he debates Brazil's future under the post–1985 democratic government. (*See* Feminism and Literature.)

BIBLIOGRAPHY: Additional selected works by Francis: *Opinião pessoal*, 1966; *Paulo Francis nu e cru*, 1976. Criticism: Silverman, Malcolm. "Intellectual Satire in the Novels of Paulo Francis." *LBR* (Winter, 1982), pp. 209–219.

LUIZA LOBO

FREIRE, LUÍS JOSÉ JUNQUEIRA (1832–1855). Bahian Junqueira Freire spent three years as a monk. The combination of strict monastic discipline and an uncertain religious faith soon gave cause for bitter regret. A congenital history of heart disease led to his death a year after abandoning the order, during which time he wrote an autobiography and published *Inspirações do claustro* (1855; Inspirations from the Cloister).

Freire belongs to the second generation of Brazilian romantics, who imitated especially the satanic and erotic sensationalism of Lord Byron, Alfred de Musset, and the Spaniard José de Espronceda (1808–1842). Nonetheless, the cultural atmosphere of Bahia largely isolated Freire from the mainstream of these developments. Consequently, his main stylistic influence was the neoclassical, arcadian tradition transmitted from Portugal by Gonçalves *Dias. (See Arcadias; Romanticism.)

Conflict is therefore characteristic of his poetry. On a thematic level, it appears in the sexual repression, the sense of revolt and remorse, and the obsession with death that were the result of his ill-chosen religious career. With regard to form, it is evident in his attempt to communicate that intensity of feeling through the hard, imageless prosaicism of neoclassical poetry. In his second collection *Con-*

tradições poéticas (n.d.; Poetic Contradictions), the disparity between form and content is least pronounced.

Freire did not achieve the popularity of someone such as Alvares de *Azevedo. Interest in his work has revived only recently after the rapid decline that followed its initial publication.

BIBLIOGRAPHY: Additional selected works by Freire: *Obras poéticas*, n.d.; *Elementos de retórica nacional*, 1869. Criticism: Cândido, Antônio. "Conflito da forma e da sensibilidade em Junqueira Freire." *Formação da literatura brasileira; momentos decisivos*. Belo Horizonte: Itatiaia, 1975, II:155–161; Pires, Homero. *Junqueira Freire, sua vida, sua época, sua obra*. Rio: A Ordem, 1929.

DAVID H. TREECE

FREYRE, GILBERTO (1900–1987). Born to a genteel family of Brazilian-Dutch background in Pernambuco State, Freyre was educated from an early age in Latin, Greek, and English and pursued higher education in the United States. He graduated with a B.A. from Baylor University and an M.A. and a Ph.D. from Columbia University in cultural anthropology. There he studied with the eminent anthropologist Franz Boas (1858–1942), the philosopher John Dewey (1859–1952), and other leading intellectuals of the time who, he openly admits, greatly influenced the direction of his life. Although Freyre preferred to devote himself to writing, he taught and lectured on Luso-Brazilian history and culture at many North American, European, and Brazilian universities. Among the many national and international *prizes he received was the French Legion of Honor in 1986.

Freyre exemplified perfectly a Brazilian tradition whereby creative literature combines with scholarly publication. Thus his studies of colonial Brazilian life (e.g., *Casa grande e senzala* [1933; *The Masters and the Slaves*, 1946, 1956]), often read like sagas, while his novels and even poems bear the mark of the professional historian.

Freyre's passion for the Brazilian Northeast led him to begin a cultural movement known as "Region-Tradition" in 1923 in Recife. (A volume of essays published in 1941 bears that title). It was, in part, a retort to the modernist movement (*see* Modernism), which had been launched in São Paulo in 1922. Freyre considered these southern writers and artists to be imitators of European styles. In the "Regionalist Manifesto" (1926), he and other major regionalist writers (e.g., José Américo de *Almeida, Jorge de *Lima, and José Lins do *Rego) outlined regionalist goals for a true, national Brazilian literature, a literature inspired by the reality of Brazil's regionalist divisions. The "Regionalist Congress," which took place later that same year, fortuitously was linked to a more general modernist movement. (*See* Regionalism.)

Less well known but worthwhile are Freyre's forays into prose fiction. The novel *Dona Sinhá e o filho padre* (1964; *Mother and Son: A Brazilian Tale*, 1967) and its continuation *O outro amor do Dr. Paulo*, (1977; Dr. Paulo's Other

Love) relate the story of a young seminarian and his love for his dedicated mother and for a no less devoted school mate, Paulo Tavares, the doctor of the sequel. Both novels blend fact and fiction to create what an American critic, John Coleman, has called "meta-literature" depicting a turbulent period of Brazilian history as the country passed from empire to republic. The setting of *O outro amor do Dr. Paulo* is mainly Paris, where Freyre imaginatively described the life of those Brazilian aristocrats who chose self-imposed exile in protest against the new republic and the disappearance of a plantation society based on slave labor.

Truly a citizen of the world, Freyre benefited from most of the major cultural movements of the twentieth century, from painting to poetry to sociology to history. Against this vast background, he has viewed both Portuguese and Brazilians as creators of a specific civilization that reflects an European substratum within a tropical setting characterized by racial and ideological diversity, as outlined in his *New World in the Tropics* (1959).

To be sure, Freyre's claim of this Luso-Brazilian "new world in the tropics" founded on racial harmony and ecological balance has been countered especially in recent years by younger anthropologists and historians less given to romantic fancy. Even so, no one disputes his place as a pioneer researcher with a talent for synthesis and probing analysis. Certainly, one of his country's most prolific writers, Freyre was a central figure on the cultural scene of modern Brazil.

BIBLIOGRAPHY: Selected additional works by Freyre: *Sobrados e mucambos*, 1936 (*The Mansions and the Shanties: The Making of Modern Brazil*, 1963); *Ordem e progresso, 1959 (Order and Progress: Brazil from Monarchy to Republic*, 1970); *Seleta para jovens de Gilberto Freyre*, 1971 (*The Gilberto Freyre Reader*, 1974). Criticism: Brookshaw; Coleman, John. "Condemned to Sainthood." *NYTBR* (May 7, 1967), p. 7 (Book review of *Mother and Son); Foster/Foster, I; Loos, Dorothy S. "Gilberto Freyre as a Literary Figure: An Introductory Study." *RHM* 34 (1968), pp. 714–720; Mazzara, Richard A. "Gilberto Freyre and José Honório Rodrigues: Old and New Horizons for Brazil." *Hispania* (May, 1964), pp. 316–325; Sayers.

RICHARD A. PRETO-RODAS

FUSCO, ROSÁRIO (1910–1977). A lawyer from Minas, Fusco participated with other *mineiro* modernists such as Francisco Inácio Peixoto (1910–1986) in the literary *review *Verde*. He later published a collection of poems, *Fruta de conde* (1929; Count's Fruit [Cherimoya]), which emphasizes his nationalistic concerns through a highly colloquial language. (*See* Modernism; Regionalism.)

In the 1940s Fusco turned to other genres. *Dia do juízo* (1961; Day of Judgment) is a novel about urban life with fine psychological depth. His play *O anel de Saturno* (1949; Saturn's Ring) was a major success owing to its graceful mixture of prose and poetic dialogue. Fusco also published literary criticism. (*See* City and Literature; Critics and Criticism; Theater History.)

BIBLIOGRAPHY: Additional selected works by Fusco: *Poemas cronológicos*, 1928; *O agressor*, 1943; *Carta à noiva*, 1954.

FUTEBOL. *See* Soccer and Literature.

FUTURISM. *See* Modernism.

G

GABEIRA, FERNANDO (b. 1943). A *mineiro*, Gabeira's rise to national fame came through his participation in the kidnapping of the American ambassador to Brazil in 1969. Arrested and tortured, Gabeira was freed in 1970 in a prisoner exchange and spent the next eight years in exile in Latin America and in Europe. He returned to Brazil in 1979, when the military dictatorship declared a general amnesty.

Since his return, he has published a series of gossipy *memoirs about the personal and political events surrounding the kidnapping, his torture, his exile, and his return to a "changed" Brazil: *O que é isso, companheiro?* (1979; What's This, Pal?) and *O crepúsculo do macho* (1980; The Sunset of the Macho). *Sinais da vida no planeta Minas* (1982; Signals of Life on the Planet Minas) is a seminovel that views *machismo* in the perspective of the women's movement against it. (*See* Dictatorship and Literature; Feminism and Literature.)

Gabeira, like other radicals of the late 1960s, is now seeking national change through more normal political channels. He campaigns for "reforms" in Brazil to promote the rights of blacks, women, and homosexuals, as well as environmental protection. Hoping to attain such goals, he ran unsuccessfully—but not unimpressively—for the governorship of Rio de Janeiro in 1986. (*See* Contemporary Black Literature; Homosexuality and Literature; New Writers.)

BIBLIOGRAPHY: Additional selected works by Gabeira: *Entradas e bandeiras*, 1981; *Diário da crise*, 1984. Criticism: Riding, Alan. "Exile, Back in Rio, Agitates for Change on the Left." *NYT* (August 5, 1985), p. A2.

GALVÃO, PATRÍCIA (1910–1962). Galvão, known as Pagu, was the subject of a poem by Raul *Bopp ("Côco de Pagu"). She became a prominent figure in *modernism through her contacts with artist Tarsila do Amaral (*see* Art and Literature), writer Oswald de *Andrade, and the modernist group in 1928. The anthropophagy platform provided a basis for the radical criticism of Brazilian society and intellectual life found in her varied journalism, which touches on literature, art, theater, politics, architecture, and related topics. In 1930 Pagu married Andrade and the following year contributed to his radical magazine *O Homem do Povo* (Man of the People) with the column "A Mulher do Povo" (Woman of the People). During the 1930s she was also a militant Marxist. (*See* Art and Literature; Feminism and Literature; Theater History.)

Pagu's "poletarian novel" *Parque industrial* (1933; Industrial Park), published under the pseudonym Mara Lobo, unites cubist prose with social portraits of the lower classes of the Brás industrial neighborhood of São Paulo. Her cinematographic, ideological flashes include the role of working women and a critique of feminine consciousness. As a counterweight to this novel, her second novel, *A famosa revista* (1945; The Famous Review), is a rejection and denunciation of the Communist party.

In the 1950s Pagu translated and produced plays by Eugène Ionesco, Fernando Arrabal, Octavio Paz, Bertolt Brecht, and young Brazilian playwrights such as Ovudaldo *Viana Filho and Plínio *Marcos. Her poetry, published under the name Solange Sohl, contains original expressions of feminist consciousness. (*See* Theater History.)

BIBLIOGRAPHY: Additional selected works by Galvão: *Verdade e liberdade*, 1950; "Antologia." In *Pagu Vida Obra*. Edited by Augusto de Campos, 1982. Criticism: Bloch, Jayne. "Patrícia Galvão: The Struggle against Conformity." *LALR* (January–June 1986), pp. 188–201; Campos, Augusto de. *Pagu Vida Obra*. São Paulo: Brasiliense, 1982; Jackson, Kenneth David. "Patrícia Galvão and the Brazilian Social Realism of the 1930's." *PPNCFL* 28 (1977), pp. 95–98.

K. DAVID JACKSON

GAMA, BASÍLIO DA (1741–1795). Gama was born in Minas and was educated by Jesuits in Rio. After the Jesuits were expelled from Brazil in 1759, he entered a Jesuit seminary in Italy. Probably owing to a Jesuit benefactor, at nineteen he became a member of the prestigious Arcadia Romana. (*See* Arcadias; Religion and Literature.)

In spite of his Jesuit training, through his readings of the eighteenth-century French philosophers, Gama became acquainted with liberal ideologies. In fact, in *O uraguai* (1769; *The Uruguay*, 1878, reprint 1972), his major literary work, Gama vehemently attacked the Jesuits. This vehemence may really have been due to his desire to escape punishment upon being arrested as a Jesuit supporter.

The Uruguay narrates scenes of the Wars of the Seven Missions of Uruguay (1750–1756). The conflict pitted the Portuguese and Spanish against the Jesuits and their Indian flock, the Tupi-Guaranis. The former sought to rest control of the Indian's tribal lands, fearing the Jesuit's desire to establish an independent nation within the colony.

Genre classification of the work has been difficult. Whereas some critics see it as the best in the series of eighteenth-century Brazilian epic poems by Friar *Durão and others, Gama's English translator, Sir Richard F. Burton (1821–1890), considered it more of a "romance," lyrical narrative, or poetic drama. "Epic" moments, he noted, are followed by long, trivial passages. Indeed, the poem combines literature with self-serving political aims. Although Gama created Indians whose roles promoted "the good-savage" theme, through his hero and heroine, Cacambo and Lindóia, he also lauded the "white-knight" nature of the marquis of Pombal's government's actions in the war. (*See* Foreign Writers and Brazil; Travel Literature.)

The romantics were influenced by Gama's use of blank verse and his characterizations of heroic Indians. They looked at *The Uruguay* as one of the first independent works of a true Brazilian literature. (*See* Indianism; Romanticism.)

BIBLIOGRAPHY: Additional selected works by Gama: Critical edition and translation of *O uraguai*, 1769 (*The Uruguay*, 1872. Translated by Sir Richard F. Burton. Edited by Frederick G. H. Garcia and Edward Stanton. Berkeley: University of California Press, 1972); *Obra poética*, 1902. Translations: Hulet. Criticism: Driver; Garcia, Frederick G. H. "Richard Burton and Basílio da Gama: The Translator and the Poet." *LBR* (Summer, 1975), pp. 34–57; Garcia, Frederick G. H., and Edward Stanton. "Introduction." *The Uruguay*. Berkeley: University of California Press, 1972, pp. 1–38.

GAMA, LUÍS (1830–1882). Luís Gonzaga Pinto da Gama was the son of an unknown Bahian nobleman of Portuguese descent and the free African Luiza Mahin. Sold to slave traders by his father, after eight years of servitude, he obtained proof of the illegality of his bondage and ran off to join the army. By the 1850s Gama had secured a civilian position in the São Paulo Police Department, initiated his abolitionist activities, and began writing poems for periodicals. (*See* Slavery and Literature.)

Gama came to be regarded as the leader of the abolitionist movement in São Paulo. In 1864 he founded the *Diabo Coxo* (Limping Devil), a humorous periodical—the first of its kind in São Paulo—publishing political and social satire as well as antislavery propaganda. Subsequently, he joined the editorial staff of the newspaper *Radical Paulistano* (São Paulo City Radical), which included other leading abolitionists such as Rui *Barbosa and Joaquim *Nabuco.

Gama's collection *Primeiras trovas burlescas de Getulino* (1859; Getulino's First Burlesque Verses) is a collection of satiric verse, in the style of Gregório de *Matos, which lampooned the pseudowhite Brazilian aristocracy for its social snobbery, European ways, and mania for whiteness. In his most widely read poem, "Quem sou eu?" ("Who Am I?"), Gama wittily claimed to have relatives among all social classes because all Brazilians, regardless of wealth and social rank, were either black or, like himself, mulatto.

BIBLIOGRAPHY: Additional selected works by Gama: *Novas trovas burlescas*, 1861 (second enlarged edition of poetry of 1859). Criticism: Brookshaw; Kennedy, James H. "Luiz Gama: Pioneer of Abolition in Brazil." *Journal of Negro History* (July, 1974), pp. 255–267; Moore, Zelbert Laurence. "Luiz Gama, Abolition and Republicanism in São Paulo, Brazil, 1870–1888." Dissertation, Temple University, 1978; Sayers.

JAMES H. KENNEDY

GIUDICE, VÍCTOR (b. 1937). Giudice grew up in Rio's picturesque Tijuca neighborhood. He interjects sly social criticism into his narratives, which are ironic allegories of industrial man in the no-exit predicament characteristic of urban life. He is especially resourceful in inverting "normal" relationships, such as that of life and death. (*See* City and Literature.)

Giudice's novel *Bolero* (1985; Bolero) is a 340-page political allegory of Brazil under twenty years of dictatorship. The main character, somewhat like Samuel Beckett's Godot, waits seven years in the waiting room of a maternity ward for his wife to give birth. When the character finally despairs and leaves the hospital, he finds a changed city. What unfolds is a satire on the politization of a character surrounded by ostensibly "adjusted" personalities who are more alienated than the protagonist himself. Despite its excellence, Giudice's work is not widely known in Brazil. (*See* Dictatorship and Literature.)

BIBLIOGRAPHY: Additional selected works by Giudice: *Necrológio*, 1972; *Os banheiros*, 1979. Translations: *Review* (Spring, 1977); *St. Louis Literary Review* (November, 1976); Tolman (1978); *Translation* (Spring, 1978). Criticism: Lowe.

ELIZABETH LOWE

GOMES, ALFREDO DIAS (b. 1924). Dias Gomes did not complete his law course in Rio; rather, he began to work in theater and later turned to radio.

Gomes's first success as a dramatist was *O pagador de promessas* (1960; *Journey to Bahia*, 1964; *Payment as Pledged*, in *Modern Stage in Latin America*, 1971), which was made into an award-winning film. Set in his native Bahia, he presented the conflicts between the simple rural life and the corrupt and corrupting urban existence. Zé do Burro's desire to fulfill his promise is exaggerated by urban society—the media and the church—into subversive political, social, and religious beliefs. The role of the Afro-Brazilian religions in the rural areas is a central theme of the drama, as is the collusion between the church and the political establishment. (*See* City and Literature; Film and Literature; Religion and Literature.)

Similar to the theater of Ariano *Suassuna, several of Gomes's other plays are inspired by and develop folkloric traditions, for example, *A revolução dos beatos* (1962; The Revolution of the Religious), which presents a religious fanatic, and his play *Vargas* (1966; Vargas), coauthored with Ferreira *Gullar, which is set during a samba school rehearsal of a carnival presentation dealing with the life of the dictator and president.

During the years of dictatorship, Gomes's plays adopted a more satirical or metaphorical political angle. *O berço do herói* (1965; The Cradle of the Hero) was prohibited because, according to the censor, "its author desired to implant a cultural dictatorship [in the nation]," and *O santo inquérito* (1966; The Holy Inquisition) invokes an inquisitorial *auto-da-fé* of the colonial period in an attempt to raise the Brazilian public's awareness through allegory of the consequences of repression. Like other dramatists, during the 1970s, many of Gomes's plays faced severe censorship problems, and he turned to writing for television. (*See* Theater History.)

After 1978 Gomes returned to the stage with fables about power and oppression, for example, *Os campeões da mundo* (1978; The World Champions). His *O bem-amado* (1980; The Beloved) has been a highly successful television satire of Brazilian political practices and politicians. The protagonist Odorico Paraguassu is the supercorrupt wheeler-dealer mayor of the town of Sucupira. Carlos Drummond de *Andrade described Gomes's character as a representative figure of the Brazilian politician, with all his hypocrisy, ambition, disloyalty and unlimited desire for power. Coined the Brazilian "Dallas," it has been one of the most successful television series in Brazilian history.

BIBLIOGRAPHY: Additional selected works by Dias: *A invasão*, 1961; *A construção*, 1969; *As primícias*, 1978; *O rei de Ramos*, 1980; *Sucupira, ame-a ou deixe-a*, 1982. Criticism: Bailey, Dale S. *"O pagador de promessas*: A Brazilian Morality Play." *LATR* (Fall, 1982), pp. 34–40; Clark, Fred. "Society and the Alienated Man in Two Plays by Alfredo Dias Gomes." *RomN* (1975), pp. 712–722; Foster/Foster, I; Lyday, Leon F. "The Theatre of Alfredo Gomes Dias." *Dramatists in Revolt: The New Latin American Theatre*. Austin: University of Texas Press, 1976, pp. 221–242.

GOMES, DUÍLIO (b. 1944). Mineiro Gomes is a lawyer. His short fiction delves into the perplexities of the human condition. "Bananas" (Bananas), from the collection *Verde suicida* (1977; Green Suicide), is an allegory of man's confrontation with the overwhelming, inexplicable realities of life. While riding in a taxi, the ambiguous character extols the virtues of bananas to the driver. As he leaves the cab, having consumed some fifty bananas, the driver (and reader) sense that they have received some oddly important revelation about life.

BIBLIOGRAPHY: Additional selected works by Gomes: *O nascimento dos leões*, 1975; *Janeiro digestivo*, 1982.

GOMES, PAULO EMÍLIO SALLES (1916–1977). Paulo Emílio began his career as a movie critic in 1941, after having studied in France. A university professor, as a result of his article "Cinema and Underdevelopment" he became very influential among Brazilian intellectuals at the time of the *cinema novo* movement in the 1960s and 1970s. (*See* Film and Literature.)

In 1977 he published *Tres mulheres de tres PPPês* (*P'.s Three Women*, 1984), a three-part book about Polidoro's battle between rationality and the flesh during his journey from youth to old age. It was hailed by many critics as a classic erotic comedy; his elegant prose and irony was compared to that of Machado de *Assis.

NAOMI HOKI MONIZ

GONÇALVES CRESPO, A. *See* Crespo, Antônio Gonçalves.

GONÇALVES DE MAGALHÃES. *See* Magalhães, Domingos José Gonçalves de.

GONÇALVES DIAS, A.   *See* Dias, Antônio Gonçalves.

GONGORISM.   *See* Baroque.

GONZAGA, TOMÁS ANTÔNIO   (1744–1810). Born in Portugal, on his paternal side Gonzaga was Brazilian. He went to Brazil in 1752 and studied at the Jesuit school in Bahia. He graduated from Coimbra in law in 1768 and became a judge, first in Portugal and then in Vila Rica, Minas. His career as a magistrate was characterized by repeated accusations of corruption, opportunism, and the open pursuit of material wealth.

A member of the so-called *Minas School of poets, Gonzaga is best known for lyrics dedicated to his beloved, the adolescent Maria Joaquina Dorotéia de Seixas, called Marília, which he published under his arcadian pseudonym Dirceu. Because of his exile, he never married his Marília; instead he continued to write (hypocritically, some say) about his "lost love." This final phase of his lyrics is rated most favorably by critics, although the attribution to him of all "his" poetry is still a matter of literary dispute. (*See* Arcadias.)

Another aspect of his literary personality is revealed in the satire of the *Cartas chilenas* (1863; Chilean Letters), which only recently have definitely been attributed to him. In these thirteen free-verse letters, not only does he attack his political enemy, Governor Cunha Meneses of Minas (who is called Fanfarrão Minésio), placing the events in Chile rather than Brazil, but he also presents a rich portrait of several levels of his contemporary society—from slaves to merchants to gold prospectors.

The only poet of the Minas School to fulfill the aims of the arcadian movement and surpass its limits, Gonzaga is considered the finest of the Brazilian preromantic poets. Indeed, his life was often invoked in works of the romantics Teixeira e *Sousa, Casimiro de *Abreu, and Castro *Alves, as well as in the poetry of the modernist generation. (*See* Modernism; Romanticism.)

BIBLIOGRAPHY: Additional selected works by Gonzaga: *Marília de Dirceu*, in three parts: 1792, 1799, 1812; modern edition: *Obras completas*. 2 vols. Edited by Manuel Rodrigues Lapa. Rio: Instituto Nacional do Livro, 1957; *Tratado de direito natural*, 1942. Translations: Hulet. Criticism: Aiex, Nola Kortner. "A Luso-Brazilian Classic: The Formal Satire of *As cartas chilenas*." *Zagadnienia Rodzajów Literackich*. Poland (1980), pp. 45–61; Sayers.

GONZAGA DUQUE.   *See* Duque, Luís Gonzaga.

GRAÇA ARANHA.   *See* Aranha, José Pereira da Graça.

GROSSMANN, JUDITH   (b. 1931). Born in the interior of the state of Rio, Grossmann is a poet, fiction writer, and critic (*see* Critics and Criticism), as well as a professor of literary theory. Her poetry is in the concretist style (*See* Postmodernism in Poetry), for example, *Linhagem de Rocinante: 55 poemas*

(1959; Heritage of Rocinante: 55 Poems). Her short fiction is semiautobiograph-
ical, owing to its introspective female protagonists-narrators, in a type of fiction
indebted, evidently, to Clarice *Lispector. Her novel, *Outros trópicos* (1980;
Other Tropics), however, has a male protagonist, the musician-engineer Simon
F., whose bizarre subjugation to another artist places his true existence in doubt.
(*See* Autobiography; Feminism and Literature.)

BIBLIOGRAPHY: Additional selected works by Grossmann: *O meio da pedra: novas
estórias genéticas*, 1970; *A noite estrelada: estórias do interior*, 1977; *Temas de teoria
literária*, 1982.

GUARNIERI, GIANFRANCESCO (b. 1934). Guarnieri's family arrived in
Brazil during his childhood. He attributed his early interest in theater to the
operas he saw as a child. He began as an actor—a career in which he continues
today—but turned to writing and producing drama. He joined the Arena Theater
of São Paulo in the mid–1950s and became one of its leading figures. (*See*
Theater History.)

The central theme of Guarnieri's early plays is the abuse and exploitation of
the shantytown dwellers (*favelados*) by the ruling class and the need for unity
of action by the former to improve their lot. A Marxist orientation is evident in
his first, and perhaps best-known, play: *Eles não usam black-tie* (1958; They
Don't Wear Tuxedos). Tião, the son of a union organizer, seeks a middle-class
life-style; thus he ignores the general strike. His behavior leads to his isolation
from his family and his class. Collective action is also an important theme of
Gimba: presidente dos valentes (1959; Gimba: President of the Valiant Ones)
and *A semente* (1962; The Seed), in which, for the first time on the Brazilian
stage, the protagonist is a Marxist union leader involved in a direct socialist
revolutionary cause.

In later dramas Guarnieri used innovative theatrical devices to examine aspects
of Brazilian culture, as well as more universal dilemmas. *Castro *Alves pede
passagem* (1971; Castro Alves Asks for Permission to Enter) narrates the life of
the celebrated abolitionist poet in the style of the television show "This Is Your
Life." The "truth behind the truth" is examined by Guarnieri, who, often
comically, warned that historical "fact" can be deceptive. *O grito parado no
ar* (1973; The Shout Holding in the Air), a subtle censure of the intense military
repression, was permitted or overlooked by the censor. Guarnieri views the role
of the actor and his profession within society. The rehearsal for a drama of the
same name brings the actors' own preoccupations into the action. In spite of
economic, political, and social pressures, they realize that their duty is to perform.
(*See* Dictatorship and Literature.)

Guarnieri, like other dramatists of his generation, such as Augusto *Boal,
aims to involve the audience emotionally in the action. Taking into account the
role of censorship, he wrote: "The spectacle belongs to the actors who at no
moment lose their personal liberty of creation. This mobility, this liberty provokes
a constant transmission of stimuli which will carry the audience to an emotional

state which will facilitate comprehension of what cannot be verbally stated."
(In *Revista Brasiliense*. [September-October, 1959], p. 124).

In 1976 Guarnieri's *Ponto de partida* (Point of Departure) was produced. It
is a strong allegorical drama protesting the regime's murder of the journalist
Wladimir Herzog one year earlier. Guarnieri himself assumed the lead role of
a shepherd who knows the real murderer of the local humanist and poet.

BIBLIOGRAPHY: Additional selected works by Guarnieri: "O teatro como expressão
da realidade," *Revista Brasiliense* (September-October, 1959) pp. 121–126; *Botequim*,
1973.

GUIMARAENS, ALPHONSUS DE [AFONSO HENRIQUES DA COSTA
GUIMARÃES] (1870–1921). A lawyer, Guimaraens served as a judge until his
death. The father of fifteen children, he led a life of sacrifice and was perhaps
monastic in his acceptance of material deprivation. Such spiritual discipline,
though, nurtured his poetry, which ignored the contemporary Brazilian reality
in favor of immensely intimate themes.

While a student in São Paulo, he first read and translated the work of *symbolism's Paul Verlaine and wrote sonnets in French describing his own lyric's
indebtedness to Stéphane Mallarmé. Although Cruz e *Sousa, the other major
symbolist, admired his work (and he was admired by Guimaraens), most of his
contemporaries were unaware of his poetry. In fact, the modernists, notably
Manuel *Bandeira, played a key role in "discovering" Guimaraens, whose
works today remain somewhat ignored.

Guimaraens's most important collection of poems was *Kyriale* (1902; Kyriale),
published in Portugal and at his own expense. His poetry is distinguished by its
keen sense of musicality and creation of neologisms based on linguistic archaisms. The most recurrent images include churchbells, flowers, religious processions, dead virgins, and late afternoons, reflecting the colonial towns of Ouro
Preto and Mariana, in Minas, as well as the tragic death of his fiancée, his cousin
Constança (*Dona Mística* [1899; Miss Mystic]). "A Catedral" (The Cathedral),
whose refrain echoes with the line "Poor Alphonsus, Poor Alphonsus," and
"Ismália" (Ismalia) are considered the gems of his creative production, a large
part of which was gathered and published posthumously.

Guimaraens's brother, a symbolist poet who used the artistic name Archangelus de Guimaraens (1872–1934), wrote the collection *Coroa de espinhos* (1955;
Crown of Thorns), and Guimaraens's son is Alphonsus de Guimarães Filho (b.
1918), a postmodernist poet (for his translations, *see* "Key to Bibliographical
References," Hulet). (*See* Postmodernism in Poetry.)

BIBLIOGRAPHY: *Poesias*, 1938; *Obra completa*, 1960. Translations: Hulet; Woodbridge. Criticism: Daniel, Mary Lou. "Alphonsus de Guimaraens: Litany, Liturgy, and
Literature." *New Perspectives in Brazilian Literary Studies: Symbolism*. Edited by Darlene Sadlier. Bloomington: Indiana University, 1984, pp. 19–35.

MARIA ANGÉLICA GUIMARÃES LOPES

GUIMARÃES, BERNARDO   (1825–1884). Born in Minas, Guimarães received a law degree at the Faculty of São Paulo (1852), where he and his friends Alvares de *Azevedo and Aureliano Lessa (*see* Romanticism) founded the Epicurean Society, earning a reputation for both their bohemian escapades and their poetry. After graduation, he briefly and unsuccessfully held appointments in Minas as a judge and and a schoolteacher. From 1858 to 1861 he worked as a journalist in Rio, where he made friends with Machado de *Assis.

Although Guimarães is recognized as a significant minor romantic poet, his best-known work, though far from his artistic best, is *A escrava Isaura* (1875; The Slave Girl Isaura), recently adapted for an extremely popular film and television serial. Behind a transparently thin novelistic disguise, this is an abolitionist polemic, successful enough in its day to have been called "the Brazilian *Uncle Tom's Cabin*." (*See* Film and Literature; Romanticism; Slavery and Literature.)

Guimarães's prose usually reveals his romantic heritage through characters who personify universal human values and through the Kantian ethical imperative as a source of dramatic tension. As an Indianist, for example, he sometimes joined José de *Alencar in presenting the noble savage, as in his novel *O ermitão de Muquém* (1866; The Hermit of Muquém). In the same work, however, and in others, he is a major precursor of *regionalism through his vivid characterizations of the backlandsman of mixed, part-Indian blood and other authentic rural types. (*See* Indianism.)

Guimarães's innovations extend also to his anticipation of *naturalism, as evidenced in his novels *A filha do fazendeiro* (1872; The Rancher's Daughter), which exhibits physiological origination of emotion, and *O seminarista* (1872; The Seminarian), in which biological and environmental determinism produces a clinical case study. Complemented later by Herculano Inglês de *Sousa, Guimarães established in the novel a recognizable form of native Brazilian naturalism, during the 1870s, the decade when romanticism was dying and European naturalism had not yet been imported to replace it.

BIBLIOGRAPHY: Additional selected works by Guimarães: *Cantos de solidão*, 1852; *Obras completas*, 13 vols., 1941; *Poesias completas*, 1959. Criticism: Andrews, Norwood, Jr., "Early Anticipation of Naturalism in Brazil: The Dramatic Novels of Bernardo Guimarães." *PLL* (Fall, 1982), pp. 395–414; idem. "A Modern Classification of Bernardo Guimarães's Prose Narratives." *LBR* (Winter, 1966), pp. 59–82; idem. "Two Nineteenth-Century Brazilian Polemics: A Critical Appraisal of Bernardo Guimarães's *A escrava Isaura* and *Rosaura, a enjeitada*." *RLA* 8–9 (1966), pp. 233–272; Brookshaw; Sayers.

NORWOOD ANDREWS, JR.

GUIMARÃES, JOSUÉ   (1921–1986). Guimarães was a journalist, novelist, and author of *children's literature in his native Rio Grande do Sul State. In 1972 he began a proposed trilogy of novels about the colonization of his home state under the general title "A ferro e fogo" (By Iron and Fire): *Tempo de solidão* (1972; Time of Solitude) and *Tempo de guerra* (1975; Time of War).

These works are notable for their astute presentation of the intricate international political and socioeconomic power plays that brought about the unification of the southern territory with the nation between 1824 and 1845. The important role of German immigrants to Brazil is highlighted throughout. This literary project might be paralleled to that of his state compatriot Érico *Veríssimo.

His 1980 novel *Camilo Mortágua* (Camilo Mortagua) is set during the period immediately following the military coup of 1964 and narrates the decadence of the well-to-do *gaúcho* families against the backdrop of the dictatorship. Guimarães himself was forced into exile in Portugal during the early years of the military regime. (*See* Dictatorship and Literature).

BIBLIOGRAPHY: Additional selected works by Guimarães: *Depois do último trem*, 1973; *Lisboa, Urgente*, 1975; É tarde para saber, 1977; *Dona Anja*, 1978; *O gato no escuro*, 1982.

GUIMARÃES ROSA. *See* Rosa, João Guimarães.

GULLAR, FERREIRA [JOSÉ RIBAMAR FERREIRA] (b. 1930). Although born and brought up in Maranhão, Ferreira Gullar has lived in Rio since the 1950s. During his teens he was a disk jockey, and he has been a dynamic journalist, poet, and playwright.

Gullar's first collection of poems, *Um pouco acima do chão* (1949; A Little Above the Earth), idealizes his native city of São Luís. It was followed by another collection, *A luta corporal* (1954; The Bodily Struggle). An early adherent to concretism (*see* Postmodernism in Poetry) and one of its most successful poets, he later founded a less mathematically oriented version of the movement, neoconcretism (*see* Postmodernism in Poetry), but abandoned this type of poetry in 1960 in favor of "participatory poetry" inspired by popular traditions and forms, such as the *literatura de cordel*, for example, *Quem matou Aparecida?* (1962; Who Killed Aparecida?) (*See* Folklore and Literature.)

After 1964 Gullar became more deeply involved in social causes. He was one of the founding members of the Opinião Theater group, and with Oduvaldo *Viana Filho, he wrote one of the group's most successful plays based on popular northeastern traditions applied to the then current Brazilian sociopolitical situation: *Se correr o bicho pega, se ficar o bicho come* (1966; If You Run the Animal Beats You Up, If You Stay the Animal Eats You) and *Rubi no umbigo* (1978; Ruby in the Novel). (*See* Dictatorship and Literature; Theater History.)

His poetry in *Dentro da noite veloz* (1975; Within the Swift Night) raises specific social and political issues regarding the role of a dictatorship in society, such as in "Maio 1964" (May, 1964), which attacks the military's regime's procedure of ruling by Institutional Acts: "I am 33 years old and I have gastritis. I love life / which is full of children, flowers / women, life. This right of being in the world / having two feet and hands, a face / and a hunger for everything, hope.That right of everyone / which no institutional nor constitutional act / can remove or decree." Gullar's outspoken, accusatory tone toward the military dictatorship led to his being jailed in 1968, along with Paulo *Francis and the promoters-singers of *tropicalismo*, Caetano Veloso and Gilberto Gil, and to his exile in Buenos Aires between 1971 and 1977.

In 1976 Gullar published his longest poem, *Poema sujo* (Dirty Poem), which is an occasionally violent autobiographical paean to his native São Luís. In it the author openly lamented the inhumane treatment accorded the people by their rulers, the squalor of the impoverished existence of the city's inhabitants, and his own exile in Buenos Aires: "A man is in the city / like something is in another / and the city is in the man / who is in another city." Many critics (*see* Critics and Criticism) and writers view this poem as a summation of the status of "homo brasiliensis" during the dictatorship years. (*See* Autobiography.)

Gullar has also collaborated with Dias *Gomes on plays, and he has published important essays on social attitudes toward literature, most notably *Vanguarda e subdesenvolvimento* (1969; The Vanguard and Underdevelopment).

BIBLIOGRAPHY: Additional selected works by Gullar: *Cultura posta em questão*, 1964; *Por você, por mim*, 1968; *Crime na flora*, 1986. Translations: Bishop/Brasil; Brasil/Smith.

H

HILST, HILDA   (b. 1930). A lawyer born and educated in São Paulo, Hilst is a poet, dramatist, and fiction writer. She is also a practicing clairvoyant. A member of the Generation of 1945 (*see* Postmodernism in Poetry), Hilst has been preoccupied with her highly personal search for divine truth. In *Trovas de muito amor para um amado senhor* (1959; Profound Love Poems for a Beloved Lord), she pursued this theme within the structure of medieval poetic forms.

Although she has written many dramas, produced but not as yet published, in recent years she has turned to fiction. *Fluxo-Foema* (1970; Fluxo-Foema) is structured around the concept of "three"—conventional man, man in love, and repressed man—and presents the duality of man in these various stages of his existence. Uniting a myriad of real and imaginary philosophies, eroticism, scatology, and exoticism, Hilst's unique style has garnered critical but not popular attention.

BIBLIOGRAPHY: Additional selected works by Hilst: *Pressagio*, 1950; *A possessa*, 1967; *Qadós*, 1973; *Júbilo memória noviciado da paixão*, 1974; *Com meus olhos de cão e outras novelas*, 1986. Translations: Tolman (1978). Criticism: Ribeiro, Léo Gilson. "Apresentação." In *Ficções* by Hilda Hilst. São Paulo: Edições Quíron, 1977, pp. ix–xii.

HISTORIOGRAPHY.   Brazilian historiography moved leisurely from its preoccupation with factual narrative to a concern with interpretation. Churchmen and patricians dominated the writing of history for four centuries. Only by the midtwentieth century did significant numbers of professional historians begin to appear. For the past four decades, they have reshaped the study of the past, expanding the topics under study, broadening the use of documentation, devising new periodizations, and infusing myriad theoretical considerations. Consequently, a more complex and sophisticated historiography has emerged. However, it maintains the nationalism (the nativism of the colonial period) traditionally present in Brazilian historiography. (*See Ufanismo.*)

Chroniclers recorded the discovery and colonization of Brazil. Observant, literate men on the scene bore witness to the events they described. They kept a simple record of acts, arranging them in order of time; they did not try to reconstruct the past. A drama of flesh and blood, their accounts remained undisturbed by the compilation of documents, analysis, or interpretation. They were most active in the sixteenth and seventeenth centuries.

In his unique letter of May 1, 1500, to King Manuel I, Pero Vaz de *Caminha witnessed the discovery of Brazil and painted a verbal picture of the shore the Portuguese first visited, testifying to the beauty of the land. In its rhapsodic passages on the Indians, it exemplifies the early romantic attitudes toward them. Pero Lopes de Sousa (c. 1501–c. 1542) in his *Diário da navegação armada que foi à terra do Brasil* (1530; Navigational Diary of the Armada that Went to Brazil) recorded the first efforts at colonization. The historiography of the first century of settlement owes much to the Jesuits, particularly to Father Manuel da *Nóbrega and Father José de *Anchieta. Those indefatigable correspondents began to write as soon as they arrived in 1549; their rambling, garrulous, and highly informative letters span the remaining half century. (*See* Indianism; Portugal and Brazil; Literary Relations.)

In his *Tratado da terra do Brasil* (c. 1569; published in 1826; Treatise on the Land of Brazil) and *História da província de Santa Cruz* (1576; History of the Province of Santa Cruz), Pero de Magalhães Gandavo (?–1576) offered the first complete description of Brazil. Picturing it as a land of abundance, he described the terrain, Indians, flora, fauna, and growing number of settlements scattered along several thousands of miles of coast. The romantic notions about the Indians had disappeared by this time. Father Fernão Cardim (1540–1625), who arrived in the New World in 1583, continued the tradition established by Gandavo. His three descriptive works have been brought together under the title *Tratados da terra e gente do Brasil* (published in 1939; Treatises on the Land and People of Brasil). The *Tratado descritivo do Brasilem 1587* (Descriptive Treatise about Brazil in 1587) by Gabriel Soares de *Sousa is the last of the important sixteenth-century chronicles. Displaying an optimism pervading Brazilian historiography, he prophesied, "This land is capable of becoming a great empire."

The seventeenth century witnessed the appearance of an increased nativistic character in the chronicles. Many of the authors of that century were *mazombos*, men born in Brazil of Portuguese lineage. As native sons, they displayed an intense love of and devotion to the land of their birth. That pride contrasts with the more detached enthusiasm of their predecessors. *Os diálogos das grandezas do Brasil* (1618; Dialogues about the Wealth of Brazil) aptly illustrates that pride. Although apparently born in Portugal, Ambrósio Fernandes Brandão (c. 1560–c. 1630), a New Christian (converted Jew), found Brazil to be a haven from possible persecution and repaid the benign attitude of the colony with his loyalty and devotion, amply evident in his book. Other chronicles of the century reflect the epic territorial push of the Luso-Brazilians into the heartland of South America, expanding the boundaries of empire to both local and Portuguese satisfaction. (*See* Religion and Literature.)

Cultura e opulência do Brasil (1711; Agriculture and Wealth of Brazil) by Father André João Antonil (pseudonym of João Antônio Andreoni) (1650–1716) ranks as the last important chronicle. The Jesuit father divided his book into four studies, each dedicated to one of the main industries of the colony: sugar, tobacco, mining, and cattle. He pointed out the fortune that Brazil annually provided Portugal. *Cultura* contains less of the defensive explanation found in Brandão's *Os diálogos* and more boasting. It reflects the psychological change in the Brazilians brought about by their defeat of the Dutch and conquest of the interior. It set the stage for the rising tide of nativism that engulfed the eighteenth-century Brazilians.

The first history, which aimed to recreate and interpret the past, appeared in 1627, when Frei Vicente do Salvador (1564–1639) finished his *História do Brasil* (published in 1889; History of Brazil). He described events from the discovery to the struggle against the Dutch. The foundation of literary and scientific *academies in the eighteenth century encouraged the study of history. From one of them emerged Brazil's foremost colonial historian, Sebastião da Rocha Pita (1660–1738). Association with the Academia dos Esquecidos (Academy of the Forgotten) encouraged Rocha Pita to write his *História de América portuguesa* (1730; History of Portuguese America). The Bahian's optimism, praise of Brazil, pride in being Brazilian, and descriptions of the beauty and fertility of the land established a pattern subsequent historians would follow.

Although the nationalism encouraged by the literati played a role in Brazil's declaration of independence from Portugal in 1822, historians did not fully exercise their responsibility of explaining the past, rationalizing independence and glorifying the emerging national state until the 1830s. The foundation in 1839 of the prestigious Brazilian Historical and Geographical Institute marked the official intention of fledgling historians to assume those responsibilities. Thereafter the institute served as a mighty impetus to the study of the Brazilian past. Regional historical institutes appeared later in the century. Today, every state capital is the seat of such an institute, and most cities of any size boast similar ones. A major contribution of all of these institutes has been their diligent search for, preservation of, and publication of documents.

The institute sponsored a competition in 1840 on the challenging question of how best to write national history. A foreigner but corresponding member of the institute, Karl Friedrich Philipp von Martius (1794–1868), submitted the most convincing reply. He displayed a remarkably clear vision of the uniqueness of Brazil with its amalgamation of the three races and their contribution to a single civilization. He also discussed the phenomenon of unity through diversity, a vast nation remained unified despite powerful centrifugal temptations. In short, von Martius singled out significant historical themes that have dominated Brazilian historiography ever since.

Two intellectual giants dominated nineteenth-century Brazilian historiography: Francisco Adolfo de Varnhagen (1816–1878) and João Capistrano de Abreu (1853–1927). Taking advantage of his travels as a diplomat, Varnhagen spent much time in foreign libraries and archives. He discovered significant documents that shed new light on the colonial past. Without doubt, his foremost work is the *História geral do Brasil* (A General History of Brazil) in two volumes, 1854 and 1857, respectively. In detailed narrative, he recounted events from the discovery to the declaration of independence. He also prepared a significant critical edition of the epic poems by *Durão and B. da *Gama: *Épicos brasileiros* (1845; Brazilian Epics).

"Capistrano de Abreu became a legend in the field of historiography," concluded José Honório Rodrigues (In *Correspondência de Capistrano de Abreu.* [Rio, 1954], p. LV), one of the most distinguished of Brazil's contemporary historians. Few quibble with that conclusion. Eschewing narrative for interpretive history, Capistrano de Abreu displayed a remarkable ability to see beyond facts to their meaning and significance. He was not a prolific historian but everything he wrote was important. His principal works are *O caminhos antigos e o povoamento do Brazil* (1889; published 1930; Old Roads and the Settlement of Brazil); *Os capítulos de história colonial* (1907; Chapters of Colonial History); a critical edition of Frei Vicente de Salvador's *História do Brasil* (1886–87), and a critical edition of Varnhagen's *História geral do Brasil* (1907). Capistrano de Abreu initiated an extremely important movement of historical revision by calling attention to the importance of the Brazilian interior and its impact on national formation. In 1889, four years before Frederick Jackson Turner read his address to the American Historical Association on the impact of the frontier on U.S. history, the Brazilian's *O caminhos antigos* . . . set forth the theory of the importance of the frontier in the shaping of Brazil and national character. A self-taught historian from the provinces, he continues to be one of the most perceptive historians who has written about Brazil's past.

Along with Capistrano de Abreu, Silvio *Romero emerged as a pioneer in interpreting the Brazilian past, and, as with his peer, Romero's interpretations influenced succeeding generations of historians. A prolific writer, Romero's foremost work remains the *História da literatura brasileira*, a vast and penetrating social history. Amplifying a theme suggested by von Martius, Romero emphasized how miscegenation created both the Brazilians and their civilization.

Responding to maturing and intensifying nationalism in the twentieth century, cogently expressed during the Week of Modern Art of 1922 (*see* Modernism), historians during the twentieth century place greater emphasis on the interpretation of national character and destiny. The interpretations constitute a significant contribution to Brazilian historiography and are best represented by Paulo *Prado in his *Retrato do Brasil*, Gilberto *Freyre in *Casa grande e senzala*, Sérgio Buarque de Hollanda in *Raízes do Brasil* (1936; The Roots of Brazil), Nelson Werneck Sodré (*See* Critics and Criticism) in *Formação da sociedade brasileira* (1944; Formation of Brazilian Society), and José Honório Rodrigues (b. 1913) in *Aspirações nacionais* (1962; National Aspirations).

The establishment of chairs of history in Brazilian universities starting in the 1930s and the subsequent formation of departments of history, eventually in all the major universities, encouraged the appearance and growth of careers as professional historians, those who earn their livelihood through the teaching and writing of history. Gradually, the focal point for the study and writing of history moved from the historical institutes to the universities. The results have been a proliferation of professional journals of which the *Revista de História*, edited at the University of São Paulo, served as a model; increasingly frequent regional and national historical conferences; impressive publication programs; and the emergence of a group of outstanding historians whose research and writing rank internationally with the best anywhere. The multivolume, multiauthored *História geral da civilização brasileira* illustrates the breadth, depth, and diversity of contemporary Brazilian historiography.

BIBLIOGRAPHY: Criticism: Burns, E. Bradford, ed. *Perspectives on Brazilian History*. New York: Columbia University Press, 1967; Eakin, Marshall C. "Race and Identity: Sílvio Romero, Science, and Social Thought in Late Nineteenth-Century Brazil," *LBR* (Winter, 1985), pp. 151–174; Fringer, Katherine. "The Contribution of Capistrano de Abreu to Brazilian Historiography," *JIAS* (April, 1971), pp. 258–278; Lombardi, Mary. "The Frontier in Brazilian History: An Historiographical Essay," *Pacific Historical Review* (November, 1975), pp. 437–457; Schwartz, Stuart B. "Francisco Adolfo de Varhagen: Diplomat, Patriot, Historian." HAHR (May, 1967), pp. 185–202; Skidmore, Thomas E. "The Historiography of Brazil," *HAHR*, Part I (November, 1975), pp. 716–748; Part II (February, 1976), pp. 81–109; Stein, Stanley, J. "The Historiography of Brazil, 1808–1889." HAHR (May, 1960), pp. 234–278.

E. BRADFORD BURNS

HOMEM, HOMERO (b. 1921). Journalist and university professor in Rio, Homem was born in Rio Grande do Norte. He has been active in writers' associations and has received many literary *prizes.

Homem is primarily a poet unrelated to any of the postmodernist movements. His most widely known collection is *Calendário marinheiro* (1958; Maritime Calendar), which includes a section of poems dedicated to fishing. Other poems deal with sociopolitical themes such as life in Rio and the human condition, for example, *Canto nacional e Abecedário da Transamazônica* (1971; National Poem and Alphabet of the Trans-Amazon Highway) and *Afetogramas* (1973; Affectiongrams), poems addressed to his friends and to other poets. (*See* Postmodernism in Poetry; Regionalism.)

Homem's prose works include documentary-style reports on soccer, several stories and novels dealing with the theme (e.g., *O moço da camisa 10* [1979; The Player in Shirt Number 10]), as well as *children's literature. His novel *Cabra das rocas* (1966; Toughguy of the Rocks) falls within the category of regionalist fiction, whereas *Menino de asas* (1976; Boy with Wings) is an allegorial tale verging on science fiction. (*See* Regionalism; Soccer and Literature.)

BIBLIOGRAPHY: *O agrimensor da aurora* (complete poetry), 1981.

HOMOSEXUALITY AND LITERATURE. The first Latin American novel with a homosexual theme was Adolfo *Caminha's *Bom Crioulo*. Bom Crioulo's passion for and murder of Aleixo is described in graphic detail characteristic of *naturalism. Although characters with homosexual tendencies appear in many other works of fiction, from Raul *Pompéia's *O ateneu* to the novels of the *social novelists of the 1930s and Antônio *Callado's *Assunção de Salviano*, as well as in *Qorpo-Santo's and Nelson *Rodrigues's dramas.

Writers returned to this theme most directly in the 1970s. Gasparino Damata (pseudonym of Gasparino Da Mata) had (b. 1918) two important anthologies of gay literature of the 1940s and 1950s published: *Histórias do amor maldito* (1969; Stories of the Forbidden Love) and, with Walmir *Ayala, *Poemas do amor maldito* (1970; Poetry of the Forbidden Love). Damata has also produced his own stories, *Os solteirões* (1976; The Confirmed Bachelors), and in 1978 founded *Lampião*, a gay cultural newspaper. Fernando de Melo's play *Greta Garbo, quem diria, acabou no Irajá* (1973; Greta Garbo, Who Would Imagine It, Ended up at the Irajá) and the gay theater group "Dzi Croquetes" were also successful. (*See* Theater History.)

The period of the *abertura* has witnessed an immense increase in gay literature both in short fiction and theater. Homosexuals do not appear only as sexual beings but often as another repressed minority of Brazilian society comparable to blacks and women. Contemporaries whose works have dealt with aspects of the homosexual life-style in Brazil include Darcy Penteado (b. 1926), Caio Fernando *Abreu, Aguinaldo *Silva, Silviano *Santiago, Plínio *Marcos, Cassandra Rios, whose works deal with lesbianism and female bisexuality, Edilberto *Coutinho, Luiz Fernando *Emediato, Domingos *Pellegrini, Jr., Glauco Mattoso and João Silvério Trevisan (b. 1944), author of *Testamento de Jônatas deixado a David* (1976; Will of Jonatas to David), *Em nome do desejo* (1983; In the Name of Desire), and *Vagas notícias de Melinha Marchiotti* (1984; Vague News about Melinha Marchiotti), and a sociocultural history of homosexuality in Brazil: *Devassos no paraíso* (1986; *Perverts in Paradise* 1986). (*See* Autobiography.)

BIBLIOGRAPHY: Selected works of Brazilian gay literature in translation appear in *Gay Sunshine* 26/27 (1976); 38/39 (1979); *Now the Volcano*. Edited by Winston Leyland. San Francisco: Gay Sunshine Press, 1979. Criticism: Canales, Luis. "O homossexualismo como tema no moderno teatro brasileiro." *LBR* (Summer, 1981), pp. 173–182; Lacey, E. A. "Latin America: Myths and Realities." *Gay Sunshine* 40/41 (1979), pp. 22–31.

I, J, K

IMMIGRANTS AND LITERATURE. Brazil, like the United States, is a nation of immigrants. Since the 1820s, in addition to Portuguese settlers, waves of Germans, Italians, Spaniards, Middle Easterners, and Orientals have settled in many different areas of their adopted nation.

There is a literary tradition in Brazil dating from the nineteenth century whose topic is the immigrant and his experience as well as a portrayal of social conditions. The writers are most often Brazilian, and although they tried to depict honestly and realistically the conditions of life and the macaronic Portuguese language of the various groups of immigrants, their views reflected those of the dominant social group. These are the work of writers like Alfredo *Taunay in his *Inocência*; Aluísio *Azevedo; Lima *Barreto; Oswald de *Andrade in *Revolução melancólica* (1942; The Melancholic Revolution), which deals with Japanese migration to Brazil; Graça *Aranha; Plínio *Salgado; Alcântara *Machado; Cecílio J. Carneiro (b. 1911) in *A fogueira* (1939; *The Bonfire*, 1944), which deals with Syrian immigration; and Juó Bananére in the ''Italo-Portuguese dialect'' of São Paulo.

However, a neglected chapter in the intellectual history of Brazil is that of the important role of literature produced by the immigrants and their descendants. It portrays the trials, sufferings, and humiliations they have endured. It describes the clash of generations, the marginal relation of immigrants to Brazilian culture, the problems of assimilation, and the search for social justice and happiness.

A study of their literature reveals a growth process in various stages that culminates in cultural interaction and subsequently in cultural assimilation. These stages comprehend: (a) the period of narratives that describe the problems immigrants faced with the unfamiliar Brazilian culture and landscape; (b) the period of adjustment characterized by isolation, alienation, the need for assimilation, rejection of the old culture, and the fulfillment of their dreams; and (c) the final stage that depicts the attitude and needs of the immigrants' descendants. There is often in this final phase a ''return-to-the-roots'' syndrome, a nostalgic glance, a thematic use of the immigrants' experience as a legitimate part of Brazilian history.

The chronological development of immigrants' literature can be roughly divided into two periods: books published between 1939 and 1956 and books published from 1956 on. This division is adopted here because Samuel *Rawet's *Contos do imigrante*, published in 1956, is the first to examine immigrants' experience in depth, going beyond a depiction of their life and social conditions in the different regions of Brazil. (*See* Regionalism.)

1939–1956. The works of the first period are all relevant to the realities of immigrants' lives and are directly linked to historical circumstances that affected them. For example, *Um rio imita o Reno* (1939) by Viana *Moog deals with the social and political conditions in Brazil in the 1930s under the strong nationalistic movement galvanized by Vargas. In this period the Brazilian government undertook actions promoting cultural nationalism and antiforeign campaigns against "ethnic enclaves," especially German and Japanese and, to a lesser extent, Italians. Moog's position is explanatory, conciliatory, almost apologetic; he tried to bridge the gap of misunderstanding between the two sides in the novel—the German and the Brazilians in conflict in a small town in southern Brazil.

In 1941 Tito Batini published *E agora, quê fazer?* (And Now, What's There To Do?), supposedly written while he was imprisoned in 1924. If this is true, it makes Batini one of the earliest writers in Brazil to explore the dramatic reality of Brazilian social problems, in particular proletarian living conditions. His other novels, for example, *Entre o chão e as estrelas* (1943; Between the Earth and the Stars) and *Inácio, pastor das nuvens* (1961; *Ignatius, Shepherd of Clouds*), portray the participation of the masses in the historical changes in Brazil. In fact, Batini is a member of a rare species in Brazilian literature—the proletarian writer.

The novels by Sara Novak, *Levanta-te e luta!* (1944; Stand Up and Fight!), and by Elisa Lispector (sister of Clarice *Lispector), *No exílio* (1948; In Exile), have similar plots. They both concern survivors of the persecution of Jews in Russia early in this century, memoirs that are revived by events of World War II. Novak's novel is more an analysis of a woman confronted with the question of her Jewishness and the pronounced antisemitism in Brazil during the 1930s. Lispector's novel is the tale of a survivor of pogroms. Her purpose is to bear witness, to testify about the incredible events that led her family to flee Europe and immigrate to Brazil under difficult conditions. (*See* Feminism and Literature; Religion and Literature.)

Mansueto Bernardi, from Rio Grande do Sul, is known for his *Poemas imigrantistas* (1947; Immigrant's Poems), dedicated to the early Italian immigrants. He spoke of the rural life and the hardships of working the land. His poem "Convite à superação" (Invitation to Overcome) calls for all of the Aryan groups—Portuguese, German, Italian, and others—to join together in the Brazilian melting pot and consciously leave out other ethnic groups.

Post–1956. In the second period of immigrants' literature, the autobiographies or themes of personal recall continue. (*See* Autobiography.) But contrary to the first period, the second focuses not on experience per se but on the meaning the writer gives to it. The writer can tell his experiences or those of his ancestors with objectivity, detachment, and humor. The basic impulse is the search for identity, the need to proceed with the process of self-discovery. The writer dwells increasingly on the individual predicament. The immigrants are portrayed as exiles from their culture and their past, and the writer attempts to use his art to draw the parallel between alienation and the immigrants' dispossession, between the universal and the particular experience of human loss.

The novel by Augusto Sylvio Prödohl (b. 1916) *Às margens do Cachoeira* (1961; *At the Shores of Cachoeira*) was published first in Germany in 1958. It is a fictionalization of Viana Moog's ideas contained in the essay about the differences between Brazilian and North American colonization, *Bandeirantes e pioneiros*. In 1967 Ricardo Hoffmann's *A Superfície* (The Surface) was published. The author drew characters from the German community in which he grew up and presented the psychological aspects of that environment.

Carlos Heitor *Cony is of French Moroccan and semitic origin and was brought up in Rio. Although he does not consider himself Jewish, his political novel *Pessach: a travessia* (1967) is an example of Judaic expression since it uses symbols of the Jewish experience (Passover and Exodus). Its protagonist is a bourgeois writer of Jewish origin who has denied his heritage and is politically indifferent to the appearance of a military regime. This semiautobiographical novel is a modern allegorical representation of Brazil. José Mucinic's *Menino israelita* (1954; Jewish Boy) dealt more specifically with the problem of the immigrants' adaptation to Brazil and the problems of prejudice among the immigrants themselves in the Northeast. In 1969 Zevi Ghivelder's *As seis pontas da estrela* (The Six Points of the Star) was published, the first novel to portray a large cross-section of Jewish immigrants in Brazil. Alberto Dines in his essays, and Michael Bruckner in his short fiction, *Shema Israel* (*Oure O Israel*) (1972; Hear, Oh Israel), have also touched on this theme. (*See* Dictatorship and Literature.)

In 1968 Moacir Scliar's *O carnaval dos animais* was published as a collection of short stories that introduces into Brazilian literature the techniques and tone of Jewish black humor predominant in the United States since the 1960s. He also fully realized a depiction of Jewish characters in novels such as *A guerra no bom fim* and *O exército de um homem só*. He has cleared the way for a literature that is not strictly derived from traditional Luso-Brazilian experience. However, the presence of the immigrant and the Jew in his novels is also his manner of examining the ascendancy of Brazilian bourgeoisie.

In the 1970s and 1980s more women writers have started to mark their presence with novels that talk about the immigrant experience in Brazil. Nélida *Piñon's *A república dos sonhos* is a story of her own family beginning in Galicia, Spain, and the dreams, losses, and successes of her ancestors as they established themselves in Brazil. Zélia Gattai wrote about her Italian family's experience and political involvement in the turmoil of the early decades of the twentieth century in *Anarquistas, graças a Deus* (1979; Anarchists, Thank God). Lya *Luft, among the prominent women writers in contemporary Brazil, uses her powerful imagery and prose to describe the lives of women who, like herself, were raised in German households in the South. (*See* Memoirs.)

Among many trends in Brazilian literature, the phenomenom of immigrants' literature has not exhausted its possibilities. Younger writers dealing with the theme include Paulo Jacob (*see* Regionalism); Sílvio Fiorani (b. 1943) (for his translations, *see Ploughshares* [Winter, 1986], in his *A herança de Lündstrom* [1984; The Lündstrom Inheritance]); and Alfredo Sirkis's *Corredor polonês* (1983; Polish Corridor), dealing with Poland of the past and Poland and Brazil of the present. Immigration has also been a successful theme in film, for example, Tizuka Yamasaki's *Gaijin*, dealing with the first Japanese to arrive in Brazil at the turn of the century.

Not all of the "hyphenated Brazilians" have told their stories; the challenge to explore ethnic roots as part of the large current search for fuller consciousness of the Brazilian identity will continue. (*See* Contemporary Black Literature; Philosophy of National Identity.)

BIBLIOGRAPHY: Criticism: Vieira, Nelson H. "Post-Holocaust Literature in Brazil: Jewish Resistance and Resurgence as Literary Metaphors for Brazilian Society and Politics." *MLS* (Winter, 1986), pp. 62–70.

NAOMI HOKI MONIZ

IMPRESSIONISM. Inspired by the highly subjective movement in the plastic arts of the midnineteenth century, which aimed at fleeting yet intense glimpses of reality, impressionism in Brazilian literature was evident in the style of Raul *Pompéia, Graça *Aranha, Gonzaga *Duque, and Adelino Magalhães (1897–1987), who is also considered a forerunner of *surrealism. Impressionist techniques were also adopted by *modernism's Oswald de *Andrade, Plínio *Salgado, and Alcântara *Machado in order to give their prose works a "modern" flavor of "velocity."

BIBLIOGRAPHY: Criticism: Coutinho/Rabassa; Placer, Xavier. In Coutinho, III.

INDIAN LANGUAGES

Contemporary Situation. The variety of indigenous languages in Brazil today is as great as that of Mexico and the United States combined. Approximately 170 Indian languages are spoken in Brazil: most are found in the northern and western states and territories (Maranhão, Pará, Amapá, Amazonas, Roraima, Acre, Rondônia, Mato Grosso, Goiás, and Mato Grosso do Sul); a few in the southern states (São Paulo, Paraná, Santa Catarina, Rio Grande do Sul); two languages in Minas (Mashakalí and Krenak-Nakrehé); and two in the northeastern state of Pernambuco (Yathé or Fulnió).

Of a total population of 185,500 Indians, about 30,500 are monolingual in

Portuguese. The remaining 155,000 speakers of native languages are dispro-
portionately divided among the 170 languages, for example, Tukúna with 18,000,
Makushí with 14,500, Kaingang and Guarani with about 10,000 each. According
to recent surveys, there are 36 Indian languages with fewer than 100 speakers
and, among them, 14 languages with fewer than 50 speakers. Two-thirds of the
indigenous languages of Brazil are affiliated with one of the five larger linguistic
stocks identified in the country: Tupi, Macro-Jê, Carib, Arawak, and Pano. The
other one-third, about 60 languages, either belong to smaller linguistic families
or are not yet properly classified.

Origin of the Indian Languages in the Literature. Studies of Brazilian
Indian languages can be traced to the sixteenth-century expeditions of explorers,
in whose papers names of tribes, languages, and short word lists are found. By
1542 manuscripts of vocabularies and partial grammars had already appeared.
In 1595 Father José de *Anchieta published a grammar of Tupi or *língua geral*.
(*See* Historiography; Portuguese Language of Brazil; Religion and Literature.)

The better known works of the seventeenth century were mostly written by
missionaries. Included in this category are the Tupi catechism of Araújo (1618),
the grammars and vocabularies of Bettendorf (1687) and Figueira (1681) for
Tupi; of Breton (1665), Biet (1664), and Davis (1666) for Carib; of Montoya
(1639) for Guarani; and of Blanco (1683), Tauste (1680), and Yangues (1683)
for Carib (Cumanagota, Chayma).

For the eighteenth century we have the works of Gilij (1782), who noted
resemblances among languages mainly around the Orinoco River area, and the
classificatory works of Hervas and Panduro (1784–1787). In the nineteenth century the principal authors of works on Brazilian Indian languages were German:
von Martius (1863–1867) analyzed the languages and culture of the Indians with
whom he had made contact during his trip to Brazil with the zoologist Spix;
Steinem (1892) classified the Bakairí language as Carib, and Paul Ehrenreich
(1894) dealt with the mythology of linguistically distinct groups: Tupi-Guarani,
Arawak, and Carib. A notable Brazilian contribution was Gonçalves *Dias's
Dicionário da lingua tupi (1876; Dictionary of the Tupi Language). (*See* Folklore
and Literature; Travel Literature.)

Curt Nimuendaju, who bridged the nineteenth and early twentieth centuries,
produced a map of languages spoken at the turn of the century, linguistic classifications, and several vocabularies. Theodor Koch-Grünberg (1906, 1927) presented linguistic data from northern Amazonia, as well as another classification
of Brazilian indigenous languages. The most impressive work by a Brazilian in
this period was that of Capistrano de Abreu (*See* Historiography) (1914) on
Cashinawa.

There are several non-Brazilian scholars who, in the second third of this
century, produced major works: Jules Henry on Shokleng, Olive Shell on Krahó,
Neil Hawkins on Waiwái, and Paul Garvin using Levi-Strauss's material on
Nambiquara. A large part of the linguistic output since the 1950s has come from
the missionaries of the Summer Institute of Linguistics (SIL). Two academic

institutions also produce much of the contemporary work: the Museu Nacional (Yvonne Leite on Tapirapé, Charlotte Emmerich on Xinguan languages, Miriam Lemle on comparative Tupian) and the Universidade Estadual de Campinas (UNICAMP), with which Aryon Rodrigues, known for his studies on Tupian languages and for his classification of indigenous languages of Brazil, is affiliated. Contemporary foreign linguists include Aurore Monod-Bequelin on Trumai, Ernesto Migliazza on Yanomam, David Price on Nambiquara, and Denny Moore on Gavião.

Significance of Indian Languages for Brazilian Literature and Culture. Long a part of Brazilian vocabulary have been the various terms, especially for flora and fauna, borrowed from the many indigenous languages discussed above. Words such as *arapaima, jabiru, piranha, tapioca*, have entered Brazilian Portuguese and foreign languages from Tupian languages. (*See* Indianism.)

Indigenous literature still does not participate in the mainstream of Brazilian writing. However, the oral genre, in which indigenous myths, legends, and political thinking is expressed, is as metaphorically rich and complex in style as the written literature of any society. Finally, in the transition from the native to the national culture, some Indians who speak a little Portuguese and their own language are taught to read and write their maternal tongue. They are encouraged to express in writing their own culture so as to produce a rich and culturally relevant type of literature. (*See* Folklore and Literature.)

BIBLIOGRAPHY: Criticism: *Handbook of Amazonian Languages*. Vol. I. Edited by Desmond C. Derbyshire and Geoffrey K. Pullum. Berlin: Mouton de Gruyter, 1986; *Indians of Brazil in the Twentieth Century*. Edited by Janice H. Hopper. Washington, D.C.: Institute for Cross-Cultural Research, 1967; *Native South American Discourse*. Edited by Joel Sherzer and Greg Urban. Berlin: Mouton de Gruter, 1986; *South American Indian Languages*. Edited by Harriet E. Manelis Klein and Louisa R. Stark. Austin: University of Texas Press, 1985.

HARRIET E. MANELIS KLEIN

INDIANISM. The theme of the native American Indian had risen to prominence in European literature and thought toward the end of the eighteenth century, as the culmination of a philosophical tradition that embraces Sir Thomas More's (1478–1535) *Utopia*, Michel Montaigne's (1533–1592) essay "Des Cannibales" (1580), and Jean-Jacques Rousseau's (1712–1778) *Discourse sur l'origine et les fondements de l'inégalité parmi les hommes* (1755). Simultaneously, in colonial Brazil Father Antônio *Vieira and Friar Loreto Couto (eighteenth century) raised practical issues about the Indians' destiny. In the early nineteenth century specific social and political conditions, namely, the country's recent independence from Portugal (1822) and the existence of a native Indian population, gave Brazilian Indianism the special character of a self-conscious movement with important political implications. (*See* Portugal and Brazil: Literary Relations.)

The Brazilian Indianist movement lasted some fifty years, from 1835 to the end of the empire (1889), and produced more than thirty novels, plays, and works of poetry whose central theme is the Indian. In 1826, in an extremely influential study of the existing tradition of literature in Portuguese, Ferdinand Denis (*see* Critics and Criticism; Travel Literature) singled out two epic Indianist poems from the eighteenth century, Santa Rita *Durão's Caramuru* and Basílio da *Gama's O uraguai*, as manifestations of an emergent spirit of cultural independence. Whereas Brazil, newly emancipated from European rule, possessed no national cultural heritage, it could, according to Denis, rediscover, reinvent, and adopt the "history" and traditions of its indigenous peoples as its own. This assumed heritage would supply Brazilian artists with the mythical, heroic values that European romantics, such as Walter Scott, were deriving from medieval history of the Old World. Ironically, then, the very ethnic group whose territorial and cultural rights had been most abused and that was most alienated from Brazilian society, became the token symbol of Brazilian nationalism and independence. The movement was not limited to literature but extended to the visual arts and to other disciplines. In 1839 the Brazilian Historical and Geographical Institute was founded, one of its principal tasks being to document and publish material on the remaining indigenous populations in the country. The Tupi language became an object of study; newspapers adopted Indian titles, such as *O Tamoio*; Gonçalves *Dias's Tupi-Portuguese dictionary was published; and patriots exchanged their Portuguese names for indigenous ones. (*See* Art and Literature; Indian Languages; Portuguese Language of Brazil; Romanticism.)

In its initial stages, then, Indianism sought to identify land and nation by means of pseudoindigenous myth, for example, Ladislau dos Santos's (1801–1861) "Metamorfose original-Moema e Camorogi" (1835; Original Metamorphosis: Moema and Camorogi). But the richer and more typical writing of the first phase of the movement (1835–1850) arose out of a different theme: the imminence of conquest, the impending destruction of the Indians' timeless, mythical world. On the most obviously political level, this supplied the independence cause with an ideological and historical legitimacy, by identifying the interests of Indian and Brazilian in their struggle against Portuguese colonial oppression. More broadly, the predominantly combative spirit of this first phase, with its masculine cult of war, reflects a general atmosphere of social and political conflict in Brazil during a period of violent liberal and regionalist uprisings. Like the poetry of Gonçalves Dias, *Os tres dias de um noivado* (1844) by the mulatto writer Teixeira e *Sousa reveals an acute awareness of the meaning of social marginalization not only for the country's indigenous populations but also for a whole dispossessed class of whites and mestizos within Brazilian society. (*See* Philosophy of National Identity.)

Until 1856 Indianism had been almost exclusively the domain of poetry. The last complete Indianist epic of the movement was Gonçalves de *Magalhães's *A confederação dos tamoios*. Reactionary in its attitudes and style, the poem became a target for a number of critics, including the future novelist José de *Alencar, who published his objections in a series of letters. The literary polemic was symptomatic of a crisis of credibility regarding the function of the Indianist theme; the image of the defiant, exiled Indian warrior, symbol of freedom and independence, had outlived its usefulness.

The new lead given by Alencar in his works that were published between 1857 and 1874 and the predominantly novelistic Indianist output of other writers during that period represent a significant shift of emphasis. Works such as Joaquim Felício dos Santos's (1828–1895) *Acayaca* (1866; Acayaca), Araripe Júnior's (*see* Critics and Criticism) *Jacina, a marabà* (1870; Jacina, the Crossbred Indian), and the Amazonian writer Araújo Amazonas's (1803–c. 1864) *Simá* (1857; Sima), are concerned no longer with themes of conflict, genocide, and the military ideal but rather with the interracial encounter and dialogue that led to the formation of a peculiarly Brazilian people, indigenous culture, and psychology, and their effect on the Portuguese language as spoken in Brazil, themes of sexual and social intercourse that might be suggested by female characters— in short, the cultural and socioeconomic foundations of imperial society. (*See* Portuguese Language of Brazil.)

By the 1870s, however, those foundations, as well as the assumptions of romantic Indianism until then, were being seriously questioned by the growing movements of republicanism, abolitionism, and *realism in literature. Critical voices such as Bernardo *Guimarães began to reject the mythical, idealized Indianism of Alencar's *O guarani* and *Iracema* and to explore a more worldly, contemporary landscape inhabited by real human beings. Nevertheless, this did not prevent other writers, such as Machado de *Assis, Luís Delfino dos Santos (*see* Symbolism), and *Sousândrade, from attempting to breathe new life into the forms and themes of the classic Indianist period. (*See* Slavery and Literature.)

The Indianist movement is therefore a varied and complex artistic tradition, an indicator of some of the major sociopolitical and cultural developments experienced by Brazil in the nineteenth century, as well the country's first coherent and vigorous expression of nationalist identity. It has provided Brazilian literature with some of its most durable and popular works. Indianism has also helped to reinforce some of Brazil's most deeply embedded racial myths and stereotypes, for example, the aristocratic ancestry of the tribal warrior, as opposed to the more ignoble blood of the African slave. It is a measure of its influence that subsequent writing on Indians, such as that of the modernists, including Mário de *Andrade and Oswald de *Andrade, Raul *Bopp, and Cassiano *Ricardo, as well as the neo-Indianist tradition in contemporary fiction, led by Antônio *Callado and Darcy *Ribeiro, have had to define themselves first in relation to the nineteenth-century Indianist tradition. (*See* Film and Literature; Modernism.)

BIBLIOGRAPHY: Criticism: Brookshaw; Driver, David. *The Indian in Brazilian Literature*. New York: Hispanic Institute in the United States, 1942; Sodré, Nelson Werneck. "As razões do indianismo: o indianismo e a sociedade brasileira." *História da literatura brasileira: seus fundamentos econômicos*. 4th ed. Rio: Civilização Brasileira, 1964, pp. 255–294; Treece, David H. "Victims, Allies, Rebels: Towards a New History of Nineteenth-Century Indianism in Brazil." *Portuguese Studies* (1985–1986), pp. 56–98.

DAVID H. TREECE

IVO, LEDO   (b. 1924; BAL: 1987). Born in Alagoas, Ivo was educated in Recife, where he began his literary career as a poet. A leading figure of the Generation of 1945 (*see* Postmodernism in Poetry), he was a member of the editorial board of the *review *Orfeu*. Ivo's first collection of poems, *As imaginações* (1944; The Imaginations), attracted wide attention and was followed by *Ode e elegia* (1945; Ode and Elegy), which is considered a turning point in the generation's poetical orientation. Twelve collections of verse followed through 1964, and they were published in his collected works *O sinal semafórico* (1974; The Semaphoric Sign).

Ivo's lyrical voice throughout his career has touched on themes of childhood, fantasy, women, and the city, as well as the poet's art. Stylistically, these themes—which have been developed in both rhymed verse and prose verse— accepted the liberties attained by the modernists but also reflected the passion inherited from the romantics. This is revealed in one of his most impressive poems, "Elegia didáctica" (Didactic Elegy) from *Ode e elegia*: "Think about everything and everyone, and after the remembrances go / flying like the birds and the leaves, sand and voices / full of confidence in life and in the world / feeling yourself linked to all men and all things / bend over the body of the woman you love / or awake to the triumphal happiness of only one verse." Ivo's *Calabar* (1985; Calabar) technically invokes both the Luso-Brazilian epic tradition and Brazilian *regionalism in a dramatic historical poem about a forgotten figure of Brazilian history who becomes a symbol for the plight of contemporary Brazil. (*See* Children's Literature; Feminism and Literature; Portugal and Brazil: Literary Relations.)

Ivo has also had a successful career as a prize-winning novelist. (*See* Prizes.) *As alianças* (1947; The Alliances) narrates personal lives in Rio of the 1940s with interesting psychological detail. Perhaps his most successful work of fiction is *Ninho de cobras* (1973; *Snakes' Nest*, 1981). Set in Alagoas in the 1940s, *Snakes' Nest* is a dissertation on totalitarianism. The backdrop of the Vargas regime serves only as an allegory for contemporary Brazilian politics—the repressive extremes of the Brazilian military dictatorship during the early 1970s. About the subtitle, "A Tale Badly Told," Ivo explained: "During a dictatorship, all narratives are poorly told, since a dictatorship is a Kingdom of Lies and cannot tolerate the truth." (Cited in front flap of bookjacket of *Snakes' Nest*). A more recent novel, *A morte do Brasil* (1981; The Death of Brazil), is a pessimistic view of the nation's future during the depths of its socioeconomic and political plight of the early 1980s. (*See* Dictatorship and Literature.)

BIBLIOGRAPHY: Additional selected works by Ivo: *Finisterra*, 1972; *Confissões de um poeta*, 1979; *A noite misteriosa*, 1982. Translations: Hulet. Criticism: Montemayor, Carlos."Prólogo." In *La imaginaria ventana abierta*, by Ledo Ivo. Mexico, D. F.: Premia Editores, 1980, pp. 7–24; Tolman, Jon M. "Introduction." *Snakes' Nest*, by Ledo Ivo. Translated by Kern Krapohl. New York: New Directions, 1981, pp. v–viii.

JARDIM, LUÍS (b. 1901). From Pernambuco, Jardim had his education cut short by illness. While working in Recife, he met Joaquim *Cardozo and Gilberto *Freyre, who encouraged his writing. Jardim has had short fiction, novels, and dramas published. His most admired work is *As confissões do meu tio Gonzaga* (1949; Confessions of My Uncle Gonzaga), a psychological novel about the life of a man who allows chance to rule his existence. Set in a small interior city, the confession unravels in short introspective chunks, reminiscent of the style of Machado de *Assis. (*See* City and Literature; Regionalism.)

Jardim has also gained fame as a water colorist, an art critic, and the author of *children's literature. These careers were combined for his very successful narrative of a traditional folktale with plates: *O tatu e o macaco* (1940; *The Armadillo and the Monkey*, 1942). A volume of *memoirs, *O meu pequeno mundo* (1976; My Small World), is also of note. (*See* Art and Literature; Folklore and Literature.)

BIBLIOGRAPHY: Additional selected works by Jardim: *Maria Perigosa*, 1939; *Isabel do sertão*, 1959; *Aventuras do Menino Chico de Assis*, 1971; *O ajudante do mentiroso*, 1980. Translations: Grossman.

JARDIM, RACHEL (b. 193?). Jardim's short and long fiction dwells on the relationship between reality and imagination. *Os anos 40 (A ficção e o real de uma época)* (1973; The 1940s [Fiction and Reality of an Era]) verges on auto-biographical memoir. The descriptions of relatives, friends, favorite movies of the time and the changes in the city of Belo Horizonte itself are the backdrop for her rejection of woman's status in Brazilian society. (*See*: Autobiography; Memoirs; Feminism and Literature.)

Jardim's later fiction returns to these existential themes. In the novel *Inventário das cinzas* (1980; Inventory of the Ashes), the "author's" own emotional state is presented in the novel in the perspective of her fiction about the protagonist's dilemmas. Jardim claims that her ultimate search is for an explanation of the *mineiro* neuroses.

BIBLIOGRAPHY: Additional selected works by Jardim: *Cheiros e ruidos, estórias*, 1975; *A cristaleira invisível*, 1982; *O penhoar chinês*, 1985.

JOÃO DO RIO. *See* Rio, João do.

JOSÉ AMÉRICO. *See* Almeida, José Américo de.

JOSÉ BONIFÁCIO. *See* Silva, José Bonifácio de Andrada e.

JOSÉ BONIFÁCIO (THE YOUNGER). *See* Silva (The Younger), José Bonifácio de Andrada e.

JOSÉ, ELIAS (b. 1936). José is a college teacher in Minas. From his first collection of short stories, *A mal amada* (1970; The Badly Loved One), to his most recent, *O grito dos torturados* (1985; The Cry of the Tortured), José has demonstrated a keen ear for language and a lively imagination.

José's stories are often presented through a most intriguing use of a second-person narration, which creates a closer link between the author and his readers. The stories frequently possess a magical quality, in part due to the poetic language used, but principally because of the oneiric quality that pervades several of the pieces. Furthermore, his protagonists, mostly males, are unconventional personalities. For example, "Um estrangeiro muito estranho" (A Very Strange Foreigner), from the collection *Um pássaro em pânico* (1977; A Bird in Panic), presents an Englishman's visit to a bizarre Brazilian family, which fails to recognize its situation. Albert, the protagonist, discovers himself caught in their fantasy and struggles to get out. No matter how magical many stories may seem, however, the absurd reality of daily life and its problems are usually just below the surface, frequently being exposed just at the moment when escape from such reality seems complete.

José is a truly entertaining, even captivating, writer. Although his works have won a number of literary *prizes, they have not received the critical attention they merit.

BIBLIOGRAPHY: Additional selected works by José: *As curtições de Pitu*, 1976; *Inventário do inútil*, 1978. Translations: Tolman (1984). Criticism: Tolman (1984).

KEITH H. BROWER

JÚLIA, FRANCISCA [FRANCISCA JÚLIA DA SILVA MUNSTER] (1871–1920). Born in the interior of São Paulo, Júlia's *Mármores* (1895: Marble Tablets) was heralded as "the most skillful poetry" of the moment. Her poems faithfully followed *Parnassianism's dictum of "art for art's sake." They are impersonal, perfectly structured poems. Her best-known sonnet, "Musa impassivel" (Impassive Muse), reflects her typical form and content. Her only other collection, *Esfinges* (1903; Sphinxes), included many of the earlier poems and revealed symbolist tendencies common to many Parnassians. (*See* Symbolism.)

After her marriage in 1909, she dropped out of an active literary role and became deeply involved in what she called "mystic" beliefs. Several posthumously published sonnets written during her last years reveal a deep melancholy with the recurring theme of death. The circumstances of her own death—accidental or a suicide—remain a mystery today.

BIBLIOGRAPHY: Additional selected works by Júlia: *Livro da infância*, 1899; *Poesias*, 1961. Translations: Hulet. Criticism: Jordan, Dawn M. "Building a History of Women's Literature in Brazil." *Plaza* (Fall, 1981), (Fall, 1982).

JUNQUEIRA FREIRE. *See* Freire, Luís José Junqueira.

JURANDIR, DALCÍDIO (1908–1982?). From Marajó, an island off the coast of the state of Pará, Jurandir led a nomadic existence through the mid–1930s. In 1936 he was jailed for his participation in leftist politics. In Rio he dedicated himself to literature and political journalism. His novel *Linha do parque* (1958; Park Line) is based upon his reporting of a workers' strike in Rio Grande do Sul in the 1950s.

Although he began to write fiction in the 1930s, his first major work, *Chove nos campos da Cachoeira* (It's Raining in Cachoeira's Fields), was published in 1941. It was the first of a planned cycle of nine regionalist novels describing life, since the 1920s, in Marajó and in the state capital, Belém. Based upon his childhood memories, his primary concern is portraying in sociological detail the local color and language of this Amazonian region. *Chão dos lobos* (1976; Wolves' Land), for example, narrates Alfredo's (the cycle protagonist's) city and jungle experiences while a student in Belém. (*See* Regionalism.)

The importance of Jurandir fiction was recognized early on by the folklorist Luis de Câmara Cascudo. Jurandir's complete works were awarded the Machado de *Assis Prize (*see* Prizes) of the *Brazilian Academy of Letters. (*See* Folklore and Literature.)

BIBLIOGRAPHY: Additional selected works by Jurandir: *Marajó*, 1947; *Tres casas e um rio*, 1958; *Passagem dos inocentes*, 1963. Criticism: Adonias Filho. *Modernos ficcionistas brasileiros*. Second series. Rio, 1965; Pérez, Renard. *Escritores brasileiros contemporâneos*. Second series. Rio: Civilização Brasileira, 1964.

L

LADEIRA, JULIETA DE GODOY (b. 1935). Ladeira studied humanities and languages and lived in Belo Horizonte, Rio, and São Paulo, where she worked in advertising and publicity. Her first book, *Passe as férias em Nassau* (1962; *Spend Your Vacation in Nassau*), won the prestigious Jabuti *Prize (*see* Prizes) and elicited a perceptive review from Osman *Lins. Two years later Lins became her husband; they collaborated on many works.

The urban middle class provides the milieu for Ladeira's fiction and short stories, for example, *Era sempre feriado nacional* (1984; It was Always a National Holiday). Her fiction shows mastery of techniques such as stream of consciousness. Ladeira portrays contemporary problems and doubts with a command of both language and structure. (*See* City and Literature.)

Ladeira was one of the contributors to the six reworkings of Machado de *Assis's classic story "Missa do galo" (Christmas Eve Mass), which was organized by Lins in 1977. She has also organized and contributed to *Espelho mágico* (1985; Magic Mirror), a collection of *children's literature rewritten for adults.

BIBLIOGRAPHY: Additional selected works by Ladeira: *La Paz existe?* 1977; *Dia de matar o patrão*, 1978. Criticism: Dimmick, Ralph E. Notice in *HLAS*. No. 28 (1966); No. 36 (1974); Teixeira, Vera Regina. Review of *Missa do galo*. *WLT* (Winter, 1979), p. 88.

EDGAR C. KNOWLTON, JR.

LEONARDOS, STELLA [STELLA LEONARDOS DA SILVA LIMA] (b. 1923). Primarily a poet and author of *children's literature, Leonardos has collaborated with Maria Clara Machado (*see* Children's Literature) on many dramatic productions. She has also had fiction published.

The glorification of the city of Rio and Brazilian life in general are constant themes of her work. For example, in her *Romanceiro de Estácio* (1960; Songbook of Estácio), she recounted the life and times of the founder of Rio, Captain Estácio de Sá (c. 1520–1567), reworking popular poetry of the time. The lyrics of her *Geolírica* (1966; Geolyrics) are based upon popular regional Brazilian music *cordel* (*see* Folklore and Literature) and traditions researched by Luís de Câmara Cascudo. She dedicated the work to Mário de *Andrade. (*See* Historiography; Regionalism.)

A notable departure from the above theme appears in her novel *Estátua de sal* (1961; Statue of Salt). In it she described the status of a social pariah of a *desquitada*, a woman legally separated from her husband in predivorce Brazilian society. (*See* Feminism and Literature.)

BIBLIOGRAPHY: Additional selected works by Leonardos: *Passos na areia*, 1940; *Poesia em tres tempos*, 1957; *Rio cancioneiro*, 1960; *Teatro para crianças*, 1964; *Teatro em dois tempos*, 1972.

LESSA, ORÍGENES (1903–1986; BAL: 1981). Lessa was a well-known writer of short fiction and *children's literature, most notably *Memórias de um cabo de vassoura* (1970–1972; Memories of a Broomstick Handle). Although he was born in São Paulo, he spent his childhood in Maranhão. He has worked in advertising and as a journalist.

Lessa's short fiction is direct and humorous and often possesses an anecdoctal quality. For example, the story "Madrugada" (Dawn) from his collection *Balbino, homem do mar* (1960; Balbino, a Man of the Sea) narrates a man's early morning walk accompanied by a stray dog, an event that turns out to be an educational experience for him. Lessa also wrote *O feijão e o sonho* (1938; Black Beans and the Dream), an extremely successful novel about poverty, sacrifice, and the literary life, which was made into a popular television serial. Lessa also authored science fiction.

Collections of his journalistic writings about the 1930s revolutions were published, as was *O.K. América* (1945; Okay America), which describes his residence in the United States as an employee of the Department of Inter-American Affairs.

BIBLIOGRAPHY: Additional selected works by Lessa: *Omelete de Bombaim*, 1946; *A noite sem homem*, 1968; *O evangelho de Lázaro*, 1972; *Simão Cireneu*, 1986. Translations: *Review* 23 (1978).

LIMA, ALCEU AMOROSO [TRISTÃO DE ATAÍDE] (1893–1984; BAL: 1935). Considered during his lifetime as the dean of modern Brazilian literary critics (*see* Critics and Criticism), Lima began writing literary criticism in 1919 upon graduation from law school in Rio. Subsequently, he taught at several Brazilian universities in Rio after his reconciliation with Christianity in 1928 within the Catholic Social Action Movement in Brazil. He was a member of the Brazilian Academy of Philosophy. (*See* Religion and Literature).

During the first phase of his professional life (1919–1930), Lima practiced a kind of aesthetic, expressionist criticism under the influence of the writings of Benedetto Croce and Henri Bergson. His most decisive phase of literary criticism (1930–1965), conditioned by his contact with the Brazilian poet-philosopher

Jackson de *Figueiredo and his readings of works by Jacques Maritain and Georges Bernanos, was marked by an emphasis on moral and ethical values. During this period he came to be recognized as the official critic of Brazilian *modernism and drew attention to northeastern *regionalism. (*See* Foreign Writers and Brazil.)

Lima propounded a "globalist" theory of literary criticism free from strict ties to any one school or approach. His "Ten Commandments for Critics" stressed the superiority of the critic over criticism itself. After 1965 he concentrated less on literary criticism, expanding his focus to include wider concerns of a philosophical, political, religious, and pedagogical nature and devoting increasing numbers of essays to a formulation of his theories concerning nationalism, social democracy, and Christian humanism. (*See* Philosophy of National Identity.)

Lima defined himself as a pacifist and antiauthoritarian and maintained a moderately liberal stance on most issues. Although he symbolized a middle-of-the-road, thoroughly Catholic equilibrium within the context of Brazilian national life, several contemporaries have attributed to him the origins of liberation theology. Lima was awarded the Marie Moors Cabot Prize for Journalism by Columbia University in 1969.

BIBLIOGRAPHY: Additional selected works by Lima: *Afonso Arinos*, 1922; *Problema da burguesa*, 1932; *O espírito e o mundo*, 1936; *Contribuição à história do modernismo*, 1939; *Poesia brasileira contemporânea*, 1941; *Tres ensaios sobre Machado de Assis*, 1941; *O existencialismo*, 1951; "Art and Liberty." In *Responsible Freedoms in the Americas*. Edited by Ángel del Rio. New York: Doubleday, 1955, pp. 463–474; *A crítica literária no Brasil*. 1959; *Manuel Bandeira*, 1970. Criticism: Barbosa, Francisco de Assis. *Alceu Amoroso Lima: Memorando dos 90*. Rio: Nova Fronteira, 1984; O'Neill, A. Ancilla. *Tristão de Ataíde and the Catholic Social Movement in Brazil*. Washington, D.C.: Catholic University of America, 1939.

MARY L. DANIEL

LIMA, GERALDO FRANÇA DE (b. 1914). A *mineiro* lawyer and teacher, Lima was secretary to Georges Bernanos during his stay in Brazil. Lima's first novel, *Serras azuis* (1961; Blue Hills), presents life in an imaginary small town of the interior of Minas, which has a cast of fascinating inhabitants, including Gaius Gutemburg Roldão, whose loves and hatreds are comparable to a Shakespearean creation. Lima's *O nó cego* (1973; The Blind Knot) is a straightforward narrative, characterized by the traditional *mineiro* qualities: the profound Roman Catholic beliefs and the importance of family life and honor. Olímpio, the protagonist, is fascinated by his employee Fifita, an infatuation that leads him to the discovery that she is his wife's illegitimate daughter. (*See* Foreign Writers and Brazil; Regionalism.)

BIBLIOGRAPHY: Additional selected works by Lima: *Brejo alegre*, 1964; *Branca bela*, 1965; *Jazigo dos vivos*, 1969; *A herança de Adão*, 1984.

LIMA, JORGE DE (1895–1953). Born in Alagoas to a Pernambucan family that had been active in the abolitionist movement, Lima faced a career choice between two callings: medicine and the priesthood. Opting for medical studies, he specialized in public hygiene. Upon moving to Rio in 1930, he dedicated himself to medicine, taught at the University of Brazil, and was active in political causes. (*See* Slavery and Literature.)

Lima shows a wide range of literary influences, ranging from *Parnassianism through *symbolism to *modernism and *surrealism. His personal frame of reference includes the strong presence of northeastern *regionalism—especially the life and customs of plantation blacks—and a profound, quasi-mystical Christian devotion. The content and metaphorical language of much of his poetry may be traced to his own childhood experiences, amplified by his avowed intention to "restore poetry in Christ." His name is closely linked to that of José Lins do *Rego in the founding of the northeastern regionalist movement and to that of Murilo *Mendes in his poetic collaboration of a religious nature, especially the volume *Tempo e eternidade* (1935; Time and Eternity). (*See* Religion and Literature.)

The polivalent character of Lima's fiction and verse is best perceived by a brief glance at his best-known titles. *XIV Alexandrinos* (1914; *XIV Alexandrian Verses*), his first published collection of poetry, is clearly Parnassian, whereas *O mundo do menino impossível* (1925; The World of the Impossible Boy) shows a passage into a robust, nationalistic modernism. *Essa negra Fulô* (1928; That Black Girl Fulô), perhaps his best-known work, is representative of his humorous, yet tender, "black poetry," continued in *Poemas negros* (1947; Black Poems), which evidences proletarian political concerns.

Tempo e eternidade and *A túnica inconsútil* (1938; The Seamless Tunic) contain the most representative poems of his Christian devotion, and *Anunciação e encontro de Mira-Celi* (1950; Annunciation and Meeting of Mira-Celi) incorporates surrealistic elements into an essentially metaphysical matrix. A return to standard versification may be noted in the poet's *Livro de sonetos* (1949; Book of Sonnets), whereas his *Invenção de Orfeu* (1952; Invention of Orpheus), subtitled "Epic Biography," combines numerous verse forms in a subdivided, ten-canto superpoem.

Although Lima's fiction is less copious than his poetry, the same broad gamut of style and concerns may be noted in a comparison of *Calunga* (1935; Calunga), a novel of regional and social concerns, with *O anjo* (1934; The Angel) and *A mulher obscura* (1939; The Obscure Woman), both possessing a more metaphysical and surrealistic nature.

Lima's wide and fluctuating range of interests (he was a recognized, accomplished artist), styles, and thematic concerns—including biographies (*see* Biography and Biographers), *children's literature, and art criticism have given rise to varied critical opinions. Although acclaimed as one of the most spontaneous natural poetic geniuses of Brazilian literature, he is considered by some to be a perpetually dissatisfied poet in search of new worlds to conquer and never content with his own brilliant performance. (*See* Art and Literature.)

BIBLIOGRAPHY: Additional selected works by Lima: *Quatro poemas negros*, 1937; *Obra completa*, 1958–1959. Translations: *Brazilian Psalm*. New York: G. Schirmer, 1941; Hulet; Woodbridge. Criticism: Brookshaw; Kasdorf, Hans. "Jorge de Lima: The Medical Poet-Priest of Northeastern Brazil." *RLV* (1970), pp. 295–305; Kennedy, James H. "Jorge de Lima: Brazilian Poet." *Black World* (September, 1973), pp. 18–23; Pinto, Júlio. "Jorge de Lima's 'Unexpected Being': The Transfiguration of Matrix in *Anunciação e encontro de Mira-Celi.*" *RomN* (Fall, 1984), pp. 3–10.

MARY L. DANIEL

LIMA BARRETO. *See* Barreto, Afonso Henriques de Lima.

LINS, OSMAN (1924–1978). Born in Permanbuco, Lins was brought up by his grandmother, who later appeared as one of his fictional characters. A solitary childhood gave him the introspective nature that was an essential element in his literary career.

The main theme of Lins's fiction concerns the role of the writer in society and the liberating function of literature in a rapidly changing society. Lins followed and adapted literary traditions of writers such as Machado de *Assis, Jorge Luis Borges, and Julio Cortázar in their common perspective of creating while criticizing, of writing while being their own readers. This double perspective was especially developed in his essay-novel *Guerra sem testemunhas* (1969; War without Witnesses), which serves as a guide to the evolution of his fiction. The primary emphasis of this work is the three stages of struggle between the artist and society: search, encounter, and plenitude. These stages coincide with Lins's own artistic development. In the first stage, the author's search moves from an inarticulate, inchoate form of literary expression, what he called "gestures" in *Os gestos* (1957; Gestures), to a more meaningful and conscious use of words, as in his *O visitante* (1955; The Visitor). Both gestures and words become a means to free the main characters from their social constraints and allow them to acquire a creative or generative force through a critical view of themselves. In the novel *O fiel e a pedra* (1961; The Faithful and the Stone), Lins's social criticism derives from the *Aeneid*: a new Aeneas opposes the injustices of society in northeastern Brazil.

The second stage, encounter, represented by the short stories in *Nove, novena* (1966; Nine, Novena) also reflects the world of social injustice, but the main difference is that Lins discovered new literary techniques. For example, in it he broke with a tradition of fiction typified by the use of the omniscient narrator. Instead, he focused his fiction on the development of narrative structures and thus was able to begin establishing the relationship between an ethical and an esthetic view of the world.

In the third and final phase, plenitude, the novel *Avalovara* (1973; *Avalovara*, 1980) presents an allegory of the art of the novel and is the synthesis and epitome of all of Lins's previous fiction. Through an extended metaphor of the sexual act, writing itself in *Avalovara* is represented as a necessary regeneration of a dying world. In this sense, the novel accomplishes the author's desires, indicated twenty-three years earlier: "the creation of a literary work which, in its totality, is not only able to transmit both a singular and intense vision of the universe but, at the same time, is also the live history of the conquering of this vision."

The critic (*see* Critics and Criticism) Antônio Cândido called attention to the reversibility between world and fiction contained in *Avalovara*. The sense of reversibility is provided by a palindromic artifice, an ancient reversible sentence in Latin—'Sator arepo tenent opera rotas'—on which the whole structure of the book is based. The sentence serves as a metaphor for creation as Lins translated it to "The plowman carefully sustains the world in its orbit." As the narrator-writer falls in love three times, he is also traveling through the eight narrative lines that constitute the palindrome's letters. *Avalovara*'s narrative lines provide an ingeniously interwoven network that constantly reminds the reader that the process of writing fiction is more "real" than "fiction" per se, that the character's romance is nothing but a pretext to show the writer's process of translation of the world into words.

Most of Lins's fiction was written under the military dictatorship that came to power in 1964. This may help explain his rejection of a consumer-oriented public that passively accepts its role as reader and the text's role as authority. Instead, his preference is to plot hidden meanings in his work, through carefully built allegories, metaphors, and symbols, so that the reader participates in the unraveling of the writing process itself. He has exerted significant stylistic influence on many younger writers. (*See* Dictatorship and Literature; New Writers.)

BIBLIOGRAPHY: Additional selected works by Lins: *Marinheiro de primeira viagem*, 1963; *Lisbela e o prisioneiro*, 1964; *Lima Barreto e o espaço romanesco*, 1974; *A rainha dos cárceres da Grécia*, 1976. Translations: Donoso/Henkin. Criticism: Andrade, Ana Luiza. "Crítica e criação: as narrativas de Osman Lins." Doctoral thesis, University of Texas, Austin, 1982; Daniel, Mary Lou. "Through the Looking Glass: Mirror Play in Two Works of João Guimarães Rosa and Osman Lins." *LBR* (Summer, 1976), pp. 19–34; Rabassa, Gregory. "The Shape and Shaping of the Novel." *WLT* (Winter, 1979), pp. 30–35; Severino, Alexandrino. "Osman Lins: *A rainha dos cárceres da Grécia*" (book review). *WLT* (Winter, 1978), p. 97; Rosenfeld, Anatole. "The Creative Narrative Process of Osman Lins." *SSF* (Winter, 1971), pp. 230–244; Slater, Candace. "A Play of Voices. The Theatre of Osman Lins." *HR* (Summer, 1981), pp. 285–295.

ANA LUIZA ANDRADE

LINS DO REGO, JOSÉ. *See* Rego, José Lins do.

LISBOA, HENRIQUETA (1903–1985). Lisboa, from Minas, combined poetic activity with a career in teaching and educational administration.

In her early poetry, such as the volume *Enternecimento* (1929; Endearment), traditional lyric themes (childhood, the longing for love) are cast in a neosymbolist language that favors the erudite word. In later collections, such as *Madrinha lua* (1952; Godmother Moon), her concerns include historic events and places of Minas, an obsessive meditation on death and the celebration of a Christian spirituality. Her poetry registers the emotional reverberations of a sensitive psyche but avoids the confessional and often the outright lyric "I." (*See* Regionalism; Religion and Literature; Symbolism.)

Women of Lisboa's generation (e.g., Cecilia *Meireles, Rachel de *Queiroz, and the critic Lúcia Miguel-Pereira [*see* Critics and Criticism]) were the first to participate actively in Brazilian literary life when women in Brazil first acquired the right to vote (1932). References to the female condition occur, though mutedly, in Lisboa's poems. She alluded to the conflicting claims for women of biological versus artistic creation. In a few poems, she cast a cold eye on the supposed comforts of female domesticity and, in turn, on the cost of its renunciation. (*See* Feminism and Literature.)

Lisboa remained on the sidelines of *modernism and postmodernism. (*See* Postmodernism in Poetry.) Nonetheless, she has incorporated from them a colloquial diction and an attentiveness to the poetic potential of the word as a signifier. But mainly, with unswerving devotion, she constructed her rarified web of images, serious in tone, measured in diction, woven to capture the beauty of words and the world.

BIBLIOGRAPHY: Additional selected works by Lisboa: *Velário*, 1936; *O menino poeta*, 1943; *Montanha viva: Caraça*, 1959; *Belo Horizonte bem querer*, 1972; *Pousada do ser*, 1982; *Obra completa*, 1985. Translations: Hulet; Woodbridge. Criticism: Lobo Filho, Blanca. *The Poetry of Emily Dickinson and Henriqueta Lisboa*. Norwood, Pa.: Norwood Editions, 1978; Virgillo, Carmelo. "The Image of Woman in Henriqueta Lisboa's "Frutescência." *LBR* (Summer, 1986), pp. 89–106.

MARTA PEIXOTO

LISPECTOR, CLARICE (1925–1977). Lispector and her family immigrated to Brazil from the Ukraine when she was two months old. Although she traveled widely in her lifetime, she never returned to her place of birth. In 1937 Lispector moved with her family to the Tijuca neighborhood of Rio.

In the cosmopolitan atmosphere of Rio, Lispector, a precocious child, decided to become a writer. Diverse authors such as Hermann Hesse, Machado de *Assis, Fyodor Dostoyevsky, Katherine Mansfield, and Lúcio *Cardoso were early influences on her work. By 1944 Lispector had graduated from law school, had married a fellow law student, and had seen her first novel, *Perto do coração selvagem* (1944; Near the Savage Heart), awarded the prestigious Graça Aranha Prize for Fiction. (*See* Prizes.) This introspective and intensely psychological work was instrumental in helping to move Brazilian fiction away from the rote regionalism that had dominated it for so long.

One of Brazil's most important writers in the post–World War II era, Lispector (along with Guimarães *Rosa) revolutionized both the themes and techniques of Brazilian narrative. As a Brazilian writer, however, Lispector was seldom overtly nationalistic in her work. Seen in the larger context of the Western tradition, Lispector's fiction shows itself to be consistent with international trends such as the "new novel," postmodernism, and phenomenology. Yet in terms of her place in Brazilian literature, Lispector accomplished two important goals: she proved that narrative fiction in Brazil could deal as effectively with urban, feminist, and psychological issues as it had with its more traditional rural, masculine, and "realistic" issues. When examined from this perspective, Lispector and her work are clearly related to late Brazilian *modernism, which retained its creative energy through the 1940s. (*See* City and Literature; Feminism and Literature; Postmodernism in Poetry; Social Novelists of the 1930s.)

Lispector is often said to be a better short story writer than a novelist. Of her six collections of stories, none is more representative of her brilliance in this form than *Laços de familia* (1960; *Family Ties*, 1972), a work that redefined the nature of short-narrative writing in Brazil. Focusing thematically on philosophical issues such as language, consciousness, and being, the lyrically wrought stories of *Family Ties* tend to structure themselves around what Joyce described as the "epiphany," unexpected moments of intense insight and realization. Several of the pieces in this collection, such as "Love," "Family Ties," and "The Buffalo" are properly regarded as classics in the Lispectorian canon.

Although much of Lispector's best work is indeed in the short story form, she was also an accomplished novelist, especially of the kind widely known as the "lyrical" novel. Merging philosophical themes with an intensely poetic style and structure, Lispector wrote several of post–World War II Brazil's most important novels. One of them, *A maçã no escuro* (1961; *The Apple in the Dark*, 1967), typifies Lispector's lifelong fascination with the ontological problems of language and being. Martim, the novel's main character (and one of Lispector's few male protagonists), is enmeshed in a dual struggle: to reject what he perceives to be his inauthentic social existence and to create for himself a more authentic personal one. Thus the novel's conflict is psychological, involving not the external world of action and event but the inner turmoil of Martim's mind. Symbolic and poetic, *The Apple in the Dark* does not have a plot with a clearly defined beginning, middle, and end. The intentionally open-ended conclusion leaves the reader uncertain as to what Martim's future holds in store for him.

Two later works, *Uma aprendizagem ou o livro dos prazeres* (1964; *An Apprenticeship or the Book of Delights*, 1986) and *A hora da estrela* (1977; *The Time of the Star*, 1986), (recently made into an excellent film), show Lispector linking her highly internalized conflicts with themes of social significance. Outstanding among Lispector's later works is *Agua viva* (1973; Living Water), a powerful first-person account of a woman who is in the painful process of extricating herself from an unsuccessful love affair. Intensely lyrical in style and structure, *Agua viva* is one of the finest Brazilian novels of the 1970s. (*See* Film and Literature.)

Although Lispector never developed a formal critical system, she wrote a great many nonfiction pieces about how she viewed literature and about how she worked. Most of them can be found in *A legião estrangeira* (1964; *The Foreign Legion*, 1986) under the section titled "No fundo da gaveta" (In the Bottom of the Drawer). In addition to creating her stories and novels, Lispector also wrote *children's literature, worked as a journalist (she was one of Brazil's first female journalists), and did translation work.

Lispector is rightly judged to have been one of Brazil's most important and most influential writers in the closing decades of the twentieth century. Her international reputation as a challenging and innovative artist, one fully in tune with the major trends of her time, has grown steadily since her death in Rio in 1977. (*See* New Writers.)

BIBLIOGRAPHY: Additional selected works by Lispector: *O lustre*, 1946; *A cidade sitiada* 1949; *Alguns contos*, 1952; *A paixão segundo G.H.*, 1964; *Felicidade clandestina*, 1971; *Onde estivestes de noite*, 1974; *A vida íntima de Laura*, 1978; *A bela e a fera*, 1979; *A descoberta do mundo*, 1984. Translations: Fremantle; Grossman; *Pequod* 15 (1983); Tolman (1978); *Translation* (Spring, 1984); *Webster Review* (Fall, 1980). Criticism: Dixon, Paul F. "*A paixão segundo G.H.*: Kafka's Passion according to Clarice Lispector." *RomN* (Spring, 1981), pp. 298–304; Fitz, Earl E. *Clarice Lispector*. Boston: G. K. Hall, 1985; idem. "A Discourse Analysis of Clarice Lispector's *A hora da estrela*." *LBR* (Winter, 1982), pp. 195–208; Lindstrom, Naomi. "A Discourse Analysis of 'Preciosidade' by Clarice Lispector." *LBR* (Winter, 1982), pp. 187–194; Lowe, Elizabeth. "The Passion According to C.L." (Interview with Lispector). *Review*. (June, 1979), pp. 34–37; Moisés, Massaud. "Clarice Lispector: Fiction and Cosmic Vision." Translated by Sara M. McCabe. *SSF* (Winter, 1971), pp. 268–281; Nunes, Maria Luísa. "Narrative Modes in Clarice Lispector's *Laços de família*: The Rendering of Consciousness." *LBR* (Winter, 1977), pp. 174–184.

EARL E. FITZ

LOBATO, JOSÉ BENTO MONTEIRO (1882–1948). Following his graduation from the São Paulo Law School in 1904, Monteiro Lobato returned to his native northern São Paulo, where he was at first a district attorney for the town of Areias in the Paraíba Valley and from 1911 to 1917 was manager of his family's estate, Buquira. With the sale of the farm, Lobato moved back to the state capital, where he entered the publishing business through the acquisition of the respected *Revista do Brasil* and the foundation of the Monteiro Lobato and Company, Publishers, in 1919, and, following its collapse, the Companhia Editora Nacional, which failed in 1925.

From 1927 to 1931 Lobato served as Brazil's commercial attaché in New York. Greatly impressed with American economic development, Lobato started the Brazilian Petroleum Company soon after his return from the United States. A bitter disagreement with the autocratic regime of Getúlio Vargas concerning iron and petroleum exploration policies led to a three-month imprisonment in 1941 and a period of exile in Buenos Aires. Monteiro Lobato died a disillusioned man.

Lobato began to write both fiction and nonfiction as a youth under several different pen names. While at law school he joined the literary group "O Minarete" and met the minor novelist Godofredo Rangel (1884–1951) with whom he maintained an intense forty-year correspondence, later gathered in *A barca de Gleyre* (1944; The Gleyre Boat). A prolific writer until the end of his life—his complete works comprise thirty volumes—Lobato left an impressive collection of short stories, *crônicas*, essays, newspaper articles, *memoirs, letters, and *children's literature that attest to an intellectual activity hardly matched in Brazilian letters.

Like many premodernists (*see* Modernism), Lobato was still bound by the formal dictates of *naturalism and had a keen interest in rural themes. In spirit, however, he may have been much closer to the modernists than his diatribes against the younger artists suggest. In fact, a bitter feud was sparked by Lobato's review, in the *Estado de São Paulo* newspaper, of a 1917 exhibit of Anita Malfatti's (*see* Art and Literature) cubist paintings. An attack on the un-Brazilian, imported avant-garde ideas and techniques from Europe, the article was rebutted by a group of young intellectuals led by Oswald de *Andrade, who was later to acknowledge Lobato's important contributions to Brazilian literature.

In two essays, "Velha praga" (Old Plague) and "Urupês" (a type of mushroom), published in that same newspaper in 1914, Lobato denounced the pernicious farming techniques and general backwardness, apathy, and sickliness of the Brazilian *caipira* or *caboclo*, immortalized as his character Jeca Tatu—to whom he would return for different aims and with slightly different guises during his literary career. Widespread interest in the articles prompted Lobato to attempt a fictional treatment of the people and problems of that neglected milieu. With a combination of sarcasm, pessimism, and compassion, the short stories gathered in *Urupês* (1918; Urupês) and *Cidades mortas* (1919; Dead Cities) depict—thanks to the author's remarkable descriptive talent—the plight of men who are essentially indifferent to their own and their country's lot.

Whereas these first two collections of stories are distinguished by thematic and narrative cohesion, the third, *Negrinha* (1920; Little Black Girl), somewhat deficient in character analysis, already points to the future direction of Lobato's writing career, away from fiction and closer to the committed, journalistic prose that would better serve the causes he championed. Thus in *Mr. Slang e o Brasil* (1929; Mr. Slang and Brazil) and *América* (1932; America), a product of his admiration for the United States, Lobato preached the urgent adoption of automation, productivity awareness, and an overall practical mentality as the only solution to Brazil's woes. In *Ferro* (1931; Iron) and *O escândalo do petróleo* (1936; The Petroleum Scandal), taking a more militant stand, Lobato advocated the large-scale exploration of iron and oil deposits with the entailing industrialization ushering in Brazil's economic redemption. (In a very belated homage to Lobato's foresight, the first large oil field discovered in the Amazon area by Petrobrás, the Brazilian national oil company, was named Lobato).

Lobato's only novel, *O presidente negro ou o choque das raças* (1926; The Black President or Race Shock), set in North America of the future, is a disappointing attempt at combining science fiction and social criticism. Lobato's style reflects his intense reading of the world literary classics and even, now and then, some of the mannerisms and phrases of the Portuguese Eça de Queiroz or Camilo Castelo Branco. However, it was his ear for the regional *paulista* dialect that added a particular coloring and considerable originality to a style that proved to be the perfect vehicle for Lobato's talent for caricature and satire, as, for example, in "O colocador de pronomes" (The Pronoun Placer) and "O fígado indiscreto" (The Indiscret Liver). Lobato is at his best when dealing with a well-devised plot and a prolonged comic situation, which allow him to poke fun at his characters. But when he leaves the humorous and adopts a more serious tone, as in "Drama da geada" (Drama of the Frost) and "Bugio moqueado" (Roasted Monkey), the sentimental or the grotesque tend to prevail. (*See* Portugal and Brazil; Literary Relations.)

In numerous letters to Rangel and other friends, Lobato expressed his notion of style as a natural, spontaneous talent: writing, he insisted, should be nothing but the direct recording of one's thoughts in naked, uncomplicated prose. Although Lobato himself failed always to abide by his own writing ideal, we are indebted to him for what the critic Cassiano Nunes (*see* Critics and Criticism) has called Lobato's theory of style: essentially, a forceful call for Brazilian writers to shun obscure allusions, outdated constructions, and infatuation with literature and to adopt, instead, a colloquial, genuinely Brazilian vocabulary and syntax, as well as a new, more familiar, visually dynamic imagery.

Lobato gradually turned his attention to *children's literature. Aware, since as early as 1912, of the scarcity of adequate books for Brazil's young readers, Lobato resolved to remedy the situation. Although he had already adapted La Fontaine's fables to the Brazilian reality in 1919, it was not until the publication, and enormous success, of his first book for children, *Narizinho arrebitado* (1921; Little Turned Up Nose), that Lobato's project got under way. In works that were later to fill seventeen volumes, Lobato explored Brazilian folklore, Western mythology, and produced, above all, his *Sítio do pica-pau amarelo* (1939; Yellow Woodpecker Farm) with its residents, Dona Benta, Tia Nastácia, Pedrinho, Narizinho, Emília the witty doll, Rabicó the pet pig, and the Visconde de Sabugosa, a corn-cob turned pompous sage. (This volume has been the basis for an extremely popular television series of the 1980s.) Even those books—such as *História do mundo para crianças* (1933; World History for Children) and *Aritmética de Emília* (1935; Emilia's Arithmetic)—that have a strong didactic commitment display the skillful combination of reality and fantasy that became the trademark of Lobato's writings for the young. (*See* Film and Literature; Folklore and Literature.)

Perhaps the only aspect of his career that is clear of controversy is Lobato's status of virtual creator and still unsurpassed master of children's literature in Brazil. Several of his children's tales were adopted recently for "children's operas" in São Paulo. In most of his other endeavors, the preaching and the uncompromising positions of the staunchly individualistic Lobato were most often met by widespread national indifference. Since his death, Lobato's views

184 LOBATO, MANOEL

on numerous issues have been proven correct, and his unswerving nationalism has had a pronounced influence on Brazilian thought. It is now widely accepted that his ideas have become more important than his works and that the groundwork he laid for his country's future remains his most significant legacy. (*See* Philosophy of National Identity.)

BIBLIOGRAPHY: Additional selected works by Lobato: Fiction: *O macaco que se fez homem*, 1923; Nonfiction: *Ideias de Jeca Tatu*, 1919; *A onda verde*, 1921; *Mundo da lua*, 1923; *Na antevéspera*, 1933; Children's literature: *O saci*, 1921; *Fábulas*, 1922; *O marquês Rabicó*, 1922; *A caçada da onça*, 1924; *Novas reinações de Narizinho*, 1933; *Geografia de Dona Benta*, 1935; *Os doze trabalhos de Hércules*, 1944. Translations: *Brazilian Short Stories*, 1925.Criticism: *Atualidade de Monteiro Lobato*. Edited by Regina Zilberman. Porto Alegre: Mercado Aberto, 1983; Brookshaw; Brown, Timothy, Jr. "Characterization in the Stories of Monteiro Lobato." *BRMMLA* (1970), pp. 60–65; idem. "Idea and Plot in the Stories of Monteiro Lobato." *BRMMLA* (1973), pp. 174–180; idem. "Monteiro Lobato as a Novelist." *LBR* (Summer, 1965), pp. 99–104; Vasconcellos, Zilda Maria. *O universo ideológico da obra infantil de Monteiro Lobato*. São Paulo: Traço Editores, 1982.

SEVERINO JOÃO ALBUQUERQUE

LOBATO, MANOEL (b. 1925). A pharmacist in his native Minas, Lobato's short and long fiction repeatedly touches on the problem of man's deficient communication with his fellow man in a highly technological society.

Mentira dos limpos (1967; Lie of the Clean Ones), his first novel, dealt with a case of a self-tormented individual whose psychological problems are owed to his puritanic upbringing in a corrupt society. In the stories of *A flecha em repouso* (1976; The Arrow at Rest), prose assumes a poetic overtone as he examines common things—a telephone, a button, an automobile windshield—searching for a significant philosophical statement about the course of man's life.

BIBLIOGRAPHY: Additional selected works by Lobato: *A verdadeira vida do irmão Leovelfildo*, 1976.

LOPES, MOACIR C. (b. 1927). From northeastern Ceará, Lopes's first novel, *Maria de cada porto* (1959; Mary in Every Port), introduced a new theme to Brazilian fiction: the realistic sea story. Although earlier writers, such as Jorge *Amado, had presented the sea in a mythopoetic fashion, Lopes based his story on his experiences in the Brazilian navy during World War II. *A ostra e o vento* (1964; The Oyster and the Wind) is considered his finest novel, skillfully manipulating time and levels of reality. His more recent fiction has tended toward fable; consequently, it has been branded as "too erudite" by critics. (*See* Critics and Criticism.)

BIBLIOGRAPHY: Additional selected works by Lopes: *Chão dos mínimos*, 1961; *Por aqui não passaram rebanhos*, 1972. Criticism: Barrow, Leo L. "Symbol in *A ostra e o vento*." *LBR* (Spring, 1967), pp. 61–67; Fody, Michael, III. "The Creative Genius and Technique of Moacir C. Lopes." Dissertation, University of Arizona, 1974.

LOPES DE ALMEIDA.   *See* Almeida, Júlia Lopes de.

LOPES NETO, JOÃO SIMÕES   (1865–1916). Brought up on cattle ranches
in southern Rio Grande do Sul, near Brazil's border with Uruguay, Lopes Neto
gained a special insight into the existence of the *gaúcho*, the cowboy of the
prairie. Between 1878 and 1882 Lopes Neto studied at the famous Colégio Abílio
(described in Raúl *Pompéia's *O ateneu*). Afterwards illness prevented him from
completing a medical course; he spent the rest of his life in Pelotas engaged in
various occupations, particularly journalism.

Lopes Neto was the most important regionalist writer of southern Brazil at
the turn of the century. He presented an anedoctal, nostalgic, but sympathetic
depiction of the *gaúcho* and his traditions well after the figure had become more
of legend than a reality. (*See* Folklore and Literature; Regionalism.)

In 1910 his *Cancioneiro guasca* (Gaucho Songbook) was published; it is a
collection of popular, often satiric poetry of Rio Grande do Sul. *Contos gau-
chescos* (1912; Gaucho Stories) is a group of first-person narrations by Blas
Nunes, a forceful depictment of the poor *gaúcho* and an alter ego of Lopes Neto
himself. The *gaúcho* dialect used throughout is colorful but offers reading difficulty. Two of the stories have a historical setting: the Farroupilha Revolt (1835–
1845). "O Contrabandista" (The Smuggler), Lopes Neto's best-known story,
presents Jango Jorge, dean of *gaúcho* smugglers, whose quest for his daughter's
trousseau leads to his death. (*See* Portuguese Language of Brazil.)

Lendas do sul (1913; Southern Legends) includes "O negrinho do pastoreio"
(The Little Black Shepherd Boy). With roots in regional folklore, it is a tale
that illustrates Brazilian racial attitudes and diversity. It is dedicated to Lopes
Neto's favorite Brazilian writer, Henrique *Coelho Neto. Finally, the posthumous *Casos do Romualdo* (1952; Romualdo's Tales) is a collection of tall tales
told by a true antihero, Romualdo, wherein not only the *gaúcho* but also the
plants and animals amaze.

BIBLIOGRAPHY: Additional selected works by Lopes Neto: *Mixódia*, 1894–1895;
Os bacheréis, 1896; *Amores e facadas de Jojô e Jajá e não Ioiô e Iaiá*, 1901; *Educação
cívica*, 1906. Translations: Hulet.

EDGAR C. KNOWLTON, JR.

LOUZEIRO, JOSÉ   (b. 1932). From Maranhão, Louzeiro has lived in Rio
since 1954, where he is a journalist, scriptwriter, and novelist. (*See* Film and
Literature.)

Louzeiro's literary career began with short story collections, for example,
Depois da luta (1958; After the Battle). As a result of a reporting assignment
on abandoned children in the early 1970s, he wrote a "nonfiction" fictionalized
version of their existence, *Infância dos mortos* (1977; Infancy of the Dead),
which served as the basis for the film *Pixote*. He also produced similar "nonfiction" fiction about highly publicized "crimes" of the dictatorship years: *Lúcio
Flávio, o passageiro da agonia* (1975; Lucio Flavio, the Passenger of Agony)

and *Aracelli, meu amor* (1976; Aracelli, My Love). The later work was censored by the military dictatorship. Most recently, Louzeiro has turned to police-detective fiction dealing with drugs and sexual crimes. He has created the detective Jesuíno Conde and his assistant Manga Rosa in novels such as *M–20* (1981). (*See* Dictatorship and Literature.)

Louzeiro's fast-paced style, featuring slang and extensive dialog, has been adapted for *children's literature. His *A gang do beijo* (1984; The Kiss Gang) takes place in a school where a murder has occurred, and the students set out to discover the criminal.

BIBLIOGRAPHY: Additional selected works by Louzeiro: *Judas arrependido*, 1968; *Acusado de homicídio*, 1975; *Os amores da pantera*, 1977; *O bezerro de ouro*, 1986.

LOYOLA BRANDÃO. *See* Brandão, Ignácio de Loyola.

LUFT, LYA (b. 1938). Poet, novelist, and translator from Rio Grande do Sul, Luft has recently had several novels published that depict the lack of communication within families owing to the claustrophobic self-absorption of its members in their self-protective worlds.

In *Reunião de família* (1982; Family Reunion), Alice visits her aged father, her siblings, and their longtime housemaid only shockingly to discover long-hidden family truths-mysteries-lies of the past and to suffer through a strange mourning for the death of her nephew. Death itself and forms of madness also haunt *O quarto fechado* (1984; *The Island of the Dead*, 1986): Renata, the protagonist, views her life as a series of failures: failed marriage, failed careers, failed motherhood.

Luft's skillful manipulations of point of view and stream of consciousness in these intimate narrations of women's lot reveal a debt to Virginia Woolf (whom she has translated) and Clarice *Lispector. In her general feminist concerns, her fiction is similar to that of Adélia *Prado. (*See* Feminism and Literature.)

BIBLIOGRAPHY: Additional selected works by Luft: *Canções de limiar*, 1963; *As parceiras*, 1980; *A asa esquerda do anjo*, 1981; *Exílio*, 1987; *A mulher dividida* (in preparation). Criticism: Goldberg, Gerald Jay. "*The Island of the Dead*" (Book review). *NYTBR* (January 4, 1987), p. 18; Moreiras, Alberto. "Símbolo, alegoría y temporalidad en *Reunião de família* de Lya Luft." *Hispania* (May, 1987), pp. 250–56.

M

MACEDO, JOAQUIM MANUEL DE (1820–1882). This popular novelist and playwright was also a successful politician and tutor to the children of Princess Isabel, the heir presumptive of the empire. He wrote a great deal—twenty novels, twelve dramas, and ten books of minor pieces, including a guide to Rio, the city that is the backdrop for almost all of his writing. (*See* City and Literature.)

Although Macedo suffers from the typical excesses of the popular romantic authors—sentimentality, melodrama, facile moralizing—and the plots of his plays in particular are full of vile treachery, and, more often, sudden conversions from evil to good (for he is nothing if not conformist), these things are tempered by a taste for comedy and a talent for local color. (*See* Romanticism.)

A moreninha (1844; The Little Dark Complexioned Girl), his most famous novel, is also considered the first major Brazilian novel. (*See* Teixeira e *Sousa.) Largely set on Paquetá, an island in Guanabara Bay (which is, however, not named), it concerns the love of a medical student, Augusto, for the fifteen-year-old *moreninha*, Carolina. The most obviously romantic parts of the work are in fact two inserted tales, one a flashback to the childhood of the protagonists, when they exchange keepsakes over a dying poor man, who blesses them for their charity to him and his family, and an Indianist ''myth'' intended to explain the magical properties of a fountain. The rest of the story is set among the upper bourgeoisie of 1840s Rio and has a much lighter, more frivolous atmosphere; indeed, at times it is plainly intended to be titillating, and probably was successful in that regard. (*See* Indianism.)

Macedo was well aware of larger societal issues, and indeed in later works such as *As vítimas-algozes* (1869; The Victim-Hangmen), which is a series of stories about how slavery turns people into brutes, he tried to deal with them. He nevertheless (even in this work, which is at the very least double-edged in its argument for abolition), failed to transcend his period, 1840–1870, of which he was profoundly representative. (*See* Slavery and Literature.)

Although it is impossible to read Macedo today in the spirit that he intended, this does not mean that he should be ignored. José de *Alencar claimed that Macedo's success incited him to write. Machado de *Assis, while criticizing him for his transparency, inconsistent, and clumsy narrative devices, recognized him implicitly when he parodied (and so used) the plot of *A moreninha* in his own short story "A parasita azul" (1873).

BIBLIOGRAPHY: Additional selected works by Macedo: Novels: *O moço louro*, 1869; *O rio do quarto*, 1869; Drama: *Cobé*, 1849; *Lusbela*, 1863; Others: *Um passeio pela cidade do Rio de Janeiro*, 1862. Criticism: Cândido, Antônio. "O honrado e facundo Joaquim Manuel de Macedo." *Formação da literatura brasileira: momentos decisivos.* Belo Horizonte: Itatiaia, 1973, pp. 137–146; Pereira, Astrojildo. "Romancistas da cidade." *Interpretações.* Rio, 1944; Sayers.

JOHN GLEDSON

MACHADO, ANÍBAL (1894–1964). Machado graduated from law school in 1917, and he served as district attorney in the interior of his native Minas, which provided him with background for many of his short stories. In the 1920s he was associated with the Minas modernists, including Carlos Drummond de *Andrade and João *Alphonsus. (*See* Modernism; Regionalism.)

For thirty years Machado's home in Rio was a major literary salon where Brazilian and foreign writers, artists, and intellectuals gathered. Machado was also a mentor to numerous young writers, spending more time and energy on their manuscripts than on endeavoring to publish his own. (*See* Foreign Writers and Brazil.)

Machado's major work is found in the general collection of his stories from 1926, 1944, and 1959: *A morte da porta-estandarte e outras histórias* (1967; Death of the Standard-Bearer and other Stories). His strongly imaginative characters often possess a dreamy nature and sometimes are mad. Nature and natural forces—sea, sky, trees, and wind—exert a powerful influence on the characters and lend an animistic and poetical quality to the stories. Such characteristics are also found in the author's only novel, *João Ternura* (1965; John Tenderness), published posthumously.

Cadernos de João (1957; John's Notebooks), his most ambitious work, is a collection of poems, aphorisms, and vignettes that show his breadth and justify Machado's claim of being, above all, a surrealist. (*See* Surrealism.)

BIBLIOGRAPHY: Additional selected works by Machado: *Vila feliz*, 1944. Translations: Grossman. Criticism: Lopes (Dean), M. Angélica. "Perspetivas narrativas na contística de João Alphonsus e Aníbal Machado." Dissertation, University of Wisconsin, 1980; Proença, Manuel Cavalcanti. "Introdução." *A morte da porta-estandarte e outras histórias* by Aníbal Machado. Rio: José Olympio, 1967.

MARIA ANGÉLICA GUIMARÃES LOPES

MACHADO, ANTÔNIO DE ALCÂNTARA (1901–1935; BAL: 1931). Alcântara Machado graduated from the São Paulo Law School and dedicated himself to journalism. His comfortable, upper-middle-class milieu allowed for frequent voyages to Europe, notably Paris, where he participated in the premodernist activities. (*See* Modernism.)

His first book, *Pathé Baby* (1926; Pathé Baby), is a collection of impressions of his European trips, with a preface by Oswald de *Andrade. Machado was both an editor and writer for several major, although ephemeral, modernist *reviews, for example, *Terra Roxa e Outras Terras* (1926) and *Revista de Antropofaqia* (1928).

Like other modernists, he was concerned with the essence of Brazil; however, he was especially dedicated to São Paulo. For Machado, Brazil of the future would be composed of a hybrid race, new *mamelucos*, descendants of both the sixteenth century Portuguese settlers and the recently arrived Italian immigrants. To this mixture he dedicated *Braz, Bexiga e Barra Funda* (1927; Names of three neighborhoods in São Paulo). In this collection of stories—considered by some critics the most significant work of early modernist fiction—Machado presented realistic situations in cinematic "takes"; swift, precise, colloquial language; and slang. He defused the possible bathos of sad episodes with irony imbued in compassion. At times, though, the picturesque takes over and the psychological level remains superficial. Among the best stories are "Gaetano" ("Gaetaninho," in Grossman; *see* "Key to Bibliographical References"), about a poor Italian immigrant's dream, and "A sociedade" (Society). (*See* City and Literature; Film and Literature; Immigrants and Literature.)

BIBLIOGRAPHY: Additional selected works by Machado: *Laranja da China*, 1928; *Mana Maria*, 1936; *Cavaquinho e saxofone: crônicas*, 1940. Criticism: Martins.

MARIA ANGÉLICA GUIMARÃES LOPES

MACHADO, GILKA (1893–1980). An early Brazilian feminist associated with *symbolism, Machado's poems in *Cristais partidos* (1915; Broken Crystals) gained attention as a result of her outspoken view of woman's condition with distinctly erotic overtones. Sensuality allied with woman's inherent sadness became the principal ingredients of her "mystical sensuality," which reverberates throughout her other collections, for example, *Mulher nua* (1922; Nude Woman) and *Meu glorioso pecado* (1928; My Glorious Sin). (*See* Feminism and Literature.)

Her last volume, *Velha poesia* (1965; Old Poetry), has a note of contrition about her past. Long forgotten, only recently has her work resurfaced for critical attention.

BIBLIOGRAPHY: Additional selected works by Machado: *Obra completa*, 1978.

MACHADO DE ASSIS, J. M. *See* Assis, Joaquim Maria Machado de.

MAGALHÃES, DOMINGOS JOSÉ GONÇALVES DE (1811–1882). Gonçalves de Magalhães was brought up in Rio, where he studied medicine. In 1836, inspired by the example of the European romantics, he formed a literary group in Paris, founding the *review *Niterói: Revista Brasiliense* together with Araújo Porto *Alegre and others. Following his return to Brazil, heralded as the elder of the new literary school, he began a diplomatic career throughout which he enjoyed the friendship and patronage of Emperor Dom Pedro II. (*See* Romanticism.)

Friar Monte *Alverne, Magalhães longtime friend and mentor, provided him and the first romantic generation in Brazilian literature with its characteristic neoclassical (*see* Arcadias) style, including forms, rhythms of expressions, and Christian sentimentalism indebted to Vicomte Chateaubriand. On a political level, it was a romantic liberalism that accommodated itself increasingly within the inherited conservative institutions and neoclassical traditions.

Nevertheless, Magalhães's "Discurso sobre a história da literatura do Brasil" (Discourse on the Literary History of Brazil) and the introduction to his volume *Suspiros poéticos e saudades* (Poetic Sighs and Nostalgia), both published in 1836, did propose a radically new aesthetic for literature: the function of art was to be a pseudoreligious elevation of the human soul with its inspiration being the direct influence and impression of nature on the spirit of the poet. If little originality is apparent in the sentimentalized experiences and patriotic nostalgia of *Suspiros poéticos e saudades*, it should be remembered that at the time of their first appearance in Brazil they were indeed innovative.

On the other hand, Magalhães's late contribution to the Indianist movement, the epic poem *A confederação dos tamoios* (1856; The Confederation of the Tamoio Indians), exposes more clearly the limitations of his liberal and nativist sympathies toward the Brazilian landscape and its indigenous inhabitants. Against a colorless backdrop, the annihiliation of an entire tribe is effortlessly justified within a divine action whose inevitable outcome is independence and the imperial monarchy. The literary qualities of the poem were the subject of a significant polemic begun in 1856 by José de *Alencar. (*See* Indianism; *Ufanismo*.)

Magalhães's importance today resides in his historical role as a modest reformer, rather than in the doubtful, often mediocre quality of his poetry, which, after all, never freed itself from the neoclassic canon.

BIBLIOGRAPHY: Additional selected works by Magalhães: *Poesias*, 1832; *Antônio José* 1839; *Cânticos fúnebres*, 1864; *Obras completas*, 1864–1876. Translations: Hulet. Criticism: Driver; Machado, José de Alcântara. *Gonçalves de Magalhães ou o romântico arrependido*. São Paulo: Livaria Acadêmica, 1936; Sayers.

DAVID H. TREECE

MARANHÃO, HAROLDO (b. 1927). A native of Belém, Pará State, and after many years as a journalist and lawyer there, Maranhão moved to Rio in 1961. He was one of the founders, along with Mário *Faustino and Benedito Nunes (*See* Critics and Criticism), of the postmodernist review *Encontro*. In 1968 he published a collection of realistic short stories, *A estranha xícara* (The Strange Demi-Tasse Cup), and later *Vôo de galinha* (1978; Chicken's Flight), which consists of ministories dealing with surrealistic situations. Most recently, he has cultivated *children's literature. (*See* Postmodernism in Poetry; Surrealism.)

Dialogue combined with vivid, refined phrasing in a context of precise, denotative language give Maranhão's texts dramatic impact. Emotional situations are seen in the cold light of rational analysis, as in his most reprinted story "O leite em pó da bondade humana" (The Powder Milk of Human Kindness). Employing as a title a slightly altered line from the poetry of John Keats, this short story depicts the cruelty of a session of torture during the military dictatorship. (*See* Dictatorship and Literature.)

O tetraneto d'El-Rei (1982; The King's Great-Great Grandson) is a comic novel about the discovery and colonization of Brazil. Playing with the differences between history and fiction, it reveals a debt to the classics of Luso-Brazilian literature. Maranhão's latest novel, *Jogos infantis* (1986; Children's Games), is a powerful reconstruction of the erotic universe lived by children from the boy's viewpoint. (*See* Portugal and Brazil: Literary Relations.)

BIBLIOGRAPHY: Additional selected works by Maranhão: *A morte de Haroldo Maranhão*, 1981; *As peles frias*, 1983; *Os anões*, 1983; *O começo da cuca*, 1985.

LUIZA LOBO

MARCOS, PLÍNIO (b. 192?). Born into a poor family in Santos, São Paulo, Marcos was involved in leftist student causes. He developed an interest in theater in the mid-1940s, first as an actor.

Marcos's dramas describe the existence of the poor and marginalized elements of Brazilian society. The initial productions of his plays, supported by Patrícia *Galvão, met with censorship due to their coarse language and reality: *Barrela* (1956; Bang-Bang), set in a jail, and *Reportagem de um tempo mau* (1964; Report about a Bad Time). *Dois perdidos numa noite suja* (1966; Two Lost Men on a Dirty Night) describes two young men caught up in the vicious cycles of marginalization, which generate violence and murder. In *Navalha na carne* (1967; *Razor in the Flesh*, 1987), the symbiotic existence of society's outcasts— a pimp, a prostitute, and a homosexual—is their ironical defense against a society that uses them and then censures them. *Quando as máquinas param* (1967; When the Machines Stop) lambasted factory working conditions and was immensely successful with workers around São Paulo before being prohibited by the military dictatorship. (*See* Dictatorship and Literature.)

Marcos's fiction treats the disastrous lives of children born into misery and hopelessness, for example, *Uma reportagem maldita (Querô)* (1977; A Damned News Story [Querô]). It is notable that Marcos's dramas and fiction never offer solutions for problems he describes; rather he is primarily interested in provoking his audience and readers to action.

In the 1980s Marcos has reoriented his dramatic concerns toward mystical and existential themes, for example, *Jesus Homem* (The Man Jesus) and *Helena Blavatski* (Helena Blavatski). In *Balada de um palhaço* (1986; Ballad of a Clown), two clowns discuss their art, their role as artists, and their relationship with society.

Marcos's artistic orientation and social themes have profoundly affected the generation of young dramatists that followed, coming of age during the dictatorship, for example, Leilah *Assunção, Consuelo de *Castro, and *new writers such as Naum Alves de Souza, Isabel Câmara, and Maria Adelaide Amaral. (*See* Theater History.)

BIBLIOGRAPHY: Additional selected works by Marcos: *Jornada de um imbécil até o entendimento*, 1968; *Balbina de Iansã*, 1970; *Histórias das quebradas do mundaréu*, n.d.; *Na barra de Catimbó*, 1979; Criticism: Butler, Ross E. "Social Themes in Selected Contemporary Brazilian Drama." *RomN* (Autumn, 1973), pp. 52–60; Schoenbach, Peter J. "Plínio Marcos: Reporter of Bad Times." *Dramatists in Revolt: The New Latin American Theatre*. Edited by Leon F. Lyday and George W. Woodyard. Austin: University of Texas Press, 1976.

MARQUES REBELO. *See* Rebelo, Marques.

MARTINS, JÚLIO CÉSAR MONTEIRO (b. 1955). Martins, born in Rio, first gained literary attention when he contributed a story to the collection *Histórias de um novo tempo*, published during the years of military dictatorship. (*See* Dictatorship and Literature.)

In cinematographic flashes of contemporary urban Brazil, Martins reflected upon the disruption of Brazilian life as a result of the military regime's repression, as well as the generational conflicts resulting from the rapidly growing youthful population. These themes are repeatedly treated in the collection *A oeste de nada* (1981; West of Nothing). In the title story of *As forças desarmadas* (1983; The Disarmed Forces), a collection in which he expressed a debt to Clarice *Lispector, the young people inhabit a society built on drugs, poetry inspired by John Lennon, and the works of the Brazilian filmmaker Gláuber Rocha. The collection *Muamba* (1985; Marijuana) enforces these same themes with a bit more psychological depth but also offers a greater variety of thematic material. (*See* Film and Literature.)

Martins's literary style appeals to his own generation; thus in many stories he denied traditional grammar, spelling, and punctuation norms and built his stories around rapid dialogues filled with slang and scatology. One critic (*see* Critics and Criticism) has viewed Martins's stories as falling within the "carnival tradition" of Brazilian literature, initiated by Manuel Antônio de *Almeida.

BIBLIOGRAPHY: Additional selected works by Martins: *Bárbara*, 1978; *Sabe quem dançou?* 1978.

MARTINS PENA. *See* Pena, Luís Carlos Martins.

MATOS, GREGÓRIO DE (1636–1696). The son of a well-to-do Portuguese settler and an equally aristocratic Bahian woman, Matos graduated in law from Coimbra in 1661. Except for a short sojourn in Brazil, he subsequently practiced law in Portugal for more than twenty years before taking up practice in his native Bahia. The repatriated lawyer took minor religious orders but soon became best known for his bohemian life-style and his biting satires.

Unknown in Brazilian letters until the late nineteenth century, Matos was a devotee of the *baroque style so prevalent among contemporary Iberian and other Bahian writers; thus the attribution of poems to him has been a heatedly disputed task. He, like many writers of the time, used most of the baroque verse forms with their fondness for conceits, word play, and scholastic turns of thought. Among his immediate influences, sources, and plagiarisms (commonly accepted at the time), one can point to writers such as the Portuguese Luís de Camões and the Spaniards Luis de Góngora and, especially, Francisco de Quevedo. (*See* Portugal and Brazil: Literary Relations.)

As an heir of the Counter-Reformation, Matos created some compelling poetry inspired by profound religious conviction at odds with man's fallen nature and predisposition to sin (''we are all evil, all perverse''). His declarations of ascetic disenchantment with the temporal world often clash with the rationalist's advice to seize the day and the bloom of youth. Matos varied his inspiration by drawing upon the kind of conventional love poetry that ultimately derives from Petrarch. Thus one finds many sonnets dedicated to idealized flaxen-haired beauties but also women who are plausible and less revered, such as the black and mulatto temptresses of his native Bahia.

The poet-lawyer-cleric was acutely sensitive to local customs and the social injustices of colonial Brazil, and he often applied his sharp mind and penchant for satire to lampooning, often through antitheses, manners and morals, institutions and corrupt officials: ''What's lacking in this city? . . . Truth / What else to its disgrace? . . . Honor / Anything else to add? . . . Shame'' (In *Poemas escolhidos*. São Paulo: Cultrix, 1976, p. 37). These barbs eventually earned him the sobriquet ''Boca do Inferno'' (Hell's Mouth) and several years of exile in Angola (1686–1695). However, even an enforced change of residence upon his return to Brazil and an order of silence failed to intimidate the indomitable Matos.

Today the poet is generally considered Brazil's foremost baroque poet. None other expressed so movingly the social polarities of the era. Also of note is his use of colloquial language in which one detects even in the seventeenth century the stirrings of an inchoate Brazilian style and diction, later evoked during *modernism. Matos's brother, Eusébio (1629–1692), a Jesuit, musician, and poet, is called the ''father'' of Brazilian painting. (*See* Art and Literature; Music and Literature.)

BIBLIOGRAPHY: As noted above, even today there is dispute concerning attribution of some titles that figure in editions of Matos's works. Having made such an observation, one should note that the most complete edition is the seven-volume *Obra de Gregório de Matos*. Bahia: Editora Janaína, 1964. Translations: Hulet; Monegal/Colchie, I. Criticism: Aiex, Nola Kortner. ''Racial Attitudes in the Satire of Gregório de Matos.'' *Studies in Afro-Hispanic Literature*. New York: Medgar Evers College, 1977, I:89–97; Bates, Margaret. ''A Poet of Seventeenth Century Brazil: Gregório de Matos.'' *The Americas* (July, 1947), pp. 83–89; Reedy, Daniel R. ''The Quevedo of Brazil.'' *CLS* 2 (1965), pp. 241–247; Sayers.

RICHARD A. PRETO-RODAS

MEIRELES, CECÍLIA (1901–1964). Meireles is considered the most important female poet of the Portuguese language. (*See* Portuguese Language of Brazil.) She was born in Rio and, upon her parents' death, was raised by her Portuguese grandmother.

Although Meireles had several volumes published during the early phase of *modernism (*Espectros* [1919; Ghosts]); *Nunca mais . . . e Poema dos poemas* (1923; Nevermore . . . and Poem of Poems); and *Baladas para El-Rei* (1925; Ballads for the King), which she did not include in her complete work, she did not adhere to the extreme national context of the *paulista* group but instead associated herself with the so-called spiritualist or Catholic poets—Tasso da *Silveira, Andrade Murici (b. 1895), and others—of the literary *reviews *Árvore, Nova, Terra do Sol,* and *Festa*. In fact, she always viewed her literary production as free from any specific movement or clique. Furthermore, she maintained a discreet distance from the literary center stage.

The greatest influence on Meireles's art was the Brazilian symbolist João da Cruz e *Sousa; thus with few exceptions, her art is decidedly her personal adaptation of *symbolism's themes, techniques, and forms. Still within the symbolist creed was her interest in mysticism, which was crystallized further through her contacts with oriental culture and a voyage to India, which resulted in her volume *Poemas escritos na India* (1961; Poems Written in India).

Meireles considered her mature work to have begun with *Viagem* (1939; Voyage), awarded the *Brazilian Academy of Letters poetry *prize in 1938, and which had been highly praised by Mário de *Andrade. Her other major collections included *Vaga música* (1942; Vague Music); *Mar absoluto* (1945; Absolute Sea); *Canções* (1956; Songs); *Metal rosicler* (1960; Pyrargyrite); and *Solombra* (1963; Sunshade). Also published was her *Romanceiro da Inconfidência* (1953; Songbook of the Minas Conspiracy), a collection of narratives about the events and the figures of the *Mineiran Conspiracy; translations of García Lorca, Paul Verlaine, Israeli and Indian poets; as well as original *children's literature. She was an expert in Brazilian folklore and, in particular, aspects of Afro-Brazilian traditions and rites. (*See* Folklore and Literature.)

Meireles's poetry is principally preoccupied with abstract time, the fleeting events of daily life, and death, a concern attributed to the early loss of her parents. This is clearly revealed in "Motivo" (Motive), from *Viagem*: "I sing because the moment exists / and my life is complete. . . . / I know that one day I shall be mute; / —that is all." Her poetry searches to overcome fleeting time through themes of eternal nature: the sky, birds, the wind, are frequent images: "Why think about anything / if everything rests upon my soul; / wind, flowers, water, stars, / the night's musics and dawns?" ("Canção suspirada" [Sighed Song], from *Vaga música*).

Providing a tactile, sensuous side of nature are vibrant colors and shades of light: "My heart, made of flame, / instead of blood, lets flow / a long river of splendor" ("Imagem" [Image] from *Vaga música*). Meireles's ultimate search is for the state of love that rejects physical being and mortality in favor of a mystical solitude that can be obtained only through total liberty of spirit itself obtained through "self-exile": "I want a solitude, I want a silence, / a night of abyss and the seamless soul, / to forget that I am alive" (untitled from *Solombra*). Perhaps Meireles's most evident departure from the symbolist aesthetic is the note of optimism that radiates from her poetry, despite its preoccupation with death: "From these clear, smooth urns / I shall choose one for my ashes. / Yet are not the breezes / clearer, smoother, finer urns? / Will they not carry further the light ashes / that survive these brief ruins?" ("Urnas e brisas" ["Urns and Breezes"], translated by Raymond S. Sayers).

Meireles's unique poetry and position within Brazilian literature has grown stronger in recent years.

BIBLIOGRAPHY: Additional selected works by Meireles: *Poetas novos de Portugal*, 1944; *Pequeno oratório de Santa Clara*, 1955; *Ou isto ou aquilo*, 1964; *Batuque, samba e macumba*, 1983 (*Batuque, Samba, and Macumba: Drawings of Gestures and Rhythms 1926–1934*, [Rio: FUNARTE, 1983]). Translations: Bishop/Brasil; *Cecília Meireles: Poems in Translation*. Translated by Henry Keith and Raymond S. Sayers. Washington, D.C.: Brazilian American Cultural Institute, 1977; Fremantle; Hulet; Woodbridge. Criticism: Foster/Foster, II; García, Rubén. "Symbolism in the Early Works of Cecília Meireles." *RomN* 21 (1980), pp. 16–22; Keith, Henry, and Raymond S. Sayers. "Introduction." *Cecília Meireles: Poems in Translation*; Rónai, Paulo. "The Character of a Poet: Cecília Meireles and Her Work." In Tolman (1978), pp. 193–204; Sadlier, Darlene J. "Imagery and Theme in the Poetry of Cecília Meireles: A Study of *Mar Absoluto*." Maryland: Studia Humanitatis, 1983; Stackhouse, Kenneth. "The Sea in the Poetry of Cecília Meireles." *LBR* (Summer, 1981), pp. 183–196.

MELO, AMADEU THIAGO DE   (b. 1926). Thiago de Melo was born in Amazonas. After abandoning a career in medicine, he eventually entered the Brazilian foreign service and served as cultural attaché in Bolivia and Chile. After the Brazilian military coup in 1964, he was recalled and went into exile. (*See* Dictatorship and Literature.)

Melo is a member of the Generation of 1945. (*See* Postmodernism in Poetry.) His first poems reveal his concern with the craft of poetry, for example, *Silêncio e palavra* (1951; Silence and Word); however, he later turned toward a profound interest in man's social condition. His residence in Chile during the 1973 Chilean military coup against the government of Salvador Allende led him to compose what he considers one of his most important collections: *Poesia comprometida com a minha e a tua vida* (1975; Poetry Engagée with My Life and Yours). It includes verse tributes to Allende, for example, "Era o melhor" (He Was the Best Man), and to the poet-musician Victor Jara, murdered during the coup. Melo's optimism about man's future is an important note of his poetry.

Melo also has translated the poetry of Pablo Neruda, a writer he deeply admires.

BIBLIOGRAPHY: Additional selected works by Melo: *A lenda da rosa*, 1956; *Faz escuro mas eu canto porque a minha manhã vai chegar*, 1965. Translations: *The Massachusetts Review* (December, 1986); Woodbridge.

MELO NETO, JOÃO CABRAL DE   (b. 1920; BAL: 1968). João Cabral spent most of his childhood in the interior of Pernambuco, on sugarcane plantations belonging to his family. A descendant of traditional Pernambucan families, he counts among his relatives the late Gilberto *Freyre and Manuel *Bandeira.

During the Revolution of 1930, Melo Neto's father's sugar mill was sold, and the family settled in Recife. When he finished high school, ill health prevented him from attending the university. His literary education continued informally, through readings and friendships with the intellectuals of Recife, among them Joaquim *Cardozo and the surrealist painter Vicente do Rego Monteiro (b. 1899). He moved to Rio in the same year that his first book of poems, *Pedra do sono* (1942; Stone of Sleep), was published. In 1945 he entered the foreign service, and in 1947 he began his long years of foreign residence. In Europe, he lived in England, France, and Switzerland, but his first and longest stay was in Spain. Melo Neto found deep, lasting affinities in the culture and literature of Spain. Spanish landscapes, bullfighters, music, dancers, and artists figure prominently in his poetry, often in counterpoint to the geography, folklore, and culture of his native Pernambuco. (*See* Folklore and Literature.)

Melo Neto was later stationed in Paraguay and, as ambassador, in Senegal, Ecuador, Honduras, and was consul in Oporto, Portugal. He has received numerous *prizes and honors and is widely considered one of the most important Brazilian poets of the twentieth century.

Melo Neto's greatest contribution, as an innovator of poetic language, is perhaps his reformulation of the lyric. Along with Marianne Moore (1887–1972), a poet he admires, Melo Neto could say about a certain kind of poetry: "I, too, dislike it." Ill at ease with the lyric as "expression of the self" and fiercely opposed to sentimentality and to an "easy" poetry that flows along, propelled by poetic convention, Melo Neto accepted only with diffidence the designation "poet" (*poeta*), as if to underscore his redefinition of the term.

A practitioner and proponent of the rationally constructed poem, Melo Neto spoke at one point of a "construir claro / feito a partir do não" (a lucid construction / taking negation as its point of departure). ("No centenário de Mondrian" [On the Centenary of Mondrian], In *Museu de tudo*). The negation of lyricism has for Melo Neto the value of an ascetic discipline that increases a hunger for the nonself. With unswerving devotion, Melo Neto established connections between the language of poetry and the solid world of objects, landscapes, and social facts. His poetic mimesis, "fazer com que a palavra leve / pese como a coisa que diga," (to embody in words / the weight of the objects they name), ("Catecismo de Berceo" [Berceo's Catechism]), points up critically the evasiveness and limitations of language, as well as the unjust social orders that deform the world. Yet it would be a mistake to think of his poetry as unemotional. The discourse of the reticent narrator-observer, who seldom uses the first person, reveals an oblique but intense subjectivity. The search for the difficult, the survival against unpromising odds, the forcefulness acquired through discipline, the impact of harsh and tortured landscapes (objects, beings), are emotionally charged themes (*topoi*) to which he insistently returns, endowing them with meanings pertinent to social criticism, ethics, and aesthetics.

Believing in the poetic efficacy of words of concrete reference, Melo Neto has relied upon that function of language that Ezra Pound termed "phanopoeia: the casting of images upon the visual imagination." Although he dwelled on the observation of objects and conditions of the external world, his poetry does not reveal the physical world in its unpredictable variety. It investigates, rather, with tireless zeal certain of its aspects. The same key words—*stone, desert, knife, sun*—and their numerous variations recur obsessively. The repetition of these symbolic objects, in an intricate play of verbal permutations, does not entail redundance but an accumulation of new meanings.

In an international context, Melo Neto can be placed among those modern poets who have called the lyric into question while still creating within its framework. Imagism comes to mind, with its deflected subjectivity and focus on precise description. (Melo Neto has translated poems by Amy Lowell [1874–1925] and William Carlos Williams [1883–1963]). Other affinities can be found with the Chilean Pablo Neruda (1901–1973) of *Odas elementales* (1954; Elemental Odes) and, perhaps most importantly, with Marianne Moore and Francis Ponge (b. 1899).

The visual arts of the twentieth century—painting, architecture, sculpture—provide Melo Neto with metaphors, subjects, and theoretical inspiration. He has written poems about Picasso, Juan Gris, Dubuffet, and Mondrian, as well as a critical essay and a poem about Miró. "Architect" and "engineer" stand in for the poet, as they did for Paul Valéry, with whom Melo Neto shares a devotion to cerebral and conscious creation.

In Brazilian poetry, Melo Neto does not fit easily into the main currents of his own Generation of 1945. (*See* Postmodernism in Poetry). While sharing with those poets a search for formal strictures, Melo Neto dissented from their cultivation of traditional forms such as the sonnet, their focus on psychological states, and their distinguishing of a "poetic" lexicon. He also rejected the free verse and the off-hand colloquial rhythms, diction, and humor of the modernists, finding the unsentimental concision and unadorned nouns of Oswald de *Andrade and the visual sharpness of Murilo *Mendes more congenial. (*See* Modernism.)

Melo Neto's constructivism does not depend on the polishing of prestigious and difficult poetic forms. In keeping with his view of poetry as a craft, likened to manual labor, and his attachment to the harsher manifestations of the physical world, Melo Neto prefers the sharp edges of unpolished forms, irregular meters, assonant and imperfect rhymes. (Pre-Golden Age Spanish poetry, such as that of Gonzalo de Berceo [c. 1195–c. 1264]), was an important artistic discovery for Melo Neto). Whether working with quatrains and short meters or with the long stanzas and meters and dense discursive syntax of *A educação pela pedra* (1966; Education by the Stone), his formal labors seem designed to jolt the reader, who is always brought up short by encounters with the unexpected. Also constant is the metapoetic dimension of his poetry. From first to last, he discusses, alludes to, praises, or berates the act of writing. With deliberate demystification, he incorporates into the poem the process of its making (or a facsimile thereof), often analyzing words and images as he uses them.

Melo Neto's first book, *Pedra do sono* (1942; Stone of Sleep), influenced by *surrealism, stresses the oneiric and the visionary eye. Crisp visual images, juxtaposed, preclude mimetic possibilities and compose projections of a troubled mental life. In *O engenheiro* (1945; The Engineer) both the title and the epigraph by Charles LeCorbusier (1887–1965) signal the fascination with the poem as a construction built to perform a predetermined function. The three long poems of *Psicologia da composição* (1947; Psychology of Composition), with moments of intense and disheartened meditation on the lyric, probe the efficacy and limits of rational control in poetic creation.

After 1947 Melo Neto's poetry turned consistently to the landscapes and culture of his native Pernambuco. In the three long epic-dramatic poems of the 1950s, *O cão sem plumas* (1950; The Unfeathered Dog), *O rio* (1954; The River), and *Morte e vida Severina* (1956; Death and Life Severina), Melo Neto's poetic languages created representations of the grim life of the poor in the Northeast, without relinquishing the metalinguistic analyses that make those representations possible. The last of them, a play in verse with moments of Swiftian black humor, recounts the migration of Severino Retirante from the drought-ridden interior of Pernambuco to the destitute swamps (*mangues*) of Recife. Set to music by Chico *Buarque, performed in Brazil and France, and later made into a film, *Morte e vida Severina* is Melo Neto's most widely known work. (*See* Film and Literature; Regionalism.)

In two other publications of the period, *Paisagens com figuras* (1956; Landscapes with Figures) and *Uma faca só lâmina* (1956; A Knife All Blade or Usefulness of Fixed Ideas*, 1980), the landscapes of the Northeast are enriched by references to the places and popular culture of Spain. "Knife" becomes the main symbol through which the poetry alludes to its own language. A relationship of similarity prevails between poetic language and the themes of the poetry, also sharp-edged and cutting. *A Knife all Blade*, a long poem of dazzling linguistic inventiveness, is a key text. It defines and embodies the "style of knives," of lasting importance in Melo Neto's poetry, and presents an allegory of the slipperiness and evasion that permeates poetic language.

In the books of the early sixties—*Quaderna* (1960; Notebook), *Dois parlamentos* (1961; Two Parliaments), and *Serial* (1961; Serial)—long poems, often in quatrains and composed of various sections, display Melo Neto's masterly articulation of larger structures. In these collections, Pernambuco and Spain coexist. Landscapes, dancers, cemeteries, goats, Andalusian singing, tropical fruits, poets, and visual artists, the female body, sugarcane fields, and sugarcane workers come together in a poetry in which the forbidding "things of not" ("coisas de não"), of which he usually speaks, are balanced by objects whose precision and luminosity bring joyful fruition. In *A educação pela pedra*, stone becomes, with stark aggressiveness, a central symbol. Poetry now takes as its model the solid substance of stone, its self-sufficiency, its impact, in works "que se atirem como se atiram pedras" (that are thrown like people throw stones). Construction remains clearly in the foreground: in the two-part composition of every poem, in the neologisms, in the dense and laborious syntax, hinging on antitheses and paradoxes. At the same time, the poems perform a self-critical analysis of the limits of the language they propose.

After a gap of nine years, Melo Neto's *Museu de tudo* (1975; Museum of Everything) was published. In this collection and in the more recent *A escola das facas* (1980; The School of Knives) and *Agrestes* (1985; Ruralities)—mostly briefer poems, more casual in tone—he continued to define and to question the terms of his poetics and to evaluate, stringently, the languages of others. Places in Africa and the Andes join Pernambuco and Spain in providing the acerbic *locus amoenus* of his poetry. Although he relaxed the ban on the first person and even allowed autobiographical references, the lyric persists as an embattled zone, for his poem of choice is "o poema perverso, / de antilira, feito em antiverso" (the perverse poem / of antilyre, made up of antiverse). His next to the last book, *Auto de frade* (1984; One Act Play about the Friar), another play in verse, takes up again the epic-dramatic mode, with its account of the last day in the life of Brother Caneca, a rebellious priest put to death in Recife in 1825. (See *Autobiography*.)

The concrete poets (*see* Postmodernism in Poetry) of the 1950s singled out Melo Neto as one of their predecessors. The rigor of his compositions, the attention to the signifier and to poetry as invention, in fact agree with the tenets of the concretists. He did not, however, participate in that movement or bring his poetic practice in line with its theory. In contrast to their juxtaposition of words as "verbivocovisual" signs, Melo Neto continued to allow his poetry to absorb the cadences and sweep of an analytical, discursive prose.

As one of the strong voices of twentieth-century Brazilian poetry, Melo Neto's influence is pervasive. Yet in Brazil, where the lyrical overflowing ("o derramento lírico") so often prevails, Melo Neto's refashioning of the lyric, his poetics of self-containment, discipline, and outward-turned observation, goes against the grain. The unusual properties of Melo Neto's aesthetic system, along with its lucidity and rigor, also inevitably provide a model against which younger poets rebel.

BIBLIOGRAPHY: Additional selected works by Melo Neto: *Os três mal amados*, 1943. Translations: Bishop/Brasil; Hulet; *LALR* (January-June, 1986); Tolman (1978); Woodbridge. Criticism: Gledson, John A. "Sleep, Poetry, and João Cabral's 'False Book': A Reevaluation of *Pedra do sono.*" *BHS* (January, 1978), pp. 43–58; Peixoto, Marta. *Poesia com coisas: uma leitura de João Cabral de Melo Neto.* São Paulo: Perspectiva, 1983; Rodman, Selden. "The Ugly Duckling Who Became One of the Forty Immortals." *Review* (Winter, 1972), pp. 42–47; Tolman, Jon M. "An Allegorical Interpretation of João Cabral de Melo Neto's *Morte e vida Severina.*" *Hispania* (March, 1978), pp. 57–68.

MARTA PEIXOTO

MEMOIRS. Memoirs fulfill writers' needs to narrate their lives, offer opinions about their own and others' works, and comment on cultural-critical trends of the moment. They are an invaluable resource for literary and cultural historians because they offer not only a special insight into the writer's mind and artistic attitudes but additionally provide a perspicacious and often entertaining view of contemporary life. Perhaps the work most faithful to the aim of the form is *Minha vida de menina* (1942; *The Diary of Helen Morley*, 1957), Alice Dayrell Brant's (1880–1970) diary of her youth and family life in Diamantina, Minas, between 1893 and 1895. The English version was prepared by the American poet Elizabeth Bishop. (*See* Foreign Writers and Brazil.)

As a fictional technique, *memoirs* is the key term in the title of Manuel Antônio de *Almeida's masterpiece, as well as in Oswald de *Andrade's *Memórias sentimentais de João Miramar*, and other works. Almost every Brazilian writer has cultivated some form of memoirs, most notably: José de *Alencar, Joaquim *Nabuco, Graça *Aranha, Monteiro *Lobato, Medeiros e *Albuquerque, Raul *Bopp, Gilberto Amado (1887–1969; BAL) Humberto de Campos (*see* Critics and Criticism), and Manuel *Bandeira.

Since the post–1978 *abertura*, the period of political liberalization of the dictatorship, memoirs have become an essential ingredient of the nation's attempt to gain a "collective memory" of the events leading up to the dictatorship itself and the following twenty years of national existence. Pedro *Nava's memoirs stand out as the most important of this period, while memoirs of political activists of the late 1960s forced into exile have also attracted attention, for example, Fernando *Gabeira's series and Alfredo Sirkis's (b. 1951), *Os carbonários* (1980; The Carbonari). (*See* Dictatorship and Literature.)

Recent memoirs of note include Zélia Gattai's (b. 1917) remembrances of her family roots in Brazil, *Anarquistas, graças a Deus* (1980; Anarchists, Thank God), which was made into a television series, and her memoirs of her husband, Jorge *Amado, *Um chapéu para viagem* (1984; A Hat for the Voyage). Samuel Malamud's *Do arquivo e da memória* (1983; From the Archives and Memory) described, in part, Jewish artistic life in twentieth-century Brazil. Vera Brant (b. 1932), niece of Alice Dayrell Brant, recently had her own memoirs of her childhood published, reflecting the difference in time, space, and personality: *A ciclotímica* (1984; *The* Ciclotimica). Of note also, are the memoirs of Carolina Maria de Jesus's *Quarto do despejo* (1957; *Child of Darkness*, 1962), a now classic description of life in the shantytowns (*favelas*) and the diary of the household maid Francisca Souza da Silva, *Ai de vós!* (1983; Poor You!); and Paulo Collen's narration of his life as a ward of FEBEM, the national childcare agency, *Mais que a realidade* (1987; More than Reality). (*See* Autobiography; Feminism and Literature; Immigrants and Literature.)

MENDES, MURILO (1901–1975). Mendes was the most international of the Brazilian modernist poets. He maintained ties with Manuel *Bandeira, Drummond de *Andrade, and Oswald de *Andrade, but Jorge de *Lima is cited along with the artist Ismael Nery (1900–1934) as the principal influences in the poet's deepening mysticism and Catholicism. (*See* Modernism; Religion and Literature.)

In *Tempo e eternidade* (1935; Time and Eternity) he spoke of his poet's vocation: "I wasn't born at the beginning of this century / I was born in the breast of Eternity / I was born from a thousand superimposed lives / I was born from a thousand unfolding anguishes." Mendes's fascination with Italy and Spain later resulted in the poetic testimony of *Siciliana* (1959; Siciliana) and *Tempo espanhol* (1959; Spanish Time). In 1957 Mendes again traveled to Italy, where he became a professor of Brazilian literature at the University of Rome.

Mendes's European poetry opened new ground in *Murilogramas* (1965; Murilograms); *Retratos-relâmpago* (1970; Lightening Portraits), an anthology of his prose works, and *Transístor* (1980; Transistor), messages through which the poet maintains contact with the outside world. The imaginative, plastic qualities of his reflective poetry of experience resulted in his receiving the Etna-Taormina International Poetry *Prize in 1972, the first to be awarded to a Brazilian poet.

Mendes's works are more published in Europe—in Italian, French, and Spanish—than in Brazil, where his absence caused him to be somewhat neglected in the projection of national literary life. As did those of Drummond de *Andrade, however, Mendes's published *memoirs evoked the poetic qualities of land and family in Minas, characterizing himself as "universal" and "*mineiro*."

BIBLIOGRAPHY: Additional selected works by Mendes: *Poemas*, 1930; *História do Brasil*, 1932; *Mundo enigma*, 1945; *Janela do caos*, 1949; *Poesias (1922–1955)*, 1959; *Convergência*, 1970. Criticism: Araújo, Laís Correa do. *Murilo Mendes*. Petrópolis: Vozes, 1972; Bandeira, Manuel. "The Sardonic Brazilians." *Americas* (September, 1954), passim; Campos, Haroldo de. "Murilo e o mundo substantivo." *Metalinguagem*. São Paulo: Cultrix, 1976, pp. 55–65; Guimarães, Júlio Castañon. *Murilo Mendes*. Rio: 1986.

                                                               K. DAVID JACKSON

MENDES CAMPOS, PAULO.   See Campos, Paulo Mendes.

MENOTTI DEL PICCHIA.   See Picchia, Paulo Menotti del.

MEYER JR., AUGUSTO   (1882–1970; BAL: 1960). Meyer left his home state of Rio Grande do Sul to head the National Book Institute in Rio. He was an active journalist, critic (*see* Critics and Criticisms), and author of *memoirs.

Meyer and Raul Bopp are considered the leading figures of *gaucho* *modernism. Meyer's volume *Coração verde* (1926; Green Heart) presents strong nativist sentiment, often in a melancholic, ironic tone. *Poemas de Bilu* (1929; Bilu's Poems) and *Literatura e poesia* (1931; Literature and Poetry) include joke-poems (*poemas-piadas*) written in prose, such as "Discurso da mosca" ("The Speech, by a Fly," in Neistein/Cardozo; *see* "Key to Bibliographical References"). Meyer's final works were more somber in tone. He also left solid literary criticism about nineteenth-century writers, particularly Machado de *Assis, and about his contemporaries.

BIBLIOGRAPHY: Additional selected works by Meyer: *Prosa dos pagos*, 1943; *A sombra da estante*, 1947; *Poesias*, 1957; *Textos críticos*, 1986. Translations: Hulet, Neistein/Cardozo; Woodbridge. Criticism: Bandeira, Manuel. "The Sardonic Brazilians." *Americas* (September, 1954), passim; Morais, Carlos Dante de. "A poesia de Augusto Meyer e a infância." *Poesias* de Augusto Meyer. Rio, 1957.

MILANO, DANTE (b. 1899). Born in Rio into a family of musicians, Milano began to write poetry in the symbolist fashion. Although he is a much-heralded participant in *modernism, he did not adhere to the movement's literary postures. In fact, like Pedro *Nava (*see* Modernism), he did not have any collection of his poetry published until well after the movement: *Poesias* (1948; Poetry). Thus he was long considered Brazil's "great unknown" poet. He spent his professional life as a civil servant and has become a noted sculptor. (*See* Art and Literature; Music and Literature; Symbolism.)

Milano refutes linkage to any literary school or doctrine. His poetry reveals the intellectual depth of a student of Greek, Latin, and Portuguese classics. A theme often versed, according to Paulo Mendes *Campos, is lyrical despair, probably influenced by his readings and translations of Dante: "Something white / That is my desire. . . . Something white / quite close to me / For me to feel it / For me to forget myself / On this dense / cold and godless night." ("Imagem" [Image], In *Poesia e prosa*) Milano has also published literary criticism. (*See* Critics and Criticism; Portugal and Brazil: Literary Relations.)

BIBLIOGRAPHY: Additional selected works by Milano: *Tres cantos do Inferno*, 1953; *Poesia e prosa*, 1979. Translations: Hulet. Criticism: Martins.

MILLIET, SÉRGIO (1898–1966). Born in São Paulo, Milliet, a poet turned critic of art (*see* Critics and Criticism), culture, and literature was marked by his long residence in Switzerland (1912–1922), where he studied sociology in Geneva. His early lyrics in French reveal his knowledge of French poetry and contact with writers such as Romain Rolland. (*See* Art and Literature.)

His *Poemas análogos* (1923; Analogous Poems), along with the verse of Luís Aranha (*see* Modernism), is considered among the most experimental early modernist poetry. Milliet participated in the several modernist *reviews, including *Klaxon* and *Terra Roxa e Outras Terras*. *Terminus seco e outros cocktails* (1932; Dry Terminus and Other Cocktails), his first prose work, concerns his activities as a modernist in the 1920s. (*See* Modernism.)

In the 1930s Milliet dedicated himself to sociological studies (e.g., *Roteiro do café*, 1938; Coffee Itinerary). Active in the founding of the Philosophy Faculty of the University of São Paulo, Milliet influenced the following generation of critics (*see* Critics and Criticism), notably Antônio Cândido, through his pragmatic and relativist sociological philosophy. His well-known *Diário crítico* (1944–1955; Critical Diary, 10 volumes) initiates an extended last phase of critical activity, oriented by his cultured personality yet not following any systematic critical method.

BIBLIOGRAPHY: Additional selected works by Milliet: *L'oeil de boeuf*, 1923; *Ensaios*, 1938; *Pintores e pintura*, 1940; *A marginalidade da pintura moderna*, 1942; *Quinze poemas*, 1953; *40 anos de poesia*, 1964. Translations: Hulet; Woodbridge. Criticism: Cândido, Antônio. "Sérgio Milliet, o crítico." In *Diário crítico* by Sérgio Milliet. São Paulo: Martins, 1981, I:xi-xxx; Ramos, Péricles, da Silva. In Coutinho, III.

K. DAVID JACKSON

MINAS SCHOOL. Refers to the group of late eighteenth-century poets in the area of Vila Rica, modern Ouro Preto, in Minas, who were born or living at the time in what was the most important cultural and economic center of colonial Brazil. These poets—including Cláudio Manuel da *Costa, Tomás Antônio *Gonzaga, Alvarenga *Peixoto, Basílio da *Gama, and Santa Rita *Durão— were to some extent influenced by the ideas of the Enlightenment (*see* Arcadias), and several of them were participants in the *Mineiran Conspiracy. Their poetry, although in the neoclassic (*see* Arcadias) style, nonetheless betrays a notable nativist sentiment.

BIBLIOGRAPHY: Criticism: Sayers.

MINEIRAN CONSPIRACY. Schematically planned in the colonial town of Vila Rica, modern Ouro Preto, in the then province of Minas Gerais, this 1789 movement had Brazilian independence from Portugal as its aim. The "revolutionaries" were "enlightened" professionals, judges, and military men whose disapproval of the oppression of colonial rule was heightened by the successful independence of the thirteen colonies of North America from England. (*See* Arcadias; Historiography; Portugal and Brazil: Literary Relations.)

Economic factors—particularly the motherland's unjust taxation—and social injustice were among their complaints. The plot was revealed by one of the participants. The 1790 trial led to sentences of death and exile for the conspirators. Joaquim José da Silva Xavier (1746–1792) (called Tiradentes, Toothpuller, owing to his profession) assumed the major blame for the conspiracy. He was hanged, thus becoming one of the major cult figures of Brazilian independence. Literary figures were among the principal conspirators: Tomás Antônio *Gonzaga, Cláudio Manuel da *Costa and Alvarenga *Peixoto. As a theme, the romantic generation, in its search for national heroes, portrayed these figures as the martyrs of Brazilian independence, for example, the drama *Gonzaga* (1875) by Castro *Alves and poetry by Casimiro de *Abreu.

Twentieth-century writers have been inspired by the men as well as the events in both critical studies and original works of literature, for example, Oswald de *Andrade, Cecília *Meireles, and Murilo *Mendes.

MODERNISM

Premodernism: 1912–1922. Although the first decades of the twentieth century in Brazil were consumed by social and political transformations, the old Brazilian imperial elite was incapable of adapting rapidly enough to these forces of change. In the same manner, Brazilian literary and artistic processes seemed frozen in an increasingly irrelevant Parnassian-realist mode. The accumulated pressures for change reached a head first in the arts, in 1922, followed eight years later by a general political upheaval, the Revolution of 1930. (*See* Parnassianism, Realism.)

Precipitating events around which young artists and writers organized date from Oswald de *Andrade's return from Paris in 1912, imbued with the Futurist Manifesto of Felippo Tomasso Marinetti (1876–1944), which sought to create a new world order and culture through the destruction of the past. In 1913 Lasar Segall's (1891–1957) "shocking" expressionist art exhibit took place, and Anita Malfatti's (1896–1964) 1917 avant-garde art show in São Paulo was attacked by Monteiro *Lobato in his essay "Paranóia ou mistificação" (Paranoia or Mystification).

While Oswald and other young writers and intellectuals sought the support of Lima *Barreto, whom they saw as one of the "pioneers" of the new national identity, the targets of their often satirical, exaggerated barbs and attacks were the "established" members of the *Brazilian Academy of Letters. In 1917 Alberto de Oliveira (*see* Symbolism) addressed the academy, referring to the "unknown literary forms and unknown genres" that were appearing in São Paulo.

By the 1920s forces for artistic change coalesced around Oswald de Andrade and Mário de *Andrade, artist Tarsila do Amaral, sculptor Vítor Brécheret (1894–1955), and others. They decided to use the centennial celebrations of Brazilian independence (1822–1922) to launch a movement to bring the country's artistic expression into the modern age. The result was the Semana de Arte Moderna, the Week of Modern Art in February 1922. (*See* Art and Literature.)

Announced in the *O Estado de São Paulo* newspaper on January 20, 1922, the Week of Modern Art consisted of three one-day sessions on February 13, 15, and 17 at the Municipal Theatre of São Paulo. Graça *Aranha, Ronald de *Carvalho, and Menotti del *Picchia lectured on the origins and aims of the movement. Mário de Andrade, Manuel *Bandeira, Guilherme de *Almeida, Ribeiro *Couto, and Plínio *Salgado recited their "new" poetry. Oswald de Andrade read selections from his modernist novel *Os condenados*. Guiomar Novaes (1896–1979) held a recital of piano works of Heitor *Villa-Lobos and Ernani Braga (1888–1948). Di Cavalcanti's (1897–1976) and Malfatti's cubist paintings and sculptures by Brécheret were part of the art exhibit. Graça Aranha, who was at the time a member of the Brazilian Academy of Letters, lectured about all that modern art: "These are extravagant paintings, absurd sculptures, hallucinatory music; this poetry is flighty and unarticulated. A marvelous dawn! ... What we see today is not the renaissance of an art that does not exist. It is the emotional birth of art in Brazil itself." (In Pontual, Roberto. *Dicionário das artes plásticas no Brasil*. Rio: 1969). According to newspaper accounts, most of the events were booed by spectators. (*See* Music and Literature.)

Phase One: 1922–1930. Modernism's first decade found its most vital expression in an iconoclastic poetry, preoccupied with nationalistic themes and experimentation with new techniques, all part of the break with *Parnassianism's rigid rules.

The nationalistic debate concerning the best way to express the Brazilian character initially found expression in the literary *review *Klaxon* (1922), but the ideological diversity of the participants led to a split in which Oswald de Andrade's group published *Movimento Pau Brasil* (1926) and the *Revista de Antropofagia* (1928), while Plínio *Salgado's rightist group issued a succession of reviews, *Verde-Amarelo* (1926) and *Anta* (1927). At today's distance from the urgency and heat of the debate between Right and Left in São Paulo, the major difference between the two sides seems to have been that the most talented and creative writers were aligned with Andrade. For example, one of the founders of *Klaxon*, who also participated in the review *Terra Roxa e Outras Terras* (1926), is the eminent bibliographer Rubens Borba de Moraes (b. 1899), who had a collection of literary criticism (*see* Critics and Criticism), *Domingo dos séculos* (1926; Sunday of the Centuries), published as well as many other major works; another participant was Luís Aranha (b. 1901), whose poetry from 1922, for example *Poema pitágoras* (Pythagorean Poem) and *Poema giratório* (Gyrating Poem) (collected and published in *Cocktails* [Cocktails] in 1984), reveals the Futurist preoccupation with speed and science.

Meanwhile, in Rio two *reviews represented the efforts of Rio's intellectuals and writers to bring the modernist debate to the capital: *Estética* (1924–1925) was led by Graça *Aranha, Sérgio Buarque de Hollanda (*see* Historiography), and Prudente de Morais (who used the pseudonym Pedro Dantas) (b. 1904); *Festa*, a continuation of the Catholic review *A Ordem*, edited by Jackson de *Figueiredo and Francisco Karam (b. 1902), was launched under leadership of the neosymbolist Tasso da *Silveira, who led an antinationalistic, anti-iconoclastic group whose importance would be paramount among poets of the second phase of modernism: Cecília *Meireles, Murilo *Mendes, Augusto Federico *Schmidt, Adelino Magalhães (b. 1897–1987), Andrade Murici (b. 1895), and Murilo Araújo (b. 1894).

Ephemeral regional "modernist" reviews sprang up throughout the nation during the 1920s. *A Revista* (1925), in Belo Horizonte, searched the national past for new ideas and a national spirit. Its participants included Carlos Drummond de *Andrade and Emílio Moura (b. 1901) (for translations, *see* "Key to Bibliographical References": Hulet), whose melancholic poetry began to appear in collected forms in the 1930s. *Leite Crioulo* (1929) appeared in Belo Horizonte and sought "to rescue" the Brazilian from the "sad" heritage of the Portuguese, black, and Indian civilizations. *Verde* (1927) of Cataguazes, Minas, sought a new expression for Brazilian civilization, freeing it from European models—particularly the then more recently imported ones. In addition to Rosário *Fusco, other important contributors were Ascânio Lopes (1906–1927), Henrique de

Rezende (b. 1896), and Francisco Inácio Peixoto (1910–1986), whose complete short stories appeared in 1982: *Chamada geral* (General Roll Call). In Pernambuco, Joaquim Inojosa (1901–1987); in Belém, Pará, *Eneida was a founding member of the Flaminaçu group, which extolled Amazonian traditions. Other regional reviews were, in Bahia, *Arco e Flexa*, 1928, with poems by Sosígenes Costa (b. 1901); in Ceará, *Maracajá*, 1929; in Manaus, *Redenção*; in Rio Grande do Sul, *Madrugada*; and so on.

Oswald de Andrade was perhaps the major innovator and most liberated spirit of the era. Although his role was eclipsed during the 1930s and 1940s, he subsequently had a decisive influence on the new vanguard of the fifties, and more recently his plays and novels have been reevaluated for literary merit. Mário de Andrade was known as the "pope" of modernism, as a consequence of his influential essays on the movement and his work as a literary-art critic, musicographer, and short story writer. His rhapsody *Macuaníma* has been an important element in contemporary Brazilian sense of identity. Also, his correspondence with other figures of the period gives modern readers an insight into the intellectual climate of the period. Other notable poets of the moment were Cassiano *Ricardo, who was linked to Plínio Salgado's group but did not produce his best poetry until the 1940s and 1950s, when he aligned himself with postmodernist groups; Raul *Bopp, whose *Cobra Norato* is the perfect synthesis of Oswald de Andrade's anthropophagy; and Manuel *Bandeira, perhaps modernism's best free-verse composer, who, in the late 1930s, began to compose metered verse once again and is one of the restorers of the sonnet to poetic currency. (*See* Postmodernism in Poetry.)

Phase Two: 1930–1945. The 1920–1930 period was one in which a rapidly evolving literary debate about how to express the national character and language was permeated by serious ideological and political questions. A series of abortive revolts in the 1920s culminated in Getúlio Vargas's ascension to the country's presidency, and his fifteen-year exercise of authority saw the modernist generation consecrated in the arts. Cândido Portinari (*see* Art and Literature) became the regime's painter-laureate and Heitor Villa-Lobos achieved similar status in music. Many writers and artists worked for the Vargas government, whose ministers brought government sponsorship to the modernist revolution in architecture and sculpture.

The period's poetry was more introspective and did not have an experimental emphasis. Jorge de *Lima was the most malleable of the modernist poets, passing from Parnassianism to the 1920s modernism to the 1930s introspectivism without missing a beat. The problem with this most technically talented of poets is finding a core of identity in his changing styles and themes. Murilo Mendes was the only modernist poet strongly influenced by *surrealism; his poetry is notable for its vivid imagery and mystical themes. His residence in Italy resulted in his mature poetry scarcely being published in Brazil, seriously compromising an evaluation of his true stature. Cecília Meireles was the first woman to be consecrated into the Brazilian literary pantheon, and her serious, intimistic, colorist, philosophical verse has made her a favorite of contemporary readers. Augusto Federico Schmidt anticipated in his sprawling verses the themes of alienation and loneliness that would predominate in post–World War II poetry. Vinícius de *Moraes became the poet laureate of the *bossa nova*, and his lyrics were set to music by contemporary composers such as Carlos Lyra and Antônio Carlos Jobim. In the midst of this large group of writers, Carlos Drummond de *Andrade stood out as Brazil's greatest contemporary poet. Unlike the other poets of his generation, he became intensely involved in social causes, and his poetry is unique because of its concern with World War II in Europe. (*See* Music and Literature.)

Whereas prose had been of lesser importance in the first phase of modernism (e.g., the works of Alcântara *Machado or Eduardo Frieiro's (1892–1982) *O club dos gramófonos* (1927; The Gramophones' Club), it came into its own during the second phase of modernism. A well-defined northeastern regionalist group emerged, which portrayed a region in decline. Jorge *Amado focused on the underclasses of Bahia in more than twenty novels. His *Terras do sem fim* is his best early Marxist novel. José Lins do *Rego is famous for his ''sugarcane cycle'' of novels detailing the decadence of the elite of his native Paraíba and Pernambuco. Rachel de *Queiroz's early fiction is set in drought-stricken Ceará, and José Américo de *Almeida is generally credited with beginning the modern northeastern novel with his *A bagaceira*. (*See* Cycles; Regionalism; Social Novelists of the 1930s.)

The most important novelist of the 1930s is only tangentially linked to the regionalists. Graciliano *Ramos's concern with narrative innovation makes each of his novels a new experiment with the narrative process itself. Abandoning fiction altogether, his *Memórias do cárcere* is a mordant autobiographical analysis of the human condition. (*See* Autobiography.)

At least as important as the northeastern group of novelists was an outstanding generation of urban novelists who used psychological realism to portray the new Brazilian middle class. Four of them should be examined in any appraisal of the second modernist generation: Lúcio *Cardoso, Érico *Veríssimo, Dionélio Machado (1895–1985) and Mário Peixoto (b. 1918). Veríssimo is the only one of the group to have enjoyed great popularity, even though he has been ignored for thirty years. Machado, a psychiatrist and Communist party militant, was the author of eleven novels and a volume of short stories. He began to receive belated attention after 1970 for novels such as *Os ratos* (1935; The Rats), which describes twenty-four hours in the life of a lower middle-class hero, and *Desolação* (1944; Desolation). Peixoto's *O inútil de cada um* (1934; revised edition, 1984; Each One's Uselessness) was a major attempt at a highly hermetic modernist prose in the style of Proust.

Modernism is still being defined and redefined; new studies appear yearly on different aspects of the movement and its development in different regions of

Brazil. Among the notable Brazilian scholars of modernism are Mário da Silva
Brito (b. 1916), Antônio Cândido, and Wilson Martins. (*See* Critics and
Criticism.)
   BIBLIOGRAPHY: Translations: Bishop, Elizabeth, and Emanuel Brasil, eds. *An An-
thology of Twentieth-Century Brazilian Poetry.* Middletown, Conn.: Wesleyan University
Press, 1972; Neistein, José, and Manoel Cardozo. *Poesia brasileira moderna: A Bilingual
Anthology.* Washington, D.C.: Brazilian American Cultural Institute, 1972; Nist, John.
Modern Brazilian Poetry: An Anthology. Bloomington: Indiana University Press, 1962;
Ponteiro, Giovanni, ed. *An Anthology of Brazilian Modernist Poetry.* Oxford: Pergamon
Press, 1969. Criticism: Brookshaw; Ellison; Ferrua, Pietro. "Futurism in Brazil." *Neo-
helicon* 5 (1977), pp. 184–194; Jackson, Kenneth David. "A View on Brazilian Literature:
Eating the *Revista de Antropofagia.*" *LALR* (1978), pp. 1–9; Martins, Wilson. *The
Modernist Idea.* New York: New York University Press, 1970; Nist, John. *The Modernist
Movement in Brazil.* Austin: University of Texas Press, 1967; Simon, Iumna Maria.
"Poetic Evolution in the Industrial Revolution: The Brazilian Modernists." In Wirth,
John D., and Robert L. Jones, eds. *Manchester and São Paulo: Problems of Rapid Urban
Growth.* Stanford, Calif.: Stanford University Press, 1978. pp. 35–49; Sussekind, Flora.
Cinematógrafo de letras, literatura, técnica e modernizaçao no Brasil. Rio: 1987; Wis-
nick, José, M. *O coro dos contrários: a música em torno da Semana de 22.* São Paulo:
Duas Cidades, 1977.

JON M. TOLMAN

MONTE ALVERNE. *See* Alverne, Friar Francisco de Monte.

MONTEIRO LOBATO. *See* Lobato, José Bento Monteiro.

MONTELLO, JOSUÉ (b. 1917; BAL: 1954). Montello, one of the most
prolific writers of Brazilian literature, has had more than seventy titles published,
including novels, novellas, plays, criticism (*see* Critics and Criticism), history,
*children's literature, essays, and textbooks. Although he has spent most of his
life in Rio, he is intimately identified with his native state of Maranhão, the
setting of most of his works. He also authored *O Presidente Machado de Assis*
(2d ed., 1986; President Machado de Assis), which describes the founding and
the early years of the *Brazilian Academy of Letters. (*See* Regionalism; Theater
History.)
   Cais da sagração (1971; *Coronation Quay*, 1975) is typical of his art as a
storyteller. Although containing numerous subplots, it centers on Mestre Severino's decision to sail his boat "Bonança" from his small coastal town to the
capital of São Luís one last time to prove that, in spite of old age and a failing
heart, he is still a skilled boatsman, as well as to initiate his grandson Pedro
into the life of the sea. Upon arriving in São Luís, his grandson becomes involved
with a homosexual. Because of this, Severino plans to kill Pedro on the return
trip; however, events take a startling turn, and Pedro proves his manhood to his
grandfather. (*See* Homosexuality and Literature.)
   As elsewhere in Montello's fiction, *Coronation Quay* is marked by a dual

interest in sociological documentation and psychological analysis and held together by a delicate balance between regionalist representation and the development of universal themes. Montello's technique is largely traditional. Nevertheless, an emphasis on the role of memory and the subjective dimension of time, as well as the deft use of indirect narrated monologue, lend his fiction a modern quality.

Montello is also known for using his fiction to record the past of his native Maranhão. Such is the case of *Os tambores de São Luís* (1975; The Drums of São Luis), which reconstructs the history of slavery and racial discrimination from 1838 through 1915. Although the novel contains an indictment of the injustice of slavery and prejudice, its insistence on the accomplishments of the main character, Damião, a former slave; its affirmation of Afro-Brazilian ethnic pride; and the unquestionable presence of human decency create a positive atmosphere characteristic of Montello's worldview, in which the forces of good generally triumph over the forces of evil. (*See* Contemporary Black Literature; Slavery and Literature.)

BIBLIOGRAPHY: Additional selected works by Montello: *Janelas fechadas*, 1941; *O labirinto de espelhos*, 1952; *O fio de meada*, 1955; *Uma tarde, outra tarde*, 1968; *A noite sobre Alcântara*, 1978; *Pedra viva*, 1983; *Perto da meia noite*, 1985; *Antes que os pássaros acordem*, 1987; *A última convidada*, 1988. Criticism: Mello, Bandeira de. In Coutinho, V; Silverman, Malcolm. "A ficção sociológica e introspectiva de Josué Montello." *Moderna ficção brasileira 2*. Rio: Civilização Brasileira, 1981, pp. 111–161.

LUIZ FERNANDO VALENTE

MOOG, CLODOMIR VIANA (b. 1906; BAL: 1945). Viana Moog has practiced law, has been a journalist, and has served in various diplomatic functions, including at the United Nations. Born in Rio Grande do Sul, his writings have been primarily concerned with the interpretation of the Brazilian identity in relationship to other national identities. (*See* Philosophy of National Identity.)

His novel *Um rio imita o Reno* (1939; A River Imitates the Rhine) views the cultural dilemma faced by German *immigrants to southern Brazil, and in *Tóia* (1962; Toia) he uses his diplomatic experiences in Mexico as a basis for a love story focusing on the differences between Mexicans and Brazilians.

Moog's most famous work, however, is *Bandeirantes e pioneiros* (1954; *Bandeirantes and Pioneers*, 1964), a comparative psychosociological study of cultural, social, economic, and other differences between the United States, which he greatly admires, and Brazil. Moog's *Interpretação da literatura brasileira* (1942; *An Interpretation of Brazilian Literature*, 1951; reprint, 1970) insists upon the unity of the literature in spite of its divergent regional sources of inspiration. (*See* Regionalism.)

BIBLIOGRAPHY: Additional selected works by Moog: *Heróis da decadência*, 1934; *Uma jangada para Ulisses*, 1959.

MORAES, VINÍCIUS DE (1913–1980). The last and, according to Sérgio *Milliet, "the most brilliant of the orthodox modernists," Moraes was a poet, a playwright, a lyricist, an author of *crônicas*, a film critic, a defender of Brazilian cultural and national identity, and an outspoken critic of the military dictatorship. (*See* Dictatorship and Literature; Film and Literature; Modernism; Philosophy of National Identity.)

Born in Rio, Moraes studied law, spent an academic year at Oxford (1938–1939); served in the Brazilian diplomatic service as consul in Los Angeles, Paris, and Montevideo; and in later life dedicated himself entirely to music and poetry.

While at law school, Moraes avidly read so-called French Catholic writers—François Mauriac and Georges Bernanos—and become friends with Jorge *Amado and Otávio de *Faria. The latter played an important role in Moraes's incipient literary career; in fact, the publication of his first poem, "A transfiguração da montanha" (The Transfiguration of the Mountain), in Alceu Amoroso *Lima's Catholic *review, *A Ordem*, in 1932 was due to Faria's intervention. (*See* Foreign Writers and Brazil; Religion and Literature.)

Moraes's first collection of poems, *O caminho para a distância* (1933; The Road into the Distance), received mixed critical reviews. It was characterized by a Catholic mysticism and a pompous, complex verse style reflecting his youthful debate between "the spirit and the flesh." In *Forma e exégese* (1935; Form and Exegesis), his next collection, it is evident that he opted for "the flesh" and for a simpler verse of daily life, as exemplified in "A mulher que passa" (The Woman Passing By): "My God, I love the woman passing by. / Her cold back is a field of lilies / She has seven colors in her hair / Seven wishes on her cool lips!" *Novos poemas* (1938; New Poems) has yet another source of inspiration—the Brazilian reality. In the late thirties Moraes became fascinated with works by Machado de *Assis, Mário de *Andrade, Murilo *Mendes, and Manuel *Bandeira. It was Bandeira, along with Otávio de Faria and Aníbal *Machado, who financed the publication of Moraes's *Elegias* (1943; Elegies), which Vinícius himself considered the turning point in his poetic career. The volume reveals a stylistically simpler poetry, more worldly and bawdy.

A thriving career as film critic began in the early 1940s and brought him into contact with Orson Wells, who was in Brazil at the time. While vice-consul in Los Angeles, he became further involved in both film and jazz. His *Poemas, sonetos e baladas* (1946; Poems, Sonnets, and Ballads) was published, voicing his preoccupation with the philosophy of love, such as in the "Soneto da fidelidade" (Sonnet of Faithfulness): "I shall be attentive to my beloved in everything / Before, and with such zeal, and always, and so much. . . . / And thus, later on, when perhaps death, anguish of the living / Perhaps solitude, end of he who loves, comes looking for me / I can say about love: That it not be immortal, because it is a flame / But that it be infinite while it lasts."

Other collections of poetry followed, works written while he was attached to the Brazilian Embassy in France, including his *Antologia poética* (1955; Anthology of Poems) and *Livro de sonetos* (1956; Book of Sonnets), both of which reveal a more intense concern for social problems. Although Moraes's drama of carnival, *Orfeu da Conceição* (1965; Black Orpheus), with music by Antônio Carlos Jobim (*see* Music and Literature), received mixed reviews in Brazil, the film version by Marcel Camus brought him and Brazil worldwide attention as well as first prize at the 1959 Cannes Film Festival. (*See* Film and Literature.)

In 1962 Moraes participated in his first successful concert with Jobim and João Gilberto. (*See* Music and Literature.) After 1969, when he left the diplomatic service, he dedicated himself to music, as a singer, lyricist, and composer.

BIBLIOGRAPHY: Additional selected works by Moraes: *Para uma menina com uma flor*, 1966; *Poesia completa e prosa*, 1974. Translations: Bishop/Brasil; *The Girl from Ipanema*. Merrick, N.Y.: Cross-Cultural Communications, 1982; Hulet; Woodbridge. Criticism: Brown, Ashley. "Vinícius de Moraes (1913–1980): A Tribute." *WLT* (Summer, 1982), pp. 472–473; Foster/Foster, II.

MOTA, MAURO (b. 1912; BAL: 1969). At age twelve, Mota moved from the traditional Pernambucan sugar zone to Recife, where he completed work toward a law degree in 1937. In 1956 he was named director of the *Diário de Pernambuco*, and he initiated columns on books and authors. Around the same time he began teaching Brazilian geography at the Educational Institute of Pernambuco.

Although Mota has had fiction published, he has become known primarily as a poet ever since his first collection, *Elegias* (1952; Elegies), received *prizes from both the Pernambucan and *Brazilian Academies of Letters. He is often linked with the so-called Generation of 1945 (*see* Postmodernism in Poetry), owing to his concern for a classical form and clarity of style. He displays considerable diversity in form—ranging from the sonnet to blank verse—and in theme—ranging from pious tributes to a departed mother and wife to social criticism, erotica, and brief portraits of everyday objects such as a pencil, wall, jacket, or dog.

Although not really a regionalist in the true sense, a Northeast sensibility— perhaps the most outstanding feature of his work—is evident through a metaphoric or symbolic Pernambucan landscape, as in the collection, *Pernambucânia, ou cantos da comarca e memória* (1979; Pernambucania, or Poetry of the Neighborhood and Memory). Mota has also written works on geography, history, and sociology.

BIBLIOGRAPHY: Additional selected works by Mota: *O cajueiro nordestino*, 1954; *A tecelã*, 1956; *Paisagem das secas*, 1958; *Itinerário* (collection of all previously published poetry), 1977. Translations: Bishop/Brasil; Hulet; Woodbridge. Criticism: Pontes, Joel. "Tres aspectos da técnica de Mauro Mota." *LBR* (Summer, 1966), pp. 101–106.

PAUL DIXON

MOURÃO, RUI (b. 1929). *Mineiro* Mourão is a novelist and critic. (*See* Critics and Criticism.) His fiction is structured on mythical and biblical reincarnations within a sociopolitical backdrop of mass movements. In *Curral dos crucificados* (1970; Corral of the Crucified), Brazil's populace's internal migration to urban areas is raised to a biblical allegory, a form that became popular during the dictatorship. Jonas, the protagonist, is attracted to "paradise," the city, from the interior of Bahia. His voyage becomes a true "rite of passage," experienced by millions of his compatriots. Similar themes and techniques are used in his later novel *Jardim pagão* (1977; Pagan Garden). (*See* City and Literature; Dictatorship and Literature.)

BIBLIOGRAPHY: Additional selected works by Mourão: *As raízes*, 1956; *Cidade calabouço*, 1973; *Monólogo do escorpião*, 1983.

MUSIC AND LITERATURE. Music has been a prime channel for Brazilian esthetic energy in every era. Poetry and narrative reflect the importance of music making at all levels of society. Musical technique has influenced literary style, and the interaction between music and letters has determined cultural direction.

In the early colonial period, Father *Anchieta described a well-developed indigenous music. He used hymns and ballads in his proselytizing dramas (*autos*) to capture the attention of his native audience. Brazil kept abreast of European musical progress during the seventeenth and eighteenth centuries through Jesuit-trained church musicians. Bahian court-society balladry afforded a vehicle for gadfly satire by Gregório de *Matos. Even Manuel Botelho de *Oliveira, self-styled "first son of Brazil to publish his verses," exhibits this typical poetry-music linkage; his *Música do Parnaso* has four "choruses" of rhymes with the comic "descant."

The tragicomic opera librettos of Rio-born poet Antônio José da *Silva (The Jew) became so popular in Lisbon that they antagonized the Inquisition, which finally executed him for Judaism. But his operas survived and spread to Brazil, especially "Guerras do Alecrim e Mangerona" (War between the Rosemary and the Marjoram). Quick song artists (*repentistas*) appeared toward the end of the eighteenth century; Father Caldas *Barbosa garnered fame in Lisbon for this ability. (*See* Portugal and Brazil: Literary Relations.)

In the nineteenth century imperial and popular enthusiasm for operas, especially by Rossini but even by Silva flourished. Brazilian composer Carlos Gomes (1836–1896) was sent to Italy by Dom Pedro II and won acclaim in Europe for his opera "O Guarani" (1870), based on the novel by José de *Alencar. Alencar, Machado de *Assis, Raul *Pompéia, Henrique *Coelho Neto, and other serious writers produced valuable music journalism, and Sílvio *Romero and Melo Morais, Jr. (1844–1919), began folklore studies, publishing traditional Brazilian songs. (*See* Folklore and Literature.)

Early in the twentieth century, Lima *Barreto satirized the folklore fad in his *Triste fim de Policarpo Quaresma*, complaining that Portuguese and Amerindian aspects of Brazilian life were sentimentalized, while African contributions were both exploited and unacknowledged. In the 1920s Ronald de *Carvalho and Mário de *Andrade extolled Heitor *Villa-Lobos, who melded Brazilian folklore and European forms as a musical embodiment of the esthetic of *modernism.

Catulo da Paixão *Cearense and Ribeiro *Couto based their poetry on traditional regional songs of African origin, for example, *lundus* and *modinhas*.

Vinícius de *Moraes renewed the intimate association of poetry and music in the 1950s. Under the 1964–1985 military censorship, poets found an outlet for protest in popular songs such as Chico *Buarque's "Você" (You) or "Cálice," a Portuguese play on words and sounds, meaning at the same time both "chalice" and "be quiet," as well as in the *tropicalismo* movement, which sought to redefine Brazilian culture. (*See* Philosophy of National Identity.)

BIBLIOGRAPHY: Criticism: Appleby, David. *The Music of Brazil*. Austin, Tex.: University of Texas Press, 1983; Brookshaw; Correa de Azevedo, Luís Heitor. "Music and Society in Imperial Brazil: 1822–1889." *Portugal and Brazil in Transition*. Edited by Raymond S. Sayers. Minneapolis: University of Minnesota, 1968, pp. 303–309; Perrone, Charles A. "From *Noigandres* to 'Milagre de Alegria': The Concrete Poets and Contemporary Brazilian Popular Music." *RMLA/LAMR* (Spring-Summer, 1985), pp. 58–79; idem. "Pagings and Stagings: Musical Echoes of Literary Heritage." *LALR* (January-June, 1986), pp. 78–91; Rego, Enylton de Sá and Charles Perrone. *MPB: Contemporary Brazilian Popular Music. BSG*; Sayers, Raymond S. "Music in Machado de Assis." *REH* 34 (1966), pp. 776–90; Schoenbach, Peter J. *Classical Music of Brazil. BSG*; Vassberg, David E. "African Influences on the Music of Brazil." *LBR* (Summer, 1976), pp. 35–54; Wisnick, J. M. *O coro dos contrários: a música em torno da Semana de '22*. São Paulo: Duas Cidades, 1977.

LEE BOYD

N

NABUCO, JOAQUIM (1849–1910; BAL: 1897). A member of an important landholding, politically active family, Nabuco studied law. He was an ardent abolitionist allied with José do *Patrocínio, Castro *Alves, and Rui *Barbosa, and he authored *O abolicionismo* (1883; *Abolitionism*, 1977). Although he was a monarchist, he served the republic with great distinction as ambassador in London and Washington, where he died. (*See* Slavery and Literature.)

A minor poet, Nabuco's major works were in the fields of history, biography (*see* Biography and Biographers), and *autobiography. Aside from specifically historical essays related to Brazil and the Americas in general, Nabuco's biography of his father, Nabuco de Araújo, *Um estadista do império* (3 vols., 1897–1899; A Statesman of the Empire), is notable for its impartial view of the achievement of one of the empire's leading figures, as well as the description of political life during the era. (*See* Historiography.)

Of greater artistic importance is his autobiography *Minha formação* (1900; My Education), which reveals an admirable literary style. Also of note is the biography of him by his daughter, Carolina, *A vida de Joaquim Nabuco* (1928; *The Life of Joaquim Nabuco*, 1950), who also wrote *memoirs of her family's life, *Oito décadas* (1973; Eight Decades), and some short fiction.

Although Nabuco was truly a world citizen who admired the humane qualities of life in England, France, and the United States, he was nonetheless dedicated to social justice and the improvement of Brazil. Critic Otto Maria Carpeaux (*see* Critics and Criticism) wrote about him: "Aristocrat and champion of a generously liberal politics, highly cultured, a tolerant Christian, a writer endowed with all human and literary qualities, Nabuco was always and continues to be a Brazilian idol." (In *Pequena bibliografia crítica da literatura brasileira*. Rio: 1968, p. 132).

BIBLIOGRAPHY: Additional selected works by Nabuco: *The Spirit of Nationality in the History of Brazil*, 1908; *Obras de Joaquim Nabuco*, 14 vols., 1947–1949. Criticism: Graham, Richard. "Joaquim Nabuco, Conservative Historian." *LBR* (Summer, 1980), pp. 1–16; Munn, B. W. "Graça Aranha, Nabuco and Brazilian Rapprochement with the United States." *LBR* (December, 1969), pp. 66–72; Sayers.

NARCISA AMÁLIA. *See* Amália, Narcisa.

NASCIMENTO, ABDIAS DO (b. 1914). Playwright, artist, and political activist, Nascimento was instrumental in founding the "Teatro Experimental do Negro" (TEN), or Black Experimental Theater, in Rio in 1944. TEN's goal was to train blacks in acting and to stimulate the creation of dramatic texts reflecting black history and culture. Under Nascimento's leadership, TEN also demanded civil rights for blacks and espoused the protection of Afro-Brazilian identity as a political objective. (*See* Theater History.)

After TEN's successful production of O'Neill's *The Emperor Jones* in 1945, the group produced a series of Afro-Brazilian plays that were later published in Nascimento's anthology *Dramas para negros e prólogo para brancos* (1961; Dramas for Blacks and Prologue for Whites). Included in the anthology is Nascimento's own play *Sortilégio: mistério negro* (1960; *Sortilege: Black Mystery*, 1978), which had been banned by government censors before finally being produced in 1967. Using a black theme in a modern and aggressive manner, this work revolutionized the concepts of black theater in Brazil and, according to the French sociologist and Brazilianist Roger Bastide (1878–1974), occupies the same place in Brazilian literature that Richard Wright's (1908–1960) *Native Son* (1945) occupies in Afro-American literature. A revised version, *Sortilégio, II*, was published in 1979.

As a civil rights activist and essayist, Nascimento has had a series of treatises published exposing racism and cultural oppression and has promoted a theory of social change called *quilombismo*, which refers to the towns of runaway slaves during the era of slavery. After spending the 1970s in the United States, he returned to Brazil in 1982 and was elected to a seat in the national congress. In 1983 he founded *Afrodiáspora*, a journal of black world thought, and he published his only collection of poetry, *Axés do sangue e da esperança* (1983; Songs of Blood and Hope).

Nascimento's adamant stance against racism and his constant support of Afro-Brazilian culture have served as a great stimulus to young writers of *contemporary black literature.

BIBLIOGRAPHY: Additional selected works by Nascimento: *O negro revoltado*, 1968; *Racial Democracy in Brazil: Myth or Reality?* 1977; *Mixture or Massacre? Essays on the Genocide of a Black People*, 1979; *O quilombismo: documentos de uma militância pan-africanista*, 1980. Criticism: Brookshaw; Litto, Frederic. "Some Notes on Brazil's Black Theatre." *The Black Writer in Africa and the Americas*. Edited by Lloyd W. Brown. Los Angeles: Hennessey and Ingalls, 1973, pp. 195–221; Plumpp, Sterling. "*Racial Democracy in Brazil (Myth or Reality?)*." (review) *First World* 2 (1979), pp. 21–25.

JAMES H. KENNEDY

NASCIMENTO, ESDRAS DO (b. 1934). Born in Piauí, Nascimento's fictional world is projected through his particular version of the contemporary, urban, psychological narrative. It involves the daily trials and tribulations of struggling, archetypal middle-class professionals of both sexes whose disillusionment, frustration, hypocrisy, alienation, and, above all, solitude make for a maddening, at times shocking, metaphor of the whole Brazilian experience. Nascimento makes keen use of rotating coplots, multiple viewpoints, recurring characters from one novel to another, and repeated themes. (*See* City and Literature.)

The structure and format of his fiction since his first and most successful novel, *Solidão em família* (1963; Family Solitude), is conventional. However, two recent pieces depart radically: *Jogos da madrugada* (1983; Dawn Games) and, in a dissimilar way, his *Variante Gotemburgo* (1978; Goteburg Variant). The former portrays several London-based acquaintances whose existential dilemmas are set against a parody of Shakespeare's *King Lear*. *Variante Gotemburgo* presents its characters' dramas as if each one were a piece in the title's chess play. On a simple level, the novel is a succession of confessional depositions by characters whose interrelationships become clearer as the work unravels. More significantly, it is a chess-board game with male personages corresponding to specific white pieces, females to black ones. Character movement is the same as that on the board: when a piece advances, narrative action progresses chronologically; when it withdraws, action returns to the past; and when the piece is moved to the side, the temporal factor momentarily disappears.

Cosmopolitan and universal, Nascimento's fiction never loses its peculiar Brazilian flavor; its sparse, caustic humor; its frequent irony; or its functional eroticism. Of late, detectivesque and supernatural elements are appearing, enriching further Nascimento's hermetic, disquieting world of the contemporary Brazilian middle class.

BIBLIOGRAPHY: Additional selected works by Nascimento: *Convite ao desespero*, 1964; *Engenharia do casamento*, 1968; *Teoria de comunicação e literatura*, 1975; *Aventuras do Capitão Simplício*, 1982; *As surpresas da paixão*, 1986.

MALCOLM SILVERMAN

NASSAR, RADUAN (b. 1935). Nassar, born in the state of São Paulo, has pursued studies in a variety of areas: classical literature, law, and philosophy, but he did not receive a degree in any of them. He has worked as a journalist and in business. Currently, he divides his time between the city and a farm in the interior.

He is the author of two novels: *Lavoura arcaica* (1975; revised, 1982; Old-Fashioned Farming), which echoes the parable of the prodigal son. Nassar's version, however, is told from the point of view of the son and maintains an attitude of ambivalence regarding the family relationships. *Um copo de cólera* (1978; A Cup of Anger) also explores the psychological tensions of domestic life, this time concentrating on a few days in the existence of a married couple.

Nassar's fiction tends toward lyricism and favors interior monologue over action. When actions are narrated, they are passed through a filter of vagueness and potential allegory, so that the question of reality versus imagination becomes important. Several critics (see Critics and Criticism) view his sparse style and his use of allegory as reflections of the "strangulation" of thought during the dictatorship years. (See Dictatorship and Literature.)

BIBLIOGRAPHY: Criticism: Wolff, María Tai. "Em paga aos sermões do pai: *Lavoura arcaica* by Raduan Nassar." *LBR* (Summer, 1985), pp. 63–70.

                                                                    PAUL DIXON

NATURALISM. The term *naturalism* is used to refer to the literary movement, limited almost exclusively to prose fiction, that was founded and led in France by the novelist Émile Zola (1840–1902) and defined by him in *Le roman expérimental* (1880; *The Experimental Novel*, 1964). Based on a faith in the ability of science to provide universal answers, naturalism regarded man as a creature under the complete control of natural forces that took the form of environmental and biological determinism. In the simplest of terms, the cornerstones of the movement became the law of the influence of the environment, the law of the influence of heredity, and the law that posited the exclusively physiological origin of emotions. Literary characters took on a new kind of importance as laboratory experiments. The causes of their actions, examined "clinically" by the novelist, became as important as the actions themselves, often more important.

Naturalism is a development of *realism. Although it follows realism chronologically, it exists with it simultaneously, sharing the technique of detailed, painstakingly accurate descriptions, almost invariably with a sociological intent and frequently at great length. Naturalism, however, differs from realism in its concentration on deterministic causality. In its habitual preference for what was ugly, sordid, and even grotesque, naturalism tended toward an exaggeration of normal things and events reminiscent of *romanticism. It differs from romanticism in that the naturalist writer looked for scientific explanations, whereas the romantic writer sought transcendent principles.

Naturalism took firm root in Portugal through the works of the great Portuguese novelist José Maria Eça de Queiroz and was imported into Brazil through Eça as well as directly from France. According to one contemporary critic, Eça's *O primo Basílio* (1878; *Cousin Bazilio*, 1953) burst upon the Brazilian scene that year like a bombshell. To be sure, Bernardo *Guimarães, in particular, and Herculano Inglês de *Sousa had already produced works whose romantic heritage does not obscure their introduction of environmental determinism and the physiological origination of emotions. But they did not succeed in altering the Brazilian novel's direction, which remained essentially the same since José de *Alencar's romantic masterpiece *O guarani*. Now things were to change, radically and at once. (See Portugal and Brazil: Literary Relations.)

However, the change did not occur without protest. In a scathing review of *Cousin Bazilio*, Machado de *Assis found the female protagonist a puppet manipulated by the author rather than a victim of "forces beyond her own control." Later, near the height of the movement, Raul *Pompéia's *O ateneu* (1888; The

Athenaeum) shared naturalism's meticulous attention to descriptive detail and fondness for previously taboo subject matter, but he, like Assis, rejected its deterministic concept of the individual. Nevertheless, after Aluísio *Azevedo's *O mulato* had burst like another bombshell in 1881, naturalism was suddenly fashionable. Although the fashion would last barely a decade and a half, works adhering to the new precepts poured forth.

Despite their large quantity, including works by José *Veríssimo, Rodolfo *Teófilo, Domingos *Olímpio, and Manuel de Oliveira *Paiva, few naturalist novels of high quality were written in Brazil. The reason has been given that Brazilian authors, in their sudden attraction to the new theory, rushed to put it into practice before they had assimilated it completely. An example is Júlio *Ribeiro's *A carne*, in which simple depravity is relied upon as a substitute for biological determinism. The point has also been made that Brazilian authors generally failed to adapt naturalism to the realities of their own country, preferring instead to borrow their reality along with their techniques from Portugal (mainly through Eça's works) and France.

Against such a background it is all the more remarkable that there appeared two novels that compare favorably with the European models and that simultaneously present authentically powerful and moving pictures of Brazilian life— Aluísio *Azevedo's *O cortiço* and Adolfo *Caminha's *Bom Crioulo*. Neither Azevedo nor Caminha overpowered his readers with an excessively scientific vocabulary, often a fault in lesser writers. Both of them understood and conveyed that the victims of the deterministic forces they emphasized were human beings. Both, moreover, virtually eliminated the influence of heredity, replacing it with a greater reliance on environmental factors. Thus they asserted their ability to imitate their models creatively, rather than merely copying them, and provided the best of Brazilian naturalism with an element of autonomous identity.

Secondary novelists whose works were popular at the time included Lúcio de Mendonça (1854–1909), Horácio de Carvalho (1858–1933), Valentim de Magalhães (1859–1903), and Antônio Papi Júnior (1854–1934). According to another contemporary critic, however, naturalism had become an anachronism in Brazil by 1898. Nonetheless, distinctively regionalistic works continued to appear, some of them very good, but they received scant attention, for example, *Luzia-Homem* by Domingos *Olímpio; *O urso* (1901; The Bear) by São Paulo's Antônio de Oliveira (1874–1933); *Aves de arribação* (1902; Migratory Birds) by Ceará's Antônio Sales (1868–1940); and *Mana Silvéria* (1913; Sister Silveria) by the southerner Pedro de Castro Canto e Melo (1866–1934). Other regionalistic works were Avelino Fóscolo's (1864–1944) social fiction set in Minas, for example, *O mestiço* (1902; The Mestizo), which concerns slave plantation life, and Carmen Dolores's (pseudonym of Emília Moncorvo Bandeira de Melo) (1852–1910) posthumous novel of Brazilian women's social instability, *A luta* (1911; The Battle). (*See* Feminism and Literature; Regionalism.)

As a movement, Brazilian naturalism is, in fact, short lived and quantitatively poor in works of high quality. Even so, its importance must not be underestimated, for beyond producing two excellent novels, it firmly established the acceptance of the environment as a determinant of character and action. This major legacy, although no longer accompanied by the once popular scientific vocabulary, is clearly visible in the northeastern novel of the twentieth century, the theater of Nelson *Rodrigues, as well as, according to critic Flora Sussekind (*see* Critics and Criticism), in many of the journalistic novels (*romance-repor-tagem*) and fiction, for example, Rubem *Fonseca, which have appeared during the 1970s and 1980s. (*See* Dictatorship and Literature.)

BIBLIOGRAPHY: Criticism: Brookshaw; Coutinho/Rabassa; Montello, Josué. In Coutinho, II; Loos, Dorothy Scott. *The Naturalistic Novel of Brazil*. New York: Hispanic Institute in the United States, 1963; Moser, Gerald. "The Persistence of Naturalism in the Brazilian 'Northeastern Fiction.' " *Studies in Honor of Lloyd A. Kasten*. Madison, Wis.: Hispanic Seminary of Medieval Studies, 1975, pp. 199–208; Sussekind, Flora. *Tal Brasil, qual romance?* Rio: Achiamé, 1984.

NORWOOD ANDREWS, JR.

NAVA, PEDRO (1903–1984). Nava was a practicing rheumatologist in Minas and Rio. His involvement with literature began in Belo Horizonte. Together with Carlos Drummond de *Andrade, he was responsible for the publication of *A Revista* (1925), the first modernist *review in Minas. (*See* Modernism.)

Nava's interest in the arts was broad, and he was a painter. As a poet, Nava obeyed modernism's tenets to such an extent that Mário de *Andrade once warned him that too much concern over poetic form might lead to another type of *Parnassianism. (*See* Art and Literature.)

Toward the end of his life (he committed suicide), he began to publish his *memoirs. In them Nava played with time à la Marcel Proust (1875–1922): his narrative is anything but strictly chronological. Because Nava made time his inner space, the past is present rather than recounted, and each detail of the past is seen clearly, as if it were happening at the moment of the narration. (*See* Dictatorship and Literature.)

This approach to time is already found in *Baú de ossos* (1972; Trunk of Bones), the first of his six volumes of memoirs. The fusion of style and treatment of time serve a specific purpose: that of showing that Nava is not only telling his life, he is also reading it. The telling is accompanied by a critical reassessment of each event and his participation in it. Furthermore, this reassessment extends far beyond the anecdotal to cover the whole period in which the event took place. Hence Nava's memoirs constitute not only the narration of one man's life but also the attempt to recover and reveal a time buried in the memory of society. The lasting quality of Nava's work resides precisely in this generality.

BIBLIOGRAPHY: Additional selected works by Nava: *Balão cativo: memórias 2*, 1973; *Chão de ferro: memórias 3*, 1976; *O círio perfeito: memórias 6*, 1983. Criticism: Queiroz, Maria José de. "*Galo das trevas*: A festa da memória." *Colóquio/Letras* (September, 1982), pp. 58–60; Wlaty, Ivete Lara Camargos. "*Baú de ossos*: Um corte, uma arqueologia." *MGSL* (November 26, 1983), p. 9.

JÚLIO MACHADO PINTO

NÉJAR, CARLOS (b. 1939). Néjar studied law and has served as a judge in courts in his native Rio Grande do Sul. His law practice constitutes an important element of his poetic expression, which affords an interesting juxtaposition of lyricism and legal terminology and is characterized by extreme preciseness.

Néjar's literary debut occurred in 1960, when concretism (*see* Postmodernism in Poetry) had already established itself as the poetic vanguard, but the aura of the modernists, for example, Jorge de *Lima, was as strong as ever. Néjar, however, benefits from both currents but does not subscribe firmly to either one.

Terseness of style is an excellent means of conveying his reflections on human nature. Each one of his books is a carefully planned step of such an investigation. *Sélesis* (1960; Selesis) and his *Livro de Silbion* (1963; Book of Silbion) present poetry at the mythic level, outside of both space and time. They describe the Great Void that preceded reality with a hieratic, mystic tone. From the atemporality of the two first books, Néjar moved on to the consideration of Time in *O livro do tempo* (1965; The Book of Time), followed by the presence of man in interaction with temporal reality. In *Canga* (1971; *Yoke*, 1981) the poet's social conscience emerges as the controlling force. The same somber, ascetic examination of the human plight reappears in *Árvores do mundo* (1977; *The Tree of the World*, 1980).

The underlying unity and vast scope of Néjar's work allied to the precise simplicity of his expression contribute to making him one of the most powerful contemporary poets in Brazil with a growing reputation extending beyond national borders.

BIBLIOGRAPHY: Additional selected works by Néjar: *Ordenações I, II, III, IV, V*, 1971; *Casa dos Areeios*, 1973; *Somos poucos*, 1976; *Livro de gazéis*, 1983; *Os personae*, 1986. Criticism: Moser, Gerald M. "Carlos Néjar: *Os viventes*" (book review). *WLT* (Winter, 1980), p. 86; *Carlos Néjar, poeta e pensador*. Edited by Giovanni Pontiero. Porto Alegre: Edições Porto Alegre/Prefeitura Municipal, 1983; Tolman, Jon. "Brazilian Poetry 1945–1975." *AH* (March, 1977), pp. 2–7.

JÚLIO MACHADO PINTO

NEOCLASSICISM. *See* Arcadias.

NEOCONCRETISM. *See* Postmodernism in Poetry.

NEOREALISM. *See* Social Novelists of the 1930s.

NERY, ADALGISA (b. 1905). Born in the state of Rio, Nery was married to the modernist artist Ismael Nery, with whom she traveled to Paris and became acquainted with Heitor *Villa-Lobos. Upon Nery's death, she began to write poetry and prose and initiated a career in government service. With her second husband, a diplomat, she later resided in Canada, the United States, and Mexico.

Nery returned to Brazil in the early 1950s and was named in her own right as ambassador to Mexico. In the mid–1950s she became a political columnist for the *Última Hora* newspaper. She became known for her strong stand on moral and political issues and was then elected to Congress in the early 1960s from the then state of Guanabara. (*See* Art and Literature; Modernism.)

Poemas (1937; Poems), her first collection, possessed the subjective, romantic, sensual overtones that characterize all of her later volumes of poetry, collected in *Mundos oscilantes* (1962; Oscillating Worlds). She also had stories published in several magazines in the late 1950s and a novel, *A imaginária* (1959; The Imaginary One), whose protagonist, Berenice, suffers from doubts about herself and others. Critics have commented on the autobiographical elements of the novel. (*See* Autobiography.)

BIBLIOGRAPHY: Additional selected works by Nery: *Og*, 1943; *Erosão*, 1972; *Neblina*, 1972. Translations: Hulet.

NEW WRITERS. A preoccupation with the impact on sociopolitical and cultural life of twenty-one years of military dictatorship still hovers over Brazilian letters today; for example, Álvaro Alves de Faria's (b. 1942) very recent *Autópsia* (1986; Autopsy) which graphically narrates events of the Médici era and Luiz Gutemberg's *O jogo da gata-parida* (1987; The New Party-Girl Game). Many writers whose careers predate the dictatorship remain active, original contributors to the literary scene, for example, Antônio *Callado, Ferreira *Gullar, Dias *Gomes, Ariano *Suassuna, and Augusto de *Campos. New writers who appeared during the 1970s are now established figures, for example, Caio Fernando *Abreu, Monteiro *Martins, Adélia *Prado, and Tânia Jamardo *Faillace. Since the early 1980s, a newer generation of writers has arisen with a vitality that some critics compare to the pre–1964 period. (*See* Dictatorship and Literature.)

Poetry. Some of those poets whose careers began in the 1970s as part of the "mimeograph generation" have now achieved recognition and literary success and are published by major houses, for example, Geraldo Carneiro (b. 1943) has recently translated Shakespeare and has written song lyrics, dramas, and a study of the poetry of Vinícius de *Moraes; Chico Alvim has had *Passatempo e outros poemas* (1982; Hobby and Other Poems) published (for translations, see "Key to Bibliographical References," Monegal/Colchie); Charles has had *Coração de cavalo* (1979; Horse's Heart) published; Cacaso (Antônio Carlos de Brito) has turned to song lyrics as well as poetry; Ana Cristina César (1952–1982), whose very promising career was cut short by suicide, wrote *A teus pés* (1983; At Your Feet), and her remaining unedited works were published by Armando Freitas Filho (*see* Postmodernism in Poetry) in 1985. Other writers are Ledusha (b. 1950), who wrote *O risco no disco* (1979; The Scratch on the Record), and Carlos Saldanha, whose collections include drawings and collages, which, he stated, give his works a highly personal note: *Visões do bardo* (1980; Visions of the Bard) and *Os mistérios* (1980; The Mysteries).

In the 1980s poetry readings in bars and on television, radio, and the beach have become the order of the day. These performances, called *poesia concertanista*, or concert poetry, began in 1985 in Rio's Botanic Bar. Among the youngest poets of note are Glória Horta (b. 1954), who had *Sangria* (1984; Blood Cocktail) published; Suzana Vargas, who wrote *Sem recreio* (1983; Without Leisure) and *Sempre-noiva* (1984; Ever a Bride), which views the divorced woman's consciousness of her motherhood; Alex Hamburger, author of *Kit coleções 1980–1985* (1986; Kit Collections 1980–1985), whose poetry combines everyday impressions with media vocabulary; and the members of the *Os camaleões*, or The Chameleons—Claufe Rodrigues, Pedro Bial, and Luiz Petry—who, in their volume of the same title (1985), used English pen names and expressed their erotic feelings in verbose lines of verse and prose.

Other notable poets include Orides Fontela, who began to be published in the 1970s but only attained a wider public with her collections of intimist verse: *Alba* (1983; Dawn) and *Rosácea* (1987; Rosette); Roberto Piva (b. 1938), who began his career in 1963 unaligned with either the then current experimentalists or the neotraditionalists (*see* Postmodernism in Poetry) and whose recent collections are *20 poemas com brócoli* (20 Poems with Broccoli) and *Quizumba* (1984; Quizumba); Roberto Braga (b. 1938), who is the son of Rubem *Braga and the author of *Almanaque de amor* (1984; Love Almanac), among his many volumes; Sebastião Uchoa Leite, who is the author of *Antilogia* (1979; Anthilogy) and *Isso não é aquilo* (1982; This Is Not That); Cleonice Rainho, from Minas, who had *Vôo branco* (1979; White Flight) published, as well as short fiction—*João Mineral* (1983; John Mineral)—and *children's literature; Regis Bonvicino, who wrote *Sósia na cópia* (1983; Double in the Copy); Nelson Ascher, who wrote *Ponta da língua* (1983; Tip of the Tongue); Sebastião Nunes, who is the author of *Somos todos assassinos* (We Are All Assassins); Cyro dos Mattos (b. 1939), who had three collections of poetry and a volume of short fiction published in 1984; Hamilton Vaz Pereira, Cláudio Mello e Souza, Bernadette Lyra, and Alice Ruiz.

Fiction. Marcelo Rubens Paiva (b. 1959), the son of a politician murdered during the military dictatorship, wrote an immensely successful *memoir, *Feliz ano velho* (1982; Happy Old Year), which describes the accident that left him disabled; he recently had a science fiction novel published: *Blecaute* (1987; Black Out). Eliane Maciel (b. 1965), a young girl from the outskirts of Rio, told about her conquest of freedom from a lower-middle-class existence in her testimonial novel (*romance-testemunho*) *Com licença, eu vou à luta* (1983; Excuse Me, I'm Off to the Battle) and, afterwards, had *Corpos abertos* (1984; Open Bodies) published; Alita Sá Rego also had a testimonial novel about her life published: *Dama da noite* (1985; Lady of the Night); Lourenço Cazarré (b. 1954) wrote a satirical historical novel, *O caleidoscópio e a ampulheta* (1983; The Kaleidoscope and the Hourglass), set in Brazil of the 1950s, which received the Nestlé Prize (*see* Prizes) for fiction in 1982. Raimundo Caruso metaphorized the Latin American and Brazilian "semicolonial" situation in *Buenos días, Mr. Ludwig* (1983; Good Morning, Mr. Ludwig), a reference to the Swiss-American billionaire who promoted the questionable Jari Project in the Amazon during the 1970s and 1980s. Arnaldo Campos's (b. 1932) two major novels deal with the psychological and financial realities of Brazil today: *Réquiem para um burocrata* (1982; Requiem for a Bureaucrat) and *A boa guerra* (1986; The Good War). Sinval Medina's "epic" narrative of Brazil from the early years of the republic through the military coup of 1964 (*Memória de Santa Cruz* (1984; Memories of Santa Cruz) was in the comic serialization form popularized by Márcio *Souza. Sônia Nolasco Ferreira's *Moreno como vocês* (1984; Dark Skinned Like You) views the emotional state of Brazilians living in the never-never land of New York City as self-exiles from the turbulent socioeconomic existence of their homeland; her *Você jurou que ia ser feliz* (1986; You Swore that I Would Be Happy) also presents Brazilian exiles: Three women caught up in emotional and sensual experiences. Dinorath do Vale's (b. 1929) description of the material and emotional poverty of the inhabitants of São Paulo's interior, *Pau Brasil* (1984; Brazil Wood), is presented within a naturalistic context and was awarded the Cuban Casa de las Americas Prize in 1982. (*See* Naturalism.)

Other younger novelists of note are Zulmira Ribeiro Tavares, author of the prize-winning *O nome do bispo* (1980; The Name of the Bishop); Paulo Amador (b. 1945); Luiz Antônio Assis Brasil (b. 1945); Reinaldo Moraes (b. 1950), author of *Tanto faz* (1981; It Doesn't Make a Difference) and *Abacaxi* (1985; A Big Problem); Charles Kiefer (b. 1958); Dau Bastos (b. 1960); Marilene Felinto (*See* Feminism and Literature.); Marcelo Cerqueira, José Luis Sales, and Lila Santanna.

Short Fiction. The burst of creativity in this genre, which occurred during the 1970s, continues unabated. João Gilberto Noll (b. 1947), whose major collection of stories is his prize-winning *O cego e a dançarina* (1980; The Blind Man and the Dancer), is the leading young short fiction writer. He has also had several novels published: *Os bandoleiros* (1985; The Bandits) and *Rastros de verão* (1986; Summer Vestiges). Other important new names in the genre are Renato Modernell (b. 1953), who wrote *Che Bandoneón* (1984; Che Bandoneón), the title story of which is a pseudobiography of the popular Argentine tango musician Astor Piazzola, and *O homem do carro-motor* (1984; The Man in the Motor-Car), which was awarded the Nestlé Prize; Modesto Carone (b. 1937), who wrote *Dias melhores* (1984; Better Days), a collection of tales of violence, lunacy, and persecution set during the years of military dictatorship; Jaime Prado Gouvea's (b. 1945), whose tales also focus on similar themes: *Fichas de vitrola* (1986; Record Player Index); Roberto Bittencourt Martins, who produced a collection of brief mystery tales, *O vento nas vidraças* (1984; The Wind on the Window Panes); Anna Maria Martins, who wrote psychological episodes of family life in contemporary São Paulo: *Sala de espera* (1978; Waiting Room) and *Katmandu* (1983; Katmandu); the *mineiro* Orlando Bastos (b. 1920), who has had two collections of short fiction published that were clearly influenced by the linguistic invention of Guimarães *Rosa: *Confidências do viúvo* (1981; The Widower's Secrets) and *De repente às tres da tarde* (1984; Suddenly at Three in the Afternoon); and Miguel Jorge, who wrote the collections *Caixote* (Carton) and *Urubanda* (1984; Urubanda). Márcia Denser has become a well-known writer in a short time. Her collection of stories touch on the sexual adventures of newly liberated woman in a blatantly profane language: for example, the anthology *Muito prazer* (1982; A Pleasure to Meet You), and her own collections of stories, *Exercícios para o pecado* (1984; Exercises for Sin) and *Diana caçadora* (1986; Diana de Huntress). Other writers of short fiction include Álvaro Cardoso Gomes (b. 1944), author of *A teia da aranha* (1978; The Spider's Web); Aércio Flávio Consolin (b. 1941), author of *Mancha do sol* (1985; Sun Spot); Sérgio Faraco, author of *Manilha de espadas* (1984; Sword's Shackle); Socorro Trindade, author of *Cada cabeça uma sentença* (1978; Each Head One Sentence); Roniwalter Jatobá de Almeida (b. 1949), author of *Filhos do medo: um romance suburbano* (1979; Children of Fear: A Suburban Novel) and the stories *Pássaro selvagem* (1985; Savage Bird); Virgílio Moretzsohn Moreira, who had *Jogos do instante* (1986; Games of the Instant) published; Eric Nepomuceno (b. 1948), author of *Caderno de notas* (1979; Notebook); and Ricardo Daunt Neto. (*See* Feminism and Literature.)

Theater. Theater is experiencing one of its lowest phases in the history of Brazilian dramaturgy, principally due to the economic situation being faced by the nation in the 1980s. Furthermore, the political themes of the 1960s and 1970s, which attracted wide audiences in solidarity with playwrights attacking the regime, no longer draw a public. Naum Alves de Souza is the most significant young dramatist and director. His recent plays form a cycle of *memoirs of his youth, for example, *No Natal a gente vem te buscar* (1980; At Christmastime, We'll Come to Get You), *A aurora da minha vida* (1981; The Dawn of My Life); and *Um beijo, um abraço, um aperto da mão* (1984; A Kiss, an Embrace, a Handshake). In 1987 he wrote a dramatic biographical presentation of the life of Nijinsky. Maria Adelaide Amaral analyzed the lives of journalists during the dictatorship years in *A resistência* (written 1975; performed 1979; The Resistance) and in *Bodas de papel* (1979; Paper Wedding) described the life-style of the Brazilian executive class. She has recently written "updated" versions of classical dramas, for example Sophocles's *Electra*. Other notable figures include Paulo César Coutinho, author of *A lira dos 20 anos* (The 20 Year Old Lyre), and Luís Alberto Abreu, author of *Bella, ciao* (Bye Now, Beautiful). Several prize-winning playwrights who have not yet had productions of their works due to the economic circumstances include Wilson Sayão, Ricardo Meireles, Lauro César Muniz, Carlos Henrique Escobar, and Pedro Porfírio. Also of note is the *teatro besteiro*, or the foolishness theater, made up of short comic sketches of an impromptu nature. Among its members are Mauro Rasi (b. 1954), whose play *Tupã* (The Indian God Tupã) attacks the state of Brazilian culture; Miguel Fallabella (b. 1948); and Gerald Thomas (b. 1955), a director who has produced punk versions of classical dramas, for example *Electra com Creta* (1987; Electra with Crete).

BIBLIOGRAPHY: Additional selected works by new writers: *Anuário de poetas do Brasil* (Rio), 1977– ; *Em revista* (São Paulo), 1976– ; *Geração '80*. Edited by M. da G.

Bordini and R. Zilberman. Porto Alegre: Mercado Aberto, 1984. (Young writers from Rio Grande do Sul State); *A nova literatura brasileira* (Rio), 1983–; *Quer que eu te conte um conto?* Rio: Achiamé, 1984.

LUIZA LOBO and IRWIN STERN

NÓBREGA, FATHER MANUEL DA   (1519–1570). A Portuguese Jesuit, Nóbrega went to Brazil in 1549 and remained there until his death. He established schools for the Indians and is regarded as the founder of São Paulo. Like Father *Anchieta, with whom he was often associated, he was instrumental in organizing resistance to French attempts at colonization in Rio de Janeiro (1555–1567). (*See* Historiography; Portugal and Brazil: Literary Relations; Religion and Literature.)

Nóbrega left a body of letters that are indispensable to the study of Brazilian intellectual history: *Cartas avulsas* (1550–1558; General Letters) and *Cartas do Brasil* (1549–1550; Letters from Brazil) (modern editions, 1931). Among them is his defense of freedom for the Indians against unlawful enslavement, delivered before a royal commission in 1566. The first example of Brazilian jurisprudence, it simultaneously initiated the line of abolitionist thought. (*See* Indianism; Philosophy of National Identity.)

Nóbrega's single literary contribution is his *Diálogo sobre a conversão do gentio* (c. 1557; Dialogue Concerning the Conversion of the Gentiles) (modern editions, 1954, 1968). The first Brazilian literary work in prose, it is plainly didactic in its intent to inform other missionaries, especially Jesuits, about the real problems involved in catechizing Indians. Nevertheless, it belongs to a well-established literary tradition, the formal dialogue, thus anticipating Ambrósio Fernandes Brandão's *Diálogos das grandezas do Brasil*. (*See* Historiography.)

The dialectal structure of Nóbrega's *Diálogo* abounds with ingenious *baroque comparisons and contrasts. Its humor recalls the Portuguese poet and playwright Gil Vicente. However, although it ends on an appropriately positive note by positing the full conversion of the Indians in God's own time, it depicts their current state as bestial, thus marking Nóbrega as an early, forceful opponent of the "noble savage" myth popularized during *romanticism.

BIBLIOGRAPHY: Criticism: Burns, E. Bradford. "Introduction to Brazilian Jesuit Letters." *Mid-America* (July, 1962), pp. 181–186; Carvalho, Armando de. In Coutinho, I; Jacobsen, Jerome V. "Nóbrega of Brazil." *Mid-America* (July, 1942), pp. 3–26.

NORWOOD ANDREWS, JR.

NOVAES, CARLOS EDUARDO   (b. 1940). One of the leading contemporary purveyors of the comic *crônica and ministry in the tradition of Sérgio *Porto and Millôr *Fernandes, Rio-born Novaes targeted the *carioca* and urban and national headlines for his side-splitting black-comedy view of Brazil's sociopolitical reality during and after the military regime. (*See* City and Literature; Dictatorship and Literature.)

Several of Novães's collections have gained best-seller status, for example,

O caos nosso de cada dia (1973; Our Daily Chaos). In *A história de Cândido Urbano Urubu* (1975; The Story of Candido Urban Vulture)—according to Drummond de *Andrade, a parody on the title of the very popular *Jonathan Livingston Seagull*—Cândido's daily confrontation with generals, traffic, and bureaucracy launches him into "theoretical" discussions of religion (e.g., Christ's preference for turkey), political corruption—an endemic national disease—and Marxism. In *O Day-After do carioca* (1985; The Carioca's Day After) he included the tale "Meu Brasil brasileiro" (My Brazilian Brazil), in which a *carioca* returning from abroad knows he's home when he's conned at the airport while waiting—for hours—to pass through passport control.

The success of Novaes's *crônicas* and stories, no doubt, is due to playful puns and double entendres but also to the complementary drawings by Vilmar. (*See* Art and Literature.)

BIBLIOGRAPHY: Additional selected works by Novaes: *Os mistérios do aquém*, 1976; *Capitalismo para principiantes*, 1983; *Deus é brasileiro?* 1984; *O cruzado de direita*, 1987. Translations: *Atlas Review*.

O

OLÍMPIO, DOMINGOS (1850–1906). From Ceará, Olímpio studied law in Recife. In 1879 he began a career in journalism and republican and abolitionist politics in Pará. (*See* Slavery and Literature.)

He is known for his regionalist novel *Luzia-Homem* (1903; Luzia-Man), which critics consider a major contribution to the fiction of northeastern droughts. Unlike the exaggerated or detached portraits of the effects of the droughts written by the naturalists, such as Rodolfo *Teófilo or Antônio Papi Júnior, Olímpio's novel, with some evident romantic touches, achieved a balanced background through its unique, although occasionally fatalistic and grotesque, presentation of the social outcasts created by the major drought of 1877. Luzia, the protagonist, is an exceptional woman, a modern Greek heroine of the *sertão*, drawn to both good and evil and ultimately to her own death. Olímpio's novel raised regionalism to a universal plane. (*See* Cycles; Naturalism; Regionalism; Romanticism.)

BIBLIOGRAPHY: Additional selected works by Olímpio: *O almirante* (serialized), 1904–1906; *O uirapuru* (incomplete). Criticism: Brookshaw; Loos.

OLINTO, ANTÔNIO (b. 1919). Olinto, a *mineiro*, studied at several Catholic seminaries before beginning a career as a journalist, literary critic (*see* Critics and Criticism), and university professor. In addition to lecturing extensively in Europe, Africa, and the United States, he has served as Brazil's cultural attaché in London and Lagos.

Although he wrote several narratives in his early twenties, Olinto did not have a novel published until 1969. *A casa da água* (1969; *The Water House*, 1970) was influenced by the author's sojourn in Nigeria. It chronicles, over a period of seventy years, the struggles of a family of former Brazilian slaves who, upon returning to Africa, must adapt themselves to the new realities. His subsequent novels have had less success: *O cinema de Ubá* (1972; Ubá's Movie House) describes life as seen by a six-year-old boy in Olinto's native city of Uba; *Copacabana* (1975; Copacabana) contrasts lower- and upper-class values against the backdrop of the 1970 Soccer World Cup; and *O rei de Keto* (1980; The King of Keto) registers the experiences and recollections of Abionan, a West African merchant who peddles her wares in a different village each day of the week.

Olinto's short and longer poems reveal him to be an intellectual poet, for example, *Teorias* (1967; *Theories and Other Poems*, 1972) and *Teorias novas e antigas* (1974; New and Old Theories). Olinto also wrote a highly regarded literary column in *O Globo* newspaper examining a wide range of subjects, from William Blake to Graham Greene and from Carlos Drummond de *Andrade to Carlos *Néjar.

BIBLIOGRAPHY: Additional selected works by Olinto: Poetry: *Presença*, 1949; *O dia da ira*, 1958; *A paixão segundo Antônio*, 1967. Critical essays: *Brasileiros na África*, 1964; *População indígena brasileira de nossos dias*, 1972; *A invenção da verdade: crítica de poesia*, 1983 *Trono de vidro*, 1987. Criticism: Leonardos, Stella. "Antônio Olinto e a casa da poesia." *Jornal de letras* (Rio) 262 (1962), p. 2.

SEVERINO JOÃO ALBUQUERQUE

OLIVEIRA, MANUEL BOTELHO DE (1636–1711). Botelho de Oliveira completed the law course at Coimbra and returned to the family sugar plantation, from which he practiced law and entered politics.

Oliveira wrote poetry in Portuguese, Spanish, Latin, and Italian while at Coimbra (not unusual for the time) and had it published in his *Música do Parnaso* (1705; Music from Parnassus). He represents the late *baroque tradition in poetry, in which versatility with metrics and images took precedence over poetic creativity, inventiveness, and emotion. Only one section of his poetry, "Poemas de amor a Anarda" (Love Poems to Anarda), allows for the slightest personal sentiment. Similarly, Oliveira assumed an intellectual distance from Brazilian nativist sentiment. (*See* Music and Literature; *Ufanismo*.)

Oliveira also wrote religious verse and several dramas, none of which is outstanding. His major claim to fame is that he was "Brazil's first son" to have a complete volume of poetry published. (*See* Religion and Literature; Theater History.)

BIBLIOGRAPHY: Additional selected works by Oliveira: *Lira sacra*, 1791. Criticism: López, Enrique Martínez. "Poesía religiosa de Manuel Botelho de Oliveira." *RI* (May-August, 1969), pp. 303–327; Martins, Wilson. "O barroco literário menor." *JIAS* (January, 1970).

OLIVEIRA PAIVA. *See* Paiva, Manuel de Oliveira.

ORTA, TERESA MARGARIDA DA SILVA E (1711–1793). Sister of Matias *Aires, Orta belonged to a prominent Portuguese family. Born in Brazil to a Brazilian mother, she spent most of her adult life in Portugal. She is most often classified as a Luso-Brazilian writer. (*See* Portugal and Brazil: Literary Relations.)

Orta is considered Brazil's first woman novelist. In 1752 *As aventuras de Diófanes* (The Adventures of Diophanes) was published in Lisbon; the work is an imitation of François Fénelon's didactic novel *Adventures of Telemachus* (1699). Written under a pseudonymous anagram, Dorotéia Engrássia Tavarede Dalmira and dedicated to Princess Maria of Portugal, the novel aimed to instruct the ruler how to govern in order to achieve a perfect society.

In addition to Fénelon's influence, Orta's other literary sources were the Iberian Peninsula's pastoral and Byzantine novels, as well as ideas of the Enlightenment (*see* Arcadias), for example, the virtue of country life over the corrupting life of the city. She was against slavery, enthusiastic about science, and believed in the education of the common people. She was somewhat ambivalent in her fictional portrayal of women but treated feminine problems with a realism based on experience. (*See* Feminism and Literature.)

Although Orta's novel had no direct impact on the development of the genre in Brazil, it has a great deal of historical interest and appeal based on its feminism *avant-la-lettre*.

BIBLIOGRAPHY: Additional selected works by Orta: *Relação abreviada*, 1777. Criticism: Sousa, Ronald W. "The Divided Discourse of *As aventuras de Diófanes* and Its Socio-Historical Implication." *Problems of the Enlightenment in Portugal: Essays*. Minneapolis/St. Paul, Minn.: Institute of Ideologies and Literature, University of Minnesota, 1984, pp. 77–88; Versiani, Ivana. "The New World's First Novelist." *The Brazilian Novel*. Edited by Heitor Martins. Bloomington, Indiana: Indiana University Publications, 1976, pp. 15–27.

MARIA LUÍSA NUNES

P

PAIVA, MANUEL DE OLIVEIRA (1861–1892). Oliveira Paiva's fiction focuses on his native Ceará. His major novel, *Dona Guidinha do Poço* (1899; Miss Guidinha of Poço Plantation), was only partially published by José *Veríssimo in 1889. It remained forgotten until critic Lúcia Miguel-Pereira (*see* Critics and Criticism) republished the whole manuscript in 1952.

In this matter of fact narration of a true crime of passion, which occurred in the interior of Ceará in 1853, Dona Guidinha is presented as "possessing the devil," which leads her to the seduction of her nephew and to her own ultimate degradation. Although the work is uneven, it is an important contribution to Brazilian *realism and *regionalism owing to Paiva's effective re-creation of life in the *sertão* and his use of regional language as a tool for characterization.

BIBLIOGRAPHY: Additional selected works by Paiva: *A afilhada*, 1899; *Contos*, 1976. Criticism: Loos.

PALMÉRIO, MARIO (b. 1916; BAL: 1968). After teaching in São Paulo in the early 1940s, Palmério returned to Uberaba in the southwestern part of his native Minas. There he established several schools and founded the area's first university. He served as a three-term congressman, from 1950 to 1962, and was ambassador to Paraguay from 1962 until the 1964 military coup. (*See* Dictatorship and Literature.)

Palmério's approach to fiction writing requires long periods of careful research and meticulous composition. Thus his literary output is limited in number although certainly not in quality. The first of his two novels, *Vila dos confins* (1956; Border Town), reflects the trend away from social involvement, which had characterized the regionalist novel since the 1930s. The work's powerfulness stems not from its chronicle of corrupt *sertão* politics but from the region's human types, which it so genuinely portrays, and the "backlands knowledge"— elaborate fishing and hunting stories—which he faithfully reproduces in the regional language. (*See* Portuguese Language of Brazil; Regionalism; Social Novelists of the 1930s.)

Although Palmério's work has often been compared to that of Guimarães
*Rosa (whose chair he occupies in the *Brazilian Academy of Letters), his
represented world lacks the greater complexity and transcendence of Rosa's
backlands. This becomes more evident with his second novel, *Chapadão do
bugre* (1965; Hamlet of Bugre), in which an excessive preoccupation with documentary exactitude hampers the fictional potential of a violent vendetta involving political leaders (*coronéis*) and backlands bandits (*jagunços*). (*See*
Cycles.)

BIBLIOGRAPHY: Criticism: Proença, Ivan Cavalcanti. "Literatura das vilas e cha-
padões." *Mário Palmério: Seleta*. Rio: José Olympio, 1973, pp. 165–182.

SEVERINO JOÃO ALBUQUERQUE

PARNASSIANISM. In the history of Brazilian literature, Parnassianism—the
term deriving from Mount Parnassus, believed to be the home of the mythological
Muses—is the name given to the school of poetry that came to the forefront in
the 1880s, the last decade of the empire, continued in a dominating position
through the stormy years of the republic, and whose influence was still great
until the end of World War I. It dominated the literary establishment to the
extent that three of the four leading Parnassians—Olavo *Bilac, Raimundo *Correia, and Alberto de Oliveira (1857–1937; BAL: 1897) (for translations, *see*
"Key to Bibliographical References": Hulet)—were founding members of the
*Brazilian Academy of Letters, and the fourth—Vicente de Carvalho (1866–
1924; BAL: 1909)—was elected not much later. The two leading symbolists,
however, João da Cruz e *Sousa and Alphonsus de *Guimaraens, who are
arguably superior poets, were never awarded that recognition. (*See* Symbolism.)

Unlike the terms *romanticism* and *symbolism*, which were applied to literary
movements throughout most of Europe as well as in Brazil, the term *Parnassianism* is used only in connection with French, Brazilian, and to a minor extent
Portuguese poetry. Parnassianism was a response in opposition to earlier literary
movements, especially its great predecessor romanticism, which in Brazil had
held almost unchallenged sway for fifty years. The new poets recoiled from the
romantics' pleasure in unbridled expression of personal emotion, their depiction
of the world in terms of their own response to it, their emphasis on improvisation
and spontaneity, their predilection for grandiloquence and hyperbole, and their
carelessness and looseness of form.

The Parnassians sought objectivity, repression of emotion, and impassiveness
in relation to their subjects. They stressed the need to remember always that
writing is an art that demands extreme care and polish if it is to be elegant and
correct in form and language. If the romantics regarded music as the kindred
art of poetry because of its continuous movement in time, the Parnassians preferred the stasis of sculpture and especially that achieved by the craftsman who
worked in precious metals and gems and could achieve miniature masterpieces
of jewelry. They were repelled by the romantics' poems and dramas of epic
scope, but they did write some fine short narrative poems.

The word *Parnassianism* came directly from the three Parisian anthologies titled *Le Parnasse contemporain* (1866, 1871, and 1876; Contemporary Parnassus), which contained works of the poets who were to dominate the French literary scene until the beginning of the twentieth century. Besides Paul Verlaine (1844–1896) and Stéphane Mallarmé (1842–1898), who were leaders of the symbolist movement, there were those who were to be called *Parnassiens*, such as Leconte de Lisle (1818–1894), José Maria de Heredia (1842–1905), and Catulle Mendès (1841–1909). All admired Charles Baudelaire (1821–1867), the influence of whose multifaceted art is felt in symbolists and Parnassians alike, but the latter chose as their mentor Théophile Gautier (1811–1872), who, many years earlier, had adopted the creed of "art for art's sake" and whose important book of poems, *Emaux et camées* (1852; Enamels and Cameos), is a collection of short lyrics on "little subjects" worked on "gold or copper with the lively colors of enamel."

Brazil's connection with the Parnassians began when a minor literary figure, Arthur de Oliveira (1851–1882), returned to Rio from a long stay in Paris, where he had met and become the friend of Gautier and other leading *Parnassiens*. An interesting, charming conversationalist, he infected the young Brazilians with his enthusiasm. Poems that may be called Parnassian began to appear in the late 1870s. In 1878 the "Battle of Parnassus"—against romanticism—was fought in verse on the pages of the *Diário do Rio de Janeiro* newspaper. The three books that gave the movement its great prestige date from the 1880s: Raimundo Correia's *Sinfonias* (1883; Symphonies), Alberto de Oliveira's *Meridionais* (1884; Meridians), and Olavo Bilac's *Poesias* (1888; Poems). In 1892 Carvalho's first volume of poems was published, *Rosa rosa de amor* (Rose, Rose of Love), which may properly be called Parnassian.

As among the French poets, among the Brazilians there were individual differences, too, but they were united in their belief that art has its own life and that artistic achievement is dearly bought. All of these writers were at their best working in short forms, especially in the sonnet: the sonnet was a paradigm of brevity; it had a comparatively fixed rhyme scheme and a set metrical scheme. In addition, it provided the opportunity for elegant workmanship, and it could end spectacularly with a climactic line of *chave de ouro*, golden key. Alberto de Oliveira's "Vaso grego" (Greek Vase), Correia's "As pombas" (The Doves), Bilac's "Lingua portuguesa" (The Portuguese Language), and his sequence of sonnets, "Via Láctea" (The Milky Way) are among the best in the language.

All Parnassians have a tendency toward pessimism, but they had varying degrees of success in their attempt to confront life impassively and objectively. Alberto de Oliveira's poems became increasingly pessimistic over the years, that is, in the latter phase of his writing. He became more willing to express his personal feelings, more interested in writing about daily life, and more appreciative of the beauty of nature in Brazil. At the same time, he was becoming more rigid in his approach to form and language. Correia's work is suffused with a deep pessimism and melancholy that is not completely attributable to his study of Arthur Schopenhauer (1788–1860). He was essentially a poet of ideas, for whom the only possible God was an impassive, unconcerned one. He believed that man's destiny was nirvana, which is the title of one of his poems, and that all in life is transitory; even man's great development of scientific knowledge leads only to disillusionment. Vicente de Carvalho is called the poet of nature. In his work nature and the sea come to possess a cosmic significance that they could have had only for one who felt God in all nature, a pantheism that is revealed in "Sonho póstumo" (Posthumous Dream), in which he sees his death as a transformation into air and light. Revealing his stress on artistic perfection, in the collective editions of his poems, *Poemas e canções* (1919; Poems and Songs), he polished those previously published and included new ones.

Bilac may be considered the most representative Parnassian, the poet whose work as a whole exhibits the qualities of the school to the best possible advantage. He had a complete mastery of poetic technique and the expressive capabilities of the Portuguese language. Like the other Parnassians, he was at his best in short forms, but he was able to compose longer poems that sustain tension for several pages, like "O caçador de esmeraldas" (The Emerald Hunter), an epic fragment in forty-six six-line stanzas on the heroism of the *bandeirantes*, the pioneers who penetrated and conquered the Brazilian interior.

There are other Parnassians and late Parnassians worthy of mention and some excellent poets who may be associated with the school, although their work also shows strong tendencies toward romanticism, scientific poetry, and symbolism: Luís Delfino dos Santos (1834–1910), Teófilo Dias (1857–1889) (for translations, *see* "Key to Bibliographic References": Hulet), B. Lopes (1859–1916), Luís Murat (1861–1929; BAL: 1897), Adelino Fontoura (1859–1884), Domício da Gama (1862–1925; BAL: 1896), Guimarães Passos (1867–1909), Venceslau de Queirós (1865–1921), Carlos de Azeredo (1872–1963; BAL: 1897), Júlio Salusse (1872–1948), Amadeu Amaral (1875–1929; BAL: 1919), Goulart de Andrade (1881–1936; BAL: 1915), José Albano (1882–1923), Raul de Leoni (1895–1926), Moacir de Almeida (1902–1925), and Humberto de Campos (1886–1934; BAL: 1919). There were also women poets of note—Francisca *Júlia, whose poetry was widely read, and Júlia Cortines (1868–?)—and writers of prose who were kindred spirits of the Parnassians. They were deeply concerned with developing an elegant, rich prose style. They are remembered among other things for their dazzling descriptions and rich vocabularies.

Although after *modernism the Parnassians seemed to have been suffocated and buried, in more recent years the continued appearance of new printings and editions of their works shows that they still have an important place in the national literature.

BIBLIOGRAPHY: Collection: *Poesia parnasiana*. Edited by Péricles da Silva Ramos. São Paulo: Melhoramentos, 1967. Criticism: Coutinho/Rabassa; Haberly, David. "Luís Delfino and the Parnassian Revolution." *LBR* (December, 1969), pp. 44–54; Le Gentil, Georges. "L'Influence Parnassienne au Brésil." *RLC* 11 (1931), pp. 23–43; Ramos, Péricles da Silva. In Coutinho, III.

RAYMOND S. SAYERS

PATROCÍNIO, JOSÉ DO   (1853–1905; BAL: 1897). Known as the "Tiger of Abolition," Patrocínio led an exciting life dedicated entirely to Brazil. Born into a poor family in the interior of Rio State, upon witnessing a slave being severely punished, he swore to dedicate his life to the abolitionist cause. Patrocínio first became a pharmacist but soon began a career in journalism, using his pen in the abolitionist cause.

The owner of the *Gazeta de Tarde* newspaper, which was at the forefront of the movement, Patrocínio was also active in the republican movement and was involved in the drafting of the actual decree of the republic. His disagreement with the dictator Floriano Peixoto (a figure satirized in Lima *Barreto's *Triste fim de Policarpo Quaresma*) led to a short exile in the Amazon. In his later years, he studied flight and built himself an early flying machine.

Patrocínio was the author of three novels, the finest of which is *Mota Coqueiro* (1877; Mota Coqueiro). With the backdrop of a midnineteenth-century plantation, Patrocínio narrated the unjust hanging of a benevolent slaveowner, Mota Coqueiro, as a result of passions and jealousies of his slaves and his fellow slaveholders. The novel has many interesting black characters but suffers from too much moralizing and romantic exaggeration. In *Os retirantes* (1879; The Refugees) he presented one of the first fictional views of the northeastern drought of 1877. *Pedro Espanhol* (1884; Spanish Pedro), his final novel, is a vivid portrait of lower-class Negro life in eighteenth-century Rio. Patrocínio was greatly admired by his contemporaries. Although he died in poverty, some ten thousand people participated in the funeral cortege. (*See* Cycles; Slavery and Literature.)

BIBLIOGRAPHY: Criticism: Sayers.

PEIXOTO, AFRÂNIO   (1876–1947; BAL: 1910). Bahian Peixoto was a noted doctor and hygienist, who was also widely known in Portugal and Brazil as a critic (*see* Critics and Criticism) of the works of Luís de Camões. (*See* Portugal and Brazil; Literary Relations.)

Peixoto viewed himself as a continuator of the style of Flaubert; thus his prime fictional interest was in women's lives in the city or in the *sertão* of Bahia. Most of his novels possess a similar superficial psychological level and are set within the political and artistic atmosphere of the *belle-époque*. Critic Massaud Moisés (*see* Critics and Criticism) stated that Peixoto continually rewrote the same novel in a slightly different setting and made Lúcia, the protagonist of *A esfinge* (1911; The Sphinx), the prototype of all of his heroines. *Fruta do mato* (1920; Fruit of the Forest), a regionalistic novel, is generally considered his finest achievement, although the heroine, Joaninha, possesses intellectual qualities generally not associated with a *sertaneja*. (*See* City and Literature; Regionalism.)

A distinguished novelist before *modernism, his fame declined substantially afterwards.

BIBLIOGRAPHY: Additional selected works by Peixoto: *Maria Bonita*, 1914; *Uma mulher como as outras*, 1928; *Sinhazinha*, 1929; "American Social and Literary Influences in Brazil." *BA* (Winter, 1935), pp. 3–5; (Spring, 1935), pp. 127–129. Criticism: Brookshaw.

PEIXOTO, INÁCIO JOSÉ DE ALVARENGA   (1744–1793). Alvarenga Peixoto traveled frequently between Brazil and Portugal during his childhood. In 1767 he graduated from Coimbra and began a career as judge in Portugal and later in Brazil, where he became involved in a torrid love affair, land disputes, and other political and personal difficulties. Married to Bárbara *Eliodora, he was a member of the *Mineiran Conspiracy and supposedly the author of the motto of the movement's flag: "Libertas que sera tamen." Peixoto was exiled to Angola in 1792 and died soon after of tropical fever. (*See* Minas School; Portugal and Brazil: Literary Relations.)

Peixoto had only three poems published during his lifetime, one of which preceded Basilio da *Gama's *O uraguai*. His complete works, some of which were discovered in the twentieth century, consist of thirty-three poems. He was an occasional poet who commemorated personal and national events in a polished style that falls within neoclassicism. (*See* Arcadias.) Nonetheless, in several of his sonnets, an artistic purpose and manner resound; on these rests his fame.

BIBLIOGRAPHY: Additional selected works by Peixoto: *Vida e obra de Alvarenga Peixoto*. Edited by M. Rodrigues Lapa. Rio: Instituto Nacional do Livro, 1960. Criticism: Silva, Domingos Carvalho da. *Gonzaga e outros poetas*. Rio: Orfeu, 1970.

PELLEGRINI JR., DOMINGOS   (b. 1949). Pellegrini, a *gaúcho*, began his career as a social poet. In 1977 he turned to short fiction and was awarded the Jabuti Prize (*see* Prizes) for his collection *O homem vermelho* (1977; The Red Man). Although some of the stories have a regionalist bent, "A maior ponte do mundo" (The Biggest Bridge in the World, in Tolman [1984]; *see* "Key to Bibliographical References") deals with the construction of the Rio-Niterói bridge, in which the machinery has as important a role as the different classes of workers and supervisors. The stories and novellas in *As sete pragas* (1979; The Seven Plagues) viewed the Brazilian sociopolitical situation: oppression under the military regime. Each story deals with the dilemmas faced by another sector of Brazilian society. (*See* Dictatorship and Literature; Regionalism.)

Pellegrini's most recent collection, *Paixões* (1984; Passions), contains scenes of contemporary Brazilian life in tales about drugs, generational conflicts, sexual violence, and homosexuality, as well as political cynicism. Pellegrini's style is based on popular speech and is replete in dialogues. He has also dabbled in *children's literature. (*See* Homosexuality and Literature.)

BIBLIOGRAPHY: Additional selected works by Pellegrini: *Os meninos*, 1977.

PENA, CORNÉLIO   (1896–1958). Pena was an accomplished artist who abandoned this career to dedicate himself to fiction. The settings of his novels are the small towns of his native Minas, although he lived in Rio as an employee of the Ministry of Justice from 1927. (*See* Art and Literature; Regionalism.)

Unlike the *social novelists of the 1930s, whose works dominated fiction, Pena turned to an extremely introspective style of writing. *Fronteira* (1935; *Threshold*, 1975) evokes a long-gone personal past that still exists in the fantasy and madness of the narrator and characters. In fact, this novel as well as *Repouso* (1948; Repose) and *A menina morta* (1954; The Dead Girl) are concerned with highly personal spiritual quests. Nonetheless, they preserve a uniquely Brazilian atmosphere through their exploration of the psyche of the inhabitants of these small towns.

A psychological writer like Machado de *Assis and Raul *Pompéia, Pena is also linked with the so-called French Catholic novelists—François Mauriac, Georges Bernanos—and with the Brazilian Otávio de *Faria. (*See* Foreign Writers and Brazil.)

BIBLIOGRAPHY: Additional selected works by Pena: *Dois romances de Nico Horta*, 1939. Criticism: Riggio, Edward. "Afterword." *Threshold*. Philadelphia: Franklin Publishing Company, 1975, pp. 90–100.

PENA, LUÍS CARLOS MARTINS (1815–1848). The "founder" of the Brazilian theater, with the aid of Gonçalves de *Magalhães and the Brazilian actor João Caetano dos Santos (*see* Theater History), Martins Pena presented his first play in 1838. Between that year and his death in Lisbon, from tuberculosis, he wrote twenty-eight known plays—twenty-two comedies and six dramas.

Pena "spontaneously" began to write plays about 1832, probably under the influence of popular French imports and, according to some critics (*see* Critics and Criticism), the theater of Antônio José da *Silva (The Jew). His first comedy is considered the classic model for all of his others, as well as for much of nineteenth-century Brazilian theater: *O juiz de paz na roça* (presented 1838; published 1842; *The Rural Justice of the Peace*, in *Poet Lore* [Summer, 1948], pp. 99–119). Consisting of a series of scenes of contemporary life in the interior, the "conflicts" of the comedy concern minor, often absurd problems—mostly related to marriage—and set Brazilian against "Portuguese" (reflecting the anti-Portuguese sentiment of the postindependence period), the city dweller against the country folk.

Pena's dramatic techniques include verbal wit, such as puns, caricatures, and the near tragedy that results in the traditional "happy ending." Among his other best-known comedies are *O Judas em sábado de aleluia* (1842; The Judas on Hallelujah Saturday); *O noviço* (presented in 1845; published in 1853; The Novice); *Quem casa, quer casa* (presented in 1845; published in 1847; Whoever Marries, Wants a House).

Pena's dramas are less interesting, primarily because they are set outside Brazil and deal with foreign events; for example, *O Nero da Espanha* (1840; The Nero of Spain) deals with Spanish history. Furthermore, in these dramas, the romantic situations—mysterious appearances and disappearance, exaggerated anger, and so on—tend to reveal a less skilled artist, one who is in less control of his art, for example, the Indianist drama *Itaminda* (1858; Itaminda). (*See* Indianism; Romanticism.)

Pena dedicated himself solely to theater, unlike his literary contemporaries and followers. Although critics complain that he turned toward weak farces in his last works, his comedies had great influence on José Joaquim da *França Jr., Artur *Azevedo, and other dramatists. They are still presented today to applauding audiences.

BIBLIOGRAPHY: Additional selected works by Pena: *Teatro de Martins Pena*. Critical edition edited by Darcy Damasceno and Maria Filgueiras, 1958. Criticism: Aiex, Nola Kortner. "Martins Pena: Parodist." *LBR* (Summer, 1981), pp. 155–160; Driver; Lyday, Leon F. "Satire in the Comedies of Martins Pena." *LBR* (December, 1968), pp. 63–70; Pierson, Colin. "Martins Pena: A View of Character Types." *LATR* (Spring, 1978), pp. 41–48.

PHILOSOPHY OF NATIONAL IDENTITY. Since the rise of romantic nationalism in the last century, national philosophies have been a controversial issue. After realizing that British philosophy was empiricist, that German philosophy was idealist, and that French philosophy was rationalist, philosophers in other countries inferred from such broad generalizations that philosophy could not be universal and reached the conclusion that in each culture philosophy could and should pursue its own path.

There is an ongoing debate about whether or not there is a Spanish or a Portuguese philosophy (as opposed to philosophy in Portugal or Spain), but there is an even hotter debate about the existence of a Latin American philosophy. Mexico has been its leading advocate, under the guidance of Leopoldo Zea (b. 1912).

Brazil is seldom included in this debate, in which "Latin American philosophy" means "Spanish American." Nonetheless, the issue of Brazilian philosophy is recurrent in Brazil. Brazil has witnessed much philosophical activity in the traditional sense, but the general agreement among historians of philosophy is that imitation and eclectic assimilation of European currents are the characterizing features of Brazilian thought. The most influential European intellectual tradition is not even philosophical but sociological: positivism. Of the strictly philosophical movements, there seems to be an agreement that Neo-Thomism has had the strongest influence on Brazilian intellectual life. (*See* Positivism and Literature.)

Actually, the richest series of attempts at understanding a national history and culture have occurred in Brazil; yet such efforts have not claimed the status of philosophy. They present themselves as explanations of the Brazilian idiosyncrasy, its cultural (behavioral) patterns, generally as a tool for understanding the Brazilian developmental gap in regard to Europe, until the beginning of this century, and in regard to North America, for most of this century.

Silvio *Romero located the beginning of these attempts in the second half of the nineteenth century, the period of "the most profound commotion in the national soul.'' He himself is one of the leading thinkers about the identity question on a list that includes, among many names of different political persuasions, the philosopher Farias de Brito (1862–1917), whose works were used by Plínio *Salgado's Integralist movement; Graça *Aranha, who even proposed a Brazilian metaphysics; Viscount Afonso Celso (1860–1938; BAL: 1897), a Parnassian poet and novelist who promoted *ufanismo as the key to the Brazilian character in his *Por que me ufano do meu país* (1901; Why I Am so Proud of My Country); Sérgio Buarque de Hollanda (*see* Historiography); Euclides da *Cunha; Gilberto *Freyre; Paulo *Prado; Viana *Moog; João Cruz Costa; and Caio Prado Júnior. Dante Moreira Leite was the most accomplished critic of such a tradition but also its best exponent. His *O caráter nacional brasileiro: história de uma ideologia* (1976; The Brazilian National Character: History of an Ideology) exercised a powerful influence and put a temporary stop to the tradition of Brazilian self-analysis in terms of collective psychological character. Recently, however, the thread of that tradition was picked up once again by the anthropologist Roberto da Matta, who organized a television program about Brazilian "roots" called "The Brazilians," and by Darcy *Ribeiro. (*See* Parnassianism.)

Mention should be made of two significant collective attempts at interpreting and guiding action: one, in the 1930s, was the "authoritarian thought group," with Oliveira Vianna (1883–1951; BAL: 1937) as the major figure; the other group was associated with the Institute of Brazilian Studies (IESB) in the 1950s, which included Nelson Werneck Sodré (*see* Critics and Criticism) and Álvaro Vieira Pinto.

In the more strictly defined area of philosophy, a pluralistic coexistence of practically all European and North American trends prevails. Some of these trends, however, have attempted a particular grasp of Brazilian realities. Once again, they are represented by philosophers of both the conservative and the most politicized traditions: such as Miguel Reale (b. 1910; BAL: 1975) and Antônio Paim, for the former, and J. Arthur Giannoti, for the latter. Paulo Freire (b. 1921), awarded by UNESCO Peace Prize in 1986, has proposed a philosophy of education for the oppressed within a phenomenological frame of reference but with an original approach. It has been adopted to theatrical usage by Augusto *Boal. The obsession with a national philosophy was recently revived by Roberto Gomes, who classified all Brazilian intellectual history as rhetorical—an instance of "ornamental reasons," as he put it—and called for truly national philosophy, though without providing specifics.

Brazilian writers from the arcadians to the *new writers have had an almost obsessive concern with national culture, soul, character, spirit, or whatever name it has received throughout the years, most intensely during the dictatorship and postdictatorship era. Affonso Romano de *Sant'Anna not only had a book of poems titled *Que país é este?* (*What Kind of Country Is This?*) published but also has had a collection of essays published on the same topic; all of Antônio *Callado's fiction has been preoccupied with the question of national identity and national direction; João Ubaldo *Ribeiro's intensely "national" novel *Viva o povo brasileiro* has a similar concern. Many other writers have been involved in this search. (*See* Arcadias; Dictatorship and Literature; Popular Culture.)

BIBLIOGRAPHY: Criticism: Azevedo, Fernando de. *Brazilian Culture*. New York: Macmillan, 1950: Cândido, Antônio. "Literature and the Rise of Brazilian National Self-Identity." *LBR* (June, 1968), pp. 27–44; Costa, João Cruz. *A History of Ideas in Brazil*. Berkeley: University of California Press, 1964; Freire, Paulo. *Pedagogy of the Oppressed*. New York: Seabury Press, 1970; Freyre, Gilberto. *The Master and the Slaves*. New York: Alfred A. Knopf, 1946; Haberly, David T. *Three Sad Races: Racial Identity and National Consciousness in Brazilian Literature*. Cambridge: Cambridge University Press, 1983; Hollanda, Sérgio Buarque de. *Raízes do Brasil*. Rio: Livraria José Olympio, 1936; Ribeiro, Darcy. *The Americas and Civilization*. Berkeley: University of California Press, 1971.

ONÉSIMO TEOTÓNIO ALMEIDA

PICCHIA, PAULO MENOTTI DEL (b. 1892; BAL: 1943). Menotti del Picchia, from São Paulo State, has had a variety of careers in addition to being one of the driving forces behind the Week of Modern Art, which he described in his *memoirs, *A longa viagem* (1970–1972; The Long Voyage). (*See* Modernism.)

During the premodernist epoch (*see* Modernism), he struggled to find his own literary identity. Nonetheless, he produced notable works, including his most famous: *Juca mulato* (1917; Juca the Mulatto). This tale of the impossible love of a mulatto farm hand for the plantation owner's daughter is viewed as a key transitional work between *Parnassianism and *symbolism on the one hand and modernism on the other hand. The poem remains popular today largely because of its unmitigated sentimentalism and its traditional Brazilian theme.

Picchia was one of the founders, along with Plínio *Salgado and Cassiano *Ricardo, of the right-wing, ultranationalist *verdamarelismo* (green-yellowism). The poems of his *República dos Estados Unidos do Brasil* (1928; Republic of the United States of Brazil) are so clearly jingoistic in their intent and so prosaic in their style that they are interesting today primarily as period pieces. A far more mature Picchia as poet is evident in his latter works, for example, *O deus sem rosto* (1963; A Faceless God).

Picchia's fiction had a psychosocial bent. His earliest works were considered scandalous, for example, *Flama e argila* (1920; Flame and Clay). *O homem e a morte* (1922; Man and Death) was his contribution to modernist fiction. Later prose turned to what may be called metaphorical *Indianism, for example, *Kumminká* (1938; Kumminká); his last novel, *Salomé* (1940; Salomé), portrays the inhabitants of the growing metropolis of São Paulo. Picchia's real contribution to Brazilian literature has yet to be adequately defined and appreciated. (*See* City and Literature.)

BIBLIOGRAPHY: Additional selected works by Picchia: *Poemas do vício e da virtude*, 1913; *Dente de ouro*, 1920; *Poemas transitórios*, 1938; *O árbitro e outros contos*, 1958.

Criticism: Brookshaw; Lopes, Alberto R., and D. Jacobs Willis. "Mennoti del Picchia and the Spirit of Brazil." *BA* (Summer, 1952), pp. 240–243; Rachum, Ilan. "Antropofagia vs. verdamarelo." *LALR* (Spring-Summer, 1976), pp. 67–81.

KEITH H. BROWER

PIGNATARI, DÉCIO (b. 1927). Although Pignatari is primarily identified with the concrete poetry movement and its later developments, he has simultaneously had successful careers as a university professor, master of the advertising media, literary theoretician, and culture critic. (*See* Postmodernism in Poetry.)

Pignatari abandoned the traditionalist forms and content of the Generation of 1945, for example, his *O carrossel* (1950; The Caroussel), and along with Augusto de *Campos and Haroldo de *Campos, he established, in 1956, concretism. He published most of his early poems in the five issues of the *review *Noigandres*, gradually turning toward solely visual representation. Other poems of the time appeared in ephemeral little vanguard literary reviews, for example, *Poesia em G.*, *Código*, *Através*, and *Corpo estranho*.

In 1962 Pignatari became the editor of another concrete poetry review, *Invenção*, which included not only poems but also his criticism and manifestoes. His poetry is more socially concerned than that of other concretists. For example, his visual poetry attacks the Brazilian political situation or foreign "colonization" of Brazil; most famous is his "Coca-cola" poem (for Translations, *see* "Key to Bibliographical References," Solt). In 1987 Pignatari published *Poesia. Pois é. Poesia Po&tc.* (Poetry. That's Right. Poetry Po&tc), a complete collection of his poems and advertising.

As a semiotician, a student of the cultural significance of signs, Pignatari has published theoretical works, for example, *Informação. Linguagem. Comunicação* (1968; Information. Language. Communication), as well as critical works on semiotics within a literary context as well as an underlying force within general Brazilian culture. For example, in his *O óbvio e o misterioso: a sinagem da televisão* (1984; The Obvious and the Mysterious: Television Signs), he offered, among many other things, possible interpretations for the significance of soap operas in Brazilian life.

BIBLIOGRAPHY: Additional selected works by Pignatari: *Contracomunicação*, 1971; *Semiótica e literatura*, 2d ed., 1979. Translations: Solt.

PIÑON, NÉLIDA (b. 1936). Piñón graduated from the Catholic University of Rio. She worked briefly for the newspaper *O Globo* and the journal *Cadernos Brasileiros* and has directed several creative writing workshops.

Considered one of Brazil's foremost contemporary authors of fiction, both in the novel and the short story, she writes in a dense, poetic language, characterized by unexpected lexical combinations; subtle and frequent fluctuations among narration, dialog, and interior monologue; and a peculiar, unconventional logic. Her characters are often self-conscious and obsessive.

Many of her works display a mystical tendency. Her first novel, *Guia-mapa de Gabriel Arcanjo* (1961; Guide-Map of Gabriel Archangel), treats the idea of sin, forgiveness, and mortals' relationship with God by means of an extended dialog between the female protagonist and her alter ego-guardian angel. *Madeira feita cruz* (1963; Wood for the Cross) presents a modern incarnation of four biblical characters confronting contemporary psychological and philosophical problems. A frequent eroticism in her work is best exemplified by *A casa da paixão* (1972; The House of Passion), a lyrical treatment of a young woman's sexual initiation. (*See* Feminism and Literature; Religion and Literature).

Piñon's works occasionally acquire more epic dimensions, as with *Fundador* (1969; Founder), which mixes historical and fictional characters in relating the formation of a new society, and in the semiautobiographical *A república dos sonhos* (1984; *The Republic of Dreams*, 1989), a saga about several generations of a Galician Spanish family that immigrates to Brazil. This novel, she stated, is a testament to her own deeply felt Spanish heritage. Piñon has claimed that she did not truly consider herself a Brazilian until adulthood and that this self-definition came about through her apprenticeship with the Portuguese language (*see* Portuguese Language of Brazil) when she began serious writing in 1955. (*See* Autobiography.)

During the years of the military dictatorship, Piñon was an outspoken critic of the regime, censuring the repercussions of their activities on Brazilian society in her short fiction, notably in the collection *O calor das coisas* (1980; The Warmth of Things). She also played an important role in guiding the development of the Peruvian novelist Mario Vargas Llosa's novel based on Euclides da *Cunha's *Os sertões*. (*See* Dictatorship and Literature; Foreign Writers and Brazil.)

BIBLIOGRAPHY: Additional selected works by Piñon: *Tempo das frutas*, 1966; *Sala de armas*, 1973; *Tebas no meu coração*, 1974; *A força do destino*, 1978. Translations: Tolman (1978). Criticism: Crespo, Ángel, and Pilar Gómez Bedate. "Nélida Piñon, de *Guia-mapa a Tempo das frutas*." *RCB* 7 (1967), pp. 5–27; Pontiero, Giovanni. "Notes on the Fiction of Nélida Piñon." *Review* 17 (1976), pp. 67–71.

                                                                                        PAUL DIXON

PINTO, BENTO TEIXEIRA.   *See* Teixeira, Bento.

PIROLI, WANDER   (b. 1931). Piroli holds a law degree from the Federal University of Minas Gerais; like many contemporaries, he has been a journalist. He is a member of a generation of fine short story writers from Minas, including Rubem *Fonseca, Luiz *Vilela, and Sérgio *Sant'Anna. He has also written several books ostensibly for children, although the literary quality evident in these works make them appealing to an adult public as well. (*See* Children's Literature.)

Piroli remains best known for his 1966 collection *A mãe e o filho da mãe* (The Mother and the Son of a Bitch), which, in recent editions, has been enlarged to include the stories "Camaradas" (Comrades) and "Crítica da razão pura"

(Critique of Pure Reason), both of which have won national literary *prizes. Piroli is at his best when writing about the marginal elements in society: lower-class people oppressed by a social structure that they often fail to understand completely, as in the case of "Menino da madrugada" (Dawn Boy) and "Lá no morro" (Over There on the Shantytown Hill). His stories are dominated by themes of violence, suffering, and loneliness.

Piroli's recent stories involve the subject of sex, as in the collection *Minha bela putana* (1984; My Beautiful Prostitute). Although he keeps in mind his usual concerns, he concentrates on the pain, emptiness, and violence associated with sexual experiences. Despite his choice of themes, however, Piroli does not possess a totally pessimistic worldview. His stories often depict values such as family bonds and human understanding, which seem to function as a kind of antidote against total social disintegration.

BIBLIOGRAPHY: Additional selected works by Piroli: *O menino e o pinto do menino*, 1975; *Macacos me mordam*, 1976; *A máquina de fazer amor*, 1980; *Os dois irmãos*, 1982.

LUIZ FERNANDO VALENTE

POEMA-PROCESSO/PROCESS-POEM. *See* Postmodernism in Poetry.

POMPÉIA, RAUL (1863–1895). Pompéia's early education was in small private schools near his home in Rio, where he is said to have been a loner. At the age of ten, he was sent to the important Colégio Abílio, Abílio Boarding School, run by the baron of Macaúbas (1824–1891), the most influential pedagogue of his time in Brazil. The school was attended by the sons of the influential aristocracy and the wealthy.

The shock that Pompéia suffered finding himself in an alien world, bewildered, and at the mercy of older boys who bullied the newcomers, only years later triggered his novel *O ateneu* (1888; The Athenaeum), which some Brazilian critics have called a "psychological *autobiography." Still, Pompéia made a name for himself as a serious student with a literary and artistic bent. He contributed articles and caricatures to the school newspaper, *O Archote* (The Torch). In 1876 he entered the Colégio Dom Pedro II (still Brazil's most prestigious secondary school), where he distinguished himself as an orator at the age of seventeen and had his first novel published, *Uma tragédia no Amazonas* (1880; A Tragedy in the Amazon), a romantic story of love and plunder. (*See* Art and Literature.)

In 1881 he entered the law school in São Paulo. The university was a hotbed of unrest, the battlefield where political and social skirmishes were fought by students and faculty alike. New ideologies, including positivism and republicanism, were in the air; new sciences were being advanced: psychology and sociology. *Realism and *naturalism, new literary trends, nurtured the seeds of discontent. A born rebel, Pompéia threw himself into the fray, fighting for the abolition of slavery and the republic. By so doing, he angered his conservative professors at the university, who took revenge and failed him in his studies. He was forced to continue his studies in Recife. This rejection embittered him all the more, and he took his own revenge on the university in scenes of his novel. (*See* Positivism and Literature; Slavery and Literature.)

O ateneu has also been considered a microcosm of the nineteenth-century Brazilian political and social structure ruled over by Emperor Dom Pedro II, who, along with his family, was satirized in Pompéia's novel *As jóias da coroa* (1882; The Crown Jewels). Although the emperor is viewed today as a good and enlightened ruler, during his lifetime his contemporaries saw him in a different light. Pompéia and many of the intelligensia considered the monarchy a vestige of Portuguese imperialism and the emperor a remnant of a reactionary past, someone who led a corrupt government and who made feeble attempts from time to time to free the slaves and establish much needed agrarian reform. The emperor, however, saw himself as a "moderating influence" that forced the opposing sides of the political spectrum, the liberals and the conservatives, to seek a compromise. What really happened is that the emperor was never able to gather a following and thus was continuously attacked by both sides. In the novel the emperor is personified by Aristarco, the school's headmaster, an autocratic ruler; his court and his ministers are the faculty; the monitors represent the army and the police. The great body of students are the populace, who endure the cruelty and injustices of those in power.

It may be that upon starting the novel, Pompéia meant to paint a social condemnation of the Brazilian educational system, but as the novel progresses, it becomes apparent that the author harbors a deep anger not only against his internment at the school but against the director, the teachers, and his own schoolmates, many of whom were later able to recognize themselves in print. Thematically, Pompéia may have been inspired by Thomas Hughes's (1822–1896) *Tom Brown's Schooldays* (1857), which closely follows a young boy's career at England's Rugby from his first nervous days as a newcomer in an alien world to his last cricket match as captain of the school's team. Hughes indicted the English public school system much as Pompéia was to do thirty years later in Brazil. The only difference is that Tom Brown is able to surpass his unhappy experiences at the school whereas Sérgio is crushed by them and harbors a deep resentment, finally setting fire to and destroying the building.

The caricatures are biting. Pompéia uses a poison pen often steeped in the grotesque and the perverse. He has difficulty describing good characters; only evil ones come naturally to him. There are only three characters that might be considered sympathetic, and two, Bento and Egbert, are flawed by their homosexual inclinations; the third, Dona Ema, the headmaster's wife, abandons her husband and flees with her lover. Sérgio, the protagonist, has three lovers at the school: Sanches, forced upon him during his first days because he needs a protector; the athletic Bento, who attacks Sérgio under the staircase; and Egbert, who offers a brief romantic interlude, easily won by Sérgio and just as easily forgotten. No pure friendships are to be found in the novel. Throughout, Sérgio is a loner, much as Pompéia, who committed suicide, was in real life. (*See* Homosexuality and Literature.)

The tendency to paint man with all his foibles often to the exclusion of his good qualities led a critic like Mário de *Andrade to consider him a naturalistic writer, in the way he dwells on the "human beast" dominated by evil, desire, envy, and his basest instincts. It is true that Pompéia enjoys describing the seamy side of his characters, but he does so only in a casual way. He insinuates what could be considered spicy or risqué; he does not dwell on it, as Émile Zola, the Portuguese Eça de Queiroz, and Aluisio *Azevedo did. (*See* Naturalism; Portugal and Brazil: Literary Relations.)

Pompéia found that the principles of "artistic prose," expounded in nine-teenth-century France by the Goncourt Brothers, fitted within the canons of his own philosophy of art. He insisted that only in didactic writing was it possible to use a simple style. Not only did it give color and passion to his prose, but it became highly fluent, poetic, and, at times, extravagant. His style is most brilliant when he resorts to exaggeration, sarcasm, and caricature in describing characters and situations. It has been said that the ultimate expression of the *baroque in nineteenth-century Brazil is to be found in Pompéia's prose. Modern critics (*see* Critics and Criticism) find Pompéia to be essentially an impressionist writing for the eyes. He is completely visual not only in his caricatures that illustrate the book but also in his picturesque prose. (*See* Impressionism.)

Pompéia is today considered one of Brazil's best writers and *O ateneu* one of the ten best novels. In the past few years, two definitive editions have been published based on the original text of 1888. It cannot be said that the novel has influenced Brazilian writers since Pompéia had such a personal philosophy of writing, one that reveals his personality as well as his own psychological problems. Finally, critic Nelson Werneck Sodré considered Pompéia's collection of poems, *Canções sem metro* (1881; Songs without Meter), an "exceptional moment" in Brazilian poetry.

BIBLIOGRAPHY: Additional selected works by Pompéia: *Microscópios*, 1881. Translations: Monegal/Colchie, I; Criticism: Ivo, Ledo. *O universo poético de Raul Pompéia.* Rio: São José, 1963; López-Heredia, José. *Matéria e forma narrativa de "O Ateneu."* São Paulo: MEC/INL, 1979; Pontes, Elói. *A vida inquieta de Raul Pompéia.* Rio, 1935.

JOSÉ LÓPEZ-HEREDIA

PONTE PRETA. *See* Porto, Sérgio.

POPULAR CULTURE. The study of popular culture in Latin America has boomed in recent years. Much of the debate has focused on the term *popular culture*, which in the United States has most often been used in opposition to "high culture" to signify "mass" or "consumer culture," notably the mass media. In Latin America, in contrast, "popular culture" or "cultures" has generally referred to the cultural production and practices of the popular classes, particularly forms of oral expression and religious rituals that are seen to constitute a means of political resistance to the dominant Western culture transmitted by the transnational media.

Some recent scholarship, however, contends that this definition has led to an overly simplistic view of popular culture as too easily manipulable by the dominant classes, on the one hand, or too "resistant" to their control, on the other hand. In addition, the spread of the mass media, particularly television, has extended dominant class culture and ideology to both middle- and lower-class consumers. Rather than posit a strict opposition between dominant class and popular culture, current work in the field has explored the multiple transactions between them. Studies have focused on the reception of media-transmitted messages and on everyday life practices that use existing urban sites for the benefit of the popular classes or transform hierarchical social relations in the workplace while still stopping short of workers' control. In some cases in Latin America, the state has permitted increased autonomy for the cultural practices of ethnic minorities and marginalized classes through its own institutions and cultural policies.

A brief history of the popular culture problematic in Brazil illustrates the importance of these linkages in the Brazilian case. As anthropologist Renato Ortiz (b. 1947) has pointed out, popular culture in Brazil has been historically tied to the search for national identity. In the nineteenth century critic Sílvio *Romero, among the first to study the Brazilian national character, tried to define "the people" in terms of popular culture and ethnic categories, in accordance with the prevailing concept that the Brazilians were a unique mix of white, African, and Indian racial and cultural elements. The search for the "essence of Brazilian culture" and the national character continued to focus on popular culture throughout the twentieth century, often delving into folklore derived from Indian sources but concentrating especially on Afro-Brazilian cults and rituals as the main elements of and conduits for collective and national memory. (*See* Folklore and Literature; Philosophy of National Identity; Religion and Literature.)

The questions were taken up during *modernism, particularly by Mário de *Andrade in his studies of Brazilian folklore and in his plans for a Department of Culture in São Paulo that would promote local culture alongside European imports. In the 1930s Gilberto *Freyre cited evidence from popular-culture practices to prove his theories about the "cordial" Brazilian. In the 1950s and 1960s popular culture was a focal point for more general debates raised by the onset of industrialization. Was the authentic Brazilian culture to be found in those forms of art and expression that could be associated with the anticolonial struggle in the Third World and, more explicitly, with the anti–United States, anti-imperialism stance of social groups and guerrilla movements active throughout Latin America? Or could a truly national culture in search of modernity admit the penetration of foreign capital as well as of foreign cultural models?

After the 1964 military coup, the authoritarian state sought to promote a uniform vision of national identity, largely by developing the technological and material basis for a national communications network. The military government invested heavily in a nationwide telephone and television system, satellite capability, and a national computer industry. Television, in particular, was manipulated through censorship and direct state control of licensing and financing to create a vision of Brazilian national culture that incorporated selected elements of popular culture but at the same time exploited them to glorify the 1964 "Revolution." An example is the Médici government's use of the Brazilian victory in the 1970 Soccer World Cup competition for its own propaganda purposes. (*See* Dictatorship and Literature; Soccer and Literature.)

In Brazil today, traditionally defined popular culture overlaps with the modern-culture industry. The latter is based on a North American model, but its characteristics are determined by the inequalities of Brazilian development. For example, media producers and consumers are heavily concentrated in the major cities, where the most advanced communications technologies are available. Nonetheless, television reaches more than 70 million of 140 million Brazilians, including those in rural areas, and is of primary importance in the dissemination of political information and in the formation of social attitudes and behavior.

The state is the other principal factor in the organization of cultural activity. Along with the private communications sector, state enterprises such as Embrafilme, the national film board, and Embratur, the national tourism agency, are conduits for funds and policymakers in the cultural sphere. Although the Brazilian state has appropriated popular culture practices, such as *samba* and carnival, for its own ends since the Vargas dictatorship of the 1930s and 1940s, the military regime has expanded this role. (*See* Film and Literature.)

The civilian government that came to power in March 1985, ending twenty-one years of military rule, has continued to be active in cultural affairs. The Ministry of Culture has been established and has defined its principal task as preserving the "cultural patrimony," largely defined as period architecture, handicrafts, and "folk traditions" from economically marginal regions of the country. This latest attempt by the state to identify its own version of popular culture with "national" culture has been most effectively countered by the Catholic church and other religious cults and organizations, which have provided institutional support and social space for alternative cultural practices. (*See* Philosophy of National Identity.)

BIBLIOGRAPHY: Canclini, Néstor García. "Cultura y poder: ¿Dónde está la investigación?" Paper presented at a conference sponsored by the Social Science Research Council on "Popular Culture, Resistance and Everyday Life." Columbia University. April 11–13, 1985; Franco, Jean. "What's in a Name? Popular Culture Theories and their Limitations." *SLAPC* 1 (1982), pp. 5–14; Levine, Robert. *Brazilian Reality through the Lens of Popular Culture. BSG*; idem. "Elite Intervention in Urban Popular Culture in Modern Brazil." *LBR* (Winter, 1984), pp. 9–22; Mattos, Sérgio. "The Case of Brazilian Television." *Communications Research* (April, 1984), pp. 202–220; Ortiz, Renato. *Cultura brasileira e identidade nacional*. São Paulo: Brasiliense, 1985.

                                                                    JOAN DASSIN

PORTO, SÉRGIO (1923–1968). Writing principally under the pseudonym (heteronym, according to Porto) of Stanislaw de Ponte Preta, Rio-born Porto was one of Brazil's most raucously funny authors of *crônicas*. He created legendary characters during the early 1960s—members of Stanislaw's family: Tia Zulmira, Altamirando, and Rosamundo—in the process of satirizing aspects of *carioca* life and Brazilian national figures and culture both of the past and present. In fact, every public figure in Brazil of the early years of the military dictatorship was the target of Porto's pen. (*See* Dictatorship and Literature.)

Two collections of *crônicas* dealt with the events of the FEBEAPÁ—an acronym parodying the Brazilian military government's mania for acronyms to simplify names of massive regional development projects during the mid-1960s—which was *O festival de besteira que assola o país* (1966; The Festival of Stupidity Sweeping over the Country). Porto lambasted popular events and national flaws in a style that mixed slang with the exact amount of titillation to create an endearing black comedy of Brazilian existence. (*See* Dictatorship and Literature.)

Almost always accompanied by flattering artwork, Porto's tales remain undated, delightful reading today. His comic style has been imitated by many followers, for example, Carlos Eduardo *Novaes.

BIBLIOGRAPHY: Additional selected works by Porto-Ponte Preta: *Tia Zulmira e eu.* 1961; *Rosamundo e os outros*, 1962; *A casa demolida*, 1963; *As cariocas*, 1967.

PORTUGAL AND BRAZIL: LITERARY RELATIONS. Brazilian and Portuguese literary relations began with the arrival of the Portuguese fleet of discovery in 1500 on the east coast of South America and continued and flourished as the region was explored and settled. Although the first writers were Portuguese travelers and settlers, by the seventeenth century some of the most interesting literature in Portuguese was being written by native Brazilians. However, even what they wrote was not thought of as Brazilian literature: the writers and their public considered that they and their books were Portuguese. (*See* Historiography; Travel Literature.)

Portugal until the beginning of the nineteenth century was an absolute monarchy of which Brazil was just one province governed from Lisbon, like the other parts of the Portuguese empire. Brazil was a Portuguese monopoly, economically, politically, and intellectually. Freedom of thought no more existed there than in Portugal. There was no freedom of expression, because, among other reasons, there were no printing presses. Those who wanted to study had to go to Portugal, those who wanted to read had to import their books from Portugal, and those who wanted to write had to be published there. The libraries were in Coimbra, the palace-monastery of Mafra, and in some private collections or in convents. This monopoly situation continued almost until the eve of Brazilian independence. What readers there were, outside of the clergy, were upper-class Portuguese who were curious to know what Brazil was like. At first it was a literature predominantly descriptive of Indian and plantation life and of the land itself. There was also some good historical writing. (*See* Historiography.)

The first actual account of Brazil, dating from the very moment of discovery, is the *Carta* by Pero Vaz de *Caminha. With its enthusiastic and beautiful descriptions, it was the forerunner of later panegyrics in prose and verse. Two other works in the same vein are the *Diálogo das grandezas do Brasil*, by Ambrósio Fernandes Brandão, and the *Tratado descriptivo do Brasil em 1587* by Gabriel Soares de *Sousa. Both men were plantation owners; the first was a humanist of broad learning, the second a gifted writer who had an immense curiosity about almost every aspect of the land. (*See* Historiography.)

The close relation between Brazil and the mother country is seen in the careers of the great Jesuit, Father Antônio *Vieira, and Gregório de *Matos, lawyer, judge, and public servant. Vieira, a statesman and writer, was born in Portugal and spent large parts of his life in Brazil. His sermons were the finest preached in the seventeenth century. Matos, who also divided his life between Portugal and Brazil, was a fine lyric and religious poet but is best remembered for his satires on the multiracial societies of Lisbon and Bahia.

The period from 1578, when the Portuguese suffered a military defeat in Africa, to 1661, when they definitively established their independence from Spain, was one of great disturbances for both the mother country and Brazil, much of which was occupied by Dutch invaders for almost thirty years. After stability was finally achieved, a period of prosperity returned to Brazil with the discovery of gold in what is now known as Minas. This new wealth stimulated the settlement of large parts of the province, bringing in many Portuguese. It enabled a small luxury-loving society to grow up in Vila Rica, the capital. There, a school of talented writers appeared: the three most prominent were Tomás Antônio *Gonzaga, a lyric and satirical poet; Cláudio Manuel da *Costa, best known for his lyrics; and Inácio José de Alvarenga *Peixoto, also chiefly a lyricist. These men are remembered not only for their poetry but also because they were upper-echelon civil servants who became implicated in the *Mineiran Conspiracy, the purpose of which was to bring about Brazil's independence.

In spite of this protest against Portugal, these writers (one of whom, Gonzaga, was a Portuguese by birth) were very much part of the Portuguese intellectual movement of neoclassicism. (*See* Arcadias.) A New Arcadia was founded in Lisbon in 1790 by a Brazilian mulatto, Father Domingos Caldas *Barbosa, a favorite of the Court. Caldas Barbosa was only one of many Brazilian literati who preferred Portugal to Brazil.

Much greater than the arcadias in Portuguese literary history of the seventeenth and eighteenth centuries is the tradition of the epic poem. The example of *Os lusíadas* (1572; *The Lusiads*, many English versions) by Luís de Camões (1524–1580) inspired dozens of imitations in Portugal. It was the epic of Portuguese history and of Portugal's greatest achievement, the opening up of the sea routes to the Orient. Written in ten cantos in ottava rima with the classical apparatus of Greek mythology inherent in the structure and adorned with set speeches and topics and well-crafted epic similes, it imposed itself upon literature in Portuguese. It inspired two masterpieces dealing with Brazilian history and containing inspired pictures of the landscape and the Indians. Both Basilio da *Gama, the author of *O uraguai*, and Santa Rita *Durão, the author of *Caramuru*, were natives of Brazil who went to Portugal to study and remained there. Both poems, and *O uraguai* especially, possess a numinous sense of Brazilian place that only a native could create. The two poems helped to keep alive the Portuguese epic tradition: *O uraguai* obviously influenced *O oriente* (1814; The Orient) by the Portuguese man of letters, Brother José Agostinho de Macedo (1761–1831).

The invasion of Portugal by the French caused the removal of the Portuguese royal family and its court of 16,000 nobles to Rio. This was a great stimulus to the intellectual life of Brazil, for most of Portugal's intellectuals were among the refugees. Among the Brazilians was the "father of independence," José Bonifácio de Andrada e *Silva, a notable scientist who was to be a great statesman and, during a period of exile in France, a neoclassic poet. Another brilliant patriot was Hipólito da *Costa, who went to London where he founded the *Correio Brasiliense* (1808–1822; The Brazilian Post), the first Brazilian periodical.

Brazil's independence in 1822 did not bring independence in the sphere of human relations. The ties of common culture, Portuguese relatives, a royal family of which a son ruled Brazil and his father ruled Portugal, and the constant emigration from Portugal of intellectuals who settled or remained in Brazil for long periods held the countries together; these immigrants founded literary societies (*Gabinete Português de Leitura*) in Rio (1837), Recife (1850), Bahia (1859) and elsewhere, which are still active today. Then, too, Brazil was still to depend on Portugal for its books, including translations, and for publishers who could print and distribute Brazilian authors. Although there were schools of law, medicine, and engineering in Brazil, it was unlike the former Spanish colonies in that it had no universities. The result was that there were and would continue to be many young Brazilians who would go to Portugal to study, among them the romantic poet Gonçalves *Dias and the historian Francisco Adolfo de Varnhagen. (*See* Historiography; Romanticism.)

Portuguese literature remained a staple of the new country's intellectual life, but for some time the same could not be said of Brazilian literature in Portugal, in part because books published in Brazil were hard to come by. Still, the few Brazilian books that did cross the Atlantic in the first half century of independence were read enthusiastically and praised by the influential critics and writers. Many Brazilian and Portuguese writers knew each other well, either personally or through correspondence. The Portuguese in the Brazilian cities formed literary clubs to which Brazilians were often invited. Joaquim Maria Machado de *Assis, the country's greatest writer, was on close terms with a group of Portuguese who met regularly to discuss literature. In 1826 the Portuguese poet Viscount Almeida Garrett (1799–1854) praised Brazilian literature in a long essay on Portuguese literature and called *O uraguai* the finest modern poem in the language. In 1847 Alexandre Herculano (1810–1877), the novelist, historian, and poet, wrote a famous article on Gonçalves Dias, in which he pointed to Brazil as the country of the future and praised the poet as the last hope of Portuguese culture. The Portuguese critic and poet Teófilo Braga (1843–1924) and the very popular novelist Camilo Castelo Branco (1825–1890) affirmed that the Brazilian poets were bringing a new music to Portuguese poetry; the philosopher and poet Antero de Quental (1842–1891) said that Brazilian literature was "an exotic flower blooming on an old European tree trunk" (*apud* Sayers, Raymond S. *Onze estudos de literatura brasileira*. Rio: 1983, pp. 193–94). (*See* Critics and Criticism.)

Eça de Queiroz (1845–1900), the leading Portuguese novelist, and Machado de Assis knew each other's fiction well, and in spite of Machado's unfavorable article on Eça's *O primo Basílio* (1878; *Cousin Bazilio*, 1953), they respected each other as worthy artists. It has also been argued that the critics of *Cousin Bazilio* influenced Eça's later fiction. His *naturalism stimulated the development of naturalist fiction in Brazil. Reciprocally, the colloquial ironical style of the Portuguese realist poet Cesário Verde (1855–1886) recalls certain poems by the short-lived Brazilian romantic Álvares de *Azevedo. The Brazilian Parnassian and symbolist Raimundo Correia (*see* Parnassianism) in turn learned from Verde. Symbolists in Portugal and Brazil imbibed their doctrine directly from the French, but the Brazilians profited from their acquaintance with Portuguese such as Eugénio de Castro (1869–1944), poet and dramatist, and António Nobre (1867–1900), poet. The latter absorbed much from the symbolism of "As pombas" in Correia's *Sinfonias*. The Brazilian symbolist Alphonsus de *Guimaraens, who loved medieval Portuguese tradition, read Nobre. (*See* Symbolism.)

Through the nineteenth and early twentieth centuries, Brazilians collaborated in Portuguese periodicals. In 1915 two Brazilians, Ronald de *Carvalho and Eduardo Guimarães (1892–1928), collaborated in *Orpheu*, to which the Portuguese Mário de Sá-Carneiro (1890–1916) and Fernando Pessoa (1888–1935) contributed.

Even though contact diminished after World War II, Portugal still retained its appeal for Brazilian poets such as Cecilia *Meireles, and Ribeiro *Couto. The influence of the traditional Portuguese theater and especially of Gil Vicente (1485–1535) is to be seen in the contemporary dramatists of Brazil's Northeast: Dias *Gomes and Ariano *Suassuna. The powerful Portuguese neorealist novelists of the 1940s admired the Brazilian *social novelists of the 1930s. During the dictatorships of Salazar in Portugal and Vargas in Brazil, Brazilians like Gilberto *Freyre took refuge in Portugal, and Portuguese like Jorge de Sena (1919–1978) and Castro Soromenho (1910–1968) took refuge in Brazil. During the recently ended military dictatorship, many Brazilians fled to Portugal, for example, Josué *Guimarães and Augusto *Boal. The first Portuguese edition of Ignácio de Loyola *Brandão's *Zero* appeared in Portugal, upon being prohibited in Brazil.

Most recently, the cultural relationship has been rocky. Popular works of Brazilian literature adapted to television have been immensely popular in Portugal, and contemporary Portuguese and Brazilian writers' works are appearing in the other country, owing to the initiative of the Brazilian Nova Fronteira publishing house. Nonetheless, critic Afrânio Coutinho (*see* Critics and Criticism), taking a nationalistic stance, has led a campaign to omit a requirement in Portuguese literature from the Brazilian school system, and the Portuguese are agreeing to radical changes in their language usage to accommodate the reality of their cultural situation. (*See* Portuguese Language of Brazil.)

BIBLIOGRAPHY: Criticism: Sayers, Raymond S. "The Impact of Symbolism in Portugal and Brazil." *Waiting for Pegasus*. Edited by Roland Grass and William R. Risley. Macomb, Ill.: Western Illinois University Press, 1979, pp. 125–141; idem. "Machado de Assis in Nineteenth-Century Portugal." *Studies in Honor of Lloyd A. Kasten.* Madison, Wisc.: Hispanic Seminary, 1980, pp. 235–247; idem. "A reputação de Castro Alves no Portugal oitocentista," pp. 115–122; "Relações entre a literatura brasileira e a portuguesa no século XIX," pp. 191–200; and "A literatura brasileira no Portugal oitocentista," pp. 201–232, in *Onze estudos de literatura brasileira*. Rio: Civilização Brasileira/INL, 1983.

RAYMOND S. SAYERS

PORTUGUESE LANGUAGE OF BRAZIL. The language of Brazil is the expression of the dynamic forces that shaped its history, its people, and its culture: the Indian's condition, the Portuguese legacy, and the African rhythm. As the Portuguese language of the first colonizers (different from contemporary Portuguese of Portugal) slowly evolved in Brazil to the state in which it is found today, it has directly reflected the internal forces—political, social, economic, and linguistic—at work in the country. (*See* Indian Languages.)

Lexical contributions to its Portuguese base can be found in the minority groups of Brazil, mostly from: (a) the native Indian Tupi tribes; for example, the words *carioca* (home of the white man), used to refer to an inhabitant or life-style of the city of Rio; *caju* (cashew); and (b) the large population of slaves of African origin transported to the country in the colonial days: *moleque* (boy); *batucada* (drum beating). Prestige factors influenced the borrowings from the French; *maiô* (bathing suit), and from the American English: *creme rinse* (cream rinse), *rock and roll*, as well as the development of a specialized vocabulary used in areas such as computer technology or the surfer cult of the *carioca* youths. The innovations of *gíria* (slang) continue to add vitality to the language.

Several formal features of colloquial Brazilian Portuguese (BP) set the language apart from the Continental Portuguese (CP) of today. The phonology of BP illustrates several instances of linguistic development from its CP origins. The most notable changes can perhaps be classified in three major categories: reduction, dipthongization, and palatalization. Among consonantal reductions are: medial -ly->-l- or -y-: *mulher* (woman) [*mulé(r)*] or [*muyé(r)*]; syllable-final -s and -r> ø: *mesmo* (same) [*mem(o)*], *fazer* (to do) [*fazê*]. Vocablic reduction is seen, for example, in the diphthong ei>e: *feira* (fair) [*fera*]. Dipthongization, on the other hand, sometimes occurs in certain dialects in a>ai and e>ei: *às dez* (at ten o'clock) [*aiz deis*], and vowels are expressed in unstressed syllables: *semana* (week), CP [*s'mana*] or BP [*semana*]; or raised in unstressed final position, as in -e or -∂>i: *fonte* (source, fountain) [*fonti*]. The last example creates a situation for palatalization, in which ti or di>ĉi or ĵi: *mentira* (lie) [*menĉira*]; *medida* (measure) [*meĵida*]. A case of final sibilant backing in some dialects includes -š or -ž>-s or -z: *mais* (more) [*maiš*] [*maiž*], and we see velarization in the unvoiced tense R> velar unvoiced or weakly unvoiced h: Rio, (*hiu*). Other differences from CP are the following: the vocalization of final -l>-u: Brasil, (*braziu*); the insertion of -i- in certain consonant clusters: *advogado* (lawyer) [*adivogado*]; the addition of -i after syllable-final stops: *clube* (club); and the tendency not to weaken voiced stops /b,d,g/ between vowels: *cidade* (city), CP [*siđađə*] or BP [*sidaĵi*].

BP morphology in colloquial speech also reflects the linguistic process of reduction in language change, seen clearly in the pronominal morphology. The subject pronouns most commonly used are *eu* (I), *você* (you), *ele* (he), *ela* (she), *a gente/nós* (people/we), *vocês* (you, *pl.*), *eles* (they, *m.*), and *elas* (they, *f.*). Clitic pronouns are largely reserved for formal or literary use, as the accusative function is filled by the subject pronouns: *Vi ele na praia* (I saw him on the beach). However, *te* often replaces *você* in object position: *Você sabe que ele te ama* (You know that he loves you). *Mim* (me) is frequently employed as the subject of an infinitive headed by the complementizer *para* (for): *É para mim comer* (It is for me to eat). The verb paradigm is also simplified if one considers the general preference for the subject pronoun *a gente* (people) over *nós* (we) in colloquial speech. Thus the inflectional endings for the verb *amar* (to love) in the present indicative tense would be *amo, ama, ama, amam*. Even the latter is sometimes omitted in the paradigm among the less-educated speakers: *eles ama* (they love). The third-person indicative form, for example, *fala* (speak), is widely used in an imperative function, further simplifying the paradigm.

The syntax of BP in colloquial speech also shows the processes of regularization in linguistic change. Pronouns in an accusative or dative function are nearly always placed before the verb: *Me diz uma coisa* (Tell me something), or CP [*Diz-me*], and when an auxiliary and infinitive combination is used, the pronoun is placed between the two: BP *Você poderia me dar* (You could give me), or [*Você me poderia dar*] or [*Poderia dar-me*]. Perhaps one of the most notable syntactic differences between BP and CP is the Brazilian preference for the periphrastic gerund construction: BP's *Está fazendo* or CP's *Está a fazer*.

The actual study of Brazilian dialectology was begun early in the modernist period by Amadeu Amaral (1875–1929) with his *O dialeto caipira* (1920; The Hillbilly Dialect), followed by Antenor Nascentes's (1886–1972) *O linguajar carioca* (1922; Carioca Language) and Mário Marroquim's *A lingua do nordeste* (1934; The Northeastern Language). Mário Souto Maior has dedicated many works to the regionalisms of Pernambuco and the Northeast. Among the most notable twentieth-century philologists, linguists, and lexicographers are Fausto Barreto (1852–1915); João Ribeiro (1860–1934); Laudelino Freire (1873–1937); Joaquim Mattoso Câmara (1904–1970); Aires da Mata Machado Filho (1909–1985; BAL: 1923); Aurélio Buarque de Hollanda (b. 1910; BAL: 1961), the editor of the standard Brazilian dictionary (2d ed., 150,000 entries, 1986) (for translations, *see* "Key to Bibliographical References": Grossman); Antônio Houaiss (b. 1915; BAL: 1971); and Celso Pedro Luft. A Brazilian Academy of Philology with forty members was established in 1944 in Rio.

The recognition of Brazil as an emerging power with its own identity, and not merely as a former colony of Portugal, resulted in the recognition of its language not as a simple dialect of Portuguese but as a vital means of communication with its own characteristics to make it uniquely Brazilian. In fact, although the growing differentiation in vocabulary between BP and CP has been a feature of Luso-Brazilian culture since colonial times, polemics about "the Brazilian language" have occurred between the Portuguese and Brazilians throughout the nineteenth and twentieth centuries. The most vituperous one was between the Brazilian polemicist Carlos de Laet (1847–1927; BAL: 1897) and the Portuguese novelist Camilo Castelo Branco. A new orthographical treaty among the Portuguese-speaking nations of the world was recently debated and approved, thus unifying spelling patterns of the Portuguese language. Many Brazilian writers since the nineteenth century have made a point of using a truly Brazilian language.

In Brazil today, various polemics have recently taken place about what should be considered "correct" Brazilian Portuguese: the language traditionally taught in the schools or the language as it is spoken and written under the influence of the mass media. Although each variety has its defenders, the general consensus is that there is room for both.

BIBLIOGRAPHY: Criticism: Chamberlain, Bobby, and Ronald Harmon. *A Dictionary of Informal Brazilian Portuguese*. Washington, D.C.: Georgetown University Press, 1983; Christie, Christina. "African Influences in the Brazilian Portuguese and Literature." *Hispania* (October, 1943), pp. 259–266; Mattoso Câmara, J. *The Portuguese Language*. Chicago: University of Chicago Press, 1977; Rodrigues, José Honório. "The Victory of the Portuguese Language in Colonial Brazil." In Hower/Preto-Rodas; Silva Neto, S. Da. *Introdução ao estudo da língua portuguesa no Brasil*. Rio: Instituto Nacional do Livro, 1963.

DALE A. KOIKE

POSITIVISM AND LITERATURE. Positivism, "a philosophy of the history of the mind through sciences," was founded by the Frenchman Auguste Comte (1798–1857) and appeared in Brazil in the mid-1850s. It was the essential philosophy in abolitionism and in the development of the republic (1889), which employed Comte's motto—"Order and Progress"—as its own. Nurtured principally at the Military School of Rio by Benjamin Constant Botelho de Magalhães (1836–1891) and by Luís Pereira Barreto (1840–1923), it was carried to the state of a "pure" religion—the Positivistic Apostolate of Brazil—by Miguel Lemos (1854–1917) and his disciple Raimundo Teixeira Mendes, while combated by the members of the *Recife School. (*See* Philosophy of National Identity; Slavery and Literature.)

Many literary figures were adherents to the tenets and the sociopolitical and racial ramifications of positivism, among them José *Veríssimo, Rui *Barbosa, Júlio *Ribeiro, Euclides da *Cunha, Lima *Barreto, and João do *Rio. The writer José Isidoro Martins Júnior (1860–1904), attacked *Parnassianism and *symbolism for their "archaic" concerns but failed in his attempt to develop a literary theory and literature based on positivistic ideals. The poet Martins Fontes (1884–1937) was only slightly more successful. Nísia Floresta [Nísia Floresta Brasileira Augusta] (1809–1885) was a Brazilian friend of Comte in France. Among her publications are *Opúsculo humanitário* (1853; Humanitarian Opuscule), an essay on women's right to education. (*See* Feminism and Literature.)

Discussions of positivism as a philosophy and a guiding principle for Brazil appear in the dialogues and through the activities of characters in the works of many writers since the late nineteenth century, including Machado de *Assis, Visconde de *Taunay, and Aluísio *Azevedo and notably in Lima *Barreto's *Triste fim de Policarpo Quaresma*, in Viana *Moog's novels, and in Érico *Veríssimo's trilogy *O tempo e o vento*.

BIBLIOGRAPHY: Criticism: Brookshaw: Costa, João Cruz. "The Advent of Positivism." In *A History of Ideas in Brazil*. Berkeley: University of California Press, 1964, pp. 82–175; Lins, Ivan. *História do positivismo no Brasil*. São Paulo: Companhia Editora Nacional, 1966: Zea, Leopoldo. "Ideas and Ideologues in Latin America." *The Nineteenth-Century World*. Edited by Guy S. Metraux and François Crouzet. New York: Mentor Books, 1963, pp. 485–508.

POSTMODERNISM IN POETRY. Two years—1945 and 1956—are considered the essential turning points in the development of the great variety of trends of postmodernism in Brazilian poetry. The death of Mário de *Andrade in 1945 signaled for many critics the end of *modernism and the beginning of a new era in poetry. (*See* Critics and Criticism.)

1945–1956. Postmodernism was viewed by critics of the midforties as either a response against modernism's stylistic excesses or as a legitimate outgrowth from them. Both Alceu Amoroso *Lima (Tristão de Athayde) and Sérgio *Milliet commented in 1946–1947 about the evident change in poetic direction. Milliet affirmed that poetry was "not returning to Parnassian flowerings" but to "balanced compositions which will endure throughout time." He viewed the new poets as seeking "to reclaim the poetic aspect of poetry," which the modernists had disrespected. (In Campos, Milton de Godoy, "Introdução," *Antologia poética da geração de '45*. São Paulo: 1966, pp. 11–12, 14). The poet and critic Péricles Eugênio da Silva Ramos (b. 1919) summarized the objectives of the new poetry in the first issue of the *review *Revista Brasileira de Poesia* (1947) in an article now considered the "manifesto" of the first postmodernist generation, the so-called Generation of 1945. Other regional reviews appeared throughout the country expressing similar artistic aims, for example, *Joaquim* in Curitiba (1946–1948), organized by Dalton *Trevisan; *Revista Branca* and *Orfeu* (1947) in Rio, with the latter publication organized by poet Fernando Ferreira de Loanda

(b. 1924) (for translations, *see* "Key to Bibliographical References": Hulet), with contributions by the critic Wilson *Martins (*see* Critics and Criticism), an editorial-manifesto by Ledo *Ivo, and various works of others: *José* and *Clã* in Ceará; *Ilha* in Maranhão; *Região* and *Nordeste* in Recife; *Os Cadernos da Bahia* in Bahia; and *Edifício* in Minas. (*See* Regionalism.)

With the aid of hindsight, recent critics consider several important phenomena of the early 1940s as shaping the new generations: (1) several "poetry congresses" of the early 1940s in Recife, São Paulo, and Ceará; (2) the publication of a series of articles by Mário Neme on contemporary intellectual attitudes during those years in São Paulo; and (3) the ideological debates over fascism versus democracy and socialism versus communism during the years of World War II and the repressive Vargas regime. All of these events caused Brazilian intellectual consciousness to return to international issues rather than solely national ones. Also, several important collections of verse appeared in 1945: João Cabral de *Melo Neto's *O engenheiro*; Ledo Ivo's *Ode e elegia*; and Domingos Carvalho da Silva's (b. 1915) *Rosa extinta* (Extinguished Rose) (for translations, *see* "Key to Bibliographical References": Hulet; Nist). Silva was at the time and continues today to be one of the strongest polemicists and promotors of the Generation of 1945's identity as a poetic movement. He was a cofounder of the *Revista Brasileira de Poesia*, and he is also a short story writer, an essayist, and a critic.

A negative response to these postmodernists from the hard-line modernists— Oswald de *Andrade and Sérgio Buarque de Hollanda (*see* Historiography)— subsided by the early 1950s. Indeed, the linguistic and thematic influence of some of the modernists on the postmodernists became clear by this time; most notably in the case of João Cabral de Melo Neto, who stands out from all of his contemporaries for his skillful conciliation of the aims of both schools. Many literary careers through the mid-1960s began under the umbrella of the Generation of 1945: Bueno de Rivera (1914–1982); Afrânio Zuccolotto (b. 1913) (for translations, *see* "Key to Bibliographical References": Hulet), Antônio *Olinto, Geir *Campos, Hilda *Hilst, Dantas Mota (b. 1913), Moacyr Félix (b. 1926), Afonso Félix de Sousa (b. 1925) (for translations, *see* "Key to Bibliographical References": Hulet; Solt), Marcos Konder *Reis, Mauro *Mota, Paulo Mendes *Campos, Darcy Damasceno (b. 1922), Renata Pallottini (b. 1927) (for translations, *see* "Key to Bibliographical References": Hulet), Stella *Leonardos, Thiago de *Melo, Walmir *Ayala, and Foed Castro Chamma (b. 1927), among many others.

These poets dabbled in many different literary areas: hermeticism in poetry was popular once again; some returned to symbolism or neosymbolism in the style of Cecilia *Meireles; others turned to *surrealism; many cultivated the sonnet or the forms of medieval Galaico-Portuguese romances; still others picked up the threads of the modernists' achievements and dwelled on sociopolitical issues. (*See* Portugal and Brazil: Literary Relations.)

Experimentalism in poetry, 1956–1974: Concretism, Neoconcretism, Praxism, Semiotics, Process-Poem. The year 1956 is looked upon as the major turning point in the direction of postmodernism. Three factors are often cited: Guimarães *Rosa's Grande sertão: veredas* was published; a new attitude toward literary criticism began to take roots; and, most significantly for poetry, concretism was launched in São Paulo. Among the original members of the Generation of 1945 who broke with it in 1956 were Augusto de *Campos, Haroldo de *Campos, Décio *Pignatari, and Ferreira *Gullar. Inspired by the international context of modern poetry, specifically the works of Stéphane Mallarmé (1842–1898) and Ezra Pound (1885–1972), as well as the avant-garde activities of modernist Oswald de Andrade, they established an experimental movement called concretism in the early 1950s, publishing the *review *Noigandres* (a nonsense word taken from Pound's *Cantos*). After a series of attacks on the reigning neotraditionalists in the Sunday Supplement of the *Jornal do Brasil* in 1956, they organized an art and literary exhibition in São Paulo that celebrated their relationship with artists and musicians, invoking the 1922 Week of Modern Art (*see* Modernism); the exhibition traveled to Rio in 1957. *Concrete poetry* was defined in their manifesto of 1958 as ''a product of a critical evolution of forms, considering the historical cycle of verse (rhythmic-formal unity) as having ended, concrete poetry begins to become aware of the graphic space as a structural agent.'' (*See* Art and Literature; Music and Literature.)

Not all of the concretists supported this manifesto. In 1958 Ferreira Gullar and other poets (e.g., Theon Spanudis [b. 1915]), artists, and sculptors established neoconcretism. Their 1959 manifesto denied the sole mathematical and graphic quality attributed to poetry by the concretists. It declared the hierarchical role of subjectivity, language over space, and emphasized language's ''national'' origin. Neoconcretism was short lived. Nonetheless, Gullar went on to become a prominent social poet and surely one of the greatest influences on *new writers.

In 1961, still within its experimental, avant-garde configurations, another retort to concretism appeared. Mário *Chamie established *poema praxis*. The praxis poem movement differed from concretism in that it had a social aim as defined by Chamie in his collection of poetry *Lavra-lavra* (*Plowing-Plowing*):

What is the praxis-poem? It is what a located reality esthetically puts together according to three conditions: a. the art of composition; b. the area where the composition is achieved; c. the act of consuming the work. . . . If a praxis-poem is a field for the defense of the word's value, praxis-literature is the general field for the defense of human values against the alienation of a society which must transform itself to conquer itself.

Praxism has achieved a relatively important body of works. Other poets of the school are Yone Gianetti Fonseca, author of *A fala e a forma* (1963; Speech and Form); Mauro Gama (b. 1938), whose works include *Corpo verbal* (1964; Verbal Body) and *Expresso na noite (1968–1976)* (1982; Expressed at Night [1968–1976]); Camargo Meyer, author of *Cartilha* (1964; Primer); Antônio Carlos Cabral, who published the *Diadiário cotidiano* (1964; Daily Daydiary); and

Armando Freitas Filho, among whose works are *Palavra* (1963; Word), *Longa vida* (1983; Long Life) and 3 × 4 (1986; 3 × 4).

A second phase of concretism also began in 1961. It offered poetry in the fashion of Apollinaire's (1880–1918) *Calligrames* (1918), while citing the Russian poet Vladimir Mayakovski (1894–1930) as its inspiration: "Without a revolutionary form there can be no revolutionary literature." Stung by the criticism of their "irrelevancy to Brazil," the concretists joined with the *mineiro* group of the *review *Tendência* (e.g., Affonso *Avila, Silviano *Santiago, critic Fábio Lucas [*see* Critics and Criticism]) and briefly assumed a more social orientation. In 1964 yet another phase of concretism was the semiotic poetry movement, which presented poetry devoid of words, preferring "code-poems" or collages. It was officially launched in a 1964 issue of the *review *Invenção* by Décio *Pignatari, Luís Ângelo Pinto (b. 1941) (for translations, *see* "Key to Bibliographical References": Hulet), and José Luís Grünewald (b. 1931), author of *Um e dois* (1958; One and Two) (for translations, *see* "Key to Bibliographical References": Solt), who, in 1986, published a Portuguese version of Pound's *Cantos*. The semiotic movement called "New Language, New Poetry" (*Nova linguagem, nova poesia*), was based on the "Theory of Signs" owed to the American philosopher and mathematician Charles S. Peirce. This movement is often cited as a precursor to the current interest in semiotics in literary criticism in Brazil. Its theoretical basis was defended by the modernist Cassiano *Ricardo, who was involved in many postmodernist movements, and by the poet Edgard Braga (b. 1897) (for translations, *see* "Key to Bibliographical References": Hulet). The year 1964 is considered the zenith of postmodernist experimental movements. The *Times Literary Supplement* of London dedicated two issues—August and September 1964—to the movements and their ramifications.

The process poem movement (*poema processo*), yet another outgrowth of concretism, began in 1967 with a manifesto by Wladimir Dias-Pino (b. 1927), who wrote *A ave* (1956; The Bird) and *Processo, linguagem e comunicação* (2d ed., 1973; Process, Language and Communication); Moacy Cirne; Sanderson Negreiros; and Álvaro de Sá: "The process poem inaugurates informational processes with each new experience. That information be aesthetic or not: the important thing is that it be functional and, therefore, consumed. The poem resolves itself by itself . . . not requiring interpretation for its justification." (In Silva, A. Vasconcelos da. *Lírica modernista e percurso literário brasileiro*. Rio: 1978, p. 63). Visual objects dominate or obviate verbal ones. The poets declared the autonomy of the poem over its being written or being read. Dias-Pino, Sá and other poets, for example, Ronaldo Azeredo (b. 1937) (for translations, *see* "Key to Bibliographical References": Hulet; Solt) and Pedro Xisto (b. 1900) (for translations, *see* "Key to Bibliographical References": Hulet) closed the movement in another manifesto published in 1972.

Three important experimental poetry "exhibitions"—the "Expoesia I" in 1972, the "Poemação" in 1973, and another in 1974—set the stage for the regrouping of the poets. The Campos brothers, Pignatari, and others are still today deeply involved in experimental poetry's search for original ways of capturing and expressing reality within an international context. Augusto de Campos's publication of his poem 'Póstudo'' (Posteverything) in 1985 began a polemic among Brazilian intellectuals that has yet to wane. Other poetic movements that have appeared since the late 1960s include "Comic Strip Poems," led by Álvaro de Sá; "Visual Anthropophagy," organized by José de Arimathea Soares Carvalho; "Material as Sign," led by Neide Dias de Sá; and "Postcard Poems," by Falves Silva. Among the recent experimentalists who have roots in earlier movements are Paulo Leminski (b. 1945), who writes both poetry and prose, for example, *Caprichos e relaxos* (1983; Whims and Relaxations); *Agora é que são elas* (1985; Now I Have to Face the Music) and *Catatau* (1976; Catatau); as well as Waly Salomão, considered a post-tropicalist writer. (*See Tropicalismo.*)

Post–1956 Poets. All of the highly intellectualized vanguard positions formed around the word-spatial relationship have not totally dominated the postmodernist literary scene since 1956. The neotraditionalists of the Generation of 1945 have continued to publish and often dabbled in the experimental forms, for example, José Paulo Paes's complete works, *Um por todos* (1986; One for All) (for translations, *see* "Key to Bibliographical References": Solt).

Young poets did not reject the varieties of concretism but neither did they abandon myth, Christian doctrine, metaphysics, or social questions. Excellent poetry has been produced by writers such as Carlos *Nejar, Affonso Romano de *Sant'Anna, Affonso *Ávila, and Lindolf *Bell. Other important figures include Celso Japiassu (b. 1939), whose recent collection is *O último número* (1986; The Last Number); Armindo Trevisan (b. 1933), author of *A mesa do silêncio* (1982; The Table of Silence); Marly de Oliveira (for translations, *see* "Key to Bibliographical References": Woodbridge), who has published *Aliança* (1979; Alliance) and *Retrato* (1987; Portrait); Lélia Coelho Frota (for translations, *see* "Key to Bibliographical References": Woodbridge), author of *Caprichoso desacerto* (1965; Whimsical Mistake); Alberto da Costa e Silva (b. 1931), son of the symbolist poet and author of several collections of verse; Helena Parente Cunha, who wrote *Corpo no cerco* (1978; Fenced in Body); Regina Célia Colônia, whose poetry explored Amerindian myth and folklore, for example, *Sumaimana* (1975; Sumaimana); Eduardo Alves da Costa, who wrote *No caminho com Maiakowski* (1964; On the Road with Mayacovski) and *Salamargo* (1983; Bittersalt); and José Alcides Pinto (b. 1933), a selection of whose early poetry was published in *Antologia poética* (1984; Anthology of Poetry) and who has published the "prose-poem novel" *O amolador de punhais* (1986; The Dagger Grinder).

The "Street Guitar" movement (*Violão da Rua*) organized by Moacyr Félix began in the early sixties. It was oriented toward mass participation and comprehension of poetry: "*Violão da Rua* is a gesture resulting from poetry seen as a way of knowledge about the world and serving, therefore, towards the effort for a conscious awareness of the latest realities which define us within this world." (In Silva, A. Vasconcelos da. *Lírica modernista e percurso literário brasileiro*, p. 86). Its participants included some of the modernists (e.g., Vinícius de *Moraes, Cassiano Ricardo, Joaquim *Cardozo), as well as members of the original Generation of 1945 (e.g., Geir Campos and Paulo Mendes Campos). In its desire to "recuperate reality through verse," it was in opposition to the vanguard movements. Regionalist poets appearing in the 1960s fell within the neotraditionalist position: the Pernambuco Generation of 1965 was led by the philosophical verses of Marcus Accioly (b. 1943), whose volume of poems *Ó(DE) ITABIRA* (1980: Hey You (Ode), From Itabira) was published in celebration of Carlos Drummond de *Andrade, was followed by *Narciso* (1984; Narcissus); as well as by Maurício Mota and others. The Pocket Lyre group (*Lira do Bolso*) of Salvador, Bahia, included Ruy Espinheira Filho (b. 1942), who penned *Morte secreta e poesia anterior* (1984; Secret Death and Earlier Poetry) and the recent novel *Angela Seabra desce nos infernos* (1986; Angela Seabra Goes Down to Hell); Cid Seixas Fraga (b. 1948), author of *Fonte de pedras* (1979; Fountain of Stones); and others. (*See* Regionalism.)

From the late sixties through 1972 *tropicalismo* predominated. It was, to a certain extent, co-opted and promoted by the internationalist concretists as a further continuation of the literary heritage of Oswald de *Andrade. With the repression of the military dictatorship during the early to mid-1970s, and a consequent downturn in publishing outlets, the poetry of the "marginalized" elements of society appeared. Free of manifestoes, individualism flourished. The poets used any school of poetics, even the vanguardist ones, to express their view of the Brazilian reality. They became known as the "Mimeograph Generation" because they distributed their own poems produced on dittoes for free. Poets who garnered fame at the time were included in the anthology *26 poetas hoje*, for example, the late Ana Cristina César, Antônio Carlos de Brito, and Chacal. (*See* New Writers.) Still other poetic voices have appeared and flourished independently, for example, Adélia *Prado; Antônio Carlos Secchim (b. 1952), author of *Ária da estação* (1973; Aria of the Season); Leonardo Fróes, who has had several collections published: *Vida em comum* (1968; Life in Common), *Esqueci de avisar que estou vivo* (1973; I Forgot to Let You Know That I'm Alive), and *Assim* (1986; Thus) (for translations, *see* "Key to Bibliographical References": Woodbridge; Tolman [1978]); Ivan Junqueira, who recently translated works by T. S. Eliot; and Leila Miccolis, who wrote *O impróprio para menores de dezoito anos* (1977; Inappropriate for Minors). (*See* Critics and Criticism; Dictatorship and Literature; Theater History; New Writers.)

BIBLIOGRAPHY: Translations: Brasil/Smith. Criticism: Braga, M. Lúcia Santaella, ed. "Semiotics and Poetics in Brazil." Special Issue of *Dispositio* (Summer-Fall, 1981), articles by Haroldo de Campos and Décio Pignatari as well as other Brazilian semioticians; Campos, Haroldo de. "Structuralism and Semiotics in Brazil: Retrospect and Prospect." *Dispositio* (Spring-Summer, 1978), pp. 175–187; Chilcote, Ronald H. "Poetics and Ideology in the Pop Poetry of Brazil." *SLAPC* 2 (1983), pp. 28–98; Müller-Bergh, Claus. "Feijoada, Coke, and the Urbanoid: Brazilian Poetry Since 1945." *WLT* (Winter, 1979), pp. 22–30; Solt, Mary Ellen. "A World Look at Concrete Poetry." *Concrete Poetry: A World View*. Bloomington: Indiana University Press, 1968, pp. 7–66; Thompson, Douglas. "Pound and Brazilian Concretism." *Paideuma* (Winter, 1977), pp. 279–294; Tolman, Jon M. "Brazilian Poetry: 1945–1975." *AH* (March, 1977), pp. 1–8.

PRADO, ADÉLIA (b. 1935). Prado's roots are in Divinópolis, Minas, where she teaches philosophy. The life of the town's inhabitants is the source of inspiration for her poetry and fiction. (*See* Regionalism.).

Bagagem (1976; Baggage), her first collection of poems, is made up of stark, spiritual verses often touching on woman's lot within human existence. Her citations of the Bible and the admitted linguistic debt to Guimarães *Rosa further create the rural mystical aura that characterizes her writings. Another collection of poems, *Terra de Santa Cruz* (1982; Land of the Holy Cross), carries these literary concerns to an intensely national plane. (*See* Religion and Literature.)

Prado's fiction adapts many of her poetic techniques and is faithful to the psychological tradition of Clarice *Lispector. Her narratives relate a mystical-magical world full of intimate details of the Brazilian woman's existence. Stream of consciousness is the technique she most often uses in an unstructured, highly colloquial, "sacredly" scatalogical narration. The female protagonists of *Cacos para um vitral* (1980; Smithereens for a Strained Glass Window) and *Os componentes da banda* (1984; The Members of the Band) are semiportraits of Prado herself, who is guided by firm, practical religious beliefs in her search for spiritual truth within her bourgeois existence.

Prado is an important voice in contemporary Brazilian literature. (*See* Feminism and Literature.)

BIBLIOGRAPHY: Additional selected works by Prado: *O coração disparado*, 1978; *Solte os cachorros*, 1979; *O pelicano*, 1987. Translations: *The Massachusetts Review* (December, 1986). Criticism: Richmond, Carolyn. "The Lyrical Voice of Adélia Prado: An Analysis of Themes and Structures in *Bagagem*." *LBR* (June, 1978), pp. 90–109.

PRADO, PAULO (1869–1934). Prado was born into a traditional, well-to-do *paulista* coffee family. Although he spent his life in the business, he was deeply commited to and involved in the political, social, and cultural progress of Brazil. Prado traveled to Europe frequently. On one trip, he purchased in Paris and brought back to Brazil an important vanguard work by the cubist Fernand Léger. He supported the young *paulista* modernists both financially and morally during the Week of Modern Art. (*See* Modernism.)

Prado wrote an important and polemical study about the development of the Brazilian identity and psyche: *Retrato do Brasil: ensaio sobre a tristeza brasileira* (1928; Portrait of Brazil: An Essay on the Brazilian Sadness). Like many of his contemporaries, he sought the remote roots of his nation's backwardness. These he found in the lustful existence and the greed of the early settlers and in the easy life-style and quick profit for certain classes through slavery. Prado's work and opinions are still debated today. (*See* Philosophy of National Identity.)

BIBLIOGRAPHY: Additional selected works by Prado: *Paulística*, 1925.

PRAXISM.   *See* Postmodernism in Poetry.

PREROMANTICISM.   *See* Romanticism.

PRIZES.   Prizes for literary and cultural achievement are awarded by the federal government, some state and local governments, the *Brazilian Academy of Letters, and private cultural organizations and foundations set up by large Brazilian or multinational industries. Most of these prizes are annual and include a monetary award.

The Brazilian government offers the National Cultural Awards through the Ministry of Education and Culture in literature, art, film, and folklore. The National Book Institute, a federal agency, also offers prizes for published or unpublished manuscripts. The Ministry of Foreign Affairs awards the Brazilian Theater Prize for the best play by a Latin American writer. The most famous state prize was for many years the Paraná State Short Story Prize, which is offered for an unpublished collection of stories. Winning it has launched the career of many distinguished writers: Dalton *Trevisan, Rubem *Fonseca, Luiz *Vilela, Lygia Fagundes *Telles, Roberto *Drummond, and Luiz Fernando *Emediato, among others. The Brasília city government offers a prize for literature. (*See* Art and Literature; Film and Literature; Folklore and Literature.)

The Brazilian Academy of Letters offers the following annual prizes: the Machado de *Assis Prize—considered one of Brazil's highest literary awards—for a writer's complete works, the Afonso *Arinos Prize for Fiction, the Artur *Azevedo Prize for Drama and Theatrical Criticism, the Olavo *Bilac Prize for Poetry, the Monteiro *Lobato Prize for *Children's Literature, the Júlia Lopes de *Almeida Prize for the best novel or collection of short stories by a woman writer, the Odorico Mendes (*see* Romanticism) Prize for Translation into Portuguese, the Silvio *Romero Prize for Literary Criticism, the Antônio Larragoiti Prize for the best work on a Luso-Brazilian theme, and the José *Veríssimo Prize for the best work of scholarship. (*See* Portugal and Brazil: Literary Relations.)

Among the prizes awarded by a variety of private literary groups are the Walmap Prize for Fiction, the Chinaglia Prize, the Jabuti Prize, the Goethe Institute Prize for Fiction, the Molière Theater Prize, and the PEN Club's Graça *Aranha Prize for Fiction. Prizes are awarded by different professional authors' and critics' societies, for example, the Brazilian Association of Theatre Critics. The Brazilian Union of Writers offers the ''Brazilian Intellectual of the Year'' award; Antônio *Callado was the recipient in 1986. The Moinho Santista Foundation, established by the textile operation, offers what is considered the Brazilian ''Nobel Prize'' in two fields in a seven-year rotation. The Nestlé Prize is awarded for unpublished fiction. The Esso Prize is awarded for journalism. The Saci Prize is awarded for theater, and the Tucano de Outro Prize is for cinematographic achievement. (*See* Theater History; Film and Literature.)

PROCESS-POEM.   *See* Postmodernism in Poetry.

Q

QORPO-SANTO [JOSÉ JOAQUIM DE CAMPOS LEÃO] (1829–1883). A public schoolteacher in Rio Grande do Sul, Qorpo-Santo suffered some form of mental illness in the 1860s. He wrote comedies as a form of self-therapy and vengeance against society. (*See* Theater History.)

Similar to the art of *Sousândrade, Qorpo-Santo's art was outside the literary limits of his time, although he might be called a prenaturalist. Thematically, his plays dwell on sexual themes (e.g., the homosexual life-style in A *separação dos dois esposos* (The Separation of the Two Spouses) or psychological themes (e.g., *Hoje sou um; amanhã sou outro* (1866; Today I'm One; Tomorrow Another). His language and orthography are uniquely his own; action is stressed over the concept of literary creation. One comedy, however, falls within the satirical trend of his contemporary Martins *Pena: *Um credor da fazenda nacional* (A Creditor of the National Treasury). (*See* Homosexuality and Literature; Naturalism; Realism; Romanticism.)

In the 1920s Qorpo-Santo's works were mentioned as the predecessor to the "unliterary" productions of *modernism's Mário de *Andrade and Oswald de *Andrade. The poet and critic Guilhermino César (b. 1908) (*see* Critics and Criticism) collected Qorpo-Santo's works after several university productions of them in the 1960s.

BIBLIOGRAPHY: Additional selected works by Qorpo-Santo: *Teatro completo de Qorpo-Santo*, 1980. Criticism: César, Guilhermino. "Introdução" *Teatro completo de Qorpo-Santo*. Rio: MEC/SNT, 1980.

QUEIROZ, DINAH SILVEIRA DE (1910–1983; BAL: 1980). Queiroz was one of Brazil's most popular novelists. A descendant of an important pioneer (*bandeirante*) family in São Paulo, her family is active in the arts, for example, Valdomiro *Silveira, the novelist and short fiction writer Helena Silveira (b. 1911), the publisher Énio Silveira, and an author of *children's literature, Isa Silveira Leal. The second woman elected to the *Brazilian Academy of Letters, Queiroz occupied diplomatic posts that took her to Europe and Russia.

Floradas na serra (1939; Blossoms on the Mountain), Queiroz's first novel, is a love story set in a tuberculosis sanitarium in Campos de Jordão, São Paulo State. It was, and continues to be, a major best-seller, and was made into a very successful film (1955) with Cacilda Becker and Jardel Filho. In 1954 Queiroz published *A muralha* (The Wall), an epic historical novel about the founding of São Paulo, including characters inspired by her ancestors. It also was made into a television series with actress Fernanda Montenegro in the leading role. (*See* Film and Literature.)

Queiroz adapted the fictional technique of the "new novel" for *Verão dos infiéis* (1968; Summer of the Unfaithful), which deals with a mysterious death during the days of the suicide of Getúlio Vargas. Queiroz also wrote fiction about Christ, stories, science fiction, a drama (*O oitavo dia* (1956; The Eighth Day), as well as **crônicas* and children's literature. She was awarded the Machado de Assis Prize (*see* Prizes) for her complete works in 1954. (*See* Religion and Literature; Theater History.)

BIBLIOGRAPHY: Additional selected works by Queiroz: *Margarida La Rocque*, 1949; *Eles herdarão a terra*, 1960; *Café da manhã*, 1969; *Eu, venho* (1974; *I, Christ, I'm Coming*, 1977). Translations: Grossman. Criticism: Leal, María Teresa. "Dinah Silveira de Queiroz: An Innovator in Brazilian Literature." *Rice University Studies* (1980), pp. 81–88.

QUEIROZ, RACHEL DE (b. 1910; BAL: 1978). As the first woman to be admitted to the *Brazilian Academy of Letters, Queiroz is also a forerunner of those novelists who now dramatize women's conflicts in terms of family, schooling, milieu, and society. A major figure of the northeastern regionalist novel and a member of the group of *social novelists of the 1930s, Queiroz conveys in a neonaturalist style a profound understanding of the *sertão*, while addressing the major sociopolitical issues in question during the first half of this century. (*See* Feminism and Literature; Naturalism; Regionalism.)

Although many of her novels include Rio as part of their scenario, it is the Northeast that is an indelible source of inspiration for her portrayals of women who search for an understanding of their role in life and society. Her first novel, *O Quinze* (1930; The Year Nineteen Fifteen), was published when she was only twenty years old. It described the disastrous drought of that year in her native Ceará. *As tres Marias* (1939; *The Three Marias*, 1963) presents the constant frustrations faced by the protagonists who attempt to come to grips with sexual inequality, provincial life, lack of education, their roles as mothers and wives, their own sexual feelings, and their hopes for some form of self-realization.

Dora, Doralina (1975; *Dora Doralina*, 1984), written almost forty years later, casts her heroine in a similar conflict. But in contrast to the earlier portrayals, Queiroz drew her as a woman who eventually is free to feel independent, sexually fulfilled, and responsible. Told in a retrospective first-person voice, the novel is divided into three books that record the various stages of her life and her coming to terms with the "demons" of the past. In this novel, the heroine matures to the point of transcending the social trappings and bondage customarily linked to women by standing on her own, above all, as a human being.

Throughout her career, Queiroz has written theater and *crônicas*, which have appeared in the major Brazilian newspapers and magazines. She is a writer socially committed to questions of human rights and women's advancement. Queiroz has also written on popular northeastern folklore. (*See* Folklore and Literature.)

BIBLIOGRAPHY: Additional selected works by Queiroz: *João Miguel*, 1930; *Caminho de pedras*, 1937; *Lampião*, 1953; *A beata Maria do Egito*, 1959; *O caçador de Tatu*, 1967; *O jogador de sinuca e mais historinhas*, 1980. Translations: Grossman. Criticism: Courteau, Joanna. "*A beata Maria do Egito*: Anatomy of Tyranny." *Chasqui* (February-May, 1984), pp. 3–12; Ellison; Foster/Foster, II; Woodbridge, Benjamin, Jr. "The Art of Rachel de Queiroz." *Hispania* (May, 1957), pp. 144–148.

NELSON H. VIEIRA

QUINTANA, MÁRIO   (b. 1906). Born in the interior of Rio Grande do Sul, the son of a pharmacist who endeavored to divert him from poetry to medicine, Quintana received his only formal education at the Military School of Porto Alegre. In 1929 he began a career in journalism. He spent six months in Rio in the mid-1930s and became acquainted with the poet Cecília *Meireles. In 1934 he became a translator for the Editora Globo and rendered into Portuguese classic works by Guy de Maupassant, André Gide, Pierre Beaumarchais, Virginia Woolf, Marcel Proust, Aldous Huxley, Somerset Maugham, and others.

Quintana's first collection of poetry, *A rua dos cataventos* (1940; Weathervane Street), marked him as a poet writing counter to the then still strong modernist current. In the very traditional form of these sonnets, themes unconcerned with either the national question of collective identity or with social issues, Quintana asserted himself in opposition to the free verse then in mode and to the concept of the poet as a social and political voice. (*See* Modernism.)

Quintana's works range from volumes of short, lyrical prose-poems in *Sapato florido* (1948; Flourishing Shoe) to the aphoristic *Espelho mágico* (1951; Magic Mirror) to the collection of newspaper columns in *Caderno H* (1973; Chew Me Up Slowly, 1978), which includes a manifesto: "Carta a um jovem poeta" (Letter to a Young Poet). His verse is marked by an ironic lyricism and by a poetic metaphysics of quotidian images often taken from commonplace local settings. He has also produced *children's literature.

In 1980 Quintana was awarded the Machado de Assis Prize (*see* Prizes) of the *Brazilian Academy of Letters for his life's work. He is regarded as southern Brazil's most prominent modern poet on the national scene. (*See* Regionalism.)

BIBLIOGRAPHY: Additional selected works by Quintana: *Canções*, 1946; *O aprendiz do feiticeiro*, 1950; *Apontamentos de história sobrenatural*, 1976; *Quintanares*, 1976; *Esconderijo*, 1980; *Da preguiça como método de trabalho*, 1987. Translations: Hulet; Woodbridge. Criticism: Távora, Araken. *Encontro marcado com Mário Quintana*. Porto Alegre: L & PM Editores, 1986.

JAIME H. DA SILVA

R

RAMOS, GRACILIANO (1892–1953). At the age of two Graciliano was taken by his family from his native state of Alagoas to a farm in the *sertão* of Pernambuco. These first contacts with the dryness of northeastern Brazil and the severe droughts that impoverish its people left a lasting impression on him. They not only are remembered in his *memoirs *Infância* (1945; *Childhood,* 1979) but also represent the main impulse for his fiction: the austereness of the region and its economic impasse breeds the extreme pessimism that permeates the world of his characters.

Very early on his father was unable to interest him in the dry-goods business, noting his son's preference for literature. The young Ramos began formal study in Viçosa and, later, in Maceió, Alagoas, but he never finished secondary school. His independent readings provided the background influence for his later writings. Accessible to him in Viçosa was a library of Brazilian classics, which the young Ramos supplemented with additional volumes bought by mail. His favorite literature included works by *naturalism's Émile Zola and the Portuguese Eça de Queiroz, as well as translations of Russian authors. Like the Russian Maxim Gorky, Ramos focused on the degredation, ugliness, and immorality of social injustice. (*See* Portugal and Brazil: Literary Relations.)

In 1914 Ramos went to Rio, where he became a proofreader for newspapers. A year later he returned to his family in Palmeira dos Índios to find that the bubonic plague had killed two of his sisters, a brother, and a cousin. Necessity finally forced him to follow his father's footsteps in the dry-goods shop. He soon married, but his first wife died five years later in childbirth, leaving Ramos with four children, one of which is the writer Ricardo *Ramos. During this time he continued writing *crônicas* for local newspapers and began to work on a book. After his second marriage, in 1933, his first novel *Caetés* (Caeté Indians) was published by Augusto Federico *Schmidt. In that same decade his other works appeared in rapid succession: *São Bernardo* (1934; *São Bernardo*, 1975);

Angústia (1936; *Anguish*, 1946); and *Vidas secas* (1938; *Barren Lives*, 1968).

Ramos's activity on behalf of educational reform never ceased throughout his life. For example, he was elected president of the school board in Palmeira dos Índios. He had earlier exerted his influence in this area, when upon having been selected mayor in 1928, he opened new schools in the vicinity. In 1936 he was accused in Maceió of Communist activities and was imprisoned in Rio. The posthumous work *Memórias do cárcere* (4 vols.; 1953; Jail Memoirs) tells the story of his moral and physical degradation while imprisoned; it is also a major denunciation of the Brazilian reality under the Vargas dictatorship. After leaving prison in 1937, he remained in Rio, where he was named inspector of secondary education. There he received several *prizes. In 1945 he became a member of the Communist party, and in 1952 he and his wife traveled in the USSR. Soon after his return, Ramos was taken ill and died of cancer in 1953.

Some critics (*see* Critics and Criticism) have seen Ramos's fiction as a reflection of the political novel of the 1930s. It is their view that he was simply portraying the deterministic effects of a static capitalist world. Whereas it is true that Ramos was aware of the political dimension, his writings convey more than just a political message. After 1928 the Northeast was one of the centers of literary inspiration with the formation of the group of *social novelists of the 1930s, all of whom held one concept in common: the depiction of a troubled national reality. The theme of the drought had been explored in the nineteenth century by José do *Patrocínio, Domingos *Olímpio, and Euclides da *Cunha. José Américo de *Almeida continued the stimulus. It was up to Ramos, however, to evolve the theme with his unique aesthetic focus and technical precision. (*See* Cycles.)

Ramos occupies a notable place in this generation of writers not only for his study of the sociological reality of the Northeast but also for his penetrating analysis of the inner consciousness of the *sertanejo*. His writings may be divided into three basic categories: first-person narratives: *Caetés, São Bernardo,* and *Anguish*; third-person narrations: *Barren Lives* and the short stories of *Insônia* (1947; Insomnia); and autobiographical recollections: *Childhood* and *Memórias do cárcere*. (*See* Autobiography; Memoirs.)

In *Caetés* the narrator-protagonist João Valério writes a history of the Caeté Indians, a cannabilistic tribe from colonial times. As his historical analysis progresses, he realizes his own and his society's cannabilistic qualities: "What am I if not a savage, slightly polished with a layer of varnish? Four hundred years of civilization, other races, other customs. And I said that I did not know what was happening in the soul of a Caeté? Probably what's happening in mine, with a couple of differences."

The consensus of critical opinions gives both *São Bernardo* and *Barren Lives* the ranking of literary masterpieces for their technical excellence and careful narrative structure. *São Bernardo* is the story of Paulo Honório, who, in his memoirs, registers his own rise from worker to owner of a cattle ranch near

Viçosa. It records the social contradictions and tensions of the end of an era—the decadence of the landed aristocracy—while previewing the oncoming Revolution of 1930. It is not the social message nor the political spectrum, however, that claim the author's attention here but rather the depiction of the tortuous psychological dynamics of the ruthless protagonist in conflict with the humanitarian Madalena, his wife. His blind obsession, the thirst for power that dominated his life, leads to tragic consequences.

In *Barren Lives* Ramos reached the apogee in his writing career. In this, his last novel, he depicted the lives of Fabiano; his wife, Vitória; their two children; and the unforgettable dog Baleia. Set in the drought-ridden interior of the Northeast, the structure of the narrative is cyclical, beginning with migration of the family pursued by the drought. The story of the inarticulate herdsman and his family, who barely survive their impoverished environment, is one that strikes human compassion. The problem of educational reforms is brought to the surface often, not only in the dialogic paucity of the family's brief conversations but as a byproduct of the *sertanejo's* awareness of his place in society. Fabiano's world is ruled by a feudal mentality that reduces his condition to that of slavery. The family's frustration is augmented by the fatalistic presentiment that their children will suffer the same consequences. In spite of their heroic efforts, they are reduced to subhuman forms of existence.

This neonaturalistic thesis is rendered technically by the author's economy of style, by his insistence, even as a third-person narrator, on depicting the animistic mentality of his characters; they do not converse, they grunt and gesture so as to reflect their subhuman condition. Very often Ramos resorts to animal imagery in the metaphorical process of character development. In this manner the author emphasizes the primitive circumstance of Fabiano and his lot: "He was a poor devil; like a dog, all he got was bones."

Translations and even film versions of his works have given Ramos the exposure that he well deserves. His moral position as an intellectual jailed for his beliefs during the Vargas dictatorship was directly remembered during the most recent dictatorship, in particular in Silviano *Santiago's essay-novel-diary-creation *Em liberdade*, falsely attributed to Ramos. (*See* Dictatorship and Literature; Film and Literature.)

BIBLIOGRAPHY: Additional selected works by Ramos: *A terra dos meninos pelados*, 1941; *Histórias de Alexandre*, 1944; *Dois dedos*, 1945; *Linhas tortas*, 1962; *Viventes de Alagoas: quadros e costumes do nordeste*, 1962. Translations: Grossman; Tolman (1978). Criticism: Cerqueira, Nelson. "*Vidas secas*: A Deconstructable Novel?" *Chiricú* 67 (1982), pp. 57–81; Ellison; Foster/Foster, II; Hamilton, Russell. "Character and Idea in Ramos's *Vidas secas*." *LBR* (June, 1968), pp. 86–92; Mazzara, Richard A. *Graciliano Ramos*. New York: Twayne Publishers, 1974; Sovereign, Marie. "Pessimism in Graciliano Ramos." *LBR* (Summer, 1970), pp. 57–63; Viera, David J. "Wastelands and Backlands: John dos Passos' *Manhattan Transfer* and Graciliano Ramos' *Angústia*." *Hispania* (September, 1984), pp. 377–382.

RENÉ P. GARAY

RAMOS, RICARDO (b. 1929). Ramos, the son of Graciliano *Ramos, was born and brought up in Alagoas. He studied law in Rio and began a career in journalism.

Although Ramos has had several novels published—most notably *As fúrias invisíveis* (1974; The Invisible Furies)—his short fiction has garnered fame and significant *prizes for him. Since his early collection of regionalist fiction, *Tempo de espera* (1954; Waiting Time), he has captured the harsh, ironic realities of modern urban life (*See* City and Literature; Regionalism.)

The story "Reconhecimento" (Recognition), from his recent collection *O sobrevivente* (1984; The Survivor), is typical of his literary technique. Narrating through informal essay, verging on allegory, and imaginary dialogue, Ramos philosophized about the changes in Brazilian life over the last decades and the "national amnesia" about the past. The dialogue, in a terse, often symbolic language, is never really with another character but rather with what may be considered a sounding board. (*See* Dictatorship and Literature.)

BIBLIOGRAPHY: Additional selected works by Ramos: *Os desertos*, 1961; *Circuito fechado*, 1972; *Toada para surdos*, 1979; *Os inventores estão vivos*, 1980.

RAWET, SAMUEL (1929–1985). Born in Poland, Rawet was an engineer. In *Contos do imigrante* (1956; Tales of the Immigrant) he poetically analyzed the situation of uprooted men who attempt to comprehend and adapt to a new life. From this specific issue, his next collections, *Diálogo* (1963; Dialogue) and *O terreno de uma polegada quadrada* (1969; A Square Inch of Land), turned to a more intellectual narrative voice that debates man's relationship with the real world and the author's role in his literary creation. The influence of the Argentine Jorge Luis Borges or Hermann Hesse is evident in his writings, such as in the stories "Johnny Golem" and "Kalovim." The novelette *Viagem de Ahasverus* (1970; Ahasverus's Trip) raises the theme of the wandering Jew to a highly intellectual plane at which he crystallized many of his thoughts about migration within a Brazilian reality. (*See* Immigrants and Literature; Religion and Literature.)

In his later stories and essays, for example, *Eu-Tu-Ele* (1972; I-You-He), Rawet turned to the Brazilian social reality.

BIBLIOGRAPHY: Additional selected works by Rawet: *Os sete sonhos*, 1967. Translations: Tolman (1984). Criticism: Tolman (1984).

REALISM. In a broad critical sense, the term *realism* refers to art's attempts to represent or imitate nature with truth and adequacy. In literary history, it is specifically used to designate the midnineteenth-century movement usually associated with writers such as Stendhal (1783–1842), Balzac (1799–1850), and Flaubert (1821–1880) in France and Dostoevsky (1821–1881) and Tolstoy (1828–1910) in Russia, who rebelled against the conventions of both the *academies and the romantics. (*See* Romanticism.)

Realism aspires to "the objective representation of contemporary social reality,'' according to critic René Wellek. It presents both ''great intellectual and spiritual forces'' and ''concrete social existence,'' as in its use of the literary ''type'' (Gyorgy Lukács). Even as they represent great social stereotypes and are affected by historical issues, characters remain self-determining individuals. The realistic novel, heir of the epic, features a coherent narrative that does not become ''mere'' description. Finally, implicit in realism's critical portrait of man and society is a call for social change. These traits distinguish realism from romanticism's emphasis on sentiment and the experience of the isolated individual and also from *naturalism's stance of ''scientific'' observation and a more deterministic view of the individual and society.

Several factors complicate a study of realism in Brazilian literature. Although we can date realism from the mid-1870s through about 1905 (from the activities of the *Recife School through the late novels of Machado de *Assis), this does not mean that the movement was exclusive or even dominant during those decades. In the study of the late nineteenth-century novel, the distinction between realism and naturalism is often not completely clear. In Brazil naturalism did not so much follow realism as exist contemporaneously with it and, perhaps, even ''overshadow'' it. Historians of Brazilian literature generally consider realism together with naturalism and focus their discussions of the novel on the latter movement. Naturalism, indeed, seems a more suitable designation for the highly colored social exposés of Aluísio *Azevedo, Herculano Inglês de *Sousa, and Adolfo *Caminha, as well as other novelists of the time.

Realism first appears as a rebellion against the prolonged reign of romanticism. In the 1870s in an intellectual climate enriched by new interest in the social and biological sciences, by positivism in philosophy, and by political currents such as abolitionism, journalists and creative writers proclaimed their dissatisfaction with the antiquated and sterile forms of that movement. (*See* Positivism and Literature; Slavery and Literature.)

Here the intellectual community of Recife had an important role. Its major figure, Sílvio *Romero, called for change and renewal in Brazilian literature. Writers such as Machado de Assis and Teófilo Dias (*see* Parnassianism) attacked stagnant romanticism in the papers and magazines of Rio. Suprisingly, the most programmatic response to these critical demands came in poetry. In the 1870s writers such as José Isidoro Martins Júnior (1860–1904; BAL: 1902), Celso de Magalhães (1849–1879), José Ezequiel Freire de Lima (1849–1891), and Lúcio de Mendonça (1854–1909) produced ''political,'' ''scientific,'' and ''sociorealistic'' poetry. Of little literary merit, these innovations are most important as they challenged the romantic tradition and set the scene for *Parnassianism, a poetic movement that featured a new austerity and precision in form, even as it remained romantic in content.

In prose we find no well-defined realistic movement. Although a number of major novels were published between 1870 and 1905, it is difficult to characterize any as truly realistic. First, although many writers depict urban or rural reality, they seldom achieve (or perhaps even aspire to) works in the mold of the great writers of European realism. Furthermore, in many novels, the attempt at an "objective presentation" of society coexists with elements of other schools. Some writers were unable to leave behind the rhetoric and melodrama of romanticism. In the works of others, the depiction of society gives way to naturalism's exhaustive description and its emphasis on social and biological determinism.

Thus notes and reservations accompany a list of realist writers in Brazil. Joaquim Maria Machado de *Assis is universally acknowledged as Brazil's major realist writer; nevertheless, the technical innovations that allow him to present his critical portrait of urban society also remove him from the mainstream of European realism. A discussion of realism must consider José de *Alencar and Raul *Pompéia, although neither one can be properly included under this heading. One senses the presence of Balzac in Alencar's romantic-realist urban novel *Senhora*, and there are certainly critical, nonromantic elements in his rural novels. Pompéia's impressionistic *O ateneu* also scrutinizes contemporary society, although in terms of literary schools he remains difficult to classify. Manuel Antônio de *Almeida's picaresque *Memórias de um sargento de milícias* is an important precursor of realism in Brazil. (*See* Impressionism.)

We can mention other writers and works of considerably lesser literary quality. Otto Maria Carpeaux (*see* Immigrants and Literature) includes the Viscount de *Taunay among realist writers, pointing out the realism of the descriptive passages of his largely romantic *Inocência*. Franklin *Távora attempted to create a "literature of the North" in several works of historical fiction, for example, *O matuto* and *O cabeleira*. (*See* Regionalism.)

Yet perhaps the impact of realism on Brazilian literature is greater than this list suggests. Rather than search for works that follow the models of European realism, we might focus on writers who took the response against romanticism as a starting point for the development of new fictional forms. Whereas romanticism had already inspired Brazilian writers to depict their country's varied landscapes, realism curbed the artistic excesses of that movement and brought a new energy to the development of regionalism. Contact with realism was important in the careers of José de Alencar, Raul Pompéia, and Machado de Assis. Also, three notable literary *reviews published in Rio are directly associated with the movement: *Revista Literária* (1884), *A Semana* (1885–1887, 1893–1895), and *Vida Moderna* (1886–1887).

Although it remains difficult to speak of a well-defined period of Brazilian realism in the late nineteenth century, realism played an important part in the search for an adequate literary expression of the Brazilian reality.

BIBLIOGRAPHY: Coutinho/Rabassa; Pacheco, João. *O realismo*. Volume 3 of *A literatura brasileira*. 4th ed. São Paulo: Cultrix, 1971, pp. 7–66.

MARÍA TAI WOLFF

REBELO, MARQUES [EDDY DIAS DA CRUZ] (1907–1973; BAL: 1964). After studying at the Colégio Pedro II, in his native Rio, Rebelo enrolled in the School of Medicine but pursued a career in business. Although the social novel of the Northeast held sway from the 1930s to the 1950s (*see* Social Novelists of the 1930s), Rebelo chose instead to write about urban life, following in the footsteps of Manuel Antônio de *Almeida, about whom he wrote an important biography (see Biography and Biographers); Aluísio *Azevedo; Machado de *Assis; and Lima *Barreto. (See Social Novelists of the 1930s.)

Rebelo presented the inhabitants of the working-class neighborhoods of the northern zone of Rio as his one and only subject. He had two collections of sketches, short stories, and novelettes published in the early 1930s that attracted scant attention. His first novel, Marafa (1935; Loose Living), was awarded the Machado de Assis Prize (see Prizes). A second novel, A estrela sobe (1938; The Star Rises), only belatedly won acclaim and was made into a film. Marafa treats the world of prostitution and pandering in Rio's Mangue district. It employs cinematic techniques, short chapters, multiple levels, staccatolike sentences, and a great deal of dialogue replete with so much slang that Rebelo was persuaded to include a glossary of terms in the volume's second edition. A estrela sobe is set in the radio entertainment world of the period and possesses similar stylistic devices. He became the carioca novelist par excellence and a precursor to Rubem *Fonseca and Carlos Heitor *Cony. (See City and Literature; Film and Literature; Regionalism.)

Aside from producing other collections of stories, travelogues, and a play, he had numerous works of *children's literature published. In his later years he wrote three volumes of a projected seven-volume cycle under the general series title of "O espelho partido" (The Broken Mirror) about life in Rio's then newly developing southern zone during the Vargas years.

BIBLIOGRAPHY: Additional selected works by Rebelo: Três caminhos, 1933; Stela me abriu a porta, 1942; Cortina de ferro, 1956; A guerra está em nós, 1969. Translations: Grossman. Criticism: Foster/Foster, II.

                                                                                        BOBBY J. CHAMBERLAIN

RECIFE SCHOOL.   This name, coined by Sílvio *Romero, is given to a group of intellectuals who were students of Tobias Barreto de Meneses (1839–1889) at the Recife Law School in the 1880s. Barreto adhered to French positivism and to German evolutionist theories, which affected the *realism and *Parnassianism movements of the time. Romero and Tristão de Alencar Araripe Júnior (see Critics and Criticism), who were his most avid disciples, became two of Brazil's leading literary critics at the turn of the century. Fausto Cardoso (1864–1906) was an important disciple of Barreto's in the social sciences. (See: Philosophy of National Identity; Positivism and Literature.)

BIBLIOGRAPHY: Criticism: Brookshaw; Costa, João Cruz. A History of Ideas in Brazil. Berkeley: University of California Press, 1964; Sayers.

REGIONALISM.   The term regionalism is used to refer to the style of writing that aims to reproduce the speech, customs, history, folklore, or attitudes of a distinct geographical area of a nation. Although a regionalist work may be most authentic when produced by a native son or daughter, major works have been written by authors who use a region only as a backdrop for their creation. The goals of regionalist writing are to achieve both an accurate account of a certain region and also to attain a sense of universality that links its realities to the larger human experience. Regionalism has been a major force in Brazilian literature, most consciously since the midnineteenth century. Although primarily associated with prose fiction, in the twentieth-century regionalist poetry, dramas, and essays have been vibrant fields of literary production. (*See* Folklore and Literature; Historiography; Theater History.)

Brazil is often divided geographically into five regions: North, Northeast, Center-West, Southeast, and South. The North includes the vast territory of the Amazon River basin and jungle, focused on in the works of several native sons, including Inglês de *Sousa; José *Veríssimo; *Eneida; Dalcídio *Jurandir; Paulo Jacob (b. 1923), whose novels include *Vila Rica das queimadas* (1976; Vila Rica of the Scorched Lands), dealing with Syrian immigrants, and *A noite cobria o rio caminhando* (1983; The Night Covered the Walking River); Benedicto Monteiro (b. 1924), who has produced a trilogy of novels focusing on the sociopolitical and economic realities of the area with due attention to linguistic features, for example, *Verde vago mundo* (1972; Green Vague World) and *A terceira margem* (1983; The Third Shore); Márcio *Souza, who has also written regional theater; Agildo Monteiro; and Artur Engrácio. (*See* Immigrants and Literature; Portuguese Language of Brazil; Postmodernism in Poetry.)

Two postmodernist Amazonian poets of note are Nauro Machado (b. 1935), author of *Os órgãos apocalípticos* (1976; The Apocalyptic Organs), and Max Martins, who wrote *O ovo filosófico* (1975; The Philosophic Egg). The region has served as the background for works by non-natives, including Couto de Magalhães's (1837–1898) "scientific novel" *O selvagem* (1876; The Savage); Alberto Rangel's (1871–1945) *Inferno verde* (1904; Green Hell); João Peregrino Júnior's (1898–1985; BAL: 1945) *Puçanga* (1929; Puçanga) and his short fiction; and Gastão *Cruls's fiction. Two of *modernism's most significant works were set in the Amazon: Mário de *Andrade's *Macunaíma* and Raul *Bopp's *Cobra Norato*; Darcy *Ribeiro's *Maíra* returns to the theme of the Amazonian Indian once again. (*See* Indianism.)

The Northeast encompasses the bulge of states from Ceará to Bahia and has produced the strongest regionalist literature. Franklin *Távora was the initiator of northern regionalist fiction in the 1870s, with his "Northern Literature Manifesto," an introduction to his novel *O cabeleira*, which stressed the role of regional culture within the national life. Several poets of this *sertão* also appeared: Juvenal Galeno (1836–1931), who also published a collection of stories *Cenas populares* (1871; Popular Scenes of Life) (*see* Slavery and Literature); Trajano Galvão de Carvalho (1830–1864) (*see* Slavery and Literature); Bruno Seabra (1837–1876); and Bittencourt Sampaio (1836–1895). The "Spiritual Brotherhood Movement," which began in northeastern Ceará in 1892, was the first organized literary movement to attain national prominence and was consequential in the formation of Gilberto *Freyre's Regionalist Congress of 1926. Northeastern regionalism, concerned with the urban and rural social reality and a *saudade* for the "lost past," gave rise to fictional *cycles of social and economic conditions, which became popular with the *social novelists of the 1930s. These writers are indebted to Domingos *Olímpio's impressive novel of the droughts, *Luzia-Homem,* and Mário Sete's (1886–1950) fiction of life on Pernambucan sugar plantations. Xavier Marques (1861–1942; BAL: 1919) is considered the founder of Bahian regionalism. In addition to historical fiction about colonial Bahia, his local color novels of customs were popular, most notably *Jana e Joel* (1899; Jana and Joel), presenting life among the fishermen of Ilhéus.

In addition to Freyre, native novelists, poets, and dramatists of many literary schools and techniques have adhered to northeastern regionalism since *modernism, including José Américo de *Almeida, Rachel de *Queiroz, Amando Fontes (*see* Social Novelists of the 1930s), Joaquim *Cardozo, João Cabral de *Melo Neto, Luís *Jardim, Hermilo *Borba Filho, Jorge *Amado, José *Condé, Ariano *Suassuna, Dias *Gomes, and Sônia *Coutinho.

Other contemporary northeastern regionalists of note are, from Ceará: João Clímaco Bezerra, author of *Não há estrelas no céu* (1952; There Are No Stars in the Sky); Caio Porfírio Carneiro (b. 1928), author of several collections of short stories, as well as a journalistic novel about the Brazilian "saint" Father Cícero, *Uma luz no sertão* (1973; A Light in the *sertão*); Rodrigues Marques (b. 1932), author of the novel *Duas mulheres de Terramor* (1976; Two Women from Terramor); the short fiction writer Moreira Campos (b. 1914), author of *A grande mosca no copo de leite* (1985; The Big Fly in the Cup of Milk); the late Juarez Barroso, who documented the perilous existence of Ceará in the stories *Joaquinho Gato* (1975; Joaquinho Gato) and in the posthumously published novel *Doutora Isa* (1979; Doctor Isa); and the poet and novelist José Alcides Pinto (b. 1933); from Maranhão: José Sarney (b. 1931; BAL: 1980), the first civilian president of Brazil since the end of the recent military dictatorship, a poet, and an author of short fiction, for example, *Noites das águas* (1969; *Tales of Rain and Sunlight,* 1986); the social poet José Chagas (b. 1924), for example, *Lavoura azul* (1974; Blue Agriculture); Odilo Costa Filho (1914–1979; BAL: 1969), who wrote fiction about the river people of Maranhão, *A faca e o rio* (1965; The Knife and the River), but gained greater attention for his poetry, *Cantiga incompleta* (1978; Unfinished Song); and the younger poet, Gaspar Viriato; from Piauí: O. G. Rego de Carvalho, author of the novel *Somos todos inocentes* (We Are All Innocent) and the collection of stories *Ulisses* (1953, reprinted 1972; Ulysses); from Pernambuco: the poet and critic César Leal (b. 1921) (*see* Critics and Criticism), author of *Invenções da noite menor* (1957; Inventions of a Lesser Night); Cavalcanti Borges (b. 1910) (for translations, *See* "Key to Bibliographical References": Grossman), author of the stories in *Neblina* (1940; Fog) and several plays based on works by Machado de *Assis and Gilberto *Freyre; the poets of the Pernambucan Generation of 1965, notably Marcus Accioly; and Gilvan Lemos, whose recent collection of stories is titled *Morte ao invasor* (1984; Death to the Invader); from Alagoas, Breno Accioli (1921–1966), author of short and long fiction. (*See* Folklore and Literature; Religion and Literature; Theater History.)

From Bahia, there is James Amado (b. 1922), author of the novel *Chamado do mar* (1949; Call from the Sea), as well as critical studies of Gregório de *Matos and Graciliano *Ramos; Jorge Medauar (b. 1918), initally a poet of the Generation of 1945 (*see* Postmodernism in Poetry) but now working primarily in fiction, for example, the stories of *Agua preta* (1958; Black Water); Vasconcelos Maia (b. 1923) (for translations, *see* "Key to Bibliographical References": Grossman), whose collections of stories include *O cavalo e a rosa* (1955; The Horse and the Rose); Ewelson Soares Pinto (1926–1987), author of *A crônica do valente Parintins* (1976; The Chronicle of the Brave Parintins), an impressive view and narrative of Brazil from the 1930s to the 1950s; Hélio Pólvora (b. 1928), a journalist, a novelist and a literary critic (*see* Critics and Criticism), whose collection of stories *Estranhos e assustados* (1966; Strangers and Frightened Ones) sought to raise regionalism to a metaphysical level; Telmo Padilha (b. 1930); and the Pocket Lyre poets (*Lira do Bolso*). (*See* Postmodernism in Poetry.) Other northeasterners include Neil de Castro, author of *As pelejas de Ojuara* (1986; The Battles of Ojuara); Dirceu Lindoso; and Mário Pontes (b. 1932).

Although not a northeasterner by birth, Euclides da *Cunha's *Os sertões* is set in Bahia and is considered one of the masterpieces of regionalist and all-Brazilian literature.

The Center-West area is dominated by writers of Minas. Since colonial days, Minas has been the center of an individualistic, distinguishable literature. The *Minas School played a role in the early independence movement. Bernardo *Guimarães is considered the precursor of modern *mineiro* regionalism, and he has been followed by writers such as Afonso *Arinos, Carlos Drummond de *Andrade, Anibal *Machado, the master João Guimarães *Rosa, Mário *Palmério, Fernando *Sabino, Murilo *Rubião, Ivan *Ângelo, and the poet Abgar Renault (b. 1903; BAL: 1968), a member of the *mineiro* modernist movement, who had his only collection of verse published in 1984: *A outra face da lua* (The Other Side of the Moon). Modern *mineiro* poets have actively participated in postmodernist movements, for example, Affonso *Ávila, Silviano *Santiago, and other founders of the *review *Tendência*.

Hugo Carvalho Ramos (1895–1921), from Goiás State, was recognized by Mário de *Andrade as the most important writer of the *sertão* of his state. His short fiction and one novel, *Gente de Gleba* (People of Gleba), published posthumously in 1950, offered detailed descriptions of Goianian life. Other contemporaries include Cora Coralina (pseudonym of Ana Lins dos Guimarães Peixoto Bretas), a poet and folklorist whose works include *Meu livro de cordel* (1976; My Book of *cordel*) and *Vintém de cobre* (1983; Copper Cent); Carmo Bernardes (b. 1915), who also presents life in the interior of Mato Grosso in his *crônicas* and fiction, for example, *Areia branca* (1976; White Sand), *Nunila* (1984; Nunila), and *Memórias do vento* (1986; Memoirs of the Wind); Miguel Jorge, a dramatist and novelist, author of the novel *Caixote* (1975; Carton) and the plays *O visitante* (The Visitor) and *Os angélicos* (The Angelic Ones), both published in 1970. (*See* Folklore and Literature.)

The state of Rio de Janeiro and, most specifically, the ex-national capital city (for some, still the center of national culture) dominates the southeastern region of Brazil. Among its native sons and daughters, Machado de *Assis portrayed local *carioca* life, while describing universal human experiences. Other important regionalist writers of the state and city of Rio include João do *Rio; Otávio de *Faria; the novelist and critic Miécio Tati (b. 1913), author of *Rua do Tempo-Será* (1959; Future Time Street), which is based on his childhood remembrances of Rio; Rubem *Braga; Rubem *Fonseca; and a myriad of others who have adopted Rio as their home.

Valdomiro *Silveira began modern *paulista* regionalism. The theme of *paulista* life was central to the works of Monteiro *Lobato, Mário de *Andrade, and Alcântara *Machado, as well as many contemporaries from Loyola *Brandão to Marcos *Rey. Hernani Donato (b. 1922), an essayist and biographer, has had many novels published about his state, for example, *Filhos do destino* (1951; Children of Destiny) and *Selva trágica* (1958; Tragic Jungle), which was produced as a film. (*See* Film and Literature.)

The precursor of southern regionalism was the romantic writer Apolionário Porto *Alegre. Notable writers of the history and culture of the land of the *gaúcho* include Simões *Lopes Neto, the novelist Alcides Maia (1878–1944; BAL: 1913) (for translations, *see* "Key to Bibliographical References": Grossman), whose tales mix the lyrical and the violent aspects of the *gaúcho*'s existence; and Darcy Azambuja (1903–1970) (for translations, *see* "Key to Bibliographical References": Grossman). Also pertinent are the studies of *gaúcho* life by Múcio Teixeira (1857–1928); the poetry of Augusto *Meyer; Érico *Veríssimo's sweeping panorama of southern Brazilian history, "O tempo e o vento"; and the works of Josué *Guimarães, Mário *Quintana, Carlos *Néjar, and Walmir *Ayala. Young writers like Moacir *Scliar and Ricardo L. Hoffmann (see Immigrants and Literature) deal with the immigrant experience in southern Brazil. José Clemente Pozenato's (b. 1938) recent novel *O quatrilho* (1986; The Posse) presents the theme of Italian migration to southern Brazil in the early part of the century. Ieda Inda's *Buguala: romance de rédeas e rendas* (1983: Wild Colt: A Romance of Reigns and Laces) presents contemporary life on the Argentinian border. Other southern regionalists include the short story writers Telmo Vergara, José Luís Silveira Neto, and Renato Alba. (*See* New Writers.)

Regionalism is somewhat on the wane today owing to the increasingly stronger national communications network. Nonetheless, it continues to be a powerful force in Brazilian life and culture, one that will undoubtedly continue to exert a significant influence on Brazilian literature for some time to come. (*See also* Contemporary Black Literature.)

BIBLIOGRAPHY: Criticism: Brookshaw; Carlisle, Richard Charles. "Time and the Scapegoat in Gilvan Lemos's *Emissário do diabo.*" *LBR* (Winter, 1981), pp. 323–330; Coutinho/Rabassa; Freyre, Gilberto. *Brazil: An Interpretation.* New York: Alfred A. Knopf, 1945; Martins; Mazzara, Richard. "Regionalism and Modern Brazilian Theatre." *REH* (1975), pp. 11–32; Putnam, Samuel. "The Rise of Regionalism." *Marvelous Journey.* New York: Alfred A. Knopf, 1948, pp. 152–162; Velhinho, Moisés. *Brazil South: Its Conquest and Settlement.* New York: Alfred A. Knopf, 1968; Wagley, Charles. "Regions." *An Introduction to Brazil.* New York: Columbia University Press, 1971, pp. 23–90, 265–276.

EARL E. FITZ and IRWIN STERN

REGO, JOSÉ LINS DO (1901–1957; BAL: 1955). Rego was born on his family's sugar plantation in Paraíba State of northeastern Brazil. He was orphaned at an early age and cared for by a maiden aunt. Many critics have commented on the probable impact of this family situation on his works, since nostalgia for a mother he hardly knew is a frequent motif in his works. His aunt died when Rego was just ten, and he spent the next few years in boarding schools, an experience that is also the theme of some of his novels.

At the age of eighteen he entered the School of Law in Pernambuco, where he met the famous sociologist Gilberto *Freyre, probably the most profound direct intellectual influence in his life. Freyre would soon found the "Region-Tradition" movement, a somewhat eccentric but nevertheless extremely important regionalist movement that began partially in response to what Freyre considered the frivolity and excess of the modernist movement of Rio and São Paulo. Rego began writing occasional pieces for various local newspapers and even practiced law for a brief time, but his true vocation was writing, and within a few years he had become the principal exponent of "Region-Tradition" in fiction. He eventually moved to Rio to devote himself to writing and public service. (*See* Modernism; Regionalism.)

"Region-Tradition," whose manifesto was published in 1926, was eccentric because of its extreme position in regard to the exaltation of all things local and its rejection of all things "alien." Rego fortunately avoided such extremism in his writing, but he was nevertheless a writer who found his principal inspiration in his region. By the midthirties he was recognized as one of the two principal members of the so-called Generation of 1930, a group of a half-dozen novelists whose works were at least to some degree inspired by Freyre's ideas. The novels of this group were the dominant literary mode in Brazil for a decade, and to this day the works of Rego and his contemporary Jorge *Amado are presented to Brazilian schoolchildren as examples of this century's "classics." (*See* Social Novelists of the 1930s.)

Rego is known principally as a novelist, although he had several volumes of other writings published, including speeches, *memoirs, and sketches. His most famous novels are the six of the "sugarcane *cycle," most of which were best-sellers for at least some years after publication. The cycle, much of it transparently autobiographical, is essentially a series of chapters in the life of Carlos de

Melo, like Rego the son of one of the traditional plantation families of the Northeast. The first novel of the cycle is *Menino do engenho* (1932; *Plantation Boy*, 1966), which begins with the death of the protagonist's mother when he was four and ends with his preparation to go away to boarding school at the age of twelve. *Doidinho* (literally, "crazy little guy") (1933; *Doidinho*, 1966) is Carlos's nickname in boarding school, and the book is the chronicle of the sickly and somewhat inept boy's attempts to understand life both within and outside the school. The third novel, *Bangüe* (literally, "labor-intensive plantation system") (1934; *Bangüe*, 1966), follows Carlos to Recife, where even after finishing law school the protagonist seems oddly marginal and not yet sure who he is. *O moleque Ricardo* (1935; The Boy Ricardo), though not included in the cycle by some critics, is obviously closely related to it—it is the story of the protagonist's black childhood companion Ricardo and his adventures in the city. The contrast in the fortunes of the two characters is provocative, because although Carlos is a success, he seems not to know what to make of it. Ricardo becomes a laborer and eventually ends up on the Brazilian Atlantic prison island of Fernando de Noronha for his participation in an illegal strike. The next novel of the cycle, *Usina* (literally, "mechanized sugar mill") (1936), chronicles the death of Carlos's friend Ricardo, as well as the death of the old plantation system and the emergence of a mechanized system of sugar production, which modernizes the industry but destroys a way of life in the process. (*See* Autobiography.)

A final novel of the cycle, again one not included by some critics, is *Fogo morto* (1943; Dead Fire). Why it is not included as part of the cycle is something of a mystery, since although it is not a next logical chronological step, it is arguably Rego's masterpiece, and it has many thematic similarities to the novels of the cycle. In some sense it is a rewrite of *Usina*, since, like that novel, it is about the decline of the old plantation system and the rise of the industrialized sugar mills. In that large thematic sense, it might be considered a rewrite of the entire cycle, although it lacks the personal memoir qualities of the earlier works. That lack, however, is in some ways its greatest virtue from a literary standpoint. Since most of the novels of the cycle are highly autobiographical, they ring true as a memoir but less so as art, because Rego seems more intent on getting everything down than on transforming it into a larger drama with characters who have lives of their own. But *Fogo morto* contains his best-drawn literary characters and is, in fact, structured as three character studies stitched together. The characters are José Amaro, a proud but misunderstood saddlemaker; the degenerate plantation owner Lula; and the local eccentric Vitorino. Carlos de Melo still appears in the book, but he is a minor character, and the narrator seems less interested in him than in the peculiar and sometimes oddly touching protagonists of the three parts.

Rego wrote novels about other authentically Brazilian issues, such as *Pedra Bonita* (1938; Pedra Bonita), about rural Brazil's chronic problem with messianic movements, and *Cangaceiros* (1953; Backlands Bandits), about rural banditry. But his most affecting works are those based on his own nostalgic view of a world in dissolution. The recurring themes in these novels are all viewed with a certain psychic resonance in the author's own life: the longing for maternal care, the power and mystery of sexuality, the fear of death, the conflict of urban values and rural values, and the conflict of cosmopolitan and folk worldviews. (*See* Folklore and Literature; Religion and Literature.)

The generation to which Rego belonged is usually thought of as a generation of political writers widely considered leftists. In fact, its major members were regarded as "subversives," and the Vargas government even went to the extreme of including their works in periodic public book burnings. This is particularly mysterious in the case of Rego, since he wrote only one political novel, *O moleque Ricardo*, and even it has an ambivalent message. His other novels are either portraits of a society long gone or pictures of a system in decline, and any leftism in his works would thus appear to be purely in the mind of the beholder.

Rego's works may seem a little dated now, but probably less so than that of many of his contemporaries, because their very autobiographical nature lends them an air of authenticity. His portrayal of the decline of the plantation economy is probably the best one we have today, although it lacks the charts and graphs usually associated with such a picture. Authenticity is not his only virtue as a writer, because he was not only an acute observer but a skillful narrator, noted in part for his convincing use of the Northeast oral idiom. Many of the characters in this portrait of decadence, from the mournful Carlos to the dissipated Lula and the quixotic Vitorino, are poignant and sometimes fascinating creations whose pathetic eccentricities have timeless appeal. (*See* Film and Literature; Portuguese Language of Brazil.)

BIBLIOGRAPHY: Additional selected works by Rego: *Note*: The English translation of *Plantation Boy* includes the translations of *Doidinho* and *Bangüe*. *Histórias da velha Totônia*, 1936; *Pureza*, 1937 (*Pureza*, 1948); *Riacho doce*, 1939; *Pedro Américo*, 1943; *Poesia e vida*, 1945; *Eurídice*, 1947; *Meus verdes anos*, 1956; *Presença do nordeste na literatura brasileira*, 1957; *Dias idos e vividos: antologia*, 1981. Criticism: Brookshaw; Ellison; Foster/Foster, II; Kelly, John R. "José Lins do Rego and the Ideological Origins of Brazilian Northeastern Realism (1922–1932)." *REH* (1979), pp. 201–207; Silveira, Edmund da. "Literary Aspects of José Lins do Rego's 'Sugar Cane Cycle.' " *Hispania* (December, 1955), pp. 404–413; Thompson, Franklin M. "*Fogo morto*: Epitaph of a Way of Life." *MLJ* (1950), pp. 23–28.

JON S. VINCENT

REIS, MARCOS KONDER (b. 1922). Although Reis, an engineer from Santa Catarina State, is considered a leading figure of the Generation of 1945 (*see* Postmodernism in Poetry), he is not widely known outside literary circles, owing to his hermetic verse.

From his first collection, *Tempo e milagre* (1944; Time and Miracle), to his most recent one, *A cruz vazia na encruzilhada* (1985; The Empty Cross at the Crossroads)—with some seventeen widely spaced volumes of poetry between them—Reis has focused on the themes of childhood, love, and God. Although some stylistic affects of the modernists are evident early on, he soon turned to introspective, neo-symbolist verse and forms in which themes are recurrently developed and associated through words and metaphors. (*See* Modernism; Symbolism.)

The variety of his poetic skills is evident in collections such as *Armadura de amor* (1965; Love's Armor), containing only sonnets, or in *O muro amarelo* (1965; The Yellow Wall), in which free verse predominates. In *Teoria do vôo* (1969; Theory of Flight) childhood experiences obtain the status of a religious metaphor and suggest the child's identification with the Christ figure. (*See* Religion and Literature.)

BIBLIOGRAPHY: Additional selected works by Reis: *Meninos do luto*, 1947; *Praia brava*, 1950; *Irmão da estrada*, 1978. Translations: Bishop/Brasil; Tolman (1978); Woodbridge.

RELIGION AND LITERATURE.   Three broad areas of interpenetration between religion and literature may be delineated in Brazilian literary history: (1) works of catechetical or moralistic purpose; (2) expressions of personal devotional or metaphysical experience and probing; and (3) religious practices as part of the more general cultural perspective depicted as theme or background of literary works.

During the first century of the colonial period (1500–1600), the Jesuit presence dominated the Brazilian cultural scene in both sacred and secular functions. Priests such as Father José de *Anchieta and Father Manuel da *Nóbrega laid the foundation of descriptive and informative essays concerning the new colony. They carried out linguistic investigations and published analyses of indigenous languages. The catechetical plays (*autos*) were destined for a semiliterate or illiterate Brazilian public. The Jesuits actively founded schools and established a rigorous curriculum, which eventually led to the Licentiate degree. (*See* Indian Languages; Portuguese Language of Brazil; Theater History.)

The second century of colonial administration of Brazil (1600–1700) saw a consolidation of Jesuitic activity on all fronts as exemplified in the long and fruitful career of Father Antônio *Vieira, *baroque preacher *par excellence* and fluent epistological critic of moral ills and social injustice in the colony. As in the previous century, emphasis continued to be on the communication of values from clerical writers to their lay public of hearers and readers, as can be further seen in Father Alexandre de Gusmão's (1629–1724) allegorical-moral work in prose: *História do predestinado peregrino e seu irmão Precito* (1682; Story of the Predestined Pilgrim and His Brother Precito).

The scene alters in the third century of the colonial period (1700–1800), as the clergy comes into focus as the object of literary works as well as their author. The most noteworthy examples of this trend may be seen in the area of epic poetry, where works such as *Caramuru*, authored by Friar Santa Rita *Durão, and *O uraguai*, by Basílio da *Gama, with its anti-Jesuitic thrust, show complementary, if contrastive, faces of the same genre. Still other priests and brothers prepared histories of their orders and religious activities in the colony, for example, Friar Couto Loreto's (eighteenth century) *Desagravios do Brasil e Gloria de Pernambuco* (1757; published 1902; Redress of Brazil and Glory of Pernambuco), which includes biographies of priests active in religious as well as literary functions and, of a similar nature, Friar Antônio Jaboatão's (1695–1765) *Novo orbe seráfico brasílico* (published 1889; New Seraphic World of Brazil).

With the advent of *romanticism, poetry of religious sensibility and personal devotion surged to the fore as the literary activity of professional religious orders dwindled in Brazil. God, love, and nature merged to form the core of romantic poetic expression, from the early poetry of Gonçalves de *Magalhães through the lyrical verse of Gonçalves *Dias and the subjective confessional poetry of Álvares de *Azevedo, Casimiro de *Abreu, Junqueira *Freire, and Fagundes *Varela. In almost all cases, the agony of personal suffering and depression or the empathetic response to the suffering of others (e.g., the dispossessed Indians of Gonçalves Dias's "Deprecação) finds voice in an outpouring of prayerlike verse to God as comforter and mediator of justice or as semipantheistic presence.

Although a scene of *macumba*, the Afro-Brazilian religious ritual, appears in Manuel Antônio de *Almeida's *Memórias de um sargento de milícias*, religion as a composite of practices constituting a facet of cultural behavior to be analyzed sociologically comes into focus during the period of *realism, especially in the fictional production of the last quarter of the nineteenth century. In the novels of Aluísio *Azevedo, Raul *Pompéia, Inglês de *Sousa, Machado de *Assis, and Henrique *Coelho Neto, it is most often the negative or eccentric aspects of individual and group religious conduct that are brought under examination. Coelho Neto's *Turbilhão* offers another description of a spiritist session, a detail that reappears a few years later in Lima Barreto's *Triste fim de Policarpo Quaresma*. (*See* City and Literature.)

*Symbolism in Brazilian poetry at the turn of the century and into the first quarter of the twentieth century is characterized by a distinctly religious component, specifically in the area of subjective experiential outpouring. In the poetry of Alphonsus de *Guimaraens, the confessed longings to have been born a medieval monk find expression in verses that simultaneously celebrate the Virgin Mary, the poet's departed love, and a desire for Christian mystical union. A less overtly devout, but equally aesthetic, presence of religious sentiment characterizes the poetry of Cruz e *Sousa. Farias Brito (1862–1917) and Jackson de *Figueiredo represent the neo-Catholic movement in the literary essay of the period.

With *modernism, all three areas of religious expression outlined initially may be observed. Personal devotion and subjective metaphyiscal probing are evident in the poets of the literary *review *Festa*, especially Tasso da *Silveira, Augusto Frederico *Schmidt, and Murilo *Mendes, as well as in the verse and prose of Jorge de *Lima, for example, the *Poema do cristão* (1953; Poem of the Christian); the essays of Alceu Amoroso *Lima, and the fiction of João Guimarães *Rosa, especially his *Grande sertão: veredas*. The catechetical-moralistic tradition is revived in the urban fiction of Otávio de *Faria; José Geraldo *Vieira; Cornélio *Pena; the philosophical novel of Gustavo Corção (1896–1978), *Lições de abismo* (1950; *Who If I Cry Out*, 1967); Antônio *Callado; and in the plays of Ariano *Suassuna, most significantly *Auto da compadecida*.

It is the third tendency—the depiction of group religious practices as an integral part of cultural life—that is most noteworthy in twentieth-century Brazilian literature. Since the publication of Euclides da *Cunha's *Os sertões*, the phenomena of messianism and religious syncretism (e.g., *candomblé, macumba, umbanda*) combining elements of Catholicism, African voodoo, spiritism, and indigenous animism within Brazilian culture have become increasingly popular literary themes, especially in works produced in the Northeast. Mário de *Andrade's *Macunaíma* launched this tendency in a whimsical fashion in 1928 after which it was taken up with sociological seriousness by José Lins do *Rego and by Jorge *Amado in most of his novels. Northeastern dramatists Suassuna and Dias *Gomes have incorporated similar elements as both picturesque and problematic. In general, it may be said that popular-group religious expression is treated with greater empathy by contemporary regionalists than by their predecessors, the realist-naturalists of the turn of the century. (*See* Realism; Naturalism; Regionalism.)

In the recent period of dictatorship, priests and missionaries have played an important role in leading protests against repression and torture. Friar Betto (b. 1944) was arrested for his political activities on several occasions between 1964 and 1969; his published short stories about this era in Brazil are striking. In 1986 he interviewed Fidel Castro and *Fidel Castro e a religião* (Fidel Castro and Religion), which was sucesssful throughout Latin America, was published. His first novel, *O dia de Ângelo* (1987; Ângelo's Day), places the roles of prisoners and jailers in debate.

Furthermore, in recent Brazilian literature, there has been a renaissance of the modern Jewish cultural heritage in Brazil. Fiction by Carlos Heitor *Cony, Samuel *Rawet, and Moacir *Scliar are important contributions to the theme. (*See* Immigrants and Literature; New Writers.)

BIBLIOGRAPHY: Criticism: Brownell, Virginia A. "Martyrs, Victims and Gods: A View of Religion in Contemporary Brazilian Drama." *LBR* (Summer, 1978), pp. 129–150; Brownell-Levine, Virginia A. "Religious Syncretism in Contemporary Brazilian Theatre." *LATR* (Summer, 1980), pp. 111–117; Leite, Seraphim, S. J. *História da Companhia de Jesus no Brasil*. 2 vols. Lisbon: Livraria Portugália, 1938; Levine, Robert M. "Brazil's Jews during the Vargas Era and After." *LBR* (June, 1968), pp. 45–58; Martins, Wilson. *História da inteligência brasileira*. 7 vols. São Paulo: Cultrix/Editora da Universidade de São Paulo, 1977–1978; Vieira, Nelson H. "Judaic Fiction in Brazil; To Be or Not to Be." *LALR* (July–December, 1986), pp. 31–45.

MARY L. DANIEL

RESENDE, OTTO LARA (b. 1922; BAL: 1979). A sickly child who was not expected to grow to adulthood, Resende showed scholastic and literary talent at an early age. In Belo Horizonte he collaborated as a critic (*see* Critics and Criticism) on various journals. After receiving a law degree in 1945, he briefly taught Portuguese, French, and history in a high school founded by his father. Upon moving to Rio, he worked as a reporter and editor, eventually becoming managing editor of the magazine *Manchete* in 1956. He served for three years as an attaché for the Brazilian Embassy in Brussels.

During his professional career, Resende has written short stories and one novel, *O braço direito* (1963; *The Inspector of Orphans*, 1968), about the experiences of an orphanage director. He attained considerable recognition in 1957 with the publication of his most famous collection of stories, *Boca do inferno* (Hell's Mouth), which deals with serious crimes involving children and often focuses on events for their shock value. In general, his characters live in a fatalistic world, full of conflict, violence, and totally lacking in affection. Direct or indirect interior monologue is most often used as a technique to present this estrangement.

A notable story is "Viva la patria" (Long Live the Homeland) from his collection *As pompas do mundo* (1975; Ostentations of the World). His caricature of the rise and fall of a self-important Latin-American dictator rivals descriptions of them by the Guatemalan Miguel Ángel Asturias (1899–1974) and the Mexican Carlos Fuentes (b. 1928).

BIBLIOGRAPHY: Additional selected works by Resende: *Poemas necessários*, 1944; *O lado humano*, 1952.

PAUL DIXON

REVIEWS. Journals of original poetry and prose have always played an important role in defining and orienting literary movements imported from abroad, for example, *romanticism, *symbolism, and those that were national products, for example, *modernism and concretism (*see* Postmodernism in Poetry), throughout Brazilian literary history. In addition, many of these journals also published the "manifestoes" and polemics surrounding the birth of the new movement. During the military dictatorship, literary reviews were looked upon as particularly threatening and were closed down by the regime. (*See* Critics and Criticism; Dictatorship and Literature; Parnassianism; Postmodernism in Poetry; Realism.)

BIBLIOGRAPHY: Criticism: Doyle, Plínio. *História de revistas e jornais literários*. Rio: MEC/Casa de Rui Barbosa, 1976.

REY, MARCOS (b. 1925). A journalist and television scriptwriter, Rey's popular, easy-flowing fiction focuses on daily life in his native São Paulo. His most successful novels include *Café na cama* (1960; Breakfast in Bed) and *Memórias de un gigolô* (1968; Memoirs of a Gigolo), both of which have been adapted for film. *A última corrida* (1963; The Last Horse Race) is perhaps the only Brazilian novel to focus on life among São Paulo's horsetrack society. Several of his works possess a superficial sociopolitical angle. Rey has also written *children's literature. (*See* City and Literature; Film and Literature.)

BIBLIOGRAPHY: Additional selected works by Rey: *O enterro da cafetina*, 1967; *Soy loco por ti América*, 1978; *Malditos paulistas*, 1980; *Arca dos marechais*, 1983.

RIBEIRO, DARCY (b. 1922). Anthropologist, educator, and politician, Ribeiro has for the past twenty years been in the forefront of Brazilian intellectual activity, whether as rector of the University of Brasília or minister of education during the Goulart years, as keen observer of indigenous populations and the general social and political development of Brazil and Latin America, as critical voice of conscience during his period of forced exile, or, more recently, as politician and elected public official. (*See* City and Literature; Dictatorship and Literature; Indianism.)

After publishing many well-known anthropological, sociological, and political studies dealing with the lives of Brazil's rapidly diminishing native Americans, Ribeiro made his first incursion into the fictional realms with *Maíra* (1976; *Maíra*, 1983), a novel that, along with Antônio *Callado's *Quarup*, established a critical neo-Indianism as a significant tendency in contemporary Brazilian literature. It is a type of fiction that does not idealize the Indian, as did the nineteenth-century romantics, for example, José de *Alencar and Gonçalves *Dias, or even the 1920s modernists; rather, it attempts to paint a realistic portrait of the Indians' plight, accepting their values as being equally valid to those of mainstream Brazilian society. *Maíra* draws its structure from indigenous myths, legends, and customs, creating a fragmented narrative composed of multiple perspectives to create what has been called the most complete rendering of the current situation of Indians yet accomplished in Brazilian literature. It manages to assume and transmit an indigenous worldview without condescension or paternalism. (*See* Indian Languages; Modernism.)

His second novel, *O mulo* (1982; The Mule), finds its heritage in the confessional forms of Machado de *Assis's *Dom Casmurro*, Graciliano *Ramos's *São Bernardo*, and *João Guimarães Rosa's *Grande sertão: veredas*. Dying of emphysema, the first-person narrator, Philogônio de Castro Maya, writes his confession to his chosen heir, a priest he has never met. In the setting of the rugged and primitive backlands of Goiás, he ponders his multiple identities, his often brutish and animalistic relationships with women, the constitution of power in society, and the nature of sin, will, and human destiny. (*See* Regionalism.)

Philogônio, or the Mulo, who is or at least believes himself to be sterile, carries his ambivalent nature in his various names: *Philogônio* comes from the Greek word *phylogynia*, meaning "fondness for women"; *mulo* is a mule, a sterile cross between a horse and an ass. His confession, set against the backdrop of some fifty years of recent Brazilian history, relays a self-portrait of power in the form of an authoritarian personality.

Ribeiro's most recent novel, or "fable," in the author's words, *Utopia selvagem* (1982; Savage Utopia), uses an indigenous setting to create a satire of contemporary Brazilian society, historical interpretations of Brazil, and political relationships. Rooted in the irreverent humor of Mário de *Andrade's *Macunaíma* and the aggressive irony of Oswald de *Andrade's *antropofagia*, it self-reflexively combines many different modes of literary discourse into an often hilarious, yet always critical, portrait of Brazil and its culture.

BIBLIOGRAPHY: Selected anthropological and sociological works by Ribeiro: *Línguas e culturas indígenas no Brasil*, 1957; *As Américas e a civilização*, 1970 (*The Americas and Civilization*, 1971); *Aos trancos e aos barrancos*, 1985; *Sobre o óbvio*, 1986. Criticism: Galvão, Walnice Nogueira. "Indianismo revisitado." *Esboço de figura: Homenagem a Antônio Cândido*. São Paulo: Duas Cidades, 1979; Morino, Angelo. "L'Eden nella foresta." *LATR* (Winter, 1983), pp. 123–164.

RANDAL JOHNSON

RIBEIRO, JOÃO UBALDO (b. 1940). A well-known journalist and celebrated novelist, Ubaldo Ribeiro, from Bahia, combines a deep nationalistic concern for Brazilian issues with an overt interest in formal artistic experimentation.

Ribeiro's literary career is intertwined with the ups and downs of recent Brazilian history. His first novel *Setembro não tem sentido* (1968; September Makes No Sense) is an introspective, semiautobiographical work *(Künstlerroman)* about young intellectuals searching for an identity in a then still provincial city of Salvador. Although the novel is set before 1964, it reflects the anxiety, insecurity, and hopelessness of Ribeiro's generation as Brazil is about to enter the harshest period of authoritarianism under the military dictatorship, the years 1969–1974. (*See:* Autobiography; Dictatorship and Literature.)

Sargento Getúlio (1971; *Sergeant Getulio*, 1978) and *Vencecavalo e o outro povo* (1974; Vencecavalo and the Other People) are representative of the cultural impasse of the early seventies, when writers and artists often had to resort to allegory, symbolism, and experimental literary techniques to dodge censorship. *Sergeant Getulio* is a rambling monologue by the title character, a cruel gunman for hire, who is capable of the most savage actions against his fellow human beings. Determined to carry out his assignment to capture and bring back one of his boss's political enemies, Getulio refuses to bend even as his boss changes his mind, betrays him, and sends federal troops after him to relieve him of the prisoner. This novel is thematically and formally Ribeiro's most subversive work. When the military government's propaganda aimed to create a sense of national unity and pride, Ribeiro presented a view of Brazil marked by discontinuities and misunderstanding. Moreover, by depicting Getulio's cold-blooded cruelty, the novel explodes the myth of innate Brazilian benevolence while exposing the violence of contemporary Brazilian society, a fact of particular significance at a historical moment when torture had been institutionalized in the nation.

Vencecavalo e outro povo is an iconoclastic satire that treats in a mock-heroic tone a host of "national" issues ranging from government corruption and ineptitude to authoritarianism, colonialism, and dependency; it pokes fun at many aspects of the Brazilian national character. Ribeiro's recent works are representative of the liberalization of the mid–1970s. *Vila Real* (1979; Vila Real) deals openly with a controversial socioeconomic subject—the struggle of backlanders against an all-powerful company—that would have been inconceivable during the repressive years of the military regime. Finally, *Viva o povo brasileiro*

(1984; Long Live the Brazilian People), called an antihistory of Brazil, is a massive work covering more than three centuries of Brazilian history and exploring the sensitive issue of national identity. (*See* Philosophy of National Identity.)

BIBLIOGRAPHY: Additional selected works by Ribeiro: *Livro de historinhas*, 1981; *Política*, 1981; *Vida e paixão de Pandonar, o cruel*, 1983. Translations: *The Massachusetts Review* (December, 1986). Criticism: Silverman, Malcolm. "As distintas facetas de João Ubaldo Ribeiro." *Moderna ficção brasileira 2*. Rio: Civilização Brasileira, 1981, pp. 89–109; Solomon, Barbara Probst. "Dupes of Authority." *NYTBR* (April 9, 1978), p. 11.

LUIZ FERNANDO VALENTE

RIBEIRO, JÚLIO (1845–1890). Ribeiro was the son of an immigrant North American circus performer and a Brazilian schoolteacher from whom he received his early education. Born in Minas, he attended for a time the Military Academy in Rio. He was an active freelance teacher and journalist throughout his life.

Ribeiro's scholarly interest in linguistic and grammatical concerns is revealed in his *Traços gerais da lingüística portuguesa* (1880; A General Outline of Portuguese Linguistics) and *Gramática portuguesa* (1881; Portuguese Grammar). Integral to his journalistic endeavors were his prolific and characteristically polemical contributions to liberal and republican newspapers. He also founded several short-lived papers of his own, all with the same political orientation. (*See* Portuguese Language of Brazil.)

Respected during his lifetime as a free thinker and a combative social critic, Ribeiro had his first novel published in 1876–1877: the romantic, historical, and anti-Jesuitic *O padre Belchior de Pontes* (Father Belchior de Pontes), set against the Emboaba Wars in São Paulo during the early eighteenth century. He would nevertheless receive little attention from literary historians today had he not subsequently written the most overtly shocking novel of his time, *A carne* (1888; Flesh). (*See* Religion and Literature; Romanticism.)

A carne appeared with Ribeiro's dedication to Émile Zola in French, but the most important influence on it is that of Aluísio *Azevedo's *O homem*. An enthusiastic but imperfectly formed convert to *naturalism, Ribeiro attempted to demonstrate in the novel how basic and uncontrollable biological drives—in this case, hysteria and neurosis—determine what a human being does and becomes. He failed, for what he managed to portray amounts merely to his protagonist's sudden, unexplained, and therefore illogical depravity. The sexually explicit details, however, explain the book's immediate and lasting popularity, including its adaptation to film. Furthermore, it is still the most widely read example of what happened during Brazilian naturalism, when the theory underlying the movement gained only incomplete acceptance. (*See* Film and Literature.)

BIBLIOGRAPHY: Additional selected works by Ribeiro: *Cartas sertanejas*, 1883; *Uma polêmcia célebre: discussão com o Padre Sena Freitas*, 1934. Criticism: Brookshaw; Loos; Montello, Josué, In Coutinho, II.

NORWOOD ANDREWS, JR.

RICARDO, CASSIANO   (1895–1974; BAL: 1937). Cassiano Ricardo Leite, from the rural coffee lands of São Paulo, studied law and held several governmental posts in Rio Grande do Sul and São Paulo. He was also a very active member of the *Brazilian Academy of Letters. He wrote both symbolist and Parnassian poetry early on (e.g., *Dentro da noite* (1915; Within the Night), remaining indifferent to early modernist agitation until 1923, when he had contact with Plínio *Salgado's and Menotti del *Picchia's ultranationalistic green-yellowism (*verde-amarelo*) group. (*See* Modernism; Parnassianism; Symbolism.)

In fact, Ricardo became the most important poet of the "Anta revolution," a derivative of "green-yellowism," which rejected all the "isms" from abroad and sought to define Brazil through the Amerindian contribution before the arrival of the Portuguese. In addition to being the editor of the literary *review *Anta*, Ricardo was editor of the review *Novíssima*, which published works by other Latin American poets, including the Argentine Alfonsina Storni and the Uruguayan Juana de Ibarbourou (whose poetry was translated into Portuguese by the *paulista* poet and critic Maria José de Queiroz, in 1961), as well as Blaise Cendrars. (*See* Foreign Writers and Brazil.)

Among his significant publications of the era were *Borrões de verde e amarelo* (1926; Green and Yellow Impressions) and *Vamos caçar papagaios* (1926; Let's Hunt Parrots). Perhaps his most famous work is *Martim Cererê* (1928, definitive edition, 1947; Martim Cererê), which is an Indianist epic but hardly in the romantic tradition of Gonçalves de *Magalhães or Gonçalves *Dias. It is an epic about a "race of Indian giants," the forebears of his contemporary *paulistas*: "Because it was an island they gave it the name / Island of the True Cross / Island of great charm / Island of many birds / Islands of much light." The work is often considered the poetical equivalent of Mário de *Andrade's *Macunaíma*. (*See* Indianism; Romanticism.)

In the mid-1940s Ricardo turned to more introspective themes in his poetry, for example, *Um dia depois do outro* (1947; One Day after Another). He gradually turned to forms then being popularized by the members of the Generation of 1945 and the concretists (*see* Postmodernism in Poetry), as well as social questions as in his *O arranha-céu de vidro* (1956; The Glass Skyscraper) and in his final collection, *Jeremias Sem-Chorar* (1964; Jeremiah No-Crying). Several critics cited "A canção mais recente" (The Most Recent Poem) as one of his finest works: "The poet / with his magic lantern / is always / at the beginning of things. / He's like water / eternally early rising."

BIBLIOGRAPHY: Additional selected works by Ricardo: *Evangelho de Pã*, 1917; *Canções de minha ternura*, 1930; *João Torto e a fábula*, 1956; *Montanha russa*, 1960. Translations: Bishop/Brasil; Hulet; Tolman (1978); Woodbridge. Criticism: Brookshaw; Foster/Foster, II.

RIO, JOÃO DO   [pseudonym of PAULO BARRETO] (1881–1921; BAL: 1910). João do Rio was the most important and characteristic *carioca* journalist of the early part of the twentieth century. Although he wrote a novel, a play, and some stories, his most important works are his *crônicas*, in which his sheer inquisitiveness and powers of observation counteract his superficiality. (*See* Theater History.)

Rio became famous with his series of *crônicas* published under the title *As religiões do Rio* (1900; The Religions of Rio). In them, he attempted to give a view of all minority religions of the time, not only African religions (which he was one of the first to document) but positivism, evangelical protestantism, spiritualism, and so on. This is one of the most insightful books about Rio of the time. (*See* City and Literature; Positivism and Literature; Regionalism; Religion and Literature.)

Rio was the center of much of the literary life of the national capital and conducted a series of interviews collected in *O momento literário* (1905; The Literary Moment), which are a vital source for those wishing to understand the period. He was highly successful in this world, being elected a member of the *Brazilian Academy of Letters at the age of only twenty-nine. However, Rio was not without enemies: he was homosexual, and the venom of certain comments on his personality may have to do with that fact (''perversity'' is a common accusation). Others, however, view him as a lively, kind, witty conversationalist. (*See* Homosexuality and Literature.)

Forgotten for many years after his death, Rio's work was brought back to attention by the brilliant literary critic (*see* Critics and Criticism) and historian Brito Broca in his book *1900: a vida literária no Brasil* (1960; 1900: Literary Life in Brazil).

BIBLIOGRAPHY: Additional selected works by Rio: *A alma encantadora das nuas*, 1908; *Dentro da noite*, 1910; *Psicologia urbana*, 1911. Criticism: Broca, Brito. *1900: a vida literária no Brasil*. Rio: José Olympio, 1960; Brookshaw; Martins, Luís. ''Introdução.'' *João do Rio: uma antologia*. Rio: Sabiá, 1970.

JOHN GLEDSON

RODRIGUES, NELSON (1913–1980). One of the most popular and most polemical figures of Brazilian culture of the twentieth century, Rodrigues achieved fame in several areas: from soccer journalism and drama to fiction, *crônicas, and *memoirs. In all, he was outspoken and completely indifferent to criticism of his writings, which often included the term *illiterate*. (See Soccer and Literature.)

Rodrigues was the first Brazilian dramatist to bring the life-style of the lower bourgeoisie to the stage; thus he is a precursor to the theater of Plínio *Marcos, Oduvaldo *Viana Filho, and others. He always dealt with issues associated with this class—machismo, prostitution, the no-exit situation from poverty, sexual violence and aberrations, racial conflicts, abortion, incest—from a somewhat Freudian perspective. The critic Sábato Malgadi (*see* Critics and Criticism) has divided Rodrigues's dramas into three groups—psychological dramas, mythic dramas, and *carioca* tragedies—although in reality all of the dramas are set in Rio and its poor suburbs. (*See* Theater History.)

Rodrigues's first successful play was *Vestido de noiva* (1943; *The Wedding*

Dress, 1980); it was the most important contribution to Brazilian theater following Joracy *Camargo's *Deus lhe pague*. Unlike the latter, however, Rodrigues's
play was infinitely superior owing to the complexity of narrative levels—the
past, the present, and the realm of hallucinations—as well as to the splendid
direction of the then recent immigrant director Zbigniew Ziembinski. The plays
included by Sábato Magaldi in the *"carioca* tragedies" are among Rodrigues's
most popular. *A falecida* (1953; The Dead Woman) is set in a Rio shantytown
(*favela*). Toninho lives only for his soccer matches, while his wife, Zulmira,
looks for distraction in extramarital affairs. When she falls ill, she prepares an
elegant funeral for herself, which she is never to enjoy. *Boca de ouro* (1960;
Mouth of Gold) was another great success for Rodrigues. In it, he narrated the
life and death of an important neighborhood politican and gambler, whose teeth
were made of gold. In *O beijo no asfalto* (1961; A Kiss on the Pavement) a man
is accused by "society" of homosexuality because of an act of charity to a dying
man. *Toda nudez será castigada* (1965; All Nudity Will Be Punished) presents
a widower who decides to marry a prostitute. *Os sete gatinhos* (1966; The Seven
Little Cats) describes the destruction of a family at the subsistence level of
existence. A final drama, *O anti-Nelson Rodrigues* (1974; The Anti-Nelson
Rodrigues), lacks the biting social commentaries and attacks of earlier works
and instead presents pure, honest love as a redeeming feature of man's existence.
The director Antunes Filho presented an interesting Jungian interpretation of this
work. (*See* Homosexuality and Literature.)

   In 1949 Rodrigues described his intention to write "pestilant, fetid works,
capable, by themselves, of producing typhus and malaria in the audience."
Comments on human smells—body odors; bad breath; the smell of death, blood,
and feces—were a principal part of this technique. He further believed that his
characters were "monsters," whose violation of the morals of daily existence
were natural acts. During the military regime, many of his plays were targets
of the censors, not due to any political statements but rather because of their
open treatment of sexual matters. Ironically, it was during the military years
that many of his plays were adapted for successful films, for example, *Toda
nudez será castigada* and *O beijo no asfalto*. Rodrigues had originally set out
to be a novelist and had several works published under a female pseudonym,
Suzana Flag.

   He also had several volumes of "libelous" memoirs published about his own
life and the lives of his contemporaries. The "truth" about his life was the
subject of a biography of him published by his sister, Stella. (*See* Dictatorship
and Literature.)

   BIBLIOGRAPHY: Additional selected works by Rodrigues: *Teatro completo*. Organized and introduced by Sábato Malgadi. 4 vols. Criticism: Clark, Fred M. "Introduction." *The Wedding Dress* by Nelson Rodrigues. Valencia: Albatross/Hispanófila,
1980; Johnson, Randal. "Nelson Rodrigues as Filmed by Arnaldo Jabor." *LATR* (Fall,
1982), pp. 15–28.

ROMANTICISM. Romanticism in Western culture emerged in response to the Enlightenment's (*see* Arcadias) emphasis on reason and order and to the aesthetic rigidity of neoclassicism (*see* Arcadias), which dominated the eighteenth century. In all areas, romanticism placed greater value on emotion, imagination, and freedom. Romantic art often portrayed nature in careful (almost realistic) detail but also conveyed its mystery and power and man's emotional interaction with it. (*See* Art and Literature.)

In literature, romanticism produced important thematic and formal changes. The greatest transformation came in lyric poetry, where ideas of individual genius and creative imagination find their full expression. Major poets of European romanticism include William Blake (1757–1827), William Wordsworth (1770–1850), Samuel Taylor Coleridge (1772–1834), Percy Bysshe Shelley (1792–1822), John Keats (1795–1821), and Lord Byron (1788–1824) in England; Friedrich Hölderlin (1770–1843) and Friedrich Novalis (1772–1801) in Germany; and Alphonse Lamartine (1790–1869), Victor Hugo (1802–1885), and Alfred Vigny (1797–1863) in France. Developments in romantic narrative took two major forms. Jean-Jacques Rousseau's (1712–1778) *Confessions* provided an important model for the confessional novel, a pseudoautobiographical account of an individual's experiences and emotions. Influential examples of this form included Goethe's (1749–1832) *The Sorrows of Young Werther* (1774) and Vicomte Chateaubriand's (1768–1848) *Atalá* (1801) and *René* (1805). Romanticism's interest in past life and literature produced the historical novel, best exemplified by Sir Walter Scott's (1771–1832) detailed and dramatic episodes from Scottish history. The romantic contribution to drama is relatively slight; the popular, but hackneyed, theater of melodrama remains the predominant form of this time. In France, however, romantic drama did successfully challenge the neoclassical restrictions that had dominated theater for so long.

In Brazil, romanticism began substantially later than in Europe. The accepted dates for its aesthetic reign are 1830–1870, but in some sense it dominated the remainder of the nineteenth century. For Brazilian romantic literature, the elements of nationalism and primitivism, the emphasis on the local and the popular, and the thematic and formal innovations in Western European romanticism are especially important. Yet the fact that Brazil so readily absorbed these new ideas points to another significant context for the movement in America. Romanticism in Brazil was the art of a newly independent (1822) nation, which began to turn away from Portuguese cultural influences to the ideas and literary models of England and, above all, France. Brazilian writers found in European romanticism an energy and inspiration that, matching their own, enabled them to emerge from the moribund forms of arcadianism and neoclassicism and to begin to create their own national literature, through innovation and experiment. (*See* Portugal and Brazil: Literary Relations.)

Certain critics (*see* Critics and Criticism) have identified writers of a period of transition from neoclassicism to romanticism in the poetry of the late eighteenth-century and early nineteenth-century Brazil, such as the members of the *Minas School, for example, Tomás Antônio Gonzaga, in Domingos Borges de Barros's (1779–1885) *Poesias oferecidas às senhoras brasileiras por um baiano* (1825; Poems Offered to Brazilian Women by a Bahian); the poetry of José Bonifácio de Andrada e *Silva or Natividade Saldanha (1795–1830); the sermons of Friar Monte *Alverne; the collection of maxims by the Marquis of Maricá (1773–1848), *Máximos, pensamentos e reflexos* (complete edition, 1958; Maxims, Thoughts and Reflections), in the style of La Rochefoucauld. More relevant, however, to the movement that eventually emerged are other less specifically literary developments in this period. The French critic of Portuguese literature Ferdinand Denis (*see* Travel Literature) in his *Résumé de l'Histoire littéraire du Portugal et du Brésil* (1826; Summary of Portuguese and Brazilian Literary History) and in his *Scénes de la nature sous les tropiques* (1824; Scenes of Nature in the Tropics), and the Portuguese Almeida Garrett in his introduction to an anthology of poetry in Portuguese, *Parnaso lusitano* (1826–1827; Lusitanian Parnassus), both wrote in glowing terms of Brazilian poetry and its potential for yet greater glory. Indeed, as one of the first romantic writers in Portuguese, Garrett remains a major influence for Brazilian romanticism. In 1833 The Philomathic Society was organized at the law school in São Paulo with a goal of fostering the development of Brazilian culture and civilization. All of these elements contributed to set the scene for romanticism in Brazil.

However, the preromantic movement did not definitively emerge until the mid-1830s. In 1834 three Brazilians, Gonçalves de *Magalhães, Francisco de Salles Torres Homen (1812–1876), and Araújo Porto *Alegre, delivered lectures at the Historical Institute of France in Paris. Each discussed a different aspect of Brazilian culture: Gonçalves de Magalhães spoke on literature, Torres Homem on science, and Porto Alegre on the fine arts. Each emphasized the repression of Brazilian culture during the country's colonial period and the great possibilities for a new, truly national development. This was a key episode for the beginning of Brazilian romanticism.

In 1836 these same writers helped to found the *review *Niterói: Revista Brasiliense*, which carried the slogan "Tudo pelo Brasil and para o Brasil" (Everything in behalf of Brazil and for Brazil) and which was a major vehicle of the new movement's ideas of national progress and renewal. Only two (albeit sizable) issues of *Niterói* appeared; yet they contained important articles on Brazilian culture and society. Also in 1836, Gonçalves de Magalhães's volume of verse *Suspiros poéticos e saudades* was published; its title suggests the themes that make it one of the first Brazilian romantic works. By the 1840s romanticism had achieved the literary dominance it was to retain until at least 1870. The *review *Minerva Brasiliense*, which appeared from 1843 to 1845, was another important forum for its literature and nationalist ideas, which helped consolidate romanticism's position. Two other important reviews of romanticism were *Guanabara* (1850–1855) and *Revista Brasileira* (1857–1860, first phase).

The following general tendencies characterize Brazilian romanticism, although not all appear, or appear in the same way, in its many works.

Much romantic literature reveals a strong nationalist impulse. The movement emerged as a young Brazil sought to define its own identity and establish national institutions. Other cultural events of the 1830s were inspired by aims similar to those of the incipient romantic writers. The actor João Caetano dos Santos founded the National Dramatic Company in 1833 and the National Theatre in 1834. In 1839 the Brazilian Historical and Geographical Institute was created. With romanticism, the critically conscious search for truly Brazilian literary themes and forms began in earnest. (*See* Historiography; Theater History.)

Linked to this nationalist tendency is an interest in local geography—in Brazil's cities and countryside. Even as they have adapted European literary models, Brazilian writers have chosen Brazilian settings. For example, in his historical novels José de *Alencar incorporated Brazil's past and landscape. Writers often portrayed Brazilian surroundings in copious and accurate detail; these more realistic notes prefigure the eventual transition from romanticism to *realism and *naturalism.

The exploration of nature is a frequent theme in Brazilian romantic literature. Writers aspired both to catalogue, in nearly scientific description, the riches of Brazil's landscape and, in more emotional terms, to capture its unique beauty, mystery, and power.

*Indianism is another important topic related to romanticism's nationalist impulse. The romantics exalted the inherent nobility, strength, and artistic sensibility of the Indians. In this figure, they sought a Brazilian legendary and historical past, equal to that of Europe. They also saw the Indian as Brazil's first poet and frequently incorporated indigenous myths and tales into their own works. They made the Indian the hero of their own dramas of the origins of a nation.

The moving portrait of the Indian as a heroic but somehow solitary and even tragic figure (in Alencar's *Iracema*, for example) points to another romantic tendency: this is a literature of emotion and sentiment, which focuses on the inner drama—or melodrama—of the individual. Examples of this concern range from the introspective and melancholy poetry of an Alvares de *Azevedo to the psychological studies of Alencar's urban novels.

Yet Brazilian romanticism also has an important political and social dimension; indeed, the same rhetoric that expounds the dramas of the individual expresses more public concerns. In general, the movement is allied with political liberalism. Many romantic works, such as the abolitionist poetry of Castro *Alves, voice direct social criticism. (*See* Slavery and Literature.)

The literature of Brazilian romanticism is characterized also by formal innovation, as well as by these thematic elements. Critic Afrânio Coutinho (*see* Critics and Criticism) described Brazilian writers' experiments with the epic poem (e.g., *A confederação dos tamoios* by Gonçalves de Magalhães) and the novelistic poem (e.g., *O conde Lopo* by Álvares de Azevedo); he also catalogued their innovations in verse forms and meters.

In addition to having a creative activity, Brazilian romanticism had an important critical and scholarly component: there was great interest in the new nation's literary historiography. Indeed, one could state that literary studies in Brazil effectively began with this movement, as the volumes of critical essays and articles seem to match that of poetry, drama, and narrative. Gonçalves de Magalhães's initial lecture in Paris (later published in *Niterpói*) was titled "On the History of Literature in Brazil." Other examples are works by Santiago Nunes Ribeiro (?–1847); Joaquim Norberto de Sousa de Silva (1820–1891), who was involved in a polemic with Gonçalves *Dias about the chance discovery of Brazil, and who was also a novelist and dramatist; and Antônio Macedo Soares (1838–1905). José de Alencar and Machado de *Assis also produced important statements on the problem of a national literature. These critical writings covered not only current literature but also past works. Finally, the problem of a Brazilian literary identity is also a problem of a truly Brazilian Portuguese language. Philology, orthography, and grammatical correctness are of passionate interest to writers such as Alencar. (*See* Critics and Criticism; Indian Languages; Philosophy of National Identity; Portuguese Language of Brazil.)

Scholars writing on Brazilian romanticism frequently divide its vast cast of writers into generations and assign each generation distinctive concerns and characteristics. Aside from the already-mentioned preromantic generation, the first romantic generation's major figures include Joaquim Manuel de *Macedo, Alencar, and Gonçalves Dias, writing under the influence of James Fenimore Cooper (1789–1851), Sir Walter Scott, and Eugène Sue (1804–1857), with a concern for Indianism and the Brazilian natural setting. A second romantic generation's major figures include Manuel Antônio de *Almeida, Álvares de Azevedo, Casimiro de *Abreu, Junqueira *Freire, and Fagundes *Varela, writing under the influence of Lord Byron, Alfred de Musset (1810–1857), and Alphonse Lamartine, in which individualism and subjectivity predominate. A third romantic generation's major figures include Castro Alves, Franklin Távora, and Luís Delfino dos Santos (*see* Parnanssianism), writing under the influence of Victor Hugo and *condorism, with more political and social interests. Furthermore, Afrânio Coutinho described the period from 1845 to 1865 as "ultraromantic." It is marked by a heightened individualism and a near "exacerbation of sentiment and passion."

Lesser-known poets of the transitional phase between neoclassicism and romanticism include Odorico Mendes (1799–1864), a notable translator of Greco-Latin classics, whose sparse original works reflect neoclassicism's limits; Maciel Monteiro (1804–1868), who was in Paris at the publication of *Niterói* but was not related to Gonçalves de Magalhães's group; Elói Otoni (1764–1851), who had been involved in the *Mineiran Conspiracy and went into exile in Portugal, where he was associated with neoclassic poets and was primarily influenced by the Portuguese poet Bocage (1765–1805); Lucas José de Alvarenga (1768–1831); Dutra e Melo (1823–1846); and Januário da Cunha Barbosa (1780–1846), who prepared anthologies of early Brazilian poets and was cofounder of the Brazilian Historical and Geographical Institute.

Other partially forgotten poets of the romantic generations include Francisco Otaviano (1825–1889), an eminent statesman of the empire and a Byronic poet; Laurindo Rabelo (1826–1894), often called an ultraromantic, whose poetry was notably confessional and patriotic with condorist overtones and, in his last phase, satiric, for example, *Trovas* (1853; Poems) and *Livres* (1882; Free Poems); Aureliano Lessa (1828–1861), who was associated with Bernardo *Guimarães and Álvares de Azevedo in the Epicurean Society at the University of São Paulo and was a translator of Byron, whom he imitated in his own verse; Agrário de Meneses (1834–1863), a Bahian who was a Bryonic poet and a popular dramatist of local customs; Pedro Luís (1839–1884), who was a politican and condorist poet; and Bruno Seabra (1837–1876) and Joaquim Serra (1838–1888), who were from the Northeast and developed regional themes, including poetry on the black condition and slavery. Other now forgotten poets who were popular during their lifetimes include Luís Guimarães, Jr. (1845–1898; BAL: 1897), and the very late romantic Augusto de Lima (1859–1934; BAL: 1903). Machado de *Assis should also be mentioned among the romantic poets. There remains one major, if controversial, figure of Brazilian romanticism: Joaquim de Sousa Andrade, or *Sousândrade, who defies classification with any of the "groups." (*See* Regionalism.)

Brazil's first novels were produced during romanticism. In this genre, too, we find the attempt to portray the Brazilian landscape and society: urban, rural, and tribal. Critics generally dismiss the early mediocre attempts at novels or novelettes of João Manuel Pereira da Silva (1819–1898; BAL: 1897), for example, *O aniversário de D. Miguel em 1818* (1839; Dom Miguel's 1818 Birthday); and Justiniano José da Rocha (1812–1862), for example, *Os assassínios misteriosos ou a Paixão dos diamantes* (1839; The Mysterious Assassinations or the Passion for Diamonds). Rather, they identify *O filho do pescador* (1843) by Teixeira e *Sousa as Brazil's first important novel: on its title page, the work carries the designation *romance brasileiro* (Brazilian novel), as do many of Alencar's novels. In 1844 Macedo published the sentimental, but very readable, *A moreninha*. In contrast to Macedo's banal, artificial accounts of upper-class *carioca* society, Manuel Antônio de *Almeida's *Memórias de um sargento de milícas* is a vivid, satiric portrait of lower-class life in colonial Rio. Yet despite their different styles and subjects, both Macedo and Almeida assumed the task—as did Alencar—of depicting the Brazilian reality. Alencar used different forms to capture the many facets of Brazilian life: historical novels, Indianist novels, frontier novels of the *sertão*, as well as urban novels, rich in psychological portraiture of women. Other important romantic novelists included Bernardo *Guimarães, who experimented with the historical novel and the novel of the *sertão* of Minas, although he became best known for his antislavery novel *A escrava Isaura*. Franklin Távora and the Viscount de *Taunay are romantic regionalist novelists, in whose works critics have detected the elements of *realism. Finally, despite their relative restraint in plot and rhetoric, the early novels of Machado de Assis, for example, *A mão e a luva* and *Helena*, can be considered romantic works. (*See* Regionalism.)

In a way Brazilian theater, too, is a product of the romantic period. From the 1830s onward, the nation's new acting companies staged both European and Brazilian works. The Dramatic Conservatory, founded in 1843, further enlivened theatrical activity. In the works of the period's major dramatist Martins *Pena, we find examples of the two main forms of Brazilian romantic drama: the historical drama (e.g., *D. Leonor Teles, Vitiza ou O Nero de Espanha*) and the extremely popular light treatment of urban or rural life (e.g., *O juiz de paz na roça* and *O judas em sábado de aleluia*). Writers such as Gonçalves Dias and Alencar also wrote dramas and comedies. (*See* Theater History.)

Romanticism is a stimulating period of literary activity in Brazil. Yet the quality of romantic literature is uneven. In poetry, Gonçalves Dias, Castro Alves, Sousândrade, and a few others produced thematically and formally original works; however, much Brazilian romantic poetry is derivative, banal, and melodramatic. In fiction, Manuel Antônio de Almeida's single work and Alencar's ongoing "research" in many different novelistic areas stand out. Still, romanticism's literary achievement is not limited to the works of the period but is significant for all later Brazilian literature. Several major authors—among them Machado de Assis— first worked within its aesthetic tendencies and then took its forms as a point of departure for their own experiments. The Brazilian vanguardist movements, *modernism and concretism (*see* Postmodernism in Poetry), make a critique of romanticism's concept of art and literary nationalism part of their own programs. It is a reminder of romanticism's enduring importance that they have felt compelled to define themselves against it. Because of its handful of gifted writers, and the vitality of its literary projects and ideas, the legacy of romanticism for Brazilian literature is considerable.

BIBLIOGRAPHY: Criticism: Coutinho, II; Coutinho/Rabassa; Cunha, Fausto. *O romantismo no Brasil de Castro Alves a Sousândrade*. Rio: Paz e Terra, 1971. Hazard, Paul. "Les origines du Romantisme au Brésil." *RLC* 7 (1927), pp. 111–28.

MARÍA TAI WOLFF

ROMERO, SÍLVIO (1851–1914; BAL: 1897). Born on a plantation in Sergipe, Romero studied law in Recife. Throughout his life, he insisted on the great formative influence upon him of his classmate Tobias Barreto de Meneses (*see* Recife School), whom he extolled as one of Brazil's leading philosophers.

Settling in Rio in 1879, Romero published his own poetry, which he himself praised and classified as belonging to a "scientific" school, owing to his use of "scientific" words and metaphors: *Cantos do fim do século* (1879; Poems of the Century's End). Machado de *Assis, commenting upon his poetry, wrote that although poetic ideas appear in his works, they were not poems. Romero also began a series of critical studies of Brazilian culture, which ranged from literary history through folklore, the contemporary political scene, national history, and ethnological studies, as well as *memoirs. In addition, he was a university professor, a federal legislator, and a founding member of the *Brazilian Academy of Letters. (*See* Folklore and Literature; Historiography.)

Polemical is the adjective that best characterizes Romero's personal relationships and critical writings. He lurched from one critical extreme to its exact opposite, defending each one with vigor; he would characterize a writer as exceptional on one occasion only later to rank him as mediocre. Nonetheless, in spite of this fickleness and the lack of artistic sensibility, which many critics commented upon, Romero did introduce a sociopolitical orientation into Brazilian literary criticism.

In 1873 he attacked *romanticism, particularly *Indianism, as an "idealized lie" about the Brazilian reality. Although he stressed that the African influence made Brazilian culture unique, he was unable to see beyond contemporary racial and social prejudices to evaluate fairly the works of literature rather than the racial background of the writer. This difficulty led to highly subjective analyses and, consequently, bitter personal enmities.

Among his voluminous works, his *História da literatura brasileira* (2 vols., 1888; History of Brazilian Literature) is most notable. In reality a compilation of many of his earlier studies, the first volume offers significant generalizations about Brazilian culture and literature, and the second volume, considered much inferior by critics, has analyses of individual literary personalities from colonial figures to his contemporaries based on how well each presented the "genius, character, and spirit" of the Brazilian people. In his *Da crítica e sua exata definição* (1909; On Criticism and its Exact Definition), he reflected on the origin of his critical theory based on "applied logic."

Perhaps the best prepared and most widely read of his generation of critics, which included José *Veríssimo and Araripe Júnior (*see* Critics and Criticism), Romero's recognitions of the importance of *regionalism and miscegenation in Brazilian culture were major contributions, which directly influenced Gilberto *Freyre and other later writers.

BIBLIOGRAPHY: Additional selected works by Romero: *Ensayos literarios*. Caracas: Ayacucho, 1982. Criticism: Brookshaw; Eakin, Marshall C. "Race and Identity: Sílvio Romero, Science, and Social Thought in Late Nineteenth-Century Brazil." *LBR* (Winter, 1985), pp. 151–174; MacNicoll, Murray Graeme. "Sílvio Romero and Machado de Assis: A One-Sided Rivalry (1870–1914)." *RIB* 31(1981), pp. 366–377; Sayers.

ROSA, JOÃO GUIMARÃES (1908–1967; BAL: 1963). Born in Cordisburgo, a rural town in central Minas, Rosa revealed a precocious ability with language. His insatiable linguistic interest was soon accompanied by a fascination for the study of geography and the natural sciences, especially botany and zoology. While a medical student, he published his first short stories.

As a doctor Rosa served a large rural population in the area west of Belo Horizonte for two years, after which he became a volunteer and later a medical officer in the army. During this period he mastered several foreign languages in addition to those learned in childhood and published more stories and poetry.

A collection of his verses, *Magma* (Magma), won the poetry *prize of the *Brazilian Academy of Letters in 1937 but was never published. In 1934 Rosa passed the Foreign Service Examination and entered the Ministry of Foreign Affairs. In 1938 he was named vice-consul in Hamburg, Germany. In 1942, when Brazil broke relations with that country, he was imprisoned for several months in Baden-Baden with other members of the diplomatic corps. Upon his release, he served as secretary of the Brazilian Embassy in Bogotá until 1944, when he returned to Brazil to become head of the Documentation Service of the Ministry of Foreign Affairs. Several of the stories he had written but not published in the late 1930s were gathered together under the title *Sagarana* (1946; *Sagarana*, 1966). In the same year, 1946, he was named secretary of the Brazilian delegation to the Paris Peace Conference. After directing several other very distinguished Brazilian international commissions, he returned to Rio as cabinet chief of the Ministry of Foreign Affairs in 1951, and in 1958 he was promoted to minister first class, with the rank of ambassador.

His literary production had increased in intensity during the mid-1950s. In 1956 he had two of his most ambitious works of fiction published: the novelettes *Corpo de baile* (Dance Corps) and *Grande sertão: veredas* (*The Devil to Pay in the Backlands*, 1963). His collected works received the Brazilian Academy of Letters award in 1961, and in 1962, while serving as chief of the Borders Division of the Ministry of Foreign Affairs, he had yet another volume of short stories published: *Primeiras estórias* (1962; *The Third Bank of the River and Other Stories*, 1968). He had a volume of very short stories and essaylike "prefaces" published under the title *Tutaméia* (1967; Tutameia), and in November of that year he was formally installed in the Brazilian Academy of Letters, to which he had been unanimously elected in 1963. Three days later he died. Rosa left a number of short stories, poems, and bits of fiction in systematic order for publication; they appeared in two posthumous volumes, *Estas estórias* (1969; These Stories) and *Ave, palavra* (1970; Bird, Word).

The publication of Rosa's first collection of stories, *Sagarana*, in 1946, had an explosive effect upon the Brazilian literary scene, which had comfortably adapted itself to a decade and a half of regionalist fiction based on a pictoric reproduction of rural life, use of quaint or ethnically based dialects to imitate the oral Portuguese of urban or rural popular classes, and an easily digested theoretical base of historical, political, or socioeconomic interpretation of the realities of Brazilian regional life. Rosa flouted all of the stereotypes of region-alistic fiction while obviously writing about the familiar realities treated in the works of *social novelists of the 1930s and after, who had established the paradigms of what was assumed to be twentieth-century *regionalism. Mário de *Andrade was the only literary precedent to Rosa obvious to critics. (*See* Critics and Criticism.) In his *Macunaíma* Andrade had undertaken an iconoclastic re-working of Brazilian literary language and interpretation of what might be con-sidered as "national" or "regional" life and character. (*See* City and Literature; Portuguese Language of Brazil.)

Because Rosa was a polyglot and well read in numerous foreign literatures, literary analysts began to seek parallels with what writers of certain of those literatures (particularly Anglo-American) had achieved: Rosa was likened to Melville because of his sensitive treatment of the inner-outer world and was called the "James Joyce of the Portuguese language" because of his linguistic innovations, which included widespread lexical borrowings from ancient and modern languages, the creation of neologisms, syntatic inversions, a unique "telegraphic syntax," and the consistent use of an orally based style of story-telling possessing medieval and archetypal qualities. Still other critics preferred to see him as a *sui generis* kind of writer: a "universal regionalist" or "surre-gionalist." Such terms might convey the impact of fiction whose thematic content and physical context involved almost exclusively the remote *sertão*, but which is pervaded by a metaphysical awareness resulting in high dramas of conscience and theological inquiry.

Once the initial responses of awe, puzzlement, desperation, and excitement among both lay readers and professional critics had been expressed—and they were reiterated upon the publication of each of the author's subsequent books—the first tentative steps were taken to analyze his prose.

Sagarana consists of nine short stories all set in the backlands of Minas. The protagonists include a small donkey, a wayward husband, two lifelong friends dying of malaria, a pair of vengeful males in a love triangle, chess-playing friends in a slow-moving courtship, a witch doctor and his taunting "educated" neighbor, a town bully, and the timid rival who turns the tables with the help of a spell, talking oxen, and a bully-turned-saint. The work presents the people, animals, landscapes, diversions, tensions, and problems of the backlands in a colorful and sympathetic manner. Furthermore, it reveals Rosa's profound absorption with this subject matter and his empathy for the characters he has created or depicted from among his gallery of childhood and adult acquaintances.

Corpo do baile is comprised of seven novelettes of varying length. Beginning with the third edition (1965), it was subdivided into three smaller volumes. Whereas the stories in *Sagarana* are mutually independent of one another, a certain interrelationship exists among several of the novelettes in this collection, principally with regard to a number of their protagonists, whose careers may be followed in sketchy fashion through the sequence. *Corpo de baile* offers the richest autobiographical base of the author's works (with the possible exception of the four "prefaces" of *Tutaméia*). Special mention deserves to be made of the author's extraordinary talent in creating the world of childhood as interpreted by a child's nonjudgmental mind in terms adult readers will recognize and understand. Rosa's psychological insight is revealed in his treatment of the fantasies, superstitions, fears, forebodings, erotic urges, suspense, and tenderness that surface in the collection and the oneiric, surrealist atmosphere that dominates at least half of the work. (*See*: Autogiobraphy; Children's Literature; Surrealism.)

The Devil to Pay in the Backlands, a 600-page novel uninterrupted by chapter divisions and constructed as a first-person monologue, is considered Rosa's masterpiece, and in the year of its publication, 1956, it was awarded the Machado de *Assis Prize. (*See* Prizes.) Its nuclear thematic problem is the ostensible pact made by Riobaldo (the narrator of the story), a backlands bandit chieftain (*jagunço*), with the Devil in order to kill a rival leader, Hermógenes, and vindicate the death of the honored chief Juca Ramiro. The work brings together in forceful fashion a complex of concepts regarding the existence of God and the Devil, the role of destiny in human behavior (i.e., is life guided by chance or predestination), the nature of courage, and the essence of male-female relationships.

In the external elements of description of the landscape, fauna, and flora of Minas and narration of the everyday life of an outlaw band of the backlands, the novel might well be subtitled "the Life of Riobaldo the *jagunço*" and classified as a Brazilian epic. It has been recognized as such by both critics and the reading public, for in addition to including the incidental details of regional living, it possesses the key element of a *chanson de geste* (e.g., the theme of honor, the hero inspired by thoughts of his absent love to accomplish notable feats, the homogenous action of a heterogenous group under the inspiration of a great leader, the appearance of a traitor, the democratic trial and sentencing of a brave fighter from a rival force, the purifying or toughening effect of a series of trials on the protagonists, the interpolation within the main narrative of a number of unrelated stories recounted for entertainment or for moralist purposes, the disguise of the female warrior as a male for the achievement of intimate personal goals, and the linear plot structured on the framework of a chivalric journey or *demanda*). The novel also evidences an allegorical or archetypal intent, revealed in aspects such as the parallelism of the villain Hermógenes with the Devil, the sexually enigmatic Diadorim (also called Reinaldo or Menino) with the Guardian Angel, and Riobaldo with Everyman. The work is a gold mine of theological and metaphorical concerns and has been the focus of most of the analytical comment on the author's works to date.

The Third Bank of the River and Other Stories signaled, in 1962, Rosa's return to the genre of short fiction, a preference he was to cultivate for the remainder of his life. The twenty-one stories of this collection are considerably shorter than those contained in *Sagarana* but would yet be exceeded in brevity by the minute narratives of *Tutaméia*. The varied tales of the 1962 collection are independent of one another with the exception of the first and last, which form a chronological pair with the same protagonists. The majority are structured around what may be called "epiphanies" in the lives of children and other "marginal" or relatively powerless members of society. A general glow of gentle optimism suffuses the work, in which the elements of serenity and puckish humor are not infrequent.

The forty brief "anecdotes of abstraction" comprising *Tutaméia* (subtitled "Third Tales") are arranged in alphabetical order by title (with the exception of the three given in order of the author's initials: J-G-R) and interspersed with four longer essays called "prefaces." One of them "Vermicelli and Hermeneutics," presents Rosa's definition of an *estória* (tale) and concept of figurative imagination and language; another essay, "Hipotrelicod," offers a rationale for neologisms in speech and writing; yet another, "About the Broom and Doubt," gives personal glimpses into Rosa's sources of inspiration and perspective on the essence of life. In fact, in his earliest published volume, *Sagarana*, he had interpolated in the middle of a fast-paced story ("Saint Mark") a meditation on the renewal of language and the function of neologisms, announcing the very techniques he would employ in later works. Now, in the last book published in his lifetime, he coincidentally explained and justified the most quintessentially "Rosean" of the techniques employed throughout his literary career.

The two volumes of Rosa's works published posthumously—*Estas estórias* and *Ave, palavra*—lack the cohesion of the books published during his lifetime, although the first of the two was at least partially prepared under his supervision. In terms of general character and balance, *Estas estórias* may be considered a kind of "equal opposite" to *Sagarana*, containing an identical number of stories—nine—of nearly the same length. However, several of them depart from the ambience of the *sertão* to include a trip to an Andean country and a visit to the northeastern coastal area of Brazil. The narratives of *Estas estórias*, nonetheless, echo the thematic and stylistic-linguistic density of *Sagarana*.

Ave, palavra is a miscellanea of miniessays, narratives, and poems, totaling some fifty-five separate entries that range from vignettes of zoos in Germany, Italy, France, and Brazil to glimpses of life in diverse urban surroundings and in remote Brazilian border areas, couched predominantly in the style of memoirs. This work, more than any other in the author's production, reflects his cosmopolitan diplomatic career and sense of belonging in the greater "international neighborhood."

A sequential chronological survey of Rosa's fiction seems to reveal a tendency toward increasing abstraction and decreasing orality over the thirty-five-year span of his literary career. Yet the same integration of the energy of oral tradition and aesthetic subtlety, of stylized art, may be traced throughout; the author's prose fiction is unique and clearly distinguishable from that of any Portuguese-langauge writer, past or present. An original mind at work with traditional linguistic resources, he developed an integrated, hybrid lexicon, revitalized familiar morphological patterns, created a syntax at once angular and delicately rhetorical, and engaged in a multifaceted interplay of contrasts. Any and all of his works may be read from a number of perspectives—the sociological-regionalist, the psychological, the theological-metaphysical, the linguistic-aesthetic, and so on—but are best approached from as ecletic a stance as possible in view of the multilevel design of Rosa's fictional craft. The author himself suggests a tripartite view of his work incorporating the underlying charm (enchantment), the level-lying common meaning, and the overlying metaphorical idea.

Rosa, while one of the most intellectual of Brazilian writers, considered himself a profound anti-intellectual in his worldview and literary creativity. He had as his goal the invocation, provocation, and evocation of the ineffable, and in this enterprise he summoned his readers into constant and, perhaps, exhausting collaboration. Rosa is undoubtedly the giant of Brazilian prose fiction in the twentieth century, as was Machado de *Assis for different reasons in the nineteenth century. His innovative style, based deeply in the most remotely historical of oral traditions, yet boldly personal and dynamically cosmopolitan, has changed the face of Brazilian fiction. Every writer whose literary debut postdates 1960 is tacitly obliged to take into account Rosa, whose influence continues to grow both in the Portuguese-speaking world and among Hispanic-American writers. He stands as a paragon of excellence to be revered if not emulated. (*See* Foreign Writers and Brazil.)

BIBLIOGRAPHY: Additional selected works by Rosa: Translations: Grossman; Tolman (1978); Criticism: Daniel, Mary L. *João Guimarães Rosa: travessia literária*. Rio: José Olympio Editora, 1968; idem. "João Guimarães Rosa." SSF (Winter, 1971), pp. 209–216; Foster/Foster, II; Lowe, Elizabeth. "Dialogues of *Grande sertão: veredas*." *LBR* (Winter, 1976), pp. 231–243; Merrim, Stephanie. *Logos and the Word: The Novel of Language and Linguistic Motivation in "Grande sertão: veredas" and "Tres tristes tigres."* New York: P. Lang, 1983; Vincent, Jon. "*Corpo do baile.*" *LBR* (Summer, 1977), pp. 97–117; idem. *Guimarães Rosa.* New York: Twayne Publishers, 1978.

MARY L. DANIEL

RUBIÃO, MURILO (b. 1916). Since 1946, when *mineiro* Rubião published his first book, he has dedicated himself to rewriting and refining his relatively small repertoire of short stories, numbering around thirty. It is thus common to find slight changes from one edition to another.

Rubião has always been interested in a type of short story that he alone was the first to popularize in Brazil: a blend of magical realism, science fiction, and the absurd. It is a paradoxical mixture of the mundane and the miraculous, more intent on enchantment than fright, yet whose opaqueness nonetheless deals with real, primordial human instincts. Around a contradictory axis of reality-fantasy, the author wove his deceivingly simple narratives about werewolves and dragons, magic and magicians, infinity and finitude, confusion and hallucination. All of the tales are embued with a strong if enigmatic dose of these elements and symbolism, beginning with the always-present biblical epigraph, a kind of foreboding, parabolic preface to the esoterically deciphered later on.

"O ex-mágico" (1947; "The Ex-Magician" in *The Ex-Magician and Other Stories*, 1979) is most representative of his opus. Among Rubião's other classic stories are "Os dragões" ("The Dragons") and "A Cidade" ("The City"). When several dragons appear in a town, the inhabitants decide "to civilize them," as if they were Indians. The city of Rubião's tale is hardly a hospitable place. A voyager arrives in an unfamiliar city, only to be pursued and jailed in a confusion that will be cleared up only when the real target of the populace's fear appears.

Rubião's narratives somehow resist interpretation just as they invite it. They are at once baffling, unnerving, funny, philosophic, and outrageous. Solitude, indifference, the debilitating daily routine, and the search for a definitive form all resound in Rubião's stories. With a measured style whose every word seems deliberate and whose succinctness only tightens the knowledge of inherent suspense, his fiction enjoys success inside Brazil and abroad.

BIBLIOGRAPHY: Additional selected works by Rubião: *Os dragões e outros contos*, 1965; *O pirotécnico Zacarias*, 1974; *A casa do girassol vermelho*, 1978. Criticism: Schwartz, Jorge. *Murilo Rubião: a poética do Uroboro*. São Paulo: Ática, 1981; Silverman, Malcolm. *Moderna ficção brasileira 2*. Rio: Civilização Brasileira, 1981.

MALCOLM SILVERMAN

S

SABINO, FERNANDO   (b. 1923). Sabino, from Minas, graduated from law school in Rio in 1946. He served in diplomatic positions in Rio and in New York.

He began his career in fiction with his first novel, *O encontro marcado* (1956; *A Time to Meet*, 1967), a serious *Künsterlerroman*, a semiautobiographical tale of coming of age during the years of the Vargas regime. His recent writings have been varied: *O grande mentecapto* (1979; The Great Liar) is a picaresque novel, whereas *O menino e o espelho* (1982; The Boy and the Mirror) is based on childhood experiences. In a recent collection of stories, *A faca de dois qumes* (1985; The Two-Edged Knife), he turned to the popular detective fiction mold. (*See* Autobiography.)

It has been in the unique Brazilian genre of the **crônica* that Sabino has gained wide acclaim. He narrated the daily foibles of *cariocas* in a peppy, ironic, even sarcastic style and popular language—a combination that has proven inimitable. Sabino explored what he claimed to be the Brazilian's unique characteristic, the *jeitinho*, the manner of problem solving through often ingenious, bizarre, or slightly illegal means. In "O homem nu" (The Naked Man), from the collection of the same title, he described a *carioca*'s early morning plot to outwit the bill collector by not responding to the doorbell. Typically, the plan goes awry and rudely backfires on him. This is one of the classic narrations of modern Brazilian literature.

BIBLIOGRAPHY: Additional selected works by Sabino: *Os grilos não cantam mais*, 1940; *A companheira de viagem*, 1965; *O gato sou eu*, 1983. Translations: "Roads to Minas." *NYTBR* (October, 24, 1986).

SALES, HERBERTO   (b. 1917; BAL: 1971). The author's personal experiences in his native interior of Bahia, in Salvador, in Rio, and in Brasília have marked his fiction. His style has evolved in various directions within a regionalist perspective influenced by the literary climate of the moment. Sales has had parallel success with *children's literature. (*See* Regionalism).

Cascalho (1944; Gravel) deals with the bitter life of the diamond prospector and the concomitant ills of rural bossism and hired gunfighters. *Além dos marimbus* (1961; Beyond the Bayous) reworked the telluric element entirely. In it, tropical forests mesh with the lumber industry in a lyricism ripe with detail but not social criticism. (*See* Cycles.)

The author's subsequent novels all display a decidedly satiric bent, yet remain uncompromising in their attention to detail. In the futuristic *O fruto do vosso ventre* (1976; *The Fruit of Thy Womb*, 1982), he ridiculed—through fairy tale, tongue-in-cheek jargon, and biblical parody—the evils of the totalitarian state, robotic bureaucracy, technologic defenses, and the manipulation of Malthus's (1766–1834) prophesy on population growth. In *Einstein, o minigênio* (1983; Einstein, the Minigenius), the gifted child and awe-struck adults are caricatured in a lampoon of the multinational's role in Brazil. *Os pareceres do tempo* (1984; The Opinions of Time), however, is a historical romance about colonial Brazil, supposedly based on his own family and debunking the Portuguese view of colonization. (*See* Dictatorship and Literature; Philosophy of National Identity; Portugal and Brazil: Literary Relations.)

BIBLIOGRAPHY: Additional selected works by Sales: *Dados biográficos do finado Marcelino*, 1965; *Histórias ordinárias*, 1966; *A feiticeira da Salina*, 1974; *O casamento da raposa com a galinha*, 1975; *A porta do chifre*, 1986. Criticism: Ambrogi, Marlise Vaz Bridi. *Herberto Sales: literatura comentada*. São Paulo: Editora Abril, 1983; Silverman, Malcolm. *Moderna ficção brasileira*. Rio: Civilização Brasileira, 1978.

MALCOLM SILVERMAN

SALGADO, PLÍNIO (1895–1975). Salgado's literary accomplishments are overshadowed by his long, tempestuous political career, which began in 1933, when he founded the ultranationalistic, right-wing Ação Integralista Brasileira (Brazilian Integralist Action party), in open imitation of European fascist models. Its motto was "God, Nation, and Family." After this party participated in the attempt to overthrow Getúlio Vargas, Salgado was exiled. He was a member of the Chamber of Deputies in the post-1964 military dictatorship representing the progovernment Arena party. (*See* Dictatorship and Literature.)

Salgado was an early modernist, reading his poetry during the Week of Modern Art. His first novel, *O estrangeiro* (1926; The Foreigner), became a best-seller. It was an attempt to apply the modernist esthetics to prose fiction. Written in a fast-moving, fragmented style, interspersed with numerous extra-literary excerpts (letters, anthems, historical accounts, onomatopoeic sounds, and so on), he anticipated to some extent the literary "collages" of his ideological nemesis Oswald de *Andrade. (*See* Modernism.)

In 1926, along with Menotti del *Picchia and Cassiano *Ricardo, he cofounded *verde-amarelismo*, green-yellowism, a reference to the colors of the Brazilian flag, which espoused a nationalistic literature combining a folkloric, quasi-mystical glorification of the Brazilian past—especially its Indian origins—with a celebration of the "more authentically Brazilian" traditions of the hinterland

and a rejection of the cultural importations emanating from Europe. The *anta* (tapir) was presented as the symbol of this newly acquired cultural independence. In *O estrangeiro* as well as in his other novels, Salgado sought to put these ideas into practice, manipulating characters, plots, and Brazilian folklore to argue for greater nationalism, a moral reawakening, and increased regimentation as the only feasible solutions for the national situation. (*See* Folklore and Literature.)

Salgado failed to evolve over the years as a novelist. He dedicated himself to monologic political and sociological essays to such an extent that he may well be relegated to the ranks of authors (like José Américo de *Almeida) who are credited with having historical rather than profoundly literary influence.

BIBLIOGRAPHY: Additional selected works by Salgado: *O curupira e o carão*, 1927; *O esperado*, 1931; *O cavaleiro de Itararé*, 1932; *o que é o integralismo*, 1933; *Cartas aos camisas-verdes*, 1937; *Primeiro, Cristo*! 1946; *Tripandé*, 1972. Criticism: Ellison; Rachum, Ilan. "Antropofagia vs. Verdeamarelo." *LALR*. (Spring-Summer, 1976), pp. 67–81.

BOBBY J. CHAMBERLAIN

SALLES GOMES. *See* Gomes, Paulo Emílio Salles.

SANT'ANNA, AFFONSO ROMANO DE   (b. 1937). Born in Belo Horizonte, Sant'Anna began his career as a journalist in Minas at the age of seventeen. He is now a professor of Brazilian literature at the Pontifical Catholic University of Rio.

Sant'Anna is a poet, writer of fiction, and essayist. He has tried to build a popular and outward image of himself as a poet, in opposition to the controlled and cool style developed by Haroldo de *Campos and Augusto de *Campos, all of whom participated in the concretist movement. (*See* Postmodernism in Poetry.)

Sant'Anna's popularity was enhanced by the publication of "Que país é este?" ("What Kind of Nation Is This?"), a poem appearing on the political page of the *Jornal do Brasil* on January 6, 1980 (In *LALR* [January-June, 1986], pp. 106–110). In it, he questioned the role of the dictatorship's censorship and the identity of Brazil as a nation. Since 1984 he has been writing poems for videos of car races and soccer games broadcast by Globo television network. (*See* Dictatorship and Literature; Soccer and Literature.)

As an essayist and critic (*see* Critics and Criticism), Sant'Anna has had works published on Carlos Drummond de *Andrade and contemporary Brazilian fiction. In his *Música popular e moderna poesia brasileira* (1978; Popular Music and Modern Brazilian Poetry), he recognized that during the years of the military dictatorship, when many intellectuals left the country as political exiles, the lyrics of popular music not only filled the critical void left by their absence but also performed poetry's many characteristic social and artistic functions—a phenomenon no longer apparent in the post-1978 period of liberalization and democracy. A recent work of criticism, *O canibalismo amoroso* (1984; Loving

310

Cannibalism), presents his psychoanalytical reading of the theme of love in poetry of the Western world. (*See* Music and Literature: Postmodernism in Poetry; *Tropicalismo.*)

BIBLIOGRAPHY: Additional selected works by Sant'Anna: *Poesia sobre poesia*, 1975; *Por um novo conceito de literatura brasileira*, 1977; *Política e paixão*, 1984; *A catedral de Colônia e outros poemas*, 1985; *A mulher madura*, 1986.

LUIZA LOBO

SANT'ANNA, SÉRGIO (b. 1941). Sant'Anna began his literary career in Belo Horizonte, where he lived for seventeen years after leaving his native Rio in the 1960s. He began to write as a member of the *mineiro* literary group that debuted in the *Literary Supplement of Minas Gerais* (SLMG) and also founded the magazine of experimental fiction, *Estória*, later closed down by the military regime. (*See* Dictatorship and Literature.)

One of the many young writers who developed amidst the barrage of ideas emerging from the international counterculture currents of the 1960s and 1970s, albeit a decidedly repressive period for Brazil, Sant'Anna represents the search for artistic openness and innovation. Influenced as well by the Beat Generation, Sant'Anna manifested that necessary urge "to invent" a new form of reality, one that is reshaped from his imaginative vision of historical reality. As a result, he may be identified with the Brazilian vanguard spirit of the 1970s, the over-preoccupation with aesthetic form, and the proclivity toward revolutionary ideology with its anarchical implications.

In terms of inventiveness, Sant'Anna's first novel *Confissões de Ralfo* (1975; Confessions of Ralfo) constitutes a daring departure from traditional narration, given its protean structure and hero, depicting various contradictory aspects of Brazilian society and politics and also suggestive of a middle-class Latin American voice and a self-conscious writer, both of whom are questioning the role of traditional literature as an effective means of communicating reality.

A soap-opera parody of the anxieties and confusions plaguing Brazil's new republic of the 1980s, *Amazona* (1986; Amazona), winner of the 1986 Jabuti Prize (*see* Prizes) for fiction, continues Sant'Anna's mordant satire of Brazilian society. In this case feminism, the *esquerda festiva* ("festive leftists"), the police, and the oppressive elite are humorously depicted but not without incisive insights into the problematic nature of the Brazilian contemporary scene. Both of Sant'Anna's novels are important for understanding present-day Brazil as well as one of its most provocative writers of the avant-garde. (*See* Feminism and Literature; Philosophy of National Identity.)

BIBLIOGRAPHY: Additional selected works by Sant'Anna: *Notas de Manfredo Rangel, Repórter (a respeito de Kramer)*, 1973; *O concerto de João Gilberto no Rio de Janeiro*, 1982; *Junk-Box, uma tragicomédia nos tristes trópicos*, 1984; *A tragédia brasileira*, 1987. Translations: Tolman (1984). Criticism: Silverman, Malcolm. *Moderna ficção brasileira 2*. Rio: Civilização Brasileira, 1981, pp. 278–310; Vieira, Nelson H. "The Autobiographical Spirit in Modern Brazilian Literature." *Identity in Portuguese and Brazilian Literature*. Edited by Maria Luísa Nunes. Pittsburgh: University of Pittsburgh, 1982, pp. 58–69.

NELSON H. VIEIRA

SANTA RITA DURÃO. *See* Durão, Friar José de Santa Rita.

SANTIAGO, SILVIANO (b. 1936). A *mineiro*, Santiago is a poet, novelist, and university professor who has taught in France, the United States, and Brazil. He is considered a leading Brazilian authority on French literature and criticism.

During the late 1950s Santiago was a founding member of the *review Tendência*, whose goals are revealed even in his most recent poetry, for example, *Crescendo durante a guerra numa província ultramarina* (1978; Growing Up During the War in an Overseas Province). As an essayist, Santiago has authored major comparative literary studies and analyses of postmodernism (*see* Postmodernism in Poetry), cultural dependency, and the Brazilian cultural situation, which are included in his collection of essays *Uma literatura nos trópicos* (1978; A Literature in the Tropics) and *Vale quanto pesa* (1982; You Get What You Pay For). The first collection includes the essay "O entre-lugar do discurso latino-americano" ("The Space in Between in Latin American Discourse"), which analyzes Brazilian literature in relation to its cultural dependence on Europe and the autonomy it can develop within South America. (*See* Popular Culture.)

One of Santiago's most outstanding fictional works is his *Em liberdade* (1981; At Liberty), which he calls an essay-novel. A falsified continuation of Graciliano *Ramos*'s *Memórias do cárcere*, it explores the same theme as the original work but at different crossroads in Brazilian history: the role of the artist in a society under a dictatorship. His latest novel, *Stella Manhattan* (1985; Stella Manhattan), is set in New York City and presents the interplay between sexual and ethnic minorities through the eyes of a Brazilian homosexual. (*See* Dictatorship and Literature; Homosexuality and Literature.)

BIBLIOGRAPHY: Additional selected works by Santiago: *O banquete*, 1970; *Latin American Literature: The Space In Between*. Translated by Steve Moscov and Judith Mayne. Buffalo, N.Y.: SUNY-Council on International Studies, 1973; *O olhar*, 1974; Translations: *LALR* (January-June, 1986), pp. 202–206 Criticism: Walty, Ivete Lara Camargos. "Vozes em contraponto." *SLMG*. June 30, 1984, pp. 10–11.

LUIZA LOBO

SAUDADE. A variant form of the old Portuguese word *solidão* (loneliness) *saudade* first appeared as a literary concept—the sadness of separation from a loved one—in the medieval Portuguese songbooks. Generalized through the centuries as a feeling of nostalgia for a long-gone lover or the past in general, in the early twentieth century it was expounded into a nebulous mystical philosophy, *saudosismo*, by the Portuguese poet Teixeira de Pascoaes (1877–1952) to explain the nature of the Portuguese existence. (*See* Philosophy of National Identity; Portugal and Brazil: Literary Relations.)

In Brazil the original concept—sadness at the separation from a beloved—appeared in the poetry of Gregório de *Matos and the *Minas School. *Romanticism's writers broadened *saudade* to refer to a melancholic longing for childhood (e.g., Casimiro de *Abreu and Alvares de *Azevedo) or to a painful sensation of separation from Brazil itself when abroad (e.g., Gonçalves *Dias). *Parnassianism and *modernism and postmodernism (*see* Postmodernism in Poetry) have also dealt with variations—often parodies—of this theme.

In fiction, *saudade* has mainly been confined to writers who described their emotional and psychological attachment to aspects of the Brazilian or their own past, for example, Machado de *Assis, Raul *Pompéia, Lima *Barreto, José Lins do *Rego, Otávio de *Faria and Gilberto *Freyre.

BIBLIOGRAPHY: Criticism: Orico, Osvaldo. *A saudade brasileira*. Rio: Editora A Noite, 1940.

SAVARY, OLGA (b. 1933). Born in Belém, Pará, Savary has been, since the early 1970s, an independent poet, unaligned with any of postmodernism's movements. (*See* Postmodernism in Poetry.)

Espelho provisório (1970; Provisionary Mirror) brought together her poetry published over a period of twenty years in newspapers and magazines of Rio, Belém, and Belo Horizonte, some under the pseudonym Olenka. The volume was awarded the Jabuti Prize (*see* Prizes) in 1971, followed by other prizes in subsequent years. As the title suggests, many of the poems are autobiographical. They reflect the poet's search for an acceptable reality: "Besides me / —and between me and my dessert—I want only silence / absolute accomplice of my verse, / weaving the web of vestiges with the care of a spider" ("Quero apenas" [I Want Only]). Savary invoked Carlos Drummond de *Andrade, Cecília *Meireles, Emily Dickinson, and T. S. Eliot as mentors for her poems, many of which were adapted for concert performances in the early 1970s. A more recent collection returns to these themes but also dwells on new ones. *Magma* (1982; Magma) has highly erotic love poetry verging on pornography, which is tempered with classical references and suggestions. (*See* Feminism and Literature.)

Savary has also been a very active literary columnist for several Brazilian newspapers and reviews, as well as a prize-winning translator of major Latin American writers of fiction and poetry, for example, Pablo Neruda and Octavio Paz. She received the *Brazilian Academy of Letters prize for her 1978 translation into Portuguese of the Peruvian Mario Vargas Llosa's *Conversation in the Cathedral* ([Spanish, 1969]; 1975). (*See* Foreign Writers and Brazil.)

BIBLIOGRAPHY: Additional selected works by Savary: *Sumidouro*, 1977; *Altaonda*, 1979; *Hai-Kais de Olga Savary*. Criticism: Lobo Filho, Blanca. "*Altaonda*" (book review). *WLT* (October, 1980), p. 610.

SCHMIDT, AUGUSTO FREDERICO (1906–1965). Schmidt, born in Rio, was forced to abandon school due to his health. He worked in both Rio and São Paulo in the 1920s. In the 1930s he led a publishing house, which brought forth major works by Graciliano *Ramos, Otávio de *Faria, Gilberto *Freyre, Jorge *Amado, Vinícius de *Moraes, and others. In later life, Schmidt was a diplomat.

Schmidt initially supported *modernism's thematic goals; however, his first collection of poetry, *Canto do brasileiro Augusto Frederico Schmidt* (1928; Song of the Brazilian Augusto Frederico Schmidt), appears to reject their dogmatism: "I no longer want love, / Neither do I want to sing of my country any longer. / I am lost in this world. / I don't love Brazil any longer. / I don't want geography any longer / Nor the picturesque." In fact, his works reflect the more introspective, often romantic, and, in his case, Catholic-oriented phase of modernism. Schmidt's often-versed themes—human justice, the mystery of night, the sea, and silence—all in relation to death, predominate in *Canto da noite* (1930; Song of the Night), *Fonte invisível* (1949; Invisible Fountain), and his last collection, *O caminho do frio* (1964; The Cold Road). A representative poem is "Paz dos túmulos" (The Peace of the Graves): "Oh wind which kills the roses, cold wind! / When will you carry me off changed into dust? / When will you carry me off through the streets / when will you carry me off changed in myself / To the great sea, the great sea, the great sea."

Schmidt's prose works include a volume of *memoirs, *O galo Branco* (1948; 1957; Whitey the Rooster [his parrot's name]), and journalistic pieces of his impressions of people and places in Brazil and abroad, all of which possess a distinct poetic tenor.

BIBLIOGRAPHY: Additional selected works by Schmidt: *Poesias completas*, 1956; *Sonetos*, 1965. Translations: Hulet. *Mundius Artium* (1976); *Poet-Lore* (Spring, 1976); Woodbridge. Criticism: Andrade, Mário de. *Aspectos da literatura brasileira.* 2nd ed. São Paulo: Martins, n.d., pp. 37–41.

SCLIAR, MOACIR (b. 1937). A descendant of Russian Jews who came to Brazil in the early part of the century, Scliar lived as a child in the Jewish community of Bom Fim, a neighborhood that was to be the setting for many of his narratives about Brazilian Jews. He received a medical degree in 1962 but since then has divided his time between medicine and literature. His first collection, *O carnaval dos animais* (1968; *The Carnival of the Animals*, 1985), received a literary *prize. Since then he has written almost one title a year. (*See* Immigrants and Literature; Religion and Literature.)

With Jewish themes as his main inspirational source, Scliar recreated his own Jewish-Brazilian experiences and cultural legacy in stories that recall biblical parables, moral tales, and humorous anecdotes richly imbued with Jewish folklore, customs, and fantasy. Considered by some critics (*see* Critics and Criticism) to exemplify the magical or fantastic realism characteristic of modern Latin American prose, Scliar's fiction draws upon folklore in order to capture a paradoxical reality that is often perplexing but nonetheless real, such as *gaúchos* (cowboys) drinking mate tea and speaking Yiddish or Jewish children learning Catholic dogma. With humor, irony, and an anguished sense of hopelessness, Scliar's narratives are at times reminiscent of the prose of the American Philip Roth and the Canadian Mordecai Richler. Through Kafka's sense of the absurd and a unique brand of magical realism, Scliar created his own type of magic to express his marginal condition of being Jewish alongside the spirit of being a nationalist. (*See* Folklore and Literature; Philosophy of National Identity.)

His first full-fledged novel, *O centauro no jardim* (1980; *The Centaur in the Garden*, 1984), harbors regional, national, and universal perspectives. Narrated in the first person with flashbacks of Brazilian life from the 1940s to the early 1970s, the story of Guedali Tartakovsky, a Jewish centaur, interweaves Jewish customs and Greek mythology with modern, capitalist Brazilian experience to tell the tale of a new Brazilian hero, a latter-day Macunaíma. (*See* Mário de Andrade.) Transformed into a two-legged man due to the miracle of modern science, Guedali gradually becomes uneasy about his linkage to Brazil's "economic miracle" and its consumer-oriented, fast-paced, pressured urbanity. Steeped in contemporary Brazilian culture with its institutionalized norms, the novel portrays a kaleidoscopic Brazilian reality through the magical lens of cultural legends, allegory, myths, and folklore.

Scliar has paved the way for the novel of Jewish-Brazilian expression, but, above all, he has contributed to a new view of the social novel in which middle- and lower-class characters afford a singular perspective for understanding the Brazilian national reality.

BIBLIOGRAPHY: Additional selected works by Scliar: *O exército de um homem só*, 1973 (*The One-Man Army*, 1986); *Os deuses de Raquel*, 1975 (*The Gods of Raquel*, 1986); *A balada do falso Messias* 1976; *Os voluntários*, 1979; *A estranha nação de Rafael Mendes*, 1983; *A massagista japonesa*, 1984; *O olho enigmático*, 1986. Translations: Tolman (1984). Criticism: Day, Douglas. "The Beast in Us." *NYTBR* (May 4, 1986), p. 34; Glickman, Nora. "*Os voluntários*: A Jewish-Brazilian Pilgrimage." *Yiddish* (Winter, 1982), pp. 58–64; Lindstrom, Naomi. "Oracular Jewish Tradition in Two Works by Moacyr Scliar." *LBR* (Winter, 1984), pp. 23–33; Manguel, Alberto. "Ghostwriting for God: Moacyr Scliar's Divine Fables." *VV* (December 16, 1986), p. 65.

NELSON H. VIEIRA

SEMIOTICS.   *See* Postmodernism in Poetry.

SETÚBAL, PAULO   (1893–1937; BAL: 1934). Setúbal, a *paulista* lawyer, gave up politics to pursue a career in literature—fiction, poetry, and *memoirs— particularly regionalist fiction about popular figures and events of São Paulo's history. (*See* Regionalism.)

A marqueza de Santos (1925; *Domitila: The Romance of an Emperor's Mistress*, 1930), his most successful novel, dealt with Emperor Pedro I's (ruled 1822–1831) widely known love affair. Although this novel was immensely popular in the 1930s, most of Setúbal's other works were overshadowed by the lively modernist prose, as well as the social concerns and psychological trends of fiction of the late 1920s and 1930s (*See* Modernism; Social Novelists of the 1930s.)

BIBLIOGRAPHY: Additional selected works by Setúbal: *Alma cabocla*, 1920; *Os maluquices do imperador*, 1927; *O romance da Prata*, 1935. Criticism: *NYTBR* (August 24, 1930), p. 14.

SILVA, AGUINALDO (b. 1944). From Pernambuco, since 1964 Silva has lived in Rio, where he is a journalist, novelist, and television scriptwriter. He was also an editor of the gay cultural newspaper *Lampião*. (*See* Homosexuality and Literature.)

Silva's journalistic beat—the poor, the corrupt, and the demimonde of society—has carried over into his fiction. The lives of the socially, politically, and sexually marginalized—factory workers, homosexuals, prostitutes, drag queens—as well as the symbiotic relationship between the crime network and the police, are recurrent themes of his writings. *A república dos assassinos* (1976; The Republic of Assassins), recently made into a film, has been his most successful novel. This fictionalized account of the police corruption and participation in the vigilantelike Death Squad (*Esquadrão da Morte*) of the 1968–1972 period of the military dictatorship is a bold indictment and political statement for its time, achieved through a stylistic collage of monologues, letters, and memoirs. A similar theme is developed in his most recent novel, *O homem que comprou o Rio* (1986; The Man Who Bought Rio). (*See* City and Literature; Dictatorship and Literature; Film and Literature.)

BIBLIOGRAPHY: Additional selected works by Silva: *Redenção para Job*, 1961; *Geografia do ventre*, 1968; *Primeira carta aos andróginos*, 1975; *Padre Cícero* (with Doc Comparato), 1985. Translations: *Now the Volcano*, 1979.

SILVA (THE JEW), ANTÔNIO JOSÉ DA (1705–1739). Born in Rio, Silva went to Lisbon with his parents. There he was repeatedly persecuted for his Judaism by the Holy Inquisition. He was finally burned at the stake along with his mother and wife. (*See* Portugal and Brazil: Literary Relations; Religion and Literature.)

During his short life, Silva wrote and produced several extremely popular comic operas that reflected the foibles of contemporary Lisbon society, based on the medieval theater tradition of Gil Vicente. Although a distinctly *baroque attitude is evident in the turns and twists of his plots and prose dialog, Silva added lively stylistic influences indebted to contemporary Spanish, French, and Italian theater, for example, *opera buffa*. *Guerras do alecrim e manjerona* (1737; Wars of the Alecrin and the Marjoram) stands outs as his most perfect satire of Portuguese life. Two rival carnival groups battle over the flower that will represent them. (*See* Music and Literature.)

No nativist Brazilian element is apparent in these plays. Nonetheless, his life story was adapted for patriotic dramas by the Brazilian romantics, for example, *Antônio José ou o poeta e a inquisição*, by Gonçalves de Magalhães. (*See* Romanticism.)

BIBLIOGRAPHY: Additional selected works by Silva: *Vida do grande Dom Quixote de la Mancha e do gordo Sancho Pança*, 1733; *Esopaida ou vida de Esopo*, 1734; *Teatro cômico português*, 2 vols., 1744. Criticism: Juca Filho, Cândido. *Antônio José, O Judeu.* Rio: Civilização Brasileira, 1940.

SILVA, DEONĪSIO DA (b. 1948). Silva is from Santa Catarina State and is now a university professor of literature in the interior of São Paulo. Most of his popular short fiction is set in an imaginary town, Sanga da Amizade, in the interior and focuses on family relationships and school-life situations.

Exposição dos motivos (1976; Exposition of the Motives), awarded the Brasília Prize for Literature (*see* Prizes) in 1977, narrates the lives and adventures of the town's gallery of inhabitants, among them adulterous wives, suffering teachers, and lunatics. Silva's narrative approach is varied. He uses first-person and third-person narrators; his language is highly colloquial and fast paced; irony blends well with his satires.

Silva's recent works have continued this satiric trend. *A mulher silenciosa* (1981; The Silent Woman) is a murder mystery, the solution to which unites giant agro-business industry with university professors. *Livrai-me das tentações* (1984; Free Me from Temptations) returns to his analyses of life's contradictions in Sanga da Amizade.

BIBLIOGRAPHY: Additional selected works by Silva: *Estudo sobre a carne humana*, 1975; *Cenas indecorosas*, 1976; *A ferramenta do escritor*, 1978; *A cidade dos padres*, 1986.

SILVA, JOSÉ BONIFÁCIO DE ANDRADA E (1765–1838). Scion of a noble family, José Bonifácio figures among the best-educated Brazilians of his time. Regarded as the "Patriarch of Brazilian Independence," Silva guided the young Prince Pedro I in the latter's declaration of autonomy from Portugal in 1822; political intrigue drove him into exile in France. Upon his return, between bookish pursuits, he organized the masonic movement in Brazil.

Silva's literary formation reflects the transitional period that leads from the Enlightenment (*see* Arcadias) and its emphasis on neoclassical (*see* Arcadias) sobriety and elegance to the emergence of a romantic sensibility. In fact, the preface to his *Poesias avulsas* (1825; modern edition in 1964; Poetry), written under his arcadian pseudonym Américo Elísio, is nothing less than a preromantic manifesto in its rejection of sterile formalism and in its insistence on greater originality and the need for passionate sentiment. (*See* Arcadias; Romanticism.)

The poet's themes can be organized in three categories reflecting his classical formation, his political preoccupations, and his romantic fascination with nature as a living force attuned to the poet's own subjectivity. More topical are his odes on issues of the day, such as Greece's struggle for independence or his own response to his election as a senator from Bahia, a poem that tempers gratitude to his would-be constituents with angry resentment against Brazil's political institutions.

In a period not known for its writers of talent, Silva stands out as a significant link between the *Minas School and Brazil's first generation of romantics. His sensitivity to the inherent musicality of verse paved the way for the likes of Gonçalves *Dias and others who benefited from the example of Brazil's exemplary poet-statesman.

BIBLIOGRAPHY: Translations: Hulet. Criticism: Sayers.

RICHARD A. PRETO-RODAS

SILVA (THE YOUNGER), JOSÉ BONIFÁCIO DE ANDRADA E (1827–1886). Born in France to a family of prominent political exiles and inspired by his illustrious uncle José Bonifácio de Andrada e *Silva, whose name he bore, Silva (The Younger) received a degree in law at São Paulo and subsequently embarked upon a career in public service.

As a man of letters, Silva delved into historiography and political debate. Like his uncle, he cultivated verse either as an avocation or as an activity aimed at furthering his public life and his causes. Influenced in particular by the Portuguese romantics and ultraromantics of the midcentury, he contributed yet another collection of verse to *romanticism's lengthy list of titles evocative of bouquets, gardens, and nosegays with his *Rosas e goivos* (1848; Roses and Clove Blossoms). (*See* Portugal and Brazil: Literary Relations.)

To his credit, however, Silva transcended the limitations of literary derivation by imbuing many of his later poems with the passion born of committed action. Thus his poetical denunciation of slavery (e.g., ''A saudade do escravo'' [The Slave's Nostalgia]) struck a chord among readers and listeners at abolitionist rallies, as did his ringing appeals for democratic freedoms (e.g., ''Liberdade'' [Liberty]). (*See* Slavery and Literature.)

Indeed, Silva's wedding of lofty vision and rhetorical grandeur contributed to the formation of a peculiarly Brazilian verse style known as *condorism.

BIBLIOGRAPHY: Selected works by and criticism on Silva: Alfredo Bosi and Nilo Sclazo, eds. *José Bonifácio, o Moço: Poesias.* São Paulo: 1962.

RICHARD A. PRETO-RODAS

SILVA ALVARENGA. *See* Alvarenga, Manuel da Silva.

SILVEIRA, TASSO DA (1895–1968). Born in Paraná State, Silveira studied law and social sciences but eventually taught Portuguese and comparative literature. He participated in *modernism as a poet, but he was also active as a journalist, critic (*see* Critics and Criticism), essayist, and novelist. Silveira was the principal spokesman of the Rio modernist *review *Festa,* founded in 1927. It was the organ of the spiritualist trend in modernist poetry. (*See* Modernism; Religion and Literature.)

Silveira wrote poem-manifestoes in addition to conceptual essays. He advocated poetry based on "velocidade, totalidade, brasilidade e universalidade" (velocity, totality, Brazilian heritage, and universality). His "velocity" is not drawn from Marinetti's futurism but consists of an unexpected, emotional expressivity. "Totality" implies the material and spiritual, the human and transcendent. The third term shows the common modernist concern with illuminating national reality. "Universality" means showing Brazil as an integrated partner in the exchange of "interior forces" between peoples.

In his 1932 essay, "Definition of Brazilian Modernism," Silveira argued that his *Festa* group constituted the central force in the modernist renovation of Brazilian letters through their earlier reviews, *América Latina* (1919; Latin America) and *Árvore Nova* (1922; New Tree). This claim has been disputed by most critics, including Mário de *Andrade.

Silveira's early poetry, included in *Fio d'água* (1918; Stream of Water), continued structured symbolist modes; he did not adopt free verse until the late 1920s. He favored clarity and simplicity to express moralistic, civic, and religious concerns. Didacticism often overshadows aesthetic elaboration, and traditional Catholicism informs recurring themes and attitudes. (*See* Symbolism.)

BIBLIOGRAPHY: Additional selected works by Silveira: *Canto do Cristo do Corcovado*, 1931; *Contemplação do eterno*, 1952; *Canções a Curitiba*, 1955; *Sombra no caos*, 1958. Translations: Hulet. Criticism: Azevedo Filho, Leodegário A. de. *Tasso da Silveira e o seu universo poético*. Rio, 1963.

CHARLES A. PERRONE

SILVEIRA, VALDOMIRO (1873–1941). A *paulista*, Silveira became intensely interested in the life of the *caipiras*, the poor people from the interior of the state, and began to write stories about them in 1894. (*See* Regionalism.)

Initially, he viewed the *caipira* from a folkloric angle, although he later focused on social phenomena surrounding their existence. His later stories (e.g., the collection *Leréias* [1945; Idle Chatter]) possess greater dramatic power, but they still reveal the author's distance from his subject. (*See* Folklore and Literature.)

Some critics (*see* Critics and Criticism) have credited his works with a socioanthropological value, owing to his details of cultural patterns and language usage. He shares with Afonso *Arinos the title of founder of modern *paulista* regionalism. (*See* Portuguese Language of Brazil.)

BIBLIOGRAPHY: Additional selected works by Silveira: *Os caboclos*, 1920; *Mixuangos*, 1937. Criticism: Riedel, Dirce Cortes. "Introdução crítica a Valdomiro Silveira." *Os caboclos*. Rio, 1962.

SIMÕES LOPES NETO. *See* Lopes Neto, João Simões.

SLAVERY AND LITERATURE. Black slavery and the abolitionist movement had traumatic impacts upon Western culture. Although Brazil was one of the few countries in the Western Hemisphere to allow slavery and the last to abolish it (1888), the antislavery sentiment has been present in Brazilian literature since the eighteenth century. During the abolitionist campaign, literature in all of its forms was pressed into the service of abolitionists—black as well as white.

African slaves were first shipped to Brazil as early as 1539 and continued to arrive until the middle of the nineteenth century. The economic consequence of their work and their cultural contribution to Brazilian civilization during these 350 years has been recognized by both social scientists and cultural historians. Several frustrated attempts at ending slavery occurred in the early nineteenth century, particularly after 1830. Economic interests of the sugar-plantation oligarchy intensified slave traffic until an 1850 law finally banned it completely. In 1871 the Free Womb Law declared all children of slaves to be free. In 1879 the Abolitionist Confederation established by André Rebouças (1838–1898) and others, as well as the political activities of Joaquim *Nabuco and José do *Patrocínio, spearheaded the drive against slavery. Rebouças's series of antislavery essays in the *Gazeta da Tarde* newspaper articulated the distressing state of the slaves and the nation. (*See* Historiography.)

The recognition of the slave's status in Brazilian society and the call for abolition of slavery were first viewed in the poem *Etíope resgatado* (1757; Ethiopia Redeemed) by Father Manuel Ribeiro da Rocha (eighteenth century). He, as did Hipólito da *Costa and José Bonifácio de Andrada e Silva a half century later, called for the gradual freedom of the slaves. Among the numerous proabolition periodicals published in the early nineteenth century was *O Homem de Côr* (later called *O Mulato*), edited by the mulatto Paula Brito (1809–1861) and featuring factual articles, numerous items of fiction, and poetry focusing on black themes and personages. The theme of *quilombos*, runaway slaves' republics, especially the seventeenth-century *quilombo* of Palmares, served as the subject for a number of poems published in the 1850s. The figure of Zumbi, the legendary leader of Palmares, was glorified in heroic proportions typical of *romanticism. The image of Palmares and Zumbi has even served for the basis of many works of contemporary culture, including the very popular theatrical production of the Arena Theatre of São Paulo, *Arena conta Zumbi*, of the late 1960s, and Carlos Diegues's film *Quilombo*. (*See* Film and Literature; Theater History.)

Antislavery sentiment was not limited to any one literary school. The romantic poet Gonçalves *Dias wrote an important poem, "A escrava" (The Slave), in essence a slave girl's dream of Africa, but dealt at length with slavery only in a translation of a portion of Hugo's *Bug-Jargal* (1831), which deals with a leader of the Haitian revolution against France.

In response to the romantics who depicted the slave as a melancholy dreamer, a patriotic symbol, or a historical figure, in the 1850s a group of regionalist poets attempted to create a more realistic image of blacks and described aspects of their life on large plantations, particularly those in the northeastern backlands of the country. The poetry of these writers—Juvenal Galeno (1836–1931), Trajano Galvão de Carvalho (1830–1864), Francisco Leite Bittencourt Sampaio

(1834–1895), and Joaquim Serra (1838–1895)—were realistic in intent, yet romantic in their abolitionist fervor. (*See* Regionalism.)

It was during this period of regionalism that abolitionist poetry took direction and gained strength. By 1865 the theme of emancipation had gained eminence within Brazilian poetry. Along with the continuing image of black heroes, there appeared poetry in which black women were treated as objects of deep feelings of sincere love on the part of the poet. Typical of such love poems are the verses titled "Meus amores" (My Loves) and "A cativa" (The Captive) by Luís *Gama. An ex-slave, Gama is better known as the author of verses that derided snobbish mulattoes and insisted that all Brazilians were related because they all shared some degree of African ancestry—a concept that in itself constituted a rational contribution to abolitionist ideas.

By far the most outstanding poet of the antislavery movement was Antônio de Castro *Alves, whose passion for words and grandiloquence led his lofty style to be termed *condorism* by analogy with the majestic, high-soaring condor. The two other members of this group were Fagundes *Varela and Tobias Barreto de Meneses. (*See* Recife School.) Fagundes Varela devoted few poems to slavery; one of the most significant is his lone narrative work "Mauro o escravo" (Mauro the Slave), which describes a strong, heroic, and revengeful slave in the tradition of Hugo's Bug-Jargal. The poetic output of Tobias Barreto was relatively small; he devoted himself more to jurisprudence and literary and philosophical criticism. A mulatto who was apparently intent on solidifying his ties with the middle class, Barreto attacked slavery in only one poem, "A escravidão" (Slavery).

After the death of Castro Alves, Celso de Magalhães (1849–1879) and José Ezequiel Freire de Lima (1849–1891), both poets of the realist school, wrote a number of poems that dealt with the issue of slavery. These works were followed by those of the Parnassian poets of the 1880s, notably Raimundo *Correia and Gonçalves *Crespo. (*See* Parnassianism; Realism.)

Drama developed slowly in Brazil and did not produce great work in support of the abolitionist cause; rather, plays included black characters because slaves were an integral part of Brazilian society. Nonetheless, two important antislavery dramas are José de *Alencar's *O demônio familiar* (1858; The Family Devil) and *Mãe* (1859; Mother), which depict, respectively, the evil effects of slavery on the slave-owning family and the personal tragedy of the slave. Other social dramas of abolitionist sentiment are *História de uma moça rica* (1861; Story of a Rich Girl) by Francisco Pinheiro Guimarães (1832–1877), *Os cancros sociais* (1866; Social Cancers) by Maria Ribeiro (1829–1880), and *O escravocrata* (1884; The Slavocrat) by Artur *Azevedo and Urbano Duarte de Oliveira (1855–1902). *O escravocrata* presented the most sensational theme of the period: the sexual relations between a white woman and her slave. In other plays, particularly the comedies of Artur Azevedo and Joaquim José da *França Júnior, slaves appeared in minor roles and were frequently portrayed as picaresque characters or comic figures. (*See* Theater History.)

Prose fiction of the second half of the century often dealt with the great social issues facing the nation. In so doing, numerous historical and regional novels, serialized romances, and particularly realistic novels reflected the public's interest in the question of slavery, which constituted the most burning social issue of the time. Abolitionist novels were anticipated by works in which black characters were elevated from their previous roles as simple background figures. The serialized novel *Maria ou a menina roubada* (1852; Maria or the Stolen Girl) by Antônio Teixeira e *Sousa, though of little literary merit, is significant in that it is the first novel in which slaves play important roles; in fact, the black characters are more important to the plot than any of the white characters. The first true notes of abolitionist sentiment are found in Pinheiro Guimarães's serialized romance, *O comendador* (1856; The Commander), which is the first novel to depict the lives of rural slaves.

Harriet Beecher Stowe's *Uncle Tom's Cabin* was translated into Portuguese and published in Brazil in the early 1860s. It served as an incentive for Brazilian authors to focus on similar circumstances in their own country and to denounce unequivocally the institution of slavery. Subsequently, there appeared a series of novels that, although of superficial literary worth, were antislavery in spirit: *As vítimas algozes* (1869; The Hangmen Victims), a trilogy by Joaquim Manuel de *Macedo; *Os homens de sangue ou os sofrimentos da escravidão* (1873; Men of Blood or the Sufferings of Slavery), and *A escrava Isaura* (1875; The Slave Girl Isaura), by Bernardo * Guimarães. One of the most impressive works of the period is *Mota Coqueiro* (1877; Mota Coqueiro), which was written by José do *Patrocínio, an Afro-Brazilian who was one of the principal leaders of the movement for emancipation.

By the late 1870s interest in *naturalism under the influence of Émile Zola and Eça de Queiroz drew Brazilian writers to focus on the environmental roots of the poor man's plight. Unlike the works of Macedo and Castro Alves, naturalists in Brazil depicted not only the life of the rural poor but also that of the urban lower classes. Consequently, slaves as well as free blacks were portrayed in a truer light. The novels *O cacaulista* and *O coronel Sangrado* by Inglês de *Sousa and *O mulato* by Aluísio *Azevedo presented a new theme in Brazilian fiction: the dilemma of the successful mulatto in a less-than-friendly environment. (*See* Portugal and Brazil: Literary Relations.)

In retrospect, the literature of slavery produced up to emancipation (1888) and after (e.g., the novels of Henrique *Coelho Neto or João Felício dos Santos's historical novels *Ganga Zumba* (1962; Ganga Zumba) and *Benedita Torreão da Sangria Desatada* (1983; Benedita Torreão of Sangria Desatada), which, respectively, focus on the Palmares revolt and a slave rebellion in 1849), included not only stock figures such as the evil master and the cruel overseer but an array of black characters: the tragic mulatto, the brute suitable only for hard labor, the faithful servant, and the heroic figure struggling against unjust servitude. In addition to having been used as a vehicle for social reform, this important body of literature is significant as a reflection of slave life, the attitudes of blacks and whites toward one another, and their views on slavery. (*See* Contemporary Black Literature.)

BIBLIOGRAPHY: Criticism: *Afro-Braziliana: A Working Bibliography*. Compiled by Dorothy B. Porter. Boston: G. K. Hall, 1978; Brookshaw, David. *Race and Color in Brazilian Literature*. Metuchen, N.J.: Scarecrow Press, 1986; Conrad, Robert. *Children of God's Fire: A Documentary History of Black Slavery in Brazil*. Princeton, N.J.: Princeton University Press, 1983; Haberly, David T. *Three Sad Races: Racial Identity and National Consciousness in Brazilian Literature*. Cambridge: Cambridge University Press, 1983; Olinto, Antônio. "The Negro Writer and the Negro Influence in Brazilian Literature." *African Forum* (Spring, 1967), pp. 5–19; Rabassa, Gregory. "Negro Themes and Characters in Brazilian Literature." *African Forum* (Spring, 1967), pp. 20–34; Ramos, Arthur. *The Negro in Brazil*. Philadelphia: Porcupine Press, 1980 (reprint edition); Sayers, Raymond S. *The Negro in Brazilian Literature*. New York: Hispanic Institute in the United States, 1956.

JAMES H. KENNEDY

SOCCER AND LITERATURE. Soccer (*futebol*), the Brazilian national pastime, has often garnered international headlines for Brazil owing to its World Cup-winning teams. Pelé, Brazil's star player of the 1970s, became a widely recognized celebrity and has helped to popularize the sport in the United States.

Soccer has been not only a popular literary theme but an important avocation for Brazilian writers since the turn of the century. For example, Henrique *Coelho Neto, while president of the *Brazilian Academy of Letters, was simultaneously president of the Fluminense Soccer Club. José Lins do *Rego, between novels, managed a European tour of the Rio's Gávea soccer team. The dramatist Nelson *Rodrigues was better known to rooters (*torcedores*) as an important soccer journalist for many years.

As a literary theme, soccer appears in the works of major writers. Carlos Drummond de *Andrade and João Cabral de *Melo Neto, who played on a championship "little league" soccer team in Recife, often use soccer as a theme in their poetry, as did Vinícius de *Moraes. Jorge *Amado has written *children's literature about soccer. The national emotional depression after Brazil's loss in the 1950 World Cup was described in a script by Ferreira *Gullar and, it is rumored, caused Carlos Heitor *Cony to abandon his religious inclinations. In the 1980s Afonso Romano de *Sant'Anna has been writing poetry to be read during soccer games.

The sport has captured the interest of a myriad of writers of poetry, prose, and drama: Gilberto *Freyre, Otávio de *Faria, Joaquim *Cardozo, Murilo *Mendes, Lúcio *Cardoso, Paulo Mendes *Campos, Fernando *Sabino, Rubem *Fonseca, Décio *Pignatari, Homero *Homem, Gianfrancesco *Guarnieri, Oduvaldo *Viana Filho, and others. Edilberto *Coutinho's stories describing the glories and tragedies of the soccer player's life, *Maracanã, Adeus*, was awarded the Cuban Casa de las Américas Prize for short fiction in 1981, and Flávio Moreira da *Costa organized a collection, *Onze em campo* (1986; Eleven on the

Field), of eleven short stories viewing soccer from different perspectives written by Carlos Eduardo *Novaes, Edla van *Steen, João *Antônio, Luiz *Vilela, Ricardo *Ramos, Sérgio *Sant'Anna, and other *new writers.

Also of note are Macedo Miranda's (b. 1920) *O sol oscuro* (1968; The Dark Sun), Nelson Motta's *Brasil F.C.* (Brazil Soccer Club), and Sérgio Ortiz Prado's (b. 1930) *O sol e o verde* (1983; The Sun and the Green).

BIBLIOGRAPHY: Criticism: Levine, Robert M. "Sport and Society: The Case of Brazilian *Futebol.*" *LBR* (Winter, 1980), pp 233–252.

SOCIAL NOVELISTS OF THE 1930s. The social novels of the 1930s and after in Brazil correspond chronologically to what has been called neorealism in other literatures. These novels focus on the exploitation of workers by land-owners, the decadence of the sugar mills and plantations of the Northeast, and the effects of the droughts on the rural population and the nation as a whole. Many of these themes have developed into important literary *cycles.

The Background. The political conflicts and events that prevail in the plots of these novels can be traced to a series of rebellions (*tenentismo*), between 1922 and 1926, led by military lieutenants against the privileges in the high ranks of the military and in the rural and bourgeois oligarchies. The upheaval culminated with the Prestes Column march from north to south, looking for support for the Communist cause. In the 1930 elections, the Aliança Liberal (Liberal Alliance), the union of Paraíba, São Paulo, and Rio Grande do Sul, launched the platform of Getúlio Vargas (1883–1954) and João Pessoa as candidates for the presidency and vice-presidency, respectively, of Brazil.

These opposition candidates defended nationalist policies, the broad partici-pation of all of the states in the country's leadership, and a process of modern-ization based on the aspirations of the urban middle sectors—liberal professionals, small merchants, and manufacturers. The murder of João Pessoa on July 26, 1930, led to the "1930 Revolt" and to Vargas's ascension to power. After the 1935 Communist rebellion failed, Vargas declared a state of dictatorship in 1937, known as the New State (*Estado Novo*), inspired by Mussolini's in-tegralist movement (1937–1945).

The Writers. The conflicts between landowners and workers are the per-vasive themes in most of the famous novels of this era. José Américo de *Almeida initiated the social novel of the 1930s cycles with *A bagaceira* (1928). It was published soon after the Regionalist Congress of 1928 in Recife, a ramification of *modernism in the Northeast. (*See* Regionalism.)

Rachel de *Queiroz wrote her first novel about the drought and its social consequences in her native Ceará, *O quinze*, in 1930. Amando Fontes's (1899–1967) *Os Corumbas* (1933; The Corumbas) also views the drama of the refugees (*retirantes*). A family migrates from the dry *sertão* to the city of Aracaju, Sergipe, only to face moral degradations and tuberculosis and to see their children turn to prostitution, which is the theme of Fontes's other social novel, *Rua do Siriri* (1937; Siriri Street). Graciliano *Ramos is probably the most important author of the 1930s. His two masterpieces, *São Bernardo* (1934) and *Vidas secas* (1938), denounced the economic exploitation of the poor in Alagoas, his native state, in a harsh, cold style. José Lins do *Rego, from Paraíba, also focused on the problems of rural Brazil in his sugarcane cycle, for example, *Menino do engenho* (1932) and the most important of all later novels, *Fogo morto* (1947), which reflects the technological changes that small mills underwent when transformed into industrial mills, leading to further unemployment and social crisis. Jorge *Amado, in Bahia, had two novels published that are also part of these rural cycles: *Terras do sem fim* (1942) and *São Jorge dos Ilhéus* (1944). Like Ramos, he was *engagé* in his view of life and literature.

Before the 1930s the Brazilian novel had never attained such a level of emotional intensity, stylistic quality, or sociopolitical orientation. These writers have left an indelible impression on Brazilian literature and society.

BIBLIOGRAPHY: Criticism: Putnam, Samuel. "The Brazilian Social Novel: 1935–1940." *Inter-American Quarterly* (April, 1940), pp. 5–12; Toop, Walter R. "Amando Fontes: Time and Chronology." *LBR* (June, 1969), pp. 60–84.

LUIZA LOBO

SOUSA, ANTONIO TEIXEIRA E (1812–1861). A humble mestizo carpenter, Teixeira e Sousa became a primary schoolteacher and, later, a court secretary. He was an avid follower of Gonçalves de *Magalhães, and as such he published drama and poetry in a neoclassical (*See* Arcadias) vein with some touches of the incipient romantic school. His poem *Os tres dias dum noivado* (1844; The Three Days of an Engagement) is considered by critic David Treece an important contribution to the comprehension of *Indianism in Brazilian literature. (*See* Romanticism.)

Sousa is known as the author of Brazil's first popular novel, *O filho do pescador* (1843; The Fisherman's Son), published one year earlier than Joaquim Manuel de *Macedo's *A moreninha*. A series of novels with complicated plots and rhetorical diatribes followed, notably, a historical novel, *Gonzaga ou a conjuração de Tiradentes* (1848, 1851; Gonzaga or Tiradentes's Conspiracy), and *Maria ou a menina roubada* (1852–1853; Maria or the Stolen Girl), which was the first novel to give a substantial role to black characters. The appearance of Macedo's and José de *Alencar's fiction, which appealed more to middle-class tastes, tolled the end of Sousa's popularity. (*See* Minas Conspiracy; Slavery and Literature.)

BIBLIOGRAPHY: Additional selected works by Sousa: *As fatalidades de dois jovens*, 1856. Criticism: Driver; Sayers.

SOUSA, GABRIEL SOARES DE (1540–1591). In the 1560s Sousa arrived at Bahia, where he subsequently made a fortune as a sugarcane planter. After his brother allegedly discovered mines in the backlands of Bahia, Sousa went to Madrid to obtain permission to prospect for gold, silver, and precious stones.

While in Madrid (1584–1587) he wrote his *Tratado descritivo do Brasil em 1587* (Descriptive Treatise about Brazil in 1587).

The *Tratado* is divided into two parts: the first deals with history and geography and the second with the greatness of Brazil. First published in 1851, it offers a detailed account of the land, its people, the flora and fauna, and the region's physical and economic geography. It strongly reflects the author's enthusiastic attitude toward the new land and its future—pure *ufanismo*.

Assuming a broad definition of literature, the treatise can be considered one of the early milestones in the development of Brazilian literature with great interest for historians, geographers, anthropologists, and other specialists. (*See* Historiography.)

BIBLIOGRAPHY: Criticism: Varnhagen, Franciso Adolfo de. "Ao Instituto Histórico do Brasil" and "Aditamento." *Tratado descritivo do Brasil em 1587*, by Gabriel Soares de Sousa. São Paulo: Companhia Editora Nacional, 1938, pp. ix–xxxvii
JAMES H. KENNEDY

SOUSA, HERCULANO MARCOS INGLÊS DE (1853–1918; BAL: 1897). Sousa was born in Óbidos, central Pará. He finished work toward a law degree in São Paulo (1876), and in Recife he practiced journalism and wrote his first novel, *O cacaulista* (1876; The Cocoa Planter). Sousa entered politics, rising to the provincial governorships of Sergipe and Espírito Santo. In 1892 he moved to Rio, had his *Contos amazônicos* (1892; Amazonian Stories) published, and distinguished himself as a jurist.

Sousa, whose works were all published under the pseudonym Luís Dolzani, is best known for his novel *O missionário* (1888; The Missionary). Written after the establishment of *naturalism, this is a full-fledged, typical product of that movement. His treatment of the anticlerical theme reveals the direct influence of Eça de Queiroz and Émile Zola's *La faute de l'Abbé Mouret* (1875; *The Sinful Priest*, 1960). (*See* Portugal and Brazil: Literary Relations.)

Earlier works by Sousa, each one with the subtitle "Cenas da vida do Amazonas" (Scenes from Life in Amazonia), reveal no such influence; yet they differ greatly from the late-blooming romantic products of the 1870s. The best of them, his *O coronel Sangrado* (1877; Colonel Sangrado), set in Óbidos, conveys brilliantly the manner in which the stultifying milieu of a small town lost in the Amazonian hinterland conditions the lives of the townspeople. Moreover, it anticipates by five years the environmental determinism introduced from Europe by Aluísio *Azevedo. In this particular, technical regard, Sousa was preceded only by Bernardo *Guimarães. (*See* Realism; Romanticism.)

Sousa therefore ranks as having contributed to a recognizable variety of native Brazilian naturalism, one that flowered briefly before the European variety arrived to supplant it, even, ironically, in Sousa's own *O missionário*.

BIBLIOGRAPHY: Additional selected works by Sousa: *História de um pescador*, 1876. Criticism: Driver; Loos; Sayers; Walther, Don H. "The Critics and *O missionário*." *Romance Studies Presented to William Morton Dey*. Chapel Hill, N.C.: University of North Carolina Press, 1950, pp. 171–173.
NORWOOD ANDREWS, JR.

SOUSA, JOÃO DA CRUZ E (1861–1898). Born in Santa Catarina to freed slaves, Cruz e Sousa became the first and foremost Brazilian symbolist poet. His parents' master became his protector. After graduating from high school in 1874, he gave private lessons, and in 1881 he traveled throughout Brazil in a dramatic troupe. His first poems, in the Parnassian mold, appeared during these years. (*See* Parnassianism; Slavery and Literature; Symbolism.)

His travels through Brazil brought him into contact with the conditions of his black brothers still in slavery, which would be a constant theme of his writings. In fact, from 1882 to 1889 he published *A Tribuna Popular* (The People's Tribune), a proabolition and prorepublic newspaper, along with the poet and novelist Virgílio Várzea (1863–1941). Várzea also collaborated with him in the collection of poems in prose and short narrations of *Tropos e fantasias* (1885; Tropes and Fantasies). The volume evidences the influence of the "scientific poetry" of *naturalism and Parnassianism.

A move to Rio in 1890, where Sousa began to work as the archivist for the railroad, led him to the major Parnassian poets of the time, as well as to the works of Edgar Allan Poe, Joris-Karl Huysmans, Charles Baudelaire and others and, consequently, to the symbolist aesthetic. With the poetry of *Broquéis* (1893; Constellation) and the prose poems of *Missal* (1893; Prayer Book), he launched symbolism in Brazilian letters and became the leader of the group of young poets. His life took a drastic turn when his father died; his wife, Gavita, went mad; and he came down with tuberculosis, which had already claimed his four children.

Critics (*See* Critics and Criticism) divide Sousa's works into three phases. In his early poetry, the social *romanticism of Castro *Alves's appeals for liberty, justice, and social reform still throbs. *Tropos e fantasias*, however, begins his initiation into a vague, intimist poetry, which culminates with his primary use of the sonnet form and his thematic preoccupation with pantheism, mysticism, sensualism, and the symbolist's idealization of the word itself. The color white, symbol of purity so idealized by the symbolists, found resonance throughout Sousa's works in references to swans, lilies, and so on. In fact, this has led several critics to call him the *cisne negro*, black swan, viewing him as a black who desired to be white.

"Antífona" (Antiphony), the first poem of *Broquéis*, is dedicated to his wife, Gavita, on their wedding day; it is also a declaration of adherence to the symbolist school. Nonetheless, pain and suffering would be the dominant themes of his final works, and they are already evident in *Broquéis*: "Acrobata de dor" (Acrobat of Pain), for example, is a morbid view of the clown's life. As tragedy involved him, the theme of personal and national suffering—particularly of his fellow blacks—appears repeatedly in the poems posthumously collected in *Evocações* (1898; Evocations) and *Faróis* (1920; Searchlights). An example is "Litania dos pobres" (Litany of the Poor): "The miserable, the broken down / are the flowers of the sewage. / They are implacable ghosts / the broken down, the miserable."

Often linked with Augusto dos *Anjos and the Portuguese poet Antero de
Quental, Sousa is ranked as an eminent figure of Brazilian literature. Nonetheless,
his poetry has still to be comprehensively evaluated and appreciated today. (*See*
Portugal and Brazil: Literary Relations.)

BIBLIOGRAPHY: Additional selected works by Sousa: *Últimos sonetos*, 1905; *O
livro derradeiro*, 1945; *Obra completa*, 1945. Criticism: Brookshaw; Martins, Heitor.
"White on Black in Cruz e Sousa." *New Perspectives in Brazilian Literary Studies:
Symbolism Today*. Edited by Darlene J. Sadlier. Bloomington: University of Indiana,
1984, pp. 7–18; Sayers, Raymond S. "The Black Poet in Brazil: The Case of Cruz e
Sousa." *LBR* (Summer, 1978), pp. 175–180; Whitmore, Don. "Cruz e Sousa's Musical
References." *LBR* (Summer, 1978), pp. 63–68.

LUIZA LOBO

SOUSÂNDRADE [JOAQUIM DE SOUSA ANDRADE] (1833–1902). Born
in Maranhão, Sousândrade stands out from among the members of the second
romantic generation, to which he logically belongs, owing to his unusual life
and amazingly original literary work. He traveled through the Amazon, Latin
America, Central America, and Europe and lived in New York City, where he
began to have his complete works published. Upon his return to Brazil, he avidly
supported the republican cause and became embroiled in other national issues.
The modern Brazilian flag is based on his design. (*See* Romanticism.)

Harpas selvagens (1857; Savage Harps), his first published collection, reflects
the *baroque linguistic and semantic style characteristic of all of his writings,
placing them well outside contemporary trends. *Guesa errante* (1874–1877; The
Mythical Wandering Colombian Bird), his masterpiece, is a thirteen-canto narrative without any clearly logical organization; rather, it is structured around the
myth of the *guesa*—a cyclical sacrifice of a child indoctrinated into a cult—and
employs imagistic techniques and linguistic deconstruction of culture, which
places him among the direct predecessors of twentieth-century poets, including
the Brazilian modernists and Ezra Pound. Canto Ten of the narrative includes
"O inferno de Wall Street" ("The Inferno of Wall Street," in *LALR* [January-
June, 1986], pp. 92–99)—a result of his residence in New York—in which he
censures the open, greedy pursuit of wealth that dominated society in the late
nineteenth century. Among those he saw as being sacrificed in this pursuit were
Sousândrade himself, as a poet in an alien society, and also the Brazilian Indians,
gradually being destroyed by the dominating classes—the nobles and the clergy.

Sílvio *Romero described Sousândrade's poetry as "barely intelligible"; however, after fifty years of oblivion, which Sousândrade himself had predicted for
his work, he was rediscovered and his works were favorably reevaluated by
Haroldo de *Campos and Augusto de *Campos.

BIBLIOGRAPHY: Additional selected works by Sousândrade: *Novo Éden*, 1893. Criticism: Campos, Augusto de Campos and Haroldo de Campos. *Re/Visão de Sousândrade*.
São Paulo: Edições Iniciação, 1964; Driver; Lobo, Luiza. *Épica e modernidade em*

Sousândrade. São Paulo: Presença/EDUSP, 1986; Williams, Frederick. " 'The Wall Street Inferno': A Poetic Rendering of the Gilded Age.'' *Chasqui* (February, 1976), pp. 15–32.

SOUZA, MÁRCIO (b. 1946). Novelist, playwright, and essayist, Souza grew up in Manaus, capital of the state of Amazonas, the setting for many of his literary works. He began writing film criticism at the age of thirteen. In 1972 he directed his only feature-length film, *A selva*, based on the homonymous work by the Portuguese novelist Ferreira de Castro. (*See* Film and Literature; Portugal and Brazil: Literary Relations; Regionalism.)

Souza's works reflect Oswald de *Andrade's mordant, satirical sense of humor, which transmits a highly critical political vision of Brazilian society. All of his novels have a strong historical component. *Galvez, Imperador do Acre* (1976; *The Emperor of the Amazon*, 1980), a trenchant critique of cultural colonialism, describes in a burlesque fashion Brazil's occupation of the Acre territory at the turn of the century; *Mad Maria* (1980; *Mad Maria*, 1985) focuses on the turn-of-the-century construction of the Madeira-Marmoré railway in northwestern Brazil, a monumental example of neocolonialism; *A resistível ascensão do Boto Tucuxi* (1982; The Resistible Ascension of Boto Tucuxi) weaves Amazonian myths and legends with social satire.

Souza's subsequent novels relate political themes—coup d'etat, counterinsurgency, terrorism—in fast-moving narratives that combine adventure, science fiction, international espionage (e.g., *A ordem do dia* [1983; The Order of the Day, 1986]), and detective fiction with the literary thriller. *Operação silêncio* (1979; Operation Silence) is perhaps his most overlooked and yet most fascinating novel. It is a veritable essay on the relationship between art and politics, between theory and action, between intellectuals and the state. Set in São Paulo, Lima, and Paris, its fragmented narrative follows the path of filmmaker Paulo Conti as he remembers his experiences of the late 1960s and early 1970s, a period when many people were forced by political circumstances into tragic options. (See Dictatorship and Literature.)

Although his more recent fiction lacks the biting satire of earlier works, with his critical vision and fast-moving narratives, Souza has firmly placed himself at the forefront of Brazilian fiction today.

BIBLIOGRAPHY: Additional selected works by Souza: *A expressão amazonense: do colonialismo ao neo-colonialismo*, 1978; *Teatro indígena do Amazonas*, 1979; *Tem piranha no piracuru* and *As folhas do latex*, 1979; *A condolência*, 1984; *O palco verde*, 1984; *O brasileiro voador*, 1986; *Ação entre amigos*, 1986. Criticism: Dorfman, Ariel. "Rubber Soul." *VV* (January 14, 1986), p. 47; Franco, Jean. "It's a Jungle Out There" (Review of *Mad Maria*). *NYTBR* (January 19, 1986), p. 10; Moisés, Carlos Felipe. "Adventurers and Adventurists." *Americas* (May, 1981), pp. 25–26.

RANDAL JOHNSON

STEEN, EDLA VAN (b. 1936). Born in Santa Catarina, Steen now lives in São Paulo, where she has been active in film, literature, and feminist causes. She has organized many anthologies around these topics, for example, *O papel do amor* (1978; The Role of Love), *O conto da mulher brasileira* (1978; The Short Story about the Brazilian Woman), and *O erotismo no conto brasileiro* (Eroticism in the Brazilian Short Story). (*See* Feminism and Literature; Film and Literature.)

Steen's own short stories and novels deal with situations in which lives, principally women's lives, have gone awry. In her novel *Corações mordidos* (1983; Bitten Hearts), for example, men are only vague images in a town where the dead arise from their graves. The story "Que horas são?" (What Time Is It?), from the collection *Até sempre* (1985; Forever), presents the angered wife of a failed soccer player who imagines that she has decapitated her husband and scored a goal by successfully kicking his head into the goal, the wastebasket, while she is actually preparing a chicken for dinner. In "A bela adormecida" (The Sleeping Beauty), with reminiscences of Machado de *Assis's *Memórias póstumas de Brás Cubas*, a dead woman who committed suicide views her funeral and reviews her life of failures through multiple flashbacks.

BIBLIOGRAPHY: Additional selected works by Steen: *Cio*, 1965; *Memórias do medo*, 1974; *Antes do amanhecer*, 1977; Translations: *LALR* (January-June, 1986); Tolman (1984). Criticism: Tolman (1984).

SUASSUNA, ARIANO (b. 1927). One of Brazil's most noted dramatists, Suassuna's works combine the theatrical form of religious plays of the medieval European theater, for example, the Portuguese Gil Vicente; the theater of Spanish Renaissance, for example, Calderón de la Barca (1600–1681); and the Italian *commedia dell'arte* with folkloric tales of his native northeastern Brazil to achieve one of the finest examples of a truly national literature. (*See* Folklore and Literature; Portugal and Brazil: Literary Relations; Theater History.)

Although Suassuna studied law, his interest in drama and folklore took priority. In 1946 he founded the Pernambuco Student Theater and wrote his first play, *Uma mulher vestida de sol* (1947; A Woman Dressed in the Sun), based on legends of the northeastern popular songbooks (*romanceiro*). The *romanceiro* has provided the material for his most successful dramas. *Auto da compadecida* (1956; *The Rogue's Trial*, 1963) mixes Christian traditions with popular religion of the Northeast in a comic situation with important allegorical, social, and nationalist overtones. *O santo e a porca* (1957; The Saint and the Pig) is also placed in the *sertão*, with its culture, language, humor, and tragedy serving as the thematic basis.

In 1970 Suassuna organized all artists interested in the maintenance and promulgation of regional popular literature (*cordel*) to join the Armorial movement. He himself turned toward fiction and began a trilogy of historical novels based on popular backlands traditions: *Romance d'a pedra do reino* (1971; Romance of the Kingdom's Stone), which was followed by *História do rei degolado nas* *caatingas do sertão* (1977; Story of the King Beheaded in the Sagebrush of the Backlands). João Cabral do *Melo Neto dedicated a poem, "A Pedra do Reino" (The Kingdom's Stone, in *A escola de facas*), to Suassuna to honor his contribution to folklore.

BIBLIOGRAPHY: Additional selected works by Suassuna: *A pena e a lei*, 1971; *Farsa da boa preguiça*, 1974. Criticism: Foster/Foster, II; Lyday, Leon F. "The *Barcas* and the *Compadecida*: *Autos* Past and Present." *LBR* (Summer, 1974), pp. 84–88; Mazzara, Richard A. "Poetic Humor and Universality in Suassuna's *Compadecida*." *BSUF* 10 (1969), pp. 25–30; Ratcliff, Dillwyn. "Folklore and Satire in a Brazilian Comedy." *Hispania* (March, 1961), pp. 282–284.

SURREALISM. As described by André Breton (1896–1966) in his *Manifeste du surréalisme* (1924), surrealism sought to express artistically the real workings of thought, free of controls placed on it by reason, aesthetics, or morality.

Surrealism's appearance almost coincides with Brazilian *modernism, which in its own way adapted and overshadowed it. Nonetheless, Adelino Magalhães (1887–1987) is considered to be a precursor of the French movement in Brazil, as well as its major national exponent. His prose and poetic work, written in the 1920s and 1930s, seems to possess an unfinished quality achieved through linguistic, stylistic, and thematic devices. Several other Brazilian writers indicate a debt to surrealism, including Aníbal *Machado, Jones Rocha, Murilo *Mendes, Jorge de *Lima, João Cabral de *Melo Neto, Murilo *Rubião, and Ledo *Ivo. Surrealism still has its contemporary adherents, for example, the poetry of Denise Emmer, *A equação da noite* (The Night Equation), and stories by Marina *Colasanti. (*See* New Writers.)

SYMBOLISM. A worldwide artistic movement that grew out of *romanticism, symbolism was strongly influenced by Edgar Allen Poe (1809–1849) and Charles Baudelaire (1821–1887). In Brazil, at least, it was almost coetaneous with the less universal movement of *Parnassianism. In fact, Brazilian Parnassian poets often tended toward symbolist techniques and themes to such an extent that the poet's true affiliation was murky.

Symbolism's philosophy was Platonism; it sought to see the idea that exists beyond the world of superficial reality. Although it is not an exclusively literary movement, it attained its greatest glory in literature and its aesthetic is literary. It puts forward the theory that although the limits of denotative language are finite, the artist through the imaginative use of connotative language may go beyond rational boundaries to seek truths that descriptive and expository discourse cannot reach. The writer employs symbols that are in fact extended metaphors and that through their suggestive power present realities of a kind akin to those of dreams, reveries, and mystical visions.

Plumbing the depths of the unconscious, the symbolist poets and other artists were drawn to religious symbolism as found in the rituals of the Catholic religion, and they scrutinized theosophy and other Eastern philosophies and religions.

Conceiving of their art as the sister of music, they tried to achieve the quality of music through intense use of the sound effects produced by repetition, which they believed would reinforce the messages of their symbols. In their desire to find new music, the Brazilian poets were led to experimenting with metrical patterns that were foreign to the tradition of poetry of the Portuguese language, and their innovations in metrics, and subject matter, opened the way for the great poetic revolution of the twentieth century.

The influence of Baudelaire was not limited to the idea of the power of the symbol but also included his fascination with "decadence"—all aspects of corruption, whether physical or moral—as well as his Satanism. For this reason the symbolists were first called decadents (*decadentistas*). In fact, the first collection of poetry in Brazil that may be called symbolist is *Canções da decadência* (1887; Songs of Decadence) by Medeiros e *Albuquerque. As a group, these poets may no more be called poets of the ivory tower than Baudelaire; in some, at least, the note of social criticism is strong. João da Cruz e *Sousa, the greatest Brazilian symbolist, in his early career had written abolitionist verse and participated actively in the antislavery movement, and after the cause was victorious in 1888, he continued to express his anguish at the position of blacks, as in the poems "Crianças negras" (Black Children) or in his prose poem "Emparedado" (Walled In), in which he presented himself as the prisoner of social incomprehension and prejudice. There were other social critics such as Emiliano Perneta (1866–1921) from the state of Paraná, the author of *Ilusão* (1911; Illusion), who was associated in the pioneer symbolist literary *review *Folha Popular* (1893; The People's Journal). A second well-known poet who collaborated in this magazine was B. Lopes (1859–1915), who published a symbolist collection, *Sinhá Flor* (1899; Miss Flower), and who was from the state of Rio. (*See* Slavery and Literature.)

Symbolist poets and reviews flourished in all of the populated parts of the republic at the turn of the century. Among the most notable were *Horus* (1902), founded by Azevedo Viana (1882–1936); *A Rua de Ouvidor* (Rio, 1889–1917); *Revista Americana* (Rio, 1909–1919); and *Revista do Brasil* (Rio, 1916–1928). The *carioca* Mário Pederneiras (1868–1915), the author of *Agonia* (1900; Agony), exercised strong influence on the movement through his widely sold magazine *Fon-Fon!*, founded in 1908 and in existence for many years. Also associated with *Fon-Fon!* was Eduardo Guimaraens (1892–1928), from Rio Grande do Sul, who was consistently and splendidly a symbolist and who is considered, along with Cruz e Sousa and Alphonsus de *Guimaraens, to be one of the leaders of the movement. Very much in the tradition of the French symbolists, he embodies in his work symbolist qualities such as the use of soft colors, halftones, and imprecise outlines and a consistent tendency to melancholy. *Divina quimera* (1916; Divine Chimera) is the title of a volume of his poems and also of his collected verse.

The religious tendency, the mysticism, and, in short, the spirituality of symbolism, as well as its medievalism and its traditionalism, are found in the poetry of Alphonsus de Guimaraens. His preoccupation with religious themes is evident in the titles of his books, for example, *Setenário das dores de Nossa Senhora* (1899; The Seven Day Feast of Our Lady of Sorrows).

Alphonsus de Guimaraens, Eduardo de Guimaraens, and Cruz e Sousa are by far the greatest of the symbolists, but the number of fairly good symbolist writers is legion. Among them are Pethion de Vilar (1870–1924), Pedro Kilkerry (1885–1914), both from Bahia; Guerra Durval (1872–1947), from Rio Grande do Sul; and (Antônio Francisco) Da Costa e Silva (1885–1950), from Piauí. Augusto dos *Anjos from Paraíba has been variously classified as a Parnassian, a symbolist, and a "scientific" poet: as a Parnassian because of his forms and metrics, as a "scientific" poet because of a vocabulary that is largely drawn from that of the organic sciences, and more correctly as a symbolist because of the brooding, mysterious quality and the fascination with decadent themes evident in his volume *Eu*. A slightly later poet who belongs to the transition from the *fin de siècle* period to that of *modernism is Raul de Leoni (1895–1926), from the state of Rio. Most famous for *Ode a um poeta morto* (1919: Ode to a Dead Poet), about the great Parnassian Olavo *Bilac, and for *Luz mediterrânea* (1922; Mediterranean Light), he has been called a Parnassian, but this attribution is contradicted by his unswerving Platonism, actually the theme of many of his poems. His melancholy; his evocation of old, unhappy, far-off things; and his crepuscularism should convince the reader that he is a symbolist. It should be interesting to note that there were two prominent women symbolists, *Francisca *Júlia and Gilka *Machado. (*See* Feminism and Literature.)

Symbolism in literature was not confined to verse; there are some interesting symbolist novels and dramas. Henrique *Coelho Neto's symbolist novels include *Rei negro*, which deals with life on a great plantation during the days of slavery. Gonzaga *Duque's *Mocidade morta* is set in Rio's society of rarified artists. José Graça *Aranha depicted a future Brazil in symbolist terms in his *Canaã*. He also wrote a symbolist play, *Malasarte* (1911). José Rocha Pombo (1857–1933), a noted historian from Paraná, wrote *No hospício* (1905; In the Asylum), which is one of the first introductions into literature of the theme of the insane asylum as a symbol of the world. Nestor Vítor dos Santos was the "official critic" of the movement and also had published *Signos* (1897; Signs), symbolist stories that use interior monologues. (*See* Critics and Criticism; Theater History.)

The influence of symbolism continued well into the early twentieth century. Ronald de *Carvalho characterized this last phase of the movement as "penumbrism," in a reference to the works of Ribeiro *Couto, which "fled from the sun into the shade, the crepuscular." In fact, some of the early modernists, such as Guilherme de *Almeida, were symbolist poets of this type. Even in the great literary revival of modernism, symbolism has flourished in the works of Clarice *Lispector and Cecília *Meireles, who is usually considered a neosymbolist, as well as in the poetry of members of the Generation of 1945. (*See* Postmodernism in Poetry.)

BIBLIOGRAPHY: Criticism: Coutinho/Rabassa; Jackson, K. David. "Hallucinated Bahia: Prefigurations of Modernism in Pedro Kilkerry." *New Perspectives in Brazilian Literary Studies: Symbolism Today.* Edited by Darlene Sadlier. Indiana: Indiana University, 1984, pp. 36–47; Sayers, Raymond S. "The Impact of Symbolism in Portugal and Brazil." *Writing for Pegasus.* Edited by Roland Grass and William R. Risley. Macomb, Ill.: Western Illinois University, 1979, pp. 125–141.

RAYMOND S. SAYERS

T

TAUNAY, ALFREDO D'ESCRAGNOLLE, VISCOUNT OF (1843–1899; BAL: 1897). Taunay's father, Nicolas Antoine Taunay, was a French landscape painter who immigrated to Brazil in 1868 with Jean-Baptiste Debret (*see* Art and Literature). He enlisted in the army in 1861 and took part in the Paraguayan War (1864–1870), most notably in the retreat from the Laguna, which he wrote about in a volume originally published in French, *La retraite de la lagune* (1871; The Retreat from Laguna), and which was translated into Portuguese by his son, the historian and lexicographer Afonso d'Escragnolle Taunay (1876–1958; BAL: 1929). He was a prominent political figure in the later years of the empire, one who argued strongly for liberal reform and European immigration. He wrote under several pseudonyms, principally Sílvio Dinarte. (*See* Historiography.)

His fame as a novelist rests almost entirely on *Inocência* (1872; *Innocence*, 1946). It is set in the distant *sertão* of Mato Grosso. Remarkably, however, this is not a fictional jungle popularized by Vicomte Chateaubriand, James Fenimore Cooper, or José de *Alencar; rather, it is the real interior (which Taunay himself knew from his military experience), where people fall victims to malaria or leprosy, and traditional attitudes toward women cause loving fathers to keep their daughters in total ignorance as well as innocence, literally believing that women are close to being works of the Devil. Although its plot is still traditionally romantic—the love between an innocent girl and an ardent (if not impeccable) young traveling doctor, which is thwarted by her tyrannical father, who wishes to dispose of her to her cousin in time-honored fashion—reading it, one realizes that it retains a good deal of original freshness.

Innocence is on the boundary between *romanticism and *realism, very characteristic of the moment when it was published: the first hesitant efforts of Brazilian fiction to break with idealization. Its success is also due in large part to the personal experience of the author, who drew on people he had actually met to construct characters and their speech, which is remarkably natural and not caricatural. It has further literary importance in that it deals, for instance, with the all-powerful father, a vital theme in the Brazilian novel as a whole, and in the figure of Meyer, the (admittedly too comic) German butterfly hunter, and it confronts the primitive interior of Brazil with the "civilized" outside world. Small wonder that *Innocence* has recently been made into a very faithful and successful film by Walter Lima, Jr. (*See* Film and Literature.)

None of Taunay's other fictional work achieved the impact of *Innocence*. The most interesting is the novel *O encilhamento* (1893; Inflation), an attack on the financial scandals of the early years of the republic, which combines a thin plot with heavy-handed satire.

BIBLIOGRAPHY: Criticism: Driver.

JOHN GLEDSON

TÁVORA, FRANKLIN (1843–1888). Born in Ceará, Távora lived in Recife except for the last few years of his life. Aside from his early Indianist novel, his regionalist fiction appeared during the transition from *romanticism to *realism. (*See* Indianism; Regionalism.)

Távora's fame is due in part to his vociferous, unjustified attack on the language of José de *Alencar's fiction. He promoted the concept of "literature of the North" as the most faithful representation of pure Brazilian traditions. *Um casamento no arrabalde* (1869; A Marriage Ceremony in the Interior) presents the customs of rural marriage within the idealized framework of the romantic realists. His regional historical novels include *O cabeleira* (1876; The Cabeleira), which deals with a folkloric *jagunço* (backlands bandit); and the series, *O matuto* (1878; The Hillbilly) and *Lourenço* (1881; Lourenzo), which present the development of a religious fanatic. (*See* Folklore and Literature; Religion and Literature.)

Although some of these novels are still read today, they present a simplistic view of the Brazilian reality of the author's time through an artificially regionalistic language. (*See* Portuguese Language of Brazil.)

BIBLIOGRAPHY: Criticism: Brookshaw; Cartwright, Cecília Altuna. "The *cangaceiro* as a Fictional Character in the Novels of Franklin Távora, Rodolfo Teófilo, and José Lins do Rego." Dissertation, University of Wisconsin, 1974; Driver; Sayers.

TEIXEIRA, BENTO (1565–1600?). Born in Oporto, Portugal, Teixeira fled to Brazil with his family to escape the Inquisition. Educated by the Jesuits, he gave private lessons. After murdering his adulterous wife, he was returned to Lisbon, where he died.

Scholars have recently determined that Teixeira was the author of only one work, *Prosopopéia* (1601: Personification), an epic poem in ninety-four stanzas narrating the settlement of the captaincy of Pernambuco. A very poor imitation of Luís de Camões's *Os lusíadas* (1578), in spite of its slight nativist theme, the poem is of greater historical than literary interest. (*See* Historiography; Portugal and Brazil: Literary Relations; *Ufanismo*.)

BIBLIOGRAPHY: Criticism: Cunha, Celso, and Carlos Durval. "Introdução." *Prosopopéia*. Rio: Instituto Nacional do Livro, 1972.

TEIXEIRA E SOUSA. *See* Sousa, Antônio Teixeira e.

TELLES, LYGIA FAGUNDES (b. 1923). Telles attributes her interest in writing to the fascinating stories she heard during her childhood in São Paulo.

As a law student, she had her first book published, a collection of short stories: *Praia viva* (1944; Living Beach). A second collection of stories, *O cacto vermelho* (1949; The Red Cactus), was soon followed by her first novel, *Ciranda de pedra* (1954; *The Marble Dance*, 1986), which established Telles as an "intimist," a psychological writer in whose work women and the ensuing imprisonment of their family relationships would become the central theme. Her second novel, *Verão no aquário* (1963; Summer in the Aquarium), continued the theme of entrapment with the metaphorical aquarium of the heroine's childhood as the obstacle to her liberation. In 1969 her story "Antes do baile verde" (Before the Green Dance) won the prestigious Grand Prize (*See* Prizes) for Short Fiction at Cannes. (*See* Feminism and Literature.)

Telles's prose creates an atmosphere in which feelings of frustration, solitude, desperation, and incommunicability plague her female protagonists, who invariably are caught in a modern society in which established conventions and social norms limit their field of activity and power. As a picture of the moral, and frequently economic, decadence of the bourgeoisie and of families of past wealth, Telles's fiction underscores the conflicts and feelings of enclosure that women in such a world encounter as they attempt to adjust to the changes of modern society.

Her most famous novel, *As meninas* (1973; *The Girl in the Photograph*, 1982), published during the darkest period of Brazil's recent military rule, is, on the one hand, a courageous testimony to that time of censorship and repression and, on the other hand, a continuation of her perspective on women who are attempting to break the limits and boundaries imposed upon them by a society of tradition, exacerbated by the added pressures of an authoritarian regime. If her first two novels, narrated conventionally, can be labeled works of psychological realism, *The Girl in the Photograph* announces new directions in form and content. Told by shifting points of view and multiple narrators, often changing abruptly within the same paragraph, this book deals with the lives of three very different women struggling with the issues of love, revolution, drugs, sex, technology, and conventions. Although dramatically portrayed for the most part within the space of their rooms in a boardinghouse run by nuns, these three girls-sisters-women are no longer physically within the confines of the family home. Told with humor and stylistic and structural innovation, as well as a degree of metafictional commentary, the novel stands as a dynamic example of Telles's penetrating psychology and social commitment. Above all, however, it announced the direction that novels by Brazilian women are developing. (*See* Dictatorship and Literature.)

BIBLIOGRAPHY: Additional selected works by Telles: *Histórias do desencontro*, 1958; *Seminário dos ratos*, 1977 (*Tigrela and Other Stories*, 1986); *A disciplina do amor*, 1980; *Mistérios*, 1981. Translations: Tolman (1978). Criticism: Burgin, Richard. "*Tigrela and Other Stories*" (book review). *NYTBR* (May 4, 1986), p. 40; Silverman, Malcolm. "O mundo ficcional de Lygia Fagundes Telles." *Moderna ficção brasileira 2*. Rio: Civilização Brasileira, 1981, pp. 162–184; Tolman, Jon H. "New Fiction: Lygia Fagundes Telles." *Review* 30 (1981), pp. 65–70.

NELSON H. VIEIRA

TEÓFILO, RODOLFO (1853–1932). As a newborn, Teófilo was taken from Bahia to Ceará, where his father practiced medicine. In 1875 he received the diploma of pharmacist. He witnessed the famous 1877–1879 drought in Ceará, which left indelible impressions upon him. An abolitionist and professor of natural history, he was also a member of Ceará's Spiritual Brotherhood, the first important northeastern regionalist group. (*See* Cycles; Regionalism; Slavery and Literature.)

His devotion to Ceará combined with his scientific knowledge and a somewhat distorted view of *naturalism in literature inspired his most renowned works, a trilogy documenting that famous drought. *A Fome* (c. 1890; Hunger) depicts the plight of a well-to-do rural family that is forced to migrate to the city as a result of the economic and social disaster. One section dwells on the question of slavery. In *Os brilhantes* (1895; The Diamonds), Ceará's interior is the backdrop for the story of Jesuíno Soares, a backlands bandit (*cangaceiro*). *O paroara* (1899; The Northeastener in Amazonia) follows the exodus of another *retirante*, a refugee from the drought, who seeks a future "in exile" in the Amazon.

Teófilo's fiction is preoccupied with documentary rather than artistic aims. His characters are representatives of mass situations rather than individuals, a characteristic also found in the works of another naturalist, Aluísio *Azevedo. Characters and situations often lack depth and are illogical. Furthermore, what appears to be naturalistic detail (e.g., scientific descriptions) is nothing more than Teófilo flaunting terminology related to his profession.

Aside from writing the trilogy and other "utopian science fiction," Teófilo had scientific treatises on the drought and poems published. New critical editions of his works that appeared in the 1970s recognized their virtues.

BIBLIOGRAPHY: Additional selected works by Teófilo: *Violação*, 1898; *Memórias de um engrossador*, 1912; *Telesias: versos*, 1913; *O reino de Kiato*, 1922. Criticism: Cartwright, Cecília Altuna. "The *cangaceiro* as a Fictional Character in the Novels of Franklin Távora, Rodolfo Teófilo, and José Lins do Rego." Dissertation, University of Wisconsin, 1974; Loos.

EDGAR C. KNOWLTON, JR.

TERESA MARGARIDA. *See* Orta, Teresa Margarida da Silva e.

THEATER HISTORY. This history stresses the interchange between theatrical practice and dramatic literature from the sixteenth century until the present. As in much of Brazil's cultural production—as well as that of the rest of Latin America—the theater is marked by the invention and valorization of national themes and autochthonous traditions in constant dialogue with European, and later American, drama and theatrical conventions.

The first documented manifestations of theater in Brazil are those of the *teatro de catequese*, the Jesuit catechistic theater of the sixteenth century. Adapting the medieval structures of Spanish and Portuguese theater of religious instruction—mainly the *auto*—to the social realities of the conquest, these plays served to proselityze the Indians in both the religious and political sense and provide a sense of community in the Portuguese settlements. Father José de *Anchieta's best plays, *Auto de São Lourenço* and *Auto de Natal*, are vivid spectacles whose theatrical rhythm is punctuated by music and dance and rapid confrontations between "good and evil" and is marked by visual contrasts of light and dark. (*See* Portugal and Brazil: Literary Relations; Religion and Literature.)

This tradition of religious theater was curtailed with the expulsion of the Jesuits in 1759. In terms of secular theater, there was little documented theater of note in Brazil until the surge of nationalist spirit that coincided with the imperial epoch and *romanticism. Critic Sábato Magaldi (*See* Critics and Criticism) conjectured this lack of national dramaturgy to be due to the precarious conditions of colonization—the threat of French or Dutch attack added to the difficulties of reaching a social stability necessary for any continuous theater practice—and to the colonial tendency to adhere to European literary models.

However, two figures should be mentioned: Manuel Botelho de *Oliveira and Antônio José da *Silva (The Jew). Oliveira's most famous play, *Hay amigo para amigo*, was written in response to the Spanish playwright Francisco de Rojas Zorrilla's (1607–1648) comedy *No hay amigo para amigo*. Although his plays were written in Spanish and were stylistically derivative of the Spanish *comedia*, Oliveira is considered by some critics as the first Brazilian author of comedies. Silva became "brazilianized" when Gonçalves de *Magalhães dramatized his personal tragedy in *Antônio José ou o poeta e a inquisição*. This play, whose author proclaimed it the first tragedy written by a Brazilian and the first one to treat a national theme, did mark the beginning of the romantic drama. *Antônio José* was a resounding success with a public primed for theater with national themes.

The surge of public interest in Brazilian theater that we find at this time should not be wholly attributed to the nationalist fervor of romanticism. It also has to do with the creation, for the first time, of a solid infrastructure for theater: theaters, theatrical companies that gave a degree of financial stability and apprenticeship opportunities to actors, and some institutional funding that helped to create an ambience that attracted authors to try their hand at theater. The person most involved in making theater the principal diversion of the public was João Caetano dos Santos (1808–1863). A charismatic actor and impresario, he was instrumental in the growth of municipal and local theater in Brazil. His book *Lições dramáticas* (Dramatic Lessons) details an acting method in which voice training, respiration, and presence of the actor are primary. Although his method of professional declamatory style was based on a European level of artistic accomplishment (and continental Portuguese pronunciation), it served to help standardize and professionalize the Brazilian stage. (*See* Portuguese Language of Brazil.)

A half-year after their production of *Antônio José*, João Caetano's company produced Martins *Pena's first comedy, *O juiz de paz na roça*. Whereas tracing the origins of Brazilian theater to particularized forms such as Anchieta's *autos* or citing dubious claims to Oliveira or even Magalhães has much to do with the theater historian's legitimate desire to find or valorize a continuity in theatrical traditions as with the intrinsic value of those texts, there is no question that Pena's scenes-of-local-life (*costumbrista*) plays established a tradition in dramatic literature while also forming a school of theatrical conventions (portrayal of types, gests, and so on).

The backbone of the midnineteenth century theater was the *costumbrista* comedy and the romantic melodrama of Brazilian themes, with an occasional play that mixes the two, for example, the practically forgotten theater of Luís Antônio Burgaín (1812–1877) and of Quintino Bocaiúva (1836–1916), a republican politician and drama critic who wrote about imperial life, for example, *A família* (The Family) and *Os mineiros da desgraça* (1862; The Disgraced *mineiros*). A notable exception was the poet Gonçalves *Dias, whose historical dramas (e.g., the rarely performed *Leonor de Mendonça*) reached for the elevated style of classical European tragedy.

Most of the extant plays of this period were written by authors more famous for other genres, perhaps attracted to the stage for its popularity or power of communication on social issues. Joaquim Manuel de *Macedo staged his novel *A moreninha* but achieved better dramatic success with ''serious'' comedies that satirized the existing social and political institutions and attitudes he considered dangerous to the nation.

Following in the critical vein of the necessity of social reform, José de *Alencar wrote plays that, although highly melodramatic, were important for their elements of social condemnation and their progressive sense of nationality and call to national unity. His best play, *Mãe*, remains an important abolitionist statement. Of note also is Paulo Eiró's (1836–1871) abolitionist drama *Sangue limpo* (1863; Clean Blood). (*See* Slavery and Literature.)

Two significant divergences from the general trend can be found in the works of Álvares de *Azevedo and *Qorpo-Santo. Azevedo's *Macário* is a somewhat surrealistic romantic fantasy with allegorical figures (Satan and others) whose hero has the energy of a Brazilian Calabar. The staging suggested by the play, the surrealistic tone, and the allegorical figures would become popular conventions of the end of the century. Qorpo-Santo, although one of the few thoroughly original dramatic and theatrical creators of the Brazilian stage, is rarely produced and received no recognition in his lifetime. (*See* Surrealism.)

By the end of the century, the melodrama was decidedly secondary to the comedy. José Joaquim da *França Júnior, whose comedies are among the best in Brazilian dramatic literature, owes much to Pena, as can be seen in his well-constructed social critiques. However—sign of the times—Pena's ebullient and often naive romantic playfulness is replaced in França Júnior's works by an acerbic and sometimes vulgar humor structured by attention to realistic detail in his satires of institutions and social customs.

The *revista*—satirical sketches influenced in Brazil by the English music hall and French and American vaudevilles—and the *chanchada*—the satiric version of a serious, usually foreign, drama—took over the Brazilian stage at the time. Artur *Azevedo created the *revista do ano*, yearly *revista*, beginning in 1877. In this style, but more intellectually *fin de siècle*, are João do *Rio's comedies of metropolitan decadence, for example, *A bela madame Vargas*. The intellectual farce had another practitioner in Henrique *Coelho Neto, whose thematic penchant for spiritualist themes (and satire of same) and preference for symbolic imagery added another dimension to this comedy, for example, *O diabo no corpo; O pedido*.

The end of the empire and the beginning of the republic marked the rise of the actor as the major factor in the growth of Brazilian theatrical tradition. In the confusion and enthusiasm of the newly founded republic, the careful and classic declamatory style of João Caetano degenerated, or at best was reformulated into burlesque buffonery. By the end of World War I, which served to isolate Brazil from Europe, the actor reigned by personality as never before.

Actors in the 1920s and 1930s became popular idols. Plays were written expressly for the purpose of keeping the principal actor always in center stage, for example, Joracy *Camargo's *Deus lhe pague* with Procópio Ferreira (1898–1979). The two most important theater groups, directed by the histrionic actors Procópio Ferreira and Jayme Costa, specialized in light comedy, a major theme being the life of the lower middle class in suburban Rio or São Paulo and satires of the middle class and its pretensions.

In Rio activity involved the Trianon Theater, where both Procópio and Costa did many plays. The major playwrights in what was posteriorly called the "Trianon" group were Gastão Tojeiro (1880–1965), author of *Onde canta o sabiá* (Where the Sabiá Bird Sings); Roberto Gomes, author of *Berenice* (Berenice); Oduvaldo Viana, dramatist of *Manhãs do sol* (Sunny Mornings); and Joracy Camargo. The Trianon style was predominant in Rio, and indeed in the rest of the country, until the late 1940s, when industrial and governmental patronism gave rise to professional and university theater groups.

In São Paulo the Week of Modern Art (*see* Modernism) included only one theater piece of minimal theatrical value, *As experiências* (The Experiments) by Flávio Carvalho (1899–1973), who was also a notable modernist architect. Possibly, the aestheticism of the Week of Modern Art did not lend itself to the inclusion of theater, since Brazilian theater was at that time already strongly rooted in the popular tradition of the *revista* and *chanchada*. The amateur theater in the homes of wealthy *paulistas* (e.g., the "Toy Theater" of Álvaro Moraes), however, acted as an important stimulus among the industrialists to patronize university groups and later professional groups. Oswald de *Andrade's plays, although written in the 1930s, were not produced at this time. Viriato Correia's (1884–1967) historical dramas (e.g., *Tiradentes; O grande amor de Gonçalves Dias*), as well as his weak urban social satires, were constantly on the scene during the 1930s and 1940s.

The critic Gustavo Dória correctly stressed the importance of the interchange between amateur, student, and professional groups in the growth of the theatrical traditionals in Brazil. The Brazilian Student Theater (TEB), founded in 1938 by the promotor and impresario Paschoal Carlos Magno (1906–1980), became a primary training ground for actors, emphasizing classical texts such as *Hamlet* but also stimulating interest in finding serious (as opposed to *revista*) national texts. Under Carlos Magno's tireless efforts in organizing festivals and finding financial support, TEB branches spread throughout Brazil. The University Theater, under the leadership of the actress Jerusa Camões, also played an important part in the movement. In 1948 Alfredo Mesquita (b. 1907) formed the Brazilian School of Dramatic Art, in São Paulo, which schooled actors, playwrights, and directors who fed the professional movement of the late 1940s and 1950s.

The influx of theater talent fleeing World War II did much to renovate the Brazilian theater and bring it back into a dialogue with European theatrical experimentation: Ruggero Jacobbi from Italy and Zbigniew Ziembinski (1908–1978) from Poland, both directors and actors, dedicated their talents to the Brazilian stage. Ziembinski's innovative and highly expressionistic staging of Nelson *Rodrigues's *Vestido de noiva* is considered by most critics as the beginning of modern theater in Brazil, marking a renovation in concepts of staging, scenic design, and production. *Vestido de noiva* was put on in Rio by an amateur group, Os Comediantes (The Comedians). As a result of this success and the continued direction of Ziembinski, Os Comediantes became a professional group in 1945, with a regularly produced repertory of plays. (*See* Immigrants and Literature.)

The economic expansion that accompanied industrialization in the 1940s paved the way, in the early 1950s, to a cosmopolitan urban theater. The light comedies and *revistas* of the Trianon era gave way to the sophisticated modern comedies of authors such as Guilherme de *Figueiredo; Raimundo Magalhães Jr. (*See* Biography and Biographers); Silveira Sampaio (1914–1965), author of *Flagrantes do Rio* (Flashes of Rio), and Pedro *Bloch. Furthermore, the enthusiasm of the development of nationalistic policies during the Kubitschek years (1956–1961) shifted the focus of the professional theater to the social drama. This transition is best exemplified in the works of the Brazilian Comedy Theater (TBC). Founded by the Italo-Brazilian industrialist Franco Zampari, the TBC—the prototype of liberal professional theater in Brazil—was São Paulo's most successful theater from 1948 through 1964. The scant TBC repertory of Brazilian plays from 1948 to 1958 relied almost exclusively on the urban comedies of Abílio Pereira de Almeida (1906–1977), for example, *Rua São Luiz, 27-8°* (27 São Luiz Street, Eighth Floor) or *Santa Marta Fabril, S.A.* (Santa Marta Factory, Inc.). It concentrated on admirable productions of European plays (by Carlo

Goldoni, John Priestley, Luigi Pirandello, Noel Coward, Jean-Paul Sartre) and staged the social and psychological dramas of the American playwrights—Tennessee Williams, Eugene O'Neill, and Arthur Miller. Only with the 1958 production of Jorge *Andrade's *Pedreira das almas* did the TBC focus a limited attention on the recent—but already successful—serious Brazilian playwrights. From 1958 until 1964 TBC produced plays by Andrade, Dias *Gomes, and Gianfrancesco *Guarnieri.

This relative lack of attention to national dramatists was partially responsible for the formation of the other major group of the 1950s, the Arena Theater of São Paulo. In 1954 José Renato formed the Arena Theater as an experimental group, an aesthetic answer to the spatial circumscription of proscenium theaters in the intimate staging of theater-in-the-round, as well as an alternative to the high-cost professional productions of the TBC. Around 1956, with the inclusion of the politically active Guarnieri, Oduvaldo *Viana Filho, and Augusto *Boal, Arena began to emphasize the search for a dramatic form that would speak to the social problems of Brazil. The creation of the Dramatic Seminars, in 1958, which elaborated plays of individual authors within the content of collective discussion, dealt directly with the problem of finding national texts. Guarnieri's *Eles não usam black-tie* and Viana Filho's *Chapetuba Futebol Clube*, the two major plays of the seminars, reflect the social realism of this tendency.

The boom of the 1950s in national theater and dramatists had one of its most fecund expressions in the Northeast, particularly in Pernambuco, where student groups were already well established. Taking themes from folklore—often from *cordel*—and using medieval theatrical forms, such as the *auto*, and the *bumba-meu-boi*, to portray the wealth of popular culture and analyze the social conditions of the region, playwrights created a renaissance of popular theater that continues to be a primary force in all of Brazilian theater (not just relegated to the Northeast or interior regions of Brazil). Also, the puppet theater (*mamulengo*), found in the Northeast, has been a significant—although somewhat peripheral—contribution to the theatrical traditions of Brazil. The most important dramatist of this movement was, and remains, Ariano *Suassuna. The plays of Hermilo *Borba Filho, who is also a theater historian; Joaquim *Cardozo; Rachel de *Queiroz; and Dias *Gomes are also of note for their use of northeastern theme, setting, and popular verse form. (*See* Folklore and Literature.)

Imitating the success of Arena and the groups of the Northeast (e.g., The Popular Northeastern Theater), political radicalization around the question of national identity found voice in other forms of theater. As in the new theater of the rest of Latin America—stimulated by the Cuban Revolution—groups in the early 1960s (and later some alternative groups of the 1970s) opted for varying degrees of collective creation in text and for alternative space of production as a political statement, considering this a step in translation of modes of theatrical production from the capitalist model toward the socialist. The theaters of the Popular Culture Centers (CPC), the cultural arm of the National Students' Union, and the Popular Culture movement (MPC) in Pernambuco, whose practice was informed by the theories of Paulo Freire (*See* Philosophy of National Identity), performed their thematically leftist plays and sketches (again with the conventions of popular theater) in union halls, schools, working-class neighborhoods, slums, parks, and rural zones as part of their program of political mobilization.

The military coup in 1964 curtailed the work of the CPC and MPC. Theaters' response to the increasing censorship and political repression of the military regime resulted in several important theatrical conventions that significantly influenced the Brazilian stage. (*See* Dictatorship and Literature).

The Grupo Opinião (Opinion Group), formed by ex-integrants of the CPC, elaborated a series of dramatic musical shows. The *Show Opinião*, put on in December of 1964 (and organized by Viana Filho), interwove song and testimony of three singers into a statement of protest through the valorization of the popular music of Brazil. *Liberdade, liberdade*, text by Flávio Rangel and Millôr *Fernandes, protested political closure through a mixture of song and statement (parts of speeches, poetry, and so on) that sketched the trajectory of occidental democracy. Although the use of music as political and social commentary was not new (it had been used in the *revista*), the collage technique employed in these shows initiated a tight method of incorporating music into dramatic structure. (*See* Music and Literature.)

Arena Theater, under the direction of Augusto Boal, developed the joker (*coringa*) system, in which tales of past national heroes were told through music and verse. The character of the joker, acting as narrator-moderator-interpreter of the events on stage functioned to reinterpret history and give perspective to the ideological presuppositions that underpin what Boal considered previous historical myth. Both Arena and Opinião, along with many other Brazilian playwrights, directors, and actors, acknowledge a strong debt to the theater of Bertolt Brecht.

Perhaps the most significant innovation in terms of later theater was done by the director José Celso Martinez with his group Oficina. Founded in 1958, Oficina came to the forefront of the theatrical scene with its 1967 production of Oswald de Andrade's play *O rei da vela*. Based on the cannabilist aesthetic of the 1920s, this production proposed a political aesthetic of aggression, which differed from that of the Americans (e.g., Living Theater) and Europeans (e.g., Peter Brook) in its underscoring of Brazilian stereotypical images—the grotesque caricaturing of the exotic (*exótica*) that, originating in a foreign or alienated Brazilian conception of Brazilian reality, had become internalized and assimilated into Brazilian culture. This emphasis on spectacle and image was the theatrical precursor of *tropicalismo*.

Brazilian theater flourished between 1964 and 1968. The relatively open cultural space of the first years of the dictatorship still allowed expression of the inventiveness of theater's response to political changes. Also, the possibilities of direct and immediate communication of theater made it the preferred and most effective cultural voice of these years.

The promulgation of the Fifth Institutional Act of December 1968 instituted a period of severe censorship and repression that, continuing until 1979, has had lasting repercussions on the theater. Because of economic pressures, Opinião had already effectively disbanded in 1968, although its work was carried on into the 1980s by the playwright João das Neves, author of *O último carro: anti-tragédia brasileira* (1974; The Last Car: A Brazilian Anti-Tragedy) and *Mural mulher* (1979; Mural Woman). Boal and José Celso went into exile in the early 1970s.

Professional theater, which in the late 1950s and early 1960s had built a solid base on the social dramas of the major Brazilian playwrights, suffered a radical change in the 1970s. Heavy and often arbitrary censorship, along with the economic problems of production caused by this censorship, caused many playwrights to turn their energies to writing soap operas (*telenovelas*) and television specials. In texts written for the stage, metaphor became the dominant dramatic mode—sometimes to the point of incomprehensibility—in the attempt to evade censorship. The musical metaphor—exemplified by works of Chico *Buarque and Ruy Guerra (b. 1931)—folded under the economic pressures of censorship. By the end of the 1970s professional theater was relying mainly on light comedy, for example, João *Bethencourt, foreign imports, or small-cast works whose possible forced cancellation would not occasion economic disaster.

On the other hand, the 1970s saw the rise of small independent groups whose works fed the theatrical scene of redemocratization after 1979. Taking advantage of spaces opened by the related national cultural policy of 1974, which emphasized popular culture (theater festivals became outlets for the exchange of ideas in the 1970s) or operating outside of the mainstream, these groups reinterpreted the legacy of the 1960s, creating a parallel or alternative theater.

Independent political theater found renewed expression in the traditions of popular theater (e.g., *Teatro União e Olho Vivo*). Under the direction of its principal playwright César Vieira, it was able to perform in the working-class neighborhoods of São Paulo, developing its plays in response to the critical arguments of its public. Formed in 1971, the Ipanema Theater became the veritable temple of *tropicalismo*'s youth with its production of José Vicente's (b. 1945) *Hoje é dia de rock* (1972; Rock's on Today). The group *Asdrubal Trouxe o Trombone* (Asdrubal Brought His Trombone) followed in this line. Directors whose apprenticeships had been in professional theater (Almir Haddad; Antunes Filho) invested their time and talent in alternative theater.

Antunes Filho's landmark 1978 adaptation of Mário de *Andrade's *Macunaíma*, begun as a group project in theatrical experimentation in 1976 and still performed nationally and internationally, has rightfully brought worldwide acclaim to the Brazilian theater. Using the basic legends, characters, and episodes that inform Andrade's vision of modernity and national identity, the play shifts to more contemporary images while perserving the rhapsodic flow of the original text. This highly visual spectacle builds its theatricality on superb acting, gest, and suprisingly simple scene solutions that provide a sense of cultural movement. For example, Antunes Filho organized stage movement to suggest the carnival groups (*blocos*), having the actors, in groups, move in diagonals across the stage as action and dialogue occur. There is no scenery or stage set. Props are few—newspaper pages, a long strip of cloth, a mobile bed—and used multireferentially. This inventive staging converts a lack of economic resources into an aesthetic plus. Also remarkable is the play's spatial versatility: it can transform the large empty stage of a municipal theater or the more intimate space of a small neighborhood theater into equal magic.

As indicated, the evolution of contemporary Brazilian theater involved the work of groups and directors more than that of individual dramatists. However, if we look at this period from the point of view of dramatic literature, we also see an overriding thematic concern for social issues and an intention to write "Brazilian plays" within the plurality of tendencies that mark Brazilian drama. Since not all contemporary dramatists maintained an integral association with a group, a brief recapitulation of the period in terms of its major writers will help to complete this perspective.

Considered by many the best contemporary playwright, Nelson *Rodrigues's lacerating studies of suburban life do not fit into a mold. Jorge *Andrade's major theme discusses the breakdown of the rural oligarchy in the state of São Paulo. The problems of the urban working class are treated in Guarnieri's dramas, while Viana Filho's best plays detail the social and political alienation of the urban middle and lower middle class. Plínio *Marcos's naturalistic yet lyrical works focus on the lives of the outcast, the criminal, and the marginals of Brazilian society. The best of Dias Gomes's existential-political plays take the Northeast as a theme and setting, as do Ariano Suassuna's social-religious parables. Abdias do *Nascimento, both with his plays and his work with the TEN, made an important contribution to Brazilian theater in his exploration of Afro-Brazilian culture. Children's theater also began to flourish in the late 1950s: Maria Clara Machado, the major Brazilian practitioner of this genre, has received international attention for her dramas. (*See* Children's Literature; Contemporary Black Literature; Naturalism.)

Despite the difficult times, the last years of the 1960s and the early 1970s have yielded new writers, most of whom are still writing and reaching maturity as dramatists. Chico Buarque still writes musicals based on social critique. Leilah *Assunção and Consuelo de *Castro, as well as Isabel Câmara, author of *As moças* (1968; The Girls), give contemporary dramatic space to the female protagonist. The following young writers are also of note: Roberto Austregésilo de Athayde (b. 1949), whose major work is *Apareceu a Margarida* (1973; *Miss Margarida's Way*), which views the military regime's "big brother" tactics and was extremely successful in Brazil and on Broadway with the actress Estelle Parsons; Antônio Bivar (b. 1939), author of *Cordélia Brasil* (Cordélia Brasil), which treats the desperate no-exit situation of Brazilian life during the 1970s, as well as *Alzira Power* (1971; Alzira Power) and *Alice que delícia!* (1987; Alice What a Delight); Mário Prata, author of *O cordão umbilical* (1971; The Umbilical Cord) and *Fábrica de chocolate* (1979; Chocolate Factory); João Ribeiro Chaves

Netto, author of *A patética* (written 1977; produced 1980; The Pathetic One), initially prohibited by censorship; and Vital Santos, author of *As sete luas de barro* (1980; The Seven Clay Moons).

The months directly following the political opening of 1979 were euphoric ones for theater. Texts that had been censored, or totally *engavetados* (shoved in the censor's drawers), were staged and became, like *Rasga coração* by Viana Filho, banners of democratic reaffirmation and national identity, as well as box-office smashes. New plays, geared for big stage production, such as Dias Gomes's *Campeões do mundo*, were written and purposefully structured as historical mosaics designed to recover a sense of history—of the time lost since 1968—in Brazilian drama. Carlos Alberto Soffredini's *Na carreira do divino* (1979; In the Divine Race), which received several *prizes, narrated the lives of a *caipira* family fighting for its traditions against encroaching capitalism. The smaller and younger groups (O Pessoal do Despertar, O Pessoal do Cabaré) tended to do more intimate stage pieces that investigated their sense of being—in essence, a lost generation—staging plays that poignantly captured the shadow life of adolescents living under repression. In both small theater spaces and in the larger commercial theaters, dozens of plays were produced that discussed themes of torture, guerrilla warfare, and social revindication: themes prohibited since the midsixties.

However, despite the richness of themes, the proliferation of new drama and groups, and the large quantity of previously censored texts now available for production, little has surfaced of real dramatic merit in the texts of this period. The most notable exception to this pessimistic picture is the continuing work of Antunes Filho with the Research Theater of the SESC, which is made up of a group of businesses actively supporting cultural activities. His recent productions of Nelson Rodrigues and adaptation of *Matraga* by Guimarães *Rosa show a unity of concept and style truly original and distinctly Brazilian. One hopes that, as in the past, the strength of autochthonous theatrical conventions will beget a corresponding surge of dramatic literature when economic conditions ameliorate.

The aesthetic quality of dramatic literature and of the stage has varied greatly in the 400 years' history of Brazilian theater. However, theater should be seen at least as much as a "process" as a "product." At best, theatrical communication depends on convention and consensus in immediate interchange with the concerns and expectations of its public. Perhaps more than any other of the arts, theater has maintained a steady hand on the cultural pulse of the nation, reflecting the values of politics and institutions that have informed Brazilian society.

BIBLIOGRAPHY: Criticism: Brownell, Virginia A. "Martyrs, Victims and Gods: A View of Religion in Contemporary Brazilian Drama." *LBR* (Summer, 1978), pp. 129–150; Butler, Ross E., Jr. "*Jeito* in Contemporary Brazilian Theater." *PPNCFL* (1973), pp. 303–309; idem. "Social Themes in Selected Contemporary Brazilian Dramas." *RomN* (Autumn, 1973), pp. 52–60; Driskell, Charles B. "The *Teatro de Arena* of São Paulo: An Innovative Professional Theater for the People." *Popular Theater for Social Change in Latin America*. Los Angeles: University of California, Los Angeles, Latin American

348

TORRES, ANTÔNIO

Studies Center, 1978, pp. 270–280; Fernández, Oscar. "Brazil's New Social Theater." *LATR* (Fall, 1960), pp. 15–30; George, David. "The Staging of *Macunaíma* and the Search for National Theater." *LATR* (Fall, 1983), pp. 47–58; Mazzara, Richard. "Regionalism and Modern Brazilian Theater." *REH* (1975), pp. 11–32; Michalski, Yan. *O teatro sob repressão*. Rio: Zahar, 1985; Prado, Décio de Almeida. *Apresentação do teatro moderno brasileiro: crítica teatral 1947–1955*. São Paulo: Martins, 1956; Sousa, José Galante de. *História do teatro no Brasil* (many editions); Unruh, Vicky. "Language and Power in *Miss Margarida's Way* and *The Lesson*." *LALR* (January-June, 1986), pp. 117–125.

LESLIE DAMASCENO

TORRES, ANTÔNIO (b. 1940). A Bahian, Torres was a journalist in Bahia and São Paulo and later worked in advertising in São Paulo, Portugal, and Rio.

Since the 1970s he has written six novels. The action in *Um cão uivando para a lua* (1972; A Dog Howling at the Moon) is set in an insane asylum, where a reporter recollects his past life in the interior of Bahia and then in the state capital, Salvador. The topic of craziness was a crucial one in the 1970s, not only because of individual life experiences but also because of the repression and censorship enforced by the military dictatorship, which led many young intellectuals into political exile or to psychiatric treatment. (*See* Dictatorship and Literature.)

In *Essa terra* (1976; *This Land*, 1987), Torres viewed the conflicts experienced by immigrants from the interior to the developed urban centers of Brazil through the double voiced narrator: Totohim, in Bahia, and Nelo, in São Paulo. An epigraph from William Faulkner's *The Sound and the Fury* reveals Torres's source for his stylistic innovations. The conflict between rural and urban Brazil also appears in *Carta ao bispo* (1979; Letter to the Bishop), while *Os homens dos pés redondos* (1973; The Men with Round Feet) tells of Torres's experiences in Portugal during the dictatorship of Antônio de Oliveira Salazar. (*See* Portugal and Brazil: Literary Relations.)

In some ways Torres's latest novel, *Balada da infância perdida* (1980; Ballad of the Lost Childhood), picks up earlier themes. The protagonist's hallucination brings up Brazil's political past, this time from a Spanish-American perspective.

BIBLIOGRAPHY: Additional selected works by Torres: *Adeus velho*, 1981. Translations: Tolman (1984). Criticism: Leite, Lígia Chiappini Moraes. "Prefácio." *Essa terra*. São Paulo: Ática, 1986; Tolman (1984).

LUIZA LOBO

TRAVEL LITERATURE. Picturesque and often detailed or insightful personal accounts of experiences, places, and life in colonial Brazil were written by foreign sailors, soldiers, explorers, civil servants, clerics, missionaries, poets, scientists, mechanics, doctors, pirates, convicts, and smugglers. The best-known sixteenth-century authors included André Thevet, Jean de Léry, Hans Staden, and Antony Knivet. Staden's narrative (Marpurg, 1557; translation, London, 1874), about his captivity among Brazilian Indians, provided a storyline for the

1971 film *Como era gostoso o meu francês* (*How Tasty Was My Little Frenchman*). Some major seventeenth-century travel writers treating Brazil were Olivier van Noort, Claude d'Abbeville, Richard Flecknoe, François Froger, and Antony Sepp von Rechegg. Among many others, Charles Marie de la Condamine, de la Flotte, Louis de Bougainville, Evariste Parny, John White, George Stauton, and James Semple-Lisle wrote relevant travel books in the eighteenth century. The sections pertaining to Brazil, however, tended to be short. (*See* Film and Literature; Historiography; Religion and Literature.)

The lifting of Portuguese mercantilist restrictions affecting Brazil in the first decade of the nineteenth century, the diffusion of news about the economic potential of the new empire, and the greater facility of transportation as the century progressed all resulted in geometric increases in the number of educated foreigners who went to Brazil and, thus, in the travel books that were produced. Most of these nineteenth-century books about Brazil did not treat additional countries. Nevertheless, as had occurred in earlier times, many of them were reprinted or translated into foreign languages. In fact, dozens of these books reappeared in Portuguese between the 1930s and 1970s, in testimony to their permanent value.

As had been the case in the colonial period, the reflective but diverse travel writers of the nineteenth century were generally in Brazil for reasons related to their professions. Most resided there for some years. Besides some adventurous vacationers, they included working businessmen, scientists, seamen, diplomats, churchmen, engineers, novelists and poets, artists, and local English-language newspaper editors. Their documentaries were not exclusively travelogues; many of the authors recorded, occasionally in technical terms, what they saw and achieved during their normal engagements in Brazil. Naturally, they had individual biases and limitations, sometimes including an inadequate knowledge of Portuguese. (*See* Art and Literature; Foreign Writers and Brazil.)

A. Curtis Wilgus (New Jersey, 1973) identified some 90 percent of the full-length nineteenth-century travel books about Brazil in English; he listed 42 by Americans, 81 by Britons, and two by Canadians. Alicia Tjarks (*Revista de História de América*, vol. 83) listed 140 travel books by writers of other languages. Various nineteenth-century authors each produced two or more of such books on Brazil. More than half of the works exceeded 400 pages, many occupying two or three volumes.

Some major nineteenth-century continental European travel writers on Brazil were Auguste Saint-Hilaire, Jean-Baptiste Debret (*see* Art and Literature), Ferdinand Denis (*see* Critics and Criticism), Robert Avé-Lallemant, Charles Ribeyrolles, Charles Expilly, Jean Reclus, and Max Leclerc, all of whom published in French; and Wilhelm von Eschwege, Carl Seidler, Hermann Burmeister, Johann von Tschudi, Oscar Canstatt, Karl von den Steinen, and Karl von Koseritz, who wrote in German. About a dozen travel books on nineteenth-century Brazil were translated into English, the outstanding ones being by Prince von Wied-Neuwied (London, 1820), Johann von Spix and Karl von Martius (London,

1824) (*see* Historiography), Prince Adalbert of Prussia (London, 1849), Emperor Maximilian I of Mexico (London, 1868), Franz Keller-Leuzinger (London and New York, 1874), and Adele Toussaint-Samson (Boston, 1891).

Only broad generalizations can be made about the themes and subject matter of so large a body of works, spanning a full century. All of the authors recounted personal experiences, including journeys, individuals they met, and historical events that they witnessed. Virtually all described Brazilian scenes and life-styles or customs (sometimes including forms of religious observance) in the places and among the social groups that they observed. Many writers remarked upon the country's social structure and racial and ethnic multiplicity, as well as upon the slave trade and the nature of Brazilian slavery; they expressed a wide range of views about slavery. A number of the foreign commentators emphasized Brazil's material and cultural "progress" or "prospects" and wrote about particular examples or sectors of the economy. Some authors assessed public policies or addressed the issue of Brazil's relative political stability and unity under its monarchy, compared to the frequent civil warfare suffered by the Spanish American republics. Later writers discussed the abolition of slavery and establishment of a republican government in Brazil.

Brazil's extraordinary physical environment attracted naturalists and geologists, and Emperor Pedro II encouraged and supported scientific exploration and reporting. There are thus multiple foreign accounts of the country's climatic and geographic features and contrasts; the immense variety of its geology, fauna, and flora; and the conditions of Indian tribes in the Amazon.

The following authors wrote outstanding nineteenth-century English-language travel books about Brazil. The cities (with the dates) in which their works were first published indicate the authors' nationalities. A dozen women wrote Brazilian travel books in English in the last century.

The attempt of the merchant Thomas Lindley (London, 1805) to smuggle goods into and out of Brazil, in 1802, ended with his imprisonment for a year by the Portuguese in the northeastern captaincy of Bahia. Although Lindley was required to spend his nights in jail, he was allowed to walk about the city of Salvador during the day. He recorded his detailed observations of the city, including its commerce, monuments, and forts. He also described the homes, customs, behavior, and intimate lives of the townspeople.

A merchant and wool dealer, John Luccock (London, 1820) described the "material, moral, and intellectual state" of Rio at the time of the Portuguese court's arrival in 1808. He then depicted the capital's "rapid progress toward civilization" during the next ten years. Luccock wrote about local customs, sensed the rise of Brazilian nationalism, and discussed the institution of slavery. He extended his treatment to Minas and to Rio Grande do Sul, which he visited several times.

The mineralogist and seaman John Mawe (London, 1812) wrote the first firsthand descriptions in English of Brazil's gold and diamond mines and camps, including the tools and procedures that were used. He recounted his travels of

1809–1810 in Minas and the interior of São Paulo, where the mines were located, and in Santa Catarina and Rio. Mawe reported on the climate, agriculture, commerce, population, manners, and customs.

Henry Koster (London, 1816) moved to Pernambuco in 1809, after living in Portugal and contracting tuberculosis in England. He traveled in Paraíba, Maranhão, Ceará, and Rio Grande do Norte and tried to grow sugarcane in Pernambuco. What he more successfully cultivated there was the friendship of leading native Brazilians. Koster wrote down his experiences and well-reasoned opinions and described socioeconomic conditions in copious detail; he focused in part on the status of freedmen and slaves. His own drawings served as illustrations for his book, which enjoyed great popularity.

Maria Graham (London, 1824) recorded her strong impressions of life in the coastal cities of Recife, Salvador, and Rio, which she visited between 1821 and 1823. She was a talented and penetrating writer and, like Koster, used her own drawings to illustrate her book. Graham returned to Brazil in 1824 to become a governess and tutor to the daughter of Emperor Pedro I. (*See* Art and Literature.)

The Reverends Daniel Kidder and James Fletcher (Philadelphia, 1845; 1857) were Methodist missionaries who worked in Brazil between the 1830s and 1860s. They wrote about their "residence and [wide] travels," described Brazilian life and customs in detail, and supplied historical and geographical information.

The eminent entomologist Henry Bates (London, 1863) described "habits of animals, Brazilian and Indian life," and his own adventures during eleven years of research and travel in the Amazon, beginning in 1848. Charles Darwin had encouraged Bates to write his classic book, which supports Darwin's and Alfred Wallace's theory of evolution by natural selection.

A visiting inventor and manufacturer, Thomas Ewbank (New York, 1856), presented a kaleidoscopic picture of life in Rio in the early 1850s. He described places, individuals, social conditions, habits and norms, religious life, popular art forms, foods, tools and illnesses. Ewbank's views were sometimes critical, and he was deeply disturbed by the abuse of slaves and by the loose personal morals of the clergy.

With the end of slavery in the United States South, the Reverend Ballard Dunn (New York, 1866) described the visit he and others paid to the province of São Paulo in order to study the prospects and pave the way for immigration by ex-Confederates. Dunn's book contains several of his own reports, including statistics, about social, economic, and agricultural conditions in Brazil.

John Codman (Boston, 1867) was the captain of the merchant ship that transported Dunn to Brazil. The ship called at southern Brazilian ports, and Codman took advantage of opportunities to travel inland. In the province of Rio, he toured the mountain town of Petrópolis, where members of the Brazilian court and government and the *carioca* elite spent their summer months. He also visited several plantations, including that of Dom Pedro II. Codman not only described these excursions but also supplied general information about production, commerce, and so on in Brazil. Moreover, he presented his observations and opinions about Brazil's central role in the long Paraguayan War.

The "Thayer expedition" to the Amazon in the mid-1860s, led by the celebrated Swiss-American naturalist Louis Agassiz, who was accompanied by his wife, Elizabeth (Boston, 1868), was recorded mainly by Mrs. Agassiz, a sharp observer and gifted writer. The couple also visited the Rio area and Ceará. The book is strongest in the areas of geography, botany, zoology, and ethnology.

Britain's consul at Santos, São Paulo, Captain Richard Burton (London, 1869), described his late-1860s journey from Rio to Minas, including his exploration of the central highlands and his visits to gold and diamond mines. He also recounted his 1,500-mile canoe trip down the São Francisco River. Independently, Burton translated several works of Brazilian literature, including Basílio da *Gama's O uraguai. (See Foreign Writers and Brazil.)

The scientist Herbert Smith (New York, 1879) took part in the "Morgan expedition" to Brazil in 1870, and he was entrusted, in 1874, with exploration of some of the tributaries of the Amazon and Tapajós Rivers. His landmark book described the Amazon and the coast and presented an eyewitness account of the devastating northeastern drought of 1877–1879. It also contained Smith's political and economic ideas concerning Brazil.

Michael and Edward Mulhall (Buenos Aires, 1877), owners and editors of an English-language newspaper in Argentina, wrote a Brazilian "handbook" containing the former's detailed account of his 1870s journeys to the interior province of Mato Grosso and to the southern province of Rio Grande do Sul, including its colony of German settlers.

Hastings Dent (London, 1886) recounted his year of residence and research in several parts of Brazil. He compared the planter (*fazendeiro*) class of the rural interior to the English gentry. Dent discussed religion in Brazil, the movement to abolish slavery, and the state of the nation's finances, as well as meteorological conditions and natural history.

The United States consul-general in Rio from 1882 to 1885, Christopher Andrews (New York, 1887; 1891), discussed Brazil's "conditions and prospects" and gave an account of the downfall of the empire and establishment of the republic.

Marie Wright (Philadelphia, 1901) described her two years of travel in Brazil, "covering thousands of miles." She wrote about the "new" postabolition republic and its industries, resources, and "attractions" at the end of the nineteenth century. Other important nineteenth-century works were written by George Gardner (London, 1846), Alfred Wallace (London, 1853), Edward Wilberforce (London, 1856), Thomas Cochrane (London, 1859), James Wetherell (Liverpool, 1860), Thomas Bigg-Wither (London, 1878), and James Wells (Philadelphia, 1886).

In the twentieth century, European and North American journalists and social scientists were regularly sent to South America, and travel books consequently became less central to foreign knowledge about Brazil. Nevertheless, when two statesmen of international stature visited Brazil and each published a volume about it, the reading public of their countries, and beyond, took note. The former (and future) prime minister of France, Georges Clemenceau (Paris, 1911), described his tour of South America.

Theodore Roosevelt (New York, 1914) reached Brazil's boundary on the Paraguay River in mid-December 1913 to take part in the "Roosevelt-Rondon expedition." For nearly five months the group journeyed through Mato Grosso and the Amazon. The former American president, a naturalist, chronicled the group's progress, commenting always about the geography and terrain, fauna and flora, individuals and cultures, and the hardships and dangers that the expedition encountered. Colonel Cândido Rondon was the principal surveyor and mapped the "chief affluent of the Madeira, which is itself the chief affluent of the Amazon." During the expedition the river was given the official name Rio Roosevelt, subsequently modified to Rio Teodoro.

Another twentieth-century Brazilian travel book was widely read for a different reason: it mocked the classic adventure yarns. Peter Fleming (London, 1933), the literary editor of *The Spectator*, narrated his group's 3,000-mile search, "mostly under amusing conditions," for an eccentric explorer, Colonel Fawcett, who had reportedly disappeared in the Brazilian hinterland. Beyond "the discovery of one new tributary to a tributary to a tributary of the Amazon, nothing of importance was achieved." Fleming's book, however, was "throughout strictly truthful" and debunked some authors who "had made great play with the Terrors of the Jungle: the alligators, the snakes, the man-eating fish, the lurking savages, those dreadful insects."

Afonso d'Escragnolle Taunay (1876–1958; BAL: 1929) and Cândido de Mello-Leitão were leading scholars of Brazilian travel literature and published several works on the subject.

BIBLIOGRAPHY: Criticism: Levine, Robert M. "Contemporary Narratives." *Brazil, 1822–1930: An Annotated Bibliography for Social Historians.* New York: Garland Publishing, 1983, pp. 241–259; Moraes, Rubens Borba de. *Bibliographia Brasiliana: Rare Books about Brazil Published from 1504 to 1900 and Works by Brazilian Authors of the Colonial Period.* 2 vols. Revised and enlarged edition. Los Angeles/Rio: University of California, Los Angeles, Latin American Center Publications/Livraria Kosmos Editora, 1983; Naylor, Bernard. *Accounts of Nineteenth-Century South America: An Annotated Checklist of Works by British and United States Observers.* London: Athlone Press, 1969.

FRANCES ELIZABETH RAND

TREVISAN, DALTON (b. 1925). Considered one of Brazil's most preeminent modern short stories writers, Trevisan, a lawyer by profession, was born and has always lived in his native city of Curitiba, Paraná State, which also provided the background for his writings.

Trevisan's stories first appeared in the *review *Joaquim* (1946–1948), which he founded and which was one of the principal publications of early postmodernism (*See* Postmodernism in Poetry), and in locally published collections. He gained national attention when his *Novelas nada exemplares* (1959; Not at All Exemplary Novels) appeared in Rio. His career has flourished through many subsequent collections of stories, notably *Cemitério de elefantes* (1964; The Elephants' Graveyard), *A guerra conjugal* (1969; The Conjugal War), and *Abismo de rosas* (1976; Abyss of Roses).

The characters of Trevisan's Curitiba are lower-middle-class antiheroes and antiheroines, whose lives center around sex: any kind, any place, any time. Trevisan captures the psychology and language of their existence with shrewd expertise. His characters are symbolically named João e Maria (John and Mary), two very common Portuguese names. Women characters in many stories are often used and abused but can also, on occasion, be as brutal as their macho husbands, boyfriends, lovers and Johns, as in the story "A mão e o punhal," (The Hand and the Dagger) from *Novelas nada exemplares*.

"O vampiro de Curitiba" (The Vampire of Curitiba) from *O vampiro de Curitiba* (1965; *The Vampire of Curitiba and Other Stories*, 1972) is considered one of his classic tales. Nelsinho, the protagonist of the stories, is so obsessed with sex that he pursues the women of Curitiba at night, comparing himself to a vampire who must drink blood to survive. Although he discovers some disagreeable aspects of life in this pursuit (e.g., the aging of his favorite teacher), he nonetheless culminates the sex act and through it passes on this vampire's existence to others. Trevisan's most recent novel, *A polaquinha* (1985; The Little Prostitute) narrates the total debauchery of a lower-middle-class girl. It has been called pornography by more than one critic. (*See* Critics and Criticism.)

In exploiting the sensual realm, Trevisan presents a somber caricature of man's existence that is often filled with sardonic humor. With subtlety and the conciseness that defines his style, Trevisan is able to defamiliarize the stereotypic relationships that alienate people. In treating the sordidness and banality of the ordinary, he holds a mirror to contemporary Brazilian society.

BIBLIOGRAPHY: Additional selected works by Trevisan: *Desastres do amor*, 1968; *A faca no coração*, 1975; *O meu querido assassino*, 1983. Translations: Donoso/Henkin; *Exile* (1976); Fremantle; *LALR* (January-June, 1986). Tolman (1978); *The Vampire of Curitiba and Other Stories*. New York: Alfred A. Knopf, 1972. Criticism: Burrell, Karen. "Social Prejudice Examined in Dalton Trevisan's "O ciclista." *BRMMLA* (1982), pp. 111–118; Lask, Thomas. "The Soil and Some of its Fruits." *NYTBR* (December 12, 1972), p. 6; Rabassa, Gregory. "Introduction." *The Vampire of Curitiba and Other Stories*. New York: Alfred A. Knopf, 1972, pp. ix–xiii; Vieira, Nelson H. "João e Maria: Dalton Trevisan's Eponymous Heroes." *Hispania* (March, 1986), pp. 45–52.

RENÉ P. GARAY

TROPICALISMO (TROPICÁLIA). Divided by its founders into two phases, *tropicalismo* (1967–1968) and post-*tropicalismo* (1969 and later), this brief but tremendously influential movement in popular music of the late 1960s is regarded by some analysts as a more general cultural movement involving art, film, theater, and the other literary genres for example, the film *Macunaíma*, based on Mário de *Andrade's novel. (*See* Art and Literature; Film and Literature; Music and Literature; Theater History.)

Songwriters Caetano Veloso (b. 1942) and Gilberto Gil (b. 1942), later followed by the poet-lyricists Torquato Neto (b. 1944), author of *Os últimos dias da paupéria* (1982; The Last Days of Poverty), José Carlos Capinan (b. 1941), and the poet and novelist Jorge Mautner (b. 1941) (for translations, *see* "Key to Bibliographical References": Brasil/Smith), proposed a critical review of national culture through song and blurred distinctions between "committed nationalistic" and "alienated" art. Reformulating Oswald de *Andrade's *antropofagia* in the context of song, the tropicalists contrasted, often in parody, antiquated cultural relics with modern, technologically advanced phenomena.

Veloso's song "Tropicália" is the prototypical composition. The manifesto and sole realization of the collective is the historical LP record "Tropicália ou panis et circensis" (Philips R76514L, 1968; Tropicalia or Bread and Circus). The critic Augusto de *Campos's avid reception of the group's theory, in his *Balanço da bossa e outras bossas* (1974), brought a wave of critical response.

Waly Salomão, author of *Me segura que vou dar um troço* (1972; Hold Me Because I Am Going to Have an Attack) and *Gigolô de bibelô* (1983; Gigolo of Knickknacks), is considered the leading figure of post-*tropicalismo*.

BIBLIOGRAPHY: Additional selected works of *Tropicalismo*: Veloso, Caetano. *Alegria, alegria*. Rio: P. Q. Ronca, 1977. Criticism: Béhague, Gérard. "Popular Music in Latin America." *SLAPC* 5 (1986), pp 56–67; Brookshaw; Chilcote, Ronald H. "Poetics and Ideology in the Pop Poetry of Brazil." *SLAPC* 2 (1983), pp. 28–98; Favaretto, Celso. *Tropicália: alegoria alegria*. São Paulo: Kairós, 1979; Perrone, Charles A. "Lyric and Lyrics: The Poetry of Song in Brazil." Dissertation, University of Texas, 1984; Stein, Stephanie. "Brazilian Waves: The Tide of Brazilian Artists." *Upbeat* (August–September, 1986), pp. 42–45.

CHARLES A. PERRONE

U

UBALDO RIBEIRO, J. *See* Ribeiro, João Ubaldo.

UFANISMO.   Viscount Afonso Celso (*see* Philosophy of National Identity) coined the word *ufanismo* from the Latin word *ufanus* (happy) and applied it to an encomiastic attitude toward a description of Brazil's overwhelming size, its imposing beauty, and the great variety of flora, fauna, and natural resources, all of which have left discoverers and generations of travelers and immigrants utterly bedazzled. (*See* Historiography; Immigrants and Literature; Travel Literature.)

Pero Vaz de *Caminha exudes this nativist sensation in his letter of the discovery of Brazil, as do all the early chroniclers and narrators of discovery. *Romanticism rekindled *ufanismo* as part of the search for a true national heritage. Gonçalves *Dias's "Canção de exílio" (Song of Exile) is considered the epitome of *ufanismo* in verse. *Modernism picked it up again for both serious and parodic ends, in an attempt to individualize modern Brazil from European culture.

Ufanismo remains today an essential ingredient in the optimism about the nation's future, sustaining Brazilians in times of political, social, and economic turmoil.

BIBLIOGRAPHY: Additional selected works on *Ufanismo*: Celso, Afonso. *Porque me ufano do Brasil*. Rio, 1901.

ULTRAROMANTICISM.   *See* Romanticism.

V

VARELA, LUÍS NICOLAU FAGUNDES (1841–1875). A moody young man of delicate constitution, Fagundes Varela undertook an unfortunate first marriage, suffering the loss of a baby son. This marked the beginning of an erratic life of alcoholism and financial insecurity.

Together with Castro *Alves, Varela led the third generation of romantics who wrote mainly during the 1860s. From the poets of previous decades, for example, Casimiro de *Abreu, they inherited an often facile sentimentalism and musicality. However, the political developments of the period—abolitionism, republicanism, and the Paraguayan War (1864–1870)—offered new themes for a social and humanitarian poetry celebrating American liberty and democracy. (*See* Romanticism; Slavery and Literature.)

Varela's work comprises roughly two phases, the culmination of the first being *Cantos e fantasias* (1865; Poems and Fantasies). In it, he still explored the established paths of romanticism but introduced to them an epic and narrative lyricism. In poems such as "Cântico do calvário" (Chant of the Cavalry), to the memory of his son, personal experience acquires a large human dimension through his use of biblical metaphors and evocations of nature.

The second phase, beginning with *Cantos dos ermos e da cidade* (1869; Poems of the Wilderness and the City), continues with the earlier social themes but is more typically a poetry of pastoral idyll. The notion of flight from urban society is linked to the spiritual crisis that probably produced *Anchieta ou O evangelho na selva* (1875; Anchieta or The Gospel in the Jungle), an Indianist epic celebrating the evangelical mission. (*See* City and Literature; Indianism.)

Varela's poetry represents both a synthesis of the earlier romantic tendencies and a transition toward Castro Alves. Early interest in his student life and personal lyric output has been followed more recently by a reevaluation of his elegiac and religious poems.

BIBLIOGRAPHY: Additional selected works by Varela: *Noturnas*, 1861; *Vozes de América*, 1864; *Cantos religiosos*, 1878. Translations: Hulet. Criticism: Brookshaw; Cavalheiro, Edgard. *Fagundes Varela*. São Paulo: Martins, 1958; Driver; Sayers.

DAVID H. TREECE

VASCONCELOS, JOSÉ MAURO DE (1920–1984). An immensely popular novelist of the 1960s—except with critics—Vasconcelos was also a film and television actor. Born in the state of Rio of part Indian blood, he was brought up in Rio Grande do Norte. As a teenager, he was a sailor, a boxer, a farmer, a dancer, and an artist's model. He was also a dedicated employee of the Indian Protection Service.

Vasconcelos's novels are based on his childhood and adult experiences. For example, *Banana brava* (1942; Wild Bananas) evokes his work on a banana plantation. Many other novels followed, the content and style of which were debated and often censured for their poor construction, weak characterization, and emotional simplicity. In spite of these critical attacks, Vasconcelos's *Meu pé de laranja lima* (1968; *My Sweet-Orange Tree*, 1970) gained huge commercial success. The poor children-protagonists—Zezé and Portuga—became even greater national heroes in a highly successful television serialization. Although Vasconcelos continued to write afterwards, including neo-Indianist fiction, he never again matched that success. (*See* Children's Literature; Film and Literature; Indianism.)

BIBLIOGRAPHY: Additional selected works by Vasconcelos: *Rosinha, minha canoa*, 1962; *O palácio japonês*, 1969; *O veleiro de cristal*, 1973; *Kuryala, capitão e carajá*, 1979.

VAZ DE CAMINHA. *See* Caminha, Pero Vaz de.

VEIGA, JOSÉ J. (b. 1915). Veiga was born in the interior of Goiás State, whose rusticity would later serve, in part, as inspiration for his fiction. (*See* Regionalism.)

Veiga, with Murilo *Rubião, is considered Brazil's foremost practitioner of magic realism. However, unlike Rubião, Veiga's world is clearly Brazilian in setting and colloquial in language. All his pieces share a rural or small-town locale, populated by unpretentious, mostly male characters, often in a realm of the absurd. People can be seen flying just as animals can take over a town! Similarly, his neologisms, most frequent in the exotic timelessness of novels like *Os pecados da tribo* (1980; The Sins of the Tribe) and *Aquele mundo de Vasabarros* (1982; That World of Vasabarros), defy easy categorization.

The apparent simplicity of plot is further accentuated by the often puerile attitudes assumed by (narrator)-characters, some of whom are children. Once this literal or superficial level is penetrated, a parallel philosophical plane comes into imprecise view, centering around the multiple facets of contemporary Brazilian social and political reality. The author's premise—the relativity of what is or is not real—is enveloped in somewhat of a paradox. (*See* Dictatorship and Literature.)

The logical and the lyrical coexist and complement each other. The resulting symmetry, a blend of *goiano* regionalism, somber introspection, and (not so) innocent fantasy, aptly characterize Veiga's *prize-winning success.

BIBLIOGRAPHY: Additional selected works by Veiga: *A hora dos ruminantes*, 1966 (*The Three Trials of Manirema*, 1979); *A máquina extraviada*, 1968 (*The Misplaced Machine and Other Stories*, 1970); *De jogos e festas*, 1980; *Torvelinho dia e noite*, 1985; Criticism: Monegal, Emir Rodríguez. *NYTBR* (Reviews of *The Three Trials of Manirema* and *The Misplaced Machine and Other Stories*) (August 30, 1970), p. 32; Silverman, Malcolm. *Moderna ficção brasileira*. Rio: Civilização Brasileira, 1978.

MALCOLM SILVERMAN

VERÍSSIMO, ÉRICO (1905–1975). Veríssimo gave up his career as a pharmacist to pursue a life of letters. Widely traveled in Brazil and abroad, he spent several periods in the United States lecturing and teaching Brazilian literature and as director of the Department of Cultural Affairs of the Pan American Union (1953–1956). Aside from creating many works of fiction, he wrote travel literature and *children's stories.

Veríssimo's literary tastes were influenced by the British writers of his youth, particularly Aldous Huxley; Somerset Maugham, whose works he translated into Portuguese; and Oscar Wilde. Other direct influences acknowledged by the author include Anatole France, Henrik Ibsen, and Machado de *Assis. His preference for urban, middle-class themes evidenced itself in the 1930s precisely when rural-based *regionalism, which emphasized concerns of socioeconomic injustice and decadence, was establishing itself as the more typical trend in Brazilian literature.

In that decade of political polarization, he maintained a middle-of-the-road tolerance of differences that sought above all the reconciliation of misunderstandings and practice of fraternal humanitarianism, a stance he was able to maintain throughout his career. Veríssimo's novels typically contain frequent, sometimes lengthy, discussions of social philosophy and political history presented in the form of dialogue and interior monologue; this is the aspect of his work that has been most subject to criticism from the point of view of textual cohesiveness. (*See* Social Novelists of the 1930s.)

Veríssimo's fictional works may be divided into three periods both chronologically and thematically. The first, extending through the early forties, comprises a series of short novels, including *Caminhos cruzados* (1935; *Crossroads*, 1943) and *Um lugar ao sol* (1936; A Place in the Sun), designed as an integrated series. They accompany the same nucleus of predominantly young and urban middle-class characters through adolescence and early adulthood against the backdrop of national and international affairs of the period. Two novels written during the same time—*Olhai os lírios do campo* (1938; *Consider the Lilies of the Field*, 1947) and *O resto é silêncio* (1943; *The Rest Is Silence*, 1946)—expand the gallery of characters beyond the scope of the aforementioned series and explore humanitarian and personal aspects of the professional lives of doctors and writers vis-à-vis their public.

The second phase of Veríssimo's novelistic production is made up of his epic trilogy called "O tempo e o vento" (Time and the Wind), which is a panoramic social and political history of his home state of Rio Grande do Sul between 1745 and 1945. The first volume of the trilogy, *O continente* (1951), was published in English under the title *Time and the Wind* (1951). Contrasting with his vigorous mural of strong human groups in passionate interaction is a short novellete of the mid-1950s, *Noite* (1954; *Night*, 1956), which carries the gentle psychological probing of Veríssimo's first period further into the introspectively surrealistic, a path he opted not to pursue subsequently. (*See* Surrealism.)

In his last phase, Veríssimo broadened his thematic and spatial horizons. *O senhor embaixador* (1965; *His Excellency, Mr. Ambassador*, 1967) and *Incidente em Antares* (1971; *Incident in Antares*) deal with matters as diverse as the Vietnam War, race relations, international diplomacy, terrorism, and political oppression, showing the author at his most ideologically concerned and pessimistically ironic. He ventures into the realm of magical realism to demythologize allegorically the structures and institutions—such as the political dilemma of Brazil in the 1970s—of which he was more tolerant in earlier years. (*See* Dictatorship and Literature.)

Veríssimo thought of himself as a teller of stories and a painter of people and places. His depth of human warmth and easy writing style combine to make him a perennial favorite of readers both young and old. His popularity was recently restored through a fine television serialization of *Time and the Wind*.

BIBLIOGRAPHY: Additional selected works by Veríssimo: *Fantoches*, 1932; *Clarissa*, 1933; *Meu ABC*, 1936; *Saga*, 1940; *Gato preto em campo de neve*, 1941; *Brazilian Literature: An Outline*, 1945; *México*, 1957 (*Mexico*, 1960); *Israel em abril*, 1969. Criticism: Foster/Foster, II; Garcia, Frederick. "Érico Veríssimo: Nameless Soldiers in a Nameless War." *Ensayistas* (March, 1981), pp. 75–77; *NYTBR* (book reviews) (January 24, 1943; April 20, 1949; September 23, 1951; April 1, 1969).

MARY L. DANIEL

VERÍSSIMO, JOSÉ (1857–1916; BAL: 1897). A very active ethnographer and an early anthropologist of Amazonian life, as well the author of short narrations, Pará-born Veríssimo initially studied engineering in Rio but, due to illness, returned to his native state, where he founded the *Gazeta do Norte* newspaper and was active in pedagogical matters. He eventually became the director of the prestigious Colégio Pedro II school.

Veríssimo's creative writing is in the local color style popularized during the romantic-realist period: *Cenas da vida amazônica* (1886; Scenes of Amazonian Life). He is best known as a member of the triumvirate of turn-of-the-century literary critics—along with Sílvio *Romero and Tristão de Araripe Júnior. (*See* Critics and Criticism.) His analyses of Brazilian literature, culture, and foreign literature—from colonial days through his own time—are presented in the six volumes of his *Estudos da literatura brasileira* (1901–1907). His opinions are based on solid artistic judgment and conditioned by his beliefs about the nature and direction that Brazilian literature should assume.

Although Veríssimo is somewhat forgotten today, his essays and his *História da literatura brasileira* (1916; History of Brazilian Literature) remain valuable sources of information and critical opinion.

BIBLIOGRAPHY: Additional selected works by Veríssimo: *A Amazônia: aspectos econômicos*, 1892; *Estudos brasileiros*, 1889, 1894; *Que é literatura, e outros escritos*, 1907; *Letras e literatos*, 1936. Criticism: MacNicoll, Murray Graeme. "José Veríssimo: Critic and Contemporary of Machado de Assis: 1872–1916."*KRQ* (1980), pp. 345–359.

VERÍSSIMO, LUÍS FERNANDO (b. 1936).

Veríssimo, the son of Érico *Veríssimo, is one of the best-known literary figures in Brazil today. His *crônicas* have appeared in major national publications. Since December 1982 he has been a contributor to the national weekly *Veja*, replacing fellow humorist Millôr *Fernandes. Like Fernandes, Veríssimo is a fine cartoonist, whose drawings are not mere illustrations of or commentaries on his texts but independent pieces standing in their own right.

Known for his sharp, often scabrous humor and wit, Veríssimo has given the *crônica* a new literary stature through his use of techniques normally associated with the short story and novel and, particularly, through his creation of unforgettable characters who recur in his writings: the detective Ed Mort, a paragon of incompetence; the little old lady from Taubaté, who allegedly was the last person in Brazil to believe in the government; and, above all, the celebrated psychoanalyst from Bagé, a macho, outspoken, self-styled Freudian analyst, whose unconventional methods include whipping his patients. His *O analista de Bagé* (1981; The Analyst of Bagé) is the all-time best-seller in Brazilian literary history.

A fine observer of the contemporary Brazilian urban milieu, Veríssimo, by dissecting the commonplace of daily life, reaches unexpectedly fresh insights into human foibles and reveals their absurd underside. No segment of Brazilian society escapes his mordant satire. Profiting from the relaxation in censorship since 1979, Veríssimo has been able to touch on a myriad of subjects, including social mores, violence and crime, national and local politics, inflation, corruption, urban loneliness, and sex.

BIBLIOGRAPHY: Additional selected works by Veríssimo: *A grande mulher nua*, 1975; *Amor brasileiro*, 1977; *Ed Mort e outras histórias*, 1979; *A velhinha de Taubaté*, 1983; *A mãe do Freud*, 1985. Translations: *Bits and Pieces*. Porto Alegre, Brazil, 197?.

LUIZ FERNANDO VALENTE

VIANA FILHO, ODUVALDO (1936–1974).

Viana Filho was born into a tradition of theatrical and political activism. His father, Oduvaldo Viana, was one of the most popular and successful playwrights of his generation, and his mother, Deocélia Viana, was also a writer. Both parents were active members of the Brazilian Communist party, as was Viana Filho from the age of fourteen until his death.

A key figure in the Brazilian national theater movement from his beginning

364 VIANA FILHO, ODUVALDO

work in student theater in 1954, Viana Filho worked as an author, and sometime actor, in theater, cinema, and television. Preferring to work in a collective, his history as a playwright and activist is inextricably bound with that of politically oriented theater groups. He was an early core member of the Arena Theater of São Paulo, leaving that group in 1960 to create theater within the Centro Popular de Cultura (Popular Culture Center) (CPC). After the 1964 coup, he worked with the Opinião Theater Group. With the political repression of 1968, he—like many other authors who continued to write plays that were produced when censorship permitted—turned to television scripts as his only viable source of income. (*See* Dictatorship and Literature; Theater History.)

Although Viana's main theme involves the social alienation of the urban middle class, progressively proletarianized by inflation and the economic difficulties of survival, he experimented with many dramatic forms and theatrical conventions. Examples are the social realism of betrayal in a small-town soccer team, *Chapetuba Futebol Clube* (1959; Chapetuba Soccer Club); musical shows (*Show Opinião*, 1964; Opinião [Opinion] Show); a Brechtian farce with themes from *popular culture (*Se correr o bicho pega, se ficar o bicho come*, 1965; If You Run the Animal Beats You Up, If You Stay the Animal Eats You), coauthored with Ferreira *Gullar; realistic existentialist studies of the alienated middle class (*Corpo a corpo*, 1970; Body to Body); and a parable on Latin American dictators (*Papa Highirte*, 1968; Papa Highirte). (*See* Soccer and Literature.)

His last and best play, *Rasga coração* (1974; literally, Render Heart) is considered by many critics (*See* Critics and Criticism) to be the best Brazilian play of recent past decades. A mixture of realistic theatrical conventions, Brechtian devices of "alienation," and traditions of the Brazilian musical revue, the play traces the political conflicts and personal doubts of three generations—from the 1920s to the 1970s—thereby creating a mosaic of historical fact and historical interpretation (the historical moment as lived and perceived by the characters of the play). The protagonist is Custódio Manhaes Jr., known as Manguari Pistolão, a middle-class civil servant who has dedicated his life to activism within the Communist party line. The dramatic present (1972) describes the confrontation between the protagonist's political ideals and strategies and those of his son, Luca, a hippie environmentalist. The dramatic structure is constituted by Manguari's nonchronological flashbacks into the last forty years of his private-political life. Two scenic planes of reality are presented—past and present. Dramatic action is fragmented between these two planes, often with simultaneous dialogue. This structures a collage that gives meaning to the historical and personal past juxtaposed to the pathos and doubt that mark the protagonist's determined struggle to find dignity and affirmation through his political beliefs. Viana Filho wrote *Rasga coração* in "homage to the anonymous political activists."

Besides writing plays, Viana Filho was an astute theoretician whose assessments of Brazilian theater and dramatic literature still speak directly to issues of today's debate. Although his work is often marked by a laborious scrupulousness in appraisal and revision, it is his fusion of theoretical vision regarding theater in society with his dramatic practice that places him at the center of cultural issues that inform contemporary Brazilian society.

BIBLIOGRAPHY: Additional selected works by Viana Filho: *Quatro quadras de terra*, 1963; *Moço em estado de sítio*, 1965; *Os Azeredos mais os Benevides*, 1966; *A longa noite de cristal*, 1969; *Mão na luva*, 1984; *Alegro desbum*, 1987. Criticism: Damasceno, Leslie. "Oduvaldo Vianna Filho: 'Pessedismo' and the Creation of the Anonymous Revolutionary Hero." *Literature and Contemporary Revolutionary Cultures* (January, 1986); Guimarães, Carmelinda. *Um ato de resistência: o teatro de Oduvaldo Vianna Filho*. São Paulo: MG Editores Asociados, 1984.

LESLIE DAMASCENO

VIANA MOOG. *See* Moog, Clodomir Viana.

VIEIRA, FATHER ANTÔNIO (1608–1697). Vieira was born in Lisbon and immigrated with his parents to Salvador, Bahia, in 1614. He took Jesuit orders in 1635, although he already had begun to preach two years earlier. In these first years of his career, he was a missionary among the Indians in the Amazon and the Northeast, areas to which he returned throughout his life. In Europe, from 1641 to 1652, he carried out diplomatic missions for the Portuguese Court and continued to preach. Except for a brief trip to Lisbon (1654–1655) to plead for better treatment of the Indians, Vieira spent the next nine years as a missionary in Maranhão. (*See* Portugal and Brazil: Literary Relations; Religion and Literature.)

In 1661 the colonists expelled him and his fellow Jesuits to Portugal. From 1662 to 1668 Vieira was prosecuted by the Inquisition for his "heretical" views and possible Jewish blood, after which he went to Rome, where he preached in both Portuguese and Italian. In 1681 he returned to Bahia, where he remained until his death.

Vieira is best known for his sermons consisting of fifteen volumes published between 1679 and 1748. Although primarily reflections on religious doctrine— prepared for some important church occasion—these sermons also reveal his concern with sociopolitical issues. In context and form, they are exemplarily *baroque. Vieira presented his ingenious arguments on political and religious topics and his imaginative (and often fantastic) readings of the scriptures in a rich, elaborate prose. Complex rhetorical, syntactic constructions and configurations make these texts dazzling but also difficult—even obscure. His sermons, printed as pamphlets, garnered him fame throughout Latin America and even attracted the attention of Sor Juana Inés de la Cruz (1651–1695), the Mexican nun.

Among the most notable sermons are "Sermão pelo bom sucesso das armas de Portugal contra as de Holanda" (Bahia, 1640; Sermons for the Success of Portuguese Arms against the Dutch), an exhortation to the people of Bahia when the Portuguese began to rebuff the Dutch invasion of northeastern Brazil; "Sermão de Santo Antônio'' (Maranhão, 1654; Sermon of Saint Anthony); and "Sermão da Sexagésima" (Lisbon, 1655; Sermon of Sexagesima Sunday), which includes Vieira's thoughts on rhetoric and style.

In addition, Vieira's opus includes equally eloquent *Cartas* (4 vols., 1735–1827; Letters) to kings, diplomats, Court, and church figures on political, economic, and personal topics, as well as a number of more official but incomplete texts and a series of "prophetic," religiously unorthodox works on the future of the Portuguese empire, for example, *Quinto império* (The Fifth Empire) and *História do futuro* (1718; History of the Future). (*See* Historiography.)

Beyond its value for the history of colonial Brazil, the Portuguese empire, and the Catholic church, Vieira's work is of special importance for the study of Brazilian literature. Although some scholars have claimed Vieira as a Portuguese writer for reasons of his birth and his long stays in Europe, his concern with Brazil is clearly evident. His writings reflect on linguistic problems, such as the encounter of indigenous languages with Portuguese, and the relationship between peninsular and Brazilian Portuguese. Furthermore, he enriched the Portuguese of his time with many elements of "American" origin. Finally, in their exegesis of the Old Testament, his prophetic works find significant messages not only about Portugal but also about the New World. (*See* Indian Languages; Portuguese Language of Brazil.)

BIBLIOGRAPHY: Additional selected works by Vieira: *Obras completas*, 27 vols., 1858. There are many modern Portuguese and Brazilian collections of his selected works. Translations: Monegal/Colchie, I. Criticism: Gomes, Eugênio. In Coutinho, I; Preto-Rodas, Richard A. "Anchieta and Vieira: Drama as Sermon, Sermon as Drama." *LBR* (December, 1970), pp. 96–103.

MARÍA TAI WOLFF

VIEIRA, JOSÉ GERALDO   (1897–1977). Rio-born Vieira trained in medicine, specializing in radiology. While a medical student and doctor, he published several short stories and five novels. *A mulher que fugiu de Sodoma* (1931; The Woman Who Fled from Sodom) is considered his major work of fiction of this epoch. He left medicine in the late 1940s and embarked on a career in literature, translation, and art criticism. (*See* Art and Literature.)

While other writers of the 1930s and 1940s were concerned with sociological and regionalist themes, Vieira's fiction took a significantly different direction. In *A quadragésima porta* (1943; The Fortieth Door) and in *Terreno baldío* (1961; Barren Land), he depicts Brazilians living in Paris between the war years. They are members of high society, intelligent, and psychologically complex individuals who enjoy their comfortable life-style. Revealing the inner workings of his characters, Vieira's novels are frequently very long and tightly packed with sociopolitical and religious details. Dream sequences and flashbacks also show the inner reality of his characters, in addition to shifting perspectives and a host of technical maneuvers borrowed from film. (*See* Film and Literature; Social Novelists of the 1930s.)

Unfortunately, Vieira's plots are often too thin and too unengaging to make the density of the narrative worth the reader's trouble. His works, nonetheless, provide interesting reading if for no other reason than that they portray a unique Brazilian reality.

BIBLIOGRAPHY: Additional selected works by Vieira: *Território humano*, 1936; *A ladeira da memória*, 1950; *Paralelo 16: Brasília*, 1966.

KEITH H. BROWER

VILELA, LUÍZ (b. 1942). *Mineiro* Vilela received a degree in philosophy. A journalist in São Paulo, he described the newspaperman's life in his novel *O inferno é aqui mesmo* (1979; Hell Is Right Here). He was the editor of an important short story magazine, *Estória*, suppressed during the dictatorship years. (*See* Dictatorship and Literature.)

Vilela's first collection of stories, *Tremor da terra* (1967; Earthquake), was awarded the national fiction *prize. It was followed by other short fiction and then by his novel *Os novos* (1971; The Young Ones), dealing with the illusions and disillusions of university life. His most recent fiction analyzes the undercurrents of man's existence—for example, repression, aggression, suicide—through narratives of man's—often children's—paradoxical desires and dilemmas. The story "Felicidade" (Happiness) from his collection *Tarde da noite* (1970; Late at Night) focuses on a joyous fortieth birthday party. Initial joy turns to paranoia when the honored guest is unable to cope with the intimacy and good wishes of his friends and relatives. He seeks isolation from the crowd in the bathroom. The story, one of Vilela's best, is also noted for its stylistic inventiveness—one long, unpunctuated paragraph adds to the intensity of the character's extremely conscious dilemma. (*See* Children's Literature.)

BIBLIOGRAPHY: Additional selected works by Vilela: *No bar*, 1968; *Lindas pernas*, 1979; *Entre amigos*, 1982; *O choro no travesseiro*, 1986. Translations: Fremantle; *LALR* (July-December, 1986); *Mundus Artium* (1975); *The Ohio Journal* (Summer, 1978); Tolman (1984); *Webster Review* (Fall, 1978). Criticism: Parker, John. "Intertext, Interpretant, and Ideology in Luís Vilela's *Entre amigos.*" *Portuguese Studies* 2 (1986); Tolman (1984).

VILLA-LOBOS, HEITOR (1887–1959). Villa-Lobos gave concerts of his music as part of the Week of Modern Art in 1922 (*See* Modernism). Although just one professional engagement in a lifetime of international composing and conducting successes, his identification as a Brazilian modernist was thereby secured. (*See* Music and Literature.)

In 1921 he wrote music to poetry by Mário de *Andrade and asked Ronald de *Carvalho for "some sentimental and ironical lines" for a song cycle, inspiring the latter's *Poemas irônicos e sentimentais*. Villa-Lobos composed music for poems by Carlos Drummond de *Andrade, Jorge de *Lima, Ribeiro *Couto, Manuel *Bandeira, and Dante *Milano early in their careers. Bandeira was a close friend whom the composer often asked for literary advice and song lyrics, especially to the "Dança" (Dance) for "Bachianas Brasileiras No. 5" (1945), now a signature-tune for Brazil.

Villa-Lobos wrote some of his own lyrics using the pseudonym E. Villalba Filho—(his father, Raul Villa-Lobos (1862–1899), had written histories of the 1891–1893 military rebellions under the pseudonym Epaminondas Villalba).

BIBLIOGRAPHY: Criticism: Mariz, J. Vasco. *Heitor Villa-Lobos: Brazilian Composer*. Gainesville: University of Florida Press, 1963; Kiefer, Bruno. *Villa-Lobos e o modernismo na música brasileira*, 1987; Vassberg, David. "Villa-Lobos: Music as a Tool of Nationalism." *LBR* (December, 1969), pp. 55–65; Wright, Simon J. "Villa-Lobos and the Cinema: A Note." *LBR* (Winter, 1982), pp. 243–250.

LEE BOYD

Index

This index includes all writers, themes, major literary works, literary techniques, notable literary protagonists, major place names, and major historical events and personalities referred to in this dictionary. Writers appear under their last names, composite last names, e.g., Coelho Neto or Miguel-Pereira, or the last name of their pseudonym. Where two writers possess similar names, a distinction is made through the use of the first initial, first name or composite last names. When published translations of works are available, they appear in italics in parenthesis immediately following the Portuguese title; other titles are literal translations and are not italicized. All foreign writers and personalities are listed in groups according to their nationalities; for example, Faulkner is listed under "American cultural influences." References to kings, queens and emperors are listed under the royal name. Page references to main entries appear in bold typeface.

abertura (political liberalization), xlvii, 112, 160, 200. *See also* dictatorship

abolitionism, 1, 4, 10, 54, 89, 94, 102, 108, 149, 175, 187, 215, 226, 229, 237, 245, 319, 338, 359; in Alves, 14; in Bilac, 60; *Diablo Coxo*, 145; in L. Gama, 145; in B. Guimarães, 151; *O Homen de Côr*, 319; and Indianism, 168; *O mulato*, 319; and positivism, 256; and *Radical Paulistano*, 145; in Cruz e Sousa, 326; in theater, 340. *See also* slavery

Abreu, Caio Fernando, **1**, 112, 160, 222

Abreu, Casimiro de, **2**, 14, 284, 296, 359; and Gonzaga, 148; *saudade*, 312

Abreu, João Capistrano de, 88, 96, 157–58, 203; and Indian languages, 165

Abreu, Luís Alberto, 225

Academies, xl, **2–3**, 37, 84, 157, 272; Academy of Fine Arts, 5, 37, 67; and

Arcadias, xl. *See also* Brazilian Academy of Letters

Accioli, Breno, 277

Accioly, Marcus, 262, 277

Acre, 328

Adonias, Filho, **3–4**

Afonso VI (King of Portugal), xxxix

Afro-Brazilian culture, xlv; contemporary literature, 89–90; folklore, 127, 194, 212; in Coelho Neto, 87; in Jorge Amado, 15–16, 132–33; in Montello, 209; music, 54, 118, 212–13; and A. do Nascimento, 216; in Olinto, 582; and popular 87, 248; Portuguese language, 254; and Romero, 299; and slavery, 318–22; and theater, 346. *See also* black literature; religions; slavery

Aires, Matias, **4**, 45, 55, 230

Alagoas, xxxix, 132, 169, 176, 269, 271, 324; regionalists, 277

Alba, Renato, 279
Albano, José, 236
Albuquerque, José Medeiros e, 4, 96, 200, 331
Alcântara Machado. See Machado, Antônio de Alcântara
Alegre, Apolinário Porto, 4–5, 279
Alegre, Manuel Araújo Porto, 4, 5, 13, 37, 189, 294
Aleijadinho (Antônio Francisco Lisboa), 35, 37, 55
Alencar, José de, xlv, 6–9, 11, 45, 96, 131, 200, 218, 297, 298, 324, 335, 336; opinion of Callado, 70; and crônica, 100; and C. Gomes, 212; and B. Guimarães, 151; on Macedo, 188; on Gonçalves de Magalhães, 167–68, 190; and neo-Indianism, 287; and realism, 274; and romanticism, 295, 296; and slavery, 320; theater, 298, 320, 340; works on film, 128
Alencar, Mário de, 8
allegory: in Jorge Amado, 15; in M. de Assis, 43; in Assunçao, 45; in Álvares de Azevedo, 340; in Chico Buarque, 67; in Callado, 70; in Camargo, 71; in Cony, 163; and dictatorship, 110, 111, 178; in G. Figueiredo, 127; in Giudice, 146; in Dias Gomes, 146; in Duílio Gomes, 147; in Guarnieri, 150; in Homem, 159; in Ivo, 169; Lins, 178; in Nassar, 217; of dictatorship years, 212; in Melo Neto's poetic language, 198; in M. Mota, 211; in R. Ramos, 272; and religion, 283; in Ubaldo Ribeiro, 288; in Rosa, 302; in short fiction, 111–12, 146; in Suassuna, 329; in theater, 340; in E. Veríssimo, 362
Almeida, Abílio Pereira de, 342
Almeida, Belmiro de, 37
Almeida, Filinto de, 10
Almeida, Guilherme de, 9, 26, 128, 204, 332
Almeida, José Américo de, 9–10, 139, 207, 270, 274, 277, 309, 323
Almeida, Júlia Lopes de, 10, 49, 101, 264; children's literature, 81; and feminism, 101

Almeida, Manuel Antônio de, 11–12, 61, 85, 126, 192, 200, 274, 284, 296, 297, 298; biography, 61; A. Cândido's evaluation, 11, 97
Almeida, Martins de, 20
Almeida, Moacir de, 236
Almeida, Renato de, 133
Almeida, Roniwalter Jatobá de, 225
Almeida Filho, 111
Alphonsus, João, 12, 76, 188
Alvarenga, Lucas José de, 296
Alvarenga, Manuel Inácio da Silva, 3, 12, 35
Alvarenga, Oneida, 133
Alvarenga Peixoto. See Peixoto, Inácio José de Alvarenga
Alverne, Friar Monte, 13, 190, 294
Alves, Antônio Castro, 13–15, 18, 89, 148, 203, 215, 295, 296, 297, 326, 359; theme of G. Campos play, 74; theme of Guarnieri play, 149; and slavery, 320, 321
Alvim, Francisco (Chico), 112, 222
Amado, Gilberto, 200
Amado, James, 278
Amado, Jorge, 15–17, 38, 128, 184, 207, 210, 277, 280, 285, 313, 322, 324; and film, 131; and folklore, 132–33
Amador, Paulo, 224
Amália, Narcisa, 18, 123
Amaral, Amadeu, 236, 255
Amaral, Father Prudêncio do, 35
Amaral, Maria Adelaide, 192, 225
Amaral, Tarsila do, 28, 37, 63, 143, 204
Amazon, xviii, xliv, xlv, 2, 63, 101, 130, 131, 132, 159, 165, 172, 195, 223, 237, 245, 325, 328, 338, 350–53, 365; and Fereira de Castro, 135; in modernism, 25, 118, 206; regionalists, 276; in J. Veríssimo, 362–63
Amazonas, Araújo, 168
American cultural influences: L. and E. Agassiz, 352; C. Andrews, 352; Beat Generation, 310; E. Bishop, 22, 136, 200; F. Boas, 139; J. Cage, 73; C. Chaplin, 21; J. Codman, 351; J. F. Cooper, 6, 7, 296, 335; J. Dewey,

139; E. Dickinson, 312; Reverend B. Dunn, 351; T. Ewbank, xliii, 351; W. Faulkner, 58, 66, 85, 348; Felix the Cat, 82; J. Fletcher, 351; L. Gottschalk, 134; E. Hemingway, 85, 94; D. Kidder, 351; F. Lang, 65; linguistic influence, 254; Living Theater, 344; A. Lowell, 197; H. Melville, 301; A. Miller, 343; Tom Mix, 82; M. Moore, 196, 197; C. Nimuendaju, 165; E. O'Neill, 216, 343; E. Parsons, 346; C. Peirce, 260; J. G. Percival, 93; E. A. Poe, 326, 330; E. Pound, and concretism, 75, 197, 259, 260, 327; T. Roosevelt, 353; P. Roth, 314; H. Smith, 352; H. B. Stowe, 321; S. Temple, 82; theatrical, 341; travel writers, 348–49; F. J. Turner, 158; O. Wells, and V. de Moraes, 210; W. Whitman, 74, 78; T. Williams, 343; W. C. Williams, 197; M. Wright, 352; R. Wright, 216

Amoedo, Rodolfo, 37
Amora, Antônio Soares, 100
"O analista" ("The Psychiatrist") (Machado de Assis), 41
Anchieta, Father José de, xxxviii, xxix, 18–19, 156, 226, 283; and Indian languages, 18, 165; and music, 212, 339; and theater, 339, 340; and Fagundes Varela, 359. See also Indianism
Andrada e Silva. See Silva, José Bonifácio de Andrada e
Andrada e Silva (The Younger). See Silva (The Younger), José Bonifácio de Andrada e.
Andrade, Carlos Drummond de, 12, 19–23, 51, 65, 76, 101, 188, 205, 220, 227, 229, 262, 278, 309; and E. Bishop, 23, 136; on Dias Gomes, 147; and M. Mendes, 200, 201; influence of on Savary, 312; and soccer, 322; and Villa-Lobos, 367
Andrade, Goulart de, 236
Andrade, Jeferson Ribeiro de, 112, 118
Andrade, Joaquim Pedro de, 29, 129, 130
Andrade, Jorge, 23–24, 343, 346
Andrade, Mário de, xlv, xlvi, 11, 24–27,

76, 97, 135, 174, 204, 212, 265, 276, 279, 285, 287, 290, 314, 345; on Machado de Assis, 44; on Bandeira, 51, 56; and Bopp, 63, 70; on Brazilian art, 38, 206; on P. V. de Caminha, 73; and R. de Carvalho, 79; and Cearense, 80; and city literature, 85; critics of, 98, 99; and Elis, 118; and film, 130; and Indianism, 168; and Meireles, 194; and V. de Moraes, 210; and Nava, 220; on Pompéia, 247; and popular culture, 248; and postmodernism, 257–58; and Carvalho Ramos, 278; and Rosa, 300; and T. de Silveira, 318; and tropicalismo, 354; and Villa-Lobos, 367
Andrade, Oswald de, 20, 114, 135, 182, 189, 200, 203, 204, 205, 206, 265, 287, 328; and M. de Andrade, 24, 27–29, 28, 37, 45, 53, 56, 63; A. and H. de Campos's interpretation of, 73, 75; and film, 130; and P. Galvão, 28, 143; on immigration of Japanese, 161; and impressionism, 164; and Indianism, 168; and Melo Neto, 197; and M. Mendes, 200; and postmodernism, 258, 259; and Salgado, 308; and theater, 341, 344; and tropicalismo, 262, 355
Andrade, Thales de, 81
Ângelo, Ivan, 30, 111, 278
Anísio, Chico, 30–31, 38
Anjos, Augusto dos, 31–32, 327, 332; biography, 61
Anjos, Ciro dos, 20, 32, 46
Antonil, Father André João, xl, 157
Antônio, João, 32–33, 86, 111, 323
antropofagia (anthropophagy), 143; and Bopp, 63–64, 206; and A. de Campos, 73; and film, 130; "Manifesto Antropófagio," 28; Revista de Antropofagia, 20, 37; and D. Ribeiro, 287; and tropicalismo, 130, 355; visual, 261
Antunes Filho: and Macunaíma, 345–46, 347; and N. Rodrigues, 292
Aracaju (Sergipe), 323
Aranha, José Pereira da Graça, xlv, 8, 33–34, 38, 161, 164, 200, 241, 264;

and modernism, 204, 205; and symbolism, 332
Aranha, Luís, 202, 205
Araripe Júnior, Tristão de Alencar, 96, 299, 362; and Indianism, 168; and Recife School, 275
Araújo, Murilo, 205
Araújo Porto Alegre. *See* Alegre, Manuel Araújo Porto
Arcadias, xl, 4, 12, **34–36**, 37, 46, 94, 115, 117, 138, 148, 190, 203, 231, 238, 241, 316, 324; Arcadia Romana, 144; and city literature, 84; New Arcadia, 54, 55, 251; Overseas Arcadia, 92; and romanticism, 293, 316
Arena Theater: and Boal, 62, 343, 344; and Guarnieri, 62, 149; and J. Renato, 343; and Zumbi, 319; and Viana Filho, 364
Arinos, Afonso, **36**, 117, 264, 278, 318
armorial movement (Suassuna), 329–30
Arrigucci Júnior, Davi, 98
art, **36–39**, 46, 47, 63, 105, 143, 164, 202, 293, 335, 349, 366; architecture of Minas, 21, 35, 46, 55; and Borba Filho, 64; and A. de Campos, 73; and M. Colasanti, 87; critics, 24, 114; Gonzaga Duque, 114; and Dutch influence, xxxviii, 37; and folklore, 170, 176; and J. de Lima, 176; and E. de Matos, 193; and Melo Neto, 197; and Milano, 202; and modernism, 204, 206; and Nava, 220; and Parnassianism, 234; and C. Pena, 238; and Pompéia, 245; and postmodernism, 259; and travel literature, 351; and *tropicalismo*, 354
Ascher, Nelson, 100, 223
Asdrubal Trouxe o Trombone (theater group), 345
Assis, Joaquim Maria Machado de, 7, 12, 32, **39–45**, 46, 77, 147, 151, 170, 173, 177, 179, 201, 210, 239, 264, 267, 275, 277, 284, 298, 301, 329, 361; opinion of J. de Alencar, 10; and M. A. de Almeida, 11; evaluation of by Lima Barreto, 56; biographers, 61; and Brazilian Academy of Letters, 54,

61, 67, 172, 208; and city literature, 84; *crônica*, 101; as a literary critic, 96; on Indianism, 168; and Macedo, 188; and music, 212; and Portuguese in Rio, 252; and positivism, 257; on Eça de Queiroz, 218–19, 253; and realism, 273, 274; and Rio, 279; and D. Ribeiro, 287; romanticism, 296, 297, 298; on Romero, 298; and *saudade*, 312; on É. Zola, 41
Assis, Judith Ribeiro de, 102
Assis Brasil. *See* Brasil, Assis
Assunçao, Leilah, **45**, 125, 346; and Marcos, 192
O ateneu (The Athenaeum) (Pompéia), 160, 185, 218, **245–47**, 274
Athayde, Austregésilo de, 67
Athayde, Roberto Austrégesilo de, 346
Athayde, Tristão de. *See* Lima, Alceu Amoroso
Austrian cultural influence: S. Freud, 291; S. Zweig, 53, 78, 135
autobiography, xlvii, 1, 4, 32, 40, **45–46**, 61, 63, 90, 121, 137, 138, 149, 153, 160, 163, 170, 199, 207, 212, 222, 244, 270, 293, 307, 312; by Bandeira, 53; during dictatorship, 111, 121; and memoirs, 200; and Pompéia, 245; and Lins do Rego, 280–82; and Ubaldo Ribeiro, 288; and Rosa, 301
Auto da compadecida (*The Rogue's Trial*) (Suassuna), 285, 329
Avalovara (*Avalovara*) (Lins), 178
Ave, palavra (Bird, Word) (Rosa), 300, 303
Ávila, Affonso, **46–47**, 260, 261, 278
Ayala, Walmir, 38, **47**, 160, 258, 279
Azambuja, Darci, 279
Azeredo, Carlos de, 236
Azeredo, Ronaldo, 260
Azevedo, Aluísio, xliv, 37, **47–49**, 72, 128, 161, 219, 247, 273, 275, 284, 289, 325, 338; and positivism, 257; and slavery, 321
Azevedo, Artur, 47, **49**, 61, 62, 136, 240, 264, 320, 341
Azevedo, Manuel Álvares de, 14, **49–50**, 67, 84, 139, 151, 253, 284, 295, 296,

340; and allegory, 340; and *saudade*, 312

Babo, Lamartine, 130
A bagaceira (*Trash*) (J. A. de Almeida), 10, 207, 323
Bahia, xxxviii, xl, xli, xlii, xliv, 54, 55, 62, 94, 102–105, 127, 138, 146, 148, 157, 212, 237, 251, 252, 258, 297, 307, 324, 332, 338, 348; in Adonias Filho, 3; in Jorge Amado, 15–17, 131, 207; and Durão, 115; in Dias Gomes, 146; *Lira do Bolso*, 262, 278; in G. de Matos, 84, 192; in modernism, 206; regionalists, 276–78; in Ubaldo Ribeiro, 288; in J. B. de Andrada e Silva, 317; in travel literature, 350
Bananére, Juó, 28, 161
Bandeira, Manuel, 26, 27, 38, 45, **51–53**, 101, 196, 200, 204, 206, 210; on Cearense, 80; on Gonçalves Dias, 108; and Alphonsus de Guimaraens, 150; and M. Mendes, 200; and Villa-Lobos, 367; and Zweig, 135
bandeirantes (explorers), xl; in Bilac, 60, 236
Bandeirantes e pioneiros (*Bandeirantes and Pioneers*) (Moog), 209
Barbosa, Father Domingos Caldas, xli, **54**, 90, 251; and music, 212
Barbosa, Francisco de Assis, 61
Barbosa, Januário da Cunha, 96, 296
Barbosa, João Alexandre, 98
Barbosa, Rui, **54–55**; and abolitionism, 145, 215; and A. France, 135; and positivism, 257
baroque, xxxix, 2, 4, 21, 35, 36, 37, **55–56**, 67, 69, 86, 92, 103, 113, 193, 226, 230, 247, 315, 327; and Ávila, 46; and concretism, 75; and Father A. Vieira, 365
Barreto, Afonso Henriques de Lima, 46, **56–58**, 237, 275, 284; and Antônio's fiction, 32–33; biography of, 61; and contemporary black literature, 89; and immigrants, 161; and modernism, 204; and music, 212; and positivism, 257; and *saudade*, 312

Barreto, Bruno, 128, 131
Barreto, Fausto, 255
Barreto, Luís Pereira, 256
Barreto, Tobias, 89, 275
Barros, Domingos Borges de, 294
Barroso, Juarez, 277
Barroso, Maria Alice, **58–59**, 123
Bastos, Dau, 224
Bastos, Orlando, 224
Batini, Tito, 162
Becker, Cacilda, 266
Beckmann, Manuel, xl
Beiguelman, Paula, 100
Belém, xxxviii, 63, 118, 119, 122, 172, 190, 206, 312. *See also* Pará
Bell, Lindolf, **59**, 261
Belo Horizonte, 64, 90, 170, 173, 205, 220, 285, 299, 309, 310, 312. *See also* Minas Gerais
Benedetti, Lúcia, 84
Bento (protagonist of *Dom Casmurro* by Machado de Assis), 43
Bernardes, Artur, xlv
Bernardes, Carmo, 278
Bernardi, Mansueto, 162
Bethencourt, João, **59–60**, 345
Betto, Friar, 285
Bezerra, José Clímaco, 277
Bial, Pedro, 223
biblic sources, 75, 263, 308, 366. *See also* Religion
Bilac, Olavo, **60–61**, 101, 234, 235, 236, 264, 332; M. de Andrade, opinion of, 25; and Loyola Brandão, 66; and children's literature, 81; on Patrocínio, 81, 101
Bildungsroman, 46, 65
Bins, Patrícia, 125
biography, **61**, 72, 176; of J. de Alencar, 8; of M. A. de Almeida, 61, 274–75; of Anchieta, 19; of Arinos, 36; of Machado de Assis, 40, 46; and Nabuco, 215; in post-dictatorship, 112; of religious figures, 284; of N. Rodrigues, 292
Bivar, Antônio, 346
Black Experimental Theater (*TEN*), 216, 346

black literature: children's, 82; of Coelho
    Neto, 87, 332; contemporary, **89–90**,
    143, 164, 209, 216; of J. de Lima,
    466; of A. do Nascimento, 216; and
    Patrocínio, 237; theater, 340, 346
Bloch, Pedro, **62**, 342
Boal, Augusto, xlvii, **62–63**, 110, 241,
    253, 343, 344, 345; and Guarnieri,
    149
Bocaiúva, Quintino, 39, 340
Bodansky, Jorge, 131
bodypoems (*corpoemas*) (Bell), 59
Bojunga, Lygia, 83
Bom Crioulo (*Bom Crioulo*) (A. Cam-
    inha), 72, 160, 219,
Bomfim, Manuel, 81
Bonvicino, Régis, 223
Bopp, Raul, 38, **63–64**, 132, 143, 200,
    206, 276; and Indianism, 168
Borba Filho, Hermilo, **64**, 133, 277, 343
Borges, Cavalcanti, 277
Bosco, João, 84
Bosi, Alfredo, 99
bossa nova, xlvi, 207. *See also samba*;
    music
Braga, Edgard, 260
Braga, Ernani, 204
Braga, Roberto, 223
Braga, Rubem, **64–65**, 223, 279
Braga, Sônia, 131
Brandão, Ambrósio Fernandes, 156, 226,
    251
Brandão, Ignácio de Loyola, **65–66**, 86,
    110, 128, 253, 279; as film critic, 65,
    131
Brant, Alice Dayrell, 200; and E.
    Bishop, 136, 200
Brant, Vera, 200
Brasil, Assis, **66**, 100; on Chamie, 81
Brasil, Emanuel, 136
Brasil, Luiz Antônio Assis, 224
Brasília, 245, 307, 316
Brazilian Academy of Letters, 3, 44, 54,
    61, 62, **67**, 87, 172, 194, 204, 208,
    211, 234, 264, 265, 266, 267, 290,
    291, 299, 300, 313, 322; and Graça
    Aranha, 34, 204; and Parnassianism,
    234

Brazilian Academy of Philology, 256
Brazilian Academy of Philosophy, 174
Brazilian Comedy Theater (*Teatro Brasi-
    leiro de Comédia*), 342
Brazilian Historical and Geographical In-
    stitute, xlii, 107, 157, 167, 295, 296
Brazilian School of Dramatic Art, 342
Brazilian Student Theater (*Teatro Estu-
    dantil Brasileiro*), 342
Brazilian Union of Writers, 264
Brazilian Writers Association, 127
Brécheret, Vítor, 28, 204
Brejo das almas (Fen of Souls) (Drum-
    mond de Andrade), 20
Bressane, Júlio, 130
British cultural influences, 240; J. M.
    Barrie, 82; H. Bates, 351; W. Blake,
    230, 293; P. Brook, 344; Sir Richard
    Burton, 134, 144–45, 352; Lord By-
    ron, 14, 49, 84, 138, 293, 296, 297;
    L. Carroll, 82; C. Chaplin, 21; S. T.
    Coleridge, 293; N. Coward, 343; C.
    Darwin, 351; H. Dent, 352; C. Dick-
    ens, 133; T. S. Eliot, 262, 312; P.
    Fleming, 353; M. Graham, 37, 351;
    G. Greene, 70, 122, 230; T. Hughes,
    246; A. Huxley, 267, 361; R. Kipling,
    135, 740; J. Keats, 191, 293; H. Kos-
    ter, 351; J. Lennon, 192; J. T. Lin-
    dley, 350; J. Locke, 13; J. Luccock,
    350; T. Malthus, 308; K. Mansfield,
    179; S. Maugham, 267, 361; J. Mawe,
    350; G. Meredith, 84; Sir T. More,
    166; M. and E. Mulhall, 352; G. Or-
    well, 67; philosophy, 240; J. B. Pries-
    tley, 343; Sir W. Scott, 6, 7, 8, 167,
    293, 296; W. Shakespeare, 53, 127,
    175, 217, 222, 342; P. B. Shelley,
    293; R. Southey, 134; L. Sterne, influ-
    ence on Machado de Assis, 40; J.
    Swift, 198; Times Literary Supplement
    and postmodernism, 260; travel writ-
    ers, 352; A. Wallace, 351, 352; O.
    Wilde, 361; V. Woolf, 186, 267; W.
    Wordsworth, 293
Brito, Antônio Carlos de (Cacaso), (died
    1987), 112, 222, 262
Brito, Farias de, 241, 284

Brito, Francisco de Paula, 39, 319
Brito, Mário da Silva, 208
Broca, José Brito, 97, 291
Bruckner, Michael, 163
Bruno, Haroldo, 83
Buarque, Chico, xlvii, 1, **67–68**, 126, 212; and Boal, 63; and children's literature, 68, 83; and film, 131; and Melo Neto, 198; and theater, 345, 346
Bulhões, Antônio, **68**
bumba-meu-boi, 64, 77, 126, 343. *See also* folklore.
Burgaín, Luís Antônio, 340
Byzantine novel, 231

Cabral, Antônio Carlos, 259
Cabral, Pedro Álvares, 72
Cabral de Melo Neto. *See* Melo Neto, João Cabral de
Cacaso (Antônio Carlos de Brito) (died 1987) 112, 222, 262
Caetano, João. *See* Santos, João Caetano dos
Caetés (Caete Indians) (G. Ramos), 269, 270
Cais de sagração (*Coronation Quay*) (Montello), 208–9
Calado, Friar Manuel, **69**
Calasãs, Pedro de, 89
Caldas, Father Sousa, 35
Callado, Antônio, **69–71**, 86, 110, 160, 222, 241–42, 264; and Indianism, 168; and religion, 285; and D. Ribeiro, 287
Câmara, Eugênia, 13, 14
Câmara, Isabel, 192, 346
Câmara, Joaquim Mattoso, 255
Camargo, Joracy, **71**, 292, 341
Camargo, Oswaldo de, 90
Caminha, Adolfo, **71–72**, 160, 219, 273
Caminha, Pero Vaz de, xxxvii, 19, **72–73**, 156, 251, 357
Camões, Jerusa, 342
Campello, Myriam, 125
Campos, Arnaldo, 223
Campos, Augusto de, 38, 61, **73–74**, 75, 222, 243, 259, 260, 261, 309, 327, 355
Campos, Geir, **74–75**, 258, 262

Campos, Haroldo de, 38, 73, **75–76**, 243, 259, 260, 309, 327
Campos, Humberto de, 96, 200, 236
Campos, José Maria Moreira, 277
Campos, Narcisa Amália de Oliveira. *See* Amália, Narcisa
Campos, Paulo Mendes, **76**, 258, 262; and *crônica*, 101; on Milano, 202
Campos Filho, Joaquim Jácome de Oliveira, 18
Canaã (*Canaan*) (Graça Aranha), 33, 332
Canadian cultural influences: M. Richler, 314; travel writers, 349
Cândido, Antônio, 84, 97–98; on M. A. de Almeida, 11, 97; on O. de Andrade, 29; on Lins, 178; and Milliet, 202; and modernism, 208
Cândido de Carvalho. *See* Carvalho, José Candido de
Caneca, Brother, 199
Canedo, Gregoriano, 20
Cannabrava, Euryalo, 99
Canudos, xliv, 102, 103, 104, 135. *See also* Cunha, Euclides da
Capellaro, Vittorio, 128
Capinan, José Carlos, 355
Capitães da areia (*Captains of the Sand*) (Jorge Amado), 16
Capitu (protagonist of *Dom Casmurro* by Machado de Assis), 43
Caramuru (Caramuru) (Durão), 35, 114–115, 165, 252, 283
Cardim, Father Fernão, 156
Cardoso, Fausto, 275
Cardoso, Lúcio, 3, **76–77**, 122, 128, 179, 207, 322; and children's literature, 82
Cardozo, Joaquim, **77**, 127, 170, 196, 262, 277, 322, 343,
A carne (Flesh) (J. Ribeiro), 219, 289
Carneiro, Caio Porfírio, 277
Carneiro, Cecílio J., 161
Carneiro, Edison, 133
Carneiro, Geraldo, 222
carnival, theme of in: R. Couto, 95; R. Drummond, 114; Eneida, 119; Monteiro Martins, 192; V. de Moraes, 211; A. J. da Silva, 315; theater, 345–46

Carone, Modesto, 224
Carpeaux, Otto Maria, 100, 135; on Na-
    buco, 215; on realism, 274
Carr, Stella, 83
Cartas chilenas (Chilean Letters) (Gon-
    zaga), 84, 93, 148
Caruso, Raimundo, 223
Carvalho, Flávio, 341
Carvalho, Horácio de, 219
Carvalho, José Cândido de, 77–78
Carvalho, José de Arimathea Soares, 261
Carvalho, O. G. Rego de, 277
Carvalho, Ronald de, xlv, 26, 38, 78–79,
    97, 204, 212, 253, 332; and Villa-Lo-
    bos, 367
Carvalho, Trajano Galvão de, 276, 319
Carvalho, Vicente de, 234, 235; M. de
    Andrade's evaluation of, 25,
Carvalho, Walter Campos de, 79
Carybé, 38
A casa de água (The Water House)
    (Olinto), 229
A casa da paixão (The House of Passion)
    (Piñon), 124, 244
Casa grande e senzala (The Mansions
    and the Shanties) (Freyre), 139, 158
Cascudo, Luís de Câmara, 126, 133,
    172, 174
Castello, José Aderaldo, 100
Castro, Consuelo de, 79–80, 346; and
    Marcos, 79, 192
Castro, Josué de, 46
Castro, Neil de, 278
Castro Alves. See Alves, Antônio Castro
Cavalcante, Joyce, 125
Cavalcanti, Emiliano Di, 38, 204
Cavalheiro, Edgard, 61
Cazarré, Lourengo, 223
Ceará, xxxviii, xlii, 5, 71, 105, 184,
    219, 229, 233, 258, 323, 336, 338; in
    modernism, 206, 207; regionalists,
    276–77; Spiritual Brotherhood, 276,
    338; in travel literature, 351
Cearense, Catulo da Paixão, 80, 213
Celso, Afonso, 241, 357
Celso, José, 29, 345
censorship. See dictatorship
Cerqueira, Marcelo, 101, 224

César, Ana Cristina, 112, 222, 262
César, Guilhermino, 265
Chacal, 112, 262
Chagas, José, 277
Chamie, Mário, 80–81, 259
Chamma, Foed Castro, 258
Charles, 222
Chaves Netto, João Ribeiro, 346–47
Chanchada (satiric play), 341
children's literature, 47, 60, 67, 78, 81–
    84, 88, 127, 151, 159, 169, 170, 176,
    181, 190, 208, 223, 238, 264, 265,
    266, 267, 275, 286, 301, 307, 360,
    361, 367; for adults, 173, 244; and
    Bandeira, 52; and detective fiction,
    186; and Eneida, 119; and Leonardos,
    173–74; and Lessa, 174; and Monteiro
    Lobato, 182, 183; and C. Meireles,
    194; and soccer, 322; and theater, 346
Cicero, Father, 132, 277
Cinco minutos (Five Minutes) (Alencar),
    6, 7
cinema novo (new cinema), xlvi, 128–29;
    and E. da Cunha, 105; and dictator-
    ship, 110; and Salles Gomes, 147
Ciranda de pedra (The Marble Dance)
    (L. F. Telles), 337
Cirne, Moacy, 260
city, xlvii, 32, 35, 48, 49, 68, 72, 76,
    84–86, 91, 121, 173, 212, 229–30,
    237, 272, 274, 284, 286, 291, 295,
    297, 304, 315, 359, 363; theme of: in
    J. de Alencar, 7; in Jorge Amado, 15–
    16; in crônicas, 226; in Drummond de
    Andrade, 20; in Loyola Brandão, 65–
    66; in Callado, 70–71; in A. de Cam-
    pos, 73; in children's literature, 83; in
    Condé, 88; in O. de Faria, 121–122; in
    R. Fonseca, 133–34; in Fusco, 140; in
    Giudice, 146; in C. Lispector, 179; in
    J. M. de Macedo, 187–88; in Alcân-
    tara Machado, 189; and modernism,
    207; and E. do Nascimento, 216–17;
    and popular culture, 248; and realism,
    274; See also Aracaju; Belém; Belo
    Horizonte; Brasília; Curitiba; Manaus;
    Maceió; Óbidos; Pelotas; Porto Al-
    egre; Recife; Rio; Salvador; Santos

Claro enigma (Clear Enigma) (Drummond de Andrade), 21

Cobra Norato (The Snake Norato) (Bopp), 38, 63, 132, 206, 276, "code-poems," 260

Coelho Neto, Henrique, **86–87**, 101, 185, 284; evaluation of by Lima Barreto, 56; and music, 212; and slavery theme, 321; and soccer, 322; and symbolism, 332; and theater, 341

Coimbra, University of, xl, 12, 18, 92, 93, 107, 114, 192, 230, 238, 250,

Colasanti, Marina, 83, **87–88**, 125, 330

Collen, Paulo, 200

Colônia, Regina Célia, 261

The Comedians (*Os Comediantes*), 342

comic novel, 11–12

comic-strip poetry, 261

Comparato, Doc (Luís Felipe Loureiro Comparato) 315

concretism, xlvi, 46, 148, 221, 243, 259–60, 290, 309; and Drummond de Andrade, 22; and O. de Andrade, 29; and Bandeira, 53; and Campos brothers, 38, 59, 73–74, 75–76; and Chamie, 80–81; and Faustino, 122; and Gullar, 152; and Melo Neto, 199; and neoconcretism, 152, 259; and romanticism, 298. *See also* postmodernism

Condé, Elísio, 88

Condé, João, 88

Condé, José, **88**, 277

condorism, 14, **88–89**, 296, 297, 317, 320

A confederação dos tamoios (The Confederation of the Tamoio Indians) (Gonçalves de Magalhães), 6, 71, 167, 190, 295

Confissões do Ralfo (Ralfo's Confessions) (S. Sant'Anna), 310

Congílio, Mariazinha, 101

Conselheiro, Antônio, xliv, 103–105. *See also* Cunha, Euclides da

Consolin, Aércio Flávio, 225

O continente (*Time and the Wind*) (É. Veríssimo), 361–62

Cony, Carlos Heitor, 46, **90–91**, 101, 110, 163, 275, 285, 322

Coralina, Cora, 278

Corção, Gustavo, 284–85

cordel (popular literature sold on a string), 38, 132, 152, 174, 278, 324; and theater, 343

coringa (joker): Boal, 62, 344

Corpo de baile (Dance Corps) (G. Rosa), 300, 301

corpoemas (body poems) (Bell), 59

Correia, Diogo Álvares (protagonist of *Caramuru* by Durão), 115

Correia, Raimundo, 60, **91–92**, 234, 235, 253, 320; evaluation of by M. de Andrade, 25

Correia, Viriato, 82, 342

O Correio Brasiliense (H. da Costa), 93–94, 252

O cortiço (*The Brazilian Tenement*) (Aluísio Azevedo), 48, 219

Cortines, Júlia, 236

Costa, Cláudio Manuel da, 3, 35, 55, 67, **92–93**, 203, 251,

Costa, Eduardo Alves da, 261

Costa, Flávio Moreira da, **93**, 322–23

Costa, Gal, 73

Costa, Hipólito da, xli, **93–94**, 319

Costa, Jayme, 341

Costa, João Cruz, 241

Costa, Sosígenes, 206

Costa Filho, Odilo, 277

costumbrismo (scenes of life): in theater, 339–40

Coutinho, Afrânio, 98, 99, 295, 296; and Brazilian Portuguese, 98; and Portuguese literature, 254; and romanticism, 295–96

Coutinho, Carlos Nelson, 100

Coutinho, Edilberto, **94**, 160, 322

Coutinho, Paulo César, 225

Coutinho, Sônia, **94–95**, 125, 277

Couto, Friar Loreto, 166

Couto, Rui Ribeiro, **95**, 204, 213, 253, 332; and Villa-Lobos, 367

Crespo, Antônio Gonçalves, **95–96**, 320

critics, literary: Brazilian, 96–100; foreign: J. Coleman, 140; G. Lukács, 100, 272; J. M. Massa, 61; J. M. Tol-

man, 134; D. H. Treece, 324; A. War-
ren, 98; R. Wellek, 98, 272
crônica, xliv, 20, 25, 38, 47, 49, 60, 65,
    76, 78, **100–101**, 119, 122, 126, 136,
    182, 210, 226, 250, 266, 267, 269,
    278, 290, 291, 307, 363; feminism,
    101; illustrators, 150
Crônica da casa assassinada (Chronicle
    of the Assassinated House) (L. Car-
    doso), 77
Cruls, Gastão, 38, **101–2**, 276
Cruz e Sousa. *See* Sousa, João da Cruz e
cubism, 28
Cunha, Euclides da, xliv, xlv, 10, 20,
    56, 70, 98, **102–105**, 136, 241, 244,
    270, 278, 285; and positivism, 257
Cunha, Fausto, 100
Cunha, Helena Parente, 125, 261
Cunha, Manuel Rodrigues Pimenta da,
    102
Curitiba (Parana), 353
Cuti (Luís Silva), 90
cycles, 276–77; backlands, 36, 105, 234,
    281, 302, 329, 336, 338; cocoa, 105,
    325; drought, 10, 83, 105, 229, 237,
    266, 269, 270, 277, 323–24, 338;
    gold-mining, 105, 308; *sertão*, 105,
    117; and social novel, 323–24; sugar-
    cane, 105, 207, 277, 280, 324; *Tragé-
    dia burguesa*, 122

Da Cunha, Euclides. *See* Cunha, Euclides
    da
Damasceno, Darcy, 258
Damata, Gasparino, 160
Daniel, Herbert, 46
Danish cultural influence: H. C. Ander-
    sen, 81
Dantas, Pedro, 205
Daunt Neto, Ricardo, 225
Deane, Percy, 38
death squad (*esquadrão da morte*), 315
decadentistas (decadent poets), 331. *See
    also* symbolism
Denser, Márcia, 125, 224–25
detective fiction: and Albuquerque, 4; and
    Fonseca, 134; and Louzeiro, 186; and

Sabino, 307; and D. da Silva, 316; and
    M. Souza, 328
Deus, Friar Gaspar de Madre de, 3
Deus lhe paque (May God Bless You)
    (Camargo), 71, 292
Um dia no Rio (A Day in Rio) (O.
    França Júnior), 137
Dias, Antônio Gonçalves, xliii, **107–10**,
    252, 284, 290, 317, 342; in Aluísio
    Azevedo's *O mulato*, 48; biography of,
    61, 97; "Canção do exílio," 95, 109;
    and city literature, 84; and Durão, 115;
    evaluation of by A. Herculano, 252–
    53; and folklore, 133; and Junqueira
    Freire, 138; and Indianism, 167; and
    Indian languages, 165, 167; and neo-
    Indianism, 287; and polemic on dis-
    covery of Brazil, 296; and *saudade*,
    312; and slavery, 319; and theater,
    298, 340; and *ufanismo*, 357
Dias, Cícero, 38
Dias, Teófilo, 236, 273
Dias Gomes. *See* Gomes, Alfredo Dias
Dias-Pino, Wladimir, 260
dictatorship (1964–1985), xxxvii, xlvi–
    xlvii, 98, **110–13**, 118, 121, 126, 137,
    138, 143, 146, 149–50, 152, 163, 191,
    192, 195, 220, 223, 315, 363, 364;
    and C. F. Abreu, 1; and Jorge Amado,
    15, 24, 30; and Antônio, 32–33, 45,
    46, 59; and black literature, 89–90;
    and Boal, 63; and Loyola Brandão,
    65–66; and Chico Buarque, 67; and
    Callado, 69–70; and C. de Castro, 79;
    and children's literature, 82–83; and
    city literature, 85–86, 212; and Cony,
    90–91; and criticism, 98; and *crônica*,
    226, 250; and R. Drummond, 114; and
    feminism, 124; and film, 129; and R.
    Fonseca, 133–34; and Gullar, 152–53;
    and homosexuality, 428, 451; and
    Lins, 178; and Louzeiro, 185–86; and
    Marcos, 191; memoirs of, 200; and V.
    de Moraes, 210; and Mourão, 212; and
    music, 213; and A. do Nascimento,
    216; and Nassar, 218; and Nava, 220;
    and new writers, 222; Novaes, 227;
    and Pellegrini Jr., 238; and Piñon,

244; and popular culture, 248–49; and Porto, 629; and postmodernism, 262; and R. Ramos, 272; and religion, 285; in reviews, 286, 310; and Ubaldo Ribeiro, 288; and N. Rodrigues, 292; and H. Sales, 308; and Salgado, 308; and A. R. de Sant'Anna, 309; and Santiago, 311; and M. Souza, 328; and L. F. Telles, 337; in theater, 344; and Torres, 348; and Veiga, 360; and E. Veríssimo, 362; and L. Vilela, 367

Diegues, Carlos, 129, 131, 319
Dines, Alberto, 163
Dolores, Carmen (Emília Moncorvo Bandeira de Melo), 123, 219
Dom Casmurro (*Dom Casmurro*) (Machado de Assis), 42, 287
Dona Flor e seus dois maridos (*Dona Flor and Her Two Husbands*) (Jorge Amado): on film, 131; and folklore in, 132–33
Donato, Hernani, 82, 279
Dora, Doralina (*Dora, Doralina*) (R. de Queiroz), 266
Dória, Gustavo, 342
Dourado, Autran, **113**
Os dragões ("The Dragons") (Rubião), 773–74
Drummond, Roberto, 111, **114**, 264,
Drummond de Andrade. *See* Andrade, Carlos Drummond de
Duque, Luís Gonzaga, 37, **114**, 164; and symbolism, 332
Durão, Friar José de Santa Rita, 5, 35, **114–15**, 158, 167, 203, 252, 283
Durval, Adalberto, Guerra, 332
Dutch cultural influences: invasion of Brazil, xxxviii, 69, 157, 251, 365; and M. de Nassau, xxxviii; and F. Post, 37; travel writers, 349
"Dzi Croquetes" (gay theater group), 160

Eça, Matias Aires Ramos da Silva e. *See* Aires, Matias
Eiró, Paulo, 89, 340
Eles não usam black-tie (They Don't Wear Tuxedos) (Guarnieri), 149, 343

Eliodora, Bárbara, **117**, 123, 238
Élis, Bernardo, **117–18**
Emboabas Wars, xl; in J. Ribeiro, 289
Emediato, Luiz Fernando, 110, **118**, 160, 264
Emmer, Denise, 330
O encontro marcado (*A Time to Meet*) (Sabino), 307
Eneida, **118–19**, 276; and modernism, 206
Engrácio, Artur, 276
Enlightenment, 4, 115, 203, 231, 316; and H. da Costa, 94; influence of on Arcadias, 34–35; and romanticism, 293
epic poetry, 5, 35, 92, 134, 251, 359; in Bilac, 60–61; and Calado, 69; and Durão, 114–15; and B. da Gama, 144; Indians in, 167; Ivo, 169; and Melo Neto, 198–199, 251–252; and Ricardo, 737; and *Os sertões*, 103; and B. Teixeira, 336; Varela, 359; and Varnhagen, 158
Epicurean Society (São Paulo romantic literary group), 49, 151, 297
epistolary novel, 10
Esaú e Jacó (*Esaú e Jacó*) (Machado de Assis), 43
Escobar, Carlos Henrique, 225
A escrava Isaura (The Slavegirl Isaura) (B. Guimarães), 26, 151; television serial, 131, 297
Os escravo (The Slaves) (Alves), 14
Espinheira Filho, Rui, 262
Espírito Santo, 74, 325
Espumas fluctuantes (Floating Spume) (Alves), 13
esquadrão da morte (death squad), 315
O estrangeiro (The Foreigner) (Salgado), 308–9
A estranha nação de Rafael Mendes (*The Strange Nation of Rafael Mendes*, 1988) (Scliar), 314
A estrela sobe (The Star Rises) (Rebelo), 275
Eu (*I*) (Anjos), 31
Expoesia I (poetry exhibition in 1972), 260
expressionism, 28

Uma faca só lâmina (*A Knife All Blade*) (Melo Neto), 198
Fagundes Telles. *See* Telles, Lygia Fagundes
Fagundes Varela. *See* Varela, Luís Nicolau Fagundes
Faillace, Tânia Jamardo, **121**, 125, 222
Fallabella, Miguel, 225
Faoro, Raymundo, 100
Faraco, Sérgio, 225
Faria, Álvaro Alves de, 222
Faria, Otávio de, 3, 87, **121–22**, 128, 210, 239, 279, 284, 313, 322 *saudade*, 312
Farroupilha Revolt, xlii, 5; in Lopes Neto, 185
Faustino, Mário, **122**, 190
Fazendeiro do ar (Planter of Air) (Drummond de Andrade), 21
O feijão e o sonho (Black Beans and the Dream) (Lessa), 174
Felinto, Marilene, 125, 224
Felix, Moacir, 258; and Street Guitar movement, 261
Feliz ano novo (Happy New Year) (R. Fonseca), 110, 133
feminism, 101, **123–26**, 149, 169, 170, 179, 200, 224, 244, 312; and J. de Alencar, 7, 81; and J. L. de Almeida, 10; and Jorge Amado, 16, 18, 35; and Assunção, 45; and Lima Barreto, 57, 58; and Chico Buarque, 68; and C. de Castro, 79; and city literature, 86; and Colasanti, 87–88; and S. Coutinho, 94–95; and criticism, 98; and Denser, 225; and Eneida, 119; and Faillace, 121; and J. J. França Júnior, 136; and Francis, 138; and Gabeira, 143; and P. Galvão, 74, 144; and immigrant literature, 162; in Leonardos, 174; and C. Lispector, 76, 180; and L. Luft, 186; and G. Machado, 189; and naturalism, 219; and A. Nery, 222; and Orta, 231; and Parnassianism, 236; and positivism, 257; and A. Prado, 263; and R. de Queiroz, 266; and S. Sant'Anna, 310; and Steen, 329; and symbolism,

332; and L. F. Telles, 337–38; and theater, 346; travel literature, 350, 352
Fernandes, Millôr, 38, **126**, 226, 344, 363; on Chico Buarque, 68
Ferraz, Geraldo, 27
Ferreira, Ascenso, 77, **126–27**
Ferreira, Procópio, 341
Ferreira, Sônia Nolasco, 138, 224
Ferreira Gullar. *See* Gullar, Ferreira
A festa (*The Celebration*) (Ângelo), 30
Figueiredo, Guilherme de, **127**, 342
Figueiredo, Jackson de, **127–28**, 175, 205, 284
Figueiredo, João Baptista, xlvii
film, xl, xliv, 9, 29, 30, 93, 110, 118, 122, **128–31**, 132, 151, 174, 183, 185, 210, 275, 279, 282, 286, 292, 319, 329, 336, 348–49, 360, 366–67; and Loyola Brandão, 65; and Chico Buarque, 67; and Callado and Glâuber Rocha, 229; and Salles Gomes, 147; immigration in, 164; and Indianism, 168; and Alcântara Machado, 189; and Monteiro Martins, 192; and Melo Neto, 198; and prizes, 264; and D. S. de Queiroz, 266; and R. Ramos, 271; and Aguinaldo Silva, 315; and M. Souza, 135, 328; and *tropicalismo*, 354–55
Fiorani, Sílvio, 164
Flaminaçu (Para-modernist group), 119, 206
Flag, Suzana, 46, 292
Floresta, Nísia, 257
Fogo morto (Dead Fire) (Rego), 281, 324 on film, 130
folhetim (serialized fiction) 6, 47
folklore, xlv, 15, 23, 24, 31, 47, 54, 95, 103, 126, **131–33**, 134, 152, 170, 172, 174, 185, 278, 318, 336; and art, 36–37; in children's literature, 82, 83, 84; in *Cobra Norato*, 63–64; in Dias Gomes, 146; in R. C. Colônia, 261; and Indian culture, 165–66, 287; and Jewish-Brazilian, 313–14; and Monteiro Lobato, 183; in C. Meireles, 194; in Melo Neto, 196; and music, 212; in popular culture, 248; in R. de Queiroz,

267; in Romero, 248, 298; in Salgado, 308–9; in Scliar, 313–314; in M. Souza, 328; in Suassuna, 329; and theater, 343. *See also* Afro-Brazilian culture
Fonseca, Rubem, 86, 110, **133–34**, 244, 264, 275, 279; and neonaturalism, 220
Fonseca, Yone Gianetti, 259
Fontela, Orides, 223
Fontes, Amando, 277, 323
Fontes, José Martins, 236, 257
Fontoura, Adelino, 236
foreign writers, **134–36**, 188; and travel literature, 348–53
Fortaleza, 71. *See also* Ceará
Fóscolo, Avelino, 219
Fraga, Cid Seixas, 262
França Júnior, José Joaquim da, 49, 101, 110, **136–37**, 240, 320, 340–41
França Júnior, Oswaldo, 111, **137**
Francis, Paulo, 46, **137–38**, 153
Franco, Afonso Arinos de Melo, 36
Franco, Francisco de Melo, 35
Freire, Laudelino, 255
Freire, Luís José Junqueira, 14, 45, **138– 39**, 284, 296
Freire, Paulo, 241; and theater movements, 63, 344
Freitas Filho, Armando, 222, 260
French cultural influences, xxxvii, xxxix, xl, xli, xlii, 5, 202, 218, 234–35, 239, 240, 253, 275, 311, 331, 341; Apollinaire, 260; H. Balzac, 6, 20, 133, 272, 274; C. Baudelaire, 31, 235, 326, 330, 331; R. Bastide, 216; P. Beaumarchais, 267; H. Bergson, 174; G. Bernanos, 122, 135, 175, 210, 239; S. Bernhardt, 134; L. Bloy, 122; A. Bréton, 330; M. Camus, 211; B. Cendrars (Swiss), 25, 135, 290; R. Chateaubriand, 6, 7, 107, 190, 293, 335; P. Claudel, 24; G. Clemenceau, 353; A. Comte, 256, 257; E. Condillac, 13; J. B. Debret, 5, 37, 335, 349; F. Denis, 96, 134, 167, 294, 349; D. Diderot, 40; J. Dubuffet, 197; P. Éluard, 51; F. Fénelon, 231; G. Flaubert, 237, 272; P. Fort, 24; A. France, 44, 135,

361; T. Gautier, 235; A. Gide, 267; Goncourt Brothers, 247; J. M. Heredia, 235; V. Hugo, 14, 18, 89, 107, 293, 296, 319, 320; J. K. Huysmans, 326; E. Ionesco, 144; P. Laclos, 20; J. de LaFontaine, 183; A. de Lamartine, 107, 293, 296; LaRochefoucauld, 4, 294; Leconte de Lisle, 235; C. Le-Corbusier, 198; F. Léger, 263; *Le Parnasse contemporain*, 235; J. de Léry, xxxvii, 348; C. Lévi-Strauss, 26; linguistic influence on Portuguese, 254; M. Maeterlinck (Belgian), 20; S. Mallarmé, 74, 150, 259; J. Maritain, 175; F. Mauriac, 20, 210, 239; G. de Maupassant, 4, 49, 267; C. Mendès, 235; J. B. Molière, 20, 45, 84, 127, 264; P. Mondrian, 196, 197; M. de Montaigne, 166; A. de Musset, 138, 296; philosophy, 240; F. Ponge, 197; positivism, 256–57; M. Proust, 20, 22, 85, 220, 267; provençal poetry, 74; R. Rolland, 202; J. J. Rousseau, 109, 166, 293; Saint-Hilaire, 349; G. Sand, 7; J. P. Sartre, 343; S. de Sismon di (Swiss), 93, 96; Stendhal, 272; E. Sue, 296; travel writers, 348–49; P. Verlaine, 150, 194, 235; P. Valéry, 197; A. de Vigny, 293; É. Zola, and Aluísio Azevedo, 48, 58; É. Zola, and A. Caminha, 72; É. Zola, and Brazilian naturalism, 41, 58, 72, 218, 247, 269, 289, 321; and Inglês de Sousa, 325
Freyre, Gilberto, xxxviii, xlvi, **139–40**, 158, 170, 196, 241, 248, 253, 276, 277, 280, 299, 312, 322; and *saudade*, 312; and Zweig, 135
Frieiro, Eduardo, 207
Fróes, Leonardo, 262
Frota, Lélia Coelho, 261
Fusco, Rosário, **140–41**, 205
futebol. See soccer
futurism, 24, 28, 33, 204, 205, 318; and R. de Carvalho, 78; *See also* Modernism

Gabeira, Fernando, xxxvi, 30, 46, 112, **143**, 200

Gabinete Português de Leitura, 252
Gabriela, cravo e canela (*Gabriela,
Clove and Cinammon*) (Jorge Amado),
16; and film, 131
Galeno, Juvenal, 276, 319
Galvão, Patrícia, 28, **143–44**, 191; biog-
raphy of, 61, 74
Galvão, Trajano. *See* Carvalho, Trajano
Galvão de
Galvão, Walnice, 16, 98, 105
Gama, Basílio da, 5, 35, **144–45**, 158,
167, 203, 238, 252, 283; and Sir R.
Burton, 134, 352; and Durão, 115
Gama, Domício, 236
Gama, Luís, **145**, 320
Gama, Mauro, 259
Gandavo, Pedro de Magalhães, xxxvii,
156
garimpeiro (gold prospector), xl
Gattai, Zélia, 164, 200
gaúcho (related to southern Brazil), 5,
93, 151, 185, 238; modernism, 201;
regionalists, 279; and Scliar, 313–14
Geisel, Ernesto, 133
Generation of 1945, 46, 74, 76, 155,
169, 195, 197, 211, 243, 257, 258,
259, 261, 262, 277, 282, 290, 332
German cultural influences, 240, 275; F.
Bouterwek, 96; B. Brecht, 74, 144,
344, 364; P. Ehrenreich, 441; evolu-
tionism, 240; J. W. Goethe, 75, 293;
Grimm Brothers, 81; F. Hegel, 13; H.
Hesse, 179, 272; F. Hölderlin, 293; F.
Kafka, 3, 74, 85, 314; I. Kant, 13,
151; T. Koch-Grünberg, 165; H. Mar-
cuse, 28; K. F. P. von Martius, 157,
158, 165; W. F. Murnau, 130; F.
Novalis, 293; R. Rilke, 74; J. M. Rug-
endas, 37; F. Schiller, 53; C. von
Schmid, 81; A. Schopenhauer, 236; H.
Staden, 130, 348; travel writers, 348–
49; A. von Webern, 73
Ghivelder, Zevi, 163
Giannoti, J. Arthur, 241
Gil, Gilberto, 153, 354
Gilberto, João, 211
Giudice, Víctor, 86, **146**
Goeldi, Oswaldo, 38

Goiás, 117, 287, 360; regionalists, 278
Goldstein, Norma S., 100
Gomes, Alfredo Dia, **146–47**, 222, 253,
277, 285, 343, 346, 347; and Gullar,
153
Gomes, Álvaro Cardoso, 225
Gomes, Carlos, 7, 212
Gomes, Duílio, **147**
Gomes, Paulo Emílio Salles, **147**
Gomes, Roberto, 241, 341
Gonçalves Crespo. *See* Crespo, Antônio
Gonçalves
Gonçalves de Magalhães. *See* Magalhães,
Domingos José Gonçalves de
Gonçalves Dias. *See* Dias, Antônio
Gonçalves
Gonzaga, Tomás Antônio, 12, 35, 93,
148, 203, 251, 294; in Alves's play,
14; and city literature, 84; as theme of
Casimiro de Abreu, O. de Andrade, C.
Meireles, and M. Mendes, 203; and
Teixeira e Sousa, 324
Gonzaga Duque. *See* Duque, Luís
Gonzaga
Gottlieb, Nadia B., 100
Goulart, João, xlvi, 129, 137, 287
Gouvea, Jaime Prado, 224
Graça, Aranha. *See* Aranha, José Pereira
da Graça
Grande sertão: veredas (*The Devil to Pay
in the Backlands*) (Rosa), 105, 259,
284, 287, 300, 301–2; television ver-
sion of, 131
Greek cultural influences, 9, 73, 78, 202,
225, 229, 251, 287, 296, 314, 316,
330, 332; Aesop, 127; and Parnassian-
ism, 234; Sophocles, 225
Gregori, Ana Elisa, 84
Grey, Roberto, 93
Grieco, Agrippino, 100
Grossman, Judith, **148–49**
Grünewald, José Luís, 260
O guarani (The Guarani Indian) (J. de
Alencar), 6, 7, 168, 218; on film, 128;
opera, 212
Guarnieri, Gianfrancesco, 62, **149–50**,
322, 343, 346
Guedes, Lino, 89

Guerra, Ruy, 345
A guesa errante (The Mythical Wander-
    ing Colombian Bird) (Sousândrade),
    327–328
Guimaraens, Alphonsus de, 12, 24, **150**,
    234, 253, 284, 331, 332
Guimaraens, Archangelus de, 150
Guimarães, Bernardo, 12, 26, 67, 117,
    128, **151**, 278, 297, 321, 325; and Ál-
    vares de Azevedo, 49; and film, 131;
    and naturalism, 218; and romanticism,
    297
Guimarães, Eduardo, 253, 331, 332
Guimarães, Francisco Pinheiro, 320, 321
Guimarães, Josué, **151–52**, 253, 279
Guimarães Filho, Alphonsus de, 150
Guimarães Jr., Luís, 297
Guimarães Rosa. *See* Rosa, João
    Guimarães
Gullar, Ferreira, xlvii, 29, 69, 110, **152–
    53**, 222, 259, 322; and Dias Gomes,
    146; and Viana Filho, 364
Gusmão, Alexandre de, 283
Gutemberg, Luiz, 222

Haddad, Almir, 345
haiku, 9
Hamburger, Alex, 223
Haro, Rodrigo de, 38
Herzog, Wladimir, 118; as theme of
    Guarnieri play, 150
Hilst, Hilda, **155**, 258
Hirszman, Leon, 129
História de literatura brasileira (History
    of Brazilian Literature) (Romero), 158,
    299
historiography, 69, 85, 88, 96, 115, 130,
    134, **155–59**, 165, 174, 203, 205, 213,
    226, 241, 250, 295, 319, 325, 336,
    348–49, 357, 366; *Revista de história*,
    159
Hoffmann, Ricardo L., 163, 279
Hollanda, Aurélio Buarque de, 255
Hollanda, Heloísa Buarque de, 100
Hollanda, Sérgio Buarque de, 67, 85,
    158, 205, 241; and postmodernism,
    258

Homem, Francisco Sales Torres, 5, 96,
    294
Homem, Homero, **159**, 322
homosexuality, 94, 143, **160**, as theme in
    C. F. Abreu, 1, 46, 47; A. Caminha,
    72; *Lampião*, 160; Marcos, 191; Mon-
    tello, 208; Pellegrini Jr., 238; Pom-
    péia, 246; Qorpo-Santo, 265; J. do
    Rio, 291; N. Rodrigues, 292; Santiago,
    311; Aguinaldo Silva, 315
A hora da estrela, (*The Time of the Star*)
    C. Lispector, on film, 131
Horta, Glória, 223
Houaiss, Antônio, 256

immigrants, 28, **161–64**, 209; and Ama-
    zon, 276; in Graça Aranha, 33; in Alu-
    ísio Azevedo, 48; internal, 348; in
    Alcântara Machado, 189; and memoirs,
    200; in Rawet, 272; and religion, 285;
    in Rio Grande do Sul, 152, 279; in
    Scliar, 313–14; and theater, 342; and
    ufanismo, 357
impressionism, 9, 33, 86, **164**, 247, 274;
    in literary criticism, 96
Inda, Ieda, 279
India: poetry in translation, 194
Indianism, 134, **166–68**, 276, 290, 295,
    297, 299, 308, 324, 336, 359; in J. de
    Alencar, 6–7, 18, 25, 26, 27, 35; and
    art, 37, 38, 47, 58, 63; and Felipe Ca-
    marão, 69; in P. V. de Caminha, 72–
    73; and city literature, 85; and Gon-
    çalves Dias, 107–109; and Durão, 115;
    and film, 131; and B. da Gama, 144–
    45; and B. Guimarães, 151; and J. M.
    de Macedo, 187; and Gonçalves de
    Magalhães, 190; and music, 212; and
    neo-Indianism, 287, 360; and Nóbrega,
    226; and Pedro II, 319; and Picchia,
    242; and theater, 240
Indian languages, xxxix, **164–66**, 167,
    283; and J. de Alencar, 7; and An-
    chieta, 18, 165; in M. de Andrade, 26;
    and Gonçalves Dias, 109; influence of
    on Portuguese, 254; linguists of, 164–
    66
Indians, xxxvii–xl, xlii, xlv; in J. de

on Portuguese, 254; linguists of, 164–66

Indians, xxxvii–xl, xlii, xlv; in J. de Alencar, 6–7; and art, 37; and Callado, 70; in children's literature, 82; and film, 365; languages, xxxviii, **164–66**; legends of, 47; and *Martim Cererê*, 290; music, 212; myths, 261; neo-Indianism, 287, 360; and "noble savage" theme, 73, 151, 156, 167, 226; and Picchia, 242; and popular culture, 248; religion, 285; and Romero, 299; and Sousândrade, 327; and Távora, 336; and theater, 339; in travel literature, 350

Inocência (*Innocence*) (Viscount Taunay), 161, 274, 335; on film, 128

Inojosa, Joaquim, 206

"Instinto de nacionalidade" (Instinct of Nationality) (Machado de Assis), 40

Integralism, 121, 241, 308

invisible theater (Boal), 63

Iracema (*Iracema*) (J. de Alencar), 6–7, 70, 168, 295; on film, 8, 128

Iracema (Bodansky/Senna film), 131

Irish cultural influences: S. Beckett, 146; J. Joyce, 66, 85, 180, 301; J. Joyce and concretism, 75, G. B. Shaw, 127; O. Wilde, 361

irony, 45, 53, 66, 68, 146, 147, 201; in children's literature, 83

Israeli poetry: and C. Meireles, 194

Italian cultural influences, 201; Amicis, Edmondo De, 81; *commedia dell'arte*, 329; B. Croce, 174; Dante, 74, 202; C. Goldoni, 343; F. T. Marinetti, 24, 135, 204, 318; Maquiavelli, 121; and M. Mendes's poetry, 201; Mussolini, 323; *opera buffa*, 315; Petrarch, 193; Pirandello, 135, 343; Rossini, 212

Ivo, Ledo, 101, **169**, 258, 330; evaluation of R. Correia by, 92

Jaboatão, Friar Antônio, 3, 284

Jabor, Arnaldo, 128

Jacob, Paulo, 164, 276

Jacobbi, Ruggero, 342

Jaguar, 38

Japiassu, Celso, 261

Jardel Filho, 266

Jardim, Luís, 38, 77, **170**

Jardim, Rachel, **170**, 277

Jeca Tatu (character of Monteiro Lobato), 182

Jesuits, xxxviii, xxxix, xl, 7, 144, 148, 193, 226, 336; as historians, 156–157, 283; as musicians, 212; and J. Ribeiro, 289; theater, 19, 339; and Father A. Vieira, 365–66

Jesus, Carolina Maria de, 200

Jews and Jewish themes, 91, 200, 285, 313–14, 315–16, 365. *See also* immigrants; religion

João VI (King of Portugal) xli, 11, 37

João do Rio. *See* Rio, João do

Jobim, Antônio Carlos (Tom), 84, 207, 211

joke-poem (*poema-piada*), 27, 53, 201

joker system (*coringa*): and Boal, 62, 344

Jorge, Miguel, 224, 278–79

Jorge, um brasileiro (*The Long Haul*) (O. França Jr.), 136

Jornal de Letras (Rio), 88

José, Elias, 171

José I (King of Portugal), xl, 35

José Américo. *See* Almeida, José Américo de

José Bonifácio. *See* Silva, José Bonifácio de Andrada e

José Bonifácio (The Younger). *See* Silva, José Bonifácio de Andrada, (The Younger)

Jubim, Maurício, 37

Juca Mulato (Juca the Mulatto) (Picchia), 242

O juiz de paz na roga (*The Rural Justice of the Peace*) (Pena), 239, 340

Júlia, Francisca, **171**, 236, 332; evaluation of by M. de Andrade, 25

Junqueira, Ivan, 262

Junqueira Freire. *See* Freire, Luís José Junqueira

Jurandir, Dalcídio, **172**, 276

Karam, Francisco, 205

Kiefer, Charles, 224

Kilkerry, Pedro, 74, 332
Klintowitz, Jacob, 38
Konder, Rodolfo, 111
Kubitschek, Juscelino, 113, 129, 342
Künstlerroman, 32, 46, 288, 307

Laços de família (*Family Ties*) (C. Lispector), 180
Ladeira, Julieta Godoy, **173**
Laet, Carlos de, 256
Lafetá, João Luiz, 98
Lajolo, Marisa, 100
Lampião, 160
Larragoiti, Antônio, 264
Latin American cultural influences: S. Allende, 195; M. A. Asturias, 286; J. L. Borges, 101, 177, 272; and criticism of H. de Campos, 75; Fidel Castro, 285; J. Cortázar, 30, 101, 113, 177; Sor J. I. de la Cruz, 365; Cuban Revolution and Facundo theater, 104; C. Fuentes, 286; J. de Ibarbourou, 290; V. Jara, 195; G. Mistral, 136; and Moog, 209; P. Neruda, 195, 197, 312; O. Paz, 144, 312; A. Piazzola, 224; popular culture, 247; M. Puig, 136; D. F. Sarmiento, 104; A. Storni, 290; theatrical, 364; in Torres, 348; M. Vargas Llosa, 105, 136, 244, 312; L. Zea, 240
Latin cultural influences, 202, 296, 357; *Aeneid*, 177
Lau, Percy, 38
Leal, César, 277
Leal, Isa Silveira, 82, 265
Ledusha, 125, 222
Lee, Rita, 84
Leite, Dante Moreira, 241
Leite, Lygia Chiappini Moraes, 100
Leite, Sebastião Uchoa, 223
Leme, Fernão Dias Pais, 61
Leminski, Paulo, 261
Lemos, Gilvan, 277
Lemos, Miguel, 256
Leonardos, Stella, 84, **173–74**, 258
Leoni, Raul de, 236, 332
lesbianism, 160. *See also* homosexuality
Lessa, Aureliano, 49, 151, 297

Lessa, Orígenes, **174**
Liberdade, liberdade (Liberty, Liberty) (M. Fernandes), 126, 344
Libertinagem (Libertinage) (Bandeira), 52–53
Lima, Alceu Amoroso (Tristão de Athayde), 97, 122, 127, **174–75**, 210, 284; and G. Bernanos, 135; and postmodernism, 257
Lima, Augusto de, 297
Lima, Geraldo França de, **175**; and G. Bernanos, 135
Lima, Jorge de, 38, 135, 139, **176–77**, 206, 221, 284, 330; and G. Bernanos, 135; and M. Mendes, 200; and Villa-Lobos, 367
Lima, José Ezequiel Freire de, 273, 320
Lima, Luís Costa, 99
Lima Jr., Walter, 130, 336
Lima Barreto. *See* Barreto, Afonso Henriques de Lima
Limeira, José Carlos, 90
Lindoso, Dirceu, 278
linguists: of Indian languages, 165–66; of Portuguese language, 255–56
Lins, Álvaro, 97
Lins, Osman, 1, 47, 56, 86, 173, **177–78**; and children's literature, 83
Lins do Rego. *See* Rego, José Lins do
Lisboa, Henriqueta, **178–79**
Lisbon, 4, 54, 59, 91, 95, 212, 230, 239, 250, 251, 315, 336, 365
Lispector, Clarice, 1, 47, 66, 77, 86, 99, 149, 162, **179–81**, 192; and children's literature, 83; and feminism, 123, 124–25; and film, 131; and L. Luft, 186; and A. Prado, 263; and symbolism, 332
Lispector, Elisa, 123, 162
Loanda, Francisco Ferreira de, 257–58
Lobato, José Bento Monteiro, xlv, 56, **181–84**, 200, 279; biography of, 61; and children's literature, 81–82, 264; evaluation of Élis by, 118; and film, 131; on A. Malfatti, 37
Lobato, Manoel, **184**
Lobo, Edu, 63
Lobo, Luiza, 100

Lombardi, Bruna, 125
Lopes, Ascânio, 205
Lopes, B(ernardino), 236, 331
Lopes, Moacir C., **184**
Lopes de Almeida. *See* Almeida, Júlia Lopes de
Lopes Neto, João Simões, 132, **185**, 279
Lopez, Telê Porto Ancona, 98
Loreto, Friar Couto, 283–84
Louzeiro, José, 86, 111, **185–86**; and film, 131
Loyola Brandão. *See* Brandão, Ignácio de Loyola
Lucas, Fábio, 46, 99, 260
Luft, Celso Pedro, 256
Luft, Lya, 125, 164, **186**
Luís, Pedro, 297
A luta corporal (The Bodily Struggle) (Gullar), 152
Lyra, Bernadette, 223
Lyra, Carlos, 207
Lyra, Pedro, 100
lyrical novel: C. Lispector, 188

A maça no escuro (*The Apple in the Dark*) (Lispector), 180
Macaúbas, Baron of, 245
Macedo, Joaquim Manuel de, 6, 11, 85, 100–101, **187–88**, 296, 297, 324; and film, 131; and slavery, 321; and theater, 340
Maceió (Álagoas), 269
Machado, Alexandre Ribeiro Marcondes, 28
Machado, Ana Maria, 83, 123; *Alice e Ulisses*, 125
Machado, Aníbal, **188**, 210, 278, 330
Machado, Antônio de Alcântara, 38, 164, **188–89**, 207, 279; and immigrants, 161
Machado, Dionélio, 207
Machado, Gilka, 123, **189**, 332
Machado, Maria Clara, 84, 173, 346
Machado, Nauro, 276
Machado, Rubem Mauro, 46
Machado de Assis. *See* Assis, Joaquim Maria Machado de
Machado Filho, Aires da Mata, 255

Maciel, Eliane, 223
Macunaíma (*Macunaíma*) (M. de Andrade), 25–26, 27, 38, 63, 70, 73, 99, 206, 276, 285, 287, 290, 354; dramatization, 27, 345–46; on film, 27, 130; and Rosa, 300; and Scliar, 314
Madeira feita cruz (Wood for the Cross) (Piñon), 244
Magalhães, Adelino de, 164, 205, 330
Magalhães, Benjamin Constant Botelho de, 102, 256
Magalhães, Celso de, 133, 273, 320
Magalhães, Couto de, 276
Magalhães, Domingos José Gonçalves de, xlii, 5, 6, 13, 96, 108, **189–90**, 284, 294, 295, 296, 324; and Indianism, 167, 290; and theater, 239, 240; and A. J. da Silva, 316, 339
Magalhães Junior, Raimundo de, 61, 342
Magalhães, Valentim, 219
magical realism, in: J. C. de Carvalho, 78; J. Condé, 88; M. Rubião, 304; Scliar, 314; Setúbal, 314; Veiga, 360; E. Veríssimo, 362
Magno, Paschoal Carlos, 342
Maia, Alcides, 279
Maia, Vasconcelos, 278
Maior, Mário Souto, 255
Maíra (*Maíra*) (D. Ribeiro), 276, 287
Malamud, Samuel, 200
Malfatti, Anita, 28, 37, 204; and Monteiro Lobato, 182, 204
Malgadi, Sábato, 291, 292, 339
mamulengo (puppet theater), 343
Manaus, 328; in modernism, 63, 206. *See also* Amazon
"Manifesto antropófago" (Manifesto of Anthropophagy) (O. de Andrade), 28
"Manifesto de poesia pau brasil" ("Manifesto of Pau Brasil Poetry") (O. de Andrade), 28
Manuel I (King of Portugal), 72, 156
Maranhão, xxxviii, xl, xlii, 30, 33, 47, 48, 49, 86, 91, 107, 152, 185, 190, 208–9, 258, 327, 365; regionalists, 277; in travel literature, 351
Maranhão, Haroldo, **190–91**
Marcos, Plínio, 110, 144, 160, **191–92**,

291, 346; influence of on C. de Castro, 79
marginal poetry, 112
Maria I (Queen of Portugal), xl, 12, 35; as princess, 231
Maricá, Marquis of, 294
Marília de Dirceu (Gonzaga), 148
Marinho, José Carlos, 83
Marinho, Saldanha, 39
Marins, Francisco, 82
Marques, Oswaldino, 99
Marques, Rodrigues, 277
Marques, Xavier, 277
A marquesa de Santos (*Domitila: The Romance of an Emperor's Mistress*) (Setúbal), 314
Marques Rebelo. *See* Rebelo, Marques
Marroquim, Mário, 255
Martim Cereré (Ricardo), 290
Martinez, José Celso, 344
Martins, Anna Maria, 86, 224
Martins, Júlio César Monteiro, xlvii, 86, 112, 118, **192**, 222
Martins, Luís, 38, 101
Martins, Max, 276
Martins, Roberto Bittencourt, 224
Martins, Wilson, 98–99, 208, 258
Martins Junior, José Isidoro, 257, 273
Martins Pena. *See* Pena, Luís Carlos Martins
Marxism: and Jorge Amado, 207; and O. de Andrade, 27, 28; and concretism, 75; and criticism, 99, 100; in Francis, 138; in P. Galvão, 144; in Guarnieri, 149; and Novaes, 227
Mascates War, xl
masonic movement, 316
Material as Sign (poetry movement), 261
Mato Grosso, 76, 278, 335; in travel literature, 352, 353
Matos, Eusébio de, 193
Matos, Gramiro de, 111
Matos, Gregório de, xxxix, 55, 67, 145, **192–93**, 212, 251, 278; and city literature, 84; and *saudade*, 312
Matta, Roberto da, 241
Mattos, Cyro dos, 223
Mattoso, Glauco, 160

Mautner, Jorge, 355
Medauar, Jorge, 278
Médici, Emílio, 222, 249
medieval literature, 9; and Anchieta, 18–19; and P. V. de Caminha, 73; *chason de geste*, 302; and *cordel*, 132; and Gonçalves Dias, 107–109; Portuguese songbooks, 311–12; and postmodernism, 258; and romanticism, 167; *saudade*, 311–12; Gil Vicente, 315, 329
Medina, Sinval, 224
Meireles, Cecília, 136, 179, **194–95**, 205, 206, 253, 267, 332; and children's literature, 83; and folklore, 133; and Mineiran Conspiracy, 203; influence of on Savary, 312
Meireles, Ricardo, 225
Meireles, Vítor, 37
Mello-Leitão, Cândido, 353
Melo, Amadeu Thiago de, 110, **195**, 258
Melo, Antônio de Castro Canto e, 219
Melo, Dutra e, 96, 296
Melo, Emília Moncorvo Bandeira de (Carmen Dolores), 123, 219
Melo, Fernando de, 160
Melo Neto, João Cabral de, 99, **196–99**, 277, 330; influence of on Ávila, 46; and Chico Buarque, 67; and A. de Campos, 74; and film, 131; and postmodernism, 258; and soccer, 322
memoirs, xxxvii, xlvii, 4, 10, 11, 23, 46, 47, 61, 93, 102, 134, 135, 136, 138, 170, 182, **200**, 201, 215, 220, 223, 242, 269, 270, 291, 298, 313, 314; Bopp's, on anthropophagy, 63; during dictatorship, 111, 112; on feminism, 351–52; Gabeira's, 143; of immigrants, 164; and M. Mendes, 201; Picchia's, on modernism, 242; and Lins do Rego, 281; and N. Rodrigues, 292; and N. A. de Souza's theater, 225
Memorial de Aires (*Counselor Ayres's Memoirs*) (Machado de Assis), 43
Memórias de Lázaro (*Memories of Lazarus*) (Adonias Filho), 3
Memórias de um gigolô (*Memories of a Gigolo*, 1988) (Rey), 286
Memórias de um sargento de milícias

(*Memories of a Militia Sergeant*) (M. A. de Almeida), 10, 85, 97, 297; play by M. Fernandes, 126; and realism, 274; and religions, Afro-Brazilian, 284

Memórias do cárcere (Jail Memoirs) (G. Ramos), 38, 207, 270, 311; on film, 129–30

Memórias póstumas de Brás Cubas (*Epitaph of a Small Winner*) (Machado de Assis), 40, 41, 42, 43–44

Memórias sentimentais de João Miramar (*Sentimental Memoirs of John Seaborne*), 28, 29, 200

Mendes, Raimundo Teixeira, 256

Mendes, Murilo, 38, 176, 197, **200–1**, 203, 205, 206, 210, 284, 330

Mendes, Manuel Odorico, 264, 296

Mendes Campos. *See* Campos, Paulo Mendes

Mendonça, Lúcio de, 219, 273

Meneses, Agrário, 297

Meneses, Luís da Cunha, 84, 148

Meneses, Tobias Barreto de, 89, 275, 298, 320

As meninas (*The Girl in the Photograph*) (L. F. Telles), 124, 337

Menino do engenho (*Plantation Boy*) (Rego), 280–81, 324; on film, 130

Menotti del Picchia. *See* Picchia, Paulo Menotti del

Merquior, José Guilherme, 100

Mesquita, Alfredo, 342

messianism, 103, 285; in O. de Andrade, 28; in Lins do Rego, 281

"Mestres do passado" (Masters of the Past) (M. de Andrade), 25

Meyer, Camargo, 259

Meyer Júnior, Augusto, 44, **201–2**, 279

Miccolis, Leila, 262

Miguel-Pereira, Lúcia, 61, 97, 179, 233

Milagre na cela (Mircle in the Cell) (J. Andrade), 23

Milano, Dante, **202**; and Villa-Lobos, 367

Milliet, Sérgio, 26, 38, 97, **202–3**; on V. de Moraes, 210; on postmodernism, 257

mimeograph generation, 222, 262

Minas Gerais, xl, 2, 12, 23, 24, 25, 30, 32, 35–36, 46, 55, 76, 79, 92, 99, 105, 113, 114, 117, 118, 133, 136, 140, 143, 144, 147, 150, 151, 170, 171, 175, 178, 184, 188, 200, 203, 211, 219, 220, 223, 224, 229, 233, 238, 244, 251, 258, 260, 263, 289, 297, 299, 304, 307, 309, 311, 367; and Drummond de Andrade, **19–23**; G. Bernanos, 135; black literature, 90; and city literature, 84; and modernism, 140, 201, 278; and regionalists, 278; and Rosa, 299–300; and travel literature, 350–51

Minas School, 37, 46, 92, 148, **203**, 278; and romanticism, 294, 317; and *saudade*, 213

Mineiran Conspiracy, xli, 14, 92, 117, 203, 238, 251, 296, 324; and Academies, 3; and Arcadias, 35, 36; and C. Meireles, 194

Minha formação (My Education) (Nabuco), 215

Miranda, Macedo, 323

O missionário (The Missionary) (Inglês de Sousa), 325

Modernell, Renato, 224

modernism, xlv, 8, 9, 11, 12, 20, 60, 61, 76, 77, 78–79, 87, 101, 126, 135, 136, 179, 182, 188–89, 197, 200, 202, **203–8**, 220, 221, 237, 242, 267, 282, 313, 315, 317, 332; and M. de Andrade, 24–27; and O. de Andrade, 27–29; and *Anta*, 290, 309; and Graça Aranha, 34; and art, 36–39; and Assis, 44; and Bandeira, 51–52; and Lima Barreto, 56; and Bopp, 63–64; and R. de Carvalho, 78–79; in children's literature, 82; in city literature, 84–85; and criticism, 97, 98; and dialectology, 255; in film, 129; and Gonzaga, 148; and historiography, 158; and impressionism, 164; and Indianism, 168; and A. Amorosa Lima, 175; and J. de Lima, 176; and G. de Matos, 193; and C. Meireles, 194; and music, 212; and neo-Indianism, 287; in Pará, 118; and

Parnassianism, 236; and Picchia, 242; in popular culture, 248; and postmodernism, 257, 258, 259; and P. Prado, 263; and Qorpo-Santo, 265; and regionalism, 139, 201, 205–6, 277, 280, 323–24; regional reviews of, 205–6; and religion, 127–28, 284–85; and romanticism, 298; and Salgado, 308–9; and *saudade*, 312; and Sousândrade, 327; and surrealism, 330; in theater, 341; and *ufanismo*, 357; and *verdeamarelismo*, 242, 290; and Villa-Lobos, 367

Moisés, Massaud, 99, 237

Monte Alverne. *See* Alverne, Friar Monte

Monteiro, Agildo, 276

Monteiro, Benedicto, 276

Monteiro, Maciel, 296

Monteiro, Vicente do Rego, 196

Monteiro Lobato. *See* Lobato, José Bento Monteiro

Montello, Josué, 61, **208–9**

Montenegro, Fernanda, 266

Moog, Clodomir Viana, 163, **209**, 241; and immigration, 162; and positivism, 257

Moraes, Álvaro, 341

Morães, Reinaldo, 224

Moraes, Rubens Borba de, 205

Moraes, Vinícius de, 51, 128, 207, **210–11**, 213, 222, 262, 313, 322; and children's literature, 83

Morais, Prudente de, 205

Morais Junior, Melo, 133, 212

A moratória (The Moratorium) (J. Andrade), 23

Moreira, Virgílio Moretzsohn, 225

A moreninha (The Dark Complexioned Girl) (Macedo), 85, 187, 297, 324; as a play, 340; television serial, 131

Morte e vida Severina (Death and Life Severina) (Melo Neto), 198; music in by Chico Buarque, 67; television serial, 67, 131

Mota Coqueiro (Patrocínio), 237, 321

Mota, Dantas, 258

Mota, Mauricio, 262

Mota, Mauro, **211**, 258

Mott, Odete de Barros, 82–83

Motta, Nelson, 323

Moura, Emílio, 20, 205

Mourão, Rui, 46, **211–12**,

Mucinic, José, 163

O mulato (The Mulatto) (Aluísio Azevedo), 48, 219, 321; film, 128

O mulo (*The Mule*, 1988) (D. Ribeiro), 287–88

Muniz, Lauro César, 225

Muralha, Sidônio, 83

Murat, Luís, 236

Murici, Andrade, 194, 205

music, 24, 35, 47, 55, 64, 80, 82, 126, 127, 193, **212–13**, 230; in J. Andrade, 23, 24; and Antônio, 32; and Buarque, 63, 67–68; and A. de Campos, 73; and Cardozo, 77; in children's literature, 262; and dictatorship, 110, 309; Milano, 202; and modernism, 204, 206, 207; and *modinha*, 54, 80, 95, 213; and V. de Moraes, 210–11; and A. Piazzola, 224; and postmodernism, 259; and regionalism, 173; and *repentistas*, 212; and symbolism, 331; and popular theater, 334; and *tropicalismo*, 354–55; and Villa-Lobos, 367–68

Nabuco, Carolina, 61, 215

Nabuco, Joaquim, 45, 61, 67, 145, 200, **215**, 319

Nascentes, Antenor, 135, 255

Nascimento, Abdias do, 89, **216**

Nascimento, Esdras do, **216–17**

Nassar, Raduan, 111, **217–18**

National Book Institute, 3

national identity, 8, 9, 33, 34, 36, 57, 63, 108, 114, 129, 140, 158, 164, 175, 184, **240–42**, 327; in Drummond de Andrade, 20; in Callado, 69–70; in criticism, 98; in E. da Cunha, 103; and Indianism, 166–68; in *Macunaíma*, 206; and modernism, 204–6; in Moog, 209; and modernism, 204–6; in V. de Moraes, 210; in music, 213; and popular culture, 248; Portuguese language, 256; and positivism, 256; and P. Prado, 263; and Ubaldo Ribeiro, 288–

89; and romanticism, 295; and S. Sant'Anna, 310; and Scliar, 314; and theater, 338–48
nativism, 63, 79, 92, 96, 97, 201, 230, 350; in art, 37; in baroque literature, 56; in Callado, 69; in C. M. da Costa, 92–93; and B. da Gama, 252; and historiography, 155–59, 336; and Indianism, 166–68, 190; and modernism, 203–8; and *ufanismo*, 357
naturalism, xliv, 3, 10, 40–41, 47, 48, 72, 182, **218–20**, 229, 245, 247, 253, 269, 289, 295, 326; in *A carne*, 289; in city literature, 84; and feminism, 123; and B. Guimarães, 151; and homosexuality, 160; in G. de Matos, 193; and neonaturalism, 134, 224, 266, 267; and prenaturalism, 151, 265; and realism, 273; and religion, 285; and slavery, 321; and Inglês de Sousa, 325; and Teófilo, 338; and theater, 346
Nava, Pedro, 12, 38, 111, 200, 202, **220**
Negreiros, Sanderson, 260
négritude, 89
negroidism: Lima Barreto, 58
Néjar, Carlos, **221**, 230, 261, 279
Neme, Mário, 258
neoclassicism, 34, 35, 55, 84, 138, 190, 203, 238, 251, 252, 293, 316, 324; and Gonçalves Dias, 108
neoconcretism. *See* postmodernism
neorealism. *See* social novel
neosymbolism. *See* symbolism
Neo-Thomism, 240
Nepomuceno, Eric, 225
Nery, Adalgisa, 38, **221–22**
Nery, Ismael, 38, 200, 221
Neto, Torquato, 355
Neves, João das, 345
Neves, Tancredo, 132
"new criticism," 98
"new novel," and C. Lispector, 180; and D. Silveira de Queiroz, 266
newspaper theater (*teatro jornal*): Boal, 62
New World in the Tropics (Freyre), 140
new writers, xlvii, 112, 138, 143, 181,

222–26, 241, 262, 323; and feminism, 125; and Gullar, 259; and Lins, 178
Niemeyer, Oscar, 77
Nóbrega, Father Manuel da, xxxviii, xxix, 156, **226**, 283
Noll, João Gilberto, 224
"No meio do caminho" ('In the Middle of the Road") (Drummond de Andrade), 20
Norwegian cultural influences: H. Ibsen, 361
Novaes, Carlos Eduardo, 38, 101, **226–27**, 250, 323
Novaes, Guiomar, 204
Novais, Carolina Xavier de, 39
Novak, Sara, 162
Nunes, Benedito, 99, 190
Nunes, Cassiano, 206; on Monteiro Lobato, 61, 183
Nunes, Sebastião, 223

Óbidos (Pará), 325
object poems (Bell), 59
Oficina Theater, 28, 344
Oguiam, Edu Omu, 90
Olímpio, Domingos, 219, **229**, 270, 277
Olinto, Antônio, **229–30**, 258
Oliveira, Alberto de, 37, 60, 204, 234, 235; evaluation of by M. de Andrade, 25
Oliveira, Antônio de, 219
Oliveira, Arthur de, 235
Oliveira, Eduardo de, 90
Oliveira, Franklin de, 100
Oliveira, José Carlos de, 86
Oliveira, Manuel Botelho de, 55, **230**; and music, 212; and theater, 339, 340
Oliveira, Marly de, 261
Oliveira, Urbano Duarte de, 320
Oliveira Paiva. *See* Paiva, Manuel de Oliveira
Opinião Theater, 152, 344, 345, 364
Orfeu da Conceição (Black Orpheus) (V. de Moraes), 211
Orico, Osvaldo, 82, 133; and Zweig, 135
Orta, Teresa Margarida da Silva e, 4, 123, **230–31**
Ortiz, Renato, 248

Otaviano, Francisco, 297
Otoni, Elói, 296
Ouro Preto, 92, 143, 203; and Bandeira, 186; and Alphonsus de Guimaraens, 150

Padilha, Telmo, 278
Paes, José Paulo, 83, 261
O pagador de promessas (*Journey to Bahia*) (Dias Gomes), 146
Pagu. *See* Galvão, Patrícia
Paim, Antônio, 241
Paiva, Manuel de Oliveira, 219, **233**
Paiva, Marcelo Rubens, 223
Palhares, Vitoriano, 89
Pallottini, Renata, 258
Palmares, xl, 132, 319, 321
Palmério, Mário, 117, **233–34**, 278
Papi, Júnior, Antônio, 219, 229
Pará, xxxviii, xlii, 118, 172, 190, 229, 312, 325, 362; and modernism, 118, 206
parable, 217, 364
Paraguayan War, xliii, 14, 89, 359; and Camargo, 71; and travel literature, 351; and Viscount Taunay, 335
Paraíba, 10, 94, 207, 280, 323, 324, 332; in travel literature, 351
Paraná, 98, 118, 317, 331, 332, 353
Parnassianism, xliv, 2, 24, 31, 37, 51, 52, 53, 55, 56, 60–61, 91, 92, 95, 126, 171, 175, 220, **234–36**, 241, 242, 253, 275, 290, 296; and modernism, 204–6; and positivism, 257; and post-modernism, 257; and realism, 273; and *saudade*, 312; and slavery, 320; and Cruz e Sousa, 326; and symbolism, 330
parody, 7, 28, 47, 83; of Gonçalves Dias's poem, 95, 107; of J. M. de Macedo, 188; in E. do Nascimento, 217; in S. Porto, 250; in H. Sales, 307, 308; in S. Sant'Anna, 310; and *saudade*, 312; and *ufanismo*, 357
Parreiras, Antônio, 37
Parthenon Literary Society, 4
Passos, Guimarães, 236
pastoral novel, 231

Patrocínio, José do, 215, **237**, 270, 319, 321
Paula, José Agrippino de, 110
Paulicéia desvairada (*Hallucinated City*) (M. de Andrade), 24, 85
Paulo, Damásio, 38
Pederneiras, Mário, 331
Pedra do sono (Stone of Sleep) (Melo Neto), 196, 198
Pedreiras das alma (Quarry of Souls) (J. Andrade), 23, 343
Pedro I, Emperor of Brazil, xli–xlii, 316, 351; in Setúbal fiction, 314–15
Pedro II, Emperor of Brazil, xlii–xliii, 107, 108, 109, 212, 351; and Pompéia, 246; and scientific explorations, 350
Peixoto, Afrânio, 96, **237–38**
Peixoto, Floriano, 237
Peixoto, Francisco Inácio, 140, 206
Peixoto, Inácio José de Alvarenga, xli, 35, 117, 203, **238**, 251
Peixoto, Mário, 207
Pelé, 322
Pelotas (Rio Grande do Sul), 185
Pellegrini Jr., Domingos, 112, 118, 160, **238**
Pena, Cornélio, 38, 99, 122, 133, **238–39**, 284
Pena, Luís Carlos Martins, 49, 127, 136, **239–40**, 265, 298, 340, 341
Pena Filho, Carlos, 94
Penteado, Darcy, 160
penumbrism, 9, 51, 332. *See* symbolism
Peregrino Jr., João, 276
Pereira, Antônio Olavo, 46
Pereira, Astrojildo, 99
Pereira, Hamilton Vaz, 223
performance poetry, 59
Pernambuco, xliii, 4, 31, 55, 64, 77, 88, 105, 126, 139, 170, 176, 177, 207, 211, 269, 280, 315; and Calado, 69; and Generation of 1965, 262, 277; language of, 255; and Melo Neto, 196–199; and modernism, 206; and M. Mota, 211; and regionalists, 276–77; and student theater, 329, 343; and B. Teixeira, 336; in travel literature, 351

Pernambuco, João, 80
Pernambuco Student Theater, 329, 343
Perneta, Emiliano, 331
Perto do coração selvagem (Near the
Savage Heart) (C. Lispector), 124–25,
179
Pessoa, João, 323
O Pessoal do, cabaré (theater group), 347
O Pessoal do Despertar (theater group),
347
Petalógica (literary club), 39
Petrópolis, 136, 351
Petry, Luiz, 223
phenomenology: in C. Lispector, 180
Philip II (King of Spain), xxxviii
Philomatic Society, 294
philosophers, 240–42
philosophes, xl, 144
Piauí, xlii, 66, 122, 216, 332; regional-
ists, 277
picaresque novel, 85, 307
Picchia, Paulo Menotti del, 101, 128,
204, **242**, 290, 308
Pignatari, Décio, **243**, 259, 260, 322
Pinheiro, Joaquim Fernandes, 96
Piñon, Nélida, 86, 112, 124, **243–44**;
and feminism, 123; and immigrant lit-
erature, 163
Pinsky, Mirna, 83
Pinto, Álvaro Vieira, 241
Pinto, Bento Teixeira. *See* Teixeira,
Bento
Pinto, Ewelson Soares, 278
Pinto, José Alcides, 261, 277
Pinto, Luís Angelo, 260
Pires, Cornélio, 133
Piroli, Wander, **244–45**; children's litera-
ture, 83
Pita, Sebastião da Rocha, 2, 157
Piva, Roberto, 223
Pocket Lyre, 262, 278
poem-objects (A. de Campos), 73
Poemação (poetry exhibition in 1973),
260
poema-piada (joke-poem), 27, 53, 201
poema processo (process poem), 259–60
Poema sujo (Dirty Poem) (Gullar), 153

poesia concertanista (concert poetry),
222
poesia-experiência (poetry-experiment)
(Faustino), 122
"Poesias americanas" (American Poems)
(Gonçalves Dias), 109
Poetic Catechism (Bell), 59
Pólvora, Hélio, 278
Pombal, Marquis of, xl, 12; in B. da Ga-
ma's poem, 145
Pombo, José Rocha, 332
Pompéia, Raul, 37, 46, 56, 160, 185,
218, 239, **245–47**, 284; and music,
212; and realism, 274; and *saudade*,
312
Pompeu, Renato, 111
Ponte Preta. *See* Porto, Sérgio
Pontes, Mário, 278
Pontes, Paulo, 67
popular culture, xlv, 1, 242, **247–49**,
364; and film, 131; and folklore, 132,
133
Popular Culture Centers (*CPC*), 343, 364
Popular Culture Movement (*MPC*), 343
Popular Northeastern Theater, 343
Porfírio, Pedro, 225
Portella, Eduardo, 100
Portinari, Cândido, 38, 206
Porto, Sérgio, 38, 226, 250
Porto Alegre, 90, 121, 267. *See also* Rio
Grande do Sul
Portuguese language of Brazil: xxxix,
xlv, 15, 31, 35, 78, 98, 140, 194,
233, **254–56**, 340; and African influence, 54, 55; J. de Alencar, 7–8;
Drummond de Andrade, 20; M. de
Andrade, 26; Bandeira, 52; Barreto,
56; Bilac, 236; Bopp, 63; A. de Cam-
pos, 73; Cearense, 80; Coelho Neto,
86; E. da Cunha, 105; Gonçalves Dias,
108; Élis, 118; *gaúcho* dialect, 185;
Indian influence, 18, 166; Italo-Portuguese dialect, 28, 161; *língua geral*,
xxxix, 165; Monteiro Lobato, 82; G.
de Matos, 193; Melo Neto, 199; Oliveira Paiva, 233; Palmério, 233–34;
Qorpó-Santo, 265; and regionalism,
275–80; J. Ribeiro, 289; romanticism,

296; Rosa, 301, 303; V. Silveira, 318; Sousândrade, 327; Suassuna, 329–30; Távora, 336; Tupi-Portuguese dictionary, 109; Veiga, 360; Father Vieira, 366

Portuguese writers and Brazilian literature, xxxvii–xli, 191, 202, 234, 238, 240, **250–54**, 258, 264, 296, 308, 311, 317, 339; Arcádia Lusitana, 35, 36, 37; baroque, 55–56; Bocage, 296; T. Braga, 253; C. Castelo Branco, 183, 253, 256; L. V. de Camões, 9, 35, 52, 99, 114, 122, 193, 237, 251, 336; A. F. de Castilho, 107; E. de Castro, 253; Ferreira de Castro, 135, 328; Viscount Almeida Garrett, 84, 96, 107, 252, 294; A. Herculano, 107, 252; Brother J. A. de Macedo, 252; L. de Montalvor, 78; A. Casais Monteiro, 136; A. Nobre, 52, 253; T. de Pascoaes, 311; F. Pessoa, 78, 122, 253; J. M. Eça de Queiroz, 40–41, 48, 72, 183, 218, 219, 247, 253, 269, 321, 325; A. de Quental, 31, 253, 327; M. de Sá-Carneiro, 78, 253; A. de Oliveira Salazar, 136, 253, 348; Father Sardinha, xxxvii; J. de Sena, 136, 253; Cruz e Silva, 117; Castro Soromenho, 253; *O Trovador*, 107; C. Verde, 52, 253; G. Vicente, 226, 253, 315, 329

positivism, xliv, 10, 101, 102, 240, **256–57**; and Pompéia, 245; and realism, 273; and J. do Rio, 291

postcard poems, 261

poster poems, 59

postmodernism, xlvi, 22, 29, 36, 59, 73, 74, 75, 76, 81, 83, 113, 122, 148, 150, 152, 155, 159, 169, 179, 180, 190, 195, 197, 199, 206, 211, 221, 222, 223, 243, **257–63**, 277, 278, 282, 290, 309, 311, 312, 353; and art, 37, 38, 46; and Bandeira, 53; and city literature, 85; and regionalism, 276; and romanticism, 298; and *saudade*, 312; and symbolism, 332

Poty, 38

Pozenato, José Clemente, 279

Prado, Adélia, 125, 186, 222, 262, **263**

Prado, Paulo, 38, 158, 241, **263**

Prado, Sérgio Ortiz, 323

Prado Junior, Caio, xlvi, 241

Prata, Mário, 346

praxism, 81, 259, 260. *See also* postmodernism

premodernism. *See* Modernism

preromanticism, 148, 294, 316. *See also* Arcadias, romanticism

Prestes Column, xlv, 323

Primeiras estórias (The Third Bank of the River and Other Stories) (Rosa), 300, 302

prizes, 19, 20, 62, 78, 79, 91, 114, 127, 139, 159, 169, 171, 175, 224, 245, **264**, 270, 272, 275, 313, 316, 347, 360, 367; Graça Aranha, 179; Brazilian Academy of Letters, 62, 67, 172, 194, 266, 300, 301, 312; Cannes Short Fiction, 337; Casa de las Américas, 94, 224, 322; children's literature, 83; Chinaglia, 1; Esso, 118; Etna-Taormina, 201; French Legion, 140; Goethe Institute, 70, 134; Jabuti, 95, 173, 238, 310, 312; King of Spain, 118; Molière, 45, 79; Nestlé, 223, 224; Paraná, 118; Saci, 23; Stalin, 15; UNESCO Peace, 241

process poem (*poema processo*), 259, 260

Prödohl, Augusto Sylvio, 163

Proença, Manuel Cavalcanti, 99

proletarian fiction, 144, 162

pseudonyms, 6, 12, 24, 35, 92, 144, 145, 148, 157, 205, 219, 231, 292, 312, 316, 325, 335, 368

psychological novel: 3, 12, 46, 58, 77, 137, 140, 169, 170, 216, 295, 297, 337, 362, 366; J. de Alencar, 7; A. Dourado, 113; C. Lispector, 179–81; and modernism, 207; Nassar, 217; C. Pena, 239; Pompéia, 245–47; A. Prado, 263; G. Ramos, 271; Rosa, 301–02; J. G. Vieira, 366–67

punk drama, 226

Qorpo-Santo, 160, **265**, 340

Quadros, Jânio, 129

Quarup (*Quarup*) (Callado), 70, 287
Queirós, Venceslau de, 236
Queiroz, Dinah Silveira de, **265–66**
Queiroz, Maria José de, 290
Queiroz, Rachel de, 101, 123, 179, 207, **266–67**, 277, 343; and Brazilian Academy of Letters, 67, 266
Queiroz Law, xliii
Quilomboje, 90
quilombos (runaway slave colonies): film, 319; A. do Nascimento's *quilombismo*, 216; Palmares, xxxix, xliv, 319
Quincas Borba (*Quincas Borba, Philosopher or Dog?*) (Machado de Assis), 42
Quintana, Mário, **267**, 279; and children's literature, 83
Quintella, Ary, 111
O quinze (The Year Nineteen Fifteen) (R. de Queiroz), 266, 323

Rabelo, Laurindo, 297
Rainho, Cleonice, 223
Ramos, Graciliano, 38, 118, 207, **269–71**, 278, 287, 313, 323–24; children's literature, 82; and Santiago, 271, 311; works on film, 129–30
Ramos, Hugo Carvalho, 278
Ramos, Maria Luísa, 100
Ramos, Péricles Eugênio da Silva, 257
Ramos, Ricardo, 269, **271**, 323
Rangel, Alberto, 276
Rangel, Ângela do Amaral, 2
Rangel, Flávio, 126, 344
Rangel, Godofredo, 182
Rasga coração (literally: Render Heart) (Viana Filho), 364
Rasi, Mauro, 225
Rawet, Samuel, 77, **272**, 285; and immigrant literature, 162
Reale, Miguel, 241
realism, xliv, 6, 8, 10, 47, 48, 84, 87, 233, 245, 265, **272–74**, 275, 335, 336, 362; and Indianism, 168; and naturalism, 218; and Parnassianism, 204; and religion, 284, 285; and romanticism, 6, 295, 297; and slavery, 320
Rebelo Marques, 11, 61, **274–75**
Rebouças, André, 319

Recife, 13, 31, 46, 51, 54, 63, 77, 89, 139, 169, 170, 196, 199, 211, 229, 246, 252, 273, 322, 323, 325, 336; in travel literature, 351
Recife School, 89, 96, 256, **275**; and Graça Aranha, 33; and realism, 273; and Romero, 298
redondilha: in Bandeira, 52
Regency (1831–1840), xlii, 13, 107, 108
regionalism, xlv, 3, 5, 10, 15, 17, 21, 25, 31, 36, 37, 47, 56, 67, 76, 77, 78, 83, 84, 88, 93, 94, 117, 134, 159, 162, 169, 170, 174, 175, 179, 188, 208–9, 229, 233, 237, 238, 263, 272, 274, **275–80**, 287, 318, 325, 336, 360, 361, 366; and J. de Alencar, 7; and Borba Filho, 64; in city literature, 84–85; and literary cycles, 105; and A. Dourado, 113; and B. Guimarães, 151; and historiography, 158; and Jurandir, 172; and Lopes Neto, 185; and Melo Neto, 198; and modernism, 126, 207; and national unity, 209; and naturalism, 219, 229; and Portuguese language, 255–56; and postmodernism, 262; and R. de Queiroz, 266–67; and Regionalist Manifesto, 139; and Region-Tradition, 139, 280; and Lins do Rego, 281, 285; and religion, 285; and Romero, 299; and H. Sales, 307; and Setúbal, 314; and slavery, 319–20; and social novel, 323–24. *See also* Acre; Alagoas; Amazon; Bahia; Ceará; *gaúcho*; Goiás; Mato Grosso; Minas Gerais; Maranhão; Pará; Paraíba; Paraná; Piauí; Rio de Janeiro; Rio Grande do Norte; Rio Grande do Sul; Santa Catarina; São Paulo; Sergipe
Rego, Alita Sá, 223
Rego, José Lins do, 45, 139, 176, 207, **280–82**, 285, 324; and children's literature, 82; and *saudade*, 312; and soccer, 322; works on film, 130
Rego, Norma Pereira, 85
O rei da vela (The Candle King) (O. de Andrade), 28, 29, 344
Rei Negro (Black King) (Coelho Neto), 87, 332

Reis, Marcos Konder, 258, **282–83**
Reis, Maria Firmino dos, 123
religion, xlv, 59, 69, 76, 138, 162, 226,
230, **283–85**, 336, 348–49; and Academies, 3; and Alverne, 13; and art, 37;
and Callado, 69–70; and P. V. de
Caminha, 73; and Catholic Renaissance, 127–28; and Cony, 90–91; and
Dom Vital Center, 128; and Durão,
114–115; and O. de Faria, 121–22; and
feminism, 123; and *Festa*, 317; and
Francis, 138; and Hilst, 155; and Jesuits, xxxviii, 144; and A. Amoroso
Lima, 174–75; and J. de Lima, 176–
77; and H. Lisboa, 179; and Gonçalves
de Magalhães, 190; and G. de Matos,
193; and C. Meireles, 194; and memoirs, 200; and M. Mendes, 201; and
modernism, 127; and V. de Moraes,
210; and R. Mourão, 212; and Nóbrega, 578; and *A Ordem*, 128, 205,
210; and Piñon, 244; and popular culture, 248; and A. Prado, 263; and D.
S. de Queiroz, 266; and Rawet, 272;
and regionalism, 175; and M. K. Reis,
282–83; and J. do Rio, 291; and Rosa,
300; and Schmidt, 313; and Scliar,
313–14; and Antônio José da Silva,
315–16; Tasso da Silveira, 317; Auta
de Souza, 123; Suassuna, 329; symbolism, 330; and theater, 339; Tupi catechism, 165; Varela, 359; Father Vieira,
365–66. *See also* religions, Afro-
Brazilian
religions, Afro-Brazilian, 87, 146, 194,
285, 291; *candomble*, in Jorge Amado,
15–16, 132–33; *candomblé*, in S. Coutinho, 95; *macumba*, 10, 284; *macumba*, in Bandeira, 53; *umbanda*, 285
renaissance, 99, 142, 190, 235
Renato, José, 343
Renault, Abgar, 278
republicanism, xliv, 4, 14, 54, 56, 57,
101, 237, 289, 359; and children's literature, 81; and E. da Cunha, 102–
105; and Indianism, 168; and Pompéia,
245; and positivism, 256; and travel
literature, 350, 352

Resende, Otto Lara, **285–86**
Retrato do Brasil (*Portrait of Brazil*) (P.
Prado), 158, 263
reviews, **286**; *Acadêmica*, 19; *Afrodiáspora*, 216; *América Latina*, 318; *Anta*,
205, 290; *Arco e Flexa*, 206; art, 37,
38; *Árvore*, 194; *Árvore Nova*, 318;
Através, 243; *Cadernos Brasileiros*,
243; *Os Cadernos da Bahia*, 258; *Cadernos Negros*, 90; *Cla*, 258; *Código*,
243; *Complemento*, 30; *Corpo Estranho*, 243; *Correio Brasiliense*, 93–
94, 252; *Edifício*, 113, 258; *Encontro*,
190; *Estética*, 205; *Estória*, 310, 367;
Euclydes, 19; feminist, 87; *Festa*, 194,
205, 284, 317; *Fígaro*, 47; *Flaminaçu*,
119, 206; *Floreal*, 56; *Folha Popular*,
331; *Fon-Fon!*, 47, 331; *Guanabara*,
294; *A Gazetinha de Resende*, 18; *Horus*, 331; *Ilha*, 258; *Invenção*, 46, 243,
260; *Joaquim*, 257, 353; *José*, 258;
Klaxon, 9, 56, 202, 205; *Leite
Crioulo*, 205; *Letras de Hoje*, 302; literary, 12, 100; *Madrugada*, 206; *A
Manhã*, 19; *Maracajá*, 206; *Minerva
Brasileira*, 294; *Movimento Pau Brasil*, 205; *Niterói: Revista Brasiliense*,
xlii, 5, 189, 294, 296; *Noigandres*,
243, 259; *Nordeste*, 258; *Nova*, 87,
194; *Novíssima*, 290; *A Ordem*, 128,
205, 210; *Orfeu*, 169, 257; *Orpheu*
(1915), 78, 253; *Poesia em G.*, 243;
postmodernist, 257–63; *Praxis*, 81;
Quilombhoje, 90; realist, 274; *Região*,
258; *Rendençao*, 206; *A Revista*, 20,
205, 220; *Revista Americana*, 331; *Revista Branca*, 257; *Revista Brasileira*,
67, 294; *Revista Brasileira de Poesia*,
257, 258; *Revista de Antropofagia*, 20,
63, 189, 205; *Revista do Brasil*, 181,
331; *Revista do Norte*, 77, 127; *Revista Literária*, 274; *A Rua do Ouvidor*, 331; *A Semana*, 274; *Tempo
Brasileiro*, 100; *Tendência*, 46, 260,
278, 311; *Terra do Sol*, 194; *Terra
Roxa e Outras Terras*, 12, 189, 202,
205; *Travessia*, 302; *Verde*, 140, 205;

Verde-Amarelo, 205; *Vida Moderna*, 274
revista (theatrical review), 71, 341, 342, 344, 364
Rey, Marcos, 86, 279, **286**
Rezende, Henrique de, 205–6
Ribeiro, Darcy, 276, **287–88**; and Callado, 71; and Indianism, 168
Ribeiro, João, 96, 255
Ribeiro, João Ubaldo, 242, **288–89**
Ribeiro, Júlio, 219, 257, **289**
Ribeiro, Maria, 320
Ribeiro, Santiago Nunes, 296
Ricardo, Cassiano, 99, 168, 206, 242, 262, **290**, 308; and semiotics movement, 260
Ricardo, Paulo, 84
Rio de Janeiro (city and state), xl, xli, 3, 4, 5, 6, 11, 12, 13, 18, 19, 22, 31, 39, 47, 48, 49, 51, 54, 56, 58, 59, 63, 65, 76, 77, 78, 79, 85, 86–87, 88, 90, 91, 95, 100, 101, 107, 113, 118, 121, 126, 127, 133, 134, 136, 137, 138, 143, 144, 146, 148, 151, 152, 159, 172, 173, 174, 175, 176, 179, 185, 187, 188, 189, 190, 192, 194, 196, 201, 208, 210, 220, 226, 238, 245, 250, 252, 266, 267, 274, 286, 289, 307, 309, 310, 313, 315, 331, 341, 348, 350, 366; and Brazilian Academy of Letters, 67, 68, 71, 72; and *crônica*, 100–101; and Leonardo, 173; and J. M. de Macedo, 187–88; and *Memórias de um sargento de milícias*, 11, 40; and modernism, 205; and Rebelo, 274–75; and regionalists, 279; and João do Rio, 290–91; and N. Rodrigues, 291–92
Rio, João do, 61, 101, 257, 279, **290–91**, 341; in Bressane film, 130
Rio Grande do Norte, 159, 360; in travel literature, 351
Rio Grande do Sul, xlii, 1, 4, 5, 47, 63, 121, 151, 162, 172, 185, 201, 221, 265, 267, 290, 323, 331, 332; German role, 152; Lopes Neto, 185; L. Luft, 186; modernism, 206; Moog, 209; re-

gionalists, 279; in travel literature, 350, 352; and E. Veríssimo, 362
Rios, Cassandra, 160
Rivera, Bueno de, 258
River Plate War, xliii
Rocha, Gláuber, 129, 192; and Callado, 71; and E. da Cunha, 105; and fiction, 128
Rocha, Jones, 330
Rocha, Justiniano José da, 297
Rocha, Manuel Ribeiro da, 319
Rocha, Ruth, 83
Rodrigues, Claufe, 223
Rodrigues, Eustáquio, 90
Rodrigues, João Barbosa, 133
Rodrigues, José Honório, 158
Rodrigues, Nelson, 46, 71, 128, 160, **291–92**, 342, 346, 347; and naturalism, 220; and soccer, 322
Rodrigues, Stella, 292
romance-reportagem (journalistic novel/non-fiction/fiction), 91, 111; and Louzeiro, 488; and neonaturalism, 219
romanticism, xlii, xliii, xlv, 5, 10, 11, 18, 14, 36, 53, 58, 60, 72, 87, 95, 96, 123, 145, 148, 151, 167, 203, 234, 245, 265, 289, **293–98**, 316, 317, 324, 326, 327, 335, 336, 359, 362; and C. de Abreu, 2; and J. de Alencar, 6, 8; and Alverne, 13; and Alves, 13–14; and Machado de Assis, 39–40; and Aluísio Azevedo, 47–48; in Álvares de Azevedo, 49–50; city literature, 84–85; and condorism, 88–89; and R. Correia, 91; and C. M. da Costa, 92–93; and Gonçalves Dias, 107–110; and film, 129; generations of, 107, 108, 138; and music, 234; and J. M. de Macedo, 187; Gonçalves de Magalhães, 189–90; and naturalism, 218; and "noble savage" theme, 151, 156, 167, 226; and realism, 272–74; and religion, 284; reviews of, 294; and Romero, 299; and *saudade*, 312; and slavery, 237, 319; and symbolism, 330; and theater, 239, 339; and *ufanismo*, 357
Romero, Sílvio, xliii, 78, 96, 158, 240–41, 248, 264, 275, **298–99**, 362; eval-

uation of Sousândrade by, 327; and folklore, 133; and music, 212; and realism, 273

Rónai, Paulo, 135

Rondon, Colonel Cândido, 94, 101, 135; and T. Roosevelt, 353

Rosa, João Guimarães, 38, 56, 78, 117, 179, 224, 234, 278, 284, 287, **299–304**; and E. da Cunha, 105; and film, 131; and postmodernism, 259; A. Prado, influence on, 263; and theater, 347

A rosa do povo (*The People's Rose*) (Drummond de Andrade), 21

Rosas, J. M. de (Argentine dictator), xliii

Rubião, Murilo, 76, 278, **304–5**, 330; and Veiga, 360

Ruiz, Alice, 223

Russian cultural influences: F. Dostoyevsky, 134, 179, 272; F. Dostoyevsky, and Machado de Assis, 44; M. Gorky, 269; V. Mayakovski, 75, 260; Nüinsky, 225; L. Tolstoy, 272

Sá, Álvaro de, 260, 261

Sá, Estácio de, 173

Sá, Neide Dias de, 261

Sabino, Fernando, 46, 278

Sagarana (Rosa), 38, 300, 301, 303

Saldanha, Carlos, 222

Saldanha, Natividade, 294

Sales, Antônio, 219

Sales, Herberto, **307–8**

Sales, José Luís, 224

Salgado, Plínio, 121, 290, **308–9**; and immigrants, 161; and impressionism, 164; and modernism, 204, 205, 206, 242; and national identity, 241

Salles, Fritz Teixeira de, 46

Salles Gomes. *See* Gomes, Paulo Emílio Salles

Salomão, Waly, 261, 355

Salusse, Jólio, 236

Salvador (Bahia), xli, 13, 15, 17, 84, 90, 262, 288, 307, 348, 365

Salvador, Friar Vicente do, xxxix, 157, 158

samba, xlv, xlvi, 130; and the state, 249

Sampaio, Francisco Leite Bittencourt, 276, 319

Sampaio, Silveira, 342

Santa Catarina, 59, 282, 316, 326, 329; in travel literature, 351

Santana, Lila, 224

Sant'Anna, Afonso Romano de, xxxvii, 99, 241, 261, **309–10**, 322

Sant'Anna, Sérgio, 86, 111, 244, **310–11**, 323

Santa Rita Durão. *See* Durão, Friar José de Santa Rita

Santiago, Silviano, 30, 46, 99–100, 160, 260, 278, 311; and G. Ramos, 271

Santos (São Paulo), 352

Santos, João Caetano dos: and romantic theater, 239, 295, 339–40, 341

Santos, João Felicio dos, 131, 321

Santos, Joaquim Felício dos, 168

Santos, Ladislau dos, 167

Santos, Luís Delfino dos, 168, 236, 296

Santos, Nelson Pereira dos, 129–30

Santos, Nestor Vitor dos, 96, 332

Santos, Quirino dos, 89

Santos, Vital, 347

São Bernardo (*São Bernardo*) (G. Ramos), 269, 270–71, 287, 324; on film, 129

São Luís (Maranhão), 152, 153, 209

São Paulo, xli, 1, 4, 5, 8, 10, 13, 30, 32, 49, 51, 54, 56, 59, 63, 64, 65, 79, 80, 89, 95, 102, 118, 127, 134, 136, 145, 149, 150, 151, 155, 171, 172, 174, 181, 188, 189, 191, 202, 204, 217, 224, 226, 233, 242, 245, 263, 286, 289, 290, 313, 314, 316, 323, 325, 329, 337, 341, 348, 367; and J. Andrade, 23; and M. de Andrade, 24–27; in A. and H. de Campos, 73, 75; and P. Galvão, 144; horsetrack society, 286; and modernism, 204–5; and postmodernism, 73; in D. Silveira de Queiroz, 265–66; regionalists, 279; Setúbal, 314; and theater, 342; in travel literature, 351

Sargento Getúlio (*Sergeant Getúlio*) (Ubaldo Ribeiro), 288

Sarney, José, xlvii, 67, 277

satire, in: O. de Andrade, 28, 29; Machado de Assis, 40, 60; Lima Barreto, 212; H. de Campos, 75; city literature, 84; *crônica*, 100, 126; J. J. França Júnior, 137; Francis, 382; L. Gama, 145; Giudice, 146; Dias Gomes, 147; Gonzaga, 251; in Lopes Neto, 185; G. de Matos, 192–93; new writers, 223; Pompeia, 246; Qorpo-Santo, 265; D. Ribeiro, 287; Ubaldo Ribeiro, 288; romanticism, 297; H. Sales, 308; S. Sant'Anna, 310; A. J. da Silva, 315; Deonísio da Silva, 316; slavery literature, 145; M. Souza, 328; in Suassuna, 329; Viscount Taunay, 336; in theater, 340, 341

saudade, 2, 25, 127, 276, **311**; and city literature, 85; Gonçalves Dias, 109

Savary, Olga, **312**

Sayão, Wilson, 225

Schmidt, Augusto Frederico, 205, 207, 269, 284, **313**; and Bernanos, 135

Schwartz, Ester, 100

Schwartz, Jorge, 100

Schwarz, Roberto, 39, 44, 98

science fiction, 100, 101, 159, 174, 223, 266, 328, 338

scientific poetry, 31, 236, 273, 298, 326, 332

Scliar, Moacir, 111, 163, 279, 285, **313–14**

Seabra, Bruno, 276, 297

Sebastian (king of Portugal), xxxviii

Secchim, Antônio Carlos, 262

Segall, Lasar, 38, 204

Seixas, Cid, 262

semiotics, 259, 260; and Ávila, 46; and "New Language, New Poetry," 260; and Pignatari, 243

Semog, Eli, 90

Senhora (Madam) (Alencar), 6, 7, 47, 274

Senna, Orlando, 131

Sentimento do mundo (Sentiment of the World) (Drummond de Andrade), 20

Seraphim Ponte Grande (*Seraphim Grosse Pointe*) (O. de Andrade), 28, 29

Sergipe, 127, 298, 323

Serra, Joaquim, 297, 320

sertão (hinterland), 36, 56, 70, 86, 105, 229, 233, 237, 266, 269, 276, 277, 278, 297, 301, 303, 323, 329, 335; Cearense, 80; Elis, 117–18; Palmério, 233; Rosa, 299–304

Os sertões (*Rebellion in the Backlands*) (E. da Cunha), 70, 98, 102–105, 278; and religion, 285

Sete, Mário, 277

Setúbal, Paulo, **314–15**

Sevcenko, Nicolau, 100

Sganzerla, Rogério, 100, 131

short story, xlvii, 1, 3, 4, 10, 12, 19, 24, 30, 32, 44, 47, 49, 68, 74, 87–88, 93, 94, 95, 96, 101, 113, 114, 118, 119, 121, 128, 132, 133, 137, 147, 149, 159, 163, 170, 171, 172, 174, 177, 182, 184, 185, 188, 190, 205, 206, 215, 222, 223, 226–27, 238, 243, 244, 265, 266, 272, 275, 276, 277, 278, 285, 286, 304, 316, 318, 329, 337, 363, 366, 367; allegory, 111–112; during dictatorship, 111–112; and film, 130; C. Lispector, 180; prizes, 1, 118, 264, 322; and Rosa, 300; and D. Trevisan, 353–54

Silva, Abel, 111

Silva, Aguinaldo, 111, 160, **315**; work on film, 131

Silva, Alberto da Costa e, 261

Silva, (Antônio Francisco) Da Costa e, 261, 332

Silva (The Jew), Antônio José da, **315–16**, 339; and music, 212; and Martins Pena, 239

Silva, Deonísio da, **316**

Silva, Domingos Carvalho da, 258

Silva, Falves, 261

Silva, Francisca Souza da, 200

Silva, João Manuel Pereira da, xlii, 297

Silva, Joaquim Norberto de Sousa e, 96, 296

Silva, José Bonifácio de Andrada e, xlii, 252, 294, **316–17**, 319,

Silva (The Younger), José Bonifácio de Andrada e, 89, **317**

Silva, Luís, 90
Silva Alvarenga. *See* Alvarenga, Manuel Inácio da Silva
Silveira, Énio, 265
Silveira, Helena, 101, 265
Silveira, Oliveira, 90
Silveira, Tasso da, 79, 127, 194, 205, 284, **317–18**
Silveira, Valdomiro, 265, **318**
Silveira Neto, José Luís, 279
Simões Lopes Neto. *See* Lopes Neto, João Simões
Sirkis, Alfredo, 112, 164, 200
slavery, xxxviii, xlii, xliii, 5, 10, 15, 18, 21, 26, 31, 44, 48, 49, 95, 107, 123, 140, 145, 148, 151, 215, 229, 273, 276, 317, **318–22**, 332, 338, 359; and Alves, 13; and *O ateneu*, 245; and Gonçalves Dias, 107; and Indianism, 168; and J. M. de Macedo, 187; and Montello, 209; and naturalism, 219; in Olinto, 229; and Patrocínio, 237; and Lins do Rego, 280–82; and romanticism, 297; and Cruz e Sousa, 326, 331; and theater, 340; and travel literature, 350
SLMG (*Suplemento Literário de Minas Gerais*), 310
Soares, Antônio Macedo, 296
soccer, xlvi, 33, 93, 230, **322–23**, 329; and E. Coutinho, 94; and dictatorship, 249; and Homem, 159; and Nelson Rodrigues, 291; and A. R. de Sant'Anna, 309; and Viana Filho, 364
social novel, xlvi, 3, 10, 15, 32, 58, 76, 88, 104, 207, 220, 233, 239, 266, 270, 274, 277, 280, 300, 315, **323–24**, 361, 366; and city literature, 85, 179–80; cycles, 105; and films, 129; and homosexuality, 160; and Portuguese neorealism, 253; and G. Ramos, 270
Sodré, Nelson Werneck, xlvi, 99, 158, 241, 247
Soffredini, Carlos Alberto, 347
Sortilégio: mistério negro (*Sortilege: Black Mystery*) (A. do Nascimento), 216
Sousa, Afonso Félix de, 258

Sousa, Antônio Teixeira e, 108, 187, 297, **324**; and Gonçalves Dias, 108, 167; and Indianism, 446; and slavery, 321
Sousa, Gabriel Soares de, 156, 251, **324–25**
Sousa, Herculano Inglês de, 28, 47, 65, 151, 276, 284, **325**; and naturalism, 218, 273; and slavery, 321
Sousa, João da Cruz e, 31, 37, 150, 234, **326–27**, 331, 332; and contemporary black literature, 89; and C. Meireles, 194; and religion, 284
Sousa, Pero Lopes de, 156
Sousândrade, 297, 298, **327–28**; and A. and H. de Campos, 74, 75; and Indianism, 168; and Qorpo-Santo, 265
Souza, Auta de, 123
Souza, Cláudio de Mello e, 223
Souza, Gilda de Mello e, 100
Souza, Márcio, 224, 276, **328**; *A. selva*, film version of, 128,
Souza, Naum Alves de, 192, 225
Souza, Parcifal de, 111
Spanish cultural influences, xxxviii, 57, 196, 198, 201, 239, 244, 339; F. Arrabal, 144; Father Acuña, xxxviii; Calderón de la Barca, 329; J. Benet, 105; G. de Berceo, 196, 197; M. de Cervantes, 149; M. de Cervantes, and children's literature, 82; J. de Espronceda, 138; F. García-Lorca, 20, 194; L. de Góngora, 55, 193; B. Gracián, 55; J. Gris, 197; J. Miró, 197; F. de Orellana, xxxviii; P. Picasso, 197; F. de Quevedo, 55, 193; P. Teixeira, xxxviii; F. de Rojas Zorilla, 339
Spanudis, Theon, 259
Spiritual Brotherhood of Ceará, 276, 338
Steen, Edla van, 125, 323, **329**
structuralism, 99
Studart, Heloneida, 125,
Suassuna, Ariano, 146, 222, 253, 277, 285, **329–30**, 346; and folklore, 133, 343
surrealism, 22, 60, 88, 95, 164, 175, 188, 190, 196, 198, 206, 258, 301, **330**, 340, 362

Sussekind, Carlos, 111
Sussekind, Flora, 100, 219
Swiss cultural influences: B. Cendrars, 25, 135, 290; C. Jung, 292; S. de Sismondi, 93, 96
symbolism, xliv, 9, 24, 31, 33, 37, 51, 52, 53, 60, 74, 78, 86, 92, 95, 96, 123, 171, 175, 189, 202, 253, 258, 261, 290, 318, **330–33**; and Alves, 14; and art, 114; and A. de Guimaraens, 150; and Indianism, 168; and modernism, 204, 242; and neo-symbolism, 179, 194–95, 205, 258, 282; and Parnassianism, 234; and positivism, 257; and religion, 284; and Cruz e Sousa, 326–27

Tapajós, Renato, 110
Tati, Miécio, 279
Taunay, Afonso d'Escragnolle, 335, 353
Taunay, Alfredo d'Escragnolle, Viscount of, **335–36**; and film, 128; and immigrants, 161; and positivism, 257; and realism, 274; and romanticism, 297
Taunay, Nicolas Antoine, 335
Tavares, Zulmira, Ribeiro, 224
Távora, Franklin, 105, 274, 276, 296, 297
teatro besteiro, 225
Teatro Experimental do Negro (TEN) (Black Experimental Theater), 216, 346
teatro jornal (newspaper theater), 62
Teatro Novo (New Theater), 45
Teatro Oficina (Oficina Theater Group), 28, 45
Teatro União e Olho Vivo (Union and Living Eye Theater, 345
Teixeira, Bento, 55, **336**
Teixeira, Múcio, 279
Teixeira e Sousa. *See* Sousa, Antônio Teixeira e
television: and films, 131, 266, 360, 362, 364; and popular culture, 249; and Portugal, 253; soap operas (*telenovelas*), 131, 243, 345
Telles, Gilberto Mendonça, 99

Telles, Lygia Fagundes, 86, 111, 112, 123, 124, 264, **337–38**
A tenda dos milagres (*The Tent of Miracles*) (Amado), 16–17; television version, 131
Teófilo, Rodolfo, 219, 229, **338**
Teoria da poesia concreta (Theory of Concrete Poetry) (A. and H. de Campos), 73
Teresa Margarida. *See* Orta, Teresa Margarida da Silva e
Terras do sem fim (*The Violent Land*) (Jorge Amado), 15, 207, 324
testimonial novel, 110, 223
theater, xlii, 10, 24, 27, 28, 30, 44, 47, 49, 50, 54, 64, 69, 74, 98, 110, 126, 127, 130, 136, 144, 146, 149–50, 155, 170, 187, 206, 208, 210, 220, 230, 265, 266, 267, 278–79, **338–48**; and J. de Alencar, 8; and Anchieta, 18–19, 212, 283; and J. Andrade, 23; and Arena, 149, 319; and black literature, 89–90, 216; and Bloch, 62; and Boal, 62–63; and Camargo, 71; and C. de Castro, 79–80; and children's, 84; and Gonçalves Dios, 107, 108; and folklore, 131–32; and Dias Gomes, 146–47; and Francis, 137; and Fusco, 140; and National Conservatory, 59; and P. Marcos, 191–92; and new writers, 225; and *Oficina* Theater Group, 28, 45; and *Opinião* Theater Group, 152; and Oppressed, Theater of the, 62–63; and Martins Pena, 239–40; and Pernambuco Student Theater, 329; and prizes, 127, 225, 264; and Nelson Rodrigues, 291–92; and romanticism, 295, 298; and Antônio José da Silva, 315; and slavery, 319, 320; and Suassuna, 329; and *teatro besteiro*, 577; and *teatro foro*, 63; and *Teatro Novo*, 45; and *tropicalismo*, 354–55
theater forum (*teatro foro*): and Boal, 63
Theater of the Oppressed: and Boal, 62–63
Thomas, Gerald, 225
Tiradentes, 62, 324, 342; *See also* Mineiran Conspiracy

Tojeiro, Gastão, 341
Toquinho, 84
Torres, Antônio, 86, 111, **348**
Tragédia burguesa (Bourgeois Tragedy)
(O. de Faria), 121–22
translators into Portuguese, 59, 68, 181,
297; Drummond de Andrade, 20; Ban-
deira, 51, 135; A. de Campos, 73; G.
Campos, 74; H. de Campos, 75; J. C.
de Carvalho, 78; S. Coutinho, 94; G.
Figueiredo, 127; P. Galvão, 144; L.
Luft, 186; C. Meireles, 194; Melo
Neto, 196; O. Mendes, 264, 296; prize
for, 264, 312; Quintana, 267; Savary,
312; É. Veríssimo, 361; J. G. Vieira,
366
Tratado descritivo do Brasil em 1587
(Descriptive Treatise about Brazil in
1587) (Soares de Sousa), 156, 325
travel literature, xxxvii, xliii, 37, 96,
134, 165, **348–53**, 357; and film, 130
As tres Marias (*The Three Marias*) (R.
de Queiroz), 123, 266
Trevisan, Armindo, 261
Trevisan, Dalton, 86, 264, **353–54**; and
film, 130; and *Joaquim*, 257
Trevisan, João Silvério, 160
Trindade, Socorro, 225
Trindade, Solano, 89
Triste fim de Policarpo Quaresma (*The
Patriot*) (Lima Barreto), 57, 212, 237,
257, 284
tropicalismo, 28, 38, 67, 110, 153, 309–
10, **354–55**; and A. de Campos, 73;
and R. Drummond, 114; and film, 130;
and music, 153, 213; and postmodernism, 261, 262; and theater, 344, 345
Turbilhão (Whirlpool) (Coelho Neto), 87,
284
Tutaméia (Tutaméia) (Rosa), 300, 301,
302–3

Ubaldo Ribeiro. *See* Ribeiro, João
Ubaldo
ufanismo, xxxvii, 18, 36, 56, 66, 69, 92,
115, 155, 190, 325, **357**; and P. V. de
Caminha, 19, 73; Viscount A. Celso,
241

ultraromanticism, 49, 89, 95, 296, 297.
See also romanticism
O uraguai (*The Uruguay*) (B. da Gama),
35, 144–45, 167, 252, 283, 352; and
Alvarenga Peixoto, 238; Garrett's evaluation of, 252,
Urupês (Monteiro Lobato), 182
utopia, 28, 57, 70, 338; and concretism,
75

Vaga música (Vague Music) (C. Meireles), 194
Vale, Dinorath do, 224
O vampiro de Curitiba (*The Vampire of
Curitiba*), (D. Trevisan), 354
Varela, Luís Nicolau Fagundes, 14, 19,
284, 296, 320, **359**
Vargas, Getúlio, xlvi, 118, 162, 266,
275, 307; and M. de Andrade, 26; and
Dias Gomes/F. Gullar play, 146; and
Ivo, 169; and Monteiro Lobato, 181;
and modernists, 206; and popular cul-
ture, 249; and postmodernism, 258;
and G. Ramos, 270, 271; and J. Lins
do Rego, 282; and Salgado, 308; and
social novel of the 1930s, 282, 323;
and foreign writers during World War
II, 135, 253
Vargas, Suzana, 223
Varnhagen, Francisco Adolfo, 157–58,
252
Várzea, Virgílio, 326
Vasconcellos, José Mauro de, 360
Vasconcelos, Father Simão de, 19
Vaz de Caminha. *See* Caminha, Pero Vaz
de
Veiga, José J. 111, 117, **360–61**
Veloso, Caetano, 73, 153, 354
Ventura, Adão, 90
verdamarelismo, 242, 290, 308
Vergara, Telmo, 279
Veríssimo, Érico, 59, 110, 207, 279,
361–62, 363; and positivism, 257
Veríssimo, José, 51, 67, 79, 96–97, 111,
152, 219, 233, 256, 264, 276, 299,
362–63
Veríssimo, Luís Fernando, 101, **363**

Vestido de noiva (*The Wedding Dress*)
(N. Rodrigues), 291, 342
Viana, Azevedo, 331
Viana, Deocília, 363
Viana, Oduvaldo, 341, 363
Viana, Vivina, 83
Viana Filho, Oduvaldo, 62, 110, 144,
291, 343, 346, 347, **363–65**; and Gul-
lar, 152; and soccer, 322
Viana Moog. *See* Moog, Clodomir Viana
Vianna, Francisco José Oliveira, 241
Vicente, José, 46, 345
Vida e morte de M. J. Gonzaga de Sá
(*The Life and Death of M. J. Gonzaga
de Sá*) (Lima Barreto), 57
A vida passada a limpo (Life in a New
Copy) (Drummond de Andrade), 22
Vidas secas (*Barren Lives*) (G. Ramos),
269, 271, 324; on film, 129
Vieira, Father Antônio, xxxix, 55, 75,
166, 251, 283, **365–66**
Vieira, César, 345
Vieira, João Fernandes, 69
Vieira, José Geraldo, 284, **366–67**
Vila dos confins (Border Town) (Pal-
mério), 233
Vila, Martinho da, 84
Vilar, Pethion de, 332
Vilela, Luiz, 244, 264, 323, **367**
Villaça, Antônio Carlos, 111
Villa-Lobos, Heitor, xlvi, 78, 95, 204,
206, 212, 221, **367–68**

Villa-Lobos, Raul, 368
Vilmar, 38, 227
violão da rua (street guitar movement),
361–62
Viriato, Gaspar, 277
visual anthropophagy, 261
viva o povo brasileiro (*Long Live the
Brazilian People*, 1988) (Ubaldo Ribeiro), 289

Week of Modern Art, 9, 20, 28, 34, 38,
51, 78, 158, 204, 242, 259, 263, 308,
341, 367
Wolff, Fausto, 101
World War II, xlvi, 65, 162, 179, 184,
207, 253, 258; and theater, 342

Xavier, Joaquim José da Silva (Tiradentes), 203
Xisto, Pedro, 260

Yamasaki, Tizuka, 164

Zampari, Franco, 342
Zero (*Zero*) (Loyola Brandão), 65–66,
110, 253; and film, 131
Ziembinski, Zbigniew, 292, 342
Zilberman, Regina, 100
Ziraldo, 38
Zuccolotto, Afrânio, 258
Zumbi, xl, 62, 132, 319. *See also*
Palmares